Business Accounting and Taxation

Business Accounting and Taxation

Edited by **Terry Ness**

Willford Press

New York

Published by Willford Press,
118-35 Queens Blvd., Suite 400,
Forest Hills, NY 11375, USA
www.willfordpress.com

Business Accounting and Taxation
Edited by Terry Ness

International Standard Book Number: 978-1-68285-233-0 (Hardback)

Printed in China.

Contents

Preface

This resource book aims to highlight some of the key concepts, laws, rules and accounting principles that are followed in various business enterprises across the globe. The book aims to outline various categories of corporate taxes that are imposed on business entities like income taxes, payroll taxes, excise taxes, sales taxes, vat, etc. It provides comprehensive insight on different tax computing methods, assessment of returns, fiscal neutrality, and rates & collection of taxes. This book incorporates concepts and case studies from around the world to provide an overview of contemporary practices. It will serve as a reference to a broad spectrum of readers.

This book unites the global concepts and researches in an organized manner for a comprehensive understanding of the subject. It is a ripe text for all researchers, students, scientists or anyone else who is interested in acquiring a better knowledge of this dynamic field.

I extend my sincere thanks to the contributors for such eloquent research chapters. Finally, I thank my family for being a source of support and help.

Editor

The impact of income tax rates (ITR) on the economic development of Botswana

Bonu N. S.* and Pedro Motau P.

Faculty of Business, University of Botswana, Gaborone, Botswana.

Traditional schools of thought advocated the theory of low income tax rates' influencing economic development, whereas modern schools of thought propagated the theory of higher income tax rates producing greater economic growth, especially for developed nations. In order to justify these thoughts an attempt was made taking Botswana as a case study to pin point the effect of low and high income tax rates on economic growth. In this study various parameters were taken into account including income tax rates, income tax revenue, total revenue and GDP of the country in the nominal and real value of the money. It was located that low income tax rates boosted the economic growth of Botswana.

Key words: Income tax rates, economic development, nominal, real value of money.

INTRODUCTION

Income tax is a tool to achieve economic growth in any country. Income tax is accepted not only as a means of raising the required public revenue, but also as an essential fiscal instrument for managing the economy (Burgess, 1993). Of all the taxing systems, income tax plays a major role in generation of revenue and distribution of income in any country. If income taxation is poorly designed, it may lead to fiscal imbalance, insufficient tax revenue and distortions in resource allocation that can reduce economic welfare and growth (World Bank, 1991). Hence, an ideal tax system would achieve a balance between resource allocation, income distribution and economic stabilization (Lewis, 1984).

Patterns of income taxation (both in level and in composition) differ from country to country because of economic, cultural and historical factors. Ratios of tax revenue to gross domestic product (GDP) in developing countries are typically in the range of 15 to 20%, compared with 30% in industrialized nations (World Bank, 1991). It is also established that countries have different approaches to tax administration. Maisto (1988) stated that "contradictory approaches towards the subject matter have been shown by the tax authorities of different countries because of their diverging interests".

An optimal tax rate has to compromise between the state's revenue and its economic development. A high tax rate would deter saving and development, while a lower tax rate would lead to less revenue to the state. A tax directly influences the savings of individuals and companies; it is a double edged sword used to curtail consumption activity and at the same time, allows the taxpayer to save money in different development activities (Swami, 1995). The income tax financing the current social security benefits such as health, security and provision of utilities draws heavily upon income that otherwise would have been saved. Instead of accumulating capital, this income goes to social security transfers which are probably consumed (Boadway, 1982).

LITERATURE REVIEW

Bartik (1994a and b) suggested that a 10% lowering of taxes would raise employment and investment between 1 and 6%. World Bank periodically relates that economic development is directly correlated to the level of taxation, more so in developing nations where the lower marginal tax rates have higher economic growth. In addition, policy makers in these countries have a "keen interest in the elasticity of economic activity with respect to taxes, suggesting that states and regions are interested in manipulating their tax systems in an attempt to attract business or to foster growth" (Wasylenko, 1997). On the other hand, income tax rates are increased due to factors such as enormous reduction in the purchasing power of money, heavy tax erosion, urgent need for yield and dynamic public expenditure (Fossati, 1992). While dealing with

*Corresponding author. E-mail: bonuns@mopipi.ub.bw.

the effects of income tax rates (ITR) on economic reforms, Henry and William (1996) suggested that one should evaluate the desirability of reform proposals and the impact of such reforms on individuals and businesses as a whole. They further stated that ITR change would revolve around three factors: the tax base, allowable deductions and economic development. While dealing with the ITR, it is suggested that one should study the effects created by these rates, especially the impact of ITR on economic growth (Holger, 2003).

Various governments have different approaches and methods of fixing the ITR. The French Government recently introduced preferential tax treatment by reduced I-TR for young innovative companies completely based on the economic growth. The scheme was originally proposed to the State by French biotechnology as "a way to rapid and strong economic growth" (European Chemical News, 2004).

Martin and George (2003) analyzed several tax rates and expenditure categories and concluded that the tax system has a direct impact on the growth rate of the economy of a country. Long-term economic growth has a direct link with the country's tax policy (John and Pamela, 2003). Fixation of ITR may be based on different systems of taxation. Akira (2003) demonstrated that a flatrate wage tax stimulated economic growth, while interest income taxation did not foster such growth. Tetsuo (2003) suggested that taxation based on environmental pollution factors results in two contradicting issues such as reduction in production and increase in tax revenue, but in the long run, this system will help the healthy economic growth for future generations. Olhoft (2003) is of the opinion that spending millions of taxpayers' money on tax breaks and tax incentives is most likely a misguided strategy for any State when the State is in budget deficit.

Earlier studies

There are two schools of thought in understanding the impact of ITR on the economic growth of any country, the traditional school and the modern school. Robert Barro of Harvard had an influential study several years back, which surmised that while holding other determinants of growth constant, low tax rates and low government spending were associated with higher growth (Slemrod, 2003). The higher the marginal tax rate, the greater the chances of higher income taxpayers diverting extra time from productive operations to leisure activities.

The modern school of thought revealed that the higher marginal tax rates lead to greater economic development in the long run. The government would secure a greater revenue, which when invested in the country's education and infrastructure development, will boost the economy. Slemord (2003) suggested that raising taxes and using the resultant revenue for education and infrastructure would also increase economic growth.

THEORETICAL FRAMEWORK

Problem statement

It is assumed that a higher ITR leads to a higher tax revenue collection which in turn, will enhance the economic development of any country, especially in developed nations as compared to developing or under-developed nations (Slemord, 2003). Extensive literature review revealed that higher ITR in developed countries correlated with high prosperity. This finding cannot apply to all nations, specifically not developing ones. It is the main objective of this research to locate whether there is a greater impact on the economic development by increasing ITR in a developing country such as Botswana.

Objectives

The main objectives of this study are to identify:

i) The impact of change of income tax rates on the economic development of Botswana.
ii) The correlation between the change in income tax rates with that of tax revenue.
iii) The change in the GDP with that of change in the income tax rates.
iv) The effect of inflation over the ITR and revenue.

Hypotheses

Based on the above cited research problem and objectives, the following hypotheses were developed for further study:

H1: Developed nations charged a higher ITR than developing nations.
H2: A more direct effect of income tax revenue on total revenue be located and tax collection per person in developed nations compared to developing nation.
H3: At higher tax rates, based on the nominal value of money (NVM), 1% of income tax rate (both at higher marginal tax rate (HMTR) and average tax rate (ATR) leads to higher (i) tax revenue (ii) total revenue (iii) GDP (iv) percentage tax revenue over total revenue (v) percentage of tax revenue over GDP (vi) tax collection per tax return and (vi) per person based on population.
H4: At higher tax rates, based on the real value of money (RVM), 1% of income tax rate (both at HMTR and ATR) leads to lower (i) tax revenue (ii) total revenue (iii) GDP (iv) percentage tax revenue over total revenue (v) percentage of tax revenue over GDP (vi) tax collection per tax return and (vii) per person based on population

METHODOLOGY

The extensive literature review indicated that the effect of income tax rates (ITR) over income levels and income growth (Wasylenko, 1997) have been less frequently used in the studies of state and local economic development. To fill in the gap in existing literature, a maiden venture is undertaken to locate the ITR effect on tax collection, revenue generation, GDP and related economic issues.

The research is divided into three major areas namely (i) comparative study of ITR with that of income tax revenue (ii) comparative study of ITR with that of total revenue generation and (iii) comparative study of ITR effect on GDP.

In addition to the above, the following further variables of ITR are evaluated:

(a) Higher marginal tax rate (HMTR)
(b) Average tax rate (ATR)

The average rate of income tax paid by a person is that, person's total tax divided by his or her income. The marginal rate of tax is the rate he or she would pay on another unit of income (Lipsey, 1989). These terms are used with minor modifications in this research. HMTR means the top tax rate an individual is supposed to pay at a higher brand of income. The maximum rate at which an individual is charged is taken into account and then the flat rate of company tax is considered. The average of these two is taken as HMTR. In the case of ATR, the average of the individual's minimum and top tax rates are taken, then the same is added to the company's flat tax to get the average of these two.

HMTR = (Top marginal tax rate of individual + Company flat tax rate)/2 (i)
ATR = {(Low marginal tax rate of an individual + Top marginal tax rate of individual)/2+Company flat tax rate}/2 (ii)

The effects of the above rates are studied in terms of nominal value of money (NVM) and real value of money (RVM). NVM is the money's face value whereas RVM is the intrinsic value of the money obtained after delinking the effect of inflation in the country. The following principle is applied to find out RVM:

RVM = Base Year (1982) NCOLI/(NCOLI of the current year. Where NCOLI = National Cost of Living (iii)

The year 1982 is considered as the base year for the intensive study of ITR effect in Botswana because the Income Tax Act of Botswana was overhauled in 1982 and this year was then used for a com-parative study of capital gains etc, assuming NCOLI as 100 in 1982. Hence, it is ideal and practical to apply 1982 as a base year for this research. It is also sensible to study the effect of change in income tax rates over a long period in order to find out the trends in changes of tax rates, income generated from income tax source, total revenue, GDP etc. Hence this study covers 1982 to 2002 covering two decades.

In addition, the following parameters are applied in finding out the effect of 1% tax rate at lowest tax rate and highest tax rate:

Nominal value of money (NVM) for the period 1982-2002: Effect of 1% income tax rate (ITR) at higher marginal tax rate (HMTR) and at average tax rate (ATR)

(i) Income tax revenue collected
(ii) Total revenue generated
(iii) GDP of Botswana
(iv) Percent of tax revenue over total revenue
(v) Percent of tax revenue over GDP
(vi) Tax collection per tax return
(vii) Tax collection per person based on the total population

Real value of money (RVM) for the period 1982-2002: Effect of 1 % income tax rate (ITR) at higher marginal tax rate (HMTR) and at average tax rate (ATR)

(i) Income tax revenue collected
(ii) Total revenue generated
(iii) GDP of Botswana at 1% of ITR
(iv) Percent of tax revenue over total revenue
(v) Percent of tax revenue over GDP.

The above test results will be compared at both low and high tax rates prevailing in Botswana over two decades.

Furthermore, the research entailed the collection of secondary data from published sources such as the annual reports of department of taxes, bank of Botswana and Income Tax Acts of Botswana published since 1973. Other publications include "Africa: South of the Sahara" (Europa), and publications of international monetary fund for the period covering 1982 to 2002 and other electronic sources.

Scope of the study

This study also covers the general effect of ITR on developing nations. The tax rates etc., of the selected developing nations in Southern African Developing Community (SADC) for the year 1999/2000 were used. For a comparative study, a few developed nations such as Japan, China, UK, USA and Canada were selected ensuring an East to West spectrum. For the detailed study of the effect of ITR on economic development in the developing nations, Botswana is chosen for the detailed study covering the period from 1982 to 2002.

DISCUSSION

H1: Developed nations charged higher ITR than developing nations

Many countries follow different approaches in taxing income. Earlier studies revealed that developed nations charged high tax rates than developing nations. In order to prove these statement nineteen nations were taken into account selecting fourteen developing nations in Africa and a random selection of five developed countries from east to west. Table 1 displays these nineteen nations' ITR ranging from the lowest and highest marginal tax rates of each country charged in the year 1999/2000. Table 1 further reveals the top marginal tax rates varying from 20 to 45% and low marginal tax rates varying from 5 to 20% for individual taxation and 15 to 50% for Company taxation. Out of the nineteen countries under study, Zimbabwe and South Africa charged the highest marginal tax rate of 45% in SADC, while China charged the same for individuals amongst the developed nations. The lowest tax rate at top marginal tax rates is charged by Mozambique (20%) in SADC and Canada (29%) among the developed nations.

Under the lower marginal tax rates, Botswana and Mauritius charged the lowest at 5% in SADC and China charged 5% in developed nations. The highest rate at the lower marginal tax bracket is charged by Zambia and Zimbabwe (20%) in SADC and Canada (16%) in the developed nations under study.

The above conclusions are presented in the Table 3 (a) and (b), which pinpoint the above stated results.

Table 1. Low and top marginal tax rates for individuals and tax rates for companies in selected developed and developing nations.

Country	ITR (Individuals) (%)	Company tax (%)	Source
Angola	18 to 40	50	Btinternet.com
Botswana	5 to 25	25	Income Tax : Chapter 52:01/2002
Congo	15 to 40	50	Cf.heritage.org/index/country.cfm
Lesotho	18 to 40	25	Lesotho.gov
Malawi	15 to 35	35	KPMG,
Mauritius	5 to 30	35	Lowtax.net
Mozambique	10 to 20	35	cpi.co.mz/facts_mz.htm
Namibia	18 to 36	35	mti.gov.na
Seychelles	10 to 40	15	Lowtax.net/lowtax/html/jsypetx.html
South Africa	19 to 45	35	Sars.gov.za/it/brochure_tax_in_sa.htm
Swaziland	18 to 40	37.5	Gov.swaziland
Tanzania	8 to 35	30	Tra.go.tz/tax_structure.htm
Zambia	20 to 30	35	Zic.org.zm/ipa_information.asp
Zimbabwe	20 to 45	30	Deloitte and Touche
China	5 to 45	30	Shanghaiguide.com/
Japan	10 to 37	30	Gol.com/users/jpc/japan/MALAWI taxes.htm
Uk	10 to 40	30	Inlandrevenue.gov.uk/rates/it.htm
Usa	15 to 40	35	Ctj.org/htm/margfaq.htm
Canada	16 to 29	21	Ccra-adrc.gc.ca/tax/individuals/faq/

H2: More direct effect of income tax revenue over GDP, total revenue and tax collection per person in developed nations compared to developing nations

A comparative analysis of the effect of income tax revenue on GDP and total revenue of the SADC countries and a few developed countries for the year 1999/2000 is presented in Table 2.

Impact of income revenue over GDP

Table 2 (e) reveals that the influence of income tax revenue over GDP is not much in economically advanced countries such as Japan, China, UK, USA and Canada. Among the advanced countries, Japan has 4% followed by Canada (9%), UK (10%), China (11%) and USA (12%). In developing nations, the lowest influence of income tax over the GDP is found in Mozambique (2%) followed by Mauritius (4%), Seychelles (5%), Tanzania and Zambia (6% each), Congo (7%), Lesotho (8%), Botswana (9%) whereas a greater influence is found in Malawi (50%), Angola (36%), Zimbabwe (14%), South Africa (13%) and Namibia (12%).

The above analysis is presented in Table 3 (d) in order to highlight the findings and for a comparative study. Based on the above analysis it can be stated that majority of developing nations are depending on income tax revenue for their economic development. There is no uniformity in the percentage of income tax revenue collection over GDP in the developing nations. It varied from 2 to 50%. Whereas the developed nations' income tax influences variance between the lowest and highest is not much on GDP. It ranged from 4 to 12%, whereas in developing nations the variance ranges from 2 to 50%.

Impact of income tax revenue over total revenue(Hypothesis 4)

In order to find out the influence of income tax revenue over the total revenue the income tax revenue data and total revenue data of 1999/2000 is taken into account for the analysis and determination of the results.

In the advanced countries, China collected 78% of its total revenue from income tax followed by USA (49%), Canada (48%), Japan (36%) and UK (27%) (Table 2 (f)). In the developing nations, the highest percentage of income tax revenue over the total revenue is Angola (75%), followed by South Africa (57%), Zimbabwe (51%), Malawi (42%), Zambia 36%, Namibia (30%), Swaziland (26%), Botswana (22%), Mauritius (19%), Congo (17%) and Lesotho (16%). The lowest influence of income tax revenue over the total revenue of the country is found in Seychelles (12%) and Mozambique (14%) and Tanzania (15%). Both developing and developed nations recorded the highest percentage of income tax revenue over the total revenue within a range of 75 and 78%, and the lowest is between 12 and 27% from developing and developed nations [(e)].

Income tax collected per person

In the SADC region, South Africa ($387.79) collected maximum income tax per head, followed by Botswana

Table 2. Impact of Income tax revenue over GDP and total revenue for the year (1999/2000).

(a)	(b)	(c)	(d)	(e)	(f)	(g)
Angola	930	448	337	36	75	27.57
Botswana	5340	2208	484	9	22	322.67
Congo	1937	847	145	7	17	50.52
Lesotho	640	295	48	8	16	22.77
Malawi	165	197	82	50	42	8.29
Mauritius	3272	765	144	4	19	121.67
Mozambique	2965	362	51	2	14	2.93
Namibia	2146	857	254	12	30	154.33
Seychelles	522	227	26	5	12	32.88
South Africa	125887	29651	16788	13	57	387.79
Swaziland	936	295	77	8	26	78.39
Tanzania	1963	771	119	6	15	3.61
Zambia	1497	263	95	6	36	10.81
Zimbabwe	4181	1143	579	14	51	47.10
China	989621	138264	107351	11	78	84.81
Japan	3655135	455849	162576	4	36	1283.66
Uk	1330009	519688	138060	10	27	2320.29
Usa	9299200	2191734	1078789	12	49	3956.09
Canada	586836	115021	55001	9	48	1906.63

Note: (a) Country under study (b) Gross domestic product (million) converted into a common currency (US$) based on the currency rates in 1999 (c) Total revenue of the country in US$ (million) (d) Income tax revenue in US$ (million) (e) Percent of income tax revenue over the GDP (f) Percent of income tax revenue over total revenue (g) Collection of income tax revenue per person in US$.

Table 3. Range analysis of developed and developing nations on ITR and their influence over GDP, total revenue and tax collected per person.

Range analysis	Developed nations		Developing nations	
	Highest	Lowest	Highest	Lowest
(a) % Higher marginal ITR (individuals)	China (45)	Canada (29)	RSA and Zim. (45)	Moz. (20)
(b) % Lower marginal ITR (individuals)	Canada (16)	China (5)	Zam. and Zim. (20)	Bot. and Mau. (5)
(c) % Company tax rates	USA (35)	Canada (21)	Ang. and Con. (50)	Seyche. (15)
(d) % of IT revenue over GDP	USA (12)	Japan (4)	Malawi (50)	Moz. (2)
(e) % of IT revenue over total revenue	China (78)	UK (27)	Angola (75)	Sey. (12)
(f) Collection of IT per head (US $)	USA (3956.09)	China (84.81)	RSA (387.79)	Moz. (2.93)

(Compiled from Table 2 and the analysis).

$322.67), Namibia ($154.33), Mauritius ($121.67), Swaziland ($78.39), Congo ($50.52), Zimbabwe ($47.10), Sey-chelles ($32.88) and Angola ($27.57). The lowest income tax revenue per head is collected in Mozambique ($2.93), followed by Tanzania ($3.61), Malawi ($8.29) and Zambia ($10.81).

Among the developed nations, the income tax collected per person is highest in USA ($3956.09), followed by UK ($2320.29), Canada ($1906.63), Japan ($1283.66) and China ($84.81). There is a wide disparity of income tax revenue collected per head both in the developing nations and developed nations. This range is high in the developed nations. This may be due to the huge population in China [Table 3 (f)].

ANALYSIS OF BOTSWANA INCOME TAX RATES (ITR), INCOME TAX COLLECTION, REVENUE GENERATION AND THEIR IMPACT ON GDP (ECONOMIC ACTIVITIES)

Earlier studies revealed that there will be higher economic development if income tax rates are high, more so in developed nations. The higher tax rates lead to increase in the total tax revenue, total revenue of the country and there will be direct positive effect in boosting the GDP. One should also seriously think whether the boosting of tax revenue, total revenue and GDP of the country is in terms of nominal value of money and real value after inflation adjustment. It is necessary to do an in-depth study

Table 4. Income tax rates (ITR) details in percentage

Individuals' tax rates				Company	HMTR	ATR	Threshold (Pula) (h)	No. of tax payers (i)
Year (a)	LMIITR (b)	TMIITR (c)	AIITR (b+c)/2 (d)	CTR (e)	(c+e)/2 (f)	(d+e)/2 (g)		
1982	10	65	37.5	35	50.0	36.25	0	NA
1983	5	65	35.0	35	50.0	35.00	0	NA
1984	5	60	32.5	35	47.5	33.75	0	NA
1985	5	60	32.5	35	47.5	33.75	0	NA
1986	5	60	32.5	35	47.5	33.75	0	17451
1987	5	60	32.5	35	47.5	33.75	0	NA
1988	5	60	32.5	35	47.5	33.75	0	NA
1989	5	60	32.5	35	47.5	33.75	0	NA
1990	5	60	32.5	35	47.5	33.75	0	13199
1991	5	40	22.5	40	40.0	31.25	9000	15053
1992	5	40	22.5	40	40.0	31.25	9000	13288
1993	5	40	22.5	40	40.0	31.25	9000	16884
1994	5	40	22.5	40	40.0	31.25	9000	13000
1995	5	30	17.5	25	27.5	21.25	9000	13828
1996	5	30	17.5	25	27.5	21.25	15000	17430
1997	5	25	15.0	25	25.0	20.00	15000	15569
1998	5	25	15.0	25	25.0	20.00	20000	17895
1999	5	25	15.0	25	25.0	20.00	20000	17187
2000	5	25	15.0	25	25.0	20.00	20000	18462
2001	5	25	15.0	25	25.0	20.00	20000	16414
2002	5	25	15.0	25	25.0	20.00	25000	9955

Note: (a) Year; (b) LMIITR (Low marginal individual income tax rate); (c) TMIITR (Top marginal individual income tax rate); (d) AIITR (Average individual income tax rate); (e) CTR (Company tax rate); (f) HMTR (Higher marginal tax rate); (g) ATR (average tax rate); (h) Threshold (the minimum amount not taxed); (i) Number of taxpayers in the year.

of these issues considering a developing nation like Botswana to establish whether these findings are applicable to the developing nations.

Hypothesis

H3: At higher tax rates, based on the nominal value of money (NVM), 1% of income tax rate (both at higher marginal tax rate (HMTR) and average tax rate (ATR) leads to higher

(i) tax revenue
(ii) total revenue
(iii) GDP
(iv) percentage tax revenue over total revenue
(v) percentage of tax revenue over GDP
(vi) tax collection per tax return and
(vii) tax collection per person based on population

In order to test the above hypothesis, income tax rates details are collected from the old Income Tax Acts and other sources for the period from 1982 to 2002, BoB (1985-2004) and CSO (2001). This data is presented in Table 4.

Tax information

Table 4 (b) highlights the lower marginal individual income tax rate (LMIITR) that is payable beyond the thres-hold if any and top marginal individual income tax rate (TMIITR) is that rate beyond a specific amount, an indivi-dual is liable to pay the highest tax rate. These lower and higher tax rates are on the high side during the early pe-riod of study (10-65% in 1982) and gradually reduced (5 to 25% in 2002). The average individual income tax rate is obtained by applying the principle of (LMIITR + TMIIT-R)/2. The average individual income tax rate is 37.5% in 1982 and gradually reduced to 15% by 2002 (Table 4 (d)). Companies are taxed at flat rate, which varied from 35% in 1982 to 25% in 2002 [Table 4 (e)].

The higher marginal tax rate (HMTR) is derived from the principle of (TMIITR + COMPANY FLAT RATE)/2. The year 1982 reflected as 50% HMTR (65 + 35)/2 and year 2002 as 25% (25+25)/2 as HMTR [Table 4 (f)].

Table 4 (h) indicates the various thresholds given to individuals. There was no threshold until 1991 and the tax payers were given various concessions such as the married person's allowance, education and medical allowances etc. In order to streamline and standardize the tax law, the government of Botswana replaced all these allowances with a threshold of P9000 where no tax is collected. This threshold was gradually increased to P25000 by 2002.

The number of taxpayers (tax returns assessed) is col-

Table 5. Revenue information

Year	At nominal value of money			NCOLI	At real value of money			Population
(a)	(b)	(c)	(d)	(e)	(f)	(g)	(h)	(i)
	Tax Rev	Total Rev.	GDP		Tax Rev.	Total Rev	GDP	
30-Jun	(Pm)	(Pm)	(Pm)		(Pm)	(Pm)	(Pm)	Million
1982	103.1	322.6	743.3	100.0	103	323	743	0.9
1983	98.2	392.6	920.5	109.0	90	360	844	0.9
1984	139.9	563.1	1106.0	119.1	117	473	929	0.9
1985	256.9	802.9	1170.9	130.1	197	617	900	0.9
1986	324.6	1092.2	4516.0	141.2	230	774	3198	1.3
1987	553.2	1462.9	4442.0	154.9	357	944	2868	1.3
1988	741.2	1693.5	6170.1	168.0	441	1008	3673	1.4
1989	989.8	2446.4	10038.0	187.3	528	1306	5359	1.4
1990	1038.3	2604.2	6690.5	207.2	501	1257	3229	1.4
1991	1400.4	3263.1	8343.0	232.0	604	1407	3596	1.5
1992	1201.1	3999.6	8977.6	272.3	441	1469	3297	1.5
1993	1304.8	4552.2	11257.3	311.6	419	1461	3613	1.5
1994	1428.7	5127.1	12100.0	343.1	416	1494	3527	1.5
1995	1423.0	4594.0	12530.3	377.8	377	1216	3317	1.5
1996	1160.9	5143.4	14631.0	417.0	278	1233	3509	1.5
1997	1245.5	5352.7	18015.1	454.1	274	1179	3967	1.5
1998	1947.2	7677.6	20162.6	481.0	405	1596	4192	1.5
1999	1987.0	7536.8	21523.9	514.3	386	1465	4185	1.5
2000	2592.8	11837.1	28636.5	568.8	456	2081	5035	1.5
2001	3422.4	12926.7	31922.1	602.5	568	2146	5298	1.7
2002	3703.4	14226.6	36337.5	655.9	565	2169	5540	1.8

Note: (a) Year; (b) Income tax revenue at nominal value of money; (c) Total revenue at nominal value of money; (d) GDP at nominal value of money; (e) National cost of living index; (f) Income tax revenue at real value of the money; (g) Total revenue at the real value of the money; (h) GDP at the real value of the money; (i) Population of the country.

lected from the annual reports of the department of taxes. For the years 1982-1885 and 1987-1990, the details of tax payers were not available (NA) and others are shown in Table 4 (i). The highest tax returns (18,462) were assessed in the year 2000, when HMTR and ATR were at their minimum. This may be an indication that low tax rates lead to savings, development and income generation.

Revenue information

The revenue information is classified into two categories, namely; revenue at nominal value of money and revenue at real value of money.

Table 5 (b), (c) and (d) record the tax revenue, total revenue and GDP respectively of the year. These figures show the face value of money which we call nominal value of the money. Due to inflation, the national cost of living index (NCOLI) gradually increased from 100 in 1982 to 655.9 by 2002. In other words, P6.55 in 2002 equaled P1.00 in 1982. The NCOLI was applied to the nominal values of income tax, revenue and GDP to determine the real value of money. Columns (f), (g) and (h) respectively highlight the real value of tax revenue, total revenue and GDP. Column (i) indicates the total population of the country at the specific year of study.

Income tax revenue, total revenue and GDP gradually increased in both nominal value and real value of money. Population also gradually increased. In the nominal value of money, there is an absolute increase by 35.92 times in tax revenue, 44.01 times in total revenue and 48.89 times in GDP when compared to the base year 1982 to that of the latest year under study (2002). One should not jump to the conclusion that the country has tremendously improved its tax revenue, total revenue and GDP generation. These results may be the effect of inflation that prevailed in Botswana. Hence we have to delink the effect of inflation by application of NCOLI.

Over these 21 years, the country could increase the real value of the money by 5.51 times in tax revenue, 6.72 times in total revenue and 7.46 times in GDP. Growth is noticed in all areas of study but not at a commendable scale. It was noticed that the population of the country doubled during the 21 years of study.

The main issue of this research is to find out the effect of income tax rates over generation of tax revenue, total revenue and GDP under the situations of nominal and real value of money. The study has to further classify the ef-

Table 6. Impact of high marginal and average tax rates.

Year	At higher marginal tax rates (HTMR)							At average tax rates (ATR)						
(a)	(b) (Pm)	(c) (Pm)	(d) (Pm)	(e) %	(f) %	(g) (000)	(h) (Pm)	(i) (Pm)	(j) (Pm)	(k) (Pm)	(l) %	(m) %	(n) (000)	(o) (Pm)
1982	2.06	6.5	14.9	0.6	0.3	NA	2.3	2.84	8.9	21	0.9	0.4	NA	3.2
1983	1.96	7.9	18.4	0.5	0.2	NA	2.2	2.81	11.2	26	0.7	0.3	NA	3.1
1984	2.95	11.9	23.3	0.5	0.3	NA	3.3	4.15	16.7	33	0.7	0.4	NA	4.6
1985	5.41	16.9	24.7	0.7	0.5	NA	6.0	7.61	23.8	35	0.9	0.7	NA	8.5
1986	6.83	23.0	95.1	0.6	0.2	0.4	5.3	9.62	32.4	134	0.9	0.2	0.6	7.4
1987	11.65	30.8	93.5	0.8	0.3	NA	9.0	16.39	43.3	132	1.1	0.4	NA	13
1988	15.6	35.7	129.9	0.9	0.3	NA	11.1	21.96	50.2	183	1.3	0.4	NA	16
1989	20.84	51.5	211.3	0.9	0.2	NA	14.9	29.33	72.5	297	1.2	0.3	NA	21
1990	21.86	54.8	140.9	0.8	0.3	1.7	15.6	30.76	77.2	198	1.2	0.5	2.3	22
1991	35.01	81.6	208.6	1.1	0.4	2.3	23.3	44.81	104.4	267	1.4	0.5	3.0	30
1992	30.03	100.0	224.4	0.8	0.3	2.3	20.0	38.44	128.0	287	1.0	0.4	2.9	26
1993	32.62	113.8	281.4	0.7	0.3	1.9	21.7	41.75	145.7	360	0.9	0.4	2.5	28
1994	35.72	128.2	302.5	0.7	0.3	2.7	23.8	45.72	164.1	387	0.9	0.4	3.5	31
1995	51.75	167.1	455.6	1.1	0.4	3.7	34.5	66.96	216.2	590	1.5	0.5	4.8	45
1996	42.21	187.0	532.0	0.8	0.3	2.4	28.1	54.63	242.0	689	1.1	0.4	3.1	36
1997	49.82	214.1	720.6	0.9	0.3	3.2	33.2	62.28	267.6	901	1.2	0.3	4.0	42
1998	77.89	307.1	806.5	1	0.4	4.0	51.9	97.36	383.9	1008	1.3	0.5	5.4	65
1999	79.48	301.5	861.0	1.1	0.4	4.6	53.0	99.35	376.8	1076	1.3	0.5	5.8	66
2000	103.71	473.5	1145.5	0.9	0.4	5.6	69.1	129.64	591.9	1432	1.1	0.5	7.0	86
2001	136.90	517.1	1276.9	1.1	0.4	8.3	80.5	171.12	646.3	1596	1.3	0.5	10.4	101
2002	148.14	569.1	1453.5	1	0.4	14.9	82.3	185.17	711.3	1817	1.3	0.5	18.6	103

Note: Impact of 1% of income tax rate (ITR) at nominal value of money (NVM). HMTR: (a) Year; (b) Income tax revenue; (c) Total revenue; (d) GDP; (e) Tax revenue over total revenue; (f) Tax revenue over GDP; (g) Per tax return (h) per person based on population. ATR: (i) Income tax revenue; (j) Total revenue; (k) GDP; (i) Percentage of Income tax revenue over total revenue; (m) Percentage of income tax revenue over GDP; (n) Per tax return ; (o) Per person based on population.

fect of HMTR and ATR on the tax revenue, total revenue and GDP.

Under each category of NVM and RVM, the research concentrates on the effect of 1% of ITR over income tax revenue, total revenue, GDP, percentage of tax revenue over total revenue. Percentage of tax revenue over GDP, tax collected per tax return and tax collected per person were based on the total population.

The above results will be compared when lower and higher tax rates were prevailing in Botswana during the period of study to determine whether higher tax rates lead to economic development in the developing nations of Africa, like Botswana.

Impact of income tax rates (ITR) on various factors under study at nominal value of money based on HMTR and ATR

Table 6 highlights the impact of 1% of income tax rate on the tax revenue, total revenue, GDP, percentage tax revenue over total revenue, percentage of tax revenue over GDP, tax collection per tax return and per person based on population, as based upon the nominal value of the money.

Nominal value of money at HMTR

Income tax revenue: Generally income tax revenue occupies a major role in the total revenue of the country; hence the effect of 1% of ITR at HMTR is tested and presented in Table 6 (b). The principle applied is:

1% effect of HMTR = Tax revenue/HMTR (iv)

In 1982 the effect of 1% HMTR = P103.1/50 = P2.06m
In 2002 the effect of 1% HMTR = P3703.0/25 = P148.14m

As the HMTR is reduced from 50 to 25%, the tax collection is gradually increased and it confirmed that the effect of 1% ITR is more effective at reduced HMTR.

Total revenue: Table 6 (c) reveals the effect of 1% of ITR on the total revenue generation. At higher tax rates, the revenue generation is lesser per 1% of ITR when compared to lower tax rates. The principle applied here is:

1% effect of HMTR = Total revenue/HMTR (v)

In 1982 the effect of 1% HMTR = P322.6/50 = P6.5m
In 2002 the effect of 1% HMTR = P14226.6/25 = P569.1m.

In 1982, the revenue generated per 1% of tax rate is P6.5m, whereas in 2002 it registered P569.1m at the lower tax rates. This test also indicated the higher the tax rates, the lower the total revenue and vice versa. Lower income tax rates generate higher revenue which will add to the economic development of the country.

Effect of 1% of ITR on GDP

Column (d) of Table 6 reflects the effect of 1% of ITR on GDP of Botswana. The principle applied here is:

1% effect of HTMR = GDP/HTMR (vi)

In 1982 = P743.3/50 = P14.9m
In 2002 = P36337.5/25 = P1453.5m

In this test also, the lower HMTR lead to high GDP. In the year 1982, 1% of ITR has a total of P14.9 m GDP whereas in 2002, it has achieved P1453.5 m. There is a gradual increase of GDP when ITR is gradually reduced. This test also proved that the lower the HTMR the higher the GDP through economic growth.

Effect of 1% of ITR on the tax revenue over total revenue

This test reveals the correlative effect of tax revenue over the total revenue. The principle applied here is:

{(Tax revenue/Total revenue)*100}HMTR (vii)

To test the principle years 1982 and 2002 figures of Table 5 (b) and (c) are taken:

1982 = {(103.1/322.6)*100}/50 = 0.6%
2002 = {(3703.4/14226.6)*100}25 =1%

This test also indicated that the lower the tax rate, the higher the tax collection per 1% of ITR. Column (e) of Table 6 revealed that there is a gradual increase in percentage when there is a gradual decrease in HMTR.

Effect of 1% of ITR on tax revenue over GDP

This test pinpoints the relative effect of tax revenue over GDP at 1% of tax rate. The principle applied here is:

{(Tax revenue/GDP)*100}HMTR (viii)

To test the principle years 1982 and 2002 figures of Table 5 (c) and (d) are taken.

1982 = {(103.1/743.3)*100}/50 = 0.3%
2002 = {(3703.4/36337.5)*100}25 =0.4%

This test also indicated that the lower the tax rate, the higher the revenue generation per 1% of ITR. Column (f) of Table 6 revealed that there is a gradual increase in percentage, when there is a gradual decrease in HMTR. Over 21 years the change is only 0.1%.

Effect of 1% of ITR per tax return

Number of tax returns assessed or number of persons taxed is taken as a basis for the study of effect of 1% ITR in relation to tax revenue generation. The data for the number of persons' taxed for years from 1982 to 1985 and from 1987 to 1989 was unavailable. The first available year is 1986, where 17,451 tax returns were assessed when the tax threshold is zero. Hence many more tax returns were furnished than in 2002. This is due to the high threshold given in 2002 and because the majority of small income groups were not liable to submit tax returns. Hence the tax returns almost reduced to 50%. However the principle applied here is:

(Tax revenue/No of returns assessed)/HTMR (ix)

For 1986 = {(P324 600 000/17451)/47.5 = P400
For 2002 = (3 703 400 000/9955)/25 =P14 900

In this test also, it is proved that the lower the tax rates, the higher the tax revenue per tax return.

Tax collection per 1% of HMTR /population

The effect of 1% ITR based on population is calculated as the principle:

(Tax revenue/Population)/HMTR (x)

In 1982 = (P103.1/0.9)/50 = P2.3 m
In 2002 = (P3 703m)/1.8)/25 = P82.3 m

This test also proved that lower HMTR has given rise to more tax per 1% of HMTR/per person.

As mentioned earlier, the effect of tax rate is to be tested at HMTR and ATR. So far we have seen the effect of HMTR and the following investigation is to find out the effect of 1% of ATR on all variables such as:

Real value of money (RVM) at ATR

Income tax revenue

The principle applied is:

1% effect of ATR = Tax revenue/ATR (xi)

In 1982 the effect of 1% ATR = P103.1/36.5 = P2.84m
In 2002 the effect of 1% ATR = P3703/20 = P185.17m

Total revenue

Table 7(j) reveals the effect of 1% of ITR on the total revenue generation. At higher average tax rates, the revenue

Table 7. Real value of money (RVM) at HMTR and ATR.

Year	At higher marginal income tax rates							At average income tax rates						
(a)	(b)	(c)	(d)	(e)	(f)	(g)	(h)	(i)	(j)	(k)	(l)	(m)	(n)	*(o)*
						(000)							(000)	
1982	2.06	6.5	14.9	0.6	0.3	NA	2.3	2.84	8.9	20.5	0.9	0.4	NA	3.2
1983	108	7.2	16.9	0.5	0.2	NA	2.0	2.57	10.3	24.1	0.7	0.3	NA	2.9
1984	2.47	10	19.6	0.5	0.3	NA	2.7	3.48	14.0	27.5	0.7	0.4	NA	3.9
1985	4.16	13	18.9	0.7	0.5	NA	4.6	5.85	18.3	26.7	0.9	0.6	NA	6.5
1986	4.84	16.3	67.3	0.6	0.2	0.3	3.7	6.81	22.9	94.8	0.9	0.2	0.4	5.2
1987	7.52	19.9	60.4	0.8	0.3	NA	5.8	10.58	28.0	85	1.1	0.4	NA	8.1
1988	9.29	21.2	77.3	0.9	0.3	NA	6.6	13.07	29.9	109	1.3	0.4	NA	9.3
1989	11.13	27.5	112.8	0.9	0.2	NA	7.9	15.66	38.7	159	1.2	0.3	NA	11.2
1990	10.55	26.5	68.0	0.8	0.3	0.8	7.5	14.85	37.2	95.7	1.2	0.5	1.1	10.6
1991	15.09	35.2	89.9	1.1	0.4	1.0	10.1	19.32	45.0	115	1.4	0.5	1.3	12.9
1992	11.03	36.7	82.4	0.8	0.3	0.8	7.4	14.12	47.0	106	1.0	0.4	1.1	9.4
1993	10.47	36.5	90.3	0.7	0.3	0.6	7.0	13.4	46.8	116	0.9	0.4	0.8	8.9
1994	10.41	37.4	88.2	0.7	0.3	0.8	6.9	13.33	47.8	113	0.9	0.4	1.0	8.9
1995	13.70	44.2	120.6	1.1	0.4	1.0	9.1	17.72	57.2	156	1.5	0.5	1.3	11.8
1996	10.12	44.9	127.6	0.8	0.3	0.6	6.7	13.1	58.0	165	1.1	0.4	0.8	8.7
1997	10.97	47.1	158.7	0.9	0.3	0.7	7.3	13.71	59.0	198	1.2	0.3	0.9	9.1
1998	16.19	63.8	167.7	1.0	0.4	0.9	10.8	20.24	79.8	210	1.3	0.5	1.1	13.5
1999	15.45	58.6	167.4	1.1	0.4	0.9	10.3	19.32	73.3	209	1.3	0.5	1.1	12.9
2000	18.23	83.2	201.4	0.9	0.4	1.0	12.2	22.79	104.1	252	1.1	0.5	1.2	15.2
2001	22.72	85.8	211.9	1.1	0.4	1.4	13.4	28.4	107.3	265	1.3	0.5	1.7	16.7
2002	22.59	86.8	221.6	1.0	0.4	2.4	12.6	28.23	108.5	277	1.3	0.5	2.8	15.7

Note: Impact of 1% of ITR at RVM. HMTR: (a) Year; (b) Income tax revenue; (c) Total revenue; (d) GDP; (e) Tax revenue over total revenue; (f) Tax revenue over GDP; (g) Per tax return; (h) Per person based on population. ATR: (i) Income tax revenue; (j) Total revenue; (k) GDP; (l) Percentage of Income tax revenue over total revenue; (m) Percentage of income tax revenue over GDP; (n) Per tax return; (o) Per person based on population.

generation is lesser per 1% of ITR when compared to lower tax rates. The principle applied here is:

1% effect of ATR = Total revenue/ATR (xii)

In 1982 the effect of 1% ATR = P322.6/36.5 = P8.9m
In 2002 the effect of 1% ATR = P14226.6/20 = P711.3m

Effect of 1% of ITR on GDP

Column (k) of Table 7 reflects the effect of 1% of ITR on GDP of Botswana:

1% effect of ATR =GDP/ATR (xiii)

1982: 743.3/36.5 = P21m
2002: 36337.5/20 = P1817m

Effect of 1% of ITR on the tax revenue over total revenue

This test reveals the correlative effect of tax revenue over total revenue. The principle applied here is:

{(Tax revenue/Total revenue)*100} ATR (xiv)

To test the principle years 1982 and 2002 figures of Table 5 (f) and (g) are taken;

1982 = {(103.1/323)*100}/36.5 = 0.9%
2002 = {(3703.4/14226.6)*100}20 =1.3%

This test also indicated that the lower the tax rate, the higher the tax collection per 1% of ITR. Column (k) of Table 6 revealed that there is a gradual increase in percentage when there is a gradual decrease in ATR.

Effect of 1% of ITR on total revenue over GDP

This test pinpoints the relative effect of total revenue over GDP at 1% of tax rate. The principle applied here is:

{(Total revenue/GDP)*100}ATR (xv)

To test the principle years 1982 and 2002 figures of Table 5 (c) and (d) are taken.
1982 = {(103.1/743.3)*100}/36.25 = 0.4%

2002 = {(3703.4/36337.5)*100}20 =0.5%

This test supports the earlier conclusion that the lower the tax rates, the higher the revenue generation per 1% of ITR. Column (f) of Table 6 revealed that there is a gradual increase in percentage when there is a gradual decrease in ATR. Over 21 years the change is only 0.1%

Effect of 1% of ITR per tax return:

The principle applied here is:

(Tax revenue/No of returns assessed)/ATR (xvi)

For 1986 = {(P326 600 000/17451)/33.75 = P600
For 2002 = (3 703 400 000/9955)/20 =P18600

This test also proved that lower tax rates generate, the higher the tax revenue per tax return.

Tax collection per 1% of ATR /Population

The population of the country is doubled during these 21 years period. The effect of 1% ITR based on population is calculated as the principle:

(Tax revenue/Population)/ATR (xvii)

In 1982 = (P103.1/0.9)/36.5 = P3.2
In 2002 = (P3703.4/1.8)/20 = P103m.

This test also concluded that a lower ATR has given rise to more tax per 1% of ATR/per person.

Impact of income tax rates over income tax revenue, total revenue, GDP, tax collection per person, per tax payer at real value of money

The fourth hypothesis investigates the effect of the real value of money by stating: "At the real value of money (R-VM), 1% of income tax rate (both at higher marginal tax rate (HMTR) and average tax rate (ATR) leads to lesser (a) tax revenue (b) total revenue (c) GDP and (d) tax collection per person and per taxpayer when compared to lower ITR with higher ITR" The results obtained at the nominal value of the money may be totally different when we study the application of theory of real value of money (RVM). Table 7 portrays the effect of 1% of ITR at RVM by taking the variables of HTMR and ATR.

Let us analyze the various variables by applying the principles mentioned under H3 replacing the NVM by the RVM.

EFFECT OF 1% ATR TAKING THE RVM

Real value of money (RVM) at HMTR: Income tax revenue

The tax revenue at real value in 1982 will be the same as nominal value of money; as 1982 is the base year where the NCOLI is deemed to be 100, whereas the RVM in 20-02 is P565m. At the real value the income tax collection is hardly increased by five times (Table 5 (f)). The effect of 1% of ITR at HMTR is derived by the principle:

1% effect of HMTR =Tax Revenue/HMTR (xviii)

In 1982 the effect of 1% HMTR = P103/50 = P2.06m
In 2002 the effect of 1% HMTR = P565/25 = P22.59m

As the HMTR is reduced from 50 to 25%, the tax collection at the RVM is gradually increased at a lower growth rate when compared to NVM. It is confirmed that the effect of 1% ITR is more effective at the reduced HMTR under RVM also [Table 7 (b)].

Total revenue

Table 7 (c) reveals the effect of 1% of ITR on the total revenue generation. At higher tax rates, the revenue generation is less per 1% of ITR when compared to lower tax rates. The principle applied here is:

1% effect of HMTR = Total Revenue/HMTR (xix)

In 1982 the effect of 1% HMTR = P323/50 = P6.5m
In 2002 the effect of 1% HMTR = P2169/25 = P86.8m

In 1982, the revenue generated on the basis of RVM per 1% of tax rate is P6.5m, whereas in 2002 it registered P-86.8 m at the lower tax rates. This test also indicated that the higher the tax rates, the lower the total revenue and vice versa.

Effect of 1% of ITR on GDP

Column (d) of Table 7 reflects the effect of 1% of ITR on GDP of Botswana. In this test also, the lower HMTR lead to higher GDP. In the year 1982, 1% of ITR has a total of P14.9m GDP whereas in 2002, it achieved P221.6m. The growth rate compared to NVM is not as encouraging although there is a gradual increase of GDP when ITR is gradually reduced. This test also proved that the lower the HTMR the higher the economic growth.

Effect of 1% of ITR on the tax revenue over total revenue

This test reveals the correlative effect of tax revenue on the total revenue. The principle applied here is:

{(Tax revenue/Total revenue)*100}HMTR (xx)

To test the principle years 1982 and 2002 figures of Table 5 (f) and (g) are taken.

1982 = {(103/323)*100}/50 = 0.6%
2002 = {(565/2169)*100}25 =1%

This test also indicated that the lower the tax rate, the higher the tax collection per 1% of ITR. Column (e) of Table 7 revealed that there is a gradual increase in percentage when there is a gradual decrease in HMTR.

Effect of 1% of ITR on tax revenue over GDP

This test pinpoints the relative effect of tax revenue over GDP at 1% of tax rate. The principle applied here is:

{(Tax revenue/GDP)*100}HMTR (xxi)

To test the principle years 1982 and 2002 figures of Table 5 (c) and (d) are taken.

1982 = {(103.1/743)*100}/50 = 0.3%
2002 = {(565/2169)*100}25 =0.4%

This test also indicated that the lower the tax rate, the higher the revenue generation per 1% of ITR. Column (f) of Table 7 revealed that there is a gradual increase in percentage when there is a gradual decrease in HMTR.

Effect of 1% of ITR per tax return

The principle applied:

(Tax revenue/No of returns assessed)/HTMR (xxii)

For 1986 = {(P230 000 000/17451)/47.5 = P300
For 2002 = (565 000 000/9955)/25 =P2.3

In this test also, it was proved that the lower the tax rates, the higher the tax revenue per tax return.

Tax collection per 1% of HMTR /population

The population of the country doubled during this 21 year period.

The effect of 1% ITR based on population is calculated as the principle:

(Tax revenue/population)/HMTR (xxiii)

In 1982 = (P103.1/0.9)/50 = P2.3m
In 2002 = (P565m/1.8)/25 = P12.6m.

This test also suggested that lower HMTR has given rise to more tax per 1% of HMTR per person.

As mentioned earlier, the effect of tax rate will be tested at HMTR and ATR. So far, we have seen the effect of HMTR. The following investigation is to find out the effect of 1% of ATR on all variables such as:

Real value of money at ATR

Income tax revenue: It is reiterated that income tax revenue occupies a major role in the total revenue of the country, hence the effect of 1% of ITR at ATR is tested and presented in column (i) of Table 6. The principle applied is:

1% effect of ATR = tax revenue/ATR (xiv)

In 1982 the effect of 1% ATR = P103.1/36.5 = P2.84m
In 2002 the effect of 1% ATR = P565.0/20 = P28, 23m

As the ATR is reduced from 36.5 to 20%, the tax collection is gradually increased and it confirmed that the effect of 1% ITR is more effective at a reduced ATR.

Total revenue: Table 6 (j) reveals the effect of 1% of ITR on the total re-venue generation. At higher average tax rates, the reve-nue generation is less per 1% of ITR when compared to lower tax rates. The principle applied here is:

1% effect of ATR = total revenue/ATR (xxv)

In 1982 the effect of 1% ATR = P322.6/36.5 = P8.9m
In 2002 the effect of 1% ATR = P2169/20 = P108.5m

In 1982, the revenue generated per 1% of tax rate is P8-.9m, whereas in 2002 it is registered as P711.3m at a lower tax rates. This test also indicated that higher the tax rates, the lower the total revenue and vice versa. Lower average income tax rates generate higher revenue which will add to the economic development of the country.

Effect of 1% of ITR on GDP

Column (k) of Table 6 reflects the effect of 1% of ITR on GDP of Botswana. In this test also, the lower ATR lead to a higher GDP. In the year 1982, 1% of ITR has a total of P21m GDP whereas in 2002, it has achieved P277m. There is a gradual increase of GDP when ITR is gradually reduced. This test also proved that the lower the ATR the higher the economic growth.

Effect of 1% of ITR on the tax revenue over total revenue

This test reveals the correlative effect of tax revenue over the total revenue. The principle applied here is:

{(Tax revenue/Total revenue)*100}ATR (xxvi)

To test the principle years 1982 and 2002, figures of Table 5 (b) and (c) were taken.

Table 8. Analysis of the final results at nominal and real value of money

Final test Of hypothesis for 1% of ITR	Nominal value				Real value			
	HMTR		ATR		HMTR		ATR	
	TTR	LTR	TTR	LTR	TTR	LTR	TTR	LTR
H1. Income tax revenue (Pm)	2.06	148.14	2.84	185.2	2.06	25.59	2.84	28.23
H2. Total revenue (Pm)	6.5	569.1	8.9	711.3	8.5	86.6	8.9	108.5
H3. GDP (Pm)	14.9	1453.5	21	1817	14.9	221.6	20.5	277
H4. % of TxR/TR (P'000)	0.6	1.0	0.9	1.3	0.6	1.0	0.9	1.3
H5. % of tax revenue over GDP	0.3	0.4	0.4	0.5	0.3	0.4	0.4	0.5
H6. Per tax return (P000)	0.4	14.9	0.6	18.6	0.3	2.4	0.4	2.8
H7. Per person based (Pm)	2.3	82.3	3.2	103	2.3	12.6	3.2	15.7

Note: TTR = Top tax rate; LTR = Low tax rate

1982 = {(103.1/322.6)*100}/36.5 = 0.1%
2002 = {(565/2169)*100}20 =1.3%

This test also indicated that the lower the tax rate, the higher the tax collection per 1% of ITR. Column (k) of Table 7 revealed that there is a gradual increase in percentage when there is a gradual decrease in ATR.

Effect of 1% of ITR on total revenue over GDP

This test pinpoints the relative effect of total revenue over GDP at 1% of tax rate. The principle applied here is:

{(Total revenue/GDP)*100}ATR (xxvii)

To test the principle years 1982 and 2002 figures of Table 5 (c) and (d) are taken.

1982 = {(103.1/743.3)*100}/36.25 = 0.4%
2002 = {(565/5540)*100}20 =0.5%

This test also indicated that the lower the tax rate, the higher the revenue generation per 1% of ITR. Column (f) of Table 6 revealed that there is a gradual increase in percentage when there is a gradual decrease in ATR. Over 21 years, the change is only 0.1%

Effect of 1% of ITR per tax return

Number of tax returns assessed or number of persons taxed was taken as a basis for the study of effect of 1% ITR in relation to tax revenue generation. As stated earlier, a few years' data was unavailable. The first available year is 1986 where 17451 tax returns were assessed and the threshold was zero. Hence, there will be more tax returns compared to year 2002. In the year 2002, the highest threshold was given to an individual; hence the majority of the tax payers need no subject to tax returns. Hence the tax returns almost reduced to 36.5%. However the principle applied here is:

(Tax revenue/No of returns assessed)/ATR (xxviii)

For 1986 = {(P230 000 000/17451)/33.75 = P400
For 2002 = (565 000 000/9955)/20 =P2800

In this test also, it is proved that lower the tax rates, the higher the tax revenue per tax return.

Tax collection per 1% of ATR /population

The population of the country doubled during these 21 years period.

The effect of 1% ITR based on population is calculated as the principle:

(Tax revenue/Population)/ATR (xxix)

In 1982 = (P103.1/0.9)/36.5 = P3.2m
In 2002 = (P565/1.8)/20 = P15.7m.

This test also proved that lower ATR has given rise to a higher tax per 1% of ATR per person.

Table 8 pinpoints the effect of 1% of income tax rate under nominal value and real value of money taking into account the higher marginal tax rate and average tax rate. Under each category, the high tax and low tax rate effects are also shown. In all investigations, it revealed that the low tax rates have shown better results than top tax rates.

Conclusions

Developed nations(Hypothesis 1)

The top marginal income tax rate is located in China (4-5%) and the lowest was 29% in Canada. In lower marginal tax rates, the highest was charged by Canada (16%) and lowest was in China (5%). The maximum company tax was charged by USA at 35% and the lowest was Canada at 21%.

The impact of income tax revenue over the GDP varies from 4 to 12%, lowest being from Japan and the highest was from USA. The share of income tax revenue over its total revenue is impressive in developed nations ranging from 78% (China) to 27% (UK). Income tax collection per head varies from $3956.09 (USA) to $84.81 (China). The highest income tax collection per head is recorded in USA.

It is not a universal truth that developed nations charged higher ITR. There are instances where a few developing nations such as South Africa and Zimbabwe charged top marginal tax rate at 45%. Hence the first hypothesis is nullified as developing nations have been charging higher tax rates compared to developed nations.

Developing nations(Hypothesis 2)

Except Malawi (36.5%) and Angola (36%), the impact of income tax revenue over the nations GDP is not impresssive in developing nations. The lowest impact of income tax over GDP is located in Mozambique (2%), Botswana (3%) and Malawi (4%).

High impact of income tax revenue over the total revenue of the countries is located in countries such as Angola (75%), South Africa (57%), Zimbabwe (51%), Malawi (42%), Zambia (36%), and Namibia (30%). The lowest impact of income tax over its total revenue was traced to Botswana (6%) and Namibia (6%).

Among the SADC countries, the highest income tax per head is collected in South Africa ($387.79) and the lowest is from Mozambique ($2.93). The more direct effect of income tax revenue located over the total revenue and tax collection per person in developed nations compared to developing nations. Based on the above analysis, it can be stated that the majority of developing nations are depending on income tax revenue for their economic development. There is no uniformity in the percentage of income tax revenue collection over GDP in developing nations. It varied from 2 to 50%. Whereas the developed nations' income tax influence variance between the lowest and highest does not depend as much on GDP. It ranged from 4 to 12% whereas in developing nations the variance was from 2 to 50%.

Both developing nations and developed nations recorded the highest percentage of income tax revenue over the total revenue in the range of 75 to 78% and the lowest is between 12 and 27% from developing and developed nations [Table 3 (e)].

There is a wide disparity of income tax revenue collection per head both in the developing nations and developed nations. The range is high in the developed nations. This may be due to a huge population in China [Table 3 (e)]. The majority of developing and developed nations depend on tax revenue. It was observed that developing nations compared to developed nations depend more on income tax revenue. The range of income tax influence is greater in developing nations than in developed nations.

Both types of nations (developing and developed nations recorded highest percentage of income tax reve-nue over total revenue and at the same time it was located that there is a wide variation in income tax collection per head.

Hypothesis 3

The research on hypothesis of ITR influence in developing nations taking case study that the lower the ITR at NVM under the variable of HTMR proved that the higher the tax collection, revenue generation, increase in GDP, percentage of tax revenue over total revenue, percentage of tax revenue over GDP, tax collection per tax return and tax collection per head. This hypothesis is tested at the NVM, taking HMTR and ATR. Income tax revenue, total revenue and GDP are gradually increased at NVM. When HMTR is reduced from 50 to 25%, the tax collection increased and it is confirmed that the effect of 1% of ITR is more effective at the reduced HTMR. Lower income tax rates generated more revenue for the economic development. The effect of 1% reduction of ITR has given raise to increase in tax revenue, GDP, total revenue, tax collection per return and per person at lower HTMR.
Average Tax Rates (ATR) is also taken into account to find out the effect of reduction in ATR in tax collection, revenue generation, increase in GDP, influence of 1% decrease in tax rates over revenue generation, GDP etc., it is located to confirm or to disprove the hypothesis that higher tax rates lead to higher effect is disproved. Lower tax rates have more impact on the tax collection, generation of total revenue, and increase in economic growth.

Hypothesis 4

This study the effect of RVM and assumed that higher tax rates lead to lower tax collection, revenue generation, GDP etc. Even in this study of RVM, the lower tax rates have lead to higher tax collection, revenue generation and economic development. Table 8 has given the final analysis showing that the lower tax rate (LTR) has given more effect on income tax revenue, total revenue, GDP, percentage of tax revenue over total revenue, tax revenue over GDP, tax per tax return and per person. This was proved in both nominal and real value of money in the coverage of higher marginal tax rates and average tax rates.

The above research and analysis disproves the earlier theory that higher tax rates lead to economic development. In order to disprove this theory in developing nations such as Botswana, there is a greater impact of the lower income tax rates on the economic development of the country through a higher tax revenue collection, generation of higher revenue and increase in GDP.

Limitations and suggestions for future research

The major limitation of the study is the incompleteness of data on income tax of the SADC countries under study. Nevertheless, the information available for more than 50% of the countries will represent the whole region as Bobbie (1973) observed, that a sample from a population will accurately describe the total population. A sample of one developing country like Botswana may not be a universal truth; hence it is suggested to take up a cluster of developing nations and developed nations for further research at a large scale.

REFERENCES

Akira Y (2003). Taxation and growth with overlapping generations. J. Public Financ. 87 (3/4): 467-487.

Babbie ER (1973). Survey Research Methods Wadsworth Publishing Company Inc. California.

Bank of Botswana (1985-2004), Annual Reports.

Bartik T (1994a). "Jobs, Productivity and LOCAL Economic Development: What Implications Does Economic Research have for the role of Government: National Tax. J. (47): 847-862.

Bartik T (1994b). "Taxes and Economic Development: What do we know and what can we know?" Proceedings of Eigthy Seventh Annual Conference on Taxation (Nov. 13): 102-106, Charleston, SC, National Tax Association. Tax Institute of America.

Boadway RB (1982). Public Sector Economics, Little, Brown and Company.

Burgess Ronald (1993). Public Revenue without Taxation, Shepheard-Walwyn (Publishers) Ltd, London.

Central Statistics Office (2001). Statistical Bulletin, (26,) No.1.

Department of Taxes, Botswana (1990-2004). Annual Reports

Europa Publications (1990-2004). Regional Survey of the World, Africa, South of Sahara. Taylor & Francis Group.

European Chemical News (2004). Tax Carrot hangs for Enterprise. 80 (2082): 29-34.

Fossati (1992). "From Personal to Indirect Taxation: A general Equilibrium approach", in Galeotti G, Graham J (1994). "The International Handbook of Corporate and Personal Taxes", Chapman & Hall.

Government of Botswana (1973 – 2002). Income Tax Act of 1973 and all amended Acts up to 2002.

Henry J, Aron, William G, Gale (Ed) (1996). Economic Effects of Fundamental Tax Reform. Brookings Institution Press, Washington D.C.

Holger S (2003). Capital tax reform, corporate finance, and economic growth and welfare. J. Econ. Dyn. Control 28 (3): 595-615.

Jerry MR (1983). Dictionary of Business and Management, Wiely-International, New York.

John DW, Pamela H (2003). Issues in Analyzing the Macroeconomic Effects of Tax Policy. National .Tax .J. 56 (3): 447-462.

Lewis SR Jr. (1984). Taxation for Development: Principles and Application. New York: Oxford University Press.

Lipsey RG (1989). An Introduction to Positive Economics, Weidenfeld, Nicolson, London, Seventh Edition.

Maisto G (1988). Tax Treatment of Cost-Contribution Arrangements, Kluwer Law & Taxation Publishers, Boston.

Marrelli M (1992). Design and Reform of Taxation Policy, Kluwer Academic Publishers, the Netherlands.

Martin Z, George D (2003). Fiscal Policy and Economic Growth. J. Econ. Surveys. 17 (3) 397-418.

Olhoft RS (2003). Discussion of the effect of State Income Tax Apportionment and Tax Incentives on New Capital Expenditures. J. Am. Tax. Assoc. 25: 27-32.

Slemord J (2003). The Truth about Taxes and Economic Growth. Challenge. 46 (1): 5-14.

Swami BN (1995). Taxation, Inflation, Savings and Development: Case Study of Republic of Botswana. African Review of Money, Finance and Banking – a Supplementary Issue of "Savings and Development". 1 and 2.

Tetsuo O (2003). Environmental Tax Policy and Long-Run Economic Growth. Japanese Econ. Rev. 54 (2): 203-217.

Wasylenko M (1997). "Taxation and Economic Development: The State of the Economic Literature" New England Econ. Rev. March/April, 3-53.

World Bank (1991). Lessons of Tax Reform, World Bank Washington DC.

Corporate taxation and capital gains realization in Canada

Tao Zeng

Accounting School of Business and Economics, Wilfrid Laurier University, Waterloo, Ontario, Canada, N2L 3C5. E-mail: tzeng@wlu.ca.

In this paper, an empirical work is designed to test whether corporate capital gains realization is associated with corporate tax. Under Canadian tax rules, capital gains are taxed when a taxpayer realizes them, rather than at the time that those gains accrue. It was tested whether corporate tax status, including accumulated loss-carry-overs, affects the decision to realize capital gains. Using financial statements from Canadian corporations, this study finds that, after controlling for other factors, corporate capital gains realization is positively associated with loss-carry-overs accumulated from previous years, which generally supports the argument that corporations take into account their tax status when realizing capital gains. This study also finds that firms realize capital gains for financing purposes. However, this study does not find that firms realize capital gains to manage earnings.

Key words: Capital gains realization, tax rate, loss-carry-over.

INTRODUCTION

Capital gains realization by individuals has been studied extensively throughout the years (Eichner and Sinai, 2000; Seyhun and Skinner, 1994; Burman and Randolph, 1994; Burman et al., 1994; Cook and O'Hare, 1992; Badrinath and Lewellen, 1991; Auten et al., 1989; Auten and Clotfelter, 1982; Feldstein and Yitzhaki, 1978 etc.); Odean (1998) for example, shows that investors are more likely to sell loss investments in December than in other months; Jin (2006) provides evidence that tax-sensitive investors defer selling stocks that incurred large capital gains; and Chay et al. (2006) examine a type of distribution that is taxed as capital gains, rather than as dividends and find that ex-day return behaviour reflects the value of tax-timing capital gains.

However, relatively few studies have examined corporate capital gains realization (Desai and Gentry, 2003). Desai and Gentry (2003) examine how capital gains taxes affect a firm's decision to realize capital gains. Their time-series analysis of aggregated corporate realization behaviour demonstrates that capital gains taxes are negatively associated with realized capital gains. Their firm-level analysis of realization behaviour finds similar results. Despite receiving limited researches, the volume of corporate taxable capital gains realization in Canada is substantial. For example, data shows that taxable capital gains across all industries have averaged 70% of individual taxable capital gains, over the last fifteen years (Figure 3). In addition, a corporation's capital gains can be an important component of its income. Figure 2 shows that, over the last fifteen years, capital gains income comprised about 10 - 30% of total taxable income, across all industries. In this paper, it was empirically tested whether a corporation's capital gains realization decision is associated with its tax status and whether other factors significantly impact that decision.

Before 1972, Canada did not impose income tax on capital gains. Since that time, Canada has taxed varying percentages of capital gains on the basis of the realization principle. Under this principle, capital gains are taxed in the year they are realized[a]. Capital losses, if

a From 1972 to 1987, one-half of capital gains were taxable, and one-half of capital losses were deductible against taxable capital gains. In 1988 and 1989, two-thirds of capital gains were taxable, and two thirds of capital losses were deductible against taxable capital gains. From 1989 to February 2000, three-quarters of capital gains were taxable, and three-quarters of capital losses were deductible against taxable capital gains. From March 2000 to October 18, 2000, the inclusion rate for capital gains and the deduction rate for capital losses was reduced to two-third. Finally, this inclusion deduction rate was reduced to one-half.

incurred, could only be deducted against capital gains; they may not be deducted against other types of income[b]. If there are not sufficient capital gains in the year to offset the capital losses, the excess losses can be carried backward for 3 years, or carried forward indefinitely, to be deducted against capital gains realized in those years. Unlike U.S. tax rules on capital gains or losses, Canadian tax rules do not distinguish short term, and long term, status.

As in the literature, it does not have an explicit theoretical model of capital gains behaviour. It simply follow other studies (Auten et al., 1989) and argue that realizing capital gains has some economic value (e.g., an important source of internal financing) as holding assets with accrued gains. Hence the decision to realize the capital gains depends on whether the value of realizing those gains is greater than the costs, which include the capital gains taxes.

Based on the realization tax rule for capital gains and losses, taxes are incurred when taxpayers realize capital gains or losses, not when capital gains or losses are accrued. Constantinides (1983, 1984) argues that the realization tax rule provides a tax-timing option to taxpayers to realize losses whenever they occurs, but defer gains to another time. However, tax rule and transactions costs prevent investors from exploiting this tax-timing option fully.

This study seeks to test whether a corporate capital gains realization decision can be explained by tax incentives. In particular, it was test whether a corporation's accumulated capital loss-carry-overs can affect its decision to realize capital gains. If a corporation has loss-carry-overs from the previous years, it will realize capital gains to use those losses as soon as possible.

Furthermore, one important source of financing for the corporation is the selling of properties, marketable securities, and other investments, as well as selling discontinued operations or subsidiaries (Desai and Gentry, 2003; Bates, 2005). Bates (2005) finds that sales of corporate subsidiaries usually result in substantial cash remuneration. Similar to free cash flow from operations, cash proceeds from such sales have been reallocated to unfunded projects. Since capital gains arise from selling any of the above assets, this study also expects to find that a corporation may sell assets when it needs financing. In other words, the value of proceeds from sales is inversely related to the corporation's ability to generate free cash flow.

Finally, current studies find that firms use asset sales to manage earnings; however, the results are not conclusive. For example, Bartov (1993) demonstrates that firms time the sale of assets to smooth earnings. Herrmann et al. (2001) examine Japanese managers' use of income from selling assets and marketable securities to manage earnings. They find that firms with current performance below previous forecasts manage earnings upward by reporting higher income from asset sales. Nevertheless, Black et al (1998) examine asset sales in countries where asset revaluation is allowed (such as UK, Australia, and New Zealand). They find that firms in those countries do not appear to smooth earnings through asset sales. This study will add earnings (before capital gains or losses realization) into the model. If firms use asset sales to manage income, it is expected to find that firms with low earnings before asset sales will realize more capital gains, and vice versa.

Using SEDAR Canadian corporate financial reporting data, this study finds that a corporation's capital gains realization appears to be particularly shaped by tax incentives, that is, capital gains realization is positively associated with loss-carry-overs accumulated from previous years. In addition, a corporation's capital gains are generalized for financing purposes. However, the firms were not found to realize capital gains from asset sales to manage earnings.

This study seeks to assist corporate taxpayers, tax advisers, pension consultants, and others in making decisions on capital gains realization. This study is also of interest to policy- makers, to the extent that it assists them in understanding about how a corporation's capital gains realization is affected by the capital gains taxes, since significant tax dollars are involved.

In the next section, relevant literatures on corporate capital gains or losses realization will be reviewed.

LITERATURE REVIEW

Bull et al. (2004) study both corporate and individual capital gains/losses. They use the statistics and data from the Income Division of the IRS and show that capital realizations are persistent at the aggregate, and at the individual and corporate taxpayer level. They also show that for all corporations in the US, there is a striking run-up in capital gains realization in the late 1990s and a large decline in the early 2000s. This is consistent with this study of Canadian corporations in Figure 1. However, Bull et al (2004) only study the corporate capital gains behaviour at an aggregate level and not examine what factors determine the decision to realize capital gains.

Desai and Gentry (2003) examine how capital gains taxes affect a firm's decision to realize capital gains. Their time-series analysis of aggregated corporate realization behaviour demonstrates that capital gains taxes are negatively associated with realized capital gains. Their firm-level analysis of realization behaviour finds similar results. In their firm-level analysis, they regress capital gains on marginal tax rate, Tobin's Q, and firm size.

Auten et al. (1989) argue that previous studies on capital gains realization behaviour have been hampered

[b] One except to this rule is the capital loss incurred from disposition of the shares or bonds of a small business company. This capital loss could be deducted against any types of income.

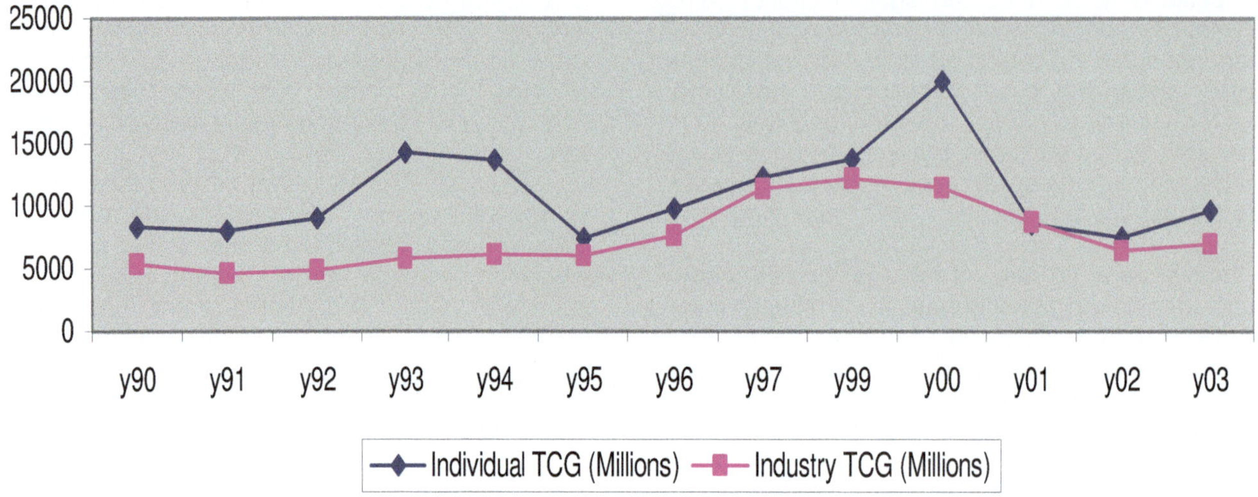

Figure 1. Individual and industrial taxation capital gains realization, 1990 - 2003.
Source: Statistics Canada.

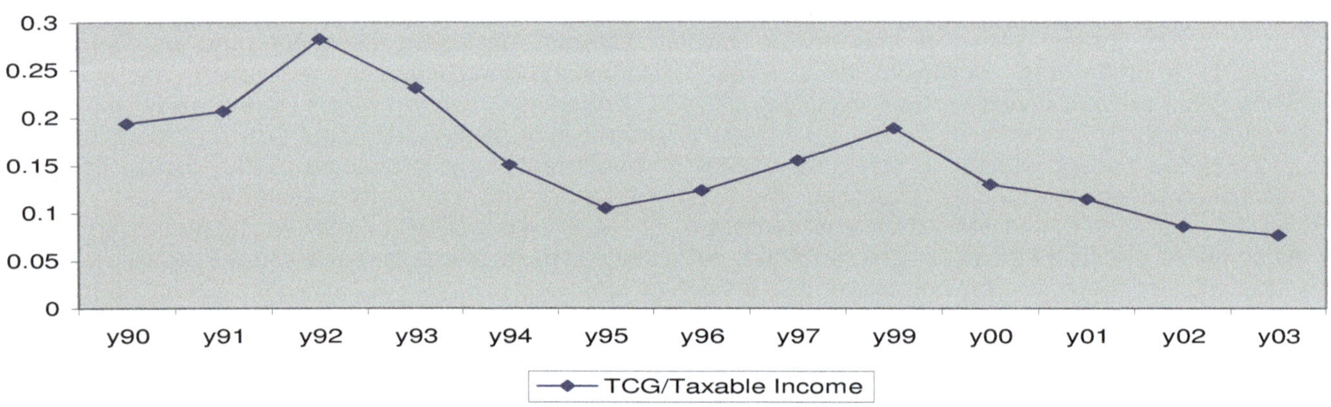

Figure 2. Ratio of Taxable Capital Gains to Taxable Income, 1990 - 2003.
Source: Statistics Canada.

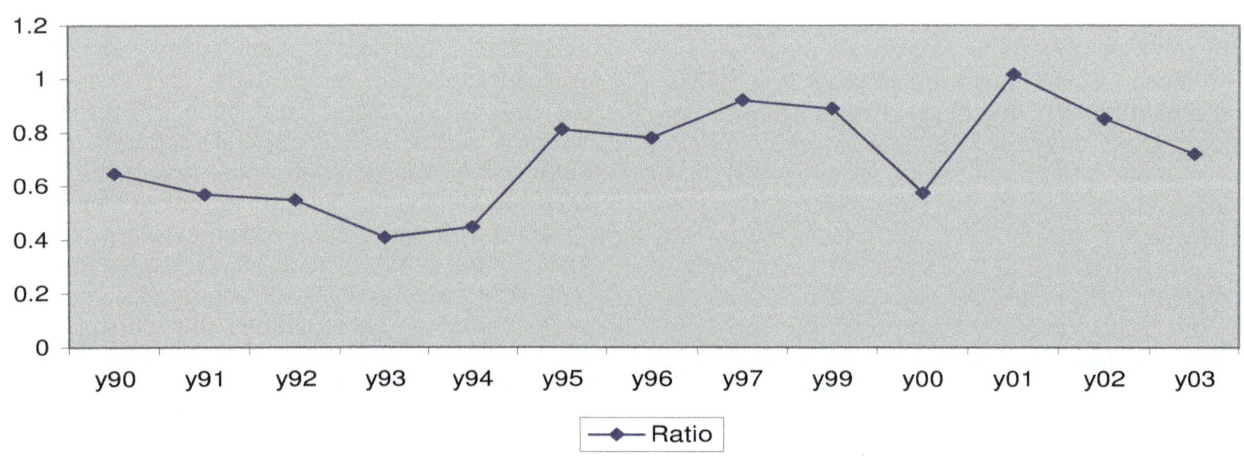

Figure 3. Ratio of industry taxable capital gains to individual taxable capital gains, 1990 - 2003.
Source: Statistics Canada.

by econometric problems. In particular, the marginal tax rate on capital gains is determined simultaneously with the level of capital gains. Desai and Gentry (2003) use the Graham's estimates of marginal tax rates (Graham, 1996) and admit that these rates are driven by the presence of non-capital losses, which are not completely divorced from the gains/losses on the investments. In other words, their marginal tax rates and gain/loss realizations are determined simultaneously.

This study overcomes this problem by using loss-carry-overs accumulated from previous years and the effective tax rate, before the effect of current gains/losses as explanatory variables. Plesko (2003) and Lisowsky (2007) find that firms' loss-carry-over positions can be used to infer firms' marginal tax rates and actual tax liability.

This study extends existing research by analyzing Canadian corporations using the SEDAR financial reporting data. In the next section, I develop the empirical tests.

EMPIRICAL TESTS

This study seeks to test whether corporate capital gains realization decision can be explained by tax incentives. In particular, whether a corporation's accumulated capital loss-carry-overs can affect its decisions to realize capital gains. If firms have loss-carry-overs from previous years, they will realize capital gains to use those losses as soon as possible.

In addition, since selling asset is an important source of internal financing, and capital gains or losses may be generated from the sale, firms may sell assets when they need financing.

Earnings (before capital gains) have been added in the model. If firms use asset sales to manage earnings, it is expected that firms will realize more capital gains from selling assets if their earnings before the sale are low, and vice versa.

Firm size was also added, firms' statutory tax rates and effective tax rates in the model.

In summary, the regression model is specified as follows:

$$CG_{it} = \alpha_0 + \alpha_1 STR_{it} + \alpha_2 ETR_{it} + \alpha_3 LCO_{it} + \alpha_4 INC_{it} + \alpha_5 CAS_{it} + \alpha_6 SIZ_{it} + \varepsilon_{it}$$

CG_{it} : Net capital gains realized for firm i in year t.

STR_{it} : Firm i's statutory tax rate in year t.

ETR_{it} : Firm i's effective tax rate in year t.

LCO_{it} : Accumulated loss-carry-overs from previous years for firm i in year t.

INC: net earnings before net capital gains for firm i in year t.

CAS: cash flow before proceeds from selling assets for firm i in year t.

SIZ: firm size for firm i in year t.

Table 1. Industry distribution.

Metal and Mining (SIC 1000 - 1299	
Industry	**Number of firms**
Consumer	36
Energy	33
Health care	9
Materials	54
Industrials	16
Information technology	10
Utilities	5
Tele communications	4
Total	167
A: Future tax assets	Amounts %

The regression was performed using two-year financial data, obtained from the System for Electronic Document Analysis and Retrieval (SEDAR)[c]. Corporations in the sample have to meet the following 3 conditions: (1) Canadian public companies with share prices listed on the TSX300 at the fiscal year end of 2005 or 2006 (a total of 271 firms); (2) available audited annual financial statements for the years 2004-2006 on SEDAR (3 firms are removed); (3) not in the banking, real estate, insurance, and financial institutions (SIC 6000-6799, 39 firms are removed) and not income trusts or funds (53 income trusts or income funds are removed).

As a result, there are 167 firms and thus 334 firm-year observations (two-year data) from 8 industries (see Table 1 for the industry distribution).

The variables for the tests are measured as follows:

The dependent variable is net capital gains, measured as capital gains net of capital losses. Firms' financial reports disclose the following four items related to capital gains/losses. Firms report their gains/losses and/or proceeds from selling the following assets: (a) property, plant and equipment (PPE); (b) marketable securities or other investments; (c) discontinued operation or subsidiaries; and (d) other miscellaneous gains/losses (see Table 2 for the categories of corporate capital gains/losses).

Table 2 shows that, in 2005, the largest capital gains resulted from the disposition of PPE. About 56% of capital gains arose from selling PPE. In 2006, the largest capital gains arose from the disposition of discontinued business, operations, or subsidiaries, representing about 53% of all capital gains.

[c] SEDAR is the system used for electronically filing most securities-related information with the Canadian securities regulatory authorities. Filing with SEDAR started January 1, 1997, and is now mandatory for most reporting issues in Canada. The SEDAR system allows users to access public company and mutual fund securities-related information (e.g., annual financial reports).

Table 2. Categories of corporate capital gains (in Millions).

		2006	2005
Disposition of PPE	Capital gains	999	4787
Disposition of PPE	Capital losses	66	112
Disposition of marketable securities/investments	Capital gains	2271	2031
Disposition of marketable securities/investments	Capital losses	218	203
Disposition of discontinued operation/subsidiaries	Capital gains	3653	1666
Disposition of discontinued operation/subsidiaries	Capital losses	44.1	48
Other	Capital gains	61	38
Other	Capital losses	0	0
Total	Capital gains	6984	8522
Total	Capital losses	328	363

Table 2 also shows that, for the years 2005 and 2006, firms realized much more capital gains than capital losses. This is consistent with Desai and Gentry (2003), who find that U.S. public firms realized more capital gains than capital losses for their sample periods (1990 - 1999).

Statutory tax rate is the combined Canadian federal and provincial income tax rates, obtained from the income tax footnote. It shows the general tax burden across firms in Canada. In this study, firms are subject to the statutory tax rates of 31 - 49%.

Effective tax rate shows the firm's specific tax burden and specific tax status. It is measured as the provision for income tax, divided by earnings before income tax and non-controlling interest (zero if no income tax is payable in that year). Effective tax rate is different from statutory tax rate since firms could claim losses in accumulated from previous years, as well as certain credits (e.g., manufacturing and processing credit, investment tax credit, etc) and resource allowance, which also reduce the effective tax rate. The firm's foreign subsidiaries are subject to the foreign tax rates, which are different from the statutory tax rates. Effective tax rates can be generally obtained from the income tax footnote. Ideally, effective tax rate should exclude taxes resulting from realizing capital gains.

Firms with the same statutory tax rate may have different effective tax rates since they each have a different tax status. Hence the effective tax rate is added in the model on the basis that it will be relevant to capital gains realization.

Loss-carry-over is measured as those losses accumulated from other years. It includes both capital losses and non-capital losses, and can be obtained from the income tax footnote.

Cash flow, proceeds from selling assets, net earnings, and total assets can all be directly obtained from financial statements. To reduce heteroskadesticity, all the variables except firm size, statutory tax rate and effective tax rate are deflated by the firm's market value. The firm's market value is measured as the number of shares outstanding, multiplied by the share price, at the fiscal year end.

TESTING RESULTS

The testing results are presented in Tables 3 to 9. Table 3 describes the statistics of the variables. It shows the variables mean, first quartile, median, third quartile, standard deviation, maximum, and minimum values. For example, the mean value of capital gains is 0.0081; the first quartile and median are zero, the third quartile value is 0.0021; the standard deviation value is 0.0521, the maximum capital gains value is 0.8405 and the minimum is -0.1324.

For the sample period, 62% of firm-year observations have realized either capital gains or capital losses or both (44% realized only capital gains, 6% realized both capital gains and capital losses, and 12% realized only capital losses). As such, capital gain/loss realization appears to be quite common over the sample period.

In addition, for all the firm-year observations, total net capital gains are more than 14% of total earnings (before gains/losses) in year 2006, and more than 11% of total earnings in year 2005. After being deflated by firm market value, total net capital gains are over 25% of total earnings (before gains/losses) in year 2006, and over 15% of total earnings in year 2005. Therefore, despite receiving limited attention, the volume of corporate capital gains is substantial, and increasing so, when compared with corporate net income.

Another variable that deserves more explanation is the variable of loss-carry-overs. The mean value is 0.1195; the first quartile value is 0.0042; the median is 0.034; the third quartile value is 0.1035; the standard deviation is 0.2401, the maximum and minimum are 1.7331 and zero respectively. Overall, for the sample period, more than 80% firm-years have accumulated losses from previous years. These losses can be used to offset income in the current or future years.

Table 3. Descriptive statistics of variables. The sample contains 334 observations.

Variables	Mean	1st Quartile	Median	3rd Quartile	Std. Dev.	Maximum	Minimum
CG	0.0081	0	0	0.0021	0.0521	0.8405	-0.1324
STR	0.3508	0.34	0.35	0.36	0.0217	0.49	0.31
ETR	0.2387	0	0.325	0.35	0.1605	0.9	0
LCO	0.1195	0.0042	0.034	0.1035	0.2401	1.7331	0
INC	0.0463	0.0036	0.034	0.0676	0.1404	1.2393	-0.5018
CAS	-0.0044	-0.0231	-0.0002	0.0192	0.1023	0.5098	-0.7095
SIZ	9.2649	8.8856	9.2051	9.6945	0.6148	10.607	7.3464

CG: total amount of capital gains, divided by market value. Market value is measured as number of shares outstanding times share price, at the fiscal year end, *STR:* statutory tax rate, collected from the income tax footnote *ETR*: effective tax rate before the effect of current capital gains (losses) realization, collected from the income tax footnote, *LCO*: accumulated loss-carry-overs incurred from previous years, divided by market value, *INC*: net earnings before capital gains (losses), divided by market value, *CAS*: cash flow before proceeds from selling assets, divided by market value, *SIZ*: firm size, measured as the log of total assets

Table 4. Pearson correlation of variables.

	CG	*SIZ*	*CAS*	*INC*	*LCO*	*ETR*	*STR*
CG	1						
SIZ	0.1349	1					
CAS	-0.4002	-0.094	1				
INC	0.1938	0.1095	0.3359	1			
LCO	0.3574	0.2194	-0.3037	-0.094	1		
ETR	0.0495	0.2566	0.025	0.2988	-0.1327	1	
STR	-0.049	0.0058	0.1043	0.0424	-0.1374	0.0279	1

Table 5. Regression results from univariate model.

	Proceeds from sales	Net capital gains	Net capital gains	Net capital gains
Intercept	0.0195(6.8857)**	0.0074 (2.8046)**	0.0047 (1.5737)	-0.0013 (-0.4329)
Cash flow w/o proceeds from sales	-0.3989 (-14.38)**	-0.2059 (-8.005)**		
Income w/o capital gains realization			0.0732 (3.6149)**	
Loss-carry-over at the beginning				0.0806 (7.1367)**
R^2	0.38	0.16	0.04	0.13
F-test	206.7	64.08	13.07	50.93

**Significant at 0.001 level.

Table 4 presents the Pearson correlations of the variables. It shows that the maximum correlation (absolute value) is between capital gains and cash flow.

The minimum correlation (absolute value) is between firm size and statutory tax rate. The correlation between capital gains and loss-carry-over is 0.3574, which generally support the tax explanation for capital gains realization. That is, firms with accumulated losses are more likely to realize capital gains.

Table 5 presents results from the univariate model. It shows that net capital gains and loss-carry-over are positively associated, which supports the expectation that a corporation's capital gains realization is shaped by tax incentives. It also shows that the net capital gains realized from asset sales are negatively associated with cash flow (before the sales), and that the proceeds from asset sales are negatively associated with cash flow (before the sales). It supports the argument that a corporation's capital gains are generalized for financing purposes. However, the Table 5 shows that net capital gains realization is positively associated with earnings. This is not consistent with the argument that firms realize capital gains from selling assets to manage earnings. Nevertheless, Table 5 shows the preliminary results from the univariate model. Next, the results from the multivariate model will be discussed.

Table 6. Regression results for total net capital gains

$$CG_{it} = \alpha_0 + \alpha_1 STR_{it} + \alpha_2 ETR_{it} + \alpha_3 LCO_{it} + \alpha_4 INC_{it} + \alpha_5 CAS_{it} + \alpha_6 SIZ_{it} + \varepsilon_{it}$$

	Co-eff.	t-test	Co-eff.	t-test
Intercept	-0.0194	-0.372	0.0239	0.292
SIZ	0.0001	0.2	0.0001	0.9
CAS	-0.2286	-8.93**	-0.322	-9.485**
INC	0.1385	7.4279**	0.2657	8.1781**
LCO	0.0556	5.19**	0.0584	4.1533**
ETR	-0.0056	-0.3512	-0.0292	-1.1946
STR	0.046	0.3852	-0.0823	-0.4733
R^2	0.34		0.48	
F-test	28.32		30.38	
Observations	334		204	

The second and third columns show the results for all firm-year observations, while the fourth and fifth columns show the results only for firms that realized capital gains/losses in that year.
**Significant at 0.001 level.

Table 6 presents the results from the multivariate model specified in Section 3 for total net capital gains. The first two columns show the results for all firm-year observations, while the third and fourth columns show the results only for firms that realized capital gains/losses in that year. The results from Table 6 are consistent with those from the univariate model. It shows that a corporation's capital gains realization is positively associated with its loss-carry-overs accumulated from previous years. It also shows that the net capital gains realized from selling assets are negatively associated with cash flow. However, net capital gains realization is positively associated with earnings, which is not consistent with the argument that firms realize capital gains from selling assets to manage earnings.

Table 6 shows that the coefficients on other control variables including firm size, effective tax rate and statutory tax rate are not significant. Tables 7 - 9 present testing results from the multivariate model for three categories of net capital gains, that is, net capital gains realized from selling PPE, net capital gains realized from selling marketable securities and other investments, and net capital gains from selling discontinued operations and subsidiaries. The first two columns show the results for all firm-year observations, while the third and fourth columns show the results only for firms that realized such capital gains/losses in that year.

The results from Tables 7 - 9 are generally consistent with those from Table 6. It shows that a corporation's net capital gains from each of the three categories are positively associated with its loss-carry-overs accumulated from previous years and negatively associated with cash flow. In addition, net capital gains from each of the three categories are positively associated with earnings.

The coefficient on statutory tax rate is not significant for all three categories of net capital gains. The coefficient on firm size is not significant for all three categories of net capital gains realizations except for net capital gains realized from selling discontinued operations or subsidiaries. Table 9 shows that firm size is negatively associated with net capital gains from selling discontinued business. That is, larger firms realize relatively less capital gains from selling discontinued business. The coefficient on effective tax rate is not significant for all three categories of net capital gains except for net capital gains from selling PPE. Table 7 shows that effective tax rate is negatively associated with net capital gains from selling PPE. That is, firms realize relatively less capital gains from PPE sales when their effective tax rates are high, and vice versa. This is consistent with the expectation that a corporation's capital gains realization is shaped by tax incentives.

The following sensitivity tests have been undertaken in this study.

First, the variables are deflated by total assets. The results (which are not presented in this paper) do not change qualitatively.

Second, 1, 3 and 5% of the capital gains outliers and loss-carry-over outliers are deleted. Again, the results do not change qualitatively.

Finally, industry dummy variables are added to the model and these do not change the results qualitatively.

In addition, I follow Desai and Gentry (2003) and add investment opportunity as an explanatory variable, measured as the proxy for a Q-ratio. However, the variable is not significant.

Conclusion and Limitations

In this paper, an empirical work is designed to test whether corporate capital gains realization is associated with corporate tax. Based on the realization tax rule, taxes are incurred when taxpayers realize capital gains/losses, not when capital gains/losses are accrued. In this study, I test whether accumulated loss-carry-overs can affect capital gains realization. Using Canadian corporations' financial statements, this study finds that, after controlling for other factors, corporate capital gains realization is positively associated with loss-carry-overs accumulated from previous years, and is negatively related to effective tax rates. It supports the argument that corporations take into account their tax status when realizing capital gains.

Furthermore, this study finds that a corporation's capital gains are generalized for financing purposes as capital gains realized from selling assets are negatively associated with a corporation's cash flow.

Table 7. Regression results for net capital gains from dispositions of PPE

$$CG_{it} = \alpha_0 + \alpha_1 STR_{it} + \alpha_2 ETR_{it} + \alpha_3 LCO_{it} + \alpha_4 INC_{it} + \alpha_5 CAS_{it} + \alpha_6 SIZ_{it} + \varepsilon_{it}$$

	Co-eff.	t-test	Co-eff.	t-test
Intercept	0.0014	0.2484	0.0024	0.3123
SIZ	0.0003	0.6573	0.0003	0.2276
CAS	0.0006	0.2353	-0.0125	-1.7942*
INC	0.0025	1.2223	0.0317	3.4618**
LCO	0.0035	3.0474**	0.0077	3.1984**
ETR	-0.003	-1.7233*	-0.0141	-3.142**
STR	-0.008	-0.6959	-0.008	-0.285
R^2	0.052		0.19	
F-test	2.974		5.22	
Observations	334		137	

The second and third columns show the results for all firm-year observations, while the fourth and fifth columns show the results only for firms that realized capital gains/losses in that year.
** Significant at 0.001 level, *significant at 0.1 level.

Table 8. Regression results for net capital gains from disposition of marketable securities or other investments.

$$CG_{it} = \alpha_0 + \alpha_1 STR_{it} + \alpha_2 ETR_{it} + \alpha_3 LCO_{it} + \alpha_4 INC_{it} + \alpha_5 CAS_{it} + \alpha_6 SIZ_{it} + \varepsilon_{it}$$

	Co eff.	t-test	Co eff.	t-test
Intercept	-0.011	-0.314	0.1866	1.2494
SIZ	0.0003	0.1091	-0.0014	-0.1379
CAS	-0.1308	-7.6225**	-0.3382	-6.3238**
INC	0.0791	6.3339**	0.2621	6.0201**
LCO	0.0307	4.2752**	0.0049	0.2029
ETR	-0.0028	-0.2538	-0.0183	-0.4653
STR	0.0121	0.1662	-0.5079	-1.5175
R^2	0.27		0.58	
F-test	20.41		14.71	
Observations	334		71	

The second and third columns show the results for all firm-year observations, while the fourth and fifth columns show the results only for firms that realized capital gains/losses in that year.
**Significant at 0.001 level.

However, no support is found for the notion that firms realize capital gains from selling assets to manage earnings as the firm's capital gains realizations are positively associated with earnings.

Nevertheless, this study provides only a preliminary conclusion. This is because public financial reports do not disclose a corporation's precise tax status, such as taxable income, tax rates, etc. In addition, the financial statements used are consolidated statements for the parent company and all its subsidiaries. For tax purposes, each company or subsidiary is an independent taxpayer. In order for the conclusions of this study to be stronger, relevant data for each independent corporate taxpayer needs to be used as such data is not available to this study.

Lastly, the gains/losses collected from financial reports do not perfectly match taxable capital gains/losses. For example, for depreciable assets and intangible assets (eligible assets), the depreciation rules, the rules on acquisition and disposition of these assets differ between accounting principles and tax law. Despite these limitations, financial reporting data can still shed light on the

Table 9. Regression results for net capital gains from disposition of discontinued operations or subsidiaries

$$CG_{it} = \alpha_0 + \alpha_1 STR_{it} + \alpha_2 ETR_{it} + \alpha_3 LCO_{it} + \alpha_4 INC_{it} + \alpha_5 CAS_{it} + \alpha_6 SIZ_{it} + \varepsilon_{it}$$

	Co eff.	t-test	Co eff.	t-test
Intercept	-0.0094	-0.3947	0.2343	1.9405*
SIZ	-0.0009	-0.4566	-0.01734	-2.6068**
CAS	-0.0923	-7.9188**	-0.1207	-3.4838**
INC	0.0522	6.1438**	0.3662	7.9779**
LCO	0.0212	4.3438**	0.0464	2.9566**
ETR	0.0026	0.361	-0.0284	-0.9803
STR	0.046	0.8457	-0.2046	-0.7608
R^2	0.28		0.74	
F-test	20.79		20.77	
Observations	334		51	

The second and third columns show the results for all firm-year observations, while the fourth and fifth columns show the results only for firms that realized capital gains/losses in that year.
** Significant at 0.001 level, * significant at 0.1 level.

determinants of corporate capital gains realization.

ACKNOWLEDGEMENT

The author thanks the participants of the 101st National Tax Association Annual Conference, the participants of the 18th International Conference of Pacific Rim Management, and anonymous reviewers for their valuable comments. The author also gratefully acknowledges the financial support for this research received from CA/Laurier Research Centre.

REFERENCE

Auten G, Clotfelter CT (1989). Permanent versus Transitory Tax Effects and the Realization of Capital Gains, Q. J. Econ. 97(4): 613-632.
Badrinath SG, Lewellen WG (1991). Evidence on Tax-Motivated Securities Trading Behaviour. J. Finan. 46(1): 369-382.
Bartov E (1993). The Timing of Asset Sales and Earning Manipulation. Account. Rev. 68(4): 840-855.
Bates TW (2005). Asset Sales, Investment Opportunities, and the Use of Proceeds. J. Finan. 60(1): 105-135.
Black EL, Sellers KF, Manly TS (1998). Earning Management Using Asset Sales: An International Study of Countries Allowing Non-current Asset Revaluation. J. Bus. Finan. Account. 25(9-10): 1287-1317.
Burman LE, Clausing KA, O'Hare JF (1994). Tax Reform and Realizations of Capital Gains in 1986, Natl. Tax J. 47: 1-19.
Burman LE, Randolph WC (1994). Measuring Permanent Responses to Capital-Gains Tax Changes in Panel Data, Am. Econ. Rev. 84(4): 794-809.
Chay JB, Choi D, Pontiff J (2006). Market Valuation of Tax-Timing Options: Evidence from Capital Gains Distributions. J. Finan. 61(2): 837-865.
Constantinides GM (1983). Capital Market Equilibrium with Personal Tax, Econometrica May 51: 611-636.
Constantinides GM, Ingersoll J (1984). Optimal Bond Trading with Personal Taxes, J. Finan. Econ. Sept. 13: 299-335.
Cook EW, Hare JFO (1992). Capital Gains Redux: Why Holding Periods Matter, National Tax Journal, Vol. XLV, No.1, 53-76 (March 1992).
Desai MA, Gentry WM (2003). The Character and Determinants of Corporate Capital Gains, Tax Policy Econ. MIT Press 18: 1-36.
Eichner M, Sinai T (2000). Capital Gains Tax Realizations and Tax Rates: New Evidence from Time Series, Natl. Tax J. 53(3): 663-681.
Feldstein M, Yitzhaki S (1978). The Effect of the Capital Gains Tax on the Selling and Switching of Common Stock, J. Pub. Econ. 9: 17-36.
Graham JR (1996). Proxies for the Corporate Marginal Tax Rate, J. Finan. Econ. 42: 187-221.
Herrmann D, Inoue T, Thomas WB (2001). The Sale of Assets to Manage Earnings in Japan, Working Paper, Oregon State University 2001.
Jin L (2006). Capital gains Tax Overhang and Price Pressure, J. Finan. June. 61(3): 1399-1431.
Lisowsky P, Inferring US (2007). Tax Liability from Financial Statement Information, Working paper, Boston University School of Management, September.
Odean T (1998). Are Investors Reluctant to Realize Their Losses? Journal of Finance 52: 1563-1588.
Plesko G (2003). An Evaluation of Alternative Measures of Corporate Tax Rates, J. Account. Econ. 35: 201-226.
Seyhun HN, Skinner DJ (1994). How Do Taxes Affect Investors= Stock Market Realizations? Evidence from Tax-Return Panel Data, J. Bus. 67(2): 231-262.

3

Investigation of the effective factors in the efficiency of tax system

Seyed Mohammad Mousavi Shahroodi

Faculty of Industrial Engineering and Management, Shahroud Industrial University, Iran.
Email:mosavi.shams@gmail.com.

In Iran, Tax Organization is in charge of collecting taxes. To have an efficient organization, we need to investigate the factors effective in the efficiency of the organization and to determine the level of their effectiveness. This study focuses on six of several factors, which may be effective in the efficiency of tax system, including information technology (IT), tax law, administrative formalities, private sector services, encouragements, tax fraud and education. This study attempts to seek the opinions of tax experts regarding the aforementioned factors.

Key words: Efficiency of tax system, allocation officers, taxpayers, per capita allocation, tax formalities.

INTRODUCTION

A tax organization, which collects the highest amount of taxes from the existing resources in the fastest possible time duration and with the lowest possible collection costs can be regarded as an efficient organization.

It is possible to come to an efficient tax system, only if we obtain a scientific attitude towards whatever comes under the category of taxation. If we want to have a macro-structural point of view towards theoretical issues in taxation, the best way is to carry out scientific and academic studies, collect data from tax officers or, in other words, those in charge of collecting taxes and taxpayers (Samiei, 1999).

In a reformed system, the tax rates should be appropriate and rational, the exemptions should be lower in amount, the tax collection organization should be more efficient, the tax burden of the indigent people should be lighter and the fight against corruption and tax evasion should be much more intense.

The tax system in developing countries imposes high expenses on the society. Low efficiency, high collection charges, waste of time for taxpayers and the staff, and the low amounts of received taxes and the deviation of optimum allocation of resources are some of the features of such systems (Farzbod, 2000).

So, one can claim that in Iran, the existing tax sources are not utilized in an appropriate manner. The process of tax collection is a long and slow one and accordingly the cost of tax collection is high. In order to create a highly efficient organization, it is necessary to carry out inclusive scientific studies and researches; this study aims to investigate some effective factors in the efficiency of the tax system, including technology, regulations, tax encouragements and frauds, private sector services and education (Nikchehreh, 2002).

Efficiency of tax organization

Today, the tax ratio and tax effort are considered as the main indicators for the measurement of the efficiency of tax system (Taghavinezhadian, 1990).

Tax efficiency is most often called as the tax effort. The main indices which are used in the analysis of the success or failure of the tax system include:

1) The ratio of the collected taxes to the allocated tax equals the amount of taxes estimated in Budget Act and ratified by the Parliament. One of the ratios used in analyzing the success of tax system is the ratio of the collected taxes to the ratified tax; if this ratio equals one, it would indicate that the tax system has been able to collect the taxes estimated in the national budget; in case the ratio is less than one, it would be the indicator of the failure of tax system in achieving the ratified budget; and in case this ratio is higher than one, it would indicate whether the budget estimation has not been based on real facts or the taxes have been collected in higher

amount than what people can afford (Masgrio and Masgrio, 1993).

2) The relative index equals the percentage of changes in the collected tax compared to that of the previous year. This index is relatively more applicable than the previous one. If this ratio is lower than one, the efficiency of the tax system decreased compared to that of the last year; in case it equals one, the efficiency of the tax system did not change compared to that of the last year; in case it is higher than one, the efficiency of the tax system has been increased compared to the last year. This index is not accurate enough to determine the level of efficiency, because it does not deal with the potential decrease or increase of income in the society;

3) The relative tax index and tax effort. The tax ratio equals the amount of taxes collected to the gross national product. The tax capacity includes the amount of taxes that the economy of a certain society may afford. Since tax capacity is directly related to the gross national product, so, tax ratio indicates the level of utilization of tax capacity.

The efficiency of tax system with tax effort shows to what extent the tax system has been able to use the existing capacity, therefore, tax system should do its best to achieve the objective, and hence tax efficiency is based on tax effort.

In case the index of tax attempt is lower than one, the tax system would be inefficient; and in case the ratio equals one, the tax system would be efficient (Taghavinezhadian, 1990, p. 168).

One of the aspects of an efficient tax system is that increase in its tax revenues should be higher and faster than the increase in gross national product. Indeed, this system should be able to appropriately respond to the increase of gross national product.

Effective factors in the financial power of individuals and the society to pay taxes

The effective factors in the power of the individuals and the society for payment of taxes are determined by two sets of structural and volitional:

1) The main structural factors that are effective on the ability of the individuals in payment of taxes include the level of per capita income of the economic texture of the society and the significance of the various kinds of economic activities as well as the macroeconomic policies adopted by the governments.

2. The effective volitional factors, which influence the ability of the individuals and the society in payment of the taxes include:

a) The level of development of a culture of tax payment in the society;

b) The position that public opinion holds about the tax system;

c) The attitude of the citizens towards the government that may be influenced by the quality of public services and the way of allocation of the tax revenues.

In general, the expansion of the culture of tax payment in the society in a way that people assume the payment of taxes as their duty, and have a proper understanding of the responsibilities and duties of the government in receiving a percentage of national products and expending it on providing the requirements of the people, would effectively influence the payment of taxes.

Effective factors in the ability of the government in tax collection

1) Enactment of appropriate tax laws;
2) The accessibility of tax bases;
3) Tax rates;
4) The number of tax sources; and
5) The executive expenditures of tax collection.

The ability of the government in tax collection depends not only on structural factors, but also on official factors. In many developing countries, the low level of tax revenues is due to the fact that the tax laws are not carried out properly and perfectly, and this, in turn, results from the inefficiency of the official system and the executive methods of allocation and collection systems (Nikchehreh, 2002).

METHODOLOGY

The statistical universe of this study includes the viewpoint of tax experts, which consist of all general auditors, chief auditors, assessors, and assistant auditors of departments of economic and financial affairs of Karaj (city of Iran).

In this study, the table of "Georges and Morgan" and "Cohen" was used for the sample volume. Moreover, for the preparation of the questionnaire appropriate for this study, some theses on the issue under investigation were studied and the supervisors and advisors of those theses were consulted and some tax experts were interviewed for their viewpoints to be understood and then the questionnaire was formulated.

For the validity of the questionnaire to be estimated, Cronbach α was used, where 0.7499 was established as α coefficient. When the data were collected, they were classified and analyzed, and then the research questions were answered based on statistical methods and so, the conclusions were drawn.

RESULTS AND DISCUSSION

The explanation of the results obtained for each of the effective factors in the tax system can be presented as follows:

1) More than 80% of the tax experts have recognized the utilization of IT as an effective factor for the efficiency of tax system. Utilization of the machinery and facilities may

promote the efficiency. Exploitation of IT may also provide the grounds for utilization of a more efficient and more advanced management system in the organizations.

2) More than 80% of the experts do not assume the present tax laws to be effective factors for the efficiency of the tax system. Even if we may have the most proper and appropriate laws, the efficiency would not be possible to achieved if these laws and regulations are not carried out properly. The studies reveal that simple, explicit, clear, and integrated laws can result in the promotion of the efficiency and satisfaction of the taxpayers.

3) More than 70% of tax experts do not consider the bureaucratic formalities as an efficient factor in the efficiency of the tax system. For a case to be dealt with, it is necessary to follow the procedures such as allocation of the tax unit, recognition of the tax amount and the tax collection; however, the length of the stage of tax collection may sometimes prevent the tax system to reach its objectives. For this reason, some arrangements have been considered for the reduction of the process of tax collection in the amendment of the laws ratified in 2001.

4) More than 70% of the tax experts do not believe in the efficiency of utilization of the private sector services. Lack of a scholarly and scientific management and the existence of traditional structure is one of the most significant factors that hinder the utilization of the services of the private sector in the tax system.

5) More than 70% of tax experts believed that tax encouragements are among the effective factors, which influence the efficiency of the tax system. Using the facilities, tax relieves, and the exemptions that are specific to the good pays can be effective factors in the promotion of the efficiency of the tax system.

6) More than 80% of the experts do not consider the tax fines as an effective factor for the efficiency of the tax system. One of the reasons for non-application of effective tax fines is the Islamic culture and the religious beliefs in the country.

7) More than 70% of the tax experts believe that application of judicial punishments is not an effective factor for the efficiency of the tax system. Lack of appropriate regulations and laws in this regard and the Islamic culture and the emphasis of Islam on the exclusion of harsh measures against those people who refrain from paying the taxes, can be among the significant factors, which cause the experts not to believe in the application of judicial punishments.

8) More than 80% of the tax experts believe that training the personnel and the taxpayers is one of the effective factors in the efficiency of the tax system.

Awareness of the experts and the taxpayers with the laws as well as their own responsibilities and duties, and the sufficient skill of the personnel of the tax system may have a great influence on the efficiency of the tax system. Education through IRIB, newspapers, as well as inclusion of the issues related to taxation in the textbooks and providing an insight in the taxation issues can play a significant role in this regard.

Conclusion

With regard to the results obtained, it was concluded from this study that factors such as tax laws, utilization of the services of private sector, tax fines, judicial fines and the formal procedures (the unnecessary bureaucratic formalities) can not be regarded as effective factors in the efficiency of tax system.

On the contrary, the utilization of IT in tax system, tax promotions, training the personnel of tax system and taxpayers can be effective factors for the efficiency of the tax system. However, other factors can also influence the tax system, which, in turn, can be discussed in the future studies.

Some suggestions have been provided by the tax experts for the improvement of the tax system:

1. Improvement of the ways of taxation;
2. Financial ability of the personnel of the tax system;
3. Utilization of IT;
4. Avoiding the interference of the departments and industrial unions in taxation;
5. Increasing the manpower in the tax organization;
5. Considering the management quality in the tax organization;
6. Hiring those employees in the tax organizations who have degrees related to the financial affairs and taxation;
7. Encouragement and punishment of the employees;
8. Collection of the levies and coordination of the levies received from different departments;
9. Utilization of mass media in order to define tax and taxation and the ways the taxes are used and teaching the course of taxation on different educational levels;
10. Presenting the statistics of tax collection to the mass media;
11. Tax inactivity of those institutions and systems, which are exempted from tax according to the rules;
12. Utilization of successful tax patterns of other countries with regard to the tax collection.

Suggestions

Some suggestions have been provided by the tax experts for the improvement of the tax system. These include:

i) Improvement of the ways of taxation;
ii) Financial ability of the personnel of the tax system;
iii) Utilization of IT;
iv) Avoiding the interference of the departments and industrial unions in taxation;

v) Increasing the manpower in the tax organization;
vi) Considering the management quality in the tax organization;
vii) Hiring those employees in the tax organizations who have degrees related to the financial affairs and taxation;
viii) Encouragement and punishment of the employees;
ix) Collection of the levies and coordination of the levies received from different departments;
x) Utilization of mass media in order to define tax and taxation and the ways the taxes are used and teaching the course of taxation on different educational levels;
xi) Presenting the statistics of tax collection to the mass media;
xii) Tax inactivity of those institutions and systems which are exempted from tax according to the rules; and
xiii) Utilization of successful tax patterns of other countries with regard to the tax collection.

REFERENCES

Farzbod J (2000). Investigation of the Effective Factors in the Tax Efficiency, M.A. thesis, Governmental Management Training Center: Tehran.

Nikchehreh GM (2002). Investigation of the Effective Factors in Tax Collection, M.A. thesis, Governmental Management Center: Tehran.

Samiei A (1999). Public Finance and Budget, 13th collection, Governmental Management Training Center: Tehran.

Taghavinezhadian SH (1990). Investigation of Effects of the Organizational Structure on the Efficiency of the Direct Taxes Organization, M.A. Thesis, Tehran University.

Strategic disclosure for political gain: The case of the corporate alternative minimum tax†

Gil B. Manzon, Jr.[1*] and George Plesko[2]

[1]Fulton Hall 536, Boston College. Boston, MA.
[2] University of Connecticut, School of Business 2100 Hillside Road, Unit 1041A Storrs, CT 06269-1041.

We examine the disclosure choices of firms subject to the Corporate Alternative Minimum Tax of the Tax Reform Act of 1986 (AMT). We find systematic differences in disclosure choices by firms subject to the AMT consistent with their attempting to influence perceptions of the effectiveness of the AMT. We believe these findings support the inference that firms will differentially respond to increased tax disclosures under Financial Interpretation 48 (FIN 48) that will require firms adopting uncertain tax positions to provide extensive disclosures for fiscal years beginning after 12/15/06.

Keywords: Tax, political gain, corporate alternative

INTRODUCTION

At a time when increased disclosure of corporate tax return information has been proposed as a mechanism to achieve greater transparency, it is important to evaluate how effective both voluntary and non-voluntary disclosure of corporations' tax attributes have been in the past. Increasing book tax differences, coupled with concerns about corporate tax compliance generally, prompted recent hearing by the Senate Finance Committee which included a discussion on the merits of requiring the disclosure of corporations' tax return information to improve the public's knowledge of firms tax position (Grassley, 2006). Similarly, concerns over the adequacy of tax contingencies have led to the issuance by the Financial Accounting Standards Board of Financial Interpretation Number 48 (FIN 48). Fin 48 will require firms subject to the SECs reporting requirements to alter their accounting for, and provide extensive footnote disclosures of uncertain tax positions (see Financial Standards Accounting Board, 2006).

With limited exceptions (Dworin,1985; Mills et al., 2003; Plesko, 2000, 2003, 2007)) little is known regarding factors that might cause or be associated with differences between actual and disclosed tax status. Nevertheless, much empirical tax research assumes transparent and complete self-disclosure of tax status. To the extent that this assumption of transparent and complete self-disclosure is invalid, inferences drawn from this literature may be misleading. In particular, disclosure choices related to firm specific characteristics may lead to confounded interpretations of the motivations for disclosure choices due to problems related to correlated

*Corresponding author. E-mail: manzong@bc.edu .

[1]We have benefited from the comments of and/or discussions with Jody Boynton, Lowell Dworin, Nick Greenia, Kathy Kiel, Nancy Nichols, Richard Sansing, Jeff Zabel, and especially Charles Boynton and Tom Omer and seminar participants at Boston College, Indiana University, Korea University, Northeastern University, Peking University, and Yale University. Assistance in the collection of the public use data was provided by Colin Hurley and Mary Morrill. The views expressed in this paper are those of the authors, and do not necessarily represent those of the IRS. We are solely responsible for any errors.

omitted variables.

In this study, we examine the disclosure choices of firms subject to the Alternative Minimum Tax (AMT). One design element of this study that distinguishes it from other disclosure studies is that we are able to observe firm disclosure for financial reporting purposes as well as disclosure for tax purposes. A second design element that distinguishes this study from other disclosure studies is that we can partition sample firms using a "bright line" rule intended to compel disclosure that allows us to effectively separate firms between those that have to disclose specific information (though many do not) from those that voluntary choose to disclose information (though many do not).

We partition our sample of firms between those that have to disclose their AMT status and those that do not have to disclose their AMT status using a "bright line" reporting rule. For firms in each group, we identify whether or not the firm actually disclosed its AMT status. For firms in each group (have to disclose and do or do no have to disclose and do or do not) we identify whether factors that proxy for costs and benefits of disclosure are significantly related to the disclosure/non-disclosure choice.

For firms that have to disclose, two factors are significantly related to the disclosure choice: NOL status and industry membership. We interpret the higher likelihood of disclosure by firms with NOLs as consistent with these firms "making the case" that they are unduly burdened by the AMT. With respect to industry membership, we interpret the higher likelihood of firm disclosure as a function of firm industry membership as consistent with the proposition that, when a large number of firms within an industry are subject to the AMT, disclosure of AMT status does not entail material incremental costs to the disclosing firm.

For firms that do not have to disclose AMT status, three factors are significantly related to the disclosure choice: the relative significance of the AMT burden, level of pretax income, and, again, NOL status. We interpret the greater likelihood of disclosure of AMT status by those firms with relatively higher AMT burdens as consistent with those firms attempting to gain positive political leverage in an effort to change the AMT. We interpret the lower likelihood of disclosure by firms with high reported incomes as consistent with these firms not volunteering information on the effectiveness of the AMT in increasing their tax burdens. Lastly, we interpret the greater likelihood of disclosure by firms with NOLs as an attempt by these firms to curry political favor, as we did for firms that had to disclose. We draw two major conclusions from this study. First, there are significant and nonrandom, factors that influence the disclosure choice. This finding is consistent with the view that those firms that disclose their AMT status are not representative of the population of firms subject to the AMT. Because the choice to disclose is related to specific factors that differ cross-sectionally across firms subject to the AMT, conclusions regarding the disclosure patterns of AMT firms' behavior based upon firms which self-disclose AMT liability should be made cautiously.

Second, our results provide insight into the role of the political process with respect to accounting disclosure. Previous analyses of political effects have focused on the role political considerations play in influencing earnings, with size hypothesized as being positively related to accounting choices that reduce reported earnings.[2] We consider the political implications of disclosing a given set of information. The results we report indicate that disclosure choices were made in a manner consistent with providing support for desired changes in the law or avoiding negative scrutiny. The voluntary disclosure of firms with high percentages of AMT to regular tax and the voluntary and mandatory disclosure of firms with NOLs appears consistent with an attempt to influence the legislative process to alter the AMT. Conversely, after controlling for other explanatory factors, voluntary disclosure by more profitable firms was less likely than for firms with less income. This pattern of disclosure is consistent with profitable firms attempting to suppress information that the AMT was effective in increasing their tax burden. Such information would have potentially been useful in blunting calls for repeal or alteration of the AMT statute.

In the next section we provide a brief description of the AMT. In section III we review the completeness of financial statement disclosure of AMT status. In section IV we describe sample identification procedures. In section V we describe the model we estimate and discuss our analysis of the results. The final section provides a brief summary.

A brief history of the AMT

The Tax Reform Act of 1986 (TRA86) created a corporate AMT that, for the first time, included financial statement income as a component of taxable income.

The primary rationale for including financial statement income as a component of the AMT was to reduce the number of instances in which firms reporting significant positive financial statement income avoided payment of significant explicit tax. For example, the Senate Finance Committee report from May 1986 that, in part, led to the

---

[2]An overview of the way accounting choices might be affected by the political process can be found in Watts and Zimmerman (1986), chapters 10 and 11.

final Tax Reform Act of 1986, stated that the committee found it "unjustifiable for some companies to report large earnings and...yet pay little or no taxes..." This book income adjustment provision motivated a number of earnings management studies that examined its effect on financial statement income (Boynton et al., 1992; Manzon, 1992; Wang, 1994; Choi et al., 2001). Book income was replaced by the adjusted current earnings adjustment for taxable years after 1989.

The corporate AMT parallels the regular corporate tax. Alternative Minimum Taxable Income (AMTI) begins with regular taxable income before Net Operating Losses (NOLs). The corporate AMT parallels the regular corporate tax. Alternative Minimum Taxable Income (AMTI) begins with regular taxable income before (NOLs). Taxpayers then Taxpayers then add back amounts to adjust for differences in accounting methods used for regular tax purposes and the AMT (e.g., less accelerated depreciation may be allowed under the AMT). In addition, various tax preferences are added to AMTI, such as percentage depletion in excess of original cost. The sum of regular taxable income before NOLs and these adjustments and preferences is AMTI before the book income adjustment.

Book income for the AMT was defined as the pretax book income of the consolidated financial entity associated with the consolidated tax entity. However, AMTI before the book income Book income for the AMT was defined as the pretax book income of the consolidated financial entity associated with the consolidated tax entity. However, AMTI before the book income adjustment would generally differ from pretax book income for financial purposes. The reasons for these differences, which can be economically large, may be as simple as differences in depreciation under each system or differences in consolidation between financial and tax reporting.[3]

For the years 1987 - 1989, one-half of the excess of book over taxable income (if positive) was included in the calculation of AMTI. AMTI in excess of a (phased-out) $40,000 exemption was taxed at a 20% rate,[4] compared to 40% under the regular tax in 1987 and 34% thereafter. The use of NOLs and foreign tax credits could offset up to 90% of the AMT, greatly reducing the amount of additional tax that a firm might pay. Firms are required to pay the greater of the regular tax or the AMT. If a firm is required to pay the AMT, timing differences (such as depreciation or the book income preference) generate a credit that can be carried forward to offset future regular tax liability. Permanent differences, such as tax-exempt interest, generate no AMT credit.

Gill and Treubert (1993) report that 17,370 firms paid the AMT in 1987, rising to 25,237 in 1989[5] with manufacturing firms responsible for the largest share of AMT payments. In 1987 direct additional tax payments attributable to the AMT were $2.2 billion out of approximately $87.0 billion in corporate tax liability and $9.1 billion for the period 1987 - 1989.[6]

Table 1 provides a distribution of returns with an AMT liability by asset size. It is evident from the data reported in this table that the incidence of the AMT is higher for larger firms, with approximately one in five firms with assets greater than $50 million dollars paying the AMT in each of the three years examined in this study. Gerardi et al. (1993) analyzed a panel of 10,000 large-corporation tax returns (assets in excess of $50 million) and found these firms paid 73% of the total AMT liability for all firms from 1987 - 1990, compared to 64% of the regular tax liability. Nearly one-half of all corporations in their sample paid the AMT in at least one year. Of those firms paying the AMT, the AMT increased total taxes paid more than 30% for firms on the AMT one or two years, and more than doubled taxes paid for the 11% of firms on the AMT for three or four years.[7]

If being subject to the AMT exposes a firm to additional economic costs, firms will find it disadvantageous to reveal their AMT payment to either competitors or to financial markets. Dworin (1987a, 1987b) suggested the AMT may reduce firms' leverage, investment and growth rates. Lyon (1990) has shown the AMT will increase firms' cost of capital, depending upon the length of time they pay the AMT and that debt is relatively more expensive for AMT firms.

AMT disclosure

Because of the negative economic consequences to firms

[3]Dworin (1985) provides a detailed examination of accounting differences using tax return information. Plesko (2002) provides tabulations of the components of differences based on firms' reconciliations on Schedule M1 of the tax return.

[4]In addition, the Environmental Tax (0.12 percent) is levied on AMTI before NOLs in excess of $2,000,000.

[5]While more than 32,000 firms paid the AMT in 1990 the number is not strictly comparable to earlier years as book income was replaced by adjusted current earnings in the calculation of alternative taxable income.

[6]The distinction of direct payment of the AMT is an important one. If firms took actions that increased their regular tax to avoid the AMT the Treasury would gain revenue from the imposition of the AMT even if no AMT were actually paid. As a result, the revenue figures for the AMT are lower bounds for the total amount of revenue generated by the AMT. To date, no studies have analyzed the extent of this activity.

[7]Gerardi et al. (1993) point out that their results probably understate the effect of the AMT since their panel did not include 1,473 firms with assets exceeding $50 million.

Table 1. Distribution of corporate returns with AMT as a percent of total returns, by asset class.

Asset Size ($ thousands)	1987	1988	1989
0 - 1,000	0.2	0.4	0.8
1,000 - 10,000	3.7	5.3	15.1
10,000 - 50,000	12.1	15.2	16.4
50,000 - 100,000	17.3	17.9	16.9
100,000 - 250,000	18.5	18.2	18.1
250,000 - 500,000	17.8	18.4	18.1
500,000 or more	21.2	21.1	19.7
Number of returns with AMT	17,400	25,200	25,300
AMT returns as a share of all returns	0.7	1.1	1.1

Source: Gerardi, Milner, and Silverstein (1993), Table 3.

on the AMT, the AMT status of a firm (both the amount of AMT payment and the preference items) is likely an important factor in an external assessment of the firm's total tax burden. Because the AMT entails payment of additional taxes (currently and potentially permanently) it represents, at a minimum, an increase in the present value of a firm's total tax liabilities, and a reduction in cash available for investors. The extent to which the present value of a firm's tax liability increases as a result of the AMT is a function of the amount of AMT payment and the length of time until any resulting AMT credits could be used to reduce the regular tax. The amount of information disclosed in the financial statement regarding the AMT could help investors determine how much the AMT affected total tax burden as well as help the general public assess the relative effectiveness of the AMT.

In 1987, firms following the guidance of APB-11 or SFAS-96 were required to disclose all significant differences between taxable income and pretax accounting income as well as identify causes of differences between the statutory rate and the firm's effective tax rate. As with many disclosure choices, however, firms face conflicting incentives, depending on expectations of how the information disclosed would be interpreted by the various financial statement users.[8]

An AMT liability was likely to be viewed differently from other federal taxes, because the intent of the AMT was to increase the tax on firms perceived as being too aggressive in using the tax code to reduce their liability. Given the political debate surrounding the AMT, well summarized in Lyon (1997), disclosing payment of the AMT might be viewed as evidence of the effectiveness of the AMT (to the extent that it resulted in the greater explicit taxation of profitable firms). Conversely, some firms complained that AMTI was too broadly defined and that, as a result, inadvertently affected many firms that were not the intended targets of the AMT. As such, firms that perceived themselves as innocent bystanders collaterally damaged by the AMT might disclose payment of the AMT as evidence that the AMT was not working as intended and, thus, in need of modification.[9]

At least two authors[10] have relied on self-disclosure to identify AMT firms, citing, for example, Accounting Series Release (ASR) 149 that requires firms to disclosure certain timing differences. Under ASR 149, firms are required to: Provide reconciliation between the amount of reported total tax expense and the amount computed by multiplying the income before tax by the applicable statutory Federal income tax rate, showing the estimated dollar amount of each of the underlying causes for the difference. If no individual reconciling item amounts to more than five percent ... and the total difference to be reconciled is less than five percent ... no reconciliation need be provided unless it would be significant in appraising the trend of earnings. Reconciling items that are individually less than five percent of the computed amount may be aggregated in the reconciliation.

Reliance on self-disclosure assumes that disclosing firms are not otherwise systematically different from non disclosing firms. If systematic differences exist between disclosing and non-disclosing firms, drawing conclusions based on the analysis of only those firms that disclose

[8]Gibbons et al. (1990) provide a framework for disclosure choices that considers both rules and a firm's strategic goals. Barth and Murphy (1994) along with Healy and Palepu (2001) (together with the commentary by Core (2001) provide overviews of required financial statement disclosures along with an analysis of their purposes. Elliott and Jacobson (1994) describe the costs and benefits of disclosures made by for-profit enterprises, and discuss the interests of the various users of disclosed information.

[9]In the Spring of 1995, Mobil Corporation devoted two of their "Sensible Solutions" advertisements, which appear in major national publications (e.g., *Time*) to advocating the repeal or modification of the corporate AMT.

[10]Manzon (1992) and Wang (1994).

can lead to incorrect inferences regarding the incidence of the AMT, the type of firms affected by the AMT and the response of those firms to the AMT. Such problems, of course, are not likely limited to the AMT disclosure case.[11] To the extent that tax disclosure choices respond to specific disclosure incentives, failure to control such incentives in any analysis will likely limit the validity of any tests and resulting conclusions reached.

METHODOLOGY

Sample identification

To determine the extent to which self-disclosure reflects firms' AMT position, we undertook a search of the text of annual reports following the procedure outlined in Wang (1994). First, 153 firms that self-disclosed they paid the AMT in 1987 were identified by a word search of NAARS using the search term "AMT or minimum tax." Data were then drawn for these firms and all others in the Compust file. This file was then matched to the 1987 Statistics of Income Corporate Source Book File, a stratified sample of approximately 80,000 income tax returns,[12] and unmatched firms were deleted. This matching resulted in a sample of 1,180 firms. From this group, we eliminated 983 firms that did not pay the AMT. The sample we use in this study consists of the remaining 197 firms that paid the AMT. Of these firms, 69 had AMT liabilities greater than 5% of their reported pretax income; 19 (28%) of these 69 reported paying the AMT in their financial statements and 128 had AMT liabilities less than 5% of reported pretax income, 23 (18%) of whom reported paying the AMT in their financial statements. These data are shown in Table 2 along with some descriptive data on the two samples.

As expected, the two samples differ significantly with respect to the amount of AMT they pay relative to a calculated statutory tax liability, with mandatorily disclosing firms (AMTPCT>5%) having a much higher percentage of their total tax liability attributable to the AMT than those for whom disclosure is voluntary. The two samples of firms have similar effective tax rates (ETR) and similar levels of total assets. Notably, firms which we determine should have been subject to mandatory disclosure of their AMT status were more profitable than firms for which disclosure was voluntary. Each sample has a comparable level of firms with NOLs. Notwithstanding the fact that the percentage of firms with AMT obligations greater than 5% of reported pretax income that reported paying the AMT (28%) is 56% higher than that of firms with AMT obligations under 5% of reported pretax income that reported paying the AMT (18%), it is far from 100%. The lack of uniform disclosure by firms with AMTPCT greater than 5% suggests that the numeric test identified in ASR 149 was either not viewed as binding by many firms or that ASR149 does a relatively poor (though not clearly biased) job in the aggregate in providing the identity of firms that, by rule, had to disclose the AMT.

Our use of matched financial-to-tax return data provides us with a unique setting in which to analyze disclosure. One shortcoming of disclosure research generally relates to the quality of the measures of disclosure (Healy and Palepu, 2001, pp. 426 - 427). In our setting we directly observe both the underlying tax status of the firm and whether there is a disclosure. Thus, we are able to minimize measurement error that could be related to our explanatory variables.

Modeling the disclosure decision

We use the following equation to estimate the significance of factors that proxy for the strategic disclosure choice of firms subject to the AMT in 1987:

$$Disclose_i = \beta_0 + \beta_1 AMTPCT_i + \beta_2\ ETR_i + \beta_3\ lnPI_i + \beta_4\ NOL_i + \beta_5\ IndProb_i + \beta_6\ Consol_i + e_i \quad (1)$$

where:

Disclose = 1 if the firm reported an AMT liability on its financial statements, 0.

AMTPCT = AMT liability (reported on the federal tax return) as a share of the statutory tax liability (pretax income * statutory tax rate).

ETR = Effective tax rate[13] (ratio of current federal taxes payable (Compustat data item 63) divided by pretax income).

lnPI = Logarithm of pretax income[14] (Compustat data item 170).

NOL = Equal to 1 if the firm has a positive federal tax expense and NOL carryforwards (Compustat data item 52), 0 otherwise

IndProb = Probability of a firm in an industry being on the AMT, measured as the number of firms on the AMT in each industry divided by the total number of returns in that industry (excluding entities unaffected by the AMT).[15]

Consol = Consolidation variables, measured as the difference between assets reported on the tax return and assets reported on the financial statement, divided by financial statement assets.

We control for the relative significance of the AMT using a variable closely related to that used in our numeric rule to distinguish between firms that had to disclose their AMT status and those that did not. Specifically, AMTPCT is the ratio of AMT tax payment to the statutory tax liability based on reported pretax income and the statutory tax rate.

The primary targets of the AMT were profitable firms that reported low ETRs. The variable lnPI reflects differences in firms' sensitivity to political scrutiny with respect to reporting their AMT status. All else equal, we expect firms with higher levels of pretax income to be subject to increased political scrutiny. We expect that these firms would benefit from not drawing attention to their AMT tax status. Specifically, reporting AMT tax status could be viewed as equivalent to saying that, were it not for the AMT, such firms would have had a significantly smaller federal tax liability. Such a disclosure could be interpreted by proponents of the AMT as consistent with the AMT's effectiveness.

---

[11] Relying on disclosure to determine the incidence of the AMT creates two problems. The first, addressed in this paper, is that many firms subject to the AMT may not disclose that information. Second, some research on the AMT has suggested that the largest responses to the AMT were made by firms that, as a result of managing accruals, were able to avoid the AMT altogether. See Boynton et al. (1992).

[12] A complete description of the 1987 SOI corporate sample can be found in IRS (1990).

[13] We follow Omer et al. (1991) in bounding ETR to the interval (-1, 1).

[14] The pretax income of firms with negative income were set to one dollar prior to taking the log.

[15] We exclude corporations statutorily unaffected by the AMT, such as subchapter S corporations.

Table 2. Actual versus Reported AMT Exposure for Firms with Different Levels of AMT Obligation Relative to Statutory Tax Obligation.

	AMTPCT>5%	AMTPCT<5%	Total
Disclose AMT Liability	19	23	42
Do Not Disclose AMT Liability	50	105	155
Total	69	128	197

Table 2b.

	AMTPCT>5%	AMTPCT<5%
Number of Firms	69	128
AMTPCT	0.161(0.12)	0.02(0.02)
ETR	0.117(0.26)	0.133(0.30)
ln (Assets)	6.040(1.72)	6.398(1.89)
ln (Pretax Income)	2.807(1.94)	1.271(6.43)
NOL	0.246(0.43)	0.242(0.430
IndProb	.0123(0.003)	0.013(0.003)

(Dollar amounts in millions, standard deviations in parentheses).

In contrast to not disclosing an AMT liability to mitigate adverse political scrutiny is disclosing an AMT liability to obtain favorable treatment via the political process.[16] We expect that firms with relatively high ETRs but subject to the AMT would be more likely to disclose their AMT status as part of an attempt to curry political favor. Other firms that could make the case that they were "inadvertently" or "inappropriately" paying the AMT would include those with NOLs that would not otherwise have an income tax liability in the current year. These firms may well view the AMT as imposing an unfair burden on their operations and make an effective case for AMT repeal. To test for the incentives of loss firms subject to the AMT we include a dummy variable, NOL, which is equal to one for any firm with a positive federal tax expense possessing NOL carry forwards.

The percentage of firms in an industry paying the minimum tax (IndProb) is expected to be positively related to the probability of disclosure because disclosure is less likely to result in a competitive disadvantage.[17] This variable is also related to the political cost variables described above, as industries targeted by the AMT, or which feel they were being unfairly penalized by the AMT, could use disclosure as part of a strategy to influence legislative changes.

We include two variables to measure consolidation differences between financial reporting and tax entities: A_{tax}-A_{book} is the amount by which tax return assets exceed financial statement assets, if positive, and zero otherwise; A_{book}-A_{tax} is the amount by which financial statement assets exceed tax return assets, if positive and zero otherwise. Both variables are scaled by financial statement assets. As A_{tax}-A_{book} increases, differences in the tax status of the entities are expected to increase, decreasing the likelihood that the reported tax status and the actual tax status will be the same. As discussed in Dworin (1985) and Plesko (2000, 2003), differences in entity are a critical factor in reconciling reported tax status with actual tax status. With respect to the AMT, tax-consolidated entities that include finance subsidiaries and generate significant preference items are more likely to be subject to the AMT than firms that do not have finance subsidiaries.[18] Also, firms that make extensive investments in tax-preferred assets or which finance using tax-preferred debt are more likely to be subject to the AMT than firms that do not make such investment and financing choices.

RESULTS AND ANALYSIS

The results of estimating equation (1) are shown in Table 3. We estimate equation (1) for two subsamples of firms: those that we estimate had to disclose AMT status and those that we estimate did not have to disclosure. Column (1) provides the results for the sub-sample of 69 firms that we estimate had to disclose an AMT liability following ASR 149. The most striking results are seen in the estimated coefficient on the first three variables, AMTPCT, ETR and lnPI, none of which is statistically significant. This implies that for firms with relatively large AMT liabilities, neither the magnitude of that liability, nor their overall tax burden, are associated with disclosure. Based on the next two coefficients, NOL and IndProb, both of which are positive and statistically significant, the only factors that appeared to play a role in the decision to disclose are whether the firm currently had an NOL and the incidence of the AMT among firms in the same

[16]The airline industry, for example, used its exposure to the AMT to lobby for changes in the AMT depreciation preference (Aviation Daily, 1993). In 1989, when hearings were held on modification to the AMT, a broad group of industries testified in favor of changes in the AMT, particularly the treatment of depreciation. These industries included petroleum, utilities, mining, computer lessors, and manufacturers.

[17]See Healy and Palepu (2001, p. 424-425) for a brief description of the research on the proprietary costs of disclosure.

[18]See Stickney et al. (1983) for a specific example of the complications introduced into the tax reporting problem by the presence of a finance subsidiary.

Table 3. Determinants of disclosure.

	AMT > 5%		AMT < 5%	
	(1)	(2)	(3)	(4)
	Coefficient estimates	**Marginal effects**	**Coefficient estimates**	**Marginal effects**
AMTPCT	3.649 (2.989)	0.636	36.197** (15.368)	3.344
ETR	-0.252 (1.215)	-0.044	-2.768** (1.140)	-0.226
ln(pretax income)	0.185 (0.175)	0.032	-0.111** (0.048)	-0.010
NOL	1.509** (0.636)	0.308	1.988*** (0.596)	0.275
Industry probability	243.195*** (78.282)	4.240	49.769 (90.490)	0.460
Tax Assets - Financial	-0.077 (0.061)	-0.013	-0.630 (0.783)	-0.058
Financial Assets - Tax	-1.096 (4.571)	-0.191	-3.489 (2.977)	-0.322
Constant	-5.548*** (1.229)		-4.539*** (1.831)	
Number of Firms	69		128	
log likelihood	-34.927		-45.243	
Π^2	18.67***		34.54***	
Predictions				
Correct disclose	0.68		0.70	
Correct non-disclose	0.66		0.74	
Correct overall	0.67		0.73	

The dependent variable is equal to 1 if the firm disclosed its AMT status, 0 otherwise. Robust standard errors are reported in parentheses. Marginal probabilities are listed in the second column of each equation. For continuous variables, the marginal probabilities represent the change in the probability a firm would disclose if the variable was increased by one percent from its mean value, calculated at the mean of the explanatory variables with dummy variables equal to zero. Marginal probabilities for share variables were calculated by increasing the share 1 percentage point. The marginal probability of a dummy variable was estimated as a change from 0 to 1. Number of observations: 197, 42 disclosing (21.3%). Significance levels: *** 1, 5 and 10%.

industry.

Column (2) reports the marginal effect of each variable.[19] In the case of NOL, the marginal effect of0.308 implies that the presence on an NOL increased the likelihood that a firm would disclose an AMT liability by slightly more than 30%. The magnitude of the estimated marginal effect for IndProb implies that a one-percentage point increase in the industry probability is associated with a 4.2% increase in the probability that a firm in the industry will disclose their AMT liability. The final two variables are statistically insignificant, suggesting that the degree of consolidation was not associated with the disclosure decision.

The bottom of Table 1 provides information n the model's success in predicting firms' disclosure choice.

Overall, the model correctly identifies 67% of firms that disclosed their AMT liability, with similar success in predicting the choices of both disclosing firms (0.68) and non-disclosing firms (0.66).

Column (3) presents the results of estimating equation (1) for AMT firms that did not have to disclosure AMT status under ASR 149's five percent rule. In contrast to the sample of firms that had to disclose their AMT status, each of the first three coefficients is statistically significant. The coefficient on AMTPCT is positive and significant. This result indicates that, as the relative significance of the AMT increased, firms were more likely to disclose that they paid the AMT even though such disclosure was not strictly required. This is in contrast to the results presented in column (1) that suggest that is the threshold at which reporting AMT status was mandatory the relative significance of the AMT obligation did not affect the likelihood of disclosure.

The coefficient on ETR is negative, indicating that low ETR firms were more likely to disclose AMT status than those with high ETRs. This finding is contrary to expectation. We anticipated that firms with low ETRs that were subject to the AMT would choose not to disclose AMT status so as to reduce the perception that the AMT was, in fact, effectively subjecting to higher immediate taxation firms that were paying a relatively low current tax as a percentage of pretax income.

[19] For continuous variables, the marginal probabilities were based on a one percent change in the value of the variable, calculated at the mean of the independent variables, with dummy variables set equal to zero. Marginal probabilities of dummy variables were calculated as a change from 0 to 1. For ease of interpretation, each estimate was multiplied by 100 so that the listed probability represents the percent change in the estimated probability a firm would disclose. In the case of pretax income, a one percent increase in the log of pretax income of a firm whose disclosure of AMT status is voluntary is estimated to decrease the probability of disclosure 0.012%.

The coefficient on the log of pretax income is negative and significant, indicating that firms with relatively low (high) pretax income were more likely to voluntarily disclose (not disclose) AMT status. This result is consistent with relatively low income firms attempting to influence political opinion with respect to the AMT.

As with the AMTPCT greater than five percent group, the coefficient on NOL is positive and significant, again consistent with the proposition that firms with NOLs that had to pay the AMT wanted to highlight that they were paying the AMT even though they did not fit the profile of firms that the AMT was intended to affect. As in column (1), we interpret the greater disclosure of AMT status by NOL firms as consistent with them pursuing a political agenda to bring about change in the AMT statute.

Taken together, our results with respect to AMTPCT, lnPI and NOL are consistent with the view that firms use disclosure to influence political action or avoid political scrutiny. The coefficient on the industry probability variable is not significant for firms that, under ASR 149, were not required to disclose AMT status. This result is consistent with the proposition that firms within a particular industry, but with less extensive AMT liabilities, did not necessarily have similar reporting objectives. Rather, variables that proxy for political costs are more significant in explaining the disclosure choices of firms that were not required to disclose AMT status than those that were required to disclose AMT status. The common disclosure patterns found in column (1) are not present among firms with lower AMT exposure. Further, as in column (1), the consolidation variables are not significant.

The tabulations presented at the bottom of Column (3) shows that this model correctly identifies 70% of disclosing firms and 74% of non-disclosing firms, with 73% of all firms' disclosure choices correctly predicted.

We draw two conclusions from our regression results. First, there are significant and nonrandom, factors that influence the disclosure choice, suggesting that those firms that disclose are not representative of the population of firms subject to the AMT. Because the choice to disclose is related to specific factors that differ cross-sectionally across firms subject to the AMT, we believe conclusions regarding the disclosure patterns of AMT firms' behavior based upon firms which self-disclose AMT liability should be made with caution.

Second, our results provide insight into the role of the political process on accounting disclosure. Our results indicate that disclosure is predicated on likely political outcomes. The voluntary disclosure of firms with a high percentage of AMT liability to regular tax liability and voluntary and mandatory disclosure of firms with NOLs appears consistent with an attempt to influence the legislative process to alter the AMT. Similarly, the selective non-disclosure of AMT status by more profitable firms appears consistent with these firms attempting to suppress information that the AMT was effective in increasing their tax burden. Presumptively, such information would potentially be useful in blunting calls for repeal or alternation of the AMT statute.

The results we report are consistent with the broadest description of the political process—that of a competition for wealth transfers—in which disclosure is an additional tool the firm can use to increase or retain wealth.[20]

Separately, these results are also consistent with the results reported by Wang (1994) on earnings management in response to the AMT and partially address the criticisms of Choi et al. (2001)[21]. Wang developed partitions of firms based on their self-disclosed AMT position. Given our results, his control sample of non-AMT firms may have contained a number of AMT firms that merely did not disclose. Partitioning on the disclosure should have created a bias against his finding statistically significant differences between the two sets of firms. Given the potential bias, his statistical results should be viewed as a lower bound on the extent of AMT- induced accruals.

DISCUSSION

In this study we examine the disclosure choices of firms paying the AMT. The AMT was designed to insure that all firms paid their "fair share" of tax, a largely political objective that grew out of highly publicized instances of profitable firms paying little or no explicit taxes.[22] Our access to proprietary IRS data allows us to determine with precision firms reported tax status as well as their actual tax status. The ability to classify with precision the required and actual disclosure status allows us to test different disclosure motivations. Our ability to identify the disclosure requirements and status of firms and develop differential reporting hypotheses as a function of a bright line reporting requirement provides us with a unique disclosure setting to study.

We show that self-disclosure of AMT tax status provides an incomplete picture of firms' actual tax status. The choice to disclose certain tax information is based, in part, on regulatory guidelines. Disclosure choices also appear to be balanced against the potential costs and benefits of disclosure. In particular, we find evidence that political considerations played an important role in firms' choice to disclose. The variables that are significant in explaining the disclosure choice are consistent with the view that firms use disclosure to pursue political goals.

The importance of political factors in firms' tax disclosure decisions has implications for firms that will soon be

[20]This is also consistent with the results of Jones (1991) who showed that firms may have managed their earning downwards during periods when they sought regulatory relief from foreign imports.

[21]Dhaliwal (2001) provides a more extensive analysis of the criticisms of Choi et al. (2001).

[22]For a brief history and assessment of the AMT from various perspectives, see, U.S. Senate (1995).

reporting under the guidance provided in FIN 48. FIN 48 requires that firms defer the recognition of tax benefits related to uncertain tax positions and to provide footnote disclosure of aggregate uncertain tax positions. Such disclosure may well expose firms to unwanted scrutiny from political actors including the SEC, the IRS and members of Congress. Firms may fail to fully comply with new disclosure requirements (as they have apparently done so with respect to AMT disclosures) or alter the aggressiveness of tax planning activities to avoid attracting unwanted attention.

REFERENCES

Air Transport Association Sets Full Agenda for New Administration. Aviation Daily. January 21, 1993.

Barth ME, Murphy CM (1994). Required Financial Statement Disclosures: Purposes, Subject, Number, and Trends. Account. Horiz. December: 1-22.

Boynton CP, Dobbins P, Plesko GA (1992). Earnings management and the corporate Alternative Minimum Tax. J. Account. Res. Suppl: 131-153.

Choi WW, Gramlich JD, Thomas JK (2001). Potential Errors in Detecting Earnings Management: Reexamining Studies Investigating the AMT of 1986. Contemp. Account. Res. Winter: 571-613.

Core JE (2001). A review of the empirical disclosure literature: discussion. J. Account. Econ. 31: 441-456.

Dhaliwal DS (2001). Discussion of 'Potential Errors in Detecting Earnings Management: Reexamining Studies Investigating the AMT of 1986. Contemp. Account. Res. Winter pp.615-623.

Dworin L (1985). On Estimating Corporate Tax Liabilities from Financial Statements. Tax Notes. December: pp.965-971.

Dworin L (1987a). Impact of the Corporate Alternative Minimum Tax. Natl. Tax J. September: pp.505-513.

Dworin L (1987b). Impact of the Corporate Alternative Minimum Tax: A Monte Carlo Simulation Study. in Compendium of Tax Research, 1987. (Washington D.C.: U.S. GPO).

Elliott RK, Jacobson PD (1994). Costs and Benefits of Business Information Disclosure. Account. Horiz.. December: pp.80-96.

Financial Standards Accounting Board (2006). Financial Interpretation 48: Accounting for uncertainty in income taxes: An interpretation of FASB Statement No. 109.

Gerardi GH, Milner H, Silverstein G (1993). Temporal Aspects of the Corporate Alternative Minimum Tax: Results from Corporate Panel Data for 1987 – 1990. in Proceedings of the Eighty-Third Annual Conference 1992. Columbus: National Tax Association - Tax Inst. Am. pp.117 - 127.

Gibbons MA, Richardson A, Waterhouse J (1990). The Management of Corporate Financial Disclosure: Opportunism, Ritualism, Policies, and Processes. J. Account. Res. Spring: 121-143.

Gill A, Treubert P (1993). The Corporate Alternative Minimum Tax: A Year-by-Year Analysis of Tax Return Data from 1987 – 1990. in Proceedings of the Eighty-Third Annual Conference 1992. Columbus: National Tax Association - Tax Inst. Am. 128-136.

Grassley C (2006). Opening Statement: 'A Tune-up on Corporate Tax Issues: What's Going on Under the Hood? U.S. Senate Committee on Finance: June 13.

Healy PM, Palepu KG (2001). Information asymmetry, corporate disclosure, and the capital markets: A review of the empirical disclosure literature. J. Account. Econ. September pp.405-440.

Internal Revenue Service (1990). Statistics of Income -1988: Corporation Income Tax Returns. Publication 16. Washington D.C.: US GPO.

Jones J (1991). Earnings management during import relief investigations. J. Account. Res. Autumn: pp.193–228.

Lyon A (1990). Investment Incentives under the Alternative Minimum Tax. National Tax J. December: pp.451-465.

Lyon A (1997). Cracking the Code: Making Sense of the Corporate Alternative Minimum Tax. (Washington, D.C.: The Brookings Institution).

Manzon GB (1992). Earnings Management of Firms Subject to the Alternative Minimum Tax. J. Am. Tax Assoc. Fall pp.88 - 111.

Mills L, Newberry KJ, Novack GF (2003). How Well Do Compustat NOL Data Identify Firms with U.S. Tax Return Loss Carryovers? J. Am. Tax Assoc. Fall pp.1 – 17.

Omer TC, Molloy KH, Ziebart DA (1991). Measurement of Effective Corporate Tax Rates Using Financial Statement Information. J. Am. Tax Assoc. Spring: 57 - 72.

Plesko G (2000). Book-Tax Differences and the Measurement of Corporate Income. in Proceedings of the Ninety-Second Annual Conference on Taxation. Washington, D.C.: Natl. Tax Assoc. pp.171-176.

Plesko G (2003). An Evaluation of Alternative Measures of Corporate Tax Rates. J. Account. Econ. April: 201-226.

Plesko G (2007). Estimates of the Magnitude of Financial and Tax Reporting Conflicts. working paper. University of Connecticut.

Stickney CP (1979). Current Issues in the Measurement and Disclosure of Corporate Income Taxes. Account. Rev. April: pp.421-433.

U.S. Senate, Committee on Finance (1995). Alternative Minimum Tax S. Hrg.. Washington D.C., U.S. GPO. pp.104-180.

Wang S (1994). The Relationship Between Financial Reporting Practices and the 1986 Alternative Minimum Tax. Account. Rev. July pp.495-506.

Watts RL, Zimmerman JL (1983). Positive Accounting Theory, Englewood Cliffs; Prentice-Hall.

5

Individual taxpayers' attitude and compliance behaviour in Nigeria: The moderating role of financial condition and risk preference

James O. Alabede*, Zaimah Zainol Ariffin and Kamil Md Idris

College of Business Universiti Utara Malaysia, Sintok, Kedah State-Malaysia.

A number of factors may be responsible for low compliance in income tax administration in Nigeria. However, taxpayers' attitude has been identified as one factor that play important role in influencing tax compliance behaviour. Besides, the influence of taxpayers' attitude on compliance behaviour may be moderated by financial condition and risk preference. This study investigated the moderating effect of financial condition and risk preference on relationship between taxpayers' attitude and compliance behaviour. The data of the study, which were collected through a survey of individual taxpayers' opinion, were treated statistically using moderated multiple regression. The result of the study indicates that taxpayer's attitude towards tax evasion is positively related to compliance behaviour. Furthermore, the study also reveals that taxpayer's risk preference has strong negative moderating impact on the relationship between attitude towards tax evasion and compliance behaviour.

Key words: Tax compliance, attitude, income tax administration.

INTRODUCTION

Income taxes are important source of revenue to government in both developing and developed countries (Teera and Hudson 2004). But the amount of revenue to be generated by government from such taxes for its expenditure programme depends among other things, on the willingness of the taxpayers to comply with tax laws of a country (Eshag, 1983). The failure to follow the tax provisions suggests that a taxpayer may be committing an act of noncompliance (Kirchler, 2007). Tax non-compliance occurs through failure to file tax return, misreporting income or misreporting allowable subtractions from taxable income or tax due (Roth et al., 1996; Soos, 1991).

Following the increasing cases of tax noncompliance, especially tax evasion and its consequences on the capacity of government to raise public revenue, great amount of attentions have been paid to the issue of tax compliance globally by public policy makers and researchers for the past few decades now. However, bulk of the researches on tax compliance is on developed countries especially the US, it is limited on developing countries (Chau and Leung, 2009; Torgler, 2003).

As part of these research efforts, Allingham and Sandmo (1972) developed a theory known as A-S models to explain tax compliance behaviour. This theory was derived from Becker's (1968) deterrence theory. The general conclusion of the theory is that compliance depends largely on tax audit and penalty. However, the theory had been criticized for paying more emphasis on economic factors and ignoring completely social and psychological perspective of tax noncompliance (Fischer, 1993). Scholars suggested that tax noncompliance decision may be affected by factors not considered in the basic model, or may be affected in ways not captured approximately by the theory (Alm, 1999; Spicer and Lundestedt, 1976).

The failure of the traditional theory to provide a comprehensive understanding of tax noncompliance created avenue for a research gap into the phenomenon. This research opportunity made many researchers (Andreoni et al., 1998; Chan et al., 2000; Jackson and

*Corresponding author. E-mail: joalabede@yahoo.com.

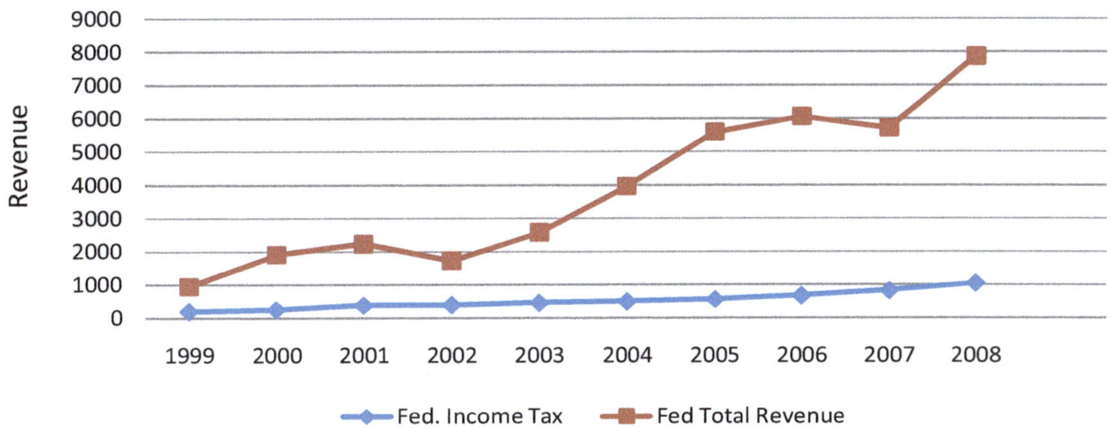

Figure 1. Nigeria's federal revenue (N'B). Note: Data for the chart derived from "Annual report and statement of account," by Central Bank of Nigeria, 2008, Abuja: Central Bank of Nigeria.

Milliron, 1986; Manaf, 2004; Yaniv, 1999; Torgler, 2003 etc) to extend A-S model to cover other factors. In the first major work on tax compliance, Jackson and Milliron (1986) identified fourteen factors as factors influencing tax compliance and these fourteen key factors were later categorized by Fisher et al. (1992) into four main determinants. However, Fischer et al. (1992) did not consider the fact that the relationship between tax compliance and some of its determinants may be moderated by other variable(s) as suggested in Kirchler et al. (2007).

The present study contributes to tax compliance literature by taking advantage of the weaknesses noted in previous studies (Allingham and Sandmo, 1972; Chan et al., 2000; Fischer et al., 1992). First, the focus of the study is on individual tax compliance behaviour in a developing economy. Secondly, the study further extended Fischer's model by incorporating the moderating effects of taxpayer's financial condition and risk preference. However, the study is primarily undertaken to determine the relationship between taxpayer's attitude and tax compliance behaviour as well as the moderating effects of taxpayer's financial condition and risk preference on the relationship.

For this purpose, the remaining part of this paper is organised as follows: the second part reviews the relevant literature while third part is on materials and methods used in the study. The result, discussion and conclusion of the study followed in the fourth, fifth and sixth part, respectively.

LITERATURE REVIEW

Tax compliance behaviour in Nigeria

Administration of income tax in Nigeria as in some other developing countries is characterised by low compliance level and despite Nigeria's human and natural endowment as well as economic potentiality, the country has continued to record one of the lowest tax compliance level in Africa (CITN, 2010). Even with all efforts through the various tax reforms[1] undertaken by Nigerian government to increase tax revenue over the years, prior statistical evidence has proven that the contribution of income taxes to the government's total revenue remained consistently low and is relatively shrinking. However, of all the taxes, personal income tax has remained the most disappointing, nonperforming, unsatisfactory and problematic in Nigerian tax system (Asada, 2005; Kiabel and Nwokah, 2009; Nzotta, 2007; Odusola, 2006; Sani, 2005). The statistical data indicated that contributions of non oil income tax to total revenue of Government in Nigeria dropped from 19.8% in 1999 to 11.7% in 2008 and the tax ratio in 2009 was 11% the lowest in West Africa and below 15% recommended for low income countries (CBN, 2008; Cobham, 2005; CITN, 2010). Specifically, the contribution of personal income tax remained marginal and comparatively low in Nigeria's tax revenue. At the state and local government levels, where the major source of internal revenue is expected to be individual income tax, its contribution to the total revenue of these levels dropped from 20.18 and 7.7% in 1999 to 12.4 and 1.6% in 2008, respectively (CBN, 2008). Figure 1, 2 and 3 show the performance of tax revenue of different level of government in Nigeria.

Taxpayers' attitude and compliance behaviour

An individual's attitude towards tax system may predict (his tax compliance behaviour. Theoretically, Ajzen 1991), Fishbein and Ajzen (1975) and Oskamp (1991)

[1] Some tax reforms in Nigeria include Structural Adjustment Program in 1986, Shehu's Task Force on Tax, 1978; Dr Sylvester's Study Group on Tax, 1999; Economic Empowering Development Strategies, 2002; Professor Dotun's Study Group on Tax, 2002.

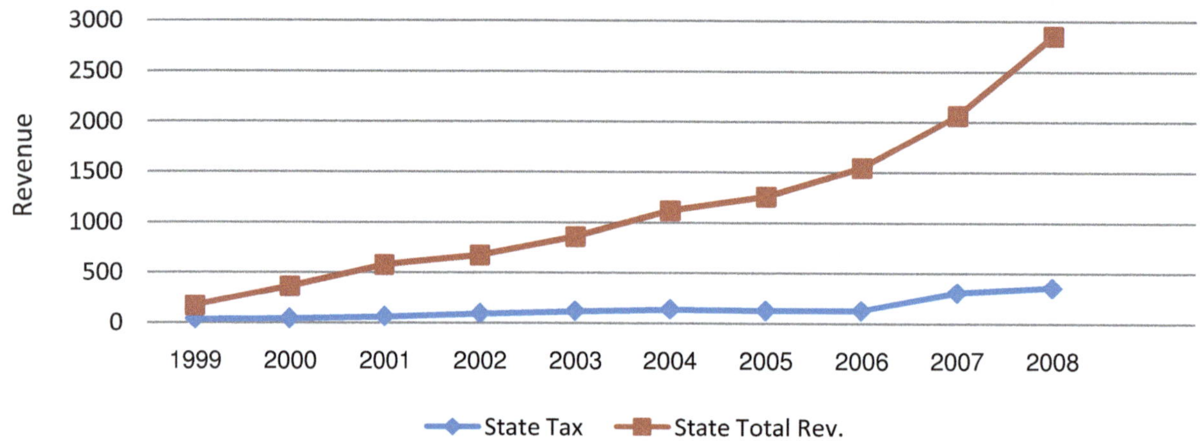

Figure 2. Nigeria states revenue (N'B). Note: Data for the chart derived from "Annual report and statement of account," by Central Bank of Nigeria, 2008, Abuja: Central Bank of Nigeria.

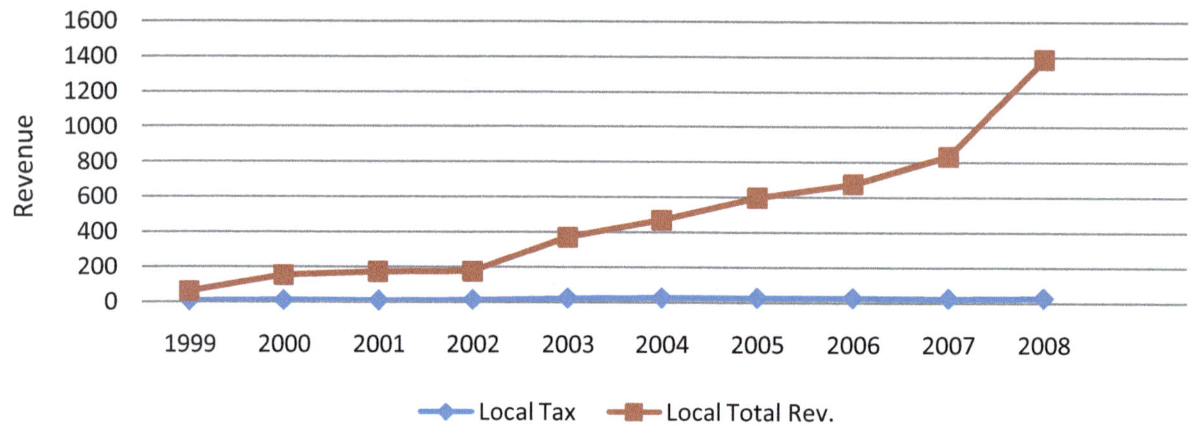

Figure 3. Nigeria's local government revenue (N'B). Note: Data for the chart derived from "Annual report and statement of account," by Central Bank of Nigeria, 2008, Abuja: Central Bank of Nigeria.

have indicated that attitude is a partial indication of behaviour. Attitude towards an event, object, function or person may be favourable or unfavourable. According to Ajzen (1991) and Fishbein and Ajzen (1975), individual evaluates an event or object positively or negatively and positive and negative evaluation is the main dominant characteristic of an individual's attitude. In agreement with the statements of Ajzen (1991) and Fishbein and Ajzen (1975), Kirchler et al. (2008) suggested that taxpayer who has favourable attitude towards tax evasion is expected to be less compliant and equally taxpayer with unfavourable attitude is likely to be more compliant. In his own submission, Bobek (1997) argued from the perspective of the theory of functional attitude that the motive of the attitude will determine whether it will be positive or negative. The taxpayer, whose motive of attitude towards tax system is to express his belief in the system, is expected to judge the fairness of the system objectively and the taxpayer whose attitude is motivated with what benefit to derive from the system may label tax system fair if he is benefiting from the system (Bobek, 1997). Eriksen and Fallan (1996) said that dimensions of attitude towards tax evasion include: attitude to one's own tax evasion which is referred to as tax ethic, fairness of tax system, attitude to other people's tax evasion and attitude to general crime.

There are empirical evidences suggesting that ethical value may play significant role in the compliance decision of an individual taxpayer. In line with this, Ho and Wong (2008) submitted that individuals with stronger ethical mind may have favourable compliance attitude as they will regard complying with rule and regulation as an obligation that must be honoured. Chau and Leung (2009) equally stated that ethical value may affect tax compliance decision of an individual. The study of Recker et al. (1994) found that tax compliance is higher where there is a stronger belief that tax evasion is unethical. The result of Bobek and Hatfield (2003) also indicated that the ethical beliefs of individuals are the best means of improving tax compliance. Manaf (2004) reported that taxpayers who see tax evasion as unethical are likely to comply more than those who regarded tax evasion as not unethical. Similar result was also reported in the study of Ho and Wong (2008).

Also, within literature of tax compliance, the perception of the taxpayers about the fairness of the tax system is recognized as an important factor that can have significant influence on tax compliance behaviour. According to Gilligan and Richardson (2005), the tax system that is perceived as unfair by the citizens may likely to be less successful and this will encourage the taxpayers to engage in noncompliant behaviour. Kirchler (2007) and Wenzel (2004) suggested that fairness can be conceptualized as distributive justice, procedural justice and retributive justice. Distributive justice is concerned with fairness in exchange of resources in both the benefit and cost, while procedural justice refers to fairness in the process of resources distribution and retributive justice is concerned with about the fairness in appropriateness of sanctions when rules are broken. However, Kirchler (2007) stated that research relating to fairness and tax compliance only focuses on distributive justice.

With regard to distributive justice, comparisons are made on the basis of individuals, groups and societal level and at individual level; taxpayers will be interested in the fairness of his tax burden, if it is perceived to be too high compare to other individuals' tax burden, his rate of compliance is likely to decrease. At the group level, the taxpayers are interested on the fairness of treating their groups compare to other groups, when a group perceived that it is not fairly treated in respect to tax burden in relation to other groups that may lead tax noncompliance in the group. At societal level, the taxpayers are concerned with the fairness of tax system of the whole society, where they perceived the tax system to be unfair, tax noncompliance is likely to increase in the society (Kirchler, 2007). The study of Spicer and Lundstedt (1976) reported that the respondents believe that when the tax system is unfair they are not more likely to comply with the tax laws. Porcano (1984) indicated that taxpayers' needs and ability to pay are the important factors that determined the fairness of tax system. Mustafa (1997) also reported that taxpayers perceived tax law to be unfair. In another study, Richardson (2006) reported a significant negative relationship tax system fairness and tax evasion.

Equally, studies have established relationship between attitudes of taxpayers and compliance. The study of Eriksen and Fallan (1996) revealed that taxpayer's attitude towards tax system has influence on reinforced desire toward tax evasion and compliance. Chan et al. (2000) reported that Hong Kong taxpayers have less favourable attitude towards tax system as a result lower level of compliance. The study of Oriviska and Hudson (2002) examined the attitudes to tax evasion and reported that evasion is condoned by large number of people who are particularly benefiting from it. Trivedi et al. (2005) also revealed that there is a relationship between attitude and compliance.

Financial condition as a moderator for attitude and tax compliance

The inconsistency of findings on the relationship between tax compliance and some of its determinants most especially the deterrents factors (Dubin et al., 1987; Dubin and Wilde,1988), has encouraged suggestion in the literature that the relationship may be moderated by certain variables (Kirchler et al., 2007). There are indications in other behavioural studies that financial condition (requirement) and family obligations moderate the relationship individuals' commitment and performance (Mathieu and Zajac, 1990; Brett et al., 1995). Empirically, some behavioural studies have shown support for the moderating effects of financial requirement on individual's behaviour (Doran et al., 1991; Brett et al., 1995).

The implication of moderating effect of individual financial condition on tax compliance and its determinants may be more obvious in the society where there is high family responsibility and poverty rate as the case in some developing countries including Nigeria (Brett et al., 1995). Therefore, financial condition of individual may have positive or negative effect on the relationship between his/her attitude and compliance behaviour. Bloomquist (2003) identified financial strain as one of the sources of taxpayer's stress and said that individual taxpayer with meagre financial resources may be tempted by his bad financial condition to be noncompliant where the expenses of his household are more than his income. In a cross national study, Stack and Kposowa (2006) reported financial dissatisfaction to be significant predictor of tax evasion.

Risk preference as a moderator for attitude and tax compliance

Risk preference is one characteristic of individual that influences his behaviour (Sitkin and Pablo, 1992). In a complete conceptualization of risk preference, three ranges are possible. These include: risk aversion, risk neutrality and risk seeking. A number of researchers and scholars have suggested that the attitude of taxpayer to risk cannot be underestimated in his/her compliance behaviour (Alm and Torgler, 2006; Hite and McGill, 1992; Torgler, 2003). Torgler (2007) submitted that individual taxpayers' decision could be affected by their attitude toward risk. Individual risk preference is one of the components of several theories relating to decision making including tax compliance theories like expected utility theory, prospect theory etc. According to Kahneman and Tversky (1979), individual tends to be inconsistent in their decision making as a result of

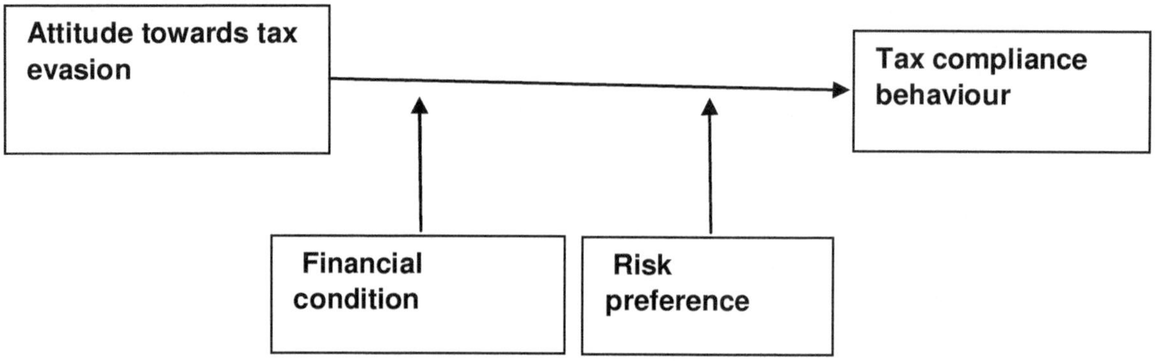

Figure 4. The research framework of tax compliance behaviour.

changing situation. Therefore, when attitude and tax compliance are predicted to have strong positive relationship it may not be so because of the effect of individual taxpayers' risk preference which varies according to situation and individual to individual.

Model and hypotheses

Based on the literature review, the tax compliance model which only incorporate individual taxpayers' attitude towards tax evasion with financial condition and risk preference as moderators is set out in Figure 4.

In the light of theoretical framework in Figure 1, the following hypotheses are developed for test:

H_1: Taxpayer with unfavourable attitude towards tax evasion is more likely to exhibit positive compliance behaviour.
H_2: Taxpayer's financial condition moderates the relationship between his/her attitude towards tax evasion and compliance behaviour.
H_3: Taxpayer's risk preference moderates the relationship between his/her attitude towards tax evasion and compliance behaviour.
H_4: The financial condition and risk preference moderate the relationship between taxpayer's attitude towards tax evasion and compliance behaviour.

MATERIALS AND METHODS

Participants

The target population of this study was individuals whose incomes are taxable under the provisions of Personal Income Tax Act Cap P8 2004[2] in Nigeria. Samples were selected from the target population using multi cluster random sampling technique. Under this technique, the samples were selected in three stages. In the first stage, the Abuja city[3] (Federal capital city of Nigeria) were selected as sampling area and in the second stage, organizations, enterprises as well as government establishments that filed tax returns and PAYE[4] to tax offices operating within the sampling area were chosen. At third stage, the individual taxpayers that participated in the study were selected from the chosen organizations and government establishments. The total population[5] of individual taxpayers in the Abuja city was 175,609 and the sample size of 382 was determined using Krejcie and Morgan's (1970) rule of thumb[6]. However, the sample size was increased to 550 to compensate for non response as suggested by Sekaran and Bougie (2010). A total of 550 questionnaires were administered to these individuals. At the end of the field work, total of 332 of usable questionnaires were retrieved representing approximately 60% response rate or 87% of predetermined sample size.

Procedure

As part of the procedure for data collection, questionnaire[7] which contains likert-type, dichotomous and categorical items was designed and subjected to content and face validity tests with the assistance of tax and research methodology experts. In addition, pre test study was conducted on the instrument using working students of a tertiary institution in Nigeria. The survey questionnaire had a cover letter which explained the purpose of the study and in order to encourage candid response to the study, the letter also explained the anonymity of the respondents would be maintained. The full survey was conducted from 17th October, 2010 to 6th December, 2010. After series of consultations with relevant Nigerian revenue officers and other individuals, the actual distribution of questionnaires to the respondents commenced through the research assistants[8] on the 8th November, 2010. Respondents were given up to 25th November 2010 to return completed questionnaires to the research assistants. However, at

[2] Personal Income Tax Act P8 LFN 2004 is the law that imposes tax on income of individuals in Nigeria.

[3] Abuja city is Nigeria capital city and has representation from every spectrum of Nigeria society.
[4] Pay as you earn (PAYE) is a scheme under which tax is deducted at point of earning income most especially by employees.
[5] The total population of individual taxpayers as at 3rd November, 2011 (Federal Inland Revenue Service).
[6] Reported in Cavana, Delahaye and Sekaran (2001).
[7] The questionnaire was written in English Language, which is the official language in Nigeria. A copy of the questionnaire can be obtained from the corresponding author
[8] A total of 22 of research assistants were appointed for the survey exercise.

Table 1. Demographic Information of the Taxpayers.

Category	Frequency (N = 332)	Percentage (Total = 100)
Gender		
Male	204	61.3
Female	128	38.6
Age groups		
20 – 30 years	75	22.6
31 – 40 years	148	44.6
41 – 50 years	85	25.6
Above 50 years	24	7.2
Education		
Primary education	7	2.1
Secondary education	58	17.5
Higher education	267	80.4
Occupation		
Professional	141	42.5
Non Professional	191	57.5
Source of income		
Public sector	171	51.5
Private sector	81	24.4
Sole proprietor	80	24.1
Income level		
Low income	218	65.7
Middle income	83	25.0
High income	31	9.3
Race		
Hausa	113	34.0
Yoruba	72	21.7
Igbo	61	18.4
Minority	86	25.9
Religion		
Islam	96	28.9
Christian	225	67.8
Traditional religion	11	3.3

the end of dateline, followed up was made for non response and the completed questionnaire forms were finally retrieved from all research assistants on the 6th December 2010.

Measures

Attitude towards tax evasion

The attitude towards tax evasion is defined as the taxpayer's disposition to respond favourably or unfavourably to tax cheat (Ajzen, 1991; Fishbein and Ajzen, 975). Attitude of the taxpayer to tax evasion comprises his belief about tax evasion; feeling about tax evasion and behaviour. The three dimensions of the taxpayer's attitude towards tax evasion were measured using 8 items. These items measured the respondents' tax ethical behaviour as well as their feeling about other tax evaders, tax system fairness and general crime. The items were structured on 5 point likert scale and they followed after the study of Eriksen and Fallan (1996). High score (above 3) is interpreted as unfavourable attitude towards tax evasion while low score (below 3) is favourable attitude towards tax evasion.

Financial condition

Personal financial condition is a moderating variable and it is defined as the extent to which the taxpayer is satisfied with his/her financial condition and that of his/her household (Lago-Penas and Lago-Penas, 2009; Torgler, 2003). It was measured categorically using options of "dissatisfy" and "satisfy" as was done in Torgler (2007) and was re-coded into dichotomous values of 0 and 1, respectively. The score of (0) indicates that the respondents are not satisfied with their financial conditions while the score of 1 suggests that they are satisfied with their financial conditions.

Risk preference

Taxpayer's risk preference is a moderating variable and it is operationally defined as risk-laden opportunities which a taxpayer considers are more desirable than other possible available choices (Atkins et al., 2005; Guthrine, 2003). The study measured the general preference of taxpayer in taking financial risk, social risk, health risk, career risk and safety risk using five items on 5 point agreed/disagree likert-scale as provided in Nicholson et al. (2005). High score (above 3) suggests that respondents are risk seeker while low score (below 3) is an indication that respondents are risk averse.

Tax compliance behaviour

Also in the context of this study, tax compliance is operationally considered as complying with tax laws in the act of true reporting of the tax base, correct computation of the tax liabilities, timely filing of tax returns and timely payment of the amount due as tax (Chatopadhyay and DasGupta, 2002; Franzoni, 2000). Any behaviour by the taxpayer contrary to the foregoing statement is noncompliant. Tax compliance behaviour was measured with four items using hypothetical scenario case as was done in Bobek (1997) and Chan et al. (2000). Respondents were asked to indicate (1) the Naira[9] amount of income and deduction they would report on their tax return if they were in a similar situation to the scenario case (2) the date they would file their income tax returns if they were in a similar situation to the scenario case (3) how many days after receiving an assessment notice it would take them to pay their income tax if they were in a similar situation to the scenario case. The score (1), (2) and (3) were assigned to the options under each items of the scenario case and the values are interpreted as somewhat compliant, moderately compliant and fully compliant.

RESULT

Respondents profile

The demographic information on the respondents as presented in Table 1 indicates that about 61% of the respondents were male leaving 39% as female and that the age grouping of majority of the respondents falls between 20 and 40 years (72.2%). Equally, approximately 80% of the respondents had higher education background either as graduates of polytechnic, university or other tertiary institutions. On occupation, the Table reveals that about 58% of the respondents were not professionals leaving 42% of the respondents as professionals. The source of income for a little more than half of the respondents was the public sector and also majority of the respondents (66%) were low income earners. Table 1 equally reveals that all the ethnic and religious groups in Nigeria were represented in the study but Hausa (34%) and Christian (67.8%) were more prominent in the study. Generally, the composition of the respondents to a greater extent fairly reflected the characteristic of population distribution of Nigeria.

Factor analysis

In order to check the construct validity of the research instrument, the items of metric latent variables were submitted to factor-analysis using principal component analysis with varimax rotation.

Attitude towards tax evasion factors

The values of Bartllet's Test of Sphericity (0.000) and KMO (0.802) as reported in Table 2 suggest that the data on attitude towards tax evasion were appropriate for factor analysis. Three factors were extracted from factor analysis using varimax rotation just as stated in the theory. These factors pulled variance explained of 29.09, 24.14 and 15.81%, respectively with eigen value of each factor greater than 1. Other results of the analysis indicate that the factor loading of items of the three factors range from 0.623 to 0.868 while the lowest values of communality and anti-image correlation coefficient were recorded on item ATT6 (0.584) and ATT1 (0.596), respectively. Furthermore, the reliability tests on the eight produced cronbach alpha of 0.740. With result of analysis presented in Table 2 the assumption of construct validity may be assumed for Attitude towards Tax Evasion.

However, this study is interested in the total scale of the taxpayer's attitude towards tax evasion rather than each of the dimensions (factors) similar to what was done in Fauzi and Kamil (2009).

Risk preference

The factor analysis on the items of risk preference yielded one factor which accounts for about 73% of the variance with eigenvalue of 3.64 (Table 3). Each of the five items has factor loading of value above 0.80 while the lowest value of communality and anti-image correlation coefficient are 0.667 and 0.672, respectively. The appropriateness of the data on Risk Preference was also assured with the values of Bartllet's Test of Sphericity (0.000) and KMO (0.846). These results also met the criteria of factor analysis and therefore provide evidence of construct validity on Risk Preference. Furthermore, the reliability test on the five items gave cronbach alpha 0.917

Tax compliance behaviour

With values of Bartllet's Test of Sphericity (0.000) and

[9] The official name for Nigeria's currency note is Naira and coin is Kobo. Naira was introduced in 1973 to replace Pound. Naira is coded as NGN and the sign is ₦. A unit of Naira is subdivided into 100 Kobo.

Table 2. Factor analysis for attitude towards tax evasion.

Factor	Code	Load	Communal	Anti-image	Total variance (%)
Factor 1					29.09
Other people underreporting their income	ATT4	0.868	0.798	0.771	
Taxpayer claiming nonexistent tax deductions	ATT2	0.805	0.709	0.815	
Feeling about other involvement in tax evasion	ATT5	0.793	0.664	0.845	
Factor 2					24.14
Seriousness of stealing money from wallet	ATT9	0.845	0.740	0.788	
Seriousness of embezzlement of funds	ATT8	0.837	0.751	0.771	
Seriousness of robbing a kiosk small amount	ATT7	0.623	0.620	0.871	
Factor 3					15.81
Taxpayer not declaring extra income	ATT1	0.808	0.656	0.596	
Defend evasion on tax system unfairness	ATT6	0.753	0.584	0.754	
KMO : 0.802			Total variance explained : 69.04%		
Bartlett's test of Sphericty: Sig 000					

Note: 1. Load = Factor loading, communal = communality, anti-image = anti-image correlation. 2. Item ATT3 was deleted in analysis.

Table 3. Factor analysis for risk preference.

Factor	Code	Load	Communal	Anti-Image	Total Variance
Factor 1					72.89%
Financial risk taking	RP1	0.888	0. 667	0.837	
Social risk taking	RP2	0.872	0.760	0.815	
Health risk taking	RP3	0.870	0.789	0.821	
Career risk taking	RP4	0.820	0.883	0.756	
Safety risk taking	RP5	0.817	0.886	0.672	
KMO : 0.846		Total variance explained : 72.89%			
Bartlett's Test of Sphericity: Sig : 000					

Note: 1. Load= factor loading, communal = communality, anti-image=anti-image correlation.

KMO (0.726), the factor analysis of the data collected on tax compliance behaviour is assumed. The analysis yielded one factor which accounts for about of 53% of the variance with Eigen value of 2.25. Item TCB4 has lowest factor loading of 0.653 while the minimum value of communality and anti-image correlation coefficient are 0.426 and 0.681, respectively. The result conforms to the minimum criteria of factor analysis and therefore supports construct validity of tax compliance behaviour. The reliability test on the 4 items gave cronbach alpha 0.740 (Table 4).

Descriptive analysis

Attitude toward tax evasion

The attitudes of the respondents towards tax evasion were evaluated in items ATT1 to ATT9 and the descriptive analysis of these items is shown in Table 5. ATT1 and 2 evaluated the ethical behaviour of the respondents and with the mean score above 3 for each of the items; it implies that the respondents had fair ethnical behaviour towards tax system. In this regarding, majority of the respondents (59% for ATT1 and 52% for ATT2) admitted that not declaring their extra income and claiming nonexistent deduction on tax return were serious offences. The feeling of the respondents towards tax fairness and tax evasion of other taxpayers were captured in item ATT4 to ATT6 and each of these items has mean scores above 3 indicating that the respondents felt bad about the involvement of others in tax evasions and tax fairness. On general crime, the majority of respondents considered stealing and embezzlement serious illegality. The attitudes of the respondents towards general crime were captured in item ATT7 to ATT9 and these items also have mean scores above 3. On the whole, going by the overall mean score of 3.58 and standard deviation of 0.90, the respondents had an

Table 4. Factor analysis for tax compliance behaviour.

Factor	Code	Load	Communal	Anti-image	Total variance
Factor 1					56.36%
Income reporting	TCB1	0.833	0.504	0.810	
Tax deductions reporting	TCB2	0.793	0.426	0.788	
Return filing	TCB3	0.710	0.629	0.695	
Tax payment	TCB4	0.653	0.694	0.681	
KMO: .726		Total Variance Explained : 56.36%			
Bartlett's test of Sphericty: Sig 000					

Note: 1. Load = factor loading, communal = communality, anti-image = anti-image correlation.

unfavourable attitude towards tax evasion.

Risk preference

The preferences of the respondents to take risk were appraised using item RP1 to RP5 and the result of the descriptive statistics on these items (Table 6) indicate that each of the items has mean score below 2. On disagreement scale, majority of the respondents (76%) did not agreed taking health risk of smoking etc (RP1) while at the agreement scale, 16% of respondents agreed to have engaged in social risk. On the whole, the overall mean score of 1.91 and standard deviation of 1.12 suggested that the respondents were risk averse.

Tax compliance behaviour

The compliance behaviour of the respondents towards tax rule and regulations are presented in Table 7. The Table reveals that about 28% of the respondents complied with tax rule and regulations in declaring their income for tax purpose and this leaves about 76% of the respondents as noncompliant. Almost the same result as in income reporting compliance was also obtained on tax claims reporting as only minority (22%) of the respondents were compliant. This result was expected considering the tax claims normally accompany income reporting. Moreover, the result reflected the fact that most of the respondents (52%) derived their income from salaries whose tax is withheld at point of payment and they did not consider it necessary to report other extra source of income for tax. Table 7 also indicates that about 48% of the respondents fully complied with tax rules regarding return filing while the remaining 52% of the respondents did not comply with the tax rule. This result is not surprising considering that a great number of the respondents were salary earners and had their taxes deducted at point of payment perhaps this might have influenced their behaviour. The descriptive statistics on tax payment compliance indicate that about 40% of the respondents fully complied and that leaves 60% as noncompliant. However, in the overall compliance, only about 11% of the respondents complied with income reporting, tax claims reporting, return filing and tax payment as stipulated by tax rule and regulations; therefore leaving majority of the respondents (89%) as noncompliant. The result indicates that tax noncompliance is a great problem in Nigeria.

Moderated multiple regression

For the purpose of testing the hypotheses of this study, moderated multiple regression analysis was adopted and used. The procedures used in the regression analysis were as recommended by Darrow and Kahl (1982), Hair et al. (2010) and supported by Evans (1987). In this case, tax compliance behaviour was regressed on Attitude towards Tax Evasion in the first stage to obtain the main effect while in the second stage; the dependent variable was regressed on independent variable, moderator(s) and the product of the independent variable and moderator(s). Before the multiple regressions, the continuous variables were centered to reduce the effect of multicollinearity as suggested by Aiken and West (1991). The results of the regression are documented in Table 8.

The result of the main effect in model 1 shows taxpayer's attitude towards tax evasion ($\beta = 0.391$; $P<0.10$) significantly positively related to compliance behaviour. In model 2, financial condition and the product term of attitude towards tax evasion and financial condition were entered and the regression result indicates that financial condition ($\beta = -0.215$; $P<0.01$) negatively related to tax compliance behaviour. The result also indicates that financial condition ($\beta = 0.032$; $P>0.10$) has insignificant positive effect on the relationship between attitude towards tax evasion and tax compliance behaviour.

Risk preference was included in model 3 as a moderator (while holding financial condition constant) and the regression result reveals a significant negative relationship between risk preference and tax compliance behaviour ($\beta = 0.126$; $P<0.05$). In addition, the result also indicates that risk preference ($\beta = -0.111$; $P<0.05$) has a

Table 5. Descriptive statistics for attitude towards tax evasion.

Code	Items	M	Std D	S A /Agree	Neutral	S D/ Disagree
ATT1.	Not declaring my extra income of NGN 20,000 on my tax return is serious offence	3.54	1.33	185 (59)	61 (18)	77(23)
ATT2.	Claiming a nonexistent deduction of NGN 5,000 on my tax return is serious offence	3.51	1.48	174 (52)	52 (16)	106 (32)
ATT4.	One can criticize a person who declares lower income than was the case on his/her tax return when there are so many others doing the same.	3.43	1.50	156 (47)	63 (19)	113 (34)
ATT5.	One can criticize others who exploit the many possibilities there are to evade taxes	2.98	1.53	136 (41)	55 (17)	141 (42)
ATT6.	You can defend people who evade taxes because the tax system is unfair	3.93	1.59	215 (65)	73 (22)	44 (13)
ATT7.	I think robbing a kiosk of NGN1,000 is a serious illegality	3.78	1.46	196 (59)	46 (14)	90 (27)
ATT8.	I think embezzling NGN 10,000 from an association which I am a member is a serious illegality	3.52	1.55	187 (56)	44 (13)	101 (31)
ATT9.	I think stealing a wallet containing NGN 500 is a serious illegality	3.93	1.43	214 (65)	34 (10)	85 (25)

Note: 1. M = Mean, Std D = standard deviation, SA = strongly agree, SD = strongly disagree. 2. Percentage in parenthesis.

Table 6. Descriptive statistics for risk preference.

Code	Items	M	Std D	S A/agree	Neutral	SD/ disagree
	Indicate the extent to which any of the following have ever applied to you.					
RP1	Health risks (eg smoking, poor diet, high alcohol consumption).	1.81	1.26	37 (11)	44 (13)	251 (76)
RP2	Financial risks (eg gambling, risky investment).	1.95	1.36	49 (15)	42 (13)	241 (72)
RP3.	Career risks (eg quitting a job without another to go to)	1.92	1.32	48 (15)	47 (14)	237 (71)
RP4.	Safety risks (eg fast driving, city cycling without a helmet)	1.96	1.34	52 (16)	46 (14)	234 (70)
RP5.	Social risks (eg standing for election, publicly challenging a rule)	1.96	1.35	53 (16)	48 (15)	231 (69)

Note: 1. M = Mean, Std D = standard deviation, SA = strongly agree, SD = strongly disagree. 2. Percentage in parenthesis.

Table 7. Descriptive statistics for tax compliance behaviour.

Component	M	SD	Noncompliance		Compliance
			Somewhat Compliance	Moderately compliance	
Income reporting	2.00	0.74	90 (27)	149 (45)	93 (28)
Tax claims reporting	1.86	0.75	120 (36)	140 (42)	72 (22)
Return filing	2.19	0.85	94 (28)	80 (24)	158 (48)
Tax payment	2.16	0.78	79 (24)	120 (36)	133 (40)
Overall	2.06	0.59	94 (28)	238 (61)	36 (11)

Note: 1. M=Mean, Std D= standard deviation, 2. Percentage in parenthesis.

Table 8. The effects of financial condition and risk preference on tax evasion and compliance behaviour.

Variable	Model 1	Model 2	Model 3	Model 4
ATT	0.139 (2.547)**	0.089 (1.206)	0.151 (2.793)*	0.118 (2.205)**
FIN CON		-0.215 (-3.993)*	-	-0.205 (-3.828)*
R P		-	0.126(2.314)**	0.114 (-2.116)*
ATT X FIN CON		0.032 (.431)	-	-
ATT X R P			-0.111(-2.045)**	-
ATT X FIN CON X RP				-0.069 (-1.290)
R^2	0.091	0.065	.051	0.085
Adjusted R^2	0.061	0.057	.043	0.073
Change R^2	0.091*	0.001	.021**	0.005
F Value	6.488*	7.660*	5.909*	7.557*

Note: (1). *p<. .01, ** p< .05,*** p< .10 (2) T Statistics in parenthesis. (3) ATT = Attitude towards tax evasion, FIN CON = Financial Condition, RP = Risk Preference.

significant negative moderating effect on relationship between attitude towards tax evasion and tax compliance behaviour.

Model 4 combines financial condition and risk preference as joint moderators and as with other models, attitude towards tax evasion is still positively related to tax compliance behaviour in the model ($\beta = 0.118$; $P<0.05$). The regression result also shows financial condition to be strongly related to tax compliance behaviour in the model ($\beta = -0.205$; $P<0.01$) .The result equally indicates that risk preference is positively related with tax compliance behaviour ($\beta = 0.114$; $P<0.10$). However, the regression analysis reveals that the joint moderating effect of financial condition and risk preference is weak ($\beta = -0.69$; $P>0.10$) on the relationship between attitude towards tax evasion and tax compliance behaviour.

DISCUSSION

Although we found evidence from the regression analysis in this study, the nature of support varies among the hypotheses. Specifically, the regression analysis provides evidence in support of the prediction in hypothesis (H_1) which indicates that taxpayers' attitude towards tax evasion is significantly positively related to their compliance behaviour and this suggests that taxpayers with unfavourable attitude towards tax evasion are more likely to show positive behaviour towards complying with tax rule and regulations. This finding is consistent with the theoretical prediction that attitude is indication of behaviour (Ajzen, 1991; Fishbein and Ajzen, 1975; Oskamp, 1991). The result equally agrees with previous studies which reported significant positive relationship between attitude to tax evasion and compliance behaviour (Eriksen and Fallan, 1996; Kirchler et al., 2008; Chan et al., 2000; Trivedi et al., 2005). However, the evidence provided by the finding indicates that the relationship between taxpayers' attitude to tax evasion and compliance behaviour is not a strong relationship. The possible explanation for the fairly strong relationship between two variables may be attributed to the fairly weak attitude of the respondents against tax evasion as well as low compliance level as indicated by descriptive statistics. This suggests that weak unfavourable attitude to tax evasion may be responsible for low compliance behaviour in Nigeria. This finding is not surprising for a developing country like Nigeria given that the attitude towards tax evasion may be influenced by other factors as corruption, lack of public accountability, religion, economic situation etc (Abdulazq, 1985; Kiable and

Nwokah, 2009). This suggests why tax evasion remains the greatest challenge confronting tax administration in Nigeria (Abdulazq, 1985; Asada, 2005; Kiable and Nwokah, 2009; Nzotta, 2007; Sani, 2005).

In testing hypothesis (H_2), there was no evidence to show that financial condition has statistically significant moderating effect on the relationship between attitude to tax evasion and compliance behaviour. This finding suggests that financial conditions do not exert significant effect on the impact of taxpayers' attitude on tax compliance. This result is contrary to the finding of Stack and Kposowa (2006) that financial dissatisfaction is significant predictor of tax evasion. The result demonstrates that the interacting effect of financial condition is not important in understanding relationship between taxpayer's attitude and tax compliance in Nigeria. The possible reason for this finding may perhaps be the reasonable number of respondents which indicated that they were satisfied with their financial condition.

However, for a country like Nigeria where more than half of its population is below poverty line, it is right to expect that financial condition would play influential role on the relationship between taxpayers' attitude towards tax evasion and compliance behaviour as suggested in the literature (Bloomquist, 2003; Stack and Kposowa 2006).

For the moderating effect of risk preference, the study provides evidence consistent with hypothesis (H_3) indicating that risk preference demonstrated significant effect on the influence of attitude towards tax evasion on tax compliance behaviour. Surprisingly, the effect of risk preference altered the direction of the relationship between the two variables from positive as previously reported to negative. This suggests that in the presence of risk preference, attitude towards tax evasion is likely to make taxpayers to be less compliant. This is an indication that the effect of risk preference renders the impact of taxpayers' attitude on tax compliance weak and unfavourably. In the light of this finding, it would appear that interacting effect of risk preference is a relevant factor for better understanding of the influence of taxpayers' attitude on tax compliance. This result equally suggests that individuals' risk preference had contributed in making taxpayers' attitude to have negative influence on compliance behaviour in Nigeria. The possible explanation for this pattern of finding may still be connected with weak attitudes of the respondents against tax evasion (Table 4).

Furthermore, contrary to the prediction of hypothesis (H_4), the regression result provides evidence showing that financial condition and risk preference jointly exerted insignificant effect on the relationship between attitude and tax compliance behaviour. This suggests that the influence of taxpayers' attitude on compliance behaviour is not significantly affected by the presence of joint effect of financial condition and risk preference.

The findings of this study have some theoretical and managerial implications. First, this study provided proof that environmental, situational, social and cultural factors may also play important role in influencing tax compliance behaviour not only economic factors as assumed in deterrence theory (Becker, 1968). As identified in Fischer et al. (1992), this study also confirms that attitude plays vital role in shaping compliance behaviour of individual taxpayers in a developing country. The most outstanding contribution from this study is its finding which demonstrated significant opposite moderating effect of risk preference on the influence of attitude on tax compliance behaviour. This finding indicates the relevance of the moderating effect of risk preference in the relationship between attitude and tax compliance behaviour and such effect cannot be underestimated theoretically. Moreover, this result provides proof to researchers that it is possible that certain factors may have moderating effects on the relationship between tax compliance and its determinants as suggested in Kirchler et al. (2007). In the light of the finding on the effect of risk preference, Fischer model would have to be extended to incorporate the moderating of risk preference on taxpayers' attitude for better understand of tax compliance behaviour.

On practical implication, the result from study suggests that policy makers, particularly those in Nigeria should adopt strategies that would prop up taxpayers' attitudes against tax evasion, such strategies would likely have positive effect on taxpayers' compliance behaviour and consequently improve tax revenue collections. Furthermore, policy makers may also be concerned with mapping out policy to mitigate the negative effect of risk preference on the relationship between attitude and tax compliance behaviour.

Conclusion

This study is undertaken primarily to determine the relationship between attitude towards tax evasion and tax compliance behaviour and how such relationship is moderated by taxpayers' financial condition and risk preference. This study has found a significant positive relationship between attitude towards tax evasion and tax compliance behaviour. It equally provides evidence showing taxpayers' risk preference strongly moderated the relationship between attitude towards tax evasion and tax compliance behaviour. Moreover, other findings of this study suggest that the effect of financial condition is not significant on relationship between attitude towards tax evasion and compliance behaviour. Similar evidence is also provided for the joint moderating effect of financial condition and risk preference.

This study has a number of limitations. In the first place, the focus of this study was on individual taxpayers but corporate taxpayers may have different opinion, perception and behaviour from the individual taxpayers. In addition, this study relied on self-reported behaviour of the taxpayers like most compliance researches. The behaviour that taxpayers portray under this method may not be truth representation of their actual behaviour (Tanzi and Shome, 1993). Also, this study only considered influence of taxpayers' attitude towards tax evasion on tax compliance behaviour but the literature has provided evidence to suggest that the influences of attitude towards government as well as the effect of individual religiosity on tax fraud are equally relevant (Stack and Kposowa, 2006).

Moreover, this study provides some guide for future research into tax compliance behaviour. More researches are needed on moderating effect of risk preference on relationship between taxpayer's attitude towards tax evasion and his/her compliance behaviour to check the consistency of the results produced by this study on this moderator. In addition, research studies are desired on taxpayers' attitude towards government and the effect of individual religiosity on tax fraud as well as on other factors influencing tax compliance behaviour particularly in developing countries.

REFERENCES

Abdulrazaq MT (1985). Judicial and legislative approaches to tax evasion and avoidance in Nigeria. J. Afr. Law, 29(1): 59-71.

Ajzen I (1991). The theory of planned behaviour. Organ. Behav. Hum. Decis. Proc., 50(2): 179-211.

Aiken LS, West SG (1991). Multiple regression: Testing and interpreting interactions. London: Sage Publication.

Allingham M, Sandmo A (1972). Income tax evasion:A theoretical analysis. J. Public Econs., 1(3-4): 323-338.

Alm J (1999). Tax compliance and tax administration. In HW Bartley, Handbook on taxation. New York: Marcel Deker.

Alm J, Torgler B (2006). Culture differences and tax morale in United States and Europe. J. Econ. Psychol., 27: 224-246.

Andreoni J, Erard B, Feinstein J (1998). Tax compliance. J. Econs. Lit., 36: 818-860.

Asada D (2005). The administration of personal income tax in Nigeria: Some problem areas. Working paper, University of Jos.

Atkins J, Goldfarb R, Kerps RE, Rogers K, Schoolman P, Van OJ (2005). Elicitation and elucidation of risk preferences. Casualty Actul. Soc. Forum. Fall, pp. 1-28.

Becker GS (1968). Crime and punishment: An economic approach. J. Pol. Econs., 76(2): 169-217.

Bloomquist KM (2003). Income inequality and tax evasion: A sysnthesis. Tax Notes Int., 31(4): 347-367.

Bobek DD (1997). How do individuals judge fairness and what effect does it have on their behaviour?(Federal income tax, Theory of planned behaviour). Ann Arbor: UMI.

Bobek DD, Hatfield RC (2003). An investigation of the theory of planned behaviour and the role of moral obligation in tax compliance. Behal Res. Acct., 15: 13-38.

Brett JF, Cron WL, Slocum JrJW (1995). Economic dependency on work: A moderator of the relationship between organizational commitment and performance. Acad. Manage. J., 38(1): 261-271.

Cavana RY, Delahaye BL, Sekaran U (2001). Applied business research:Qualitative and quantatitive methods. Milton: John Wile, Sons Australia Ltd.

Central Bank of Nigeria (2008). Annual report and statement of account. Abuja: Central Bank of Nigeria.

Chaltopadhyay S, Das-Gupta A (2002). The personal income tax in India: Compliance cost and compliance behaviour of taxpayers. New Delhi: National Institute of Public Finance and Policy.

Chan CW, Troutman CS, O'Bryan D (2000). An expanded model of taxpayer compliance: Empirical evidence from USA and Hong kong. J. Int. Acct. Audit. Taxation, 9(2): 83-103.

Chartered Institute of Taxation of Nigeria (2010). Why Nigeria's tax system is weak. Punch.

Chau G, Leung P (2009). A critical review of Fischer's tax compliance model: A research systhesis. J. Acct. Taxation, 1(2): 34-40.

Cobham A (2005). Tax evasion, tax avoidance and development. United Kingdom: Finance and Trade Policies Research Centre,University of Oxford.

Darrow A, Kahl D (1982). A comparison of moderated regression techniques: Considering strength of effects. J. Manage., 8(2): 35-47.

Doran LI, Stone VK, Brief AP, George JM (1991). Behavioural intention as predictors of job attitude: The role economic choice. J. Appl. Psychol., 76(1): 40-46.

Dubin JA, Wilde LL (1988). An empirical anaysis of federal income tax auditing and compliance. Natl. Tax J., 41(2): 61-74.

Dubin JA, Graetz MA, Wilde LL (1987). Are we a nation of tax cheater?: New econometric evidence on tax compliance. Am. Econ. Rev., 77(2): 240-245.

Eriksen K, Fallan L (1996). Tax knowledge and attitudes towards taxation: A report on a quasi-experiment. J. Econs. Psychol., 17(3): 387-408.

Eshag E (1983). Fiscal and monetary policies and problems in development countries. Cambridge: Cambridge University Press.

Evans MG (1987). Moderated regression: Legitimate disagreement, confusion and misunderstanding. J. Inft. Optim. Sci., 8(3): 293-310.

Fauzi H, Idris KM (2009).The relationship of CSR and financial performance: New evidence from Indonesian companies. Issues in Soc. Envir. Acct., 3(1): 66-87.

Federal capital city of Nigeria (2004). Personal Income Tax Act Cap8 LFN, 2004. Abuja: Government Press.

Fischer CM, Wartick M, Mark M (1992). Detection probability and tax compliance:A review of the literature. J. Acct. Lit., 11(2): 1-46.

Fishbein M, Ajzen I (1975). Belief, attitude, intention and behaviour: An introduction to theory and research- Reading. MA: Addition-Wesley.

Franzoni L (2000). Tax evasion and tax compliance. In B. Bouckaert, G. DeGeest, Encycl. Law and Econ. Cheltenham: Edward Elgar.

Gilligan G, Richardson G (2005). Perceptions of tax fairness and tax compliance in Australia and Hong Kong: A preliaminary study. J. Fin. Crime, 12(4): 331-343.

Guthrie CC (2003). Prospect theory, risk preference and the law. Northwestern Univ. Law Rev., 97: 1115-1163.

Hair JJF, Black WC, Babin BJ, Anderson RE (2010). Multivariate data analysis: A global perspective. New Jersey: Pearson Education, Inc.

Hitte PA, McGill GA (1992). An examination of taxpayer preference for aggressive tax advice. Natl Tax J., 45(4): 389-403.

Ho D, Wong B (2008). Issues on compliance and ethics in taxation: What do we know? J. Fin. Crime, 15(4): 369-382.

Jackson BR, Millron VC (1986). Tax compliance research: Finding, problem and prospects. J. Acct. Lit., 5: 125-165.

Kahneman D, Tversky A (1979). Prospect theory: An analysis of decision under risk. Econometrica, 42(1): 263-291.

Kiabel BD, Nwokah NG (2009). Curbing tax evasion and avoidance in personal Sincome tax administration: A study of the south-south states of Nigeria. European J. Econs. Fin. Admin. Sci., 15: 16-61.

Kirchler E (2007). The economic psychology of tax behaviour. Cambridge: Cambridge University Press.

Kirchler E, Muelbacher S, Kastlunger B, Wahl I (2007). Why pay taxes? A review of tax compliance decisions. Working paper, Georgia State University Altanta.

Kirchle E, Hoelzl E, Wahl I (2008). Enforced versus voluntary tax compliance: The slippery slope framework. J. Econs. Psychol., 29: 210-225.

Lago-Penas I, Lago-Penas S (2009). The determinants of tax morale in comparative perspectives:Evidence from a multilevel analysis. Spain: Instituto de Estdios fiscales.

Manaf NA (2004). Land tax administration and compliance attitude in Malaysia. Unpublished doctoral thesis, University of Nottingham, United Kingdom.

Mathieu JE, Zajac DM (1990). A review and meta-analysis of the

antecedents, correlates and consequences of organization commitment. Psychol. Bull., 108: 171-194.
Mustafa MH (1997). An evaluation of Malaysian tax administrative system and taxpayers perceptions towards assessment system, tax law fairness and tax law complexity. Unpublished doctoral thesis, Universiti Utara Malaysia.
Nicholson N, Soane E, Fenton-O'Ocreevy M, William P (2005). Personality and domain-specific risk taking. J. Risk Res., 8(2): 157-176.
Nzotta SM (2007). Tax evasion problems in Nigeria: A critique. Nig. Acct., 12(1): 40-43.
Odusola A (2006). Tax reform in Nigeria. Research paper. World Institute for Development Economic Research, United Nation University.
Orviska M, Hudson J (2002). Tax evasion, civic duty and the law abiding citizen. Eur. J. Pol. Econs., 19(1): 83-102.
Oskamp S (1991). Attitudes and opinions. Englewood Cliff: Prentice-Hall inc.
Porcano TM (1984). Distributive justice and tax policy. Acct. Rev., 59(4): 619-636.
Reckers PM, Sanders DL, Roark SJ (1994). The influence of ethical attitudes on taxpayers' compliance. Natl. Tax J., 47(4): 825-836.
Richardson G (2006). Determinants of tax evasion: A cross country investigation. J. Int. Acc. Auditing Taxation, 15(2): 150-169.
Roth JA, Scholz JT, Dry-Witte JT (1996). Taxpayer compliance: An agenda for research, volume 2. Philadelphia: University of Pennsylvania Press.
Sani A (2005). Contentious issues in tax administration and policy in Nigeria: A governor's perspective. First National Retreat on Taxation. Lagos: Joint Tax Board.
Sekaran U, Bougie R (2010). Research methods for business: A skill building approach, 5th ed. West Sussex: John Wiley and Sons Ltd.
Stack S, Kposowa A (2006). The effect of religiosity on tax fraud acceptability: A cross- national analysis. J. Sci. Study Rel., 45(3): 325-351.
Sitkin SB, Pablo AL (1992). Reconceptualising the determinants of risk behaviour. Acad. Manage. Rev., 17(1): 9-38.
Soos P (1991). Self-employed evasion and tax withholding: A comparative study and analysis of the issues. Working paper, University of California.
Spicer MW, Lundstedt SB (1976). Understanding tax evasion. Public Fin., 21(2): 295-305.
Teera JM, Hudson J (2004). Tax Performance: A Comparative Study. J. Int. Dev., 16, 785-802.
Torgler B (2007). Tax compliance and tax morale. Cheltenham: Edward Elgar Publishing Ltd.
Torgler B (2003). Tax morale: Theory and analysis of tax compliance. Unpublished doctoral dissertion, University of Zurich, Switzerland.
Trivedi VU, Shehata M, Mestelman S (2005). Attitudes,incentives and tax compliance. Canadian Tax J., 52(1): 29-61.
Wenzel M (2004). The social side of sanctions: Personal and social norms as moderators of deterrence. Law Hum. Behav., 28(5): 547-567.
Yaniv G (1999). The compliance and advance tax payment: A prospect theory analysis. Natl. Tax J., 52(4): 753-764.

6

Myth and reality of the imbricating concepts of tax avoidance and evasion

Priyesh Sharma* and Siddharth Dang

Hidaytullah National Law University (HNLU), Raipur, India.

The difference between tax avoidance and tax evasion is the thickness of a prison wall. "Human beings are greedy by nature and they want to extract the maximum out of what is potentially available to them, but there are ways of this extraction. Every way need not be wrong, though most of them are." The difference between tax avoidance and tax evasion is that tax avoidance is legally permissible by law while tax evasion is not. Judicial pronouncements within India and outside India have always marked out this distinction between the two. The predominant feature in deciding the nature of any transaction is not the underlying motive but the legality of such transaction. In India till now, the difference between tax avoidance and evasion was very clear. In India, the law is settled that tax avoidance is legal and evasion is not. A taxpayer may create a device to arrange his commercial affairs to minimize his tax liability and its acceptance is based on operation of law. But the new proposed code has blurred distinction to a great extent. This Article tries to analyze this difference and the change in the scenario as would be brought by the proposed code.

Key words: Tax Avoidance, tax evasion, legality, human nature, tax avoidance v. tax evasion, tax planning, judicial interpretation, direct tax code-India (DTC-India), objectivity, general anti-avoidance rule (GAAR).

INTRODUCTION

The difference between tax avoidance and tax evasion is the thickness of a prison wall. "Human beings are greedy by nature and they want to extract the maximum out of what is potentially available to them, but there are ways of this extraction. Every way need not be wrong, though most of them are." There are different ways by which a tax payer can escape his tax liability. But there is a thin line difference between escaping tax liability and overcoming tax burden. Everything can be done by both legal means and illegal means; consequently the outcome would also be accordingly legal and illegal respectively. One can escape from tax liability by illegal ways – this is understandable, but escaping or reducing tax liability and that too by legal manner – is it possible? Yes, it is very much possible to reduce burden of tax while remaining within the four corners of law. It is through the loopholes of which tax payers try to take the benefits for reducing their burden.

As a layman a doubt always crept into my mind that how is it possible to take that advantage of loopholes and ambiguities in the law itself to do something which is not so very much aimed by any law or law maker! Every human being no matter how honest and how law abiding he is, he always try to take the maximum benefit out of the given situation and mould the rules and regulations which suits them the best and is maximum beneficial for them. This can be done easily by illegal means. Infact for taking any advantage illegally, there is actually no requirement of moulding any law or taking privilege of any provision- it simply requires to avoid any liability and escape the law. But once again the question arises that how to do it legally? It can be done either by way of interpretation or by the provisions available in law. But how is it possible? Why would the lawmakers themselves provide the ways or provisions to escape the tax liability? Isn't it against the very concept of tax statutes? Answer is not so difficult for those who have glanced taxing statutes. Generally Tax exemptions are provided for several situations. A tax payer can mould the situation to take the benefit of this exemptions or lesser liability. Sometimes even due to improper drafting and ambiguities in the provisions tax payer escapes his liability. But again this is expected from those sitting at

*Corresponding author. E-mail: lawstudent.hnlu@gmail.com

such a high position to leave any scope of ambiguity and improper drafting. But alas! Absence of those with proper technical and professional knowledge from those positions is one of the drawbacks of our government structure. But the study does not concerned with this paper. Talking about interpretation of taking statutes, these are interpreted strictly like penal statutes. No liberal interpretation is permissible.

In India till now the difference between Tax avoidance and Evasion was very clear. In India, the law is settled that tax avoidance is legal and evasion is not. A taxpayer may create a device to arrange his commercial affairs to minimize his tax liability and its acceptance is based on operation of law. But the new proposed code has blurred distinction to a great extent. Let's try to analyze this difference and the change in the scenario as would be brought by the proposed code.

The concept of tax evasion and avoidance

Tax avoidance is the legal utilization of the tax regime to one's own advantage, to reduce the amount of tax that is payable by means that are within the law. By contrast, tax evasion is the general term for efforts not to pay taxes by illegal means.

Meaning

Tax avoidance: It refers to those cases where the tax payer has apparently circumvented the law, without giving rise to a critical offence by the use of a scheme, arrangement or devise often of a complex nature whose sole purpose is to defer, reduce or completely avoid the tax payable under the law. In other words tax avoidance is the method of reducing incidence of tax by taking advantage of certain loopholes in tax laws (hptt//en.wikipedia.org/wiki/Tax_avoidance_and_tax_evasion 2010).

Tax evasion: It is an illegal practice where a person, organization or corporation intentionally avoids paying his/her/it's true tax liability. Those caught evading taxes are generally subject to criminal charges and substantial penalties. Tax evasion is the general term for efforts by individuals, firms, trusts and other entities to evade taxes by illegal means.

Tax evasion usually entails taxpayers deliberately misrepresenting or concealing the true state of their affairs to the tax authorities to reduce their tax liability, and includes, in particular, dishonest tax reporting (such as declaring less income, profits or gains than actually earned; or overstating deductions) (http://www.investopedia.com/terms/t/taxevasion.asp 2010).

RESEARCH METHODOLOGY

Research will be more of descriptive and doctrinal research. The purpose behind the research is to bring the differences between the tax evasion and tax avoidance and analyzing them from the legal perspectives' especially in the light of coming DTC and judicial pronouncements. The data collection as such is divided into:

i) Primary data collection: Data collected through brain storming, discussion, direct interviews and information gathering.
ii) Secondary data collection: Data collected through literature survey, journals, Internet search, company records/bulletin, CD-ROM search etc.

Primary reliance has been based on internet sources like Income Tax Authorities official website and the recent news articles available. An analysis of DTC 2011 has been done.

How dangerous is tax evasion?

"The avoidance of taxes is the only intellectual pursuit that carries any reward." Tax avoidance is legally permissible hence, it does not matter how it would effect because anything which law permits is in some or the way connected with the fulfilment of some legitimate purpose or aim, so the by-products of such a purpose is not so relevant. However, tax evasion can be proved to be really dangerous. Efforts should be even made to prevent the abuse or misuse of the legal provisions. In the case of Mcdowell and co. ltd v. CTO, evil consequences of tax avoidance are summarized as follows:

1) Substantial loss of much needed public revenue;
2) Serious disturbances caused to the economy;
3) Sense of injustice and inequality;
4) Ethics of transferring the burden of tax liability to the shoulders of the guideless good citizens from those of artful dodgers.

The judicial outlook towards tax evasion clearly explains how threat full tax evasion is for the economy. First, the Supreme Court decided that the government was wrong to freeze the bank accounts of five suspected terrorists. Then the high court ruled that thousands of Britons with offshore trusts must now pay backdated tax demands imposed under retrospective legislation, introduced in the 2008 finance Act. While no one should condone tax evasion, these trusts were legal forms of tax avoidance when they were set up. All things considered, it does make one wonder who the courts regard as the real

Figure 1. Tax planning.

threat to society. (http://blogs.telegraph.co.uk/finance/ianmcowie/100003388/tax-avoidance-or-terrorism-which-is-the-biggest-threat/2010).

Tax planning versus tax evasion and avoidance

Tax planning is not tax evasion!

"Whatever is valid in the eyes of law cannot become invalid merely because it also results in tax being saved!" Tax planning, tax efficiency and tax avoidance by companies is not equal to tax evasion. These are the different approaches to the same objective that is, tax reduction (Figure 1). However, they have different characteristics and tax planning is perfectly legal as the object of tax reduction is achieved by making use of the beneficial provisions in the tax laws. On the other hand, tax avoidance is also legal though technically satisfying the requirements of law. Tax evasion is the method of evading tax by dishonest means like suppression, conscious violation of rules, etc. the prime objectives of tax planning are: reduction of tax liability, minimisation of litigation, productive investment, healthy growth of economy and economic stability. There is a very thin line of demarcation between tax avoidance and tax evasion; though both result in avoidance of tax. The distinction between the two lies in the legality of a transaction. Deliberate attempt to subvert the law or manipulation of records to obtain tax relief is an illegal act and would be regarded as tax evasion and is impermissible.

On the contrary, tax avoidance involves arranging transactions within the permissible boundaries of law to secure a tax advantage and is generally accepted as legal. The courts have attempted to provide some distinction between unacceptable tax evasion and acceptable tax avoidance, which is increasingly referred to as tax planning. However, there certainly exists a grey area between legitimate tax avoidance/ planning and illegal tax avoidance and the distinction has become increasingly blurred, in view of varying and often conflicting views of the courts. This leads to increase in uncertainty in the tax system, which is something businesses do not want (http://www.moneycontrol.com/news/management/tax-planning-is-not-tax-evasion_438940.html).

Birla controversy

This can be very well understood in the light of very recent controversy with respect to restructuring of Aditya Birla cement group resulting in some tax benefit to the group- It is a transaction that created the country's largest cement maker. In October last year, group company Grasim demerged its cement business into a wholly owned subsidiary Samruddhi cements, which was then to be merged with another group company Ultratech. This transfer of assets was undertaken to bring the group's cement operations under one legal entity and is structured as a court-approved scheme of arrangement by choosing the amalgamation route the transaction could avail of a capital gains tax exemption under section 47 of the Income Tax Act. An exemption that some experts thought would not pass muster with revenue, would the tax efficiency be interpreted as tax evasion? The issue can be settled by referring to the judicial pronouncements without much difficulty. Verdict by Apex court in A Raman and Co case supports the Birla's case. It says that "Avoidance of tax liability by so arranging commercial affairs that charge of tax is distributed is not prohibited."

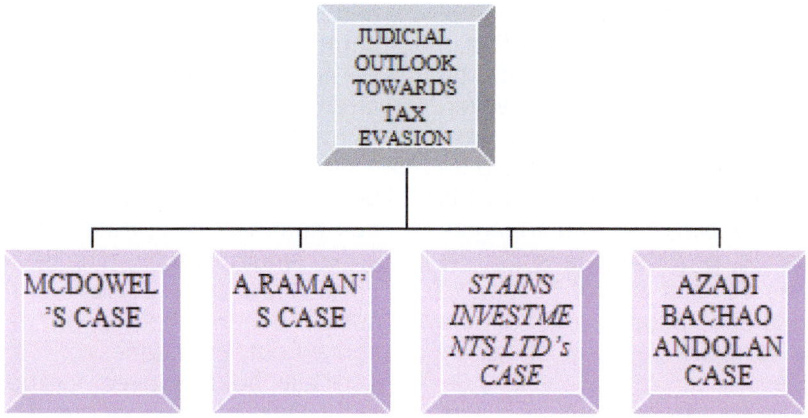

Figure 2. Judicial outlook- Indian scenario.

(http://www.moneycontrol.com/news/management/tax-planning-is-not-tax-evasion_438940.html\)

Star controversy

Yet in another recent dispute of star entertainment channels the Authority for Advance Rulings (AAR) ruled that "It is within the legitimate freedom of the contracting parties to enter into a transaction, which has the effect of extending to the party the benefit of exemption under the taxation statute. The contracting party is not bound to enter into a transaction in such a way that it results in tax liability while foregoing the benefit of exemption under law." This ruling actually addresses that fear. This ruling analyzes the fact that tax evasion and tax planning is different. If there is a genuine business transaction and tax planning happens because there are ways to structure the transaction in tax laws and land up paying no tax, then one cannot say it is tax evasion. The ruling is a welcome development and will provide guidance to evaluate acceptable tax planning in domestic and international business restructuring. (http://www.moneycontrol.com/news/management/tax-planning-is-not-tax-evasion_438940.html)

Judicial interpretation

Outlook of judiciary –outside India

Verdicts have come from different courts in various jurisdictions distinguishing tax evasion from tax avoidance or laying down the nature of these. The crux of these decisions is that "the legal right of an individual to decrease the amount of what would otherwise be his taxes or altogether avoid them, by means which the law permits, cannot be doubted."Avoidance of tax is not tax evasion and, it carries no ignominy with it, anybody can so arrange his affairs so as to reduce the burden of tax to minimum. This was held by the house of Lords in the Lord Tomlin TRC vs Duke of westminster case. The house in that case stated that the citizen has the legal right to dispose of his capital and income so as to attract upon himself the least amount of tax. Yet in another case, the W. T. Ramsay vs Inland revenue commissioners case, the house laid the principle that the fiscal consequences of a preordained series of transactions, intended to operate as such, are generally to be ascertained by considering the result of the series as a whole, and not by dissecting the scheme and considering each individual transaction separately. This case marked the significant departure of judiciary in England in their outlook towards tax avoidance schemes. The significance of Ramsay as a turning point in the interpretation of tax laws in England and the departure from the strings of westminster were explained in Inland revenue commissioners vs Burmah Oil Co. Ltd.

Judicial outlook- Indian scenario

Talking about Indian scenario and outlook of Judiciary towards these transactions three important things observed are:

1) Influence of the decisions of House of Lords;
2) The major criteria in deciding the nature of any transaction or distinguishing is the legality and permissibility of that transaction; and
3) An attempt to overcome the abuse of Law by the tax payers.

Before the decision in Mcdowell's case, the scene was that anything which in some or the other way, by restructuring, manipulation or in any manner comes within the purview of legal framework are permissible (Figure 2). In the CIT vs. A. Raman and Co. case, the Supreme Court of India observed that avoidance of tax liability by so arranging commercial affairs that charge of tax is distributed is not prohibited. Legislative injunction in taxing statutes may not, except on peril of penalty, be violated, but it may lawfully be circumvented. However, the Supreme Court in McDowell vs. CTO took the view that the legal position in case of tax avoidance should be taken as altered in the light of the judgments given by the House of Lords. With this the outlook has been changed. Tax planning may be legitimate, provided it is within the framework of law, colourable devices cannot be part of tax planning and it is wrong to encourage or entertain the belief that it is honourable to avoid payment of tax by resorting to dubious methods.

As in all areas of law, the jurisprudence developed and, the courts permitted the scheme, if there was a strong commercial motivation behind a series of transactions and tax benefit was only incidental. This was the case in Pigott vs Staines Investments Ltd which involved a company securing a tax advantage from transferring profits within a group. The court decided that the method of transferring profits was normal and commercial and the fact that a tax advantage was obtained was purely incidental. The aforestated principles and decisions were discussed in great detail by the Supreme Court in the much celebrated Azadi Bachao Aandolan case rendered in 2002, wherein the court observed: "We are unable to agree with the submission that an act which is otherwise valid in law can be treated as *non est* merely on the basis of some underlying motive supposedly resulting in some economic detriment or prejudice to the national interests, as perceived by the respondents." The Supreme Court in this case also observed that the principle laid down in the Westminster case, namely. "Every man is entitled, if he can, to order his affairs so that the tax attaching under the appropriate Acts is less than it otherwise would be", is very much alive and kicking despite the hiccups of McDowell.

Legal framework under DTC: An attempt to bring tax evasion and avoidance under the purview of any taxing statute in India!

"The direct tax code (DTC), 2009, proposes to introduce general anti-avoidance rule (GAAR), which would erase the thin line between tax avoidance and tax evasion" Under the 1961 Act there are no direct and express provisions dealing with tax evasion and tax planning. Except some special provisions relating to avoidance of tax in International transactions under chapter x, section 92 and 93. To prevent aggressive tax avoidance, which the government believes undermines the integrity and equity of the system, general anti-avoidance Rule (GAAR) has been inserted vide Section 112 of the new direct taxes code (DTC). The GAAR has defined a transaction as an "arrangement" to mean any step in, or a part or whole of, any transaction, operation, scheme, agreement or understanding, whether enforceable or not, and includes any of the foregoing involving the alienation of property.

The expression "impermissible avoidance arrangement" has also been defined under Section 113 of the DTC to mean a step in, or a part or whole of, an arrangement, whose main purpose is to obtain a tax benefit and it,- creates rights, or obligations, which would not normally be created between persons dealing at arm's length; results, directly or indirectly, in the misuse, or abuse, of the provisions of the DTC; lacks commercial substance, in whole or in part; or is entered into, or carried out, by means, or in a manner, which would not normally be employed for bona fide purposes. These definitions of "arrangement" and "impermissible avoidance arrangement" are very wide and there is a genuine apprehension in the mind of the taxpayer that it might even encompass bona fide commercial transactions.

The direct tax code, 2009, proposes to introduce General anti-avoidance rule (GAAR), which would erase the thin line between tax avoidance and tax evasion. Section 112 of the code empowers revenue authorities to declare any arrangement as 'impermissible avoidance arrangement' if it results in certain tax benefits or it creates rights or obligations which would not normally be created between persons dealing at arm's length or it results in abuse of the provisions of the code, lacks commercial substance or lacks bonafide business purpose. It allows revenue authorities to disregard, combine or re-characterize any step in any such arrangement, or re-characterize equity into debt and vice versa.

Essential features

The code allows revenue authorities to label a transaction as lacking commercial substance, if it results in significant tax benefit to a contracting party without concomitant business risks or cash flows or if the legal substance is inconsistent with the legal form or it involves round trip financing.

The code also makes a presumption in favour of the revenue that an arrangement is entered into for the tax benefit alone, unless it is rebutted by the taxpayer. The burden of proof has been shifted on to the taxpayer to establish that obtaining a tax benefit was not the main purpose of the arrangement; else the arrangement shall be presumed to have been entered into, or carried out, for the main purpose of obtaining a tax benefit. The DTC proposes to prescribe penalties and prosecution for non compliance with the tax laws. Several provisions have been spelt out in the DTC which bestow tremendous powers on the revenue authorities to initiate due diligence exercise of the international transactions relating to tax offences and penalize the tax evaders as well (http://www.thehindubusinessline.com/mentor/2009/10/19/stories/2009101950171100.htm).

Concerns

General anti-avoidance rule (GAAR) has given too many wide discretionary powers in the hands of tax authorities. Commissioner has the power to decide as to which transaction is clothed with the motive of tax avoidance and what is the main purpose behind any transaction. The Commissioner has also the powers to disregard, re-characterise, combine transaction, etc. It not only apprehends the misuse or abuse of powers, as it is well settled that 'an absolute power corrupts absolutely" but it also raise the concern as to the certainty in the tax system. Conferring so much power on the commissioner increases the level of subjectivity.

Further, the outline and the wording of GAAR induces an element of subjectivity due to the fact there is a possibility of the same being subject to different interpretation by various revenue officers, tax professionals and taxpayers. Therefore, instead of imparting certainty, which is one of the stated purposes behind DTC, more uncertainty would be introduced into the tax system, which will lead to further litigation. Unlike other jurisdictions, the DTC does not provide for any separate appeal mechanism in cases after the notice has been served to the tax payers for the invocation of GAAR. Absence of such an important provision increases the concern for more and more litigations and hardships for tax payers.

Besides that, the legislation has been over-prescriptive as to how transactions are to be re-characterised by GAAR. It has gone beyond principles laid down in Ramsay case. It even includes the incidental tax benefits. This would in a way increase the hardship of the tax payers and would interfere with the functioning of bonafide transactions. One of the major concern with the DTC, not only specific to the GAAR but in general, is the structuring and contours of this code. Existing tax code is complicated and this one has even defeated the existing one in terms of complications of the language used and the structuring of the provision. But again it would be wrong to expect a tax code without any uncomplicated approach!

Way forward

Some objectivity should be induced in the entire GAAR mechanism. Wide discretion given to the commissioner should be either curtailed down or proper checks should be imposed. This can be done by creating some supervising authority or better a proper appeal mechanism should be created. Advance ruling mechanism can act as a curb on the unbridled powers given to the commissioner to invoke GAAR. Creating a separate authority for appeal may invite the criticism of increasing the litigation and delaying the transactions of tax payers, but in the long run the advantages of this would override the anticipated evils. Not only it would induce certainty in the system but would act as a check on the powers of authorities and make them accountable. The backlog of cases must be cleared to gear up for the new bout of litigation that may arise post-implementation of GAAR. To bring objectivity and certainty proper criteria for deciding the nature of any transaction, without conferring much discretion on the commissioner in this regard should be laid down. Tax payers need not be made to wait till the completion of due diligence by the concerned authorities/officers to understand the nature of their transaction as per DTC. Unless it is implemented judiciously along with a fast track 'alternative dispute resolution' mechanism, the new regime will elevate India's position on the taxpayers' hardship index.

As seen even under the existing Act the judicial pronouncements are being influenced by the situations and pronouncements in other jurisdictions. It would be beneficial to study the experiences of other jurisdictions where the GAAR has been introduced, its effectiveness in curbing tax evasion and its impact on investment climate. Instead of experimenting the new system directly it can be adopted through a well experienced system with the required changes as per the local requirements and conditions. It should be understood that GAAR should not go against the interest of bonafide tax payers and commercial transactions. If the general anti-avoidance provisions are invoked in casual manner they would cause tremendous inconvenience and hardship to genuine and bona fide taxpayers, and undermine the confidence, faith and trust of the taxpayer in the tax administration. Restrictions should be imposed on its invocation by laying down the grounds and criteria exhaustively as far as possible. The entire structuring of the code, if not possible to be simplified, should be at least made less complicated and understandable by the layman. Although, it would not be so wise to make a fiscal law in easy and common language, but it should not be overcomplicated and technical.

Conclusion

The difference between tax avoidance and tax evasion is that tax avoidance is legally permissible by law while tax evasion is not. Judicial pronouncements within India and outside India have always marked out this distinction between the two. The predominant feature in deciding the nature of any transaction is not the underlying motive but the legality of such transaction. However, this position is now going to be changed with DTC coming into force in coming years where the distinction between tax avoidance and evasion has been blurred to a great extent in order to restrict not only tax evasions but also tax avoidance. This is correct but only to the extent that it should not make the restriction and its scope so wide so as to include tax planning also within it, which otherwise is always should be encouraged. Further, there are certain concerns with the DTC and GAAR, which should be overcome by the possible ways mentioned.

LIST OF CASES

Tomlin TRC vs Duke of Westminster, W. T. Ramsay vs Inland Revenue Commissioners, Inland Revenue Commissioners vs Burmah Oil Co. Ltd., CIT vs. A. Raman and Co, McDowell vs. CTO, Pigott vs Staines Investments Ltd, Azadi Bachao Aandolan case.

REFERENCES

http://www.investopedia.com/terms/t/taxevasion.asp

http://blogs.telegraph.co.uk/finance/ianmcowie/100003388/tax-avoidance-or-terrorism-which-is-the-biggest-threat/

http://www.moneycontrol.com/news/management/tax-planning-is-not-tax-evasion_438940.html

http://www.thehindubusinessline.com/mentor/2009/10/19/stories/2009101950171100.htm

Vyas D (2004). The law Practice of income Tax. Lexis Nexis Buttersworth, 9th Edition.

7

The effect of value added taxes on the Indian society

Ravindra Tripathi, Ambalika Sinha* and Sweta Agarwal

Department of Humanities and Social Sciences, Motilal Nehru National Institute of Technology, Allahabad, India.

Value added tax (VAT) is a type of indirect tax that is imposed on goods and services. Sometimes, when the government operates on a budget surplus or wants to increase its revenue in order to finance its budget deficit. A question that arises is whether value added tax has been a boon or misery for a developing country like India. Around 136 countries in Asia have recognized the importance of value added tax. In one of the most large scale reforms of the country's public finances in over the past 50 years, India has finally agreed the launch of its much delayed value added tax from 1st April, 2005 at a rate of 12.5%. The tax rate is fixed by meeting of different state level Finance Minister, in New Delhi, designed to make accounting more transparent, to cut short trade barriers and boost tax revenues. According to Chanakya, "A government should tax its people like a shepherd shears a flock or a bee gets nectar from a flower". The tax is levied not only on products but services that is the source of revenue for the government to plan for development activities in the country. Since, India is a developing country, the main source for revenue is generated through tax levied on the individual on the purchase of goods or services. The government imposes taxes and duty charges on the fellow people for fulfilling the infrastructural, technological, entrepreneurial demand of the country. Whether the imposition of high tax on the society is favorable or unfavorable in the present scenario to meet the technological and infrastructural demand? It has been identified that rural people are charged more tax than urban people due to subsidized rate provided to them in food products, transportation, electricity, water etc. for these facilities they are charged indirectly from their source of income like agricultural and allied activities. The question that arises is: do value added taxes promote prosperity and well being for the common men? VAT is omnipresent in all goods and services provided to the consumer. The paper aims at presenting the importance of value added tax in the Indian society, its impact and the future prospect for product and service industry in India. The data collected is secondary based from the governmental publications and standard for chartered accountants.

Key words: Value added taxes levied, socio-economic effects, role of intermediaries, Indian society, calculation of value added taxes.

INTRODUCTION

Value added tax was first introduced in France in the year 1954 and its scope was expanded to include services in 1978, agriculture in 1983 thus resulting in value added tax becoming one of the most important accounting innovations of the present century. It is presently adopted by over 115 countries all over the world. Value added tax is the abbreviated form for value added tax. For this purpose, value added is to be understood as "the value that a producer (whether a manufacturer, distributor) adds to his raw materials or purchases before selling the new or improved product or service to the user. The tax was first proposed by Dr. Wilhelm Von Siemens for Germany in 1919. The income tax, excise duty and customs duty constitute the major sources of tax revenue to the central government, the state government substantially depends on sale tax as the main source of revenue. It is implemented on all products related to food and beverages, medicines, transportation, telecommunications, amusement parks, cinema halls, properties owned etc.

Value added tax was first introduced by Maurice Maure, a French Economist and the joint director of the French tax authority in 1954. Though this tax system was first applied in France, it was soon adopted by a number of other European and Asian countries. The Indian economy is moving towards simplified and transparent

*Corresponding author. E-mail: ambalika.mnnit@gmail.com

system of indirect taxes by introducing goods and services tax in near future (Peter, 2008).

The indirect taxation, is levied on value from raw materials to the final product, at every stage, value is added to the goods and services. Initiated in France, today value added tax is widely used as a method of taxation in most of the European and Asian countries. Value added tax was first introduced in India in the year 2005. It was levied on all goods and services. Value added tax is a novelty which has claimed the international attention as more countries are adopting it in varying degrees to restructure their systems of taxation. The VAT act allow the set off of tax paid on the inputs in excess of 4% in stock transfer of goods, the same would not be useful in case where goods are transferred from non state, where similar provisions does not occur, the subsequent rates are 4 and 12.5%.

Definition – Value added tax

Value added tax in simple terms could be defined "as a tax on the value addition at different stages of manufacturing and distribution of goods and services". It is a form of indirect tax in the nature of a multi-point sales tax with a set off or credit for tax paid on purchases / services. Each transaction of goods sold in the course of business is taxed, thus providing revenue to the government on value addition at each stage.

Objectives of value added taxes

The primary objective is in the forefront of the evolution of value added tax Law, the State must ensure that barriers to inter-state trade should be eliminated in order to create a unified national market. It will agree that the VAT process must be simple, transparent, and consistent in structure and approach (NCAER, 2009).

METHOD OF COMPUTING VAT

Value added tax is levied in principle on the value of goods and services produced. Value added tax for a given period is equivalent to all income- wages and salaries, rent, interest and profit generated in the production of the aggregate output. A VAT never differs from a general tax on incomes of firms rather than individuals who ultimately receive income are responsible for paying the tax to the government. There are three methods for computing an individual firm which include the addition, the credit or invoice and subtraction method. The first method-adittion presents computing the VAT base is to sum the firm's payments of wages, salaries, interest, rent and profits.

These payments represent the firms contribution to the value of the economy's output in the period or value added. The base multiplied by the tax rate indicates the amount owed the government in value added taxes Purohit and Vishnu (2009). The second method of subtraction method computes each firms value added as sales less purchases of raw material inputs from other businesses. The third method of credit or invoice computes the tax by applying the tax rate to sales and then subtracting taxes paid on purchase of components. The computation of VAT in European countries are usually computed by the credit method (Figure 1).

The term VAT has been described as some special rate for some goods and services. Various categories of economic activity have been exempted in European countries to simplify the administrative procedure, the banking and the financial institutions offer services to which the value added concept is generally difficult to apply and are exempted from tax which includes governmental and educational services, medicine, transportation, communication products and services.

In developing countries, considered necessities of life are taxed at lower rate than the base rate while the luxury items are taxed at higher than basic rates (Rao, 1998).

Effects on the Indian society

In this diagram the Value added is the value that a producer (whether manufacturer, distributor, advertising agent, farmer etc.) adds to his raw materials, or purchases before selling the new or improved product or service. That is the inputs (the raw materials, transport, rent, advertising and so on are brought, people are paid wages to work on these inputs and when final goods and services is sold some profit is left. As the term indicates, it is a tax imposed on value addition of the goods in chain of transaction from pro duction, distribution and retail. A full fledged VAT in essence an *ad valorem* tax on domestic final consumption levied at all stages between production and final point of sale. At each stage tax is confined only to value added. So, Vat is a tax not on the total value of the goods being sold but only on the value added to it by seller. The seller is therefore liable to pay tax not on its gross value but on the net value, the gross value minus the value of input. It is a multi stage tax is being collected in instalment. Therefore, VAT may be called as modified multipoint sales tax. In this calculation starts from Rs.10/- from a trader to retailer ends in Rs. 19/- showing a difference of Rs.9 the additional value being extra charged till it reaches the consumers by the retailers.

The importance of value added tax in India and other countries are due to the following accounting standards which include:

1. Simple tax structure and transparency;
2. Neutrality of tax with respect to behaviour of consumer and of producer;
3. Transparency of tax amount in cost of goods and zero rating of tax on exports are easily identifiable.

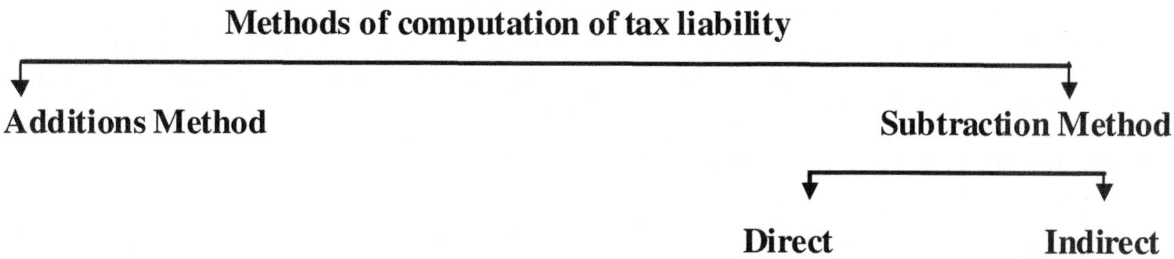

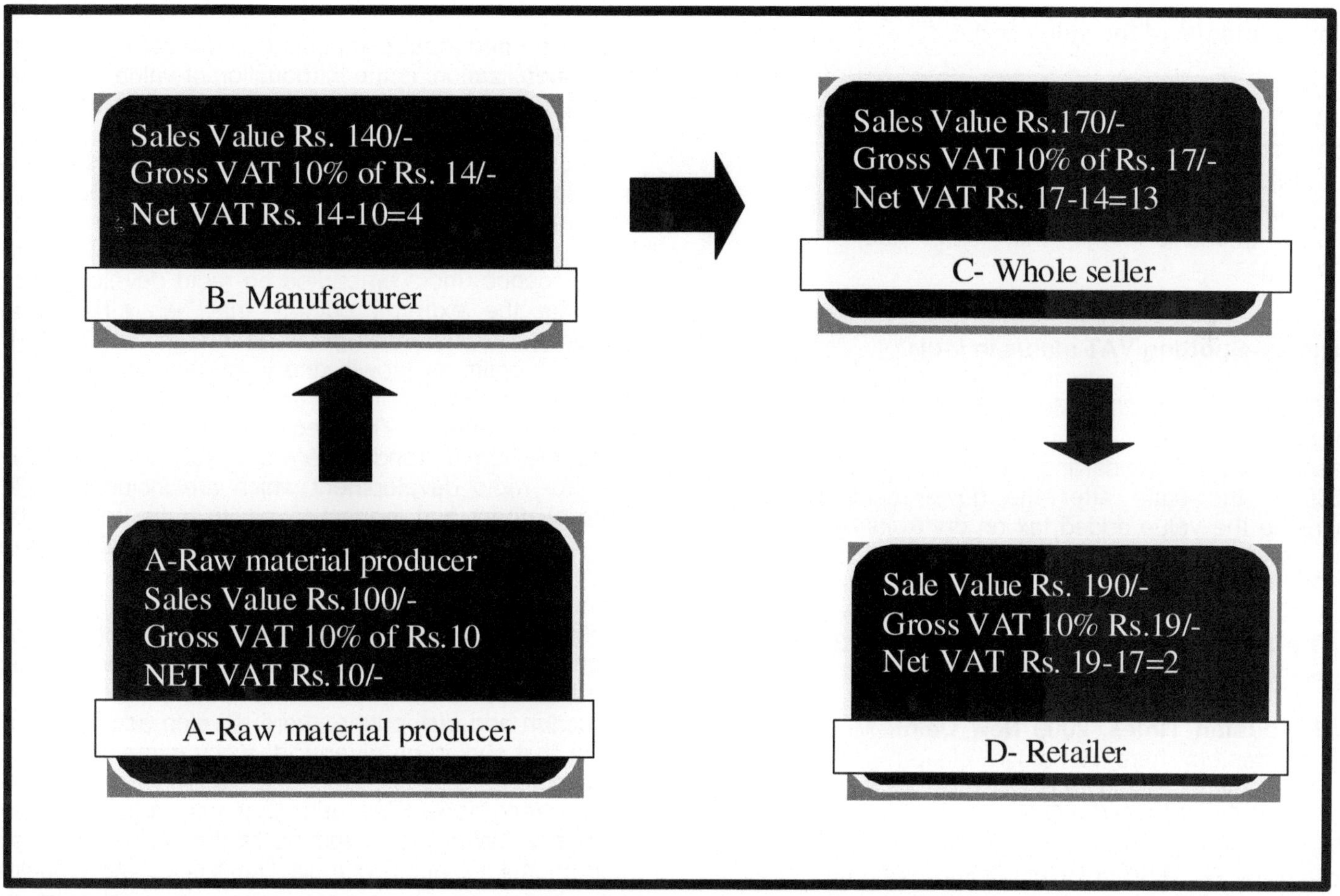

Figure 1. Diagrammatic representation – Calculating VAT. Total VAT collected at four points .Rs 10+4+ 3+2=Rs.19/- Source: A guide on Value Added Tax, Codissia (March 2003), The Coimbatore District Small Industries Association, Coimbatore.

4. Ability to provide same revenue to the Government with lower rates of tax.

Over the last few years, many attempts have been made to implement value added tax in India. Initially, all states were to move to value added tax system by 2000, but administrative problems and concern over the revenue implications of the change delayed the scheduled implementation. It has been postponed many times in the five years and was finally applicable in 2005.

IMPORTANCE OF VALUE ADDED TAX IN INDIA

If a well administered system comes in, it will not only close options for traders and business men to evade paying their taxes, but also make sure they will be compelled to keep proper records of sales and purchases. At the macro level, two issues make the production of VAT critical for India. Industry watchers believe that the value added tax system, if enforced properly, will help in addressing issues like fiscal deposits problems in India and create a high price market for the public Shankar (2005).

Summarization of the current advantages of value added taxes

1. Covering all the states in India,
2. It leads to revenue security for the government,
3. Selection of rates varies state to state due to diversified markets.

Disadvantages of the value added taxes at present:

1. VAT is recognized as an integral activity,
2. VAT is difficult to operate from the position of both administration and business,
3. Leads to business inflation,
4. It has been identified that value added tax favours capital intensive firms that can meet the global challenges.

Articles–Spotting VAT status in India

1. Times of India, 2010 Mumbai: This is a piece of news to go nuts about. The prices of dry fruits, including cashew nuts, almonds and dates, will go up by 20% to 25% in the state after the government decided to increase the value added tax on dry fruits by 8.5% from the current 4%. Once this 12.5% value added tax is levied on the nuts, prices will also soar for ayurvedic medicines, for which dry fruits is used as ingredients.

The State's decision came in on March 31, after the presentation of the budget.

2. Hindustan Times, 2009 New Delhi: More than 400 petrol dealers here remained closed on Monday in protest against the increase in the value added tax on diesel in the capital; Dealers argued that the increase in Value added tax from 12.5 to 20%, has made diesel costlier by Rs. 3.50 in Delhi, as compared with Haryana leading to a loss of almost 30 to 35% of business for petrol dealers. The worst effected were the 150 odd petrol pumps that are located to the borders of Haryana and Uttar Pradesh.

3. Express line, 2007, Jammu: With the VAT Bandh again, the medicine and chemist shops closing down from Monday till Friday. Though no prior notice has been given to the government, the chemists and druggist say that the closure has been forced, since the government is not responding and the State government has not issued any such prior notice so far regarding tax charges.

The articles in the newspaper, show how society is effected with the imposition of value added tax in India. The common people who are the daily earners are the most sufferers. Sometimes, such impositions anger burst out into the form of strike, hartal and bandh affecting peace and harmony of the society. The common people are the most sufferers as they remain entangled in meeting essential commodities for their living which include rent tax, food tax, education tax, loan tax, medicine tax, entertainment tax, fare tax etc To maintain these standards the people sometimes engage themselves into activities leading to theft, fraud, cheating, and embezzlement in the environment.

EFFECTS OF VALUE ADDED TAXES ON SOCIETY

One of the important components of tax reforms initiated since liberalization, is the introduction of value added tax. VAT is a multidimensional based system of taxation, with tax being imposed on value addition at each stage of transaction in the supply chain (Figure 2). After independence, India embarked on rapid development to eradicate the extreme poverty that has affected the transaction in the supply chain (Figure 2). After independence, India embarked on rapid development to eradicate the extreme poverty that has affected the economy. The state was given an interventionist role for achieving optimum growth and to quickly accomplish an economic transition from an underdeveloped to a developed country. This required the government to collect the surplus funds where available and to mobilize them for rapid development which are included by the name of direct and indirect taxes. In India, income tax, corporation tax, wealth tax are examples of direct taxes whereas, customs, excise and sales taxes are examples of indirect taxes.

Thus, those who are considered to be too poor to pay direct taxes because their incomes are low are also forced to pay taxes. The idea is that at each stage of production and distribution, there is value addition and a part of that should be given to the government for social development.

The rates of taxes charged differ from area to area as per policy. With the upcoming of the Mall system and International services in India like VLCC, Mc Donalds, Sub Food ways etc. charge a hefty amount from the public in the name sake charging as per government order. The medium and lower class people that are not aware of these accounting techniques face difficulties in the ascertainment of rates for a good or service. In order to maintain a better value added tax system in India, it is necessary to maintain a dual process of maintaining invoices, bills by the seller and the purchaser. "VAT is already levied differentially on food and drink; more VAT is charged to drink coffee on the premises than to take it away", writes Sheron, an adviser to the Commons health select committee's inquiry into alcohol earlier this year. "If this policy was applied to alcohol but was reversed – say, for example, reducing the VAT for on-sales from 20 to 12% – it would be possible to increase the rate of duty to

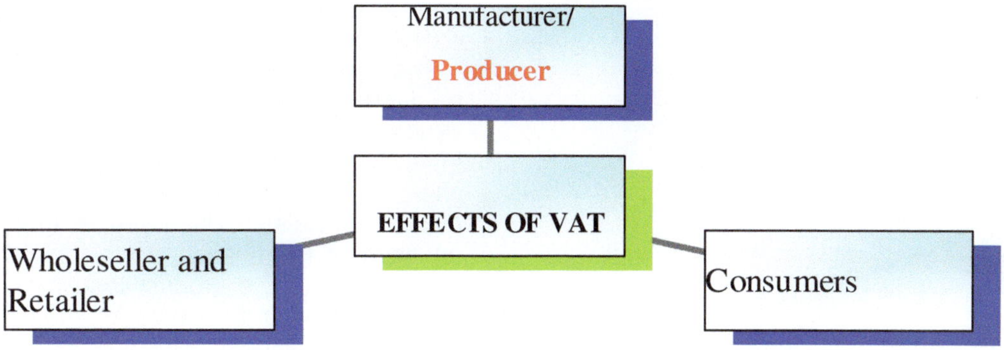

Figure 2. The effect of VAT on the Indian Society.

compensate for this without increasing the price of alcohol in pubs."

Indian position

India is a federal state. Thus, the powers of taxation are divided between the Centre and State. In India's indirect Tax system, the Central government has the authority to impose excise duties on production or manufacture while the States are assigned the power to levy sales tax. In addition, States are empowered tax on many other goods and services in the form of entry tax, octroi, entertainment tax, electricity duty, motor vehicles tax. In newspapers, we read about the high prices charged on products and services like air fares, food products, petrol, entertainment etc. is affecting people in a positive way leading to contribution for nation and humanity. The quotation of famous personalities which show the impact of value added tax in India Chidambaram to State Governments:

"on behalf of the centre, I promise to fully cooperate with you, compensate you and help in building a computer network system and resolve all problems" **(**Ramesh Chandra Secretary of the Federal Panel)

"Value added tax will be launched tomorrow (April 1) and there is absolutely no question of deferring it." (World Bank Country director Michael Carter)

"A comprehensive value added tax widens tax net, as it makes tax evasion difficult going by the experience of other countries, value added tax has proved beneficial and leads to remove buoyancy".

These comments by renowned personalities help in understanding the technicalities of the accounting and taxations.

THREATS UNDER VAT THAT IS RECOGNIZED AS PER INDIAN PERSPECTIVE

The Indian consumer is more burdened with financial crunch and price inflation. The poor are the most sufferers and their purchasing power is low. They have to earn hard to live a standard life, at ones blood and sweat. Concept of small and working family has emerged in the cities, towns and even in villages where both the partners are working to support themselves and their family. In the rural areas, the men move out to cities in search for employment and the females look after the activities of the household. In such a situation the imposition of heavy tax is feasible or the tax rates should be subsidized to avoid criminal activities such as murder, theft, fraud, embezzlement in the society. Its not only the consumer who are hit hard by the value added tax charges but the intermediaries involved in the chain, from producer to retailers have to pay taxes to the government and meet the legal and accounting standards to present a fair picture of their businesses (Hossain, 2003).

From the consumer's end:

1. Incorrect usage of non-VAT memos,
2. Use of fake bills to counter purchases made from unregistered dealers or dealers,
3. Adjustment of inter-state with purchases made local.

From the seller's end:

1. Unauthentic bills,
2. Classification of goods for applicability of special additional tax,
3. Classification of goods to identify,
4. Under pricing of goods sold.

The general public is affected by tax rates simultaneously, as rich class people are only able to bear the burden.

Issues concerning the effects of VAT

The consequences of adopting VAT or any tax change have effects on inflation, income distribution, resource allocation, economic growth and nations balance of payment depends upon the specific forms of tax and the accompanying circumstances. Many believe tax to be a

	Cash Memo **RESTAURANT**	
Bill No: 3412		
Party: Cash		
SN DESCRIPTION	QTY UNIT	PRICE (Rs.)
Masala Dosa	1cm	45.00
Add Vat @12.5%		5.62
Add Sat @ 1.00%		0.45
Less rounded off@		0.07
		....
		Rs.51

Figure 3. Cash memo of a restaurant (Example 1).

regressive tax. The objective is to encourage the economy's potential for and achieve economic growth. VAT as a direct tax tends to increase the nations exports than imports. The VAT is also considered advantageous to the balance of trades.

VALUE ADDED TAXES CAN BE ACCOUNT BASED

By the method of collection, value added tax can be accounts-based. Under the accounting method of collection, each seller charges value added tax rate on his output and passes the buyer a special invoice that indicates the amount of tax charged. Buyers who are subject to value added tax on their own sale, consider the tax on the purchase invoices as input tax and can deduct the sum from their own value added tax liability. Cash basis accounting is a very simple form of accounting. When a payment is received for the sale of goods or services, a deposit is made, and the revenue is recorded. as of the date of the receipt of funds no matter when the sale had been made "Question: A is a trader selling raw materials to a manufacturer of finished products. He imports his stock in trade, as well as purchase the same in the local markets. If the rate of VAT is assumed to be 12.50% would pay tax as under.*"

FINANCIAL IMPACT OF VALUE ADDED TAX ON DIFFERENT SECTORS- DISCUSSION

Standard value added tax rate in India

In India, the standard rate is 14%, while the reduced rates are 4, 1 and 0. Presently, there are two basic rates of VAT in India namely 4 and 12.5% effective from 1st April 2005. Apart from this, there is an exempt category and a special rate of 1% for a few selected items. In the exempt category, items of basic necessities and goods of local importance have been put up (Agha and Haughton, 1996). The value added tax is charged differently in the products/manufacturing and service industry.

The examples will provide the clear picture of VAT charges in India.

The value added tax is charged differently in the products/manufacturing and service industry. The examples will provide the clear picture of VAT charges in India. Here, the Figure 3 presents how service industry charges VAT are effecting the ignorant customers and ultimately society. The issue is that common men are unaware of the financial terminologies and calculations. In the case of the product industries the process starts from purchase of raw material, manufacturing and finally selling.

Manufacturer/Producer

The manufacturer would be required to purchase raw material after paying full tax on the rate applicable on such material. Unlike the present system wherein the manufacturer can purchase the goods at a concessional rate of tax against the declaration form no. which will be required to be issued by the manufacturer (Glen et al., 2006). The input tax suffered by him would be adjusted off from the sale of the finished product. Here, the calculation made by the manufacturer as VAT is calculated by deducting tax credit from tax collected during the payment period.

Wholesaler

The wholesaler who purchases good in large quantities form the producer or manufacturer has the responsibility in turn to charge VAT rate from the consumer for the price paid. The wholesaler sells the product at a lower price in comparison to the retail price to promote sale of the bulk commodity.

Trader / retailer

The trader would be required to collect tax on the sales made by him and the tax liability would be set off or adjusted from the purchase or input tax credit of the goods locally purchased by the consumers. The third intermediary in the supply chain has the most effective role of maintaining good relationship with the customers (Ravi, 2005). They directly deal with the regular customers the prices charged by them includes retailer, government and producer share.

Consumers

The consumers, the ender user are overburdened with the high VAT paid by them due to product or service reaching to them is through the channel of intermediaries.

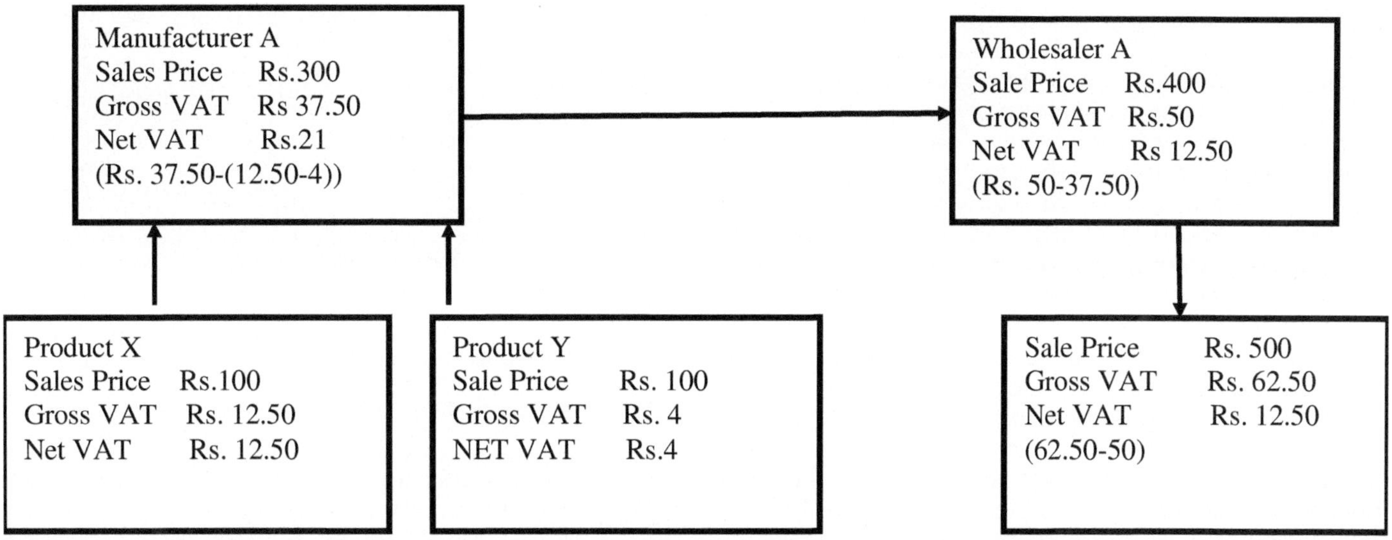

Figure 4. Different stages of VAT-results. Note: The rate of tax is assumed to be 12.5% on the transactions related to goods manufactured by A. Adopted from: Sunil P. Jain (2010), Taxonomy of VAT, Backdrop for State level VAT in India.

The common public is ignorant of the taxation techniques and find it difficult to calculate the selling price of a commodity. It is required that the customers collect invoice at every purchase to maintain an authenticity in the system (Bibi and Jean–Yves, 2004). The government has imposed VAT laws in 2006 for every individual intermediary in the supply chain to pay indirect tax as per fixed in law.

For example, in the furniture industry (product/ manufacturing industry) at every purchase by the manufacturer from raw material procurement, cutting, designing and manufacturing tax is charged at each level.

1. Raw material (wood) purchase (VAT charged),
2. Manufacturing of furniture (VAT charged again),
3. Selling price (VAT charged third time).

In the name of government law, to charge rate at every process. The price hike has emerged as a big issue in the Indian society, where people work hard to meet their daily requirements. They are charged thrice for a commodity at 12.5% (Figure 4). In todays scenario, the role of direct purchase and hyper marketing is growing in India.

The scope of direct sales through malls has emerged as a big market, leading to the elimination of intermediaries in the supply chain thus reducing the per value added services charged from the consumers. These markets are the solution to the traditional marketing system in India to overcome the hike in prices in the commodities and services. The traditional supply chain has been replaced by the new system of marketing through super bazaars, sub malls, so that consumers have more choice to buy the varied products. The price charged by them not only included the VAT charge, but also service charge and showroom costs which add more cost to the product.

These markets have emerged as a super market to the public as the role of direct selling is encouraged leading to mitigation of additional cost and risk in the process of transferring goods from one place to another (Government of India, 2005).

Stocks

Stock statement are required to be furnished as prescribed for the quarter ending and then monthly from January to March. Set-off of tax paid stocks would be given. Tax paid stocks as on march ending would be the basis for claiming set of under the new value added tax Act (Mahesh, 2001).

Export

Export would be zero rated. Tax paid on raw material used in manufacture of goods for export would be refunded by the State Government in cash \ adjustment. The exports would become more competitive in the world market as there would be no tax henceforth on raw material used for manufacture of goods for export (Kavita, 2008).

Conclusion

Value added tax would change the nature of trade in the coming years, but the medium level of trade would face problems as the companies would reduced the tier of marketing. Similarly, small retail dealers would be required to maintain more accounts or pay composition money which cannot be collected from the customers. The present provision of central sales tax and Value added tax can not go together. After the abolition of central sales tax the direct marketing concept may gain ground and the necessity of having warehouse, go downs etc. in all states may decrease or finish. Value added tax in India has been introduced in modified variants over the past two decades. However, value added tax in its original form is yet to be introduced in India, at Central or State level. After the negative and positive impact on the Indian consumers, Value added tax has been identified as the real goal maker by the Indian government in the coming years to foster growth and prosperity in the country. The change in the standard of livings has increased the purchasing power of the high class society but the medium and the poor class society has to work hard in order to achieve there living and meet extravagances.

REFERENCES

Agha A, Haughton J (1996). Designing VAT system some efficiency consideration: The review of economics and statistics. MIT Press, 78(2): 303-308.

Bibi S, Jean–Yves D (2004). "Poverty – Decreasing indirect tax reforms: Evidence from Tunisia." CIRPEE Work. Pap., 04-03, Department of Economics ,University, Laval.

Glen P, Jenkins HJ, Chun YK (2006). Is the value added tax naturally progressive? Queens Economics Department Working Paper, No. 1059.

Government of India (2005). "A white paper on State level. Value added tax" Ministry of Finance, Empowered Committee of State Finance Ministers, January.

Hossain SM (2003). " Poverty and social impact analysis: A suggested framework."IMF Working Paper, WP/03/195, October.

Kavita R (2008). Goods and services tax for India, National Institute of Public Finance and Policy, New Delhi. Work. Pap., 57: 2-6.

Mahesh CP (2001). National and sub nationals of VAT'S - A road map for India. Jstor, Econ. Polit. Wkly, p. 757.

NCAER (2009). "Moving to Goods and Services Tax in India: Impact on India's Growth and International Trade", Thirteenth Finance Commission, Government of India.

Peter (2008). "The treatment Non-Profit Bodies and Government Entities under the Empowered Committee of State Finance Ministers (2008). "A Model Roadmap for Goods and Services Tax in India." New Delhi.

Purohit MC, Vishnu KP (2009). "Goods and Services Tax in India: Estimating Revenue Implications of the Proposed GST", Thirteenth Finance Commission, Government of India.

Rao MG (1998). "Model Statute for Value Added Sales Tax in India", New Delhi. Business School, pp. 104-114.

Ravi YK (2005). Value added taxes issues and concerns. The Institute of Chartered Accountants of India, pp. 1616-1618.

Shankar (2005). "Thirty Years of Tax Reform in India." Economic and Political Weekly.

8

A comparative evaluation of South African SME financial statements against the IFRS requirements

Danie Schutte[1*] and Pieter Buys[2]

[1]North West University, Private Bag X6001, Potchefstroom, 2520, South Africa
[2]School for Accounting Sciences, Faculty of Economic and Management Sciences, North West University.

Research revealed that strong enforcement of accounting standards would improve the quality of financial reporting. As a result, information communicated by management to existing and potential shareholders should also improve. Proper financial reporting is however not necessarily an SME objective. Traditionally SME owners also fulfil a management function in the business. Moreover, little evidence exist that disclosure practices of SMEs are monitored. Notwithstanding these circumstances the IFRS for SMEs was developed for the SME sector worldwide. The relevance and adequacy of this accounting framework to the SME sector is therefore doubtful. This study compares current disclosure practices by South African SMEs against the IFRS for SMEs' illustrative financial statements. Based on a sample of financial statements from the SME sector in South Africa our results suggest to what extent the illustrative financial statements is suitable for South African SMEs.

Key words: Accounting, generally accepted accounting practice, small and medium entities, international financial reporting standards.

INTRODUCTION

When considering conventional accounting research the focus is often on the objective quantitative data that is publicly available such as from stock exchanges. Practising accountants are however also entrusted with a stewardship role and is also very much involved in the preparation of such data. Yet minimal accounting research seems to be conducted in this specific preparatory area of accounting. Although Ball and Foster (1982: 164 to 169) suggested that the financial statements exemplify the database in empirical accounting research, the focus of researchers in recent times has not been on the database or the information disclosed in the financial statements, but rather on the development of international financial reporting standards (IFRS) and more recently, on the adoption of these standards by large industrialised countries, such as the United States (US), Canada, and members of the European Union. According to Zeghal and Mhedhbi (2006: 374) empirical research on the adoption of IFRS is of a general nature only and limited to a description of particular circumstances. Early on Ball and Foster (1982: 164) identified major differences between empirical research in the field of accounting (as a social science) compared to research in the basic scientific disciplines. They advocated that accounting researchers are confronted by the imperfect match between the theoretical background of the accounting discipline and the institutional data presented by accountants. In addition they identified major differences between accounting research and work undertaken by practitioners, suggesting that "good" accounting research might not satisfy either the disciplinary purist or the practising accountant.

In addition to differences between accounting and non-accounting disciplines, evidence of diversity within the discipline of accounting also exists. A number of researchers, such as Gannon and Ashwal (2004: 43) as well as Zanzig and Flesher (2006: 1) revealed

*Corresponding author. E-mail: danie.schutte@nwu.ac.za.

JEL Classification: M41 – Accounting; **M48** – Government Policy and Regulation.

inconsistencies in national and international accounting practices. As a result many governments, accounting regulators and other governing bodies called for accounting harmonisation. Van der Tas (1988: 157) defined the term harmonisation as the coordination, or the tuning of two or more objects. Accounting harmonisation therefore implies coordination between two or more sets of financial statements. According to Van der Tas (1988: 158) accounting harmonisation can either be formal as a result of the standard setting process or spontaneous without being influenced by accounting standards. The degree of formality is further influenced by the degree of legal backing for accounting standards. Although accounting is considered to be self regulated by the professional values, ethical rules and governing bodies prescribing business practices. Willmott et al. (1992: 33) suggested that the state should be more involved in mediating the process of accounting regulation. As a result legislative backing for accounting standards was introduced in the US, United Kingdom (UK), Canada, Australia and elsewhere (Sawani, 2009: 1; Bradbury and Van Zijl, 2005: 78). Although legal backing for accounting standards and related reporting frameworks for companies was identified as one of the critical components of the corporate reform process, the situation in South Africa remains uncertain. Apart from disclosure requirements for listed companies little evidence exists that disclosure practices and related adherence to accounting standards of unlisted SMEs are monitored. We therefore suggest that the format of financial statements of the SME sector in South Africa was to a certain extent, the subject of spontaneous harmonisation due to limited enforcement and monitoring of adherence to accounting standards.

Our research was further complicated by the lack of formalities of SMEs (White, 1995: 11) as well as the fact that most information is often considered confidential. SMEs do not disclose all the information utilised in similar research projects pertaining to listed companies. Moreover, in contrast to the financial statements of listed companies, SME financial statements were not readily available. Despite these limitations we attempted to analyse disclosure practices from a sample of SME financial statements and to compare the content thereof to the illustrative financial statements of the recently announced IFRS for SMEs.

Theoretical framework

Development of the database

The accounting "database" has been the subject of major developments over the years. Companies in the US and UK were not required to compile financial statements in the nineteenth century (Watts, 1977: 58). During this period many companies voluntarily compiled financial statements comprising a balance of profit or loss as well as a balance sheet. Some companies disclosed only partial financial information and many companies did not have proper records to substantiate the financial information disclosed. In order to address this deficiency pertaining to the quality of the accounting database a number of statutory bodies were introduced in order to regulate financial reporting, for example the securities exchange commission (SEC) in the US, the Financial Reporting Review Panel in the UK and many other national monitoring bodies elsewhere (Sikka, 2001: 200). The introduction of financial reporting regularity bodies did not necessarily result in a reliable accounting database as accounting regulation has also undergone major developments in recent times. Even though IFRS was adopted by more than 100 countries, the convergence did not occur simultaneously. In 2002 the European commission (EC) issued a regulation which required listed companies from member states to prepare financial statements in accordance with IFRS as of 1 January, 2005. As a result the convergence to IFRS by European countries commenced in 2005 whilst others are planning to adopt IFRS in the near future, for example Canada, India, Japan and South Korea. In like manner the SEC outlined a roadmap that will result in mandatory transition from US generally accepted accounting principles (US GAAP) to IFRS by 2014 (Deloitte, 2009b: 1).

Major obstacles are expected in these convergence efforts, for example, without even considering other countries; there were initially approximately 200 key differences between US GAAP and IFRS alone. US GAAP contain specific rules whereas IFRS are considered to be based on principles (Gorelik, 1994: 95).

In addition to these differences, a number of new IFRSs were introduced since the formation of the international accounting standards board (IASB) in 2001. Over and above the 41 accounting standards developed from 1973 to 2001 by its predecessor, the International Accounting Standards Committee, the IASB developed a further nine accounting standards from 2001 to 2009 (IASB, 2009: 1). It appears therefore that the database of the accounting environment may not only be incompatible between different countries due to different prevailing local accounting regulations but also inconsistent from year to year due to different convergence rates to IFRS as well as new developments in IFRS.

Accountability and accounting regulation

Hope (2003: 236) suggested that strong enforcement of accounting standards would improve the quality of financial reporting. The enforcement of accounting standards is, according to the EC, dependant on transparent corporate governance systems, auditing regulation, as well as independent institutional review (CESR, 2003: 3). According to the SEC (2000: 1) a high quality financial reporting environment is dependant on a combination of efficient reporting standards and active regulatory oversight. Despite the theoretical soundness of the regularity enforcement of accounting standards, little evidence exists in connection with the effectiveness of the methods to monitor compliance of accounting standards.

Firstly, although certain countries might have systems in place to monitor compliance with prevailing accounting standards, they might not necessarily be able to monitor compliance with IFRS. The fact that, prior to the adoption of IFRS, accounting standards in many countries were rules-based might be more burdensome in practice. Furthermore, due to the fact that IFRS was only recently adopted in many countries little evidence exists in connection with the monitoring and regulation pertaining to the application of IFRS.

Benston et al. (2006: 165) warned against inconsistent accounting practices when principles-based judgments are required to measure assets and liabilities. They also proposed a true-and-fair override requirement in order to address the inconsistent application of accounting principles. In addition, if accounting practises are burdened by the application of accounting principles the regulation of accounting principles should be even more difficult to achieve. Zeff (1995: 54) highlighted difficulties experienced by accounting governing bodies to regulate principles-based terms, for example “fair presentation”.

Moreover, Kershaw (2005: 616) suggested that principles should not be taken too seriously in the process of accounting regulation and concluded that the presence of principles will not necessarily get in the way of misleading financial information. It is therefore possible that principles-based IFRS might result in inconsistent accounting practices which will in turn also complicate the process of monitoring and regulating accounting practices. In the second instance the monitoring function will be burdened by the diverse legal environments of countries across the globe. Daske et al. (2008: 2) suggested that the enforcement of IFRS will not be successful amongst countries with weak legal and enforcement regimes. Countries with stringent legal systems will therefore be more readily complying with IFRS which will in turn assist the process of monitoring compliance.

Thirdly, diverse levels of enforceability should be considered. Similar processes and practices will not necessarily be followed in the process of monitoring compliance with IFRS in different countries. The SEC will perform the monitoring function in the US, the EC will be entrusted with the function in Europe whilst the function can be conducted by securities regulators, stock exchanges or other mechanisms such as review panels in other parts of the world (Dao, 2005: 108). In addition to dissimilar processes and practices, monitoring bodies from different countries might be entrusted with different levels of enforceability. Ball et al. (2000: 4) argued that the extent to which accounting practices adhere to accounting standards varies internationally and that the incentive to follow accounting standards depends on penalties under different enforcement institutions. As a result penalties and fines for non-compliance with accounting standards may vary between countries. We therefore suggest that the process of monitoring compliance with IFRS will be inconsistent between countries due to different processes and practices as well as different levels of authority to monitor compliance with IFRS.

SME reporting

Though, Hope (2003: 236) suggested that strong enforcement of accounting standards would also increase analysts forecast accuracy it is not clear whether he envisaged all types of businesses, especially the SME sector when he made this statement. Levin and Travis (1987: 30) advocated that the financial statements of SMEs tell only half the story about private companies. The nature of SMEs (with limited investors) is substantially different than that of listed companies (with a variety of investors). The involvement of owner-managers do not warrant the same comprehensive effort by the directors to communicate financial information to multiple and diverse shareholders. Most SME owner-managers are already involved in the day-to-day operations of the businesses. Not only do they have regular access to the financial information, but they also consider certain financial information to be confidential.

Khosrow-Pour (2006: 954) suggested that issues of security and privacy are considered to be the main barriers in respect of SME research. In addition the financial statements of SMEs are not necessarily utilised for budgetary and related forecast purposes as the principal role of SME financial reporting is retrospective and confirmatory in nature (Baskerville and Cordery, 2006: 11). According to McMahon (1998: 3) the financial information of SMEs is mainly utilised to evaluate the success of past decisions and in determining the present position. Furthermore, McCahey (1986: 123) found that owner-managers are the primary users of SME statutory reports and that they do not necessarily have the ability to properly interpret them. Since the primary users of SME financial statements do not know how to interpret the information we suggest that the contents of the financial statements are also not the subject of a detailed analysis process.

In the absence of detailed analysis of SME financial statements compliance with and the related enforcement of IFRS might not be a priority for accounting regulators. Moreover, Sian and Roberts (2009: 302) found that, in addition to owner managers, tax authorities are the key recipients of SME financial statements. The likelihood that the contents and format of SME financial statements are influenced by the disclosure requirements of tax authorities, and not accounting regulators, can therefore not be ruled out. In conclusion evidence exists that the information needs of SMEs are very much different than the traditional IFRS audience.

The South African context

IFRS harmonisation in South Africa occurred from 1993 to 2004. During this period differences between South African generally accepted accounting practice (SA GAAP) and IFRS were eliminated.

The legal enforceability of SA GAAP/IFRS however remained uncertain. As a result legal backing for SA GAAP/IFRS was proposed as part of the corporate reform process (Vorster et al., 2007: 5; DTI, 2004: 1). Non-legislative measures were in place for companies listed on the JSE Ltd in the form of the GAAP Monitoring Panel who monitors disclosure practices and related compliance with IFRS. In contrast, disclosure practices of non-listed SMEs were not monitored to ensure compliance with SA GAAP/IFRS. Like their international counterparts the users of SME financial statements in South Africa will also not necessarily encourage compliance with SA GAAP/IFRS. In addition to the fact that the internal users of SME financial statements are also the owners of the business with regular access to the financial information, the financial statements of SMEs in South Africa may not always be up to date and readily available. Proper disclosure practices and compliance with accounting standards would also not necessarily address the requirements of external users. According to Collis and Jarvis (2000: 12) banking institutions and tax authorities are the main external users of SME financial statements and whilst the information needs of banking institutions and providers of finance are limited to liquidity ratios, the South African revenue service (SARS) is mainly concerned about taxable profits.

The lack of interest by SARS in a complete set of financial statements is further supported by the fact that companies are no longer required to submit financial statements, but to submit only certain tax related information for tax filing purposes (South African Revenue Service, 2010). Little evidence therefore exists that the disclosure practices of South African SMEs is in accordance with SA GAAP, IFRS or any relevant accounting framework. For this reason we suggest, based on the observations by Van der Tas (1988: 158), that the harmonisation process of SME disclosure practices in South Africa were spontaneous and not necessarily influenced by the standard setting process.

Development of hypothesis

Against the background of non-compliance with accounting standards by South African SMEs a reporting framework for the SME sector was introduced in August 2007. The exposure draft on IFRS for SMEs was adopted as the South African Statement of GAAP for SMEs without any amendments to the exposure draft on IFRS for SMEs. The IASB, after considering additional feedback, adopted the exposure draft two years later. As from 2009 a global reporting framework for the SME sector will therefore be adopted by many countries. According to the IASB the IFRS for SMEs was developed to address the reporting needs of SMEs worldwide. In developing the IFRS for SMEs the IASB conducted a number of field tests to assess the relevance of the accounting standard in different countries which encompassed the restatement of a sample of SME financial statements in accordance with the IFRS for SMEs requirements (Pacter, 2009: 30). Based on the aforementioned and in order to assess the relevance of the IFRS for SMEs in the South African context the following hypothesis was formulated:

Ho_1: In order to adopt an accounting framework for the SME sector it should be possible to restate SME financial statements in accordance with the disclosure requirements.

The hypothesis was tested by comparing the illustrative financial statements of the IFRS of SMEs against information disclosed in the financial statements of SMEs in South Africa. This comparison might be an indication of the extent to which the IFRS of SMEs is applicable and acceptable to South African SMEs.

DATA AND METHODOLOGY

The research encompassed both a literature and empirical study. The literature review considered the susceptibility of accounting standards to the SME sector. Our literature review revealed that the IFRS for SMEs was introduced despite the fact that compliance with accounting standards is not necessarily a priority of the SME sector, nor following a full review of reality. Our empirical study was conducted to analyse the contents of a sample of financial statements compiled by South African SMEs and to compare the results to the IFRS for SMEs' illustrative financial statements and other relevant disclosure requirements. The research approach followed was a content analysis, which is a well-established research method used throughout the social sciences (ACCA, 2009: 18). Content analysis can be defined as a research technique for making replicable and valid inferences from text and related data (Krippendorff, 2004: 18). In addition, although content analysis does not exclude quantitative research, the emphasis is more towards qualitative research. The focus is also on transferability, instead of generalisations, which usually limits the size of the sample (White and Marsh, 2006: 36). Although Ball and Foster (1982: 167) found that many researchers, with accounting backgrounds, focussed on the development and adoption of IFRS by large industrialised countries, a number of researchers also considered the financial information included in the financial statements of entities, or the contents thereof.

Bowman (1984: 61) advocated that content analyses of financial statements represent a fine source of data of individual firms as well as for different industries. As far as the analysis of the contents of financial statements is concerned, Spathis (2002: 179) attempted to

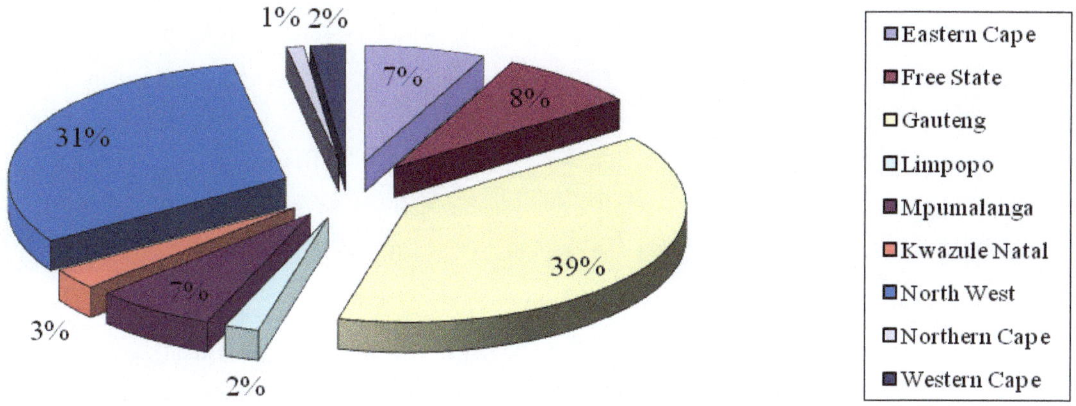

Figure 1. Classification of sample SME financial statements according to province.

develop a method to predict inaccurate financial statements from a sample of 76 Greek companies, Hernandez and Perez (2004: 126) evaluated the relevant usefulness of the various sections of the financial statements from a sample of 54 credit institutions in Spain whilst ACCA (2001: 17) constructed a disclosure index as a measure of the quality of disclosure practices for a sample of 57 UK firms. Christensen and Mohr (2003: 148) examined the financial statements of US museums and compared the results to a random sample of 50 for-profit annual reports. The contents of the IFRS for SMEs were also influenced by a number of field tests. The field tests in general encompassed compilation of financial statements in accordance with the IFRS for SMEs disclosure requirements. The IASB conducted a field test of 116 small entities from 20 different countries (Pacter, 2009: 30). ACCA (2008: 1) performed field tests of 25 companies in the UK. Their sample contained limited liability companies and one limited liability partnership ranging in sizes and sectors that are not publicly accountable. In Australia the IFRS for SMEs standard was field tested by two mid-tier medium-sized accounting firms, where each firm assessed the potential impact of the standard on the disclosure practices of three Australian entities. These entities included large proprietary companies, trusts and not-for-profit entities eligible to adopt the standard (CPA Australia and The Institute of Chartered Accountants in Australia, 2010: 12).

IFRS for SMEs in the South African context is intended for companies and other entities that are neither listed companies nor financial institutions (Heffes, 2009: 14). In contrast to the financial statements of listed companies the financial statements of SMEs were however not readily available. Where external users of SME financial statements are concerned research by Collis and Jarvis (2000: 12) suggested that tax authorities and banking institutions are the main external users of SME financial statements. Since entities in South Africa are no longer required to include financial statements when filing tax returns a sample of financial statements could not be obtained from the South African tax authority. Banking institutions could also not be considered due to contractual restrictions to share client information with third parties. Furthermore, from the perspective of SME owners the collection of financial statements might have been encumbered by issues of security and privacy considerations (Khosrow-Pour, 2006: 954). Despite these constraints a sample of financial statements from the SME sector was collected from business owners in South Africa. In an attempt to include independent data a group of fourth year accounting students assisted with the collection process. Since the IFRS for SMEs, in the South African context, is intended for entities other than listed entities and financial institutions (Heffes, 2009: 14) and owing to the fact that there is no central database available for the published financial statements of these entities, we were not aiming to include SMEs from specific industries, sizes or any other relevant classification.

According to Figure 1 the sample size consisted of 100 financial statements from the SME sector. The reporting dates were the 2008 calendar years and the majority of the reporting dates ended on the last day of February. The majority of the financial statements was from Gauteng (39%) and North West (31%). A possible explanation for this is the fact that Gauteng is described as the business Mecca of South Africa. In addition to the fact that a large portion of South African businesses reside here, Gauteng is also a neighbouring province of North West where the majority of the students was based at the time of the sample.

Furthermore, as far as the business activities of the sample are concerned we noted that the majority of the sample financial statements was from the services and retail sectors in South Africa and only a limited number of entities from the mining, transport and agriculture sectors. Another two sets of financial statements from our sample did not provide any disclosure in connection with the nature or related business activities of the entity. The distribution of the sample according to business sectors is set out in Figure 2. The financial information of all the sampled financial statements was consolidated into a single statement of balance sheet and income statement after which we compared the data to the relevant sections of the IFRS for SMEs' illustrative financial statements. The financial statements included in the sample were compiled for the 2008 financial period. Due to the fact that this period was before the effective implementation of IAS1 – presentation of financial statements/statement of GAAP for SMEs the terms "balance sheet" and "income statement" will be used in this study instead of "statement of financial position" and "statement of comprehensive income". Moreover, all the financial statements included in the sample contained the terms "balance sheet" and "income statement".

In addition to the consolidated balance sheet and income statement our analysis also contained observations in connection with the statement of changes in equity, cash flow statements and notes to the sample financial statements. The consolidation incorporated firstly the balance sheets in Table 1. The distribution of the data in Table 1 implies a fairly high degree of variability in connection with the financial data included in the sample. This variance was also supported by coefficients of variances in excess of 100% for individual line items included in the consolidated balance sheet. The dispersion of the financial data relating to non-current assets and current assets included in Table 1 is summarised in Figure 3 (Y axis presented in South African Rand values). The dispersion of financial data relating to equity, non-current liabilities and current liabilities included in Table 1 is

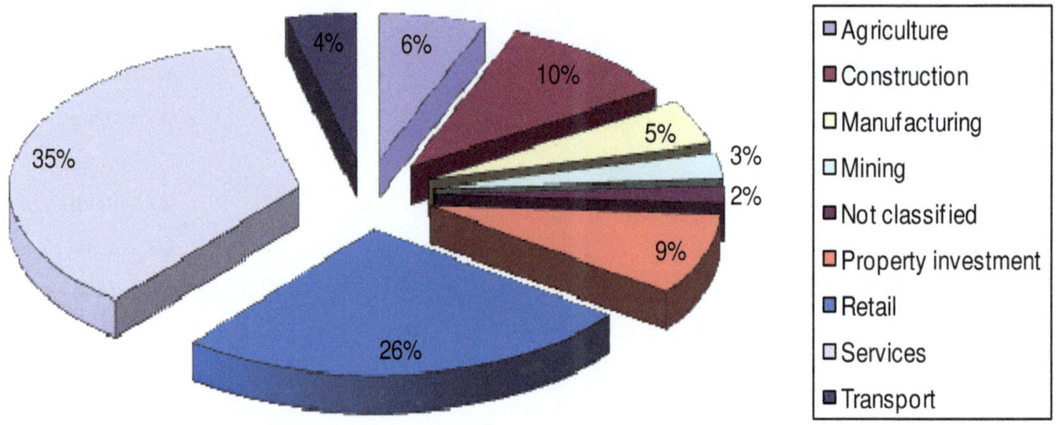

Figure 2. Distribution of sample across business sectors.

presented in Figure 4. Ninety eight percent of SMEs included statements of changes in equity, the only movement in equity for all the financial statements included in the sample however represented net profit or loss after taxation for the financial year and since this amount is included in the income statements it was decided not to consolidate the statements of changes in equity. We also decided to omit cash flow statements due to the fact that only 61% of the sample contained cash flow statements. The lack of cash flow information for certain entities might therefore distort any meaningful consolidation in this regard. In addition we analysed the notes to the sample financial statements in Table 3. The accounting policy notes are firstly presented in panel A.

Our analysis in panel A revealed that the sample financial statements contained accounting policy notes for 13 different line items in the financial statements. The number of items included in our sample is presented in the first column whereas the percentage of accounting policy notes in relation to the sections included in our sample is presented in the third column. The sections in the third column in excess of 100% (provisions, impairment of assets and foreign currency translation) implies that accounting policy notes might have been disclosed even though the relevant section was not included in the financial statements. Secondly our analysis in panel B provides a summary of additional information disclosed in the notes to the sample financial statements. These notes provide, in addition to accounting policy notes, supplementary information in connection with the balances and totals disclosed in the balance sheets and income statements. Our analysis revealed that the majority of the notes relate to the balance sheet and that a smaller number of information disclosed in the notes to the sample financial statements is applicable to the income statement. With regards to the consolidated balance sheet a number of different terms was used to describe the amounts disclosed in the sample financial statements, for example trade creditors, trade payables and accounts payable.

In addition to inconsistent descriptions several different formats were used for the income statements. Some income statements were classified by nature whilst others were classified by function. A number of entities included condensed income statements as opposed to detailed income statements. As a result it was not possible to include details of operating costs in the consolidation. Expenses were therefore classified into three different categories namely cost of sales, operating costs and finance costs. Furthermore, the three main categories in the consolidated income statement are income, expenditure and taxation. Finally our discussion covered the content and different formats of the financial statements included in our sample against the IFRS for SMEs' illustrative financial statements.

RESULTS

Consolidated balance sheet

Consolidated assets exceeded consolidated liabilities by R91 million (Table 1). Amounts disclosed as assets in the sample financial statements were between R50 for investments and R103.5 million for investment property. With reference to Figure 3 a total number of four SME financial statements contained non-current assets in excess of R20 million comprising investment property (R21.4 and R103.5 million) as well as property, plant and equipment (R43.4 million). Three of the financial statements selected contained current assets in excess of R20 million, including inventories (R26.9 million) as well as trade and other receivables (R36.9 and R46.2 million). In like manner only a few individual amounts from Figure 4 were in excess of R20 million, including long-term liabilities (R29.5, R93.3 and R63.4 million), retained earnings (R33.1, R20.8 and R48.8 million), accumulated loss (R91.8 million) as well as trade and other creditors (R28.1 million). Property, plant and equipment (87% of the sample), cash and cash equivalents (79% of the sample) as well as trade and other receivables (72% of the sample) were the main types of assets included in the financial statements. Investment property was included by only four entities ranging from R1.2 to R103.5 million with an average amount of R32.1 million per entity.

A limited number of financial statements contained goodwill (12%). Despite an accumulated loss of R91,8 million for an individual SME the consolidated retained income amounted to R64 million. Furthermore, 34% of the sample financial statements contained retained losses amounting to R135 million in total. Equity items were limited to share capital (99% of the sample), retained earnings (100%) and non-distributable reserves (11% of the sample). Liabilities were mainly long-term loans (94% of the sample) along with trade and other creditors (88% of the sample). With regards to current

Table 1. Consolidated balance sheet.

	Sum of totals (South African Rand)	Percentage of items included in sample (%)	Minimum amount disclosed	Maximum amount disclosed	Mean	Median	First quartile	Third quartile
Non-current assets	460,218,556							
Property, plant and equipment	180,648,079	87	4,426	43,358,437	2,076,415	586,172	101,617	1,840,981
Investment property	128,736,130	4	1,261,918	103,500,000	32,184,033	11,987,106	2,237,108	41,934,031
Goodwill	12,308,135	12	75,000	5,077,090	1,025,678	355,611	143,439	797,710
Investments	25,085,197	15	50	11,851,103	1,672,346	51,000	22,901	255,747
Loans receivable	108,364,582	46	1,242	26,689,215	2,355,752	396,856	114,426	1,941,377
Deferred taxation	5,076,433	14	4,240	1,849,907	362,602	53,309	15,103	474,089
Current assets	302,381,932							
Inventories	89,080,397	44	3,983	26,898,690	2,024,554	373,576	105,425	1,251,005
Trade and other receivables	167,943,035	72	375	46,248,417	2,332,542	233,693	40,581	1,504,839
Loans receivable	3,800,722	11	3,789	1,383,890	345,520	240,000	116,530	390,631
Current tax receivable	684,941	14	4,510	149,867	48,924	28,429	9,217	75,295
Cash and cash equivalents	40,872,836	79	145	9,095,130	517,378	35,867	6,785	280,072
	762,600,488							
Equity	91,286,610							
Share capital	8,130,598	99	2	7,500,000	82,127	100	100	250
Retained income	64,078,244	100	-91,796,790	48,821,142	640,782	138,921	-44,355	837,562
Non-distributable reserve	19,077,768	11	39,378	10,766,501	1,734,343	613,050	263,598	1,837,634
Non-current liabilities	410,777,210							
Long-term liabilities	381,709,145	94	506	93,289,204	4,060,736	952,388	447,557	2,274,136
Deferred taxation	29,068,065	10	17,009	14,923,198	2,906,807	355,751	72,750	3,170,149
Current liabilities	260,536,668							
Bank overdraft	54,110,374	36	3,363	14,233,203	1,503,066	121,760	30,638	905,223
Trade and other creditors	171,087,730	88	57	35,670,591	1,944,179	129,980	17,947	1,315,790
Provisions	14,415	1	14,415	14,415	14,415	14,415	14,415	14,415
Current tax payable	15,412,986	39	112	3,926,468	395,205	84,966	20,597	399,553
Deposits	1,033,927	2	33,927	1,000,000	516,964	516,964	275,445	758,482
Income received in advance	494,153	1	494,153	494,153	494,153	494,153	494,153	494,153
Short-term loans	18,383,083	21	17,154	8,776,993	875,385	328,678	80,206	678,822
	762,600,488							

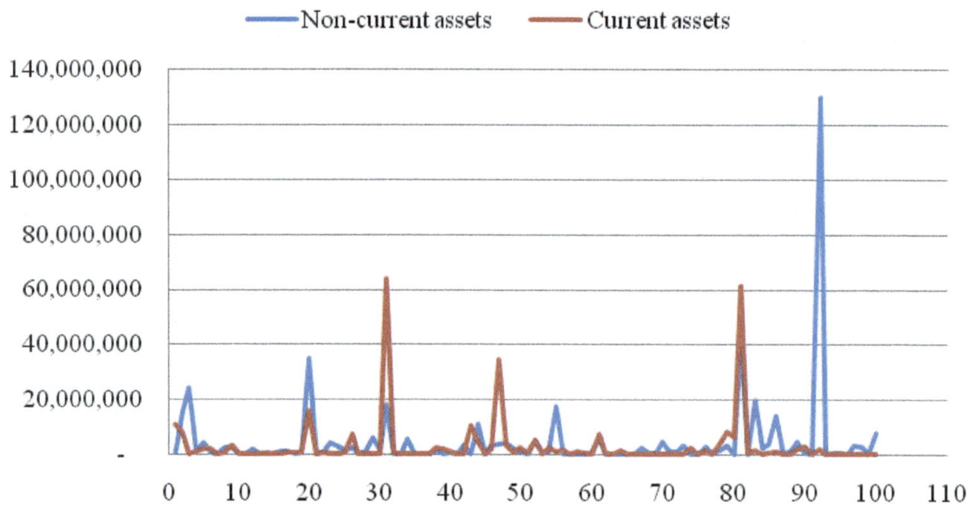

Figure 3. Analysis of assets included in sample.

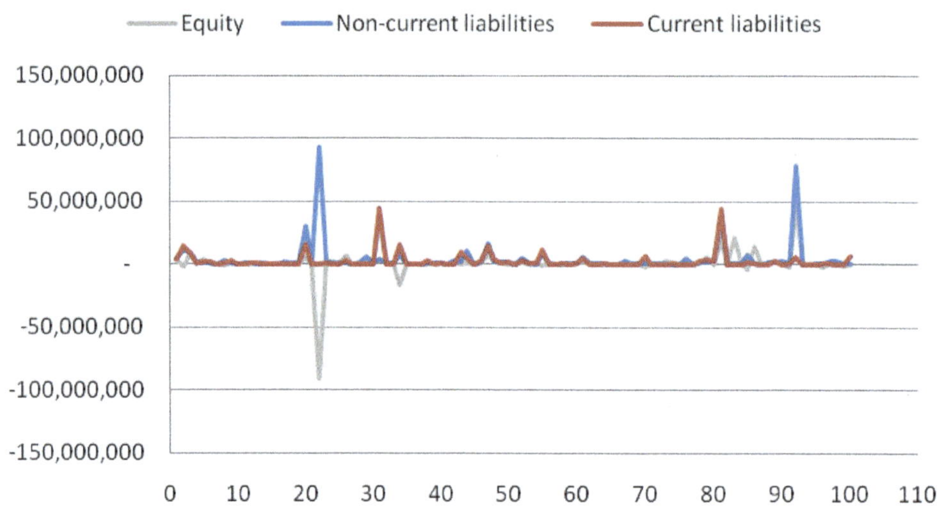

Figure 4. Analysis of equity and liabilities included in sample.

liabilities provisions (1% of the sample), deposits (2% of the sample) and income received in advance (1% of the sample) were not frequently disclosed items. With reference to Figure 4 and in addition to the aforementioned retained loss of R91,7 million a total number of five SMEs reported retained earnings under equity in excess of R20 million, A total number of four SMEs disclosed non-current liabilities in excess of R20 million while only two financial statements included in our sample contained current liabilities in excess of R20 million. As far as taxes are concerned many SMEs disclosed taxes receivable/payable separately from trade and other receivables/payables. Current tax receivable was encountered by 14% of the sample whilst 39% of SMEs disclosed current tax payable in their balance sheets. The combined total of 53% of our sample that disclosed current tax assets or liabilities as separate items in the balance sheets could be significant if the assessed losses of many SMEs are also taken into account.

On the contrary, deferred taxation was not commonly disclosed as only 14% of the entities included deferred tax assets whilst deferred tax liabilities were included by 10% of the sample.

Consolidated income statement

The consolidated profit after tax amounted to R55 million and contained profits from 65 entities (65% of sample). The remaining 35% of the sample generated losses for the period under review ranging from R175 to R16,1 million. Profits included in the sample were between R1,708 and R25 million. Most SMEs included sales (83%

Table 2. Consolidated income statement.

	Sum of totals (South African rand)	Percentage of items included in sample (%)	Minimum amount disclosed	Maximum amount disclosed	Mean	Median	First quartile	Third quartile
Income	1,371,700,511							
Sales	1,296,629,746	83	16,400	230,729,801	15,622,045	2,420,683	810,415	12,396,190
Rental income	11,174,785	9	8,350	6,579,953	1,241,643	114,035	20,000	263,158
Investment income	7,927,844	52	1	4,417,117	152,459	6,200	161	69,241
Discount received	3,503	1	3,503	3,503	3,503	3,503	3,503	3,503
Other income	55,964,633	44	8	36,063,853	1,271,923	67,543	19,209	284,008
Expenditure	1,287,548,883							
Cost of sales	852,808,895	60	3,234	163,363,757	14,213,482	2,221,706	464,410	12,438,800
Operating cost	408,527,355	97	1,308	47,135,937	4,211,622	786,364	176,814	3,312,421
Finance charges	26,212,633	72	44	7,345,089	364,064	58,758	10,447	176,649
Profit before taxation	84,151,629							
Taxation	28,860,565	75	- 1,849,907	9,123,198	384,808	9,828	-	170,910
Profit for the period	55,291,064							

of the sample) as income and operating costs (97% of the sample) as expenses. A large number of SMEs incurred finance charges (72% of the sample) and income tax (75% of the sample) in the income statements (Table 2).

Notes to the consolidated financial statements

Even though the extent to which notes were included in the financial statements was summarised in Table 3, the detail from the notes to the sample financial statements was not consolidated as part of this study. Firstly, we noted that a relatively small number of SMEs disclosed accounting policy notes. In contrast to 31 different types of accounting policy notes for listed companies (Deloitte, 2009a; PricewaterhouseCoopers, 2009) the sample contained only 13 different types of accounting policy notes. Without taking into account the amounts disclosed in the financial statements, a relatively small percentage of SMEs included accounting policy notes in their financial statements. Property, plant and equipment (71% of total sample) as well as revenue recognition (53% of total sample) were the only two types of accounting policy notes included by more than fifty percent of the sample. Accounting policy notes in connection with property, plant and equipment were limited to depreciation methods and periods and those applicable to revenue provided more information about revenue recognition criteria. If accounting policy notes are linked to items disclosed in the financial statements the following notes which provided additional information in connection with policies applied were in excess of 50%: Property, plant and equipment (82% of the sample), investment property (75% of the sample), revenue recognition (64% of the sample), and provisions (800% or 8 accounting policy notes and 1 item disclosed as provisions in sample financial statements).

Secondly, notes other than accounting policy notes pertaining to non-current assets in the balance sheet were, except for goodwill (42%), included by the majority of the SMEs included in our sample. A significant number (>75%) of the SMEs included in our sample disclosed supplementary information for property, plant and equipment, investment property, investments, loans receivable, deferred taxation, long-term liabilities and short-term loans in the notes to the financial statements. Inventories (55%) and accounts receivable (56%) were the only two types of current assets in excess of fifty percent. A higher number of notes were also included for

Table 3A. Notes to the consolidated financial statements – Panel A.

	Number of items included in the consolidated financial statements	Number of items included in the notes to the consolidated financial statements	Items included in the notes as a percentage of items included in financial statements (%)
Accounting policy notes			
Property, plant and equipment	87	71	82
Investment property	4	3	75
Goodwill	12	2	17
Financial instruments	100	23	23
Inventories	44	26	59
Provisions	1	8	> 100
Impairment of assets	0	7	> 100
Revenue recognition	83	53	64
Borrowing cost	94	11	12
Employee benefits	97	1	1
Foreign currency translation	1	2	> 100
Leases	74	7	9
Taxation	75	36	48

non-current liabilities compared to current liabilities. Under current liabilities provisions (100% of the sample) and short-term loans (100% of the sample) were in excess of fifty percent. Additional information was also disclosed for share capital (70% of the sample) whilst no notes were included for non-distributable reserves (0%) under equity in the balance sheets.

Thirdly, we observed that a low percentage of SMEs disclosed notes to the income statement. The only significant income statement items for which additional information was disclosed in the notes thereto were revenue (29%) and taxation (60%).

Illustrative financial statements

When comparing our consolidated balance sheet with the IFRS for SMEs' illustrative financial statements we noted that all the entities in our sample should include current assets/liabilities before non-current assets/liabilities. Although in a different sequence, the consolidated balance sheet could be converted into the format of the illustrative financial statements with relative ease. Investments, investment property and loans receivable were non-current assets included in our sample that are not included in the illustrative financial statements. Due to limited disclosure in this regard it was not possible to distinguish between investments in subsidiaries, investment in associates, financial assets, or any other relevant classification that may be needed in the financial statements. The majority of the long-term liabilities were classified as either loans from shareholders (60% of the sample contained loans from shareholders), loans from other related parties (40% of the sample) or instalment sale agreements (31% of the sample). A small percentage (4% of the sample) of SMEs included finance lease obligations. Furthermore, R223,8 million or 59% of the total value of long-term liabilities in Table 1 represented unsecured loans from shareholders and related parties compared to 40% secured loans amounting to R153,5 million. Eight different loans, or 1% of the long-term liabilities in value terms, did not contain any disclosure as to whether loans are secured or not. It appears as if the conversion of the income statements from our sample to the format used in the illustrative financial statements would be more burdensome than the balance sheet. Our sample consisted of both detailed and condensed income statements. The comparison of the financial statements in our sample was also complicated by the inclusion of income statements classified by nature and by function. Limited guidance is given

Table 3B. Notes to the consolidated financial statements – Panel B.

	Number of items included in the consolidated financial statements	Number of items included in the notes to the consolidated financial statements	Items included in the notes as a percentage of items included in financial statements (%)
	Notes - Consolidated balance sheet		
Non-current assets			
Property, plant and equipment	87	87	100
Investment property	4	3	75
Goodwill	12	5	42
Investments	15	12	80
Loans receivable	46	41	89
Deferred taxation	14	10	71
Current assets			
Inventories	44	24	55
Trade and other receivables	72	40	56
Loans receivable	11	2	18
Current tax receivable	14	0	0
Cash and cash equivalents	79	23	29
Equity and liabilities			
Share capital	99	69	70
Retained income	100	6	6
Non-distributable reserve	11	0	0
Non-current liabilities			
Long-term liabilities	94	84	89
Deferred taxation	10	10	100
Current liabilities			
Bank overdraft	36	11	31
Trade and other creditors	88	38	43
Provisions	1	1	100
Current tax payable	39	5	13
Deposits	2	0	0
Income received in advance	1	0	0
Short-term loans	21	21	100
	Notes - Consolidated income statement		
Revenue	83	24	29
Cost of sales	60	5	8

Table 3b. Contd.

Depreciation	97	8	8
Accounting fees	97	3	3
Employee costs	97	4	4
Finance charges	72	18	25
Taxation	75	45	60

in connection with other income as well as the distinction between the different types of revenue. Moreover, none of the income statements in our sample classified operating costs as distribution costs, administrative expenses or other expenses. Instead, in addition to SMEs disclosing detailed income statements, a number of different classifications were used to group expenses together. Clear guidance in connection with the classification of operating costs is also not provided in the illustrative financial statements.

In conclusion we noted that the majority of the SMEs included in our sample disclosed movements in retained earnings in the statement of changes in equity, as opposed to the income statement, and that these movements were limited to profits or losses pertaining to a financial year.

DISCUSSION AND CONCLUSION

Based on our literature review we found that the regulation of IFRS compliance is inconsistent between countries owing to inconsistent processes, practices as well as levels of authority and enforceability. Moreover, it appears that the monitoring of compliance with IFRS will be more acceptable to countries with politically and legally stable environments. In addition to differences in accounting regulation our literature review revealed key differences between SMEs and listed companies. Owing to these differences a number of IFRS requirements are not necessarily applicable to the SME sector. Our sample confirmed the diverse nature of SMEs in South Africa. Retained earnings were between R92 million in deficit and R49 million in surplus with share capital ranging from R2 to R7,5 million. We observed that 34% of the entities reported accumulated losses. None of the entities however accounted for impairment losses or related expenses in connection with discontinued operations and activities. Furthermore, none of the SMEs disclosed any limitations to continue as a going concern.

The absence of these items might be indicative of the close relation between the SME management role and SME ownership. Under most circumstances SME managers and SME owners are inseparable. Due to the fact that SME owners have regular access to financial and related information we suggest that SME owners also have updated information about operational and financial challenges and in contrast to listed companies SME owners/shareholders do not have to wait until impairment losses, going concern problems and related items are communicated by management in the form of the financial statements. Our observation in connection with the close relation between SME owners and SME management is further supported by a significant number of shareholders' loans (60%) included under non-current liabilities. Moreover, the majority of these loans were unsecured and interest-free with no fixed terms of repayment. The fact that SME owners are willing to finance the activities of SMEs by means of unsecured and interest-free loans provides even more evidence of the close interaction between the entity and its owners.

Our study revealed a further noteworthy difference between listed companies and SMEs. Unlike listed companies that often generate substantial funding through the listing process it appears that SMEs do not issue share capital for purposes of raising funds. The share capital of the majority of the SMEs (89%) amounted to R1,000 or less. Compared to an average amount of R4 million disclosed for long-term liabilities, the results suggest that activities are mainly financed by means of raising debt as opposed to share capital Figure 5. Further support for this observation was found in the statement of changes in equity. The only changes in equity represented accounting profits or losses for the year. The absence of dividends paid suggests that investors do not invest share capital in SMEs on which they expect a return in the form of dividends. In addition to internally generated loans from shareholders and related parties our study revealed that the majority of external loans comprised instalment sale agreements (31%) secured by underlying assets. The fact that the main type of external finance was obtained through instalment sale agreements might be

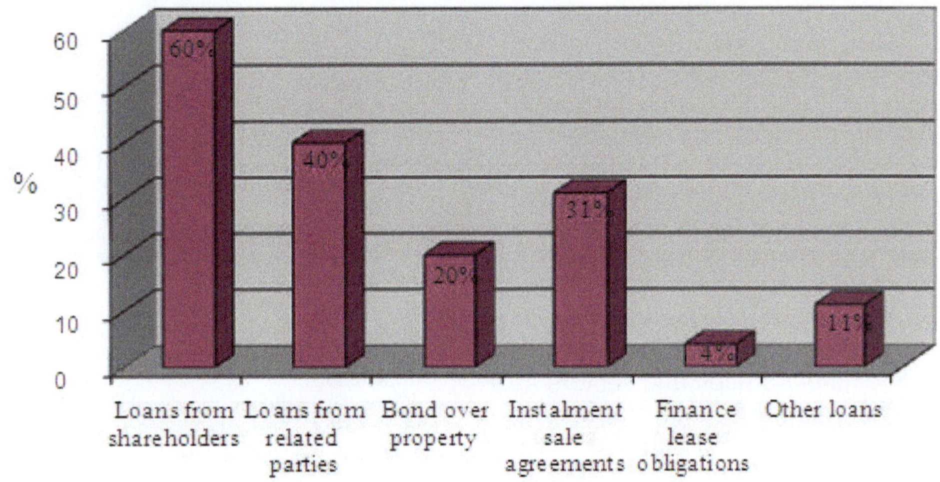

Figure 5. Analysis of long-term liabilities included in sample.

indicative of the fact that providers of finance to the SME sector are mainly concerned with the condition of the underlying assets as opposed to proper disclosure of other items included in the financial statements.

The relevant importance of non-current and other related assets was further emphasised by the fact that the majority of the sample financial statements contained property, plant and equipment (87% of the sample). Evidence that SME financial statements were compiled to address the information needs of tax authorities could be found in the fact that income taxes receivable and income taxes payable were disclosed separately from trade and other receivables/payables. A large number of SMEs also disclosed income taxes (75% of the sample) in the income statement. A small percentage of SMEs however disclosed deferred tax. Our study therefore provided evidence in connection with disclosure practices to address the needs of the two main types of external users of SME financial statements, as identified by Collis and Jarvis (2000: 12). Our research suggests that fair value accounting is not popular amongst South African SMEs. A small percentage of SMEs reported revaluations. Non-distributable reserves were disclosed by 11% of the sample whilst none of the entities disclosed additional information in connection with non-distributable reserves in the notes to the financial statements. Moreover, we observed that the majority of financial assets, for example investments are carried at cost. Despite the fact that a number of entities included rental income in the income statements, only a small percentage of SMEs classified property as investment property (4% of the sample). The practise of separating investment property from other types of property could therefore not be verified for the SME financial statements included in our sample. Even though 15% of our sample contained investments, none of the entities compiled consolidated financial statements. Due to limited disclosure in this regard we were also not able to ascertain whether these SMEs are required to prepare consolidated financial statements. In the absence of consolidated financial statements the inclusion of goodwill by 12% of our sample appears to be abnormal. Our analysis in Table 3 also revealed that limited disclosure was provided in connection with goodwill.

A limited amount of information was also disclosed in the notes to the financial statements. Less than 50% of the different types of accounting policy notes pertaining to listed companies was included in the sample. It also appeared that the notes provided a mere summary of balances and totals disclosed in the balance sheet or income statement, with very limited qualitative disclosure. Only 61% of the sample financial statements contained cash flow statements whereas disclosure in the statements of changes in equity was limited to profits or losses. In view of the fact that the illustrative financial statements include movements in accumulated profits or losses on the face of the income statement, the relevance of the statement of changes in equity in the South African context might not be certain. Finally our study revealed that the IFRS for SMEs' illustrative financial statements could be adopted without much difficulty. We found that all the main categories from the sample balance sheets and income statements were covered by the illustrative financial statements. Based on the results the hypothesis cannot be rejected. It is therefore suggested that the IFRS for SMEs could become the preferred accounting framework for SMEs in South Africa.

LIMITATIONS AND FUTURE RESEARCH RECOMMENDATIONS

Owing to the fact that our sample contained a sample of

100 SME financial statements the results might not be representative of all SMEs and other South African entities planning to adopt the IFRS for SMEs. The sample size could however favourably be compared to similar studies and more specifically the field tests conducted by the IASB.

Another limitation could be the fact that we did not involve practitioners and preparers of these financial statements. Our analysis was limited to the information disclosed in the financial statements. Due to these limitations we recommend that future research should involve the classification of entities required to adopt and apply IFRS for SMEs into different groups and sectors as well as the analysis of financial statements prepared in accordance with the IFRS for SMEs. We also recommend that the views of preparers and users of these financial statements are considered when analysing SME financial statements prepared in accordance with the IFRS for SMEs.

REFERENCES

Association of Chartered Certified Accountants (ACCA) (2001). Corporate Financial Disclosure and Analyst Forecasting Activity: Preliminary Evidence for the UK. www.accaglobal.com/general/activities/research/reports/global_integration/rr-067. Date accessed: 6 September 2010.

Association of Chartered Certified Accountants (ACCA) (2008). Summary of ACCA Field-testing on the IASB's Exposure Draft. http://www.accaglobal.com/pubs/general/activities/library/financial_reporting/other/tech-tp-sft.pdf. Date accessed: 10 September 2010.

Association of Chartered Certified Accountants (ACCA) (2009). Disclosure Practices and Policies of UK Charities. www.accaglobal.com/general/activities/research/reports/global_integration/rr_108. Date accessed: 6 September 2010.

Ball R, Foster G (1982). Corporate Financial Reporting: A Methodological Review of Empirical Research. J. Account. Res., 20(Suppl.): 161-234.

Ball R, Kothari SP, Robin A (2000). The effect of international institutional factors on properties of accounting earnings. J. Account. Econ., 29(1):1-55.

Baskerville RF, Cordery CJ (2006). Small GAAP: a large jump for the IASB. Paper presented at the Tenth Annual Conference for Financial Reporting and Business Communication, Cardiff Business School, Cardiff.

Benston GJ, Bromwich M, Wagenhofer A (2006). Principles- Versus Rules-Based Accounting Standards: The FASB's Standard Setting Strategy. Abacus, 42(2): 165-188.

Bowman E (1984). Content Analysis of Annual Reports for Corporate Strategy and Risk. Interfaces, 14(1): 61-71.

Bradbury M, Van ZT (2005). Shifting to International Financial Reporting Standards. Univ. Auckland Bus. Rev. Autumn, pp. 77-83.

Christensen AL, Mohr RM (2003). Not-for-profit annual reports: What do museum managers communicate? Financ. Account. Manage., 19(2): 139–158.

Collis J, Jarvis R (2000). How owner-managers use accounts. London: The Institute of Chartered Accountants in England and Wales.

Committee of European Securities Regulators (CESR) (2003). Standard No. 1 on Financial Information: Enforcement of Standards on Financial Information in Europe. http://www.cesr.eu/index.php?docid=214. Date accessed: 17 December 2009.

CPA Australia and The Institute of Chartered Accountants in Australia. (2010). ED192 Revised Differential Reporting Framework. http://www.cpaaustralia.com.au/cps/rde/xbcr/cpa-site/Submission_differential_reporting_2010.pdf. Date accessed: 10 September 2010.

Dao THP (2005). Monitoring Compliance with IFRS: Some Insights from the French Regulatory System. Account. Europe, 2: 107-135.

Daske H, Hail L, Leuz C, Verdi R (2008). Mandatory IFRS Reporting Around the World: Early Evidence on the Economic Consequences. http://ssrn.com/abstract=1024240. Date accessed: 30 March, 2010.

Deloitte (2009a). IFRS Model Financial Statements 2009. http://www.iasplus.com/fs/2009modelfs.pdf. Date accessed: 15 January 2010.

Deloitte (2009b). The language of business is changing. Do you speak IFRS?http://www.deloitte.com/assets/DcomUnitedStates/Local%20Assets/Documents/us_fas_ do_you_speak_ifrs_v2_150409.pdf. Date accessed: 5 December 2009.

Department of Trade and Industry (DTI) (2004). Reform of South African Company Law and its implications for the Accounting Profession. http://www.thedti.gov.za/article/articleview.asp?current=0&arttypeid=2&artid=684. Date accessed: 12 December 2009.

Gannon DJ, Ashwal A (2004). Financial Reporting Goes Global. J. Account., 198(3): 43–47.

Heffes M (2009). Early Feedback on Adoption of IFRS for SMEs. Financial Executive. www.financialexecutives.org. Date accessed: 9 September 2010.

Hernandez AML, Perez CC (2004). The relevance of Spanish local financial reporting to credit institution decisions - An empirical study. Int. J. Public Sector Manage., 17(2): 118-135.

Hope OK (2003). Disclosure practices, enforcement of accounting standards, and analysts' forecast accuracy: An international study. J. Account. Res., 41(2): 235-272.

International Accounting Standards Board (IASB) (2009). Standards IFRSs. http://www.iasb.org/IFRSs/IFRs.htm. Date accessed: 5 December 2009.

Kershaw D (2005). Evading Enron: Taking Principles Too Seriously in Accounting Regulation. Mod. Law Rev., 68(4): 594-625.

Khosrow-PM (2006). Emerging Trends And Challenges in Information Technology Management. London: IDEA Group Publishing, p. 1077.

Krippendorff K (2004). Content analysis: An introduction to its methodology (2nd ed.). Thousand Oaks, CA: Sage.

Levin RI, Travis VR (1987). Small business finance: what the books don't say. Harvard Bus. Rev., 65(6): 30-32.

McCahey JE (1986). An Appropriate Financial Reporting Framework for Small Companies. Master of Commerce Thesis, University of Melbourne, Melbourne, Victoria.

McMahon RGP (1998). Putting SME Financial Reporting into Theoretical and Practical Perspective. http://catalogue.nla.gov.au/Record/2226503?lookfor=author-browse:"McMahon,%20Richard,%201948-"&offset=1&max=26. Dateaccessed: 20 December 2009. http://www.iasplus.com/ resource /0909financialexecutivepacter.pdf. Date accessed: 10 September, 2010.

PricewaterhouseCoopers (2009). International Financial Reporting Standards – Illustrative corporate consolidated financial statements 2009. http://www.pwc.com/en_GX/gx/ifrs-reporting/pdf/Illustrative_IFRS_corporate_consolidated_financial_statements_2009.pdf. Date accessed: 15 January, 2010.

Sawani A (2009). The Changing Accounting Environment: International Accounting Standards and US implementation. J. Financ. Account., 1: 1-9.

Securities Exchange Commission (2000). SEC Concept Release: International Accounting Standards. http://www.sec.gov/rules/concept/34-42430.htm. Date accessed: 17 December, 2009.

Sian S, Roberts C (2009). UK small owner-managed businesses: accounting and financial reporting needs. J. Small Bus. Enterprise Dev., 16(2): 289–305.

Sikka P (2001). Regulation of Accountancy and the Power of Capital, Some Observations. Crit. Perspect. Account., 12(2): 199-211.

South African Revenue Service (2010). What is eFiling? http://www.sarsefiling.co.za/AboutPage.aspx. Date accessed: 15 January, 2010.

Spathis TC (2002). Detecting false financial statements using published data: Some evidence from Greece. Managerial Audit. J., 17(4): 179-

191.
Van-der TLG (1988). Measuring harmonisation of financial reporting practice. Account.Bus. Res., 18(70): 157-169.
Vorster Q, Koornhof C, Oberholster J, Koppeschaar Z, Coetzee S, Janse V, Rensburg C, Binnekade C (2007). Descriptive Accounting. Durban:LexisNexis, p. 950.
Watts RL (1977). Corporate Financial Statements, a Product of the Market and Political Processes. Australian J. Manage., 2(1): 53-75.
White MD, Marsh EE (2006) Content Analysis: A Flexible Methodology. Library Trends, 55(1): 22–45.
White Paper on National Strategy for the Development and Promotion of Small Business in South Africa (White Paper) (1995). Cape Town. http://www.info.gov.za/whitepapers/1995/smallbus.htm. Date accessed: 15 July, 2008.
Willmott HC, Puxty AG, Robson K, Cooper DJ, Lowe EA (1992). Regulation of Accountancy and Accountants: A Comparative Analysis of Accounting for Research and Development in Four Advanced Capitalist Countries. Account. Audit. Accountability J., 5(2): 32-56.
Zanzig JS, Flesher DL (2006). GAAP Requirements for Non public Companies. http://www.nysscpa.org/cpajournal/2006/506/essentials/p40.htm. Date accessed: 15 July, 2008.
Zeff SA (1995). A Perspective on the U.S. Public/Private-Sector Approach to the Regulation of Financial Reporting. Account. Horizons, 9(1): 52-70.
Zeghal D, Mhedhbi K (2006). An analysis of the factors affecting the adoption of international accounting standards by developing countries. Int. J. Account., 41: 373–386.

Design and development of credit rating model for public sector banks in India: Special reference to small and medium enterprises

Srinvas Gumparthi[1]*, Swetha Khatri[1] and V. Manickavasagam[2]

[1]SSN School of Management and Computer Applications, Chennai, India.
[2]Department of Corporate Secretaryship Alagappa University, Karaikudi, India.

This research focuses on the design and development of the credit rating model for public sector banks in India. The need to enhance the existing model and to realize the impact of BASEL II Norms was the reason for the development of the models. Also, the absence of appropriate weights in the current system triggers the need for the development of the same model. Different models were constructed using weighted average method and discriminant analysis. Under the weighted average model, various risks and their sub-parameters were identified. The parameters were classified under four heads namely: industry, business, financial and management risk. The weights developed in this study were based on a conceptual understanding and the importance attached by people that are proficient in this area. A questionnaire was developed and a judgmental survey was conducted among 15 banks with 30 credit rating managers extending the loans of small and medium enterprises (SME). A total of 35 cases were taken for the validation of the model. The new model was able to classify 32 records correctly out of the 35 cases. Further, discriminant analysis was used to classify objects/records into two or more groups based on the knowledge of some variables related to them. Under the discriminant model, the sample size taken was 100 clients of the corporate banking branch. Census was used as the sampling technique, in which 69 records were taken for the development of the model and 31 for validation. However, discriminant functions were constructed, and it was observed that the discriminant and classification scores aided in the classification of the clients. The discriminant model was able to classify 27 records correctly out of 31 cases. Thus, it was concluded that the weighted average model can be used for predicting the credit worthiness of the clients because it has higher predictive power.

Key words: Small and medium enterprise (SME), discriminant, commercial banks, credit risk, credit risk model.

INTRODUCTION

Current scenario

The Indian banking system is financially stable and resilient to the shocks that may arise due to higher non-performing assets (NPAs) and the global economic crisis.

*Corresponding author. E-mail: srigumparthi@gmail.com or srinivasg@ssn.edu.in.

A progressively growing balance sheet, higher pace of credit expansion, expanding profitability and productivity akin to banks in developed markets, lower incidence of nonperforming assets and focus on financial inclusion have contributed to making the Indian banking vibrant and strong. Indian banks have begun to revise their growth approach and re-evaluate the prospects on hand to keep the economy rolling.

The way forward for the Indian banks is to innovate to take advantage of the new business opportunities and at the same time ensure continuous assessment of risks. The most significant achievement of the financial sector reforms has been the marked improvement in the financial health of commercial banks in terms of capital adequacy, profitability and asset quality, as well as greater attention to risk management. Further, deregulation has opened up new opportunities for banks to increase revenues by diversifying into investment banking, insurance, credit cards, depository services, mortgage financing, securitisation, etc.

The last decade has seen many positive developments in the Indian banking sector. The policy makers, which comprise the reserve bank of India (RBI), Ministry of Finance and related government and financial sector regulatory entities, have made several notable efforts to improve regulation in the sector. The sector now compares favourably with banking sectors in the region on metrics like growth, profitability and non-performing assets (NPAs), while improved regulations, innovation, growth and value creation in the sector remain limited to a small part of it.

Indian banks have compared favourably on growth, asset quality and profitability with other regional banks over the last few years. Policy makers have made some notable changes in policy and regulation to help strengthen the sector. These changes include strengthening prudential norms, enhancing the payments system and integrating regulations between commercial and co-operative banks.

A rigorous evaluation of the health of commercial banks, recently undertaken by the committee on financial sector assessment (CFSA), also shows that the commercial banks are robust and versatile. The single-factor stress tests undertaken by the CFSA divulge that the banking system can endure considerable shocks arising from large possible changes in credit quality, interest rate and liquidity conditions. These stress tests for credit, market and liquidity risk show that Indian banks are by and large resilient.

However, the cost of intermediation remains high and bank penetration is limited to only a few customer segments and geographies. While bank lending has been a significant driver of GDP growth and employment, periodic instances of the "failure" of some weak banks have often threatened the stability of the system. Structural weaknesses such as a fragmented industry structure, restrictions on capital availability and deployment, lack of institutional support infrastructure, restrictive labour laws, weak corporate governance and ineffective regulations beyond scheduled commercial banks (SCBs), unless addressed, could seriously weaken the health of the sector. Further, the inability of bank managements (with some notable exceptions) to improve capital allocation, increase the productivity of their service platforms and improve the performance ethic in their organisations could seriously affect future performance.

Opportunities and challenges for banks

Indian banks have the following opportunities and challenges. First, the market sees discontinuous growth driven by new products and services to include opportunities in credit cards, consumer finance and wealth management on the retail side and fee-based income and investment banking on the wholesale banking side. These require new skills in sales and marketing, credit and operations. Secondly, banks will no longer enjoy windfall treasury gains that the decade-long secular decline in interest rates provided. This will expose the weaker banks. Thirdly, increased interest in India will only intensify the competition from foreign banks. Fourthly, given the demographic shifts resulting from changes in age profile and household income, consumers will increasingly demand enhanced institutional capabilities and service levels from banks. The extent to which Indian policy makers and complementary agenda to tackle emerging discontinuities will lay the foundations for a high-performing sector in 2010.

The main challenges facing the banking industry bank managements develop and execute such a clear and are shown in Figure 1. (http://www.gov.im/lib/docs/cso/candoeconomy2014reportappendi.pdf).

Swot analysis of the banking sector

Table 1 shows the swot analysis of the banking sector. Source: http://www.gov.im/lib/docs/cso/candoeconomy2014reportappendi.pdf.

Impact of Basel-II norms

Banking is a commodity business; as such, for banks to earn an adequate return of equity and compete for capital along with other industries, they need to be highly leveraged. The primary function of the bank's capital is to absorb any loss a bank suffers.

Norms set in the Swiss town of Basel determine the ground rules for the way banks around the world account for loans they give out. These rules were formulated by the Bank for International Settlements in 1988.

Credit risk is not the only type of risk that banks face, but also, they are faced nowadays with operational risks which are huge. The various risks that come under operational risk are competition risk, technology risk, casualty risk, crime risk, etc. The original Basel rules did

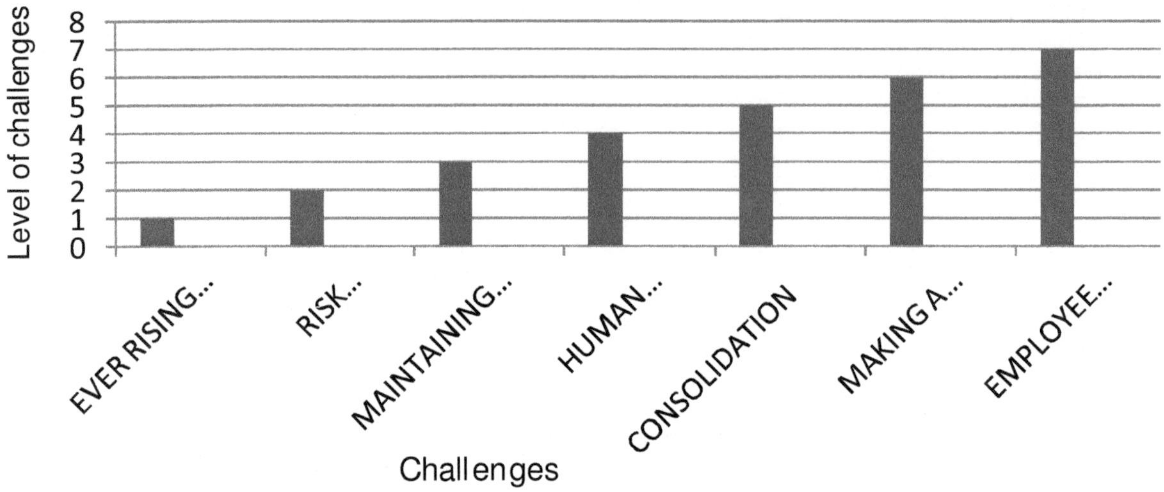

Figure 1. Challenges faced by Indian banks.

Table 1. Swot analysis of the banking sector.

Strengths	**Weaknesses**
(1) Valuable contributor to GDP over a period of 15 years and of pivotal importance to India's economy.	(1) Weak retail and mass affluent customer proposition
(2) High standard regulatory environment.	(2) Lack of competitive differential with other offshore centres
(3) Flexible work permit system.	(3) Rigid legislation that inhibits business development.
Opportunities	**Threats**
(1) Active and aggressive targeting of corporate and private clients and institutions that attract such clients.	(1) Anti-offshore regulations in foreign target markets restricting the development of products and new markets.
(2) Coordinating business relationships across the finance sector to increase revenue, thus investing in the ecosystem.	(2) Downsizing and reduction in banking operations in favour of rival jurisdictions. (3) Outsourcing to cheaper jurisdictions. (4) Subsequent impact on the finance sector ecosystem.

not take into account the operational risks. As per the Basel-II norms, banks will have to set aside 15% of their net income to protect themselves against operational risks.

Definition of key terms

Small and medium enterprise (SME)

Small and medium enterprises (SMEs), also known as small and medium businesses (SMBs) and which have other variations thereof, are companies whose headcount or turnover falls below certain limits.

SMEs always represented the model of socio-economic policies of the Government of India which emphasized the judicious use of foreign exchange for import of capital goods and inputs, labour intensive mode of production, employment generation, non concentration of diffusion of economic power in the hands of few (as in the case of big houses), discouraging monopolistic practices of production and marketing and finally, contributing effectively to foreign exchange earning of the nation with low import-intensive operations.

SMEs that have strong technological base, international business outlook, competitive spirit and willingness to restructure on their own shall withstand the present challenges and come out with shining colours to make their own contribution to the Indian economy.

Non performing assets

A loan or lease that is not meeting its stated principal and interest payments is known as non performing asset. Banks usually classify nonperforming assets as any commercial loans which are more than 90 days overdue and any consumer loans which are more than 180 days overdue. More generally, non performing assets are assets which do not produce income.

Credit risk

Probability of loss from a credit transaction is the plain-vanilla definition of credit risk. Credit risk is defined as "the risk of loss following a change in the factors that drive the credit quality of an asset". According to Basel committee, "Credit risk is most simply defined as the potential that causes a borrower or counter party not to meet its obligations in accordance with the agreed terms".

The reserve bank of India has defined credit risk as "the possibility of losses associated with diminution in the credit quality of borrowers or counterparties". Credit risk management function has become a centre of gravity, especially in a financial services industry like banking. It involves identifying and analyzing risk in credit transaction.

Credit rating

The Basel committee has defined credit rating as a 'summary indicator' of the risk inherent in individual credit, embodying an assessment of the risk of loss due to the default of a counter party by considering relevant quantitative and qualitative information.

Credit rating, through the use of symbols, can be defined as an expression of the opinion about credit quality of the issuer of securities with reference to a particular instrument. Rating is a measure of credit risk and is only one element in investment decision making. However, credit rating does not indicate market risk or predict prices or yields of credit instruments.

Credit risk model

A credit risk model is a quantitative study of credit risk, covering both good borrowers and bad borrowers. It is a mathematical model containing the loan applicant's characteristics that is either used to calculate a score representing the applicant's probability of default or to categorize borrowers into different default risk classes. A model is considered effective if a suitable validation process is also built with adequate power and calibration.

Outcomes of the risk assessment model

The following are the outcomes of the risk assessment model.

Defining the pricing bands: The grade on the rating scale is expected to define the pricing and related terms and conditions for the accepted credit exposures. As such, the higher the risk, the higher the price that could be charged.

Limits on exposure: The amount sanctioned would depend on the credit-score found on the RAM. These limits could be linked to specific parameters, like a certain percentage of the total debt required by the borrower.

Tenure of loans: The rating scale could also be used for deciding the tenure of the proposed assistance. Thus, a longer term could be offered to safe customers.

REVIEW OF LITERATURE

Small and medium enterprises (SMEs) constitute a significant part of the developing economies, and this was emphasized in the research works of Zolton and Audretsch (1993), OECD SMEs Outlook (2002) and Allen et al. (2004). Majority of these enterprises fund their capital through family or other networks; as a result, a sizeable group will borrow from traditional suppliers of credit.

In India, it is often stated that 60% of SMEs do not borrow from traditional sources. A question arises with regard to the measures that should be taken to assess the loan applications of those who borrow from traditional sources. Most of the Small and Medium Enterprises operate in a very small scale with very limited equity of the owner and more on a high cost debt fund from other sources such as external borrowing from non banking firms.

In India, the concept of small scale industry has primarily been in vogue for a long time, while the medium enterprise definition has a more recent origin. An SSI is defined on the basis of limit of historical value of investment in plant and machinery, which at present is up to Rs. 1 crore. However, with respect to some specified items, this investment limit has been hiked to Rs. 5 crore. For the recently announced small and medium enterprises fund, the Government of India has approved the limit of investment in plant and machinery to be from above Rs. 1 crore and up to Rs. 10 crore for defining a unit as a medium enterprise. Amongst the developing countries, India has been the first to display special consideration to SSIs and basic focus was on making economical use of capital and to absorb the abundant labour supply in the country. Despite its commendable contribution to the economy, MSME sector does not get the required support from the concerned government departments, banking sector, financial institutions and corporate sector, which is a obstacle in becoming more competitive in the national and international markets and which needs to be taken up for immediate and proper redressal.

MSME sector faces a number of problems, such as: absence of adequate and timely banking finance, limited knowledge and non-availability of suitable technology, low production capacity, ineffective marketing and identification of new markets, constraints on modernization and expansions, non availability of highly skilled labour at affordable cost, follow up with various agencies in solving regular activities and lack of interaction with government agencies on various matters.

Over the years, the SSI sector in India has continued to remain an important sector of the economy with its noteworthy contribution to the gross domestic product, industrial production, employment generation and exports. As per the third all India Census of SSIs (2001 to 2002), there were 10.52 million SSI units in the country, of which 1.37 were registered and 9.15 were unregistered units. For the year ended (March 2004), the said number increased to 11.52 million, providing employment to 27.40 million persons and contributing an output of over Rs. 3,480 billion in 2004.

SMEs encompass family business, small consultancies, startup companies and companies employing 100 or more employees. Hence, it is a diverse group of companies. The assessment of their likelihood of default is not immediately straightforward. The two approaches to assessment of default within companies are the accounting based approach and the Merton based approach (Merton, 1974). The Merton based approach [4] aims to compare empirically the two approaches as applied to SMEs. There is a considerable literature on accounting based approaches to assessment of companies (Beaver, 1966; Altman, 1968; Altman and Narayanan, 1997). All these research works are based on accounting concepts and generally accepted accounting principles, which are more conventional in nature. Drawback accounting based approach is predominantly historical in nature and is based on the static data provided by the clients.

Added to the historical nature, most of these accounting statements are prepared for different purpose rather than for the credit seeking purpose. For example, under mandatory disclosure, Norm companies have to publish their audited financial statement for stakeholders' purpose.

Beaver (1966) research was based on financial ratio, and in this approach, financial ratios were used as predictors of failure. However, the main focus of the study was on leverage and liquidity ratios.

Charitou et al. (2004), Keasey and Watson (1986), Lennox (1999), Ohlson (1980) and Peel et al. (1986), and recently more researchers, have acknowledged the importance of SMEs.

Keasey and Watson (1986) show that the main purpose of this paper is to review and assess the progress in developing small firm failure prediction models. It highlights a number of issues that are of particular importance in evaluating small firm failure prediction models and indicates where future research might be usefully directed. The authors conclude that while it is not yet clear whether or not they are worthwhile tools in many decision contexts, the present general models may provide material benefits as relatively cheap. Thus, it is simple to use preliminary screening devices for routine credit/lending decisions. This is because the classifications' accuracy of even relatively simple quantitative models has been shown to outperform human decision makers consistently. If, however, predictive model is required as an input into more strategic decision making, then the utility of the existing empirical models is, to a great extent, less certain.

Peel and Wilson (1986), since the seminal work of Altman (1968), and a large number of researchers have developed statistical models, derived from accounting data, with the aim of predicting corporate failure as evidenced by the event of "bankruptcy". Such models are now apparently widely and successfully used by credit/investment analysts as an aid to assessing corporate viability (Altman, 1983). However, an area which has received little attention in the management literature, but is of much importance to the analyst, is whether or not it is possible to discriminate between those financially distressed firms which fail, and those where a timely merger appears to serve as a viable alternative to corporate bankruptcy. As such, Peel and Wilson (1986) made an attempt to find some evidence on discriminating between failing and distressed acquired firms in the UK corporate sector.

Forecasted company failure in the UK using discriminant analysis and financial ratio data in the modeling of default using accounting based approach. Within this paper, the range of variables considered was extended and the standard credit scoring approaches were applied in modeling (Lin et al., 2007).

In the Merton based approach, the implementation was followed according to the method in the work of Bharath and Shumway (2004). Hence, the value of the firm is determined in terms of share price. This poses a limitation on the types of SMEs that can be considered. One could have spent time on investigating alternative valuation of the firm, but in this current research, this was not explored.

Larry and Timothy (1986), in their paper on "A note on rank transformation discriminant analysis: An alternative procedure for classifying bank holding company commercial paper ratings", made an attempt to improvise using multiple discriminant analysis. Recent studies in the financial literature have developed models to predict the rating assigned to a firm's debt by the rating agencies. However, multiple discriminant analysis (MDA) has served as the primary statistical tool.

On the other hand, the results of MDA can be biased. This study presents a less biased procedure which closely follows that suggested by the rating agencies. The improved results of the model support such a procedure.

Chandy and Duett (1990) extended the previous work in the area of commercial paper on rating models. Using the data obtained in 1985 and 1986 they rated the commercial paper as "standard, poor and moody". MDA, LOGIT and CART were the three statistical tests used. The models had a prediction rate of about 85%. It was found that in some rating categories, the quality component (judgment by analysts) played a greater role than in other categories. Variables such as sales, earning power, return on assets, and amount of equity were identified as most important in explaining the ratings of the commercial paper.

Bonds ratings by Pinches and Mingo (1973), Kaplan and Urwitz (1979), Belkaoui (1983), Kim (1993), Manzoni (2004) and Huang et al. (2004) showed that much attention was not given to the examination of individual firms' ratings, known as counterparty ratings. Although, some studies examine the ratings assigned to non-financial firms by local credit agencies (Laitinen, 1999; Doumpos and Pasiouras, 2005), evidence on the counterparty ratings assigned to banks by one of the large agencies is quite limited.

Manickavasagam and Srinivas (2009) in their research paper on risk management frame work for ITES organizations provided risk management frame work based on the operational aspects of the organization. Risk management is the process of identification, measuring or assessing the process deviations from the predetermined targets. Also, it involves developing a frame work for evaluation and quantification of deviations through mathematical modeling. Further, from a management perspective, risk management was employed to formulate the strategies used to manage it. The strategies include: transferring the risk to another party, avoiding the risk, reducing the negative effect of the risk and accepting some or all of the consequences of a particular risk. Traditional risk management focuses on risks stemming from physical or legal causes, while financial risk management, on the other hand, focuses on risks that can be managed using traded financial instruments. Preparing the risk assessment frame is the most important step in the risk management process and may also be the most difficult risk since it is prone to subjectivity and understanding of the analyst. Once uncertainties have been identified, evaluated and assessed, the steps to properly handle the risk management in ITES organizations become more systematic and programmable.

Patricia and David (2009) in their paper, seek to show that research in the risk management area has been 'framed', leading to predictable outcomes. Presentation (framing) blinkers the way a problem is perceived and reviewed. Positive labels are more likely to evoke positive associations; negative labels are more likely to evoke negative associations leading to evaluations dependent on how the situation has been labeled. A much prior literature has focused on the negative area of small business failure. An established framework is used to analyze and illustrate that framing has occurred within that literature with respect to assessment of small business failure. Many researchers have accepted that small business is likely to fail with the result that their research is aimed at supporting this contention. Such acceptance has impacts on policy decisions and decisions of venture capitalists, bankers and potential entrepreneurs.

Manickavasagam and Srinivas (2009), in their paper said that a risk assessment model (RAM) is necessary to avoid the limitations associated with a simplistic and broad classification of applicants into a "good" or "bad" category. The absence of appropriate weights in the current evaluation system triggers the need for the development of the comprehensive model based on the proven statistical application. The literature survey undertaken brought to surface 28 parameters that need to be taken into account while evaluating a prospect. These parameters were classified under four heads namely: credit, operations, liquidity and market risks. Weights developed in this study were based on a conceptual understanding and the importance attached by people that are proficient in this area. A questionnaire was developed and a judgmental survey was conducted for this purpose amongst various credit officers extending commercial vehicle and construction equipment financing. The sample size was 117 small and medium corporate clients. The existing model was able to classify 28 records correctly. So the predictive power of the original/existing model was about 80%. However, the proposed/new model is able to classify 30 records correctly. So the predictive power of the proposed/new model is 85.71%.

In a relatively recent study, ordered logistic regression was employed to examine the individual financial strength ratings assigned by Moody in a sample of 130 banks in 1997. These ratings differed in their study from those of others in several aspects. Fotios Pasiouras, Chrysovalantis Gaganis and Michael Doumpos A multicriteria was developed by a discrimination approach for the credit rating of Asian banks. In this paper, they developed a multicriteria decision aid model, to investigate whether or not it is possible to replicate the credit ratings of Fitch on Asian banks using publicly available data. The model is developed with the multi-group hierarchical discrimination (MHDIS) approach, following a tenfold cross validation procedure. Five financial variables are selected from a list of nineteen variables through factor analysis. An additional set of five non-financial variables covering ownership, corporate governance, auditing, strength of bank's franchise and its banking environment are also being used.

Manickavasagam and Srinivas (2010) risk assessment model was used for assessing NBFCs' (asset financing) customers. In this paper, the focus is on the risk model for NBFCs, though non-banking financial companies (NBFCs) form an integral part of the Indian financial system. The history of the NBFC Industry in India is a story of under-regulation, followed by over-regulation. Policy makers have swung from one extreme position to another in their attempt to set controls and then restrain them so that they do not curb the growth of the industry. This report covers the industry. Most of these NBFCs are operating with high risk of lending and more often they lend credit to small and medium size enterprises, which are categorized as high risk class of assets. To assess such high risk assets we need to have a comprehensive model. Thus, this paper aims to build risk assessment model for NBFCs' based on both qualitative and quantitative aspects of the client.

Of course, one can ultimately argue that the qualitative and quantitative aspect should jointly be used for the determination of lending decisions, in order to explore whether or not the models signal early the default made by a comparison of the predictive accuracy over a 3 year period before distress. The Merton type models are explored from the 2001 to 2004 year horizon, while the distance to default (DD) and the expected default frequency (EDF) are calculated. Accounting based (Credit scoring) models are based on a previous paper by Lin et al. (2007). Overall, the predicted correct percentages, as well as Types I and II error from various models are described. Merton models and accounting based models are compared for their ability to predict accurately different groups of SMEs. A power curve is used for measuring the predictive accuracy of models with different financial distress across groups of SMEs. Receiver operation characteristics (ROC) plots show the discrimination ability of different models. The test statistic of the areas under ROC (AUROC) is used to measure the performance of models.

Despite the fact that quite a number of studies have modeled commercial paper ratings (Peavy and Edgar, 1983, 1984; Chandy and Duett, 1990) and bonds ratings (Pinches and Mingo, 1973; Kaplan and Urwitz, 1979; Belkaoui, 1983; Kim, 1993; Manzoni, 2004; Huang et al., 2004), much attention has not been given to the examination of individual firm's ratings, known as counterparty ratings. Although, some studies examine the ratings assigned to non-financial firms by local credit agencies (Laitinen, 1999; Doumpos and Pasiouras, 2005), evidence on the counterparty ratings assigned to banks by one of the large agencies is quite limited. In a relatively recent study, employed ordered logistic regression was used to examine the individual financial strength ratings assigned by Moody's in a sample of 130 banks in 1997. Thus, we differentiate our study from that of several studies, where Fotios Pasiouras, Chrysovalantis Gaganis and Michael Doumpos A multicriteria was used to develop a discrimination approach for the credit rating of Asian banks. In this paper, they developed a multicriteria decision aid model, to investigate whether it is possible to replicate the credit ratings of Fitch on Asian banks using publicly available data. The model is developed with the multi-group hierarchical discrimination (MHDIS) approach, following a tenfold cross validation procedure. Five financial variables are selected from a list of nineteen through factor analysis. An additional set of five non-financial variables covering ownership, corporate governance, auditing, strength of bank's franchise and its banking environment was also used.

"Credit risk rating at large U.S. banks", explains how a bank's decisions about its internal rating system can have a material effect on its ability to manage credit risk. The central role of human judgment in the rating process and the variety of possible uses for ratings mean that internal incentives can influence rating decisions. Thus, careful design of controls and internal review procedures is a crucial consideration in aligning its form with function. Banks with a substantial large corporate market presence are likely to benefit from a rating system that achieves fine distinctions among relatively low-risk credits. In addition, independent credit staff are often solely responsible for rating large loans. Such an arrangement can greatly reduce potential incentive conflicts.

Manickavasagam and Srinivas (2009), in their paper "Property valuation for investment decision [with special reference to commercial mortgage backed securities (CMBS)]", showed that the discriminant model application was used to determine factors discriminating the valuation of the property. The ultimate aim of any investor is to maximize his returns and minimize his risk. In order to achieve this aim, diversification of investment is made by investors in various types of securities which may lie at a continuum between highly risky and risk free investment. Commercial mortgage backed securities (CMBS) is one of such types of instrument where people who are willing to take benefit of the real estate boom, but are not backed by real estate knowledge, can invest in these pooled and repacked loans on commercial property mortgages. The need for the study is to help the investors in better investment decision, while investing in CMBS. The level of risk involved to get an 'x' rate of yield could be determined by analyzing the various characteristics in a CMBS pool affecting the yield, thereby finding out the level of relationship between each independent variable (LTV, DSCR, loan term, amortization term, etc.) and the dependent variable (yield). This study gives an investment pattern for the investors which can be applied for property evaluation and investment decisions.

Ben et al. (2008), in their paper "The influence of the financial and accounting information adjustments on the decisions of rating agencies", show that credit rating agencies (CRA) are qualified as "auxiliaries of the financial information" by all the investors. Ratings are the results of a methodology used by CRA. Within the framework of a demystification of the agencies' method of work, the objective of this paper is to identify the importance of the accounting and financial information adjustments in the decisions of rating agencies. This allows the explanation proportion of this type of information that contributes in the development of the assigned rating to be estimated. We suggest a statistical and econometrical study that aims at determining the ratings from the accounting and financial variables adjusted by the credit rating agencies to better understand the relation between the adjustments of the ratings and the level of the ascribed score.

Young-Chan Lee, in the application of support vector machines to corporate credit rating prediction and corporate credit rating analysis, has drawn a lot of research interests in previous studies, while recent studies have shown that machine learning techniques achieved better performance than the traditional statistical ones. This paper applies support vector machines (SVMs) to the corporate credit rating problem in an attempt to suggest a new model with better explanatory power and stability. To serve this purpose, the researcher uses a grid-search technique via 5-fold cross-validation to find out the optimal parameter values of RBF kernel function of SVM. In addition, to evaluate the prediction accuracy of SVM, the researcher compares its performance with those of multiple discriminant analysis (MDA), case-based reasoning (CBR) and three-layer fully connected back-propagation neural networks (BPNs). The experiment results show that SVM outperforms the other methods.

In banking and financial markets, credit rating agencies (CRAs) have very credible and constructive role in providing the unbiased information and also helps in reducing the informative asymmetry between lenders and investors on one side, and issuers on the other side, about the credit worthiness of companies. Hence, the CRAs' role has expanded with financial globalization and has received an additional boost from Basel II which incorporates the ratings of CRAs into the rules for setting weights for credit risk. Ratings tend to be sticky, ragging markets, and overreact when they do change. This overreaction may have aggravated financial crises in the recent past, contributing to financial instability. The recent bankruptcies and in increasing of nonperforming assets of many nationalized banks have prompted scrutiny of the agencies and also banker assessment models. Criticism has been especially directed towards the high degree of concentration on qualitative and financial aspects of the company. This means that the focus is more on the financial and accounting parameters rather than the comprehensive fundamental analysis comprising economy, industry and company analysis (EIC Framework) frame work.

Credit rating agencies (subsequently denoted as CRAs) specialize in analyzing and evaluating the creditworthiness of corporate securities and issuers of debt securities. In the new financial architecture, CRAs are expected to become more important in the management of both corporate and credit risk. Their role is limited to the large scale companies and multi corporations. However, the focus of credit rating agencies was never on Small and Medium Enterprises where credit worthiness related information asymmetry was too large. On the other hand, banks were also handicapped by not having robust comprehensive models. This research attempt has been made to bridge the gap and to provide solutions to the banks. At the same time, all the banks, sooner or later, will have to adopt the rational model for assessing the credit worthiness of their clients and it will become mandatory for all banks to follow the basel committee on banking supervision (BCBS) of capital standards for banks culminating in Basel II.

The logic underlying the existence of CRAs is to solve

the problem of the informative asymmetry between lenders and borrowers regarding the creditworthiness of the latter. Issuers with lower credit ratings pay higher interest rates embodying larger risk premiums than higher rated issuers. Moreover, ratings determine the eligibility of debt and other financial instruments for the portfolios of certain institutional investors due to national regulations that restrict investment in speculative-grade bonds. The rating agencies fall into two categories: (i) recognized and (ii) non-recognized. The former are recognized by supervisors in each country for regulatory purposes. In the United States, only five CRAs of which the best among them are moody, standard and poor (S and P) are recognized by the security and exchange commission (SEC). The majority of CRAs, such as: the Economist Intelligence Unit (EIU), Institutional Investor (II) and Euro Money, are "non-recognized". There is a wide disparity among CRAs, in that they may differ in size and scope (geographical and sectoral) of coverage. There are also wide differences in their methodologies, and a definition of the default risk, which renders a comparison between them, becomes difficult.

In preparing for the formal implementation of the new Basel capital accord (Basel II) at the end of 2006, our banking sector has been studying relevant provisions and response strategies. In the hope to promote and keep our banking supervision and risk management at the international level, the bureau of monetary affairs under the financial supervisory commission (formerly the Bureau of Monetary Affairs under the Ministry of Finance) in particular has set up a new basel capital accord joint research taskforce with bankers association to study relevant regulatory and implemental issues. The banking sector is paying particular attention to the internal-ratings based (IRB) approaches for credit risk provided in Basel II. In particular, model validation has been the focus among practitioners, which plays an important role in IRB qualification by supervisors. As an introductory effort, this paper tackles the subject of credit rating model validation. In reference to current theories and practices on the subject, we examine the considerations for model validation and introduce currently adopted approaches.

However, readers should keep in mind that this paper only discusses quantitative approaches. New theories and approaches for qualitative validation will be discussed at a later date as this field of study develops. If a bank realizes the whole picture about model validation, it will facilitate the work of IRB model construction and strategic planning for its business operation. More so, if the rating system is accepted by the regulatory authority, it will certainly boost the bank's stature and market competitiveness. The following is an introduction to the minimum operational requirements for the validation of IRB model outputs suggested in the draft of Basel II, complemented with the actual case study.

The existing models are based on just financial information of the companies and very less weight age has been given to the economic issues concerning the business. Most of the models have short term assessment features and they do not look into the dynamic change process of the economy. Another concerned issue is that ranks are just valid for a certain period of time or for the particular issue. If any changes occur in the economic cycle or in government policies with respect to business or trade, the existing models do not have a mechanism to reveal the impact of such implications on the quantitative aspects of the economic decision, such as monetary policy, fiscal policy and changes in trade policies that are not integrated in any of the models which are in use. Over and above each financial institution and bank is the use of its own method in assessing credit worthiness of the customers. Credit rating agencies are also not providing comprehensive information regarding credit worthiness of the companies; hence, this research is aimed at providing solution to all concerned agencies.

RESEARCH METHODOLOGY

Need for this study

The public sector bank for which the proposed model is developed is currently using a risk score card by Crisil called the risk assessment model. For loans above Rs.10 million, only this model is used, while for loans below Rs 10 million, the bank uses its own ratings and the internal scoring model. This study is mainly done to build a model for public sector bank with various exhaustive list parameters amid different degrees of importance. This model will facilitate the bank to check the credit worthiness of the clients. Also, the bank intends to reduce the non-performing assets in SME loans.

The bank is also interested in knowing the other methods of risk assessment. All Indian banks have to adopt to the Basel II norms, which have prompted Indian overseas bank to understand how the other banks are adopting to these changes which will be implemented in the near future.

Scope of the study

The scope of this study has been restricted only to 29 variables and extraneous factors have not been considered.

1. The study is confined to identify the credit worthiness of the clients based on weighted average model and discriminant model.
2. For the weighted average model, only 15 banks have been considered and for the discriminant analysis, the bank has provided data for 100 clients.

Objective of the study

The main objective of this study is to develop a credit rating model for IOB by studying the credit rating systems of other banks and comparing it with that of the existing model of Indian overseas bank.

Limitations of the study

1. The purview of the project is limited to the Small And Medium Enterprises' (SME) division.
2. Only 15 banks have been considered for the weighted average model.

Research design

Nature of the study

The study is a descriptive design. Descriptive research is used to obtain information concerning the current status of the phenomena to describe "what exists" with respect to variables or conditions in a situation. The methods involved range from the survey which describes the status quo, and the correlation study which investigates the relationship between variables, to the developmental studies which seek to determine changes over time. Here, it involves identifying the various risks and the sub-parameters of those risks by assigning weights to all of them.

Sampling design: Weighted average model

Source of data: The type of data used in assigning appropriate weights and aiding the development of the model is the primary data. However, the various risks and their parameters were identified using secondary data.

Population: The population includes all the banks (Public, private and development banks) in Chennai who are engaged in small medium enterprise (SME) financing.

Sample size and technique: The sample size is 15 banks and the number of officers with whom judgmental survey was conducted is 30. All major players in SME financing were taken into consideration and 35 clients were taken to test the model. The sampling technique used is convenience sampling. Nonetheless, banks which offered data were selected and their data were used.

Data collection instrument: The instrument used for the survey is a questionnaire. Here, various risks and their parameters were to be rated by credit managers of different banks.

Data collection method: Personal interview method is used for collection of primary data. Here, personal interviews were conducted with the credit managers of different banks.

Data analysis tool: The weighted average method is used for data analysis, while the weighted average score helps in categorizing the various clients into different risk levels.

Discriminant model

Source of data: The data used are secondary data taken from the bank's records.

Population: The population represents all the clients of the corporate banking division.

Sample size and technique: The sample size is 100 clients of the corporate banking division. The sample consists of clients of different banks, 95% of which have good, ongoing accounts and 5% have non-performing accounts. A total of 69 clients were taken for developing the model and 31 for testing it. The sampling technique used was judgment sampling, although only those records suggested by the chief manager were taken for the development and validation of the model.

Data collection method: Data were collected from the bank's records and the secondary method was adopted.

Data analysis tool

The discriminant method was used for data analysis, and the discriminant score was used to categorize the applicants into various risk categories.

DATA ANALYSIS

Steps in development of the weighted average model

Identification of the parameters that affect SME financing

The first step in the development of the model is the identification of the various risks and parameters used in this study. For this purpose, the various manuals, websites, books and papers pertaining to the credit appraisal for small and medium enterprise were carefully studied. Also, credit appraisals done at other leading organizations were taken into consideration.

Both quantitative and qualitative aspects need to be taken into consideration while computing the risk levels. There might be certain qualitative parameters which also affect the credit worthiness of the company.

Classification of risk

Industry risk: Industry risk refers to the impact that the state's industrial policy can have on the performance of a specific industry. An industry analysis shows how diverse and different forces act on an industry, thereby creating impact on its survival and profitability. It is these risks that the companies face by virtue of the industry they operate with. For example, many REITs run the risk that despite due diligence, they will acquire properties with significant environmental issues. The parameters of industry risk are as follows:

(1) Industry cyclicality: It explains as to what stage of the life cycle the industry operates. The growth to stabilization stage can be considered as low/moderate risk stages, while the introduction and decline stages belong to the high risk categories.
(2) Demand-supply gap in the industry: Such gaps represent the relationship between the demand for a

product and the supply thereof. Thus, the higher the level of supply as compared to demand, the higher the level of the competition would be. On the other hand, the organizations in the industry having higher demand and lower supply, would find the going much easier.
(3) Government policies: The priorities of the government do affect the industry. While governments actively protect and encourage certain industries, other industries might be facing discouragement or no protection at all.
(4) Entry barriers into the industry: The possibility that new firms may enter into the industry also affects competition. Industries possess characteristics that protect the high profit levels of firms in the market and inhibit additional rivals from entering the market. It is a situation which determines the level of comfort a particular business organization can enjoy. The ease of entry leads to more competition. Also, if the ease of entry in an industry is very high, then the risk levels are low and vice versa.
(5) Growth prospects of the industry: The growth prospects for the industry refer to the outlook of the industry in both short and long term. Industry with excellent growth prospects in both short and long term are considered to be less risky, while industries with uncertainty in its growth prospects are considered to be highly risky.
(6) Technological competence: This refers to the deployment of technology in any industry. If the usage of technology is superior, then it is low/moderate risk, while technologies which are prone to fast obsolescence are highly risky.

Business risk: Business risk is defined as the probability of not attaining the expected financial results. There are several factors which contribute to business risk. Some of them are:

i. Business movement in tune with economy.
ii. Vulnerability of the business.
iii. Concentration of current assets.

The sub-parameters of business risk are as follows:

1. Client's history: This refers to the client's tenure in the business. If the client has a successful track record of more than ten years, then he will be rated high and is considered to be less risky when compared to financing a new venture which is highly risky.
2. Relationship with suppliers: It pays to invest time in building good relationships with key suppliers. If you can save money or improve the quality of the goods or services you buy from your suppliers, your business stands to gain. If the client has a long term contract with the supplier then he is less risky when compared to the one who is unimportant to the suppliers.
3. Relationship with the customers: Customer relationships are at the heart of every business, that is, how the people who keep your company afloat are treated. If the client has a long term contract with the customers, then he will be rated high and is less risky when compared to the one who is unimportant to the customers.
4. Competition: This refers to the extent of market share the client holds in the business. A client who is the local market leader is rated high and is less risky when compared to the one who is an insignificant player in the market.
5. Technology: This refers to the level of speed of innovation and time to the market. A client with very high speed of innovation and shorten time to market will be rated high and is less risky when compared to the one with no support for innovation.
6. Expertise: This refers to the level of understanding of the business process. A client who has a good business history and good professional background has high expertise and is rated high.
7. Demand for the product: This refers to the periodicity for the product. If the demand for the product the client manufactures is regular, then he is rated high and is less risky.
8. Distribution network: Distribution is the process of moving a product from its manufacturing source to its customers. This refers to the strength of the distribution network. A client who has a very good distribution network will be rated high and is less risky.

Financial risk: Financial risk is normally any risk associated with any form of financing. It is the risk that a firm will be unable to meet its financial obligations. This risk is primarily a function of the relative amount of debt that the firm uses to finance its assets. A higher proportion of debt increases the likelihood that at some point, the firm will be unable to make the required interest and principal payments. Thus, the balance sheet is a critical tool for an effective credit evaluation. Nonetheless, the sub parameters under financial risk are:

1. Liquidity: The importance of adequate liquidity is in the sense of the ability of a firm to meet current/short term obligations when they become due for payment. It is the pre requisite for the very survival of the firm. Quantity and quality of liquid assets are important and are assessed with reference to the following:

i. To understand the liquidity of the issuer, the focus of the analysis is on the maturity matching between the sources of funds and the deployment of funds.
ii. It is measured based on the current ratio. The current

ratio measures the firm's ability to meet its short term liabilities and generally, the higher the ratio, the better it is. A client with the current ratio greater than two is rated high and is less risky.
2. Leverage: The long term lenders would judge the soundness of the firm on the basis of the long-term financial strength measured in terms of its ability to pay the interest regularly as well as repay the installment of the principal on due dates or in one lump sum at the time of maturity. It represents the level of financial stake of the promoters in the business in the form of own funds, such as capital, reserve and surpluses. The highly leveraged business organization will have high debt equity ratio indicating lower financial stakes. A client with debt equity ratio lesser than 0.50 is rated high and is less risky.
3. Sales growth: It represents the percentage increase in the sales turnover as compared to that of the previous year. The higher the growth in the sales accompanied by the operating profit or net profit, the positive its indication.
4. Profitability: These are profits before depreciation, interest and tax (PBDIT). The profitability taken in this case is the relationship between operating profit and the sales. A client with PBDIT >25% is rated high and is less risky.
5. Debt service coverage ratio (DSCR): This ratio tells the repayment ability of not only the interest portion but also that of installments. As such, the higher the ratio, the better the client's rating.
6. Activity ratio: These ratios measure the speed with which various accounts/ assets are converted into sales or cash. This ratio measures the average collection period and the inventory turnover rate. A client with very low average collection period and high inventory turnover rate will be rated high.

Management risk: Management risk refers to the defects, inadequacies and lack of skill and experience in the people in key positions. The parameters used are as follows:

1. Integrity: A lender always runs the risk of dealing with a person whose integrity is doubtful or turns to be doubtful in the subsequent stage which creates a problem for the lender in the recovery of funds also. A client with highly tested and proven integrity is rated high and is less risky.
2. Family standing: A client with the good respected family standing is rated high and is less risky.
3. Financial standing: When the client has good liquidity and considerable amount of free assets, then he is rated high and is less risky when compared to the client with low liquidity.
4. Management commitment: A client with sole business and unwavering commitment is rated high and is considered to be in low/moderate risk.
5. Succession: A company with good succession plan devised by the owner is rated high and is considered to be low in risk.
6. Employee quality: Employees are the dynamic resource of any organization. A company with highly qualified and motivated employees is rated high and is considered to be low in risk.
7. Repayment record: A company with good history of repayment is rated high and is considered to be low in risk.
8. Compliance record: A client that complied with all conditions is rated high and is considered to be low in risk.

Study the weights in other banks

Once the parameters are identified, a questionnaire is prepared with all the risks and their parameters (Appendix). This is circulated among credit managers of 15 banks (Public, private and development banks) in order to find out the weights for them. However, two credit managers from each bank gave the ratings.

Assign weights to the various risk parameters

The data collected from all the banks is classified and tabulated. The average is computed for all the four risks and their sub-parameters. Since the rating is done on a ten point scale, the weights are ten percent of the individual risk scores.

The weights assigned to various parameters developed in this study are based on a conceptual understanding of the relative impact of these parameters. The weights may change if the external economic environment undergoes substantial changes. It is not possible here to claim full objectivity in assignment of different weights, which requires empirical testing of success and failure experiences of a lending organization over a substantially long period of time. The various weights assigned to different parameters are illustrated in Table 2.

Development of the risk assessment model

A comprehensive model is constructed after attaching the weights. Each client will be rated on each of the parameters based on the scorecard provided. Each score of the client will be multiplied by the corresponding weights and a weighted score will be calculated for each parameter. The weighted scores of all the parameters will be summed to arrive at the final score of each client. Based on the final score, the client is given a rating by referring to the rating scale of the model. This final score

Table 2. Various parameters and their weights.

S/N	Industry risk	[280 points]
1	Industry cycle	4.85
2	Demand -supply gap	4.71
3	Government policies	4.71
4	Entry barriers	5.13
5	Growth	4.38
6	Technology status	4.22
	Business risk	**[260 points]**
7	Client history	3.46
8	Relationship with suppliers	3
9	Relationship with customers	2.9
10	Competition	4
11	Technology	2.77
12	Expertise	2.9
13	Demand for the product	2.9
14	Strength of distribution networks	4.07
	Financial risk	**[290 points]**
15	Liquidity	5.51
16	Leverage	5.31
17	Sales growth	4.35
18	Profitability	4.54
19	Interest coverage	4.75
20	Activity ratio	4.54
	Management risk	**[170 points]**
21	Integrity	1.77
22	Family standing	2.11
23	Financial standing	1.55
24	Management commitment	2
25	Succession	2.29
26	Employee quality	1.62
27	Organization structure	1.93

decides the risk involved in operating with each client.

To aid the assessment process and to systematize the entire process, a score card has been developed in consultation with people well versed in this field. The score for each parameter in each risk category should be given based on the score card. This will then standardize the whole process.

In this model, risk rating is measured on a scale of 3 which takes into account different scoring bands beginning from 100 to 50. The first two items are in the score level of 51 categories, while the borrowers are in the five risk categories. The remaining one places the borrower in the non-performing category, based on the parameters prescribed by the bank.

Rating scale

The rating scale indicates the level of risk a particular borrowing transaction carries with it. It begins from the minimum risk category and ends with the loss asset category. A rating model helps to make distinction between various stages of loan transaction and to draw appropriate conclusions. RBI has prescribed that the overall score for risk should be placed on a numerical scale rating between 1 and 6 or 1 and 8 on the basis of the credit profile of the bank concerned. RBI usually prescribes a six point rating scale (Appendix 3), but in this model's development, the reasons for adopting a three point scale are explained in Table 3.

Reserve bank of India (RBI) has prescribed a six point rating scale, but we have condensed the rating to a three point scale. The reasons for the following are:

1. The sample size which is taken as only 30.
2. Out of the 5 NPAs, 4 have a score between 27 and 60 and only one has less than that.
3. Out of the 35 clients used for testing the model, three of them fall between the 50 and 60 ranges.
4. The six point rating scale has been condensed to a three point rating scale.

Validation of the model

For checking the consistency of performance of the model, the thirty-five existing clients were considered and rated. The comparison of the rating of the customer and the current status of the performance determines the consistency of the model.

Case 1 – EID parry (India) Ltd., Madras (Figure 2)

EID parry has the following scores:

1. It scores 107.17 on a total of 280 for industry risk.
2. It scores 107.22 on a total of 260 for business risk.
3. It scores 121.5 on a total of 290 for financial risk.
4. It scores 66.19 on a total of 170 for management risk.
5. It has an overall score of 402.08 on a total of 1000.
6. The client is put in risk category 3 which implies it belongs to NPA category.

Result: The case may not be granted credit.

Case 2 - Aban Loyd Chiles offshore Ltd., Madras (Figure 3)

Aban Loyd Chiles has the following scores:

1. It scores 210.95 on a total of 280 for industry risk.

Table 3. Rating scale.

S/N	Risk score (%)	Client risk rating	Explanation	Nature of case
1	100 to 81	1	Very low or no risk	Good
2	80 to 61	2	Tolerable risk	Moderate
3	Below 60	3	High risk	NPA

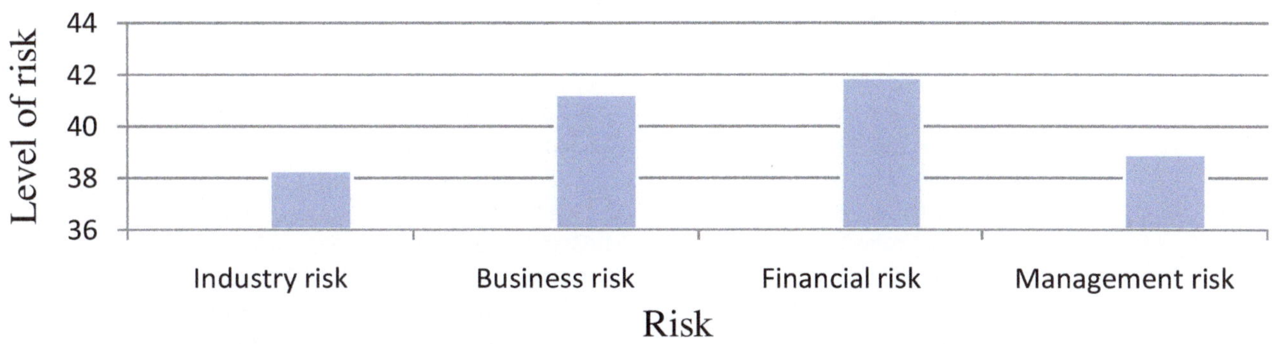

Figure 2. Validation result of EID parry.

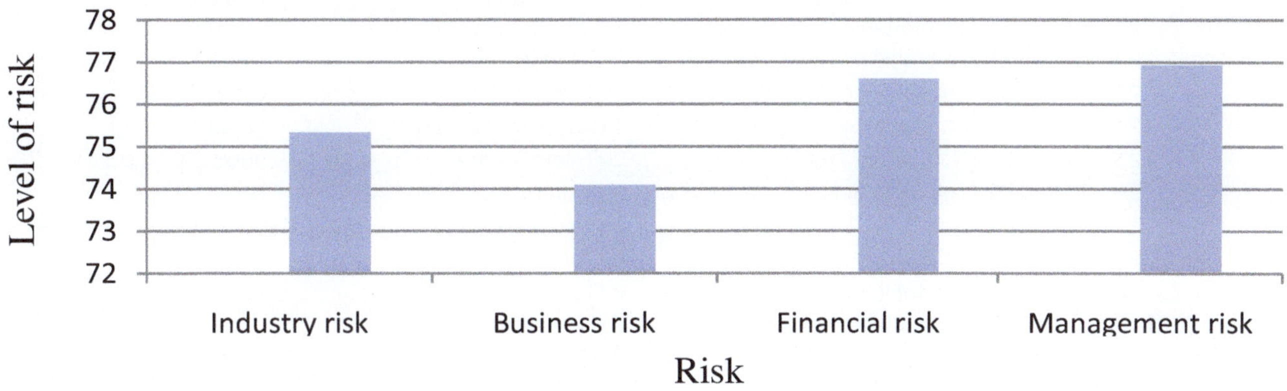

Figure 3. Validation result of Aban Lloyd.

2. It scores 192.635 on a total of 260 for business risk.
3. It scores 222.15 on a total of 290 for financial risk.
4. It scores 130.765 on a total of 170 for management risk.
5. It has an overall score of 756.5 on a total of 1000.
6. The client is put in risk category 2 which implies tolerable risk.

Result: The case may be granted credit.

Case wise statistics: A total of 35 cases were taken for the validation of the model (Table 4).

Interpretations

1. The existing model was able to classify 28 records correctly out of 35. So, the classification accuracy is 80%.
2. The new model was able to classify 32 records correctly out of 35. So, the classification accuracy is 91.42%.

Discriminant analysis

Discriminant analysis is a technique used for classifying a set of observations into predefined classes. The purpose is to determine the class of an observation based on a

Table 4. Case wise statistics.

Case number	Existing model's score	New model's score	Actual performance
1	2 (Tolerable risk)	2 (Tolerable risk)	Good
2	1(Comfortable risk)	1 (Comfortable risk)	Good
3	1 (Comfortable risk)	3 (High risk)	NPA
4	1(Comfortable risk)	1 (Comfortable risk)	Good
5	1 (Comfortable risk)	3 (High risk)	NPA
6	2 (Tolerable risk)	2 (Tolerable risk)	Good
7	3 (High risk)	1 (Comfortable risk)	Good
8	1 (Comfortable risk)	1 (Comfortable risk)	Good
9	2 (Tolerable risk)	2 (Tolerable risk)	Good
10	2 (Tolerable risk)	1 (Comfortable risk)	Good
11	2 (Tolerable risk)	2 (Tolerable risk)	Good
12	2 (Tolerable risk)	2 (Tolerable risk)	Good
13	1 (Comfortable risk)	1 (Comfortable risk)	Good
14	3 (High risk)	1 (Comfortable risk)	Good
15	2 (Tolerable risk)	2 (Tolerable risk)	Good
16	2 (Tolerable risk)	2 (Tolerable risk)	Good
17	3 (High risk)	3 (High risk)	NPA
18	3 (High risk)	3 (High risk)	Good
19	2 (Tolerable risk)	3 (High risk)	NPA
20	2 (Comfortable risk)	3 (High risk)	Good
21	1 (Comfortable risk)	1 (Comfortable risk)	Good
22	2 (Tolerable risk)	2 (Tolerable risk)	Good
23	2 (Tolerable risk)	2 (Tolerable risk)	Good
24	1 (Comfortable risk)	1 (Comfortable risk)	Good
25	1 (Comfortable risk)	2 (Tolerable risk)	good
26	2 (Tolerable risk)	3 (High risk)	NPA
27	1 (Comfortable risk)	2 (Tolerable risk)	good
28	2 (Tolerable risk)	2 (Tolerable risk)	good
29	2 (Tolerable risk)	2 (Tolerable risk)	good
30	1 (Comfortable risk)	1 (Comfortable risk)	good
31	1 (Comfortable risk)	1 (Comfortable risk)	good
32	1 (Comfortable risk)	1 (Comfortable risk)	good
33	1 (Comfortable risk)	1 (Tolerable risk)	NPA
34	2 (Tolerable risk)	2 (Tolerable risk)	good
35	3 (High risk)	3 (High risk)	NPA

set of variables known as predictors or input variables. The model is built based on a set of observations for which the classes are known. Discriminant analysis is used to classify objects/records into two or more groups based on the knowledge of some variables related to them.

Discriminant function

$Y=a+ k_1x_1 +k_2x_2 +\dots\dots\dots +k_nx_n$

where Y is a dependent variable, a is a constant, x_1, $x_2 \dots x_n$ are independent variables, and k_1 and k_2 are coefficients of the independent variables. In this case, for the development of the model, the dependent and independent variables are as follows:

1. The dependent variable (Y) is the client risk rating (CRR).
2. The independent variables (x_1, $x_2 \dots\dots x_{20}$) are as follows:

X1 = Industry cyclicality, X2 = demand-supply gap in the industry, X3 = government policies towards the industry, X4 = entry barriers in the industry, X5 = growth prospects

Table 5. Discriminant model.

Discriminant models	Function	
	1	2
Industry cycle	0.841	-0.360
Demand supply	0.369	0.034
Govt. policies	0.548	0.226
Entry barriers	-0.205	0.407
Growth prospects	-0.002	0.092
Technological competence	-0.055	-0.074
Client history	-0.069	0.688
Relationship with suppliers	0.845	-0.646
Relationship with customers	-0.087	-0.431
Competition	-0.021	0.375
Technology	0.616	-0.778
Expertise	-10.068	-0.049
Demand for the product	0.535	0.068
Strength of distribution network	0.017	0.632
Liquidity	0.177	-0.405
Leverage	0.062	0.008
Sales growth	0.280	-0.247
Profitability	0.490	-0.293
Interest coverage	-0.217	-0.333
Activity ratios	-0.112	0.132
Integrity	0.469	0.320
Family standing	-0.218	0.305
Financial standing	-0.026	0.457
Management commitment	-0.160	0.050
Succession	0.298	0.155
Employee quality	-0.597	0.153
Organisation structure	-0.015	-0.433
Repayment records	-0.226	0.430
Compliance records	0.502	0.122
(Constant)	-170.438	-10.663

for the industry, X6 = technological competence, X7 = client's history, X8 = relationship with suppliers, X9 = relationship with customers, X10 = competition, X11 = technology, X12 = expertise, X13 = demand for the product, X14 = strength of the distribution network, X15 = liquidity, X16 = leverage, X17 = sales growth, X18 = profitability, X19 = interest coverage, X20 = activity ratio, X21 = integrity, X22 = family standing, X23 = financial standing, X23 = management commitment, X24 = succession, X25 = employee quality, X26 = repayment records, X27 = compliance records and X27 = organization structure.

Building the discriminant model

To build the discriminant model, the value of the dependent and the independent variables for the 69 records are entered in the SPSS software. The discriminant scores are computed by solving all the 69 equations. Thus, the weights/coefficients for all the parameters are computed and are illustrated in Table 5.

Discriminant functions

The discriminant functions are generated from a sample of individuals (or cases), for which group membership is known. The functions can then be applied to new cases with measurements on the same set of variables, but with unknown group membership. The coefficients for the first discriminant function are derived so as to maximize the differences between the group means.

The coefficients for the second discriminant function are derived to maximize the difference between the group means, subject to the constraint that the values on the second discriminant function are not correlated with the values on the first discriminant function and so on. In other words, the second discriminant function is orthogonal to the first and the third discriminant function is orthogonal to the second, and so on.

The maximum number of unique functions that can be derived is equal to the number of groups minus one or is equal to the number of discriminating variables, which are less. The first function will be the most powerful differentiating dimension, but later functions may also represent additional significant dimensions of the differentiation.

Function 1

Y = 0.841 (industry cycle) + 0.369 (demand – supply gap) + 0.548 (government policies) - 0.205 (entry barriers) - 0.002 (growth prospects) - 0.055 (technological competence) - 0.069 (client history) + 0.845 (relationship with suppliers) - 0.087 (relationship with customers) - 0.021 (competition) + 0.616 (technology) - 1.068 (expertise) + 0.535 (demand) + 0.017 (strength of distribution network) + 0.177 (liquidity) + 0.062 (leverage) + 0.280 (sales growth) + 0.490 (profitability) - 0.217 (interest coverage) - 0.112 (activity ratios) + 0.469 (integrity) - 0.218 (family standing) - 0.026 (financial standing) - 0.160 (management commitment) + 0.298 (succession) - 0.597 (employee quality) - 0.015 (organisational structure) - 0.226 (repayment records) + 0.502 (compliance records).

Function 2

Y = - 0.360 (industry cycle) + 0.034 (demand – supplygap)

Table 6. Functions at group centroids.

Risk category	Function	
	1	2
Low risk	1.285	-0.085
Moderate risk	-0.755	0.168
High risk	-1.696	-4.816

+ 0.226 (government policies) + 0.407 (entry barriers) + 0.092 (growth prospects) - 0.074 (technological competence) + 0.688 (client history) - 0.646 (relationship with suppliers) - 0.431 (relationship with customers) + 0.375 (competition) - 0.778 (technology) - 0.049 (expertise) + 0.068 (demand) + 0.632 (strength of distribution network) - 0.405 (liquidity) + 0.008 (leverage) - 0.247 (sales growth) - 0.293 (profitability) - 0.333 (interest coverage) + 0.132 (activity ratios) + 0.320 (integrity) + 0.305 (family standing) + 0.457 (financial standing) + 0.050 (management commitment) + 0.155 (succession) + 0.153 (employee quality) - 0.433 (organizational structure) + 0.430 (repayment records) + 0.122 (compliance records).

Discriminant score

The discriminant score, also called the DA score, is the value resulting from applying a discriminant function formula to the data for a given case. The Z score is the discriminant score for the standardized data. Discriminant score derived from the two functions can be used to predict/determine the grouping of the unclassified cases.

Functions at group centroids

Functions at group centroids are the mean discriminant scores for each of the dependent variable categories for each of the discriminant functions. The centroids give the group mean on the ldf. If the two groups are of equal size, the best cutting point is half way between the values of the functions at group centroids (that is, the average). Under "functions at group centroids", we gave the group means of each of the discriminant functions (Table 6).

Classification function coefficient

Classification function coefficients are shown in Table 7.

Interpretation

1. Each column contains estimates of the coefficients for a classification function for one group.
2. The functions are used to assign or classify cases into groups.
3. To obtain a classification score for each case in each group, multiply each coefficient by the value of the corresponding variable, sum the products, and add the constant to get the score.
4. A case is predicted as being a member of the group in which the value of its classification function is largest.

Validation of the model

For checking the consistency of the model's performance, thirty-one existing clients were considered and rated. The comparison of the rating of the customer and the current status of the performance determines the consistency of the model.

Case 1- Mysore Petrochemicals Ltd., Madras

1. The discriminant score for function 1 is 0.128.
2. This lies in the moderate risk category.
3. The classification score for the moderate risk category is the highest.

Result: The client belongs to the moderate risk category and he may be given credit.

Case 2- Ultramarine and Pigments Ltd., Ranipet

1. The discriminant score for function 1 is 2.248.
2. This lies in the high risk category.
3. The classification score for the high risk category is the highest.

Result: The client belongs to the very high risk category and he may be refused credit.

Case wise statistics

Table 8 shows the case wise statistics.

Table 7. Classification function coefficients.

Discriminant functions	Risk category		
	Low risk	Moderate risk	High risk
Industry cycle	23.538	21.732	22.734
Demand supply	11.864	11.121	10.603
Government policies	33.845	32.784	31.140
Entry barriers	-9.390	-8.868	-10.702
Growth prospects	17.944	17.970	17.516
Technological competence	4.042	4.135	4.553
Client history	11.724	12.039	8.676
Suppliers	28.610	26.724	29.150
Customers	9.322	9.390	11.617
Competition	9.418	9.556	7.709
Technology	27.592	26.139	29.438
Expertise	-18.847	-16.682	-15.434
Demand	18.607	17.532	16.692
Strength	12.561	12.686	9.519
Liquidity	17.356	16.894	18.748
Leverage	1.635	1.510	1.413
Sales growth	21.294	20.661	21.628
Profitability	23.601	22.526	23.525
Interest coverage	13.378	13.736	15.602
Activity ratios	11.785	12.047	11.495
Integrity	29.515	28.640	26.602
Family standing	9.118	9.640	8.323
Financial standing	2.466	2.634	.379
Management commitment	-7.875	-7.535	-7.636
Succession	15.536	14.968	13.917
Employee quality	-14.956	-13.699	-13.900
Organisation structure	-12.413	-12.492	-10.323
Repayment records	-.471	.100	-1.828
compliance records	-.403	-1.396	-2.476
(Constant)	-930.169	-894.010	-885.790

Interpretations

1. The existing model was able to classify 25 records correctly out of 31. So, the percentage of classification accuracy is 80.6%.
2. The new model was able to classify 27 records correctly out of 31. So, the percentage of classification accuracy is 87.1% (Table 8).

FINDINGS AND SUGGESTIONS

The amount of risk assessed and which is now experienced in respect of these clients were found to be similar in the case of the weighed average model. Clients with high scores and low risk have been prompt payers on the other hand, while those with low scores and high risks were found to be defaulters. One company which was operating in tolerable or medium risk was found to have a high risk NPA. The following are the key findings of each of the model:

Weighted average model

1. Financial risk is considered to be the most significant of all risks.
2. Business risk is rated second in vitality, followed by management risk and lastly industry risk.
3. The existing model was able to classify 28 records correctly out of 35. So, the classification accuracy is 80%.
4. The new model was able to classify 32 records

Table 8. Case wise statistics.

Case no.	Existing model's score	New model's score	Actual performance
1	3 (High risk)	3 (High risk)	NPA
2	3 (High risk)	3 (High risk)	NPA
3	2 (Tolerable risk)	3(High risk)	NPA
4**	2 (Tolerable risk)	3 (High risk)	Good
5	3 (High risk)	3 (High risk)	NPA
6	2 (Tolerable risk)	2 (Tolerable risk)	Good
7	1 (Comfortable risk)	1(Comfortable risk)	Good
8**	2 (Tolerable risk)	3(High risk)	Good
9	1 (Comfortable risk)	1(Comfortable risk)	Good
10**	2 (Tolerable risk)	2(tolerable risk)	NPA
11	1 (Comfortable risk)	1 (Comfortable risk)	Good
12	2 (Tolerable risk)	2 (Tolerable risk)	Good
13	3 (High risk)	2 (Tolerable risk)	Good
14	2 (Tolerable risk)	2 (Tolerable risk)	Good
15	2 (Tolerable risk)	2 (Tolerable risk)	Good
16**	1 (Comfortable risk)	3 (High risk)	Good
17	2 (Tolerable risk)	2 (Tolerable risk)	Good
18	1 (Comfortable risk)	1 (Comfortable risk)	Good
19	1 (Comfortable risk)	1 (Comfortable risk)	Good
20	1 (Comfortable risk)	1 (Comfortable risk)	Good
21	3 (High risk)	2 (Tolerable risk)	Good
22	2 (Tolerable risk)	2 (Tolerable risk)	Good
23	2 (Tolerable risk)	2 (Tolerable risk)	Good
24	2 (Tolerable risk)	2 (Tolerable risk)	Good
25	2 (Tolerable risk)	2 (Tolerable risk)	Good
26	1 (Comfortable risk)	1 (Comfortable risk)	Good
27	3 (High risk)	2 (Tolerable risk)	Good
28	3 (High risk)	2 (Tolerable risk)	Good
29	2 (Tolerable risk)	2 (Tolerable risk)	Good
30	1 (Comfortable risk)	1 (Comfortable risk)	Good
31	1 (Comfortable risk)	1 (Comfortable risk)	Good

correctly out of 35. So, the classification accuracy is 91.42%.

Discriminant model

1. The existing model was able to classify 25 records correctly out of 31. So, the percentage of classification accuracy is 80.6%.
2. The new model was able to classify 27 records correctly out of 31. So, the percentage of classification accuracy is 87.1%.
3. All the NPAs have been correctly identified by the new model.

Suggestions

Weighted average model can be used by Indian overseas bank to check the client's credit worthiness.

Conclusion

Based on the previous findings, we can conclude that:

1. Weighted average model can be used for predicting

the credit worthiness of the clients, because it has higher predictive power.

2. The new discriminant model can be used to identify NPAs. This will help the bank to reduce their non-performing assets.

3. Qualitative factors play a major role in evaluating the credit worthiness of the clients.

REFERENCES

Allen NB, Gregory FU (2004). World Bank Conference on Small and Medium Enterprises: Overcoming Growth Constraints World Bank, MC 13-121 October 14-15, 2004.

Altman EI (1968). Financial Ratio's, Discriminant Analysis and the Prediction of Corporate Bankruptcy. J. Fin., 23: 589-609.

Altman E, Narayanan P (1997). An International Survey of Business Failure Classification Models in Financial Markets Institutions and Instruments. Malden, MA: Blackwell Publishers.

Beaver WH (1966). Financial Ratio as predictors of Failure. J. Account. Res., 4: 71-111.

Bharath ST, Shumway T (2004). Forecasting default with the KMVMerton model. University of Michigan Working Paper.

Chandy PR, Edwin HD (1990). Commercial Paper Ratings Models," Q. J. Bus. Econs., Vol. 29.

Charitou A, Neophytou E, Charalambous C (2004). Predicting Corporate Failure: Empirical Evidence from UK. Eur. Account. Rev., 13: 465-497.

ECD Small and Medium Enterprise Outlook (2002). Published by OECD Publication Services, France

Keasey K, Watson R (1986). Current Cost Accounting and the Prediction of Small Company (1991), (9)4: 11-29.

Larry GP, Timothy PC (1986). A note on rank transformation discriminant analysis: An alternative procedure for classifying bank holding company commercial paper ratings. J. Banking Fin., 10(4): 605-610.

Lennox C (1999). Identifying Failing Companies: A Re-evaluation of the Logit, Probit and DA Approaches , J. Econs. Bus. (forthcoming).

Lin SM, Ansell J, Andreeva G (2007). Predicting default of a small business using different definitions of financial distress. Proceedings of Credit Scoring and Credit Control X.

Manickavasagam V, Srinivas G (2009). Property Valuation for Investment Decision (Special Reference to Commercial Mortgage Backed Securities (CMBS)) at 2009 International Conference on Financial Theory and Engineering. Dubai, UAE. Organized by IEEE and IACSIT. Web site: http://www.iacsit.org/proceeding/icfte09.toc.pdf.

Manickavasagam V, Srinivas G (2009). Risk Management Frame Work for ITES Organizations at International Conference on Business and Information, BAI 2009 at Kuala Lumpur, Malaysia, and July 6th to 8th 2009. http://bai2009.org/file/Pages/Accounting.htm.

Manickavasagam V, Srinivas G (2010). Risk Assessment Model for Assessing NBFCs' (Asset Financing) Customers in Intl. J. Trade, Econs. Fin. (IJTEF) accepted for publishing in June, issue.

Merton RC (1974). The Pricing of Corporate Debt: The Risk Structure of Interest Rates, J. Fin., 29(2): 449-470.

Ohlson J (1980). Financial ratios and the probabilistic prediction of bankruptcy, J. Acct. Res., 18(1): 109-131.

Patricia S, David, (2009). Evaluation of small business failure and the framing problem. Intl. J. Econs. Bus. Res., 1(4): 438-453.

Peel MJ, Wilson N (1986). Some Evidence on Discriminating between Failing and Distressed Acquired Firms in the UK Corporate Sector. Omega Intl. J. Manag. Sci., 16(4): 309-318.

Financial analysis as a consideration for stock exchange investment decisions in Tanzania

A. S. Norman

Tumaini University, Tanzania or Kampala International University, Tanzania. E-mail: adamsonnorman@yahoo.com.

Stock exchange investment in Tanzania is growing fast, and many people of different varieties of income are participating in the purchase of shares commonly known as stock exchange. However, there is seemingly little concern on the use of financial analysis on the part of local individual investors when purchasing the shares. Hence, this paper presents the findings of the study on financial analysis as a consideration for stock exchange investment decision making in Tanzania. The study was conducted for four months from July to October 2006. It adopted a survey study incorporating all six registered brokers in Tanzania located in Dar es Salaam. First, the introduction was given, which provided the essentials and the need for financial statements analysis as far as decisions regarding investment is concerned, after which the literature review was done. This was followed by a presentation of the role of Dares salaam stock exchange. Subsequently, the methodology of the study was given, followed by data analysis and discussion of findings. Finally, conclusions and recommendations were given. The paper concluded that most of investors in Tanzania do not depend on the financial statements analysis of the firms when investing mainly because most of these investors have not acquired knowledge on the importance of financial statements in making decisions regarding the investment. However, big investors such as financial institutions and firms do consider financial statement analysis when investing.

Key words: Financial analysis, stock exchange, investment decisions, Tanzania.

INTRODUCTION

Financial analysis (FA) is essential for making an informed decision. The essentials increase when the FA is used as a determinant for investing, although this is not the only use of financial analysis. It is one of the tools used in evaluating a company's financial position and performance for various reasons, including for investment purposes. Thus, this study intended to examine whether people investing in stock exchange (SE) do consider financial statements analysis. Generally stock market include two main securities namely shares and bonds. Therefore the study confined with the investment in shares.

Financial statements analysis is mainly concerned with the understanding of company accounts and interpretation of the published financial statements to enable legitimate users to make informed economic decisions (Chang and Most, 1977). Since users are assumed to have a reasonable knowledge of business and economic activities and accounting and a willingness to study the information with reasonable diligence, it is anticipated that they will be deprived of their rights if body corporate do not produce such statements (Bence et al., 1995).

Financial statements are vital for making informed decisions in particular to the developing countries like Tanzania where the investments level is thin, and the general behavior to investing is immature. Normally, the presentation of the FSA is during the end of accounting period depending on the policy of the company. In this view, Abu Baker and Naser (2000), argues that, investors view the annual report as the main source of corporate information in developing countries and companies use it as a medium to disseminate information to external interested parties. The assumption is generally that the annual report reflects the commercial reality of the company concerned, and the expectation is that the reports will assist users in making informed decisions about the company and future investment options.

In Tanzania certainly, the importance of financial statements reports, and in particular the ratios drawn from these financial statements analysis, might be of greater concern compared to other countries. This is due to the level of the investment as it is no more than 20 years from mid 1990s when the policy on economic integration, in the name of trade liberalization was launched and youthfulness of the investors. In this line, therefore, the level of understanding of investors in Tanzania suggest for a study on the perception of these investors on the need for publishing accounts, and the role of the financial statements analysis. Thus, the study aims at realizing the use of the financial statements analysis when deciding to invest in stock exchange.

Background of the problem

Financial literacy is a key to saving and investing (Norman, 2003). Therefore, economic growth and transformation worldwide can be said to be dependent on the proper utilization of financial analysis information among others. Hence, before we look at the nature of the problem, the survey of stages that the economic growth of Tanzania has gone through is vital for the realization of stock exchange investment.

Economic transformation in Tanzania can be said to have undergone four important stages namely the colonial period, which was characterized with private ownership of major means of production but with thin investment level of both agricultural production and processing industries. The second is post independence but before the Arusha declaration in 1967, which was characterized with improved private sector ownership of major means of production, with agricultural products taking a leading role. The third is the period after Arusha declaration in 1967 to 1990, which was characterized with public ownership of major means of production. This resulted from nationalization of private sector in 1967, hence marking the beginning of what seemed good trend of industrial performance at the initial stages (1967 to 1980s), lasting with falling trend of production during the period of 1980s through 1990s.

The 1990 and beyond can be termed as the forth stage of economic performance as far as investment is concerned. This level of investment or economic performance was characterized with increased investment realized due to the change of economic policy from the centrally controlled economy to the open economy. Hence, most public firms were privatized. In the same vein notes that, the economic trend of most developing countries have sought dangers as many huge public investment were privatized through what was is termed at a 'giving' price.

Several reasons can be associated with the decline of industrial performance in the third period (1980s to 1990s). Such reasons include lack of sense of commitment of the Chief Executive Officers (CEOs) as were appointed to execute duties without being real owners of those firms. The decline of production necessitated the government, which was the custodian of the public firms on behalf of the people to enter into stage four (1990 and beyond) by liberalizing the economic trends through transforming the economy by changing the ownership of major means of production to private sector, while encouraging plural ownership of the firms through investing in sale and purchase of shares, commonly known as stock exchange.

In order to facilitate the stock investment, the government passed an Act of 1996 to provide room of stock exchange business in Tanzania. Thus, the Dar es Salaam stock exchange (DSE) was established in 1996 as a result of the government policy of transforming the economy, and thus marking the beginning of the people in Tanzania indulging in purchase of shares as a strategy for investing, consequently a need for proper decision making on where to invest and why.

The where and why questions are vital, in particular, when observing the performance of the companies that were the first to list shares with the DSE market and reasons backed people to invest in such companies. The first company to list its shares with the DSE was the Tanzania Oxygen Company Limited (TOL). The observation, however, reveal that those who purchased shares encountered what could be termed as loss, since the TOL share value dropped from Tshs.500 in 1998 to Tshs. 300 in 2005. On the other hand there are companies that have flourished. Such companies include the Tanzania Tea Packers Limited (TATEPA), which experienced the rise of share value from Tshs. 330 as an Initial Price Offer in the year 2000 to Tshs. 440/= in 2005. Thus the resilience of the study was on the high need for investors to effectively make decisions that would increase the prospects hence improve house hold economy. It is from that point of view, the investors should realize factors necessary for proper investing.

To make rational decisions in keeping with the objectives of the firm, the financial manager and generally investors, need to have analytical tools. The more useful tools of financial analysis possessed by an investor the more reliance on those tools for decision-making. The tools include various ratios used for realization of the performance of the industry. These ratios are essentially obtained through analyzing the financial performance of the firm. The tools thus can be summed up as financial analysis or accounts information.

Financial statement analysis therefore, is an information-processing system designed to provide data for decision-makers. The information is basically derived from published financial statements but in the process of analysis, the use is also made for non-accounting data, such as stock prices and aggregate economic indicators

Users of the financial statement information system are decision-makers concerned with evaluating the economic situation of the firm and predicting its future course.

The major group of users are investors, for making portfolio decisions, management, for evaluating the operational and financial efficiency of the firm as a whole and of subunits such as departments lenders, for determining the credit worthiness of loan applicants, labor unions for establishing an economic basis for collective bargaining, regulating agencies like TRA, EWURA for controlling the activities of subordinated units; and researchers in economics and business administration for studying firms behavior in terms of performance.

Given these varies uses and motives, it is obvious that no single information system will satisfy all the requirements. Rather, financial statement analysis should be sufficiently general and flexible to accommodate different user needs. Van (2002) indicates that, investors in a company's common stock are concerned principally with present and expected future earnings and the stability of these earnings about a trend, as well as their covariance with the earnings of other companies. As a result, investors might concentrate their analysis on a company's profitability. They would be concerned with its financial conditions in so far as it affects the ability of the company to pay dividends and to avoid bankruptcy. In order to bargain more effectively for outside funds, the management of a firm should be interested in all aspects of financial analysis that outside suppliers of capital use in evaluating the firm.

The research problem attracted the researcher in several ways; including the new-fangled venture of investment, which has attracted many Tanzanians. Secondly is the potentials vested in the entire shares business, which seem to supersede the banking interest rate at far. For example, while those invested in the Tanzania Cigarette Company (TCC) enjoyed the share value increase of about 400% from Tshs. 410/share as initial price offer (IPO) to Tshs.1650/share as closing price offer (CPO) in 2004 (DSE, 2005) and as of March 16th, 2009 stands at 1760. Such money increase, if were deposited at Commercial Banks would not earn an interest of 10%. The normal rate of most banks in Tanzania for saving accounts is between 2 to 4%. Those who invested in the Tanzania Breweries Company Limited earned about 254% in the period of about five years. Therefore, the main purpose is to set out paradox of whether those investing in shares do consider financial analysis/accounts information when investing.

Statement of the problem

In Tanzania, Stock Exchange Investment has been growing fast since its launching in 1998. For example Tanzania Oxygen Limited (TOL) listed its shares with the DSE in 1998 and attracted many people including the author of this article. Until the conduct of this study the company has not been able to give any dividend to share holders, and its share value has continued falling from Tshs. 500 as initial price offer in 1998 to Tshs. 300 in 2005 which is 40% decrease in value (DSE, 2001; DSE, 2003; DSE, 2005). The current value is TZS 290. On the other hand Twiga Cement listed its shares in 2001 and wanted to raise a capital of 31 billion shillings. With high enthusiasm of the people, the amount of money rose to 94 billion, which is about three times more than the required amount. The behavior of purchase of shares is of great concern on whether those who invest in shares have knowledge of financial analysis when investing. Since failure to understanding the financial analysis, envisage risk of loosing the capital invested.

It is important to note that the importance of financial statement analysis or simply financial analysis is independent of share price performance. In fact one may argue the poor share price performance of TOL is a reflection of poor performance that became apparent after financial analysis. Hence financial analysis is one of the tools for decision making but not the only particularly when dealing with stock exchange. Financial analysis by investor is not a shield for companies' shares price to move up or downwards. By nature investment in securities has inherent risk which the investor ought to know. It is also not correct to think that companies whose share price increased from the IPO price to the present state are risk free.

Therefore, knowing the use of financial analysis is quite potential if risk minimization is of concern. The choice of shares has been potential because it is the industry though new, yet it brings many people in owning the companies. Thus when the shares industry as far as investment is concerned is properly done; it will envisage economic improvements to many Tanzanians and thus improve the lively hood of the people.

On the contrary, if the investment done through purchase of shares would be improper, there are possibilities of many people getting into investment with suffrage. This can be substantiated through the Tanzania Oxygen Company Limited, which was the first company to list shares with the Dar es Salaam Stock Exchange, and attracted many people, thus the company raised her capital to 9.4 billion shillings (DSE, 2005:18). However the value of shares kept diminishing, and to date no dividends have been enjoyed by the people who invested. For example the value of shares have dropped from Tshs. 500 as initial price offer in 1998 to Tshs. 300 in the year 2005 which is 40% (DSE,2001, 2003, 2005) and as on March 17, 2009 the price was TZS 290. Considering the risk associated with the investment in stock shares, there is a need for the study to examine financial analysis as a consideration for investment in Tanzania a focus on Stock Exchange. It is not likely that every body investing in securities can do financial analysis. What is important is for investors in securities to invest with knowledge either through own analysis or through investment adviser.

LITERATURE REVIEW

This study avails a critical literature review on Financial Analysis as a consideration for investment. The review of literatures covers the historical perspective of the importance of financial analysis/accounts information, its development, and the recent studies on the same. It is worth noting that while it is true that the need for financial information or education is vital to investors, it is equally important to all people. The world today is full of budgets deficits and constraints and thus a need for proper financial education which will cultivate informed decision making. Thus the chapter narrates on general terms the need for financial education, and narrows to the importance of financial statements analysis (FSA).

Financial statements analysis is mainly concerned with the understanding of company accounts and interpretations of the published financial statements to enable legitimate users make informed economic decisions. Since users are assumed to have a reasonable knowledge of business and economic activities and accounting and a willingness to study the information with reasonable diligence, it is anticipated that they will be deprived their rights if body corporate do not produce such statements.

Previous research study on importance of FSA

Financial statements analyses emphasize on developing financial information within the context of formal decisions models. Consequently, financial statements analysis is regarded as data processing system designed to provide information for decision-making. In this regard, researches have been undertaken on the importance of financial statements and the importance of utilizing the same in making decisions for investors. For instance the study of Nasser and Nuseibeh (2003) on the usefulness of annual reports reveal that the user groups surveyed in the study rely mainly on information made directly available by the company and do not consult intermediary sources of corporate information in order to make informed decisions.

This may suggest that there could be same correlations if same study was to be carried in Tanzania, since, just like Saudi Arabia, Tanzania is perceived to have a limited number of listed companies and businesses and financial communities have many social and business links, resulting in relatively easy interaction between the user groups and related companies.

The expediency of information released by companies should be in a simple form and expressive language to be consumed by any client. In this dimension, suggested that to make annual reports adequate and readable, the information contained in these annual reports should be presented in an understandable manner and grouped and organized appropriately. Moreover, Epstein and Pava (1994) asserted that the language style might have a material effect on the readership, and influence the understandability of information that appears in annual reports. Wolk et al. (1992 in Nasser et al., 2003), however, suggested that even if users of annual reports are assumed to be knowledgeable, the information itself could have different degrees of comprehensibility.

In all sense, the importance of Financial Statements Analysis is inevitable to investors and most findings have indicated the imperativeness of these reports. Nasser and Nuseibeh (2003) provide a number of studies, which have investigated the usefulness of corporate information to the users and found the annual report to be important and primary source of information. These include, Mautz (1968), Briggs (1975), Lee and Tweedie (1975a,b, 1976, 1981), Epstein (1975), Anderson (1981), Arnold and Moizer (1984), Moizer and Arnold (1984), Day (1986), Gniewosz (1990), Epstein and Pava (1993), Streuly (1994), Bence et al. (1995), Anderson and Epstein (1995), Abu-Nassar and Rutherford (1996), Bartlett and Chandler (1997).

Regarding financial analysis, it shows that the managers by then lacked financial analysis skills and even if they knew not all of them were able to change corporate image. Lack of financial analysis led to the collapse of companies and privatization of those companies so as to employ people who can rescue these companies from falling apart. This action has shown that companies like Tanzania Breweries Limited (TBL), Tanzania Cigarette Corporation (TCC) to mention a few have been privatized. The impact of this is the employment of qualified people who can read and interpret ratios and determine where the company is heading.

THE DAR ES SALAAM STOCK EXCHANGE

The Capital Market and Securities Authority under the capital markets and securities (CMS) Act of 1994 established the Dar es Salaam stock exchange (DSE). The enactment of the DSE came because of government's policy of transforming its economy from public government dominated economy to private sector driven economy. The DSE was incorporated in September 1996 as a company limited by guarantee without a share a capital (DSE, 2001, 2008). It is a non-profit making organization created to facilitate the government implementations of the economic reforms in particular on enabling the private sector raise capital. The exchange became operational in April 1998 with TOL listing as the first company followed by the Tanzania Breweries Limited (TBL) during the same year. The delay was due to the necessary background operational preparations that were inevitable such as training of brokers and formulation of issuance and trading rules under the stewardship of the government through the capital markets and securities authority (CMSA, 2007).

The operation of DSE is vested in the hands of the Council, which is the Board of Directors of the company. The first Board of Directors was elected in July 1997. Further, listing of shares and bonds at the Dar es Salaam stock exchange (DSE) provides companies, the government as well as municipal authorities with a possible source of accessing funds from both the public as well as institutional investors. Listing of these securities facilitates secondary market trading of the bonds and shares and thus provides the necessary liquidity required on the market. As commonly acknowledged a market has a supply side and the demand side.

Hence, both the central government and the local government are considered supply side of the stock exchange, while the public is considered as the demand side. Therefore, the two sides meet when shares are issued for the first time. The first issuance of shares is commonly known as initial public offer (IPO). The general term of supply side does not exclude the various companies other than those owned partly or full by the government and other issuing companies. Before indulging into the procedures for listing shares and responsibilities, it is worthy understanding what is stock exchange.

Stock exchange defined

A stock exchange is a market where large and small investors can buy and sell securities (shares, bonds, etc). It is an organized market where buyers and sellers of securities meet as they are represented by dealers/brokers and acquire or dispose securities. It is a market n which securities members of the exchange who may act as both Agents (brokers) and as principal (dealers) trade.

RESEARCH METHODOLOGY

Study site

The study was conducted in Dar es Salaam. It incorporated all six brokers registered with the Dar es Salaam stock exchange (DSE).

Research design, sampling and data collection methods

The research design used in the study was the survey study design. During the collections of data the survey study was used since all six brokers were incorporated in the study. The survey study was opted to capture all the responses. It was imperative to use the survey study to articulate all necessary information for the study. Thus, the analyses were drawn from the named brokers. It can therefore, be argued that the findings of this study have been 100% of the sample. The study utilized six brokers registered with the DSE and the stock authorities namely Capital Market and Securities Authority, Unit Trust of Tanzania (UTT) and the DSE. Therefore, the unit of enquiry was Tanzania Securities Limited, Solomon Securities, Rasilimali Limited, Orbit Securities Co. Ltd., Vertex International Securities, and Core Securities Ltd. The researcher is highly convinced that these respondents were able to provide information for the study.

The sample for the study was of two types. The first sample was drawn from all six brokers registered with the DSE, hence six questionnaires were distributed. The second sample was 10 clients of each of the brokers. These are people who had shares or were seeking to buy shares from the brokers. Thus each broker was given 10 questionnaires which were given to the clients making a total of 60 clients and six brokers. Thus the total sample was 66. However the analysis has treated the two samples differently. The study adopted multiple methods of data collection namely observation, documentation, interview, and questionnaire. The data were analyzed qualitatively and quantitatively. The researcher analyzed the results of the findings in meeting its objectives and answering the research questions. Therefore charts and percentiles have been used to present the data in the manner that is desirable for understanding the data. The study composed of primary data and secondary data. Primary data was gathered from questionnaires distributed and interview carried out. Secondary data was collected through library research on scholarly information sources.

The interpretation of data on measuring knowledge level on financial analysis was based on the perception of the brokers as first respondents, and of the investors as second respondents. There has been conformity of the perceptions between the two categories.

Research questions

The study entailed to answer the following questions:

(a) Do ordinary investors understand the use of financial ratios?
(b) Which ratios are given priority by investors?
(c) Do investors consider financial ratios when investing?
(d) Is the marketing strategy done through the use of potential people in the society such as former leaders of the government one of the reason?
(e) To what extent the use of such crowned leaders (former government leaders) contribute to peoples attention and thus persuade to purchase shares in various companies?
(f) Do ordinary investors understand the use of financial ratios?
(g) Which ratios are given priority by investors?
(h) Is the marketing strategy done by potential people in the society such as former leaders of the government one of the reason?
(i) To what extent the use of such crowned leaders (former government leaders) contribute to peoples attention and thus persuade to purchase shares in various companies?

DATA ANALYSIS AND DISCUSSION OF FINDINGS

This part covers data analysis and discussion. The analysis and discussion have responded to the specific objectives and thus questions rendered through the questionnaire. The discussions cover subtopics such as the understanding of the financial analysis of the people investing in stock exchange; whether there is consideration of financial ratios when investing; ratios that are given priority if any; factors that hinder or promote the use of financial analysis by the investors, and the leading influencing factor(s) for investing in Stock Exchange.

Understanding the use of financial information

The study on financial analysis as a consideration for investment has revealed three categories of perceptions as to the understanding of the financial analysis as a consideration for investment. These are common man who are motivated by the use of potential figures in the society such as the former government leaders, and potential business men. Logical group of people, who are motivated by hearsay on the companies, eye power and show up, such as adverts of commodities sold rather than adverts on financial performance.

Finally, the third group of people who are elites on stock exchange, and potential investors such as stock exchange businessmen-people whose subscription of shares is the main source of income and thus a daily bread, and financial institutions such as PPF and NSSF.

The findings reveal that brokers perceive that most ordinary people investors do not know the use of financial analysis/accounts information when investing. Findings reveal that most of the ordinary (investors who subscribe shares below 5 milion) have no knowledge of financial information of the firms. Most of them are driven by the adverts indicating the sale of shares, potential people, in particular government leaders and businesspersons. The financial analysis knowledge of small investors as opined by brokers is gauged as 25%. Therefore, only 25% of individuals seem to be acquainted with the knowledge of investing especially the use of financial analysis information before or when investing. However, the brokers who offer the respective knowledge on proper investing bridge the gap of this category of investors.

The findings reveal further that while people are not aware of the use of accounts information/financial analysis information such as ratios yet those who purchase shares through the brokers, are advised on the financial status and at times even the anticipated payback period of the amount invested. The brokers are people with knowledge on how to trade shares, and they frequently assess the potentials of the companies listed to perform a proper role on serving people on stock exchange. The findings reveal individuals perceive that the persuasion of the brokers account about 75% of people investing. It is therefore right to say that without brokerage service, the stock exchange business cannot strive.

On the other hand, the brokers perceive that big investors such as financial institutions and potential investors whose stock exchange is the business of the day have adequate knowledge of financial analysis and thus they do use such information as a consideration for investing. These include institutions such as PPF, NSSF and LAPF. In the same category there are individuals and private firms who are elite in the business who enjoy the investing practice in shares with knowledge on financial analysis. It can thus be generalized that the big investors who invests in hundreds million and above have knowledge on financial analysis. Their knowledge is gauged at 75% and above.

Influence of potential leaders

The findings further reveal that in the past (late 1990s) the influence of potential leaders such as the government leaders, and businessmen was the key to enabling the purchase of shares. It has been indicated clearly that most of those people who purchased shares from the Tanzania Oxygen Company LTD (TOL) could be said to have been motivated by potential people such as the then President of Tanzania, His Excellency Benjamin Mkapa who officiated the sale of listed shares of TOL. Nevertheless, as time goes by the trend is being reduced. The performance of TOL seems too had been a lesson to majority investors and thus need for acquisition of financial information in particular through brokers and Stock Exchange authorities. For obvious reasons, currently the company is fairing well. The data on TOL do not reflect the current position but the position during the study and the years referred to.

Preferred ratios

The study further indicates that ratios, which are given priority when investing in various firms in particular stock exchange business, include profitability ratios, investment ratio, dividend yield ratio and earnings per share. 50 of the interviewee, which is about 83.3% of respondents, indicated that dividend ratio/earnings per share were favorable ratios when investing. Nine of the interviewee, which is about 15% of the respondents, indicated nothing as were not knowledgeable of ratios. One respondent, about 1.7% indicated liquidity ratio and profitability ratio.

There seem a little bit of confusion to the respondents, which the researcher noted when analyzing the data. The confusion is in that all the nine respondents indicated that they considered financial analysis when investing in shares. However, when asked whether they knew any ratio they all indicated that they did not know. The responses seem to envisage another important question, which is what did they mean when answered they used financial analysis when investing if they new no any ratio. When the seven out nine were interviewed, they indicated that the financial analysis to them appeared to mean the general performance of the organization as they perceive or hear from other people. This however, suggests for more education to brokers' employees

Table 1. Brokers responses on the financial analysis as a consideration for investment in stock exchange.

Name of the broker/stock exchange authorities, expert	Perception of the brokers on the use of financial analysis when investing (estimates in %)	Perception of the brokers on Individuals' consideration of financial analysis when investing (estimates in %)	Perception of individuals on the influence of brokers (estimates in %)
Orbit	75	25	75-100
Core securities	75	25	75-100
Vertex	75	25	75-100
Tanzania securities	75	25	75-100
Rasilimali securities	75	25	75-100
Umoja fund	75	25	75-100
Solomon securities	75	25	75-100
Capital market security authority	75	25	75-100
Averages	75	25	87.5

Source: Research findings on financial analysis as consideration for investment in Tanzania, responses of brokers, Dar es Salaam, 2006. The data reveals that brokers are perceived to contribute about 87.5% on decisions made by investors regarding investment, while 75% are pegged to the brokers and 25% to individuals.

sufficing the need for the investment knowledge on the types of ratios and their importance in decision-making.

Reasons persuading people to invest in stock exchange

Several reasons/factors have been mentioned as considerations for investing. The reasons range from those relating to provision of liquidity as a semi bank facility, to those of mechanism for earning profits.

Of the 60 respondents, 56 people, which are about 94%, indicated that they invest in shares for earning profit. Further, many other factors have been disclosed in relation to the earning of profits. These include increase capital from share gain essentially when shares increase value.

Investing in shares provides a room for saving money while earning profits. Unlike banks where those who invest gain very little amount of money normally between 2 to 5% for savings accounts, in shares people have had an experience of earning up to 150% per year. For example those who invested in the Umoja Trust Fund before July 2005, have earned a profit of over 50% in August 2006. Therefore, the transformation of economy with particularly shares can make one earn as much as possible.

The study has further revealed creation of employment opportunities, and generation of capital to most of the firms as one of the importance for investing in shares. To date in Tanzania there are six brokers with about 10 employees per broker (Table 1). Other authorities have also been established such as the Unit Trust Fund and capital market and securities authority (CMSA 2007) with employees about 25 each. The indicated number of employment opportunities is those, which are formally employed. However, there many employees who gain value of such employments through trickledown such as those who purchase shares in small scale and use such profit to establish Small and Medium Entrepreneurships. In so doing, many people are engaged in business. The business has also improved other business ventures such as SACCOS. Thus, the total gain in terms of employment creation is huge.

SUMMARY OF DISCUSSION AND ANALYSIS OF FINDINGS

The study has revealed that different investors perceive the consideration of financial analysis differently. There are mainly two categories of people who perceive differently and thus their level of consideration varies accordingly on the importance of Financial Analysis when or before investing.

The data indicates that about 70% of the respondents do not invest with a consideration of financial analysis. The response concurs with the perception of the brokers who felt that 75% of the

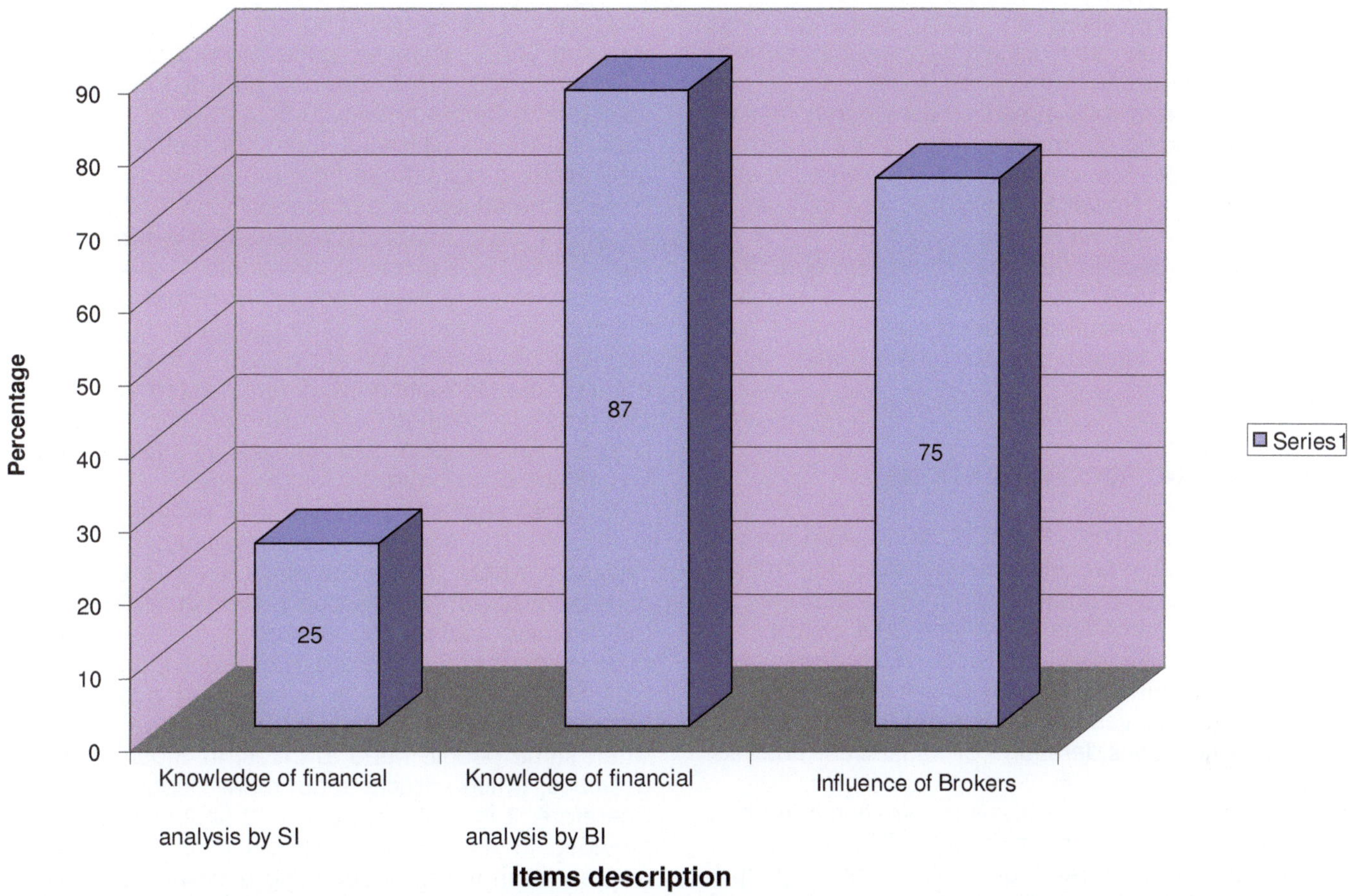

Figure 1. Level of knowledge of small investors (SI), big investors (BI) and the Influence of brokers. The figure indicates that the level of knowledge of small investors is 25%, big investors, 87% and persuasion rendered by brokers stand at 75%. Source: Research findings on financial analysis as consideration for investment, Dar es Salaam, 2006.

individual investors do not use financial statements analysis when investing. It is worth noting here that the procedures and rules for registering the firms with the DSE may connote an automatic screening of the firms listing. Since DSE would not register the firm with weak financial position in relation to the shares business. Hence, it can be assumed that although do not invest with consideration of financial analysis, yet they seem to. However, the percentage varies amongst people and time. For example, it was noted that if the study was to be conducted some five years ago that is 2000 and below, certainly most people were influenced by the potential figures/people in the society such as government leaders and businesspersons. With time, it is assumed that the DSE and brokers have played a potential role in enabling the use of financial analysis information in investing.

Further, about 26.7% of the respondents had the opinion that potential figures (Figure 1) in the society, such as government leaders and business executives influence small investors to purchase shares. This category however, as said earlier, would have captured a different opinion had such study been conducted late 1990s. The reason is that knowledge regarding investment in Stock Exchange continues to flourish. Hence, as time goes by most people are taking necessary steps to ensuring that decision making on investment is crucially dealt.

The most influencing factor is the hearsay factor and /or advert without disclosing financial position, which attained 50.3%. It is important to note that people who make decisions through the hearsay factor are essentially doing so without the consideration of financial analysis information. Equally, people who are influenced by potential figures (26.7%) are doing so without the consideration of financial analysis information. Therefore, for capturing responses in relation to whether people consider or do not consider the financial information, the categories of people can be narrowed to two main groups. That is those who consider Financial Analysis and those who do not consider. It is from that standpoint of view, the paper has narrowed the categories of people into two rather than three observed in the responses.

The categories of people are big or potential investors such as financial institutions like PPF, NSSF, and individuals who work with the brokers firms irrespective of the amount invested. This group includes people and institutions who are elites on stock exchange, and potential investors such as stock exchange businessmen-people whose subscription of shares is the main source of income and thus a daily bread. The research reveals that the understanding of Financial Analysis as perceived by the brokers for this group is 75 to 100%, hence averaging at 87.5%. However, a broader research needs to be conducted to seek responses of the firms.

The research proposed can seek to answer questions themselves rather than the perception of the brokers, which at times may result into deception. It could also involve a much bigger sample that could allow generalization.

CONCLUSION AND RECOMENDATIONS

It can be concluded that, Financial Analyses/Accounts Information are vital in providing the investors information that enables them to make informed decisions on investment. In the same line, most individual investors in Tanzania do not invest in Stock Exchange with consideration for Financial Analysis information of the firms. However, big investors such as financial institutions do invest with consideration of financial analysis information.

The use of the Financial Analysis information is termed to be associated with two main reasons. The first, is the role played by the registered brokers of educating people seeking to invest, hence enabling them acquire Financial Analysis information. The second is the performance of early listed companies such as the TOL Gas Limited, which for the first five year consecutively has failed to pay dividends to share holders, and has failed to increase value of shares at the DSE. The two reasons altogether have created a sense of alertness to investors. Thus concerted efforts should be made to ensure enlightenment of the majority people instead of getting such knowledge when they visit the brokers, who all of them are situated in Dar es Salaam hence limiting the majority population of Tanzania to attaining investment knowledge. No doubt, what has been revealed in this study cements on the importance of financial analysis as observed by many researchers. Financial Analysis is inevitable to all investors and not all people in general, even in areas, which seem need financial information education.

Nevertheless, the procedures in listing shares imply that a bad company is not likely to sell their shares in the market. No broker and bank would like to be involved in selling the shares of the company whose financial analysis indicate that is poorly performing or which its future profitability is questionable. So the fact that banks and brokers agree to be involved in the issuing of shares of a particular company implies that that company is relatively good.

Thus, though most individuals do purchase shares through hearsay and or adverts, the procedures for listing suggest that non-performing company cannot be listed with the DSE. However, good procedures executed by DSE on listing firms, do not give a loophole for the investors to ignore financial information of the firms they want to invest. There is need for further research to incorporate a big sample from more than one region and through the observance of triangulation methods to come up with more generic conclusions and recommendations such as to what extent do investors in stock exchange increase capital? What factors do hinder acquisition of financial information? What factors do promote the use of financial information? What modality is in place to ensure transfer of information from firms listed to the willing investors? In addition, what are other factors other than financial information are crucial in making informed investment decision in stock exchange?

Financial analyses (FA) are vital for making informed decisions in particular to developing countries like Tanzania where the investments level is thin, and the general behavior to investing is immature. The reality is that financial information education is a key to decision making in most daily endeavors. From planning what to eat, when, and how, one need to be acquainted with financial education. However, the need is even higher when same people need to invest in Stock Exchange a business, which attracts about many people in Tanzania. Therefore, it is recommended that financial education be provided in all levels of schools to create a sense of awareness in terms of spending and serving in all areas of business including stock exchange.

REFERENCES

Abu Baker N, Naser K (2000). Empirical evidence on corporate social disclosure (CSD) practices in Jordan. Intl. J. Commerce Manage., 10 (3/4): 18-34.

Abu-nassar M, Rutherford BA (1996). External users of financial reports in less developed countries: the case of Jordan. Br. Account. Rev., 28: 73-87.

Anderson R, Epstein M (1995). The usefulness of annual reports. Australian Accountant April, pp. 25-28.

Anderson R (1981). The usefulness of accounting and other information disclosed in corporate annual reports to institutional investors in Australia. Acct. Bus. Res. Autumn, pp. 259-265.

Arnold J, Moizer P (1984). A survey of the methods used by UK investment analysts to appraise investment inordinary shares. Accounting and Business Research Summer, 195–207.K. Naser R Nuseibeh / Br. Account. Rev., 35(2003): 129-153.

Bartlett SA, Chandler RA (1997). The corporate report and the private shareholder: Lee and Tweedie twenty years on. Br. Account. Rev., 29: 245-261.

Bence D, Hapeshi K, Hussey R (1995). Examining investment information sources for sophisticated investors using cluster analysis. Acct. Bus. Res., 26(1): 19-26.

CMSA (2007). The Capital Markets and Security Authority BI. CMSA, Dar es Salaam.

Day JFS (1986). The use of annual reports by UK investment analysts. Account. Bus. Res. Autumn, pp. 295-307.

DSE (2001). Quarterly Update. DSE, Dar es Salaam.

DSE (2003). Blue Print. Dar es Salaam Stock Exchange. Dar es Salaam.

DSE (2005). Quarterly Update. DSE, Dar es Salaam.

DSE (2008). DSE Handbook. DSE, Dar es Salaam.

DSE (2008). DSE J. 10TH Anniversary. DSE, Dar es Salaam.
Epstein MJ, Freedman M (1994). Social disclosure and individual investor'. Acct. Audit. Accountability J., 7(4): 94-109.
Epstein MJ, Pava ML (1993). The Shareholder's Use of Annual corporate Reports. Jai Press Inc, London.
Epstein MJ, Pava ML (1994). Profile of an annual report. Financial Executive Jan/Feb, pp. 41-43.
Epstein MJ, Anderson RY (1994). The usefulness of annual reports to corporate shareholders in the United States and Australia.
Epstein MJ (1975). The Usefulness of Annual Reports to Corporate Shareholders, Bureau of Business and Economic Research, California State University, Los Angeles.
Gniewosz G (1990). The share investment decision process and information use: An exploratory case study. Acct. Bus. Res., 20(79): 223-230.
Lee TA, Tweedie DP (1975a). Accounting investigation of private shareholder usage. Account. Bus. Res. Autumn, pp. 280-291.
Lee TA, Tweedie DP (1975b). Accounting investigation of private shareholder understanding. Account. Bus. Res. Winter, pp. 3-17.
Lee TA, Tweedie DP (1976). The private shareholder: his sources of financial information and his understanding of reporting practices. Account. Bus. Res. Autumn, pp. 304-314.
Lee TA, Tweedie DP (1981). The Institutional Investors and Financial Information. The Institute of chartered Accountants in England and Wales.
Mautz RK (1968). Financial Reporting by Diversified Companies. Financial Executive Research Foundations, New York.
Naser K, Nuseibeh R (2003). Quality of financial reporting: Evidence from the listed Saudi non-financial companies. Int. J. Acct., forthcoming.
Naser K, Nuseibeh R, Al-Hussaini A (2003). Users' Perception of various aspects of kuwaiti corporate reporting. Manage. Audit. J. press.
Neimark MK (1992). The Hidden Dimensions of Annual Reports. Markus Wiener Publishing Inc, New York.
Norman AS (2003). The role of financial literacy in boosting saving and investment in the Commonwealth Currents, 11(2) Marlborough, Commonwealth, London.
The Capital Markets and Securities Act (1994) (Cap. 79) (as amended) Unpublished Paper, British Accounting Association, National Conference at King Alfred's College, Winchester, March 23–25, pp. 1-24.
Van H (2002). Financial Management Policy, 12trh Ed. Pearson Ed. Inc., New Delhi, India.

A new tax technology: The Brazilian experience with a general bank transactions tax

Marcos Cintra

Rua Cesar Valejo 360, ap.191-A, São Paulo, 05685-000, São Paulo, Brazil.
E- mail: mcintra@marcoscintra.org.

This is a statement paper about tax reform. It tries to point to new trends in the world economy and to its consequences for tax practitioners', taxpayers and tax administrators. Its main conclusion is that the world needs a new tax technology, and based on the Brazilian experience, proposes that a bank transaction tax may fulfill this need. Especially in developing countries tax reform has been one of the most intensely debated topics around the world. The significance of this issue can be easily understood as developing economies, lacking strong fiscal traditions, emerge as important participants in a renovated world. Old paradigms are being constantly challenged by these new players. At the same time, their growing demand for resources necessary to meet the expectations placed on their public sector makes tax reform a crucial issue in attempting to maintain the tendency towards economic relevance which many developing countries around the world have been fiercely attempting to achieve. In Brazil, particularly, tax reform it is one of the most important items in a list of pressing domestic issues.

Key words: Tax practitioners, tax reform, tax technology, tax administrators.

INTRODUCTION

A new tax perspective

Over the past fifteen years, debate on the Brazilian tax system has been greatly intensified. It has been so intense, and at the same time, so unproductive in terms of effective results, that the Brazilian tax system has been blamed for being the most important element in slowing down the country's growth along the last two decades. But on the other hand, the debate has been very rich, and has resulted in the development of new insights on this problem.

Several propositions for tax reform have been introduced, creating a clear division of opinions between two schools of thought on the subject. On one side, stands orthodoxy, based on traditional concepts of public finance and on conventional canons of tax law. Although many of these conventional concepts on taxation have been superseded by the effects of recent technological advances -most importantly, electronic information and new means of asset transfers- they have been the main driving force observed in the tax reform proposals sponsored by the Brazilian government.

On the other side of the divide is the innovative and anti-dogmatic school of thought which proposes the elimination of conventional tax models and which is epitomized by the resurgence of the age-old concept of the Single Tax, which, in its modern version makes extensive use of non-declaratory taxes such as the bank transaction tax, and introduces electronic technology into the tax world, not as a simple mechanical improvement in gathering and auditing of data, but rather, as a conceptual building block in alternative methods and constructs about taxation and public finance. The two most significant recent contributions in this field have taken place in Brazil, (Cintra, 2009), and conceptually in the US, [FEIGE, 2000]. (Cintra, 2009; Feige, 2000; Colabella and Copinger, 1995; Coelho et al., 2001).

The first school of thought – associated with the use of conventional declaratory taxes – believes that "old taxes are good taxes". This school mistakenly sustains (so claim such conservative reformers) the continuation of paradigms which, inadvertently to them, have become outdated, and which have been superseded by the peculiar impacts of modern economies, characterized by globalization and by the overwhelming effects of the digital information age. The great Brazilian economist, diplomat, and public figure Roberto Campos, an active participant in the tax reform debate, once stated that to defend this school of thought is to engage in a melancholic exercise of trying "to perfect the obsolete."

The second school of thought calls for the elimination of declaratory taxes and for their substitution by electronic taxes operating through the bits and bytes of the data-processing centers and clearinghouses of the banking system, such as a bank transactions tax. Ultimately, because of its extensive pattern of incidence upon almost all economic transactions and therefore reaching almost all economic occurrences presently used as tax bases, this type of taxation could lead to the construction of a model with a single basic tax, an envelope tax, or the Single Tax paradigm.

The clash between these two tax paradigms, the declaratory versus the non-declaratory tax system (which might be rephrased as the "with" versus the "without" paperwork tax system) draws to the surface questions concerning not only the deep changes that are occurring within the modern world economic environment, but also the academic stance of taxation (and even of public finance) as a science.

PARADIGM CHANGE

Thomas Kuhn says that a field of study becomes a science when a community of experts consensually accepts a paradigm – that is, a set of problems and uniform standards of approach – with a foundational theory and a common set of explanatory and interpretative traditions (Kuhn, 1962; Faria, 1999). "The authority of a scientific proposition is founded on its capacity to generate consensus within a given community. This consensus, for its part, does not depend on whether the scientific propositions provide an indisputable vision of the intimate configuration of reality. It does, however, depend on whether its development has been guided by demarcation criteria that are authoritatively prevalent in the environs of that community." Kuhn goes on to state that, "It is for this reason that paradigms distinguish themselves by their incommensurability. If each paradigm sets forth the conditions of the scientific nature of the knowledge produced in its environs, the proofs invoked in favor of other paradigms tend to be disqualified a priori (Faria, 1999)." In other words, a proposal that contradicts "conventional wisdom", paraphrasing John Kenneth Galbraith (Galbraith, 1958), is summarily considered "unscientific", not because of lack of objective analysis of its scientism, but simply because it does not apply methods and models considered "correct", "truthful" or "evident".

Partly for these reasons, traditionalists say that the extensive use of a bank transactions tax as the basic pillar for a tax reform is an audacious proposition, bordering on illusion. Despite the proven capacity of such taxes to generate impressive amounts of revenue and to show an almost universal pattern of incidence and coverage, as shown by the Brazilian experience with a bank transactions tax (called IPMF/CPMF), researchers and defenders of such innovative taxation usually draw the wrath of traditionalists who oppose it. The guardians of orthodoxy, the bureaucratic establishment, and the recurrent tax evaders refuse to relinquish their decades-old professional and intellectual investments – despite the fact that all evidence proves them increasingly obsolete.

A bank transaction tax has countless advantages as a taxation system. Auditing becomes simpler; taxation criteria are more transparent; bureaucratic and compliance costs both to the public and to the private sectors are lessened. (Sandford et al., 1989; Sandford and Godwin, 1990; Bertolucci, 2001, 2005).

It is worthwhile, noting the statements made by former Secretary of Federal Revenue, Everardo Maciel, while testifying before the Comissão Parlamentar de Inquérito [Parliamentary Inquiry Committee] on May 8, 2002. The Secretary's sympathy for the CPMF (a bank transactions tax used in Brazil since 1993) is noteworthy. He said, "my presence here is solely to quickly state for the record that the bank debit transaction tax (CPMF) has been an extremely valuable instrument from a revenue collection standpoint, precisely because it manages to produce public revenue at low cost, with extreme efficiency and additionally, serves primarily as an auxiliary instrument for tax auditing."

CONSERVATIVE BACKLASH: IGNORING AN EVIDENT TRUTH

Brazilian fiscal "traditionalists," tend to reject bank transactions taxation on the pretext that, "if it were good, it would have already been adopted by more advanced economies." This sad argument acknowledges the inertial weight of entrenched concepts of tax systems or, inversely, it ignores the revolution that electronic technology has inspired in some countries (but not in all of them). For example, Brazil has a banking system that is significantly more modern than that of most of the advanced economies (including the United States), and this is the foundation that supports the paradigm shift towards the bank transactions concept. Furthermore, such an attitude ignores that there are cultural, social, political, and economic differences among countries that make some of them urgently need a new tax system, while others do not, as least not with the same intensity.

Regarding tax systems, it becomes increasingly evident that the conventional paradigm is gradually becoming exhausted. In tax matters, the conventional paradigm is following the steps described by Thomas Kuhn to justify a "scientific revolution": old beliefs become less capable of providing answers to concrete problems, and for each solved problem others appear of even greater complexity.

An illustrative example is found in the changing perception of tax administrators regarding the Income Tax. After the Second World War the global income tax became almost universally used. "This tax was an ideal instrument for the time and came to be seen by many policymakers and tax experts as a "dream tax". In the United States, 90 per cent of taxpayers had considered the income tax as a fair tax during World War Two, according to survey data published by the American Enterprise Institute (2005)". Nevertheless, perceptions about this form of taxation are gradually changing because of new circumstances present in the world, but also because of some characteristics of the income tax which were persistently ignored by policy makers. "It was considered an efficient tax because most economists dismissed its potential negative effects on work effort and incentives. Few academic articles, if any, dealt with these potential disincentives. Furthermore, though it now seems strange, books on income taxation did not even mention ´tax evasion´ or ´the underground economy´ as potential problems associated with income taxes" (Tanzi, 2006).

The conventional tax paradigm faces a serious crisis due to its incapacity to provide explanations, diagnostics, justifications, and solutions to new facts and circumstances that are rising on the contemporary economic scenario (CINTRA, 2008a, b). Indeed, what we see is the erosion of traditional mechanisms of tax collection. Such mechanisms are based on the notion (quite frequently correct) that the taxpayer is a potential defrauder, until proven otherwise, and this has led to the creation of a significant number of control, inspection procedures, auditing and surveillance systems that turn out to be expensive, complex, and highly bureaucratic, but nonetheless, incapable of preventing tax evasion and fraud.

TWO DECISIVE TURNING POINTS: GLOBALIZATION AND TECHNOLOGICAL CHANGE

In truth, the outcome of this debate on tax reform tends to become more predictable, insofar as two fundamental phenomena of modern history will impose their inevitable consequences in favor of the non-declaratory system. These two phenomena are: first, the technological revolution of the information age; and secondly (but no less important), the current globalization of world economic relations.

The information age has profoundly altered the aggregate production function of modern economies. Decision-making has been greatly streamlined by the increasing number of methods for processing massive amounts of information. Data collection and analysis have improved through increased sophistication in electronic processing. The supply and control of massive amounts of information have become key decision-making inputs for modern businesses. Furthermore, the use of paper currency is being steadily replaced by electronic money; the concept of wealth and money is being constantly redefined (Toffler and Toffler, 2006; The Economist, 2001; Cintra, 1998).

These changes bring into stark relief the precariousness of tax reporting and the handicraft mechanisms used in conventional tax systems, which, historically, were developed in response to the technological and organizational environment that existed immediately following the industrial revolution.

Furthermore, growth of the service sector's share of GDP has significantly reduced the effectiveness of the conventional tax collection, auditing, and control mechanisms. The productive sector has become ever more intangible and dematerialized, and this has only stressed the dwindling effectiveness of conventional mechanisms for tax assessment and enforcement. In fact, intangible services traded over the Internet (as for example, new accounting software, with high initial production cost but currently reduced to bits and bytes for delivery and utilization) are actually beyond the reach of tax authorities, kept outside the realm of such type of exchange. It becomes increasingly more difficult to levy specific taxes on trade of either products or services if the resulting payment transaction takes place in a tax haven, where no specified origin or destination of any good or service can be readily identified. Thus, a non-declaratory tax, such as a bank transaction tax, begins to make sense because it is levied on that agent's banking activity and not on its reported accounting statements.

Traditional tax models assume that production and its resulting taxable income, is carried out through manual production processes (or later, through mechanical production processes) concentrated within finite geographical spaces, centered in organizational structures that are autonomous, independent and subject to domestic rules established by a sovereign state. This is the world of the industrial revolution, later modified by mass production, where production and exchange are strategically concentrated on a relatively small number of large national corporations. Tax assessment and enforcement have, therefore, to be directed and adjusted to that reality (The Economist, 2000; Kellermann et al., 2007; Lebowitz, 1999).

Historically, the taxpayers' universe had previously consisted of those few large units of production and exchange that typified the early stages of the industrial economy. Soon, however, it began to encompass all businesses and individuals in modern societies. The entire universe of individuals and businesses, of all sizes and in all sectors, soon became subjected to the obligation to pay taxes. Levying taxes across the board greatly expanded the pool of taxpayers. Whereas the Tax collection, assessment, and control functions now demand operations on a scale wholly incompatible with the declaratory, bureaucratic, paper filing systems typical of the traditional tax method of "self-assessment, self-levying, self-collection, and public audits," which typify conventional declaratory tax systems.

The electronic revolution provided an indispensable new operational instrument for collecting and analyzing the enormous mass of data and information needed for tax control, monitoring, and collection processes. But such technological change is not restricted to a mere increase in speed of data processing within the old tax paradigm, although it has been successfully serving this purpose. Its main virtue, nowadays, is that it makes possible to underscore the creation of a new tax paradigm, of a new tax species, such as payment taxes, which were never possible before.

Brazil's current banking and payment systems are among the most advanced in the world and this enables them to bring about such paradigm shift. The importance of the information age is not limited to being an auxiliary method for controlling, auditing and analyzing tax data. Its importance extends beyond this, as it became a determining factor in the conceptualization of new taxation models, primarily in configuring new tax bases, such as bank transactions, electronic flows, telephone pulses, electronic wavelengths and other intangible bases, which are impossible to be reached by conventional taxes.

A second factor to demand deep changes in conventional tax models is globalization. This is a multi-faceted, complex element, which is having a strong impact on economic and social life of humankind. According to José Eduardo Faria, globalization has been responsible for the "relativity of several important concepts, principles, and categories – such as sovereignty, legality, the hierarchy of laws, subjective rights, formal equality, citizenship, balance of powers, security, and certainty – that have been heavily affected by economic, social, political, and cultural changes that have taken place largely apart from legal structures, judicial mechanisms, institutional structures, democratic procedures, and the capacity for regulation, control, management, direction, planning, and concession-granting of nation-states (Faria, 1999)."

Indeed, globalization has weakened the power of national public administrations, by decentralizing and fragmenting the decision-making capacity of traditional governments. Even more visibly, it has "debilitated the taxation and regulation capacity of governments (Faria, 1999)." José Eduardo Faria argues that, "within this highly unstable scenario, positive law... came to face a cruel dilemma: if it remains concerned with its logical integrity and with its formal rationality, in view of all these profound and intense changes, it runs the risk of not accompanying the dynamics of facts, of becoming functionally ineffective and, ultimately, socially discredited, ignored, and (in the worst case) even disposable. If it allows itself to be seduced into attempting directly to control and discipline all sectors of social, economic, and political life that are increasingly tense, unstable, unpredictable, heterogeneous, and complex... it runs the risk of becoming disfigured as a normative reference (Faria, 1999)."

The divorce between the conceptual foundations of government that emerged from the post-war period, and the realities of modern world globalization brings out what José Eduardo Faria called the "systemic ungovernability" of the traditional State (Faria, 1999). This begs the question: to what extent are traditional taxation models assimilating this new reality, marked so deeply by the information revolution and by intensive globalization? (The Economist, 1997).

The traditional tax system presupposes that the taxpayer is a nuclear firm (the same principle applies to individuals) that produces tangible goods with one or not more than a few physical facilities concentrated within a single National State (or tax territory), surrounded by suppliers and buyers that have the same basic characteristics. Figure 1 describes this situation. In this system, it is easy to assess the taxpaying capacity of the nuclear company. It is also simple to enforce tax regulations by cross-referencing data with peripheral supplier and buyer companies, or individuals. The situation is radically different, however, if the operational strategies of these businesses are executed through decentralized networks that spread across several nation-states, producing both tangible goods and, ever more frequently, services.

This new paradigm is shown in Figure 2. By their very nature, services are intangible, highly mobile and easily transported through electronic media. The illustration below shows the operational complexity of these businesses operating globally, involving federal and external variables, international trade and logistics, cross-ownership of investment capital, fast technological change and market-share strategies. These factors imply the need for increased sophistication of concepts and of operational methods that are not adequately addressed by conventional tax models. Examples of such challenges to the conventional tax paradigm are the growing incapacity of nation-states to deal with problems created by "tax havens", by increasingly complex means for laundering money, and by the uncontrolled flows of foreign funds between companies belonging to a single global conglomerate (transfer-prices) (The Economist, 2007). In testimony before the Special Commission on Cumulative Taxation in the Chamber of Deputies, on April 2, 2002, the Secretary of the *Federal Revenue*, Everardo Maciel, stated that: "the extraordinary changes occurring throughout the world also explain the large differences occurring between nations. One of these changes is globalization, which has brought very intense transformations. It is important to remember that one-third of foreign trade takes place between companies; another third is comprised of transactions within multinational corporations(...) These factors demonstrate the growing importance of these multinational firms, which raise a modern and worrisome question about the future of the corporate income tax or about the so called " transfer price" (...) Today, some countries assert the existence of transfer-prices point to the unlikely survival of taxes such as the corporate income tax in the future. Comments frequently made in the press, in international seminars, and in international tax conferences point to this fact as something new, which calls for a review of traditional tax models, most of which are of Anglo-Saxon extraction."

Globalization has, therefore, significantly changed the social, political, and economic environment in which tax systems operate. The main changes have been the extraordinary growth in international trade of goods and services, increased mobility of labor and capital, and growth of multinational, transnational and international companies. Tax administrators nowadays speak of taxation on world bases. Tax competition between countries has mushroomed. Unfortunately, such changes have gone in the direction of increasing complexity, interdependence and fiscal competition between countries. "Tax termites" (Tanzi, 2005; Tanzi, 2000) such as electronic and internet commerce, plastic and electronic money, transfer pricing, tax havens, foreign shopping, and complex financial instruments have contributed to decrease the revenue raising efficiency of national governments. "The work of ´fiscal termites´ (is) busily gnawing at the foundations of the tax systems" (Tanzi, 2000). Firms and people do not hesitate to abandon countries where they are located to seek any point on the planet that offers less progressive and lower taxes.

Tanzi believes that the effect of the fiscal termites in national economies is to decrease tax revenues. In fact, this has not been occurring. The tax burden has been increasing worldwide, but at the cost of tax shifting and increasing burden on less mobile taxpayers, such as wage earners and producers of non-tradables, worsening the domestic patterns of incidence and equity.

Strengthening the revenue-raising function on taxation

Tax officials have shown perplexity when confronted with such difficulties in preserving their national taxing capacity. Strengthening the revenue-raising function of taxation has become an absolute priority, and has led to a twofold possible solution: first is trying to typify as objectively as possible each problem or situation (which is obviously impossible to enumerate and extremely costly to operate) in order to apply appropriate taxing methods to each one of them. The problem is becoming so acute to the point of motivating governments, especially in the European Union, to discuss the creation of a super national layer of global government, capable of coordinating, or more appropriately, of attenuating, through unconditional or supervised delegation, the tensions and stresses in international tax relations among national states (Tanzi, 2007).

The other alternative is to endow tax authorities with subjective power to analyze each situation on a case by case basis, as they arise, and thereby decide what should be considered legitimate tax planning and what should be considered an illegitimate "legal" form of evasion. If the first line of conduct implies high compliance and administrative costs due to the mushrooming bureaucracy that would probably result from it, the second alternative would imply juridical insecurity and potentially mistaken or arbitrary judgments (Greco and Libertuci, 1999).

Needless to say that such "solutions" may greatly increase the compliance and administrative costs of tax systems throughout the

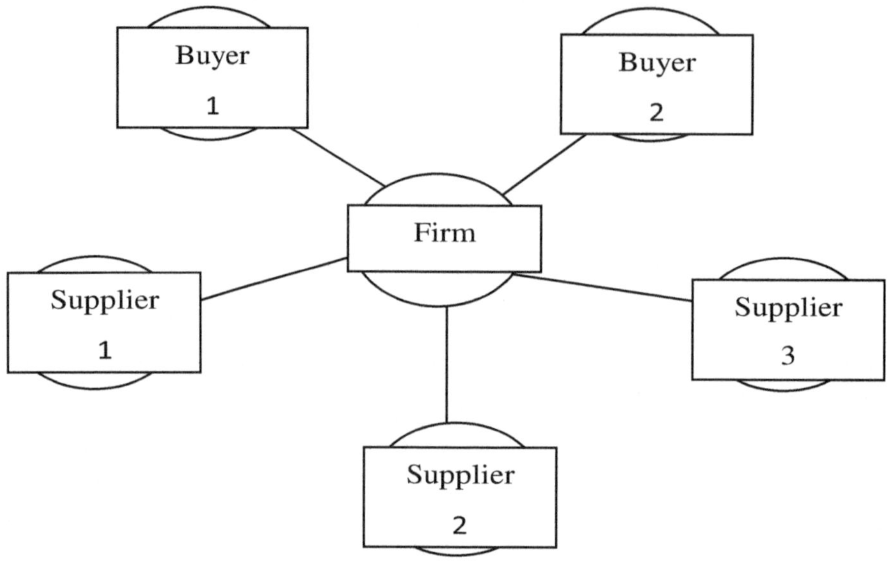

Figure 1. Traditional nuclear firm.

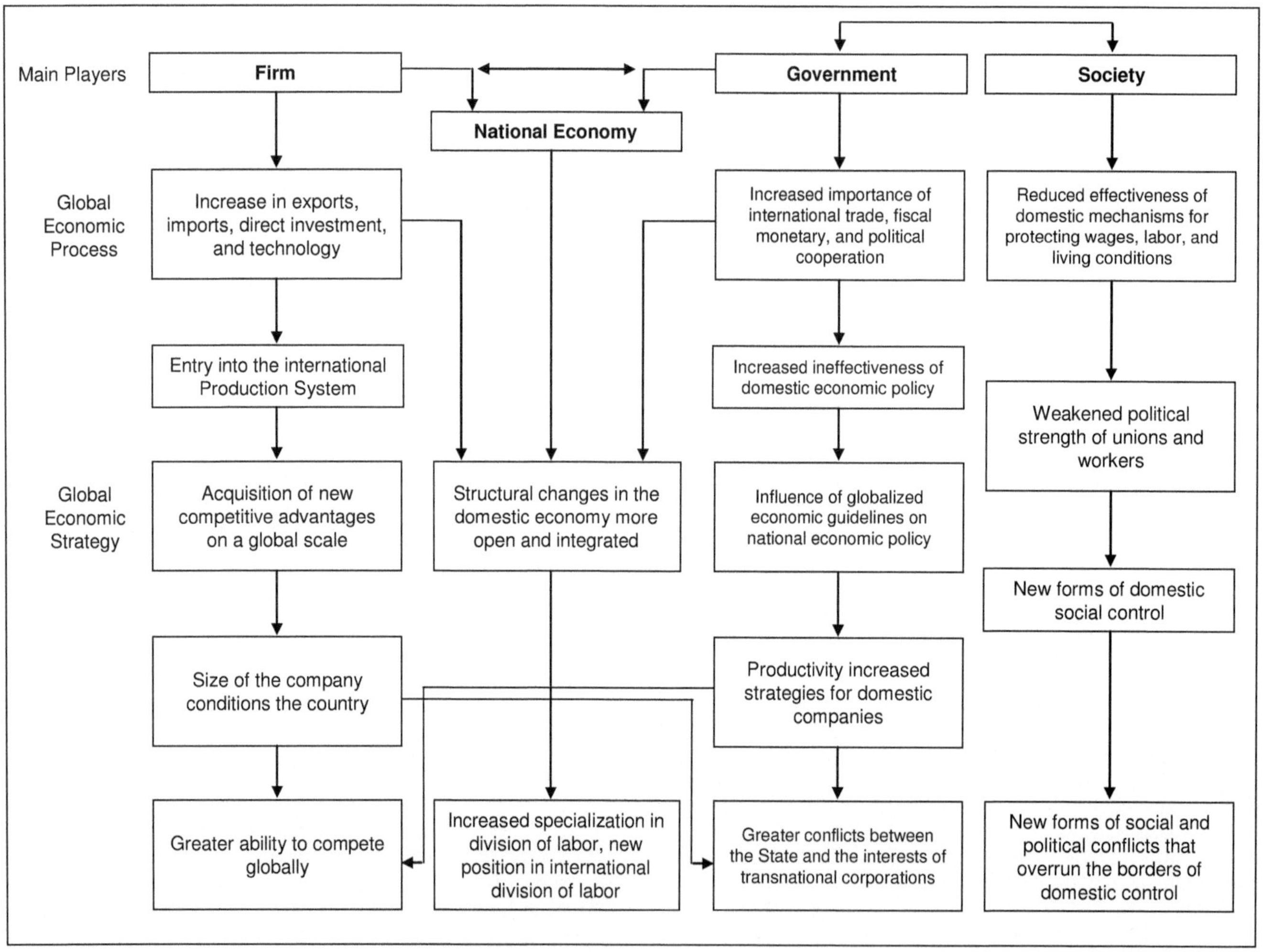

Figure 2. Processes and strategies in the globalized economy.
Source: (Faria, 1999).

world, which, in turn, could induce the growth of evasion and of the informal economy. Thus, tax evasion and the flight toward the underground economy would further reduce the taxing capacity of national governments.

Edgar Feige, a pioneer in the study and measurement of the underground economy, coined the term, *tax revolt*, stating that: "the irregular economy appears to have little respect for conventional geopolitical boundaries. Indeed, it is being increasingly noticed in almost all developed societies." Feige says further: "I wish to note that I began this investigation suspecting that the irregular economy was smaller than previous estimates had suggested. I am now convinced that the irregular economy is indeed of staggering proportions and growing rapidly (Feige, 1979)."

Tax reformers in developing countries should not become prisoners of conventional wisdom, nor be restricted to old tax models. A country's tax system must be able to adapt to thedynamics of the modern economic world. Taxation depends on ever changing economic facts, and not exclusively on consolidated juridical facts (Secretaria da receita federal, 2002).

Furthermore, it is important to get rid of traditional tax objectives to concentrate on what is essential: to collect revenue with which to finance public programs.

Romantic visions see taxation as an expression of the civic spirit of citizens, conscious of their rights and duties. Humanitarians have come to believe that the only way to redistribute wealth and income is through compensatory (or punitive) taxation of the more efficient and wealthier. Economists and political leaders seek through taxes, or through exemption from taxes, the pathway to stimulate economic growth. Ecologists and conservationists use the tax system as a form of environmental protection and of punishment of those who break preservationist rules. Urban and regional planners use taxes as inducement mechanisms to reach desirable social objectives. Farmers want to achieve land reform through taxation of large landowners. In a nutshell, everyone seeks in the tax system the solutions to their problems. As Everardo Maciel said, "this merely serves to demonstrate that the debate over taxation can take unpredictable turns, dictated by fortuitous reasons or impenetrable motives Secretaria da receita federal (2002)."

Given these multiple objectives and the inevitable indetermination that stems from the existence of more objectives than instrumental variables to achieve them, conventional tax systems have lost effectiveness in performing their essential function, that of raising public revenue.

Some taxes, to a greater or lesser degree, may perform regulatory functions. Others were created with essentially non-revenue objectives, as is the case with import taxes, which exist fundamentally as instruments of industrial policy and for protection of domestic production. Revenue from these taxes is strictly a secondary objective. Others still, such as taxes on tobacco, alcoholic beverages, or on pollution combine revenue goals with social objectives of public health and safety.

Unfortunately, this non-fiscal perspective has influenced fiscal policy so intensely that tax systems have become unintelligible and have performed poorly in its primary revenue-raising function. The multiplicity of objectives to be met by the tax system has turned it into a highly complex, bureaucratic, expensive, inefficient, and sometimes corrupt system, and has become a strong inducement to a wide variety of non-compliance and evasion tactics.

"This problem has been recently highlighted by a Report to the President of the United States on tax reform, ´Simple, Fair and Pro-Growth: Proposals to fix America´s Tax System´ prepared by the President's Advisory Panel on Federal Tax Reform (November, 2005). The Report suggests that legislators have lost sight of the fact that the fundamental purpose of the tax system is to finance public spending. Other goals have distracted the system from its fundamental purpose" (Tanzi, 2006).

From a fiscal standpoint, it is essential to collect revenue as efficiently, economically, and simply as possible. For this very same reason bank transactions taxation is continuously gaining significance as a basis for tax reform.

Theoretical formalism, which is much appreciated by staff economists who seek to identify and measure the allocative and distributive impacts of taxes with meticulous precision, is proving itself increasingly misleading as a script for tax reform, given that economic reality does not always adjust itself to the ideal economic models designed in the realm of high abstraction. In the words of Mangabeira Unger, the academic perspective unfolds in the midst of "edifying and tranquilizing illusions". But "the world is wild and obscure" (Unger, 1998). The world of perfect competition does not exist.

Along this same line of reasoning, Delfim Netto states that economic science creates the impression of being "...a body of progressive knowledge, a 'hard science'." He further says, "What all this sophistication has forgotten is that its conclusions depend upon two implicit postulates: 1) that tax evasion does not exist; in other words, that each citizen is a prisoner of rigid social rules that cast the tax evader into opprobrium, and 2) that collection of these taxes has no costs; that is, they flow naturally and smoothly to the coffers of the treasury... When one considers the falseness of these two postulates, one begins to doubt the quality of suggested recommendations and to have greater intellectual respect for 'non-declaratory tax' proposals..." (Delfim Netto, 1992).

"Governments will rediscover that the objective of taxation is to provide revenue for the state to meet its obligation and not to engage in social engineering through the tax system" (Tanzi, 2006).

TAX TECHNOLOGY AND RESPONSES TO NEW CHALLENGES FOR EFFECTIVE TAX REFORM

Tax reform, therefore, should allow for enough flexibility and realism to be able to adjust itself to a society's environment, and to its social, economic, political, and cultural characteristics.

"Since around 1980, the annoyance of taxpayers worldwide has been directed with increasing intensity not only at the high levels of taxation, but also at the complexity and instability of the tax systems. This annoyance has become a major factor in the changing attitudes of citizens towards taxation recorded in many countries during that period. In addition therefore to the level of taxation, such issues as complexity, instability and fairness of the tax systems have become important in many countries...instability, inefficiency and absence of fiscal coherence has characterized the tax systems." (Tanzi, 2006).

Such dissatisfaction with conventional tax systems that are being used extensively around the world cause even more amazement as they still find strong supporters, despite all evidence to the contrary. The amazement at this state of affairs is precisely described by the following statement: "no one would design such a system on purpose and nobody did. Only an historical explanation of how it came about can be offered as justification. That is not a justification, but a demonstration of how seemingly individually rational decisions can have absurd effects in aggregate" Kay and King, 1978; Tanzi, 2006).

In other words, citizens and policy makers are in search of a new "tax technology", paraphrasing Vito Tanzi. Maybe he is foreseeing the future, although with a certain bias in emphasis, when he mentions that "the discovery of value-added taxes in the 1950´s and its widespread use in later years must be considered the most important technological development in taxation in the past 50 years. [But also] ... gross assets taxes and taxes on financial transactions have been less important technological developments in Latin America."

The first part of his statement is gradually becoming less true, although in the past it has certainly helped to improve tax systems in the world. The second part, however, is becoming an increasingly crucial technological development in taxation.

Unfortunately, "the first law of finance is inertia", as we are painfully reminded by Prof. Richard Bird. "It is surprising that the many governments in the world, most of which are trying to raise more revenues, have not come up with more ingenious ways of doing so. The lure of the familiar and the apparent desire of most governments- like most people- not to be the first to do anything new doubtlessly account for the relative lack of fiscal innovation in the last 50 years....For the most part, however, a first lesson suggested by history is that the fiscal problems of the next 50 years will probably have to be dealt with using taxes very much like those on hand today. As with most social and political institutions, there seems to be little or no chance of a quick technological fix" (Bird, 1988).

Prof. Joseph Stiglitz seems equally skeptical about this issue when he states that "I do not see that any likely changes in technology in the near future will have a revolutionary effect on the design of our tax system" (Stiglitz, 1988). In spite of the impressive weight of such predictions, we hope the future will confirm Vito Tanzi´s remarks on the technological significance of both the electronic age and of its offspring, the financial transaction taxes, in constructing future tax systems in the world.

LESSONS LEARNED: THE BRAZILIAN EXPERIENCE WITH A DOMESTIC BANK TRANSACTIONS TAX

Billions of people throughout the world suffer the pain and misery of utmost poverty. Particularly striking and painful, is the fact that poverty flourishes in the midst of great wealth. Opulence and misery live side by side, are door to door neighbors in many developing countries. Income inequality and income concentration are nowadays two of the most common manifestations of world globalization. Countries such as Brazil now have to deal with a transitional situation which imposes great threats and challenges.

Short of official development assistance, lacking foreign aid, and unable to compete on a global level, such countries suffered a sharp fall in the rate of economic growth. Their savings rate fell dramatically, public deficit, and debt grew enormously, national industry and services were quickly taken over by multinational concerns. They now have to face the socially disrupting effects of growing inequality, such as urban violence, unemployment, swollen cities without minimum urban equipment, and dwindling social investment in sanitation, health, and education.

Emerging countries are going through a painful process of integration with the world economy and face the challenge of reaching a successful conclusion.

We do not dispute the benefits of world integration, nor do we underestimate the expected future gains that can be reaped out of growing flows of financial and commercial transactions on a global scale. But what we fear is that the process of building an integrated world economy may be aborted by the inability of the developing countries to bear the burden of such a transition to a global economy.

In response to this challenge, it is not acceptable to draw back, and to adopt the isolationist policies that typified the fifties and the sixties in the developing countries. That was a strategy that ran its course, that achieved remarkable results at its time, but that cannot be made to have the same positive effects again.

By the same token, it is not wise to allow big government to take over again, under the illusion that it can row against the tide of world integration and neutralize the prevalence of the private over the public sector. It is well known that governments make mistakes, such as mistargeting and other forms of inefficiency; governments are prone to corruption, and are easy targets for rent-seekers.

The challenge is facing us right in the eye; the bridges behind us have been burned, there is no turn around.

Based on the Brazilian experience with the use of a national transactions tax, I would like to propose the use of such tax both as an internal component of national tax systems, and as an internationally agreed toll tax in world short term capital movements.

The adoption of a transactions tax in Brazil was first proposed by me in January 1990, in the context of a modern single-tax model.

Following an old and respectable tradition in the history of economic thought, which dates back at least to the physiocratic school, the single-tax ideal was never implemented. The difficulty, which has turned the single-tax ideal into an almost utopian proposal, resides in the until now insurmountable difficulty in identifying a tax base sufficiently broad to allow the collection of enough revenues needed by governments to finance their activities, without, at the same time, requiring excessively high tax rates. As we know, evasion and its natural complement, corruption, varies in direct proportion to the nominal tax rates. Such a tax base has never been found, in the past. But now, the electronic age has opened the way for such a tax base: the set of all payments cleared through the banking system.

It is important to point out that a monetary payment has

never been used as a tax base because, before the growth of the modern banking system, payments were made through the use of commodity-based money, or, more recently, through paper money. Such means of payment implied the use of manual, or carry-on, money, and this made it impossible to implement a tax system capable of avoiding large scale tax evasion.

Nowadays, the electronic age has turned the banking system into the locus of all payment clearings. Except for small payments, most economic exchanges are made through the use of fiat money issued by the banking system, which makes possible the use of such clearing houses as the loci where tax collection can occur.

In Brazil, the long history of inflation has led to the overdevelopment of the banking system, especially to the use of sophisticated electronic means of administering bank deposits. Speed in clearing bank transactions was an essential prerequisite for high profitability in banking activities. Brazil is one of the few countries in the world that has an integrated clearing house for the whole banking sector, capable of clearing tens of millions of banking documents overnight.

At the same time, chronic inflation has caused a strong tendency for the expulsion of paper money, which not being indexed, lost purchasing power as inflation set place in Brazil, reaching in 1985, the monthly rate of 80%. The substitution of bank deposits for paper money turned Brazil into one of the most "unmonetized" economies in the world. Paper money outside the banking system accounts for less than 2% of GNP, while in other countries it rarely falls below 10% of GNP.

It should be pointed out, however, that there is a worldwide trend towards the use of electronic means of exchange -bank deposits, smart cards, on-line transactions- which leads us to believe that Keynes was right when he stated that paper money was a barbaric relic from the past and should soon be replaced by electronic means of exchange.

Such a detour into the history of money is important since it sets the ground for understanding the appearance of concrete possibilities for the achievement of the single tax ideal, based on a transactions tax.

The proposal of a single tax in Brazil raised an emotional controversy, particularly when, in 1992, and again in 1998 through 2007, Congress approved the use of such tax, although not as a single tax.

Its cumulative effects were quickly brought to the debate. Those who opposed the transactions tax pointed out its alleged negative effects on allocative efficiency. Others claimed that Brazilian exports would lose competitiveness due to the difficulties in rebating the taxes collected along the production process. Others still, pointed out the possible inducements to verticalization and banking disintermediation which could result from even modest rates on banking transactions, and that such tax would have low tax yield in stable economies, with low inflation rates.

Actually, all such criticism proved wrong. None of the negative predictions actually occurred. Quite on the contrary, the revenues collected from the transactions tax in both periods of application showed solid revenues and a universal pattern of incidence. It proved to be impossible to evade it. From the equity point of view, it turned out to be a fair tax, since the most unfair tax is that one which can be evaded

From the revenue side, each tenth of a percent (0.1%) in its rate structure resulted in revenues equivalent to 0.9% of GNP. In 1999 it collected R$ 8.5 billion with a rate of 0.2% on each bank account debit entry, both of persons or of firms. From 1999 to 2007, the rate was set at 0.38%.

The use of the transactions tax in Brazil confirmed the following advantages: it is an evasion-proof tax; it is corruption-proof; it has negligible collection cost; it is simple, non-declaratory, automatically collected, requires no bureaucratic procedures of the taxpayer, and causes no significant distortion in market functioning.

The transactions tax turned out to be both a powerful tool for achieving internal tax equity, and a source of solid revenues for the government. Although it is a turnover tax, it caused no significant distortion in the functioning of the market. It prevented tax evasion, which in many countries caused a shift of tax incidence to sectors least capable of "tax planning" or "tax avoidance", such as small and medium firms, and wage earners, with obvious negative equity impact. It also served the purpose of taxing the informal economy. It established a pattern of tax incidence, that made everybody pay, and if all pay their taxes, all should pay less.

The use of a transactions tax in Brazil was the first large scale experiment with such a tax. And it proved enormously successful. However, a few lessons were learned from it, and deserve attention from tax planners.

First, if rates are raised, a few safeguard measures should be adopted. To avoid the use of checks transfers to be used as quasi-money, they should be turned into nominal, non-endorsable orders of payment. Also, appropriate laws should require that transactions above a minimum amount should necessarily be cleared through the domestic banking system in order to acquire legal existence.

Second, the transactions tax should not be imposed on financial and capital markets. Since it is a turnover tax, at each period of maturity it would be collected on the stock of capital, thereby tending to raise the internal interest rate. This feature of the transactions tax will be further discussed below, with reference to the global Tobin tax.

Third, time and effort should be addressed to constructing input-output tables, with as many entries as possible, in order to evaluate the cost burden caused by the transactions tax in each sector of the economy. Such calculations are indispensable if exports are to be tax exempt. The Leontief tables should provide the proper levels of tax refunds to exporters. Since the transactions tax allows no tax evasion, it requires a much lower rate (2,7% in our estimates) to collect the same revenue as a conventional value-added tax with a rate of 17% as currently applied in Brazil. Therefore, a transactions tax imposes a significantly lower tax burden on all sectors of the economy, and therefore introduces less distortion in relative prices than a value-added tax.

In brief, the experiment with a transactions tax in Brazil was fully successful. It proved to be a powerful tool to raise revenues, a strong instrument to attain a more equitable pattern of income distribution, a robust deterrent of tax evasion and corruption, and at almost null collection cost.

In the light of the Brazilian transactions tax, it is important to make a few comments about the Tobin tax. The experience with a transactions tax in Brazil showed that the banking system is the unavoidable locus of all payment clearings in the modern world. It also showed that other forms of making payments, such as barter, use of paper money, or offshore facilities, usually imply higher costs than the tax economy made possible by such alternative devices. Furthermore, it became clear that some simple legislative actions would close most tax shelters.

The Brazilian experience also showed that a solid tax system, with a fair pattern of incidence, is a prerequisite for lowering income concentration and eradicating poverty.

On the other hand, a transaction tax should not reach the domestic capital markets. Especially in developing countries, where most financial transactions are short term due to the uncertainties and risks involved, a turnover tax has two effects: a) it raises the domestic interest rate, and b) it lengthens the maturity periods of financial markets.

As issues involving domestic economic policy, these two effects are usually undesirable. The higher interest rate effect reduces investment and growth; the lengthening of maturity periods, on the other hand, is more controversial. Some argue that term structure of financial markets should be left totally free to be determined solely by market forces, and therefore, should reflect the opportunity cost of money and liquidity. Others, however, argue that short term financial markets should be contained, and that a toll tax, due to its turnover characteristics, would throw some sand in the wheels of financial speculation.

It is precisely this second opinion, which led James Tobin and others to propose the introduction of a transactions tax on capital flows, on a world level. According to their opinion, trillions of dollars flow across international borders each year in search of investment opportunities. Most of it, however, is short term highly volatile capital, which many analysts believe is the main reason behind world financial instability.

Thus, a transactions tax on international capital flows would reduce the mobility of such financial flows, making capital mobility a more stable source of investment financing for the developing countries. According to this view, therefore, the transactions tax would reduce economic instability, limit the depth of international financial crisis, and would provide an alternative source of funding for eradicating world poverty.

Of course, there will be a need for multilateral coordination to implement such a tax on a world basis. Although this should turn out to be a very demanding task, it is technically viable, as the Brazilian experience has shown.

Conclusion

The transactions tax will surely be in the center of future tax systems all over the world. Both domestically (as used in Brazil) and on a world basis (as the Tobin Tax) such a tax should prove to be a valuable tool in tax reform programs around the world.

REFERENCES

Bird, Richard M (1988). Experience from a century of change. In: Stein, H. (Ed.), Tax Policy in the Twenty-First Century. New York: John Wiley and Sons.

Bertolucci, Aldo V (2001). Uma contribuição ao estudo da incidência dos custos de conformidade às leis e disposições tributárias: um panorama mundial e pesquisa de custos das empresas de capital aberto no Brasil, Master´s Thesis, FEA/USP, São Paulo.

Bertolucci, Aldo V (2005). O custo de administração dos tributos federais no Brasil: comparações internacionais e propostas para aperfeiçoamento, Ph. D Thesis, FEA/USP, São Paulo.

Cintra Marcos (1998). E-money e o imposto único. Folha de S. Paulo, São Paulo.

Cintra Marcos (2008a). Globalização, Modernização e Inovação Fiscal. In: Vasconcellos Roberto F. de (Org.). Política Fiscal, São Paulo: Editora Saraiva, Série GV-Law.

Cintra Marcos (2008b) Paradigmas tributários: do extrativismo colonial à globalização na era eletrônica. In: SANTI, Eurico MD, de (Org.). Curso de Direito Tributário e Finanças Públicas, São Paulo: Editora Saraiva.

Cintra Marcos (2009). Bank Transactions: a pathway to the Single Tax ideal. Amazon Books.

Coelho Isaias, Ebrill Liam P, Summers Victoria P (2001). Bank debit taxes in Latin America: an analysis of recent trends, Working Paper 01/67, Washington, International Monetary Fund.

Colabella Patrick R, Coppinger, Richard J (1995). Cashless taxation in the 21st Century. New York: St. John's University.

Delfim Netto Antonio (1992). Impostos não-declaratórios. Folha de S. Paulo, São Paulo.

Faria, José E (1999). O direito na economia globalizada. São Paulo: Ed. Malheiros.

Fauvet Jacques, Mendras, Henri (1958). Les paysans et la politique dans la France contemporaine. Cahiers de la Fondation Nacionale des Sciences Politiques, 94, Association Française de Sciense Politique, Paris: Librarie Armand Colin.

Feige, Edgar L (1979). How big is the irregular economy? Challenge: The Magazine of Economic Affairs, Armonk, NY.

Feige, Edgar L (2000). Taxation for the 21st century: The automated payment transaction (APT) tax, Economic Policy. Available at: www.marcoscintra.org/singletax.

Galbraith, John K (1958). The affluent Society. London: Houghton Miffin.

George, Henry (1879). Progress and Poverty. New York: Robert Schalkenbach Foundation.

Greco, Marco A, Libertuci, Elisabeth L (1999). Para uma norma geral

antielisão. IOB Cursos Empresariais, São Paulo.
Hall, Robert E, Rabushka, Alvin (1995). The flat tax. Stanford: Hoover Institution Press, Stanford University, Second Edition.
Hoffman, Stanley (1956). Le Mouvement Poujade. Cahiers de la Fondation Nacionale des Sciences Politiques, 81, Association Française de Sciense Politique, Paris: Librarie Armand Colin.
Hugon, Paul (1945). O imposto: teoria moderna e principais sistemas. São Paulo: Ed. Renascença.
Kay, John A, King, Mervyn A (1978). The British Tax System. Oxford: Open University Set Book, Fifth Edition.
Kellermann, Christian, Rixen Thomas, AHL Susanne (2007). Europeanizing corporate taxation to regain national tax policy autonomy. International Policy Analysis, Friedrich Ebert Stiftung. Available at: www.marcoscintra.org/singletax
Kuhn Thomas (1962). The Structure of Scientific Revolution. Chicago: Chicago University Press.
Lebowitz, Brian E (1999). Transfer pricing and the end of international taxation. Tax Notes International, Special Report.
Mills Dennis (1990). The single-tax. Toronto: Hemlock Press.
Sandford Cedric, Godwin Michael, Hardwick Peter (1989). Administrative and compliance costs of taxation. United Kingdom, Fiscal Publications.
Sandford, Cedric, Godwin Michael (1990). VAT administration and compliance in Britain. In: GILLES, Malcolm; SHOUP, Carl S, SICAT, Gerardo.P, Value-added taxation in developing countries. A World Bank Symposium, Washington.
Secretaria da Receita Federal (2001). Tributação da Renda no Brasil Pós-Real, Brasília, Ministério da Fazenda. Available at: www.marcoscintra.org/singletax
Secretaria da Receita Federal (2002). Condicionantes e perspectivas da tributação no Brasil. Estudos Tributários, Coordenação Geral de Política Tributária, Brasília. Estudos Tributários, n. 7. Available at: www.marcoscintra.org/singletax
Seligman, Edwin RA (1914). Essais sur l'impôt. Translation of the 8th American edition for the French by Louis Surret. Paris: Giard M,. Brière É, (Bibliothéque Internationale de Science et de le Législation Financières).p. 618.
Stiglitz, Joseph E (1988). Computerized tax collecting. In: Stein, H. (Ed.), Tax Policy in the Twenty-First Century. New York: John Wiley and Sons.
Tanzi Vito (2000). Globalization, technological developments, and the work of fiscal termites. IMF Working Paper, WP/00/181.
Tanzi Vito (2005). Globalización y Sistemas Tributarios. In: Tanzi, Vito; Barreix, Alberto; Villela, Luiz. Tributación para la integración del Mercosur. Buenos Aires: Departamento de Integración y Programas Regionales.
Tanzi Vito (2006). Death of an Illusion? Decline and fall of high tax economies. Policy Series, London: Politeia, 54: 7-8.
Tanzi Vito (2007). The future of fiscal federalism. Keynote address presented at the Conference on "New perspectives on fiscal federalism: intergovernmental relations, competition and accountability". Social Science Research Center, Berlin.
The Economist (1997). The future of state, (in the essay: A survey of the world economy). London.
The Economist (2000). Survey: globalization and tax, London. pp. 3-38.
The Economist (2001). Dreams of a cashless society. Finance and Economics, London.
The Economist (2007). A place in the Sun: a special report on offshore finance. London.
Toffler Alvin, Toffler Heidi (2006). Revolutionary Wealth. New York: Alfred A. Knopf Inc.
Unger, Roberto M (1998). Impostos e paradoxos. Folha de S. Paulo, São Paulo.
Zilveti Fernando A, Toro Carlos, Eduardo Costa MA, Britto Bianca M de (2007). Preços de transferência. In: SANTI, Eurico MD, De, Mosquera, Roberto Q, Zilveti, Fernando A (Orgs.). Direito Tributário – tributação internacional, São Paulo: Editora Saraiva, Série GVLaw.

Corporate taxation, investment and productivity: A firm level estimation

Arturo José Galindo* and Cristina Pombo

Inter-American Development Bank, Washington, DC, USA.

This paper analyses how corporate taxes can affect investment and productivity. To address this question the paper uses data from a set of 42 developing countries taken from the World Bank Business Environment Surveys and examines whether firms with different sizes are affected differently by taxation. We extend the analysis that has been carried out relating tax rates to investment into the analysis of the impact of taxation on total factor productivity. Investment and productivity are shown to respond negatively to an increase in the corporate tax rate. These effects are stronger in bigger firms.

Key words: Taxation, investment, total factor productivity.

INTRODUCTION

Many public finance economists have studied the relationship between corporate income taxes, investment and productivity, and have found evidence suggesting that excessive government regulatory and tax policies have negative consequences on the business environment and economic development. Since Hall and Jorgenson (1967) work showing that changes in the user cost of capital can explain aggregate investment reasonably well, several studies have searched for theoretical and empirical explanations for this relationship. In general, this research finds adverse effects of corporate income taxes on investment, albeit using different estimation techniques and not reaching consensus on the magnitude of such effect.[1] Recent investment models are based on the neoclassical theory that normally uses the Q-theory and the theory of the user cost of capital where a representative firm maximizes its present value. This theory relies on the assumption that aggregate investment can be expected to depend positively in a stable way on *q*, the ratio of the stock market valuation of existing capital to its replacement cost. In this context an increase in corporate taxes, by increasing the user cost of capital should have a negative impact on investment. Moreover, if productivity is imbedded in capital goods, a decline in investment should also affect productivity growth negatively. As opposed to literature on the impacts of taxes on investment, the relationship between taxes and productivity has been less studied, in part perhaps, because there is no single measure of productivity. Auerbach and Hines (2002) suggest that taxes create distortions by affecting prices and the decision making of firms and households, distorting the allocation of inputs within and between firms and thereby lowering the efficiency in the use of production inputs, thus decreasing TFP.

Numerous authors and studies have shown that the scope and nature of regulations on economic activity and factor markets can significantly and adversely impact productivity, growth and economic activity[2]. As the tax code is an important element in the map of regulations that determine the business environment, many of the ideas explored in this research can be extrapolated to tax

*Corresponding author. E-mail: ajgalindo@gmail.com.

JEL codes: E22, H2, O4.

The opinions of the authors do not reflect those of the Inter-American Development Bank or Its Board of Directors.

[1]Some examples of this are Summers (1981), Feldstein et al. (1983), Cummins et al. (1996) and Gordon and Hines (2002).

[2]Bosworth and Collins (2003), Dollar et al. (2004), Rodrik and Subramanian (2004), Loayza et al. (2004), McMillan (1998, 2004), OECD (2001), Wilkinson (2001), Alexander et al. (2004), Djankov et al. (2008), Haltiwanger (2002), He et al. (2003) and World Bank (2003, 2004a, b).

policy. The analysis of the potential links between productivity or investment and taxes is based on the idea that taxes affect productivity through different channels and that due to some relevant industry or firm specific characteristics, like the firm size, some firms and industries are essentially more affected than others. Using Djankov et al. (2010) database on taxes throughout the World and a firm level database from the World Business Environment Surveys of the World Bank (WBES), this paper estimates the impact of corporate taxation on firm level investment and total factor productivity (TFP) in emerging economies. We also explore if the previous effects identified in the literature, namely the negative impact of tax rates on investment, vary across firm sizes. Our results suggest that both investment and TFP are negatively affected by higher tax rates. This impact is greater for larger firms, that is the firms that tend to concentrate most of a country's employment and hence the drivers of growth. These results are in line with recent findings by Arnold and Schwellnus (2008) that use a data set on OECD firms to test a similar hypothesis, and find that in OECD countries, higher tax rates also reduce productivity, especially for larger firms[3].

Our paper adds to this literature by extending this result to developing countries. The rest study describes the empirical methodology and the data used in the analysis, then it presents the main results and finally the conclusion is given.

DESCRIPTION OF THE DATA AND METHODOLOGY

Using the World Business Environment Survey, a database of firm surveys assembled by the World Bank, we construct measures of investment in capital goods and total factor productivity for a sample of 42 developing countries[4]. The survey gathers information on how firms perceive the business environment and on production inputs, their costs and their outputs in a given year. The sample covers the years 2004 to 2006, but most of the sample corresponds to surveys done in 2006. The survey asks specific questions regarding investment in capital good, as well as firm sales, labor inputs and expenses in intermediate production inputs. We use the questions on capital expenditure to proxy investment and compute total factor productivity (TFP), using a Solow residual approach in which we estimate cost shares under The computation of the cost shares associated with each input in the production function is done considering three alternatives. Under the first specification we assume that they are equal for all firms in all countries and all industries. Secondly, we allow the parameters to change across industries but remaining the same different alternatives[5]. across countries. Thirdly the computation allows the parameters to differ across industries and countries.

In all specifications the cost share is computed as the average cost share of the firms in the relevant group. Once TFP is computed we estimate different specifications for the following benchmark equation:

$$X_{cij} = \beta' controls_{cij} + \psi' size_{cij} + \lambda' tx_c \times size_{cij} + \omega + \varepsilon_{cij}$$

Where, X is either the ratio of investment to the capital stock (I/K) or TFP, controls are a series of firm level controls including the ownership structure of the firm (foreign vs domestically owned), the log of the age of the firm, and a dummy indicating if the firm exports its product directly; *tx* indicates the country's corporate tax rate[6], size are dummies indicating the firm's size (micro, small, medium, large)[7] and ε is the residual[8].

In a first set of specifications, $\omega = \mu_{ci}$, where μ are country-industry fixed effects that should capture unobserved characteristics that vary at the country-industry level. Note that in this specification we cannot account for the direct impact of *tx*, since we are controlling for country-industry dummies, hence these estimates only allow us to identify the marginal effect of taxes on firms relative to the size assigned to the dummy excluded from the regression. In other words, our estimates show us if the impact of taxes is greater in small, medium and large firms, compared to micro firms (the excluded dummy). In order to account for the total impact of the tax variable we also estimate a second specification where, $\omega = \rho tx_c + \varpi' macro_c + \eta_i$. Here, macro is a vector of country-wide controls (the log of GDP per capita and the log of the Heritage Foundation's measure of economic freedom that we include as a measure of the regulatory environment) and η□ are industry level effects. The main interest of this paper is in the estimated coefficients of *tx* which the literature has suggested to be negative, and on the coefficient on the interaction of *tx* and the *size* dummies.

This coefficient shows if there is a differential effect of the corporate tax rate on investment or on TFP on firms of different sizes. Descriptive statistics of the relevant variables used in the analysis are shown in Table 1.

RESULTS

The results are reported in Table 2. The estimation of the coefficients of the firm size in all regressions is consistent

[3]Vartia (2008) finds similar results using industry level, rather than firm level information for the OECD.

[4]The sample is determined by the availability of data, and includes the following countries: Algeria, Angola, Argentina, Bangladesh, Bolivia, Botswana, Brazil, Burundi, Cambodia, Cameroon, Chile, Colombia,Congo, Ecuador, Egypt, El Salvador, Ethiopia, Ghana, Guatemala, Guinea-Bissau, Guyana, Honduras, India, Indonesia, Malawi, Mauritania, Mauritius, Mexico, Mozambique, Namibia, Nicaragua, Niger, Oman, Pakistan, Panama, Peru, Rwanda, Senegal, Tanzania, Uganda, Uruguay and Zambia.

[5]Here TFP is computed assuming a Cobb Douglas. After taking logs and rearranging we obtain an equation for A (total factor productivity) in terms of Y, K, L and M: Log (A_{cij}) = Log (Y_{cij}) – α Log (K_{cij}) – β Log (L_{cij}) – γLog (M_{cij}), where Y is output, K is capital, L is labor, M are intermediate inputs and c, i and j denote the firm j in industry i in country c.

[6]This data is taken from the World Bank's "Paying taxes" website (http://www.doingbusiness.org/exploretopics/payingtaxes/)

[7]Size is measured according to the relative size of firm's sales with respect to the distribution of sales in each country. Firms whose sales lie in the lower 25% of the distribution are considered micro enterprises, those with sales within the 25 and 50th percentile are small, between the 50 and 75th percentile are medium and above the 75th percentile are defined as large.

[8]A relevant caveat that we ought to note is that there is a possible relationship between taxes and firm size as suggested in Zimmerman (1983), Heshmati et al. (2010) and Markle and Shackelford (2011) among others. This would call for the specification of a dynamic empirical model to capture the impact of taxation on firm growth and allow for the endogeneity of the firm's size. Unfortunately, the nature of our dataset (a cross section of firms per country) does not allow us to explore this relevant dimension of the taxes productivity nexus.

Table 1. Descriptive statistics.

	Mean	Std Dev	Min	Max
I/K	0.11	0.22	0.00	1.00
TFP	1.97	1.10	-3.05	8.83
TFPj	2.41	1.80	-4.56	11.40
TFPij	2.31	1.76	-3.04	10.71
Corporate tax rate	0.20	0.10	0.03	0.73

Table 2. Regression results.

Dependent variable	(1)	(2)	(3)	(4)	(5)	(6)	(7)	(8)
	I/K	I/K	TFP	TFP	TFPj	TFPj	TFPij	TFPij
Small	0.0265**	0.0264**	0.130***	0.153***	0.150***	0.256***	0.131***	0.217***
	[0.0121]	[0.0126]	[0.0328]	[0.0484]	[0.0492]	[0.0643]	[0.0354]	[0.0737]
Medium	0.0443***	0.0417***	0.209***	0.456***	0.331***	0.691***	0.255***	0.733***
	[0.0128]	[0.0127]	[0.0382]	[0.0536]	[0.0660]	[0.0758]	[0.0414]	[0.0818]
Large	0.0685***	0.0624***	0.430***	0.675***	0.498***	0.948***	0.482***	0.955***
	[0.0132]	[0.0130]	[0.0447]	[0.0589]	[0.0709]	[0.0785]	[0.0469]	[0.0868]
Foreign	-0.000452	0.00214	0.0228	0.239***	0.0168	0.258***	0.00376	0.340***
	[0.00695]	[0.00714]	[0.0255]	[0.0339]	[0.0402]	[0.0428]	[0.0274]	[0.0505]
Log (Age)	-0.0215***	-0.0225***	-0.00435	0.00569	-0.0249**	0.0227*	0.000765	0.00765
	[0.00257]	[0.00263]	[0.00739]	[0.0106]	[0.0103]	[0.0138]	[0.00846]	[0.0161]
Export	0.00434	0.0218***	-0.021	-0.195***	0.0424*	-0.316***	0.0183	-0.359***
	[0.00524]	[0.00513]	[0.0161]	[0.0220]	[0.0228]	[0.0292]	[0.0175]	[0.0332]
Corporate tax rate		0.0253		0.0497		0.229		-0.443**
		[0.0461]		[0.168]		[0.226]		[0.224]
Corporate tax rate * small	-0.057	-0.0676	-0.108	-0.258	0.0653	-0.371	-0.229	-0.473
	[0.0622]	[0.0637]	[0.158]	[0.216]	[0.213]	[0.291]	[0.172]	[0.306]
Corporate tax rate * medium	-0.0974	-0.102*	-0.0474	-0.910***	-0.132	-1.410***	-0.405**	-1.959***
	[0.0626]	[0.0616]	[0.176]	[0.233]	[0.269]	[0.326]	[0.189]	[0.337]
Corporate tax rate * large	-0.161***	-0.165***	-0.474**	-1.368***	-0.479*	-1.760***	-1.107***	-2.800***
	[0.0600]	[0.0596]	[0.191]	[0.244]	[0.285]	[0.329]	[0.202]	[0.350]
Log (GDP per capita)		0.0236***		0.0920***		0.0999***		0.346***
		[0.00339]		[0.0136]		[0.0182]		[0.0226]
Log (Ec. freedom)		0.354***		2.862***		3.284***		3.377***
		[0.0295]		[0.107]		[0.129]		[0.181]
Observations	12211	12211	11661	11661	11662	11662	11658	11658
R-squared	0.188	0.085	0.71	0.296	0.777	0.535	0.854	0.333
Number of countries	42	42	42	42	42	42	42	42
Country-industry effects	Yes	No	Yes	No	Yes	No	Yes	No
Industry effects	No	Yes	No	Yes	No	Yes	No	Yes

with the idea that the level of investment and the level of TFP are increasing in firm size. The coefficients on firm specific characteristics (ownership, age and export orientation) vary across specifications as well as their significance. The relevant coefficients for this study suggest that the impact of corporate taxes on investment and productivity are also increasing in the size of firms. The larger the firms the bigger the negative effect of the corporate tax rate on investment and any of the measures of TFP. With respect to investment, columns (1) and (2) show that the corporate tax rate has a negative impact for medium and large firms. The estimates are not only statistically significant but are also economically important. For example, a one standard deviation increase in the corporate tax rate (0.10) would reduce I/K for large firms in 0.0165, which is close to 15% of the sample average. Columns (3) to (8) show different estimations of the impact of the corporate tax rate considering different measures of productivity. While the estimates change from one specification to the other, the result that corporate taxes hurt larger firms more than smaller ones is consistent across specifications. As mentioned earlier, the impact estimated is also economically relevant.

For example, the estimates in column (8) suggest that a one standard deviation increase in the corporate tax rate would reduce TFP in 0.8, which is equal to nearly 35% of the sample average.

Conclusions

This paper estimates the relationship between corporate taxes, investment and productivity using a data set for 42 developing countries. The main findings suggest that corporate taxes have a negative impact on investment and productivity and that the impact is bigger on larger firms which are most likely to be formal and to pay taxes anyway. These results contribute to the research in this topic and suggest that tax policies may have large consequences for the business environment as well as for economic development, since large firms tend to concentrate most of an economy's employment, and leads to the discussion of potential tradeoffs between collecting revenue and long term growth.

REFERENCES

Alexander W, Robert J, Bell JD, Knowles S (2004). Quantifying Compliance Costs of Small Businesses in New Zealand. Discussion paper, University of Otahgo.

Auerbach A and Hines J (2002). Taxation and Economic Efficiency, in Alan Auerbach and Martin Feldstein (eds.) Handbook of Public Amsterdam: North-Holland, 3: 1347-1421.

Bosworth B, Susan C (2003). The Empirics of Growth: An Update. The Brookings Institution. Washington, D.C. Manuscript.

Cummins JG, Hassett KA, Hubbard RG (1996). Tax reforms and investment: a cross-country comparison. J. Public Economics, 62: 237-273.

Djankov S, Ganser T, McLiesh C, Ramalho R, Shleifer A (2010).The effect of corporate taxes on investment and entrepreneurship American Economic J. Macroecon., 2: 31-64.

Dollar D, Mary Hallward-Driemeier, Taye M (2004). Investment Climate and International Integration. Washington, D.C., World Bank. Manuscript.

Feldstein M, Louis Dicks-Mireaux, James P (1983). "The Effective Tax Rate and the Pretax Rate of Return. J. Public Econ., 21(2): 129-158.

Gordon R, James H (2002). International Taxation, in Alan Auerbach and Martin Feldstein (eds.), Handbook of Public Economics, Amsterdam: North-Holland, 4: 1935-1995.

Hall R, Dale J (1967). Tax Policy and Investment Behavior. Am. Econ. Rev., 57(3): 391-414.

Haltiwanger J (2002). Understanding Economic Growth. The Need for Micro Evidence. New Zealand Economic Papers, 36(1): 33-58.

He KS, Morck R, Yeung B (2003). Corporate Stability and Economic Growth. William Davidson Working Paper No. 553.

Heshmati A, Johansson D, Bjuggren CM (2010). Effective Corporate Tax Rates and the Size Distribution of Firms, J. Competition Trade, 10(3): 297-317.

Loayza NV, Oviedo AM, Luis S (2004). Regulation and Macroeconomic Performance, World Bank, Washington DC. Manuscript.

Markle KS, Shackelford DA (2011). Cross-Country Comparisons of Corporate Income Taxes, NBER Working Papers 16839.

McMillan J (1998). Managing Economic Change: Lessons from New Zeland, The World Economy, 21: 827-843.

McMillan J (2004). A Flexible Economy? Entrepeneurship and Productivity in New Zeland, Working Paper, Graduate Scholl of Business, Stanford University, Stanford, CA.

Organization for Economic Cooperation and Development (2001). Businesses' Views on Red Tape, Paris, OECD.

Rodrik D, Arvind S (2004). From 'Hindu Growth to Productivity Surge: The Mystery of the Indian Growth Transition. Harvard University, Cambridge, Mass. Manuscript.

Schwellnus C, Arnold J (2008). Do Corporate Taxes Reduce Productivity and Investment at the Firm Level?: Cross-Country Evidence from the Amadeus Dataset, OECD Economics Department Working Papers, p. 641.

Summers L (1981). Taxation and Corporate Investment: A q-Theory Approach Brookings Papers on Economic Activity, 1(1): 67-127.

Wilkinson B (2001). Constraining Government Regulation. NZ Business Roundtable.

World Bank (2003). Doing Business in 2004" Understanding Regulation. Washington, D.C.World Bank.

World Bank (2004). Doing Business in 2005: Removing Obstacles to Growth. Washington, D.C. World Bank.

World Bank (2004). 2003 Annual Review of Development Effectiveness: The Effectiveness of Bank Support for Policy Reform.

Vartia L (2008). How do Taxes Affect Investment and Productivity?: An Industry-Level Analysis of OECD Countries, OECD Economics Department Working Papers 656.

Zimmerman JL (1983). Taxes and firm size, J. Accting Econs, Elsevier, 5(1): 119-149.

Investigating tax fairness in eleventh century England: Evidence from Wiltshire estates

John McDonald

Flinders Business School, Flinders University, GPO Box 2100, Adelaide 5001, Australia.
E-mail: john.mcdonald@flinders.edu.au.

The Domesday Survey of 1086 recorded a wealth of information on the Anglo-Norman tax system. The survey data includes the tax assessments, incomes and resources of most estates in England. The assessments relate to an estate tax known as the geld. Details of the way the assessments were imposed and the rationale underlying the assessment process are no longer extant, but by analysing the relationships between assessments and estate characteristics, it is possible to discover the impact of the tax on landholders and infer the main features of tax policy. An earlier paper by McDonald (2002), describes research into how Domesday taxes were levied and the characteristics of estates and tenants that received favourable tax treatment in Essex. In this paper, the research is extended to a second Domesday county, Wiltshire.

Key words: Tax fairness, Domesday book, the geld, tax frontier.

INTRODUCTION

The Domesday survey of 1086 generated a wealth of information on the Anglo-Norman tax system. Commissioned some 20 years after William, Duke of Normandy, conquered England the survey record, Domesday book, contains data on the tax assessments, incomes and resources of most estates in England. The assessments are those for an estate tax known as the geld. Details of the way the assessments were imposed and the rationale underlying the assessment process are no longer available to us, but by analysing the relationships between assessments and estate characteristics, it is possible to discover the impact of the tax on landholders and infer the main features of tax policy. An earlier paper, McDonald (2002), describes research into how Domesday taxes were levied and the characteristics of estates and tenants that received favourable tax treatment in Essex. In this paper, the research is extended to a second Domesday county, the County of Wiltshire. The evidence seems to suggest that in many respects, the tax system possessed characteristics similar to those of modern tax systems. It seems to have been constructed on a capacity to pay principle but with some unevenness in the application of the principle as a consequence of administrative practice and political considerations. This view is at odds with the ideas of Victorian historians who saw the assessments as an 'artificial' administrative creation bearing little relationship to estate income.

BACKGROUND AND RELATED RESEARCH

The Domesday survey

The Domesday survey was announced by King William at the Christmas meeting of the Great Council at Gloucester in 1085. In the following year, commissioners sent out a survey questionnaire to landholders. Their answers were reviewed in local courts and became public knowledge. The survey information was then summarized and edited at Winchester by the Exchequer to form Domesday Book. Data in Domesday book are organized by county. Within a county, the king's estates are listed first, followed by the estates of ecclesiastical tenants-in-chief and then lay tenants-in-chief. Domesday book consists of two volumes, Great and Little Domesday. Little Domesday is the survey return for the counties of Essex, Norfolk and Suffolk and Great Domesday is a summary of the returns for the other counties of England. The survey was used to document the contemporary feudal structure and revise tax assessments. Godfrey and Hooper (1996: 51) argued that, "By providing a valuation and audit of the resources of the feudal tenants-in-chief in 1086, Domesday enabled William and his successors to optimize both their wealth, through fiscal policy and efficient use of the country's resources, and their power within the feudal structure of medieval England. For the English monarchy of the period, Domesday served both accountability and decision-making needs" [1].

Earlier research on the tax assessments

The geld assessments listed in Domesday book relate to a non-feudal tax first levied by King Ethelred in 911 to fund a force to counter Danish incursions. Oldroyd (1997) describes the geld and public accounting in the Anglo-Saxon period. A land tax originally, it is thought that by Norman times it was more broadly based. It was a significant burden on landholders, being levied annually by 1086 and amounting to about 15% of the net income of the average Wiltshire lay estate. Round (1895) and the Victorian Domesday scholars saw the Domesday tax assessments as an 'artificial' administrative construct not linked to individual estate income. This view was largely based on Round's unsystematic and subjective review of the distribution of the assessments across estates, and the local government units, the vills and the hundreds of counties.

He argued that the assessments were imposed on the hundreds of the county in 100-hide units and vills in five-hide units and then apportioned to estates. As a consequence the assessments bore little relationship to the ability of the estate to pay the tax.

In McDonald and Snooks (1985a, 1986), Snooks and I argued a contrary view. Using regression methods, we showed, for example, that for Wiltshire lay estates between 74 and 80% of variation in the tax assessments could be attributed to variations in manorial net incomes (referred to in Domesday as annual values) or manorial resources, two alternative ways of measuring capacity to pay. Similar results were obtained for other counties. Capacity to pay explains from 56 to 89% of variation in individual estate assessment data for the counties of Buckinghamshire, Cambridgeshire, Essex and Wiltshire, and from 72 to 81% for aggregate data for 29 counties (McDonald and Snooks, 1987a). Influenced by this empirical evidence, we argued that similar to many modern tax systems, it was possible that the Domesday assessments reflected an attempt to collect taxes in a politically acceptable way.

We postulated that the assessments may have been based on a capacity to pay principle modified by politically expedient concessions and could be expected to exhibit some unevenness resulting from the administrative process. This uneven-ness occurred because the assessments were revised infrequently and, consequently, the link between assessment and capacity to pay became somewhat eroded. Also, it is thought assessments were revised at different times in the various counties and the hundreds of a county, and with slightly more rigour in some administrative units than others.

METHODOLOGY

Capacity to pay explains much, but not all variation in the tax assessments across estates. Were some tenants-in-chief and some kinds of estate more favourably treated than others? These questions were investigated in McDonald (2002) using data relating to the lay lords of Essex. A nonparametric measure of favourable or beneficial taxation was calculated for each estate based on the idea that an estate has received a beneficial taxation assessment if it has a lower tax assessment than another estate with the same or lower net income or annual value. More formally, the beneficial taxation index (BTI) for estate *i*, was defined as the ratio of the maximum tax assessment of all estates with the same or a lower net income than estate *i*, to the actual tax assessment of estate *i*., A BTI value of one corresponds to no beneficial taxation, and a value greater than one to some beneficial taxation[2]. In this paper, a similar analysis is carried

---

[1] Background information on Domesday England is contained in McDonald and Snooks (1986, Ch. 1 and 2; 1985a, 1985b, 1987a, 1987b and 2003) and McDonald (1998). For more comprehensive accounts of the history of the period see Brown (1984), Clanchy (1983), Loyn (1962), (1965), (1983), and Stenton (1951). Other useful references include Ballard (1906), Darby (1952), (1977), Galbraith (1961), Hollister (1965), Lennard (1959), Maitland (1897), Miller and Hatcher (1978), Postan (1966), (1972), Round (1895), (1903), the articles in Williams (1987) and references cited in McDonald and Snooks (1986). The Survey is discussed in McDonald and Snooks (1986, sec. 2.2), the references cited there, and the articles in Williams (1987). The Domesday and modern surveys are compared in McDonald and Snooks (1985c). For other studies of the Domesday economy see McDonald (1997, 2000, 2005, 2009b and 2010). Others who have made important contributions to our understanding of the Domesday economy include Miller and Hatcher (1978), Hallam (1981) and the contributors to the volume edited by Britnell and Campbell (1995).

[2] The estate BTI values correspond to efficiency measures calculated in Data Envelopment Analysis (DEA). DEA has usually been used to examine the efficiency of production units. In this study it is applied to assess how favourable estate tax assessments were given the estate net income. A major advantage of using this DEA method to calculate BTI values is that it does not assume that the tax assessment-income relationship takes a particular functional form such as the linear or log-linear forms. These ideas are discussed further in McDonald (1998).

Table 1. Mean BTI of estates of 10 largest tenants-in-chief. Wiltshire Lay estates, 1086.

Tenants-in-chief	Mean BTI	Standard deviation of mean	Deviation from overall mean	Number of estates in sample
Edward of Salisbury	2.77	1.83	0.43	39
Humfrey de Insula	1.70	0.46	-0.64	27
Ernulf of Hesdin	2.69	1.25	0.35	18
Alvred of Marlborough	1.74	0.56	-0.60	20
William of Eu	2.68	1.42	0.34	14
Waleran the huntsman	2.08	0.60	-0.26	12
Miles Crispin	1.60	0.50	-0.73	11
Osbern Gifard	2.11	0.79	-0.23	11
Ralf de Mortemer	2.27	1.08	-0.07	10
Robert fitz Girold	3.80	4.49	1.46	10
Others	2.34	1.56	0.01	161

out for the lay lords of Wiltshire and the results are compared with those of the Essex study.

RESULTS

Beneficial taxation in Wiltshire in 1086

BTIs were calculated for 333 estates of the lay lords of Wiltshire in 1086 and the way in which the BTI varied by tenant-in-chief and hundred investigated.[3] Table 1 lists the mean BTI of estates of the 10 largest tenants-in-chief. Robert fitz Girold appears to have been the most favourably treated tenant-in-chief. The mean BTI value for his 10 estates is 3.80. The deviation of this value from the overall mean (2.34) is 1.46. Notice, however, that the standard deviation of Robert's mean BTI is large (4.49). The high mean value is mainly due to the high BTIs of two of Robert's estates: Biddlesden (BTI = 16.00) and Wilsford (BTI = 6.00). Edward of Salisbury (mean BTI = 2.77) and William of Eu (mean BTI = 2.68) also have high mean BTIs.

Some who received less favourable treatment were Miles Crispin (mean BTI = 1.60), Humfrey de Insula (mean BTI=1.70) and Alvred of Marlborough (mean BTI = 1.74).

There appear to have been clear differences in the tax treatment of tenants-in-chief, and this is confirmed by formal statistical testing. A robust statistical test of the null hypothesis that the mean BTIs for the tenants-in-chief are equal, resulted in rejection of the null at the five and one percent significance level.[4] The test suggests that the tenant-in-chief was a significant factor influencing how estates were taxed.

There were 37 hundred (local government) divisions in Wiltshire. A statistical test indicated that the BHI varied significantly (at the five and one percent levels) with hundred location.[5] Hundreds for which estates received milder assessments included Ramsbury (mean BHI = 4.80), Westbury (mean BHI = 4.44), Amesbury (mean BHI = 4.14) and Elstab (mean BHI = 3.50). Some less well treated were Blackgrove (mean BHI = 1.15) and Thornhill (mean BHI = 1.20).

[3] The data file was compiled by Beverley Vickers and Eva Aker, the work being funded by Australian Research Council and Flinders University research grants. The file was compiled from Domesday Book entries in the *Victoria County History, 1900)of Wiltshire,* which were checked against a facsimile of the Latin transcript and English translations in the so-called Phillimore edition (Morris, 1975) and Alecto Historical Editions (Williams and Martin, 2003). Phillimore was used to determine the hundred locations of the estates. A general rule of thumb was developed that only entries for which (1) an annual value and a tax assessment are recorded, (2) either plough teams or some meadowland, pasture or woodland are recorded, and (3) some labour is recorded, were retained for analysis. In addition, 15 other entries were deleted either because they were implausible or incomplete. Some summary measures of the BTI distribution are: 20 or six percent of estates had a BTI=1, the first quartile of the distribution was 1.5, the median, 2.0, and the third quartile, 2.6. The estate of Biddesden had the largest index value of 16.

[4] The test was carried out by regressing the BTI on tenant-in-chief binary variables taking the value 1, if the tenant-in-chief held the estate; 0, otherwise. Regression diagnostics indicated heteroskedasticity in the disturbances and White's (1980) heteroskedasticity-consistent test was used. On the null, the test statistic is asymptotically distributed as a F-distribution with 10 and 322 degrees of freedom. The test statistic value was 4.974, which has a p-value, to four decimal places, of zero.

[5] The test was carried out in a similar way to the test for equality of the tenant-in-chief BTI means. As the hundred location of nine estates is unknown, their observations were deleted from the sample, reducing the number of observations to 324. The p-value for the test was, to four decimal places, zero.

The foregoing results suggest that all estates were not treated equally, but that tax treatment varied significantly across tenants-in-chief and the hundreds. It would be interesting to discover if the tenant-in-chief effect remains significant when we control for the hundred effect and the hundred effect is still significant when we allow for the tenant-in-chief effect. We could also ask whether the tenant-in-chief and hundred effects remain statistically significant when we control for other factors that might plausibly be expected to affect the assessments. Multiple regression was used to investigate these issues. Information is available for most estates on the size of the estate, the kind of agriculture practised and the tenure arrangement on the estate, all factors that could affect an estate's tax assessment.

Table 2 exhibits the main results of a regression of the BTI on variables measuring these characteristics.[6] Details of the imple-mentation of the geld are now largely unknown, so the regression will provide empirical evidence as to whether particular groups or activities received special treatment, and, given these special considerations, whether the assessments were evenly distributed over the county.

In the regression, the estate's tenant-in-chief was indicated by 10 binary variables (the ith, $i = 1\ldots10$, taking the value 1, if the ith largest tenant-in-chief held the estate; 0, otherwise; the intercept measuring the effect when none of the 10 largest tenants-in-chief held the estate), and the hundred location by 36 binary variables (with the intercept measuring the location effect of one hundred).

Size was measured by the single best indicator of the economic size of an estate, the estate's annual value. An index of whether production was mainly arable or grazing is given by the arable/livestock ratio, defined as the number of ploughteams on the estate divided by the total acreage of woodland, pasture and meadowland. Finally, tenure was measured by a binary variable taking the value 1, if the estate was held in demesne; 0, otherwise.

The results show that both the tenant-in-chief and hundred effects remain significant when other factors are allowed to vary in the multiple regression. Tenancy, whether an estate was held in demesne (and worked by the tenant-in-chief) or run by a tenant, was a significant factor at the five (and three) but not one percent level. Estates held in demesne were, on average, more favourably treated, having a BTI 0.61 greater than those that were sub or mesne-tenancies. Economic size (measured by the annual value of the estate) and the variable measuring the mix of arable and grazing griculture on an estate were not significant correlates.

DISCUSSION

Comparing taxation in Wiltshire with Essex

The results of the Wiltshire tax analysis can be compared with those of the earlier analysis of taxation in Essex (McDonald, 2002). The Wiltshire data are recorded in Great Domesday and are less detailed than the Essex entries that are listed in Little Domesday. In particular, livestock information is available for Essex but not Wiltshire.[7] There are other county differences. Arable farming was generally more important in eastern England (where Essex is located) than south-west England (where Wiltshire is situated), although in Essex large numbers of sheep were grazed on the extensive marshlands and their wool exported to the Continent. Also, the estate size distribution varied as between the counties. Compared with Wiltshire, Essex contained a few very large lay estates and many quite small holdings. There was much less variation in the size of Wiltshire estates.

For Wiltshire, the relationship between tax assessments and net income (annual value) is stronger (the coefficient of determination allowing for degrees of freedom is 0.75 for Wiltshire lay estates and 0.56 for Essex when the relationship is estimated in log-linear form) and for most estates the average tax rate is higher. Largely as a consequence of the stronger capacity to pay relationship for Wiltshire, BTI values tend to be lower.[8]

In the regressions of BTI on factors associated with taxation, there are some similarities between the county results and some differences (Table 2). For both, there appears to have been differential treatment of tenants-in-chief, even after other factors are controlled for.

[6] The dependent variable BTI data are restricted to lie in the interval of the real line on or above one. In McDonald (2009a), appropriate regression procedures when the dependent variable data are normalised and restricted in value are described. The simplest is least squares with standard errors calculated using White's (1980) heteroskedastic-consistent method.

[7] Wiltshire entries contain information on ploughlands. The interpretation of ploughlands is discussed in Harvey (1975, p.187) and McDonald and Snooks (1986, p.67). A minor problem of interpretation is whether or not mill renders are included in the estate's annual value. Regression evidence indicates that, because the renders are relatively small, whether they are included or not has little effect on estimated relationships, see McDonald and Snooks (1986, p. 89-90).

[8] The estimated tax relationships indicate that at all net income levels, on average, Wiltshire estates paid a higher tax. On average, for a Wiltshire estate a one percent increase in net income was associated with a 0.85 percent increase in assessment. For an Essex estate the increase was 0.71 percent. The first three quartiles of the BTI distributions were 1.5, 2.0 and 2.6, for Wiltshire estates, and 1.9, 3.1 and 4.7, for Essex estates.

Table 2. Least squres regressions of BTI on estate characteristics. Wiltshire and Essex lay estates, 1086 (heteroskedastic-consistent p-values).

Variables	Wiltshire p - values	Essex p - values
Tenant-in-chief	0.000**	0.017*
Hundred	0.000**	0.000**
Size (annual value)	0.098	0.000**
Arable/livestock mix	0.805	0.255
Tenure	0.023*	0.028*
Urban centre effect	-	0.002**
Number of observations	324	574
$\bar{R}^2$	0.17	0.17

Notes: * indicates significant at the five percent and ** significant at the one percent level.

Similarly, the hundred effect is highly significant, indicating that there was variation in tax treatment within the counties, across the local government areas. For both counties, beneficial treatment was not related to the arable/livestock mix of estate production.[9]

Two differences are apparent. First, in Essex the economic size of the estate was a factor affecting tax treatment. Smaller estates were treated more favourably, but no such association was found for Wiltshire. Secondly, for both counties, the BTI varied significantly with the tenure arrangement of the estate, but, for Wiltshire, estates worked by the tenant-in-chief were favoured above those worked by sub-tenants and for Essex the reverse was true.

Conclusion

The analysis of Domesday taxation on lay estates in Wiltshire and Essex strongly suggests that capacity of estates to pay the tax was a major factor determining the assessment – but other factors was also important. The capacity to pay relationship was stronger in Wiltshire than Essex and, as a consequence, the Wiltshire BTI values (which measure beneficial tax treatment received by estates) tended to be lower.

For both counties, some tenants-in-chief received significantly more favourable treatment. In Essex there was some evidence that the less wealthy were favoured because the regression evidence indicates that, on average, tenants-in-chief with fewer estates in the county, smaller estates, and sub-tenants, received lower tax assessments. This was not the case in Wiltshire. There, on average, estates run by sub-tenants received higher assessments, and there is no evidence that smaller estates or tenants-in-chief with fewer estates received preferential assessments. For both counties there was a statistically significant hundred assessment differential.

This suggests that administrative factors affected tax assessments, maybe because assessments were made at different times in the hundreds, or with slightly more rigor in some hundreds than others. The results also indicate different tax rates across the two counties. There is little evidence that particular estate activities were granted tax concessions. In particular, the tax system did not favour arable activity over animal husbandry or vice versa.

The details of the levying of the geld are largely lost in time, but this study shows that much can be gleaned from information contained in Domesday book. Some understanding of the tax system is emerging, but many issues remain unresolved.

ACKNOWLEDGEMENTS

The author would like to thank Eva Aker and Beverley Vickers for their excellent research assistance, colleagues and seminar participants for their comments and The Australian Research Council and the Flinders University for financial support.

[9] A variable measuring proximity to an urban centre was also entered as an explanatory variable in the Essex regression. For Essex, there were just two major urban centres, Colchester and Maldon, so it was relatively easy to locate estates close to an urban centre. In Wiltshire, there were many more boroughs (10), the situation is much more complex and hence the variable was not constructed. The proximity to an urban centre variable was significant in the Essex regression. The arable/livestock variable was also defined differently in the Essex regression. It was defined as livestock listed on the estate less cattle and beasts (which were associated with ploughing) divided by the number of ploughteams on the estate. Domesday Book does not list livestock numbers for Wiltshire estates.

REFERENCES

Ballard A (1906). The Domesday Inquest. Methuen, London. 3Britnell RH , Campbell BMS (ed) (1995). A Commercialising Economy: England 1086 to c. 1300. Manchester University Press, Manchester.
Brown RA (1984). The Normans. Boydell Press, Woodbridge.
Clanchy MT (1983). England and its Rulers, 1066-1272. Fontana, Glasgow.
Darby HC (1952). The Domesday Geography of Eastern England, reprinted 1971. Cambridge University Press, Cambridge.
Darby HC (1977). Domesday England, reprinted 1979. Cambridge University Press, Cambridge.
Galbraith VH (1961). The Making of Domesday Book. Clarendon Press, Oxford.
Godfrey A, Hooper K (1996). Accountability and Decision-making in Feudal England: Domesday Book Revisited. Acc. Hist., 1: 35-54.
Hallam HE (1981). Rural England 1066-1348. Fontana, Brighton.
Harvey SPJ (1975). Domesday Book and Anglo-Norman Governance. Transac. Royal Hist. Soc., 25: 175-193.
Hollister CW (1965). The Military Organisation of Norman England. Clarendon Press, Oxford.
Lennard R (1959). Rural England 1086-1135: A Study of Social and Agrarian Conditions. Clarendon Press, Oxford.
Loyn R (1962). Anglo-Saxon England and the Norman Conquest, reprinted 1981, Longman, London.
Loyn R (1965). The Norman Conquest. Hillary House, London.
Loyn R (1983). The Governance of Anglo-Saxon England, 500-1087. Edward Arnold, London.
Maitland FW (1897). Domesday Book and Beyond, reprinted 1921, Cambridge University Press, Cambridge.
McDonald J (1997). Manorial Efficiency in Domesday England, J. Prod. Anal., 8: 199-213.
McDonald J (1998). Production Efficiency in Domesday England. Routledge, London.
McDonald J (2000). Domesday Economy: An Analysis of the English Economy Early in the Second Millennium. Nat. Inst. Econ. Rev., 172: 105-114.
McDonald J (2002). Tax Fairness in Eleventh Century England. Account. Hist. J., 29: 173-193.
McDonald J (2005). Using William the Conqueror's Accounting Record to Assess Manorial Efficiency. Account. Hist., 10: 125-145.
McDonald J (2009a). Using Least Squares and Tobit in Second Stage DEA Efficiency Analyses. Eur. J. Operat. Res., 197: 792-798.
McDonald J (2009b). Was Tax Policy After the Norman Conquest Determined by Ability to Pay? – Using Regression and Data Envelopment Analysis to Find the Answer. Br. Tax Rev. 3: 319-324.
McDonald J (2010). Efficiency in the Domesday Economy, 1086: Evidence from Wiltshire Estates. Appl. Econ., 42: 3231-3240.
McDonald J and Snooks GD (1985a). Were the Tax Assessments of Domesday England Artificial? The Case of Essex. Econ. Hist. Rev., 38: 353-373.
McDonald J and Snooks GD (1985b). The Determinants of Manorial Income in Domesday England: Evidence from Essex. J. Econ. Hist., 45: 541-556.
McDonald J and Snooks GD (1985c). Statistical Analysis of Domesday Book (1086), J. Royal Stat. Soc. series A, 148: 147-160.
McDonald J and Snooks GD (1986). Domesday Economy: A New Approach to Anglo-Norman History. Clarendon Press, Oxford.
McDonald J and Snooks GD (1987a). The Suitability of Domesday Book for Cliometric Analysis. Econ. Hist. Rev., 40: 252-261.
McDonald J and Snooks GD (1987b) The Economics of Domesday England, in Domesday Book Studies, A. Williams (ed.), Alecto Historical Editions, London.
McDonald J and Snooks GD (2003). Domesday Economy, Oxford Scholarship Online Edition, Oxford University Press, Oxford.
Miller E, Hatcher J (1978). Medieval England: Rural Society and Economic Change 1086-1348. Longman, London.
Morris J (1975). Domesday Book: A Survey of the Counties of England. Phillimore, Chichester.
Oldroyd D (1997). Accounting in Anglo-Saxon England: Context and Evidence. Acc. Hist., 2: 7-34.
Postan MM (1966). Medieval Agrarian Society in its Prime. The Cambridge Economic History of Europe, Vol. 1, Postan MM (ed.). Cambridge University Press, Cambridge.
Postan MM (1972). The Medieval Economy and Society: An Economic History of Britain in the Middle Ages. Weidenfeld and Nicolson, London.
Round JH (1895). Feudal England: Historical Studies on the Eleventh and Twelfth Centuries, reprinted 1964. Allen & Unwin, London.
Round JH (1903). Essex Survey, in VCH Essex, Vol.1, reprinted 1977. Dawson, London.
Stenton DM (1951). English Society in the Early Middle Ages, reprinted 1983. Penguin, Harmonsworth.
Victoria County History (1900). Oxford University Press, London.
White H (1980). A Heteroskedasticity-Consistent Covariance Matrix Estimator and a Direct Test for Heteroskedasticity. Econometrica. 48: 817-838.
Williams A (ed) (1987). Domesday Book Studies. Alecto Historical Editions, London.
Williams A, Martin BH (ed) (2003). Domesday Book: A Complete Translation. Alecto Historical Editions, London.

14

Investigation of the effective factors in collection of occupation tax in Iran

Seyed Mohammad Mousavi Shahroudy

Shahrood University of Technology, Iran. E-mail: mosavi.shams@gmail.com.

Occupation tax is assumed as one of the significant sources of tax collection for the revenue sources of the government. Due to this fact, this research attempts to investigate the effective factors in the collection of the occupation tax according to the auditors as well as the taxpayers of Iran, and so identify the weak points as well as the potentialities of this field of activity, and also to help the tax system to be more efficient. It should be mentioned here that the most important factors which are investigated in this study include the computerization of the tax system, self expression program, tax laws, the field of study of the auditors, the trust of the taxpayers and auditors for each other, and tax allocation per capita (Nakhjiri, 2000). In this regard, the most fundamental objective of this study is to identify and investigate the ideas and viewpoints of the taxpayers and auditors on the issues and factors that were described earlier.

Key words: Self expression program, tax allocation per capita, allocation officers.

INTRODUCTION

The tax system as a subsystem of the executive system includes components such as human resources (managers and other employees), organization, institutions, processes and procedures, regulations, as well as facilities and resources in an organic and reciprocal relation which guides the society towards its objectives and ideals. A thorough understanding of the tax system and the principles (norms) dominating that system, as well as the contextual and internal conditions of the system can help us explain its procedural objectives and strategies as and can also help us regulate executive programs and would provide the grounds for the improvement of the tax system (Nakhjiri, 2000). Today, due to the particular internal situation, as well as the international conditions of the Islamic Republic of Iran, the need for transforming the tax system of the country is felt more than ever and it is essential to regard it as one of the most essential programs of the development of the country, considering the role an appropriate and efficient tax system can play in executing the development plans.

An analysis of this issue and the outcomes of the first and second development program indicates that in order to provide the grounds for coming to a comparison and the public trust in the management of the economic situation, as well as the financial policies at a macro level, the government needs to substantially revise its own view on the management and the issues and problems of the economical system and to clarify on its main advantages and disadvantages as well as the threats and opportunities of the domestic and international context. During the last decade, a special emphasis has been put on the financial policies appropriate for the economical development in the developing countries and among these, the attentions have been directed towards the tax policies as the main portion of the financial policies. In addition to the improvement of the tax revenues which can be obtained through an effective administration of taxation, another factor, which can strengthen the tax administration, is the inclination toward the income tax with an increasing rate, and the reasons for that can be investigated in the tax equity and the concept of the affordability as well as the increase of the income with an economical perception. If the tax auditors' field of study in tax assignment and determination; administration is not properly addressed in the tax policies, that is the tax assignment with regard to their results and consequences, the desired results can not be achieved; and the reception of new taxes as the compensation for the weaknesses and the failure in the existing tax administration would distort the equity of the tax system.

So, maintaining a dynamic tax system in the process of economical improvement is considered as a significant factor in the elimination of wealth and redistribution of the revenues and finally directing the financial courses towards the required investments in the society (Arab, 1999). With the progress and improvement of culture, science and technology as well as the development of human societies in this age, the responsibilities of the government have also been developed and duties such as providing the healthcare, education, housing and welfare providing have also been added to them, and as a result tax collection ways have also been evolved, so that the developed countries are now equipped with an appropriate and advanced tax system which not only is able to establish the social justice it can also guarantee all essential economical and social objectives (Hamidi, 1999).

With regard to the government's financial policies which are based on the gradual departure of the economical reliance of the country on the economical monopoly, taxation can be regarded as one of the main revenue sources of the country which can provide a great portion of the government's expenditure. On the other hand, it is particularly essential for the tax policymakers to look for a sound and efficient tax system which can play an active role in the development and activation of several sectors of the society. Hence, the tax system's efficiency can be improved through the investigation and analysis of the effective factors in the tax collection; and on the other hand, this tax system can be made an effective system through the implementation of a sound management and an efficient and optimized utilization (Arman, 2000) of the sources on the other hand so the purposes of this study include:

1) The investigation and analysis of the ideas and opinions of the auditors and taxpayers on the tax penalties and punishments;
2) The investigation and analysis of the ideas and opinions of the auditors and taxpayers on the taxpayers' self-expression plan;
3) The investigation and analysis of the ideas and opinions of the auditors and taxpayers on the tax allocation per capita.
4) The investigation and analysis of the ideas and opinions of the auditors and taxpayers on the computerization of the tax system;
5) The investigation and analysis of the ideas and opinions of the auditors and taxpayers on the role of the
6) The investigation and analysis of the ideas and opinions of the auditors and taxpayers on the tax law.

The research questions are:

1) Do tax penalties influence the tax collection?
2) Would the taxpayers' self-expression plan result in the establishment of tax equity?
3) Is the per capita allocation of taxes by the auditors an appropriate basis for tax assignment?
4) Does computerization of the tax system facilitate the taxation process?
5) Does the auditors' field of study influence the tax assignment?
6) Is the current tax law responsive to the requirements in the taxation affairs?

METHODOLOGY

The purpose of choosing a research method is that the researcher defines what method and approach he/she takes in order to enable him/her come to the possible answer(s) as soon, fast and economical as possible (Naderi and Seif, 1999).The present study is a descriptive research and its purpose is to describe the properties of a subject matter in an exact, true and orderly manner. The descriptive data are usually collected through questionnaires, interviews with the experienced people, observation of the events, or the documentary analysis. In other word, in descriptive surveys, the researcher focuses on the investigation and definition of the ongoing situations and sets to measure what exists and not why it exists. A survey is implemented to reveal the ideas, perceptions and preferences of the individuals. The selected universe for this study included two groups of:

(A) The society of the auditors; which included all job evaluators who were employed in the western district of Tehran (West Tax Administration); totally 250 job evaluators were determined.
(B) Taxpayers society; which included all taxpayers working in the western district of Tehran.

A random sampling was chosen in this study for the sampling as well as the members. The concept of a simplified random sampling includes the sampling in which all components of the society have enjoyed an equal chance for being selected. In this study, the sample size was estimated by Kuchran formula through the consideration of several factors and the preliminary study of the statistical universe and adopting an appropriate potential accuracy and the reliance of 95%. The instruments used for the data collection in this study include questionnaire and library. The questionnaires applied which is prepared in concordance with the purposes of the study include a questionnaire with 20 closed questions for the auditors and another questionnaire for the taxpayers with 18 closed questions. The 5-graded scale of Likert was applied for the measurement of the frequencies.

To gather the information needed for the review of the literature and the history of the related studies, a library research was used through the application of computerized research, domestic and foreign researches related to the subject of this study. The administration and distribution of the questionnaires was carried out by going to the workplaces of the auditors and handing over the questionnaires to them. The presence of the researcher at the time of the distribution and completion of the questionnaires made it possible to clarify on the original subject of the study, its purposes and significance and the way of answering the questions. In this regard, due to the existence of 19 general auditors in the western districts of Tehran, the taxpayers' questionnaires was also handed to the auditors of the district and they were asked to present them to those occupation taxpayers who had a longer years of record and are much more aware of the issues and then to receive the questionnaires after being completed and return them to the researcher.

Accordingly, out of 157 questionnaires presented to the auditors, 150 were collected after leaving out the unfinished and incomplete questionnaires. The same number was gathered for the taxpayers.

The statistical analysis in this study was carried out at two descriptive and deductive levels. At the descriptive level, the frequency, percentage, average mean and standard deviation were used, and at the deductive level, the statistical tests were used as follows, as fits the basic data and assumptions:

a) Binomial test;
b) Chi Square test (x^2);
c) Mam-Whitney U test.

The processing tools for the data included the related softwares.

Review of literature

Prior to the twentieth century and the existence of the liberal thoughts (physiocrats and classics), the governments did not directly intervene with the economic affairs and their responsibilities of the governments only included the maintenance of the external and internal security and order and the establishment of the social justice. The scientists of economy following the school of the physiocrats and the classics believed in the no-interference in economical affairs from the part of the government. The foundations of the Classic school were established on the freedom in business, and through the acceptance of this principle the classics believed that the best governments are those who rule less. They believed that the force of competition, profit seeking, and the freedom of business would automatically lead the production and the distribution of the goods and services towards the complete balance and employment of the production agents. Unlike the physiocrats who believed in a natural system for the fulfillment of the social interests, the classic folk believed in following the individual and personal interests among the social interests.

With regard to the tragic experiences of the first half of the twentieth century and the ideas of the socialists and the modern scholars of the field of economy, such as Kines, on the inability of the capitalist system of economy in guaranteeing the highest level of economic and social welfare for the society, public finance along with the duties of the government and its significance as a leader for economy and the provision of welfare became so important for all people. The policy makers and economists spent many years to regulate and establish some principles for steering the financial policies. Colbert, one of the French politicians stated:

"the art of taxation is the same as the art of plucking a goose, that is to get the highest possible amount of feathers with the least amount of cries".

It should always be focused on how to assign a tax system, so that the economic efficiency would improve and the fair distribution of the revenues would be progressed. Generally speaking, a tax is often called a fair tax when the same tax is received from the people with the same affordability; and an efficient tax system is the one that its expenditures are at the minimum level. Pitro Very says:

"it should be borne in mind that it is the people who tolerate the tax burden".

In some tax laws, the institutions and companies are considered as people. But this is not true. According to the economists, people are the shareholders, workers, the lessor, and the consumer who bear the tax burden and a company cannot; and when the politicians say that "organizations should pay their share of the tax equity" it is not clear what they mean. A nation might be directed towards a decline or downfall in two ways based on the way it administers its taxes; the first happens when the level of taxes exceeds the affordability of the nation and does not conform to the public wealth, and the second occurs when the amount of the taxes conforms to the total affordability of the nation; however, it is equally and fairly distributed among the nation. The traditional analysis of the tax systems has revealed many principles about taxation.

The taxes should enjoy both horizontal and vertical equity, should be impartial to the economical incentives, and be simple in administration of the affairs. One of the men who were truly after the establishment of a tax system with a definite horizontal equity was named Simon. He believed that the people with an equal level of income should pay an equal amount of money and at the same time should be ranked based on the principles of the vertical equity. Such a tax system required leaving out the other classes of taxes and only focusing on income taxes. Nicolas Caldor, the professor in Cambridge University strongly supports expenditure tax or consumption tax. He believes that it is consumption, and not the income that is to be considered as the basis and source for tax assignment, and that part of the income which is not consumed is added to the national wealth as a saving and would increase the total productive capacity. Jesus Honmer believes that taxes are the price for civilization; however the concern here is that who is to pay the price.

During the last years, the public finance economists have entered some particular guidelines into the principles of the welfare economy and have drawn out the criteria for an appropriate tax system. In this study, attempt has been made to investigate and analyze the problems which have been turned into real barriers for tax collection in the area of the western districts of Tehran; since the issues and concerns of the tax system are of the same nature, one can claim that the recognition of these factors in the western part of Tehran can be generalized to the whole tax system of the country, though it seems that the adjustment of some problems and issues is out of the strength and power of the officials and authorities of the western districts of Tehran and requires the consideration of the senior economic and political officials.

DISCUSSION

The results obtained from this study can be expressed as follows:

1) The results achieved on the influence of the tax punishments on the tax collection indicates that 70% of the taxpayers do not assume the punishments and fines as a factor for hasting for the payment of their taxes; and more interestingly, 76% of the tax auditors had the same opinion about the influence of the fines in the tax collection. Also, the ineffectiveness of the tax fines in the acceptance and obedience of the taxpayers was confirmed both by the taxpayers and the auditors and there was an agreement between both groups in this regard (taxpayers 79%, auditors 78%). Therefore, it can be accepted that fines and punishments are not appropriate strategies for the tax collection and the tax system has investigated the reasons for its inefficiency.

On the other hand, according to the analyses made, it was revealed that 70% of the taxpayers consider the tax incentives as an important factor in timely payment of their own taxes, while 74% of the auditors did not believe tax incentives to be appropriate tools for receiving the moneys which should be paid to the government. This distinction in the thoughts of these two groups is an indicator of a wide gap in the points of view of the auditors and the taxpayers.

2) The studies carried out showed that more than 62% of the taxpayers assume the self-expression plan, as an effective program in the collection of the taxes and nearly 53% of them have counted this plan as a positive factor for the establishment of a successful tax equity, while the belief in this plan as a tool for speeding up the tax collection process and establishment of the tax equity was 39.3 and 16.6%, respectively. So, it can be said that the perspective of both groups differed in this case and this means that the auditors did not believe in the self-expression plan as an effective tool for the establishment of tax equity and the acceleration of the tax collection process, but the tax payers have implicitly agreed with this plan. If we compare this result with the answers given to the question asked from both groups of taxpayers and auditors, that reads: "to what extent the income tax return of the taxpayers is established on documented facts?", then we would notice that 97% of the auditors consider the declarations of the taxpayers as unreal; hence, it can be said that this program has not been so much successful as an appropriate basis for the assignment and collection of taxes and until a sound bilateral relation and confidence is not formed between the auditors, as the agents of the tax organization, and the taxpayers, this plan should not be expected to have its own status in the tax system; if we are going to compare this plan with a country like U.S., we would see that in the U.S. more than 97% of the taxpayers deliver their income tax return timely to the tax administration, and this not only accelerates the collection procedure, but also reduces the expenditures both for the tax organization and for the directors.

3) The results about the per capita allocation of the taxes by the auditors shows that none of the two groups of the taxpayers and the auditors have confidence or belief in per capita allocation of taxes; in other word, approximately 80% of the taxpayers do not consider the per capita allocation of taxes as a proper criterion for the evaluation of the incomes subject to taxes, and nearly the same number of the taxpayers did not assume per capita allocation of taxes as an effective factor in establishing the tax equity. The opinion of the auditors about the per capita allocation of taxes and its conformity to the realities has been about 8.7% and about its effectiveness for the establishment of the tax equity has been 13.3%.

4) Concerning the results about the computerization of the job tax system, it was revealed that more than 70% of the taxpayers and auditors believed that computerization would accelerate the taxation affairs; however, it should be mentioned that a comprehensive information system for taxation which ensures the determination of the way of preparing and coordinating the databases, information technology and notification, has not been clearly defined and some measures which have been taken by the tax organization in a non-concentrated manner in each of the aforementioned areas do not enjoy the required coordination and overlapping and in some cases have been carried out in a parallel, repetitive, or even unnecessary manner.

5) About the tax laws, it was revealed that 78% of the taxpayers did not assume the tax laws to be sufficient for the needs and requirements of the tax system, and about 85% of them believed that the regulations in force are not clearly and explicitly defined. The opinion of the auditors about the insufficiency of the regulations for the requirements of the tax system was about 89% and about the vagueness of the regulations was about 92%. So, both groups believed that the regulations were not conforming to the requirements of the tax system both in their content and in their structure, and interestingly, this belief was stronger among the auditors than the taxpayers.

Suggestions of the research

1) Creating information services centers for training the taxpayers and familiarizing them with their duties;
2) Accelerating the creation and utilization of the comprehensive information services system for taxation;
3) Reformation of the methods and procedures for the taxation affairs;
4) Providing the conformity between the tax laws and regulations;
5) Reformation of the welfare affairs;
6) Reformation of the payment, wages and rewards system for the auditors;
7) Reformation of the appointment and promotion of the directors;
8) Reformation of the employment and selections.

LIMITATIONS OF THE STUDY

1) One of the most basic limitations in this study, other than the fact that it was a survey study, was that the tax districts were heterogeneous with regard to the kind of jobs in that geographical area. Even though we tried to deliver the questionnaires to the most experienced auditors and taxpayers who were much more aware of the issues of the day; however, the lack of a comprehensive planning system and its required essential requisites, as well as the lack of clear theoretical principles and skilled expertise in the field of taxation and the lack of protective information and researches, has inevitably resulted in some shortages in the theoretical dimensions of the concepts, drawing inferences from the realities and the analyses as well as the results and conclusions.

2) Pessimistic beliefs on the research performance at all organizational levels and among the taxpayers, and their indifference to the questionnaires and the results of the study.

3) Lack of related studies in the western districts of

Tehran and lack of reliable libraries for this field of study. 4) Doubt of some taxpayers in this fact, that answering these questions would not affect their job performances.

REFERENCES

Arab M (1999). IBFD Tax Research Institute. A. Tax J. issue, 28: 10.
Arman B, Moazen GM, Amir AA (2000). Economic Novelties. 97: 27.
Hamidi M (1999). Analysis of the Job Incomes during the second Economic Development Program, M.A. thesis, Faculty of Economic Affairs Publications: Tehran.
IBFD Tax Research Institute (2000). Translated by Arab Mazar, A. Tax J. Issue., 28: 10.
Naderi E, Seif NM (1999). Research Methodology and the Way of Its Assessment in Humanities, 16th Ed., Badr Publications: Tehran.
Nakhjiri S (2000). Effective Factors in the Success of the Occupation Tax Collection Based on the Opinions of Auditors and Taxpayers of Ardebil, M.A. Thesis, Governmental Management Training Center, P. 9.

The perception of ethics in auditing profession in Nigeria

Semiu Babatunde ADEYEMI[1]* and Temitope Olamide, FAGBEMI[2]

[1]Department of Accounting, University of Lagos, Lagos, Nigeria.
[2]Department of Accounting and Finance, University of Ilorin, Ilorin, Kwara State, Nigeria.

The purpose of the study is to provide evidence on ethics, legitimacy of auditing profession and the future outlook of the profession in Nigeria by obtaining responses from external auditors, industry and academic accountants as well as auditing students. In spite of the existence of research pointing to the link between corporate scandal and loss of public confidence, there is paucity of research focused on the future of the profession in the midst of these challenges in Nigeria. Using a survey design, the questions that were raised in the study were tested with the use of statistical tools for population means and level of significance tests. In essence, analysis of variance was carried out on the responses of the groups of respondents which were surveyed. Findings from the study show that there is no significant difference in the perception of respondent groups on the need for auditors to abide by high ethical standard and the need to shape the views of new entrants to the profession. However, respondents have different perception on the decline of core values which attracted them to the profession. The study suggests that there is the need for the profession to gear its effort towards shaping the views of new entrants to the profession in Nigeria, ensure adherence and enforcement of high ethical standard. Regulation of the profession should be targeted towards restoring the confidence of users of financial statements in financial reporting in Nigeria.

Key words: Auditing profession, ethics, public confidence, legitimacy, Nigeria.

INTRODUCTION

Background to the study

It is widely acknowledged that the accounting profession is an important facet of our society (Wyatt, 2004). Accounting emerged from the society. Hines (1988) stated that accounting is socially constructed and socially constructing. This implies that accounting influences society and accounting is influenced by society. The study noted that the public rightfully expects the accounting profession to be practical, intellectual and to have regard for the public. Cogan (1953) stated that these characteristics have been essential in defining any profession and according to Goode (1957) upholding these characteristics is how the accounting profession has been expected to serve the public interest. It becomes imperative that accounting practitioners demonstrate the attributes of objectivity and integrity and keep abreast of developments that have impact on the profession.

In the last decade, studies have shown that the auditing profession has had to deal with a lot of challenges than it has done in its lengthy history which spans over one hundred years (Smith, 2002; Mactosh et al., 2010). Failures of businesses in which deficiencies of financial reporting and corporate disclosure have figured prominently are not new phenomena. This period has

*Corresponding author. E-mail: sbaadeyemi@yahoo.co.uk.

Abbreviations: IFAC, International Federation of Accountants; **EA,** external auditors; **IA,** industry accountants; **AA,** accounting educators; **AS,** accounting students; **PCAOB,** Public Company Accounting Oversight Board; **SEC,** securities and exchange commission; **ANOVA,** analysis of variance.

been characterized by series of business failures, ethical negligence and accounting scandals both in developed economies and developing economies. Publicized cases of the recent past, such as Satyam, Enron, WorldCom, Global Crossing, Adelphia Communications, HIH, Tyco, and Vivendi, Royal Ahold and HealthSouth together with a host of companies from Nigeria (such as, Cadbury and NAMPAK), have drawn increasing attention to the auditing profession. This has had a negative and cumulative impact on the way informed opinion views financial reporting and the auditing profession. There has been great apprehension regarding the fairness of the operation of a market system where shareholders, employees in general, and pensioners have lost large sums, while those running companies, and seen as responsible for those losses, have enriched themselves as the businesses collapsed. Accountants and particularly auditors, in economies of the world such as the United States of America (USA), United Kingdom (UK), and India have all been experiencing these challenges which question the trustworthiness and integrity of the profession (Economist, 2002). This, according to Hale et al., (2005), has been eroding the confidence that the public repose on the auditing profession.

Regulatory initiatives have been put in place in developed economies to deal with the poignant erosion of ethical standards in corporate governance, financial reporting and auditing. For example, in the United States of America, the Sarbanes Oxley Act was passed into law in 2002. The International Federation of Accountants (IFAC) has also supported the formulation of auditing guidelines to enhance the reliability of corporate financial statements. The International Accounting Standards Board has consistently stressed the need for global adoption of the International Financial Reporting Standards. However, in developing economies, including Nigeria, there has been little or no efforts at positively addressing the challenges posed by non-adherence to corporate governance principles and ethical guidelines. For example, Nigeria is yet to review its Companies and Allied Matters Act 1990 (as amended) which has become more or less anachronistic in view of dynamic corporate events, globalization and the impact of information technology. Pragmatic solutions should normally be research-driven. Bakre (2007) reported that investors in Nigeria have lost several billions of dollars through the collusion of accountants and external auditors with companies' management and directors to falsify and deliberately overstate companies' accounts.

Adelaja (2009) in evaluating the perception of auditor independence in Nigeria concludes that all efforts must be made to assist the auditing profession to remain afloat on matters of ethics and independence. It is, however, in doubt if Nigerian related research efforts are adequate to fully address the challenges of enforcing ethical guidelines in financial reporting and auditing. It is also not clear whether the stakeholders are having the right perspectives about the influence of ethics on auditing which is a primary prerequisite for an enduring corporate governance culture in the country. This area remains evergreen to accounting research and therefore forms the primary focus of this study.

Statement of the problem

The various corporate collapses have led to increased scrutiny of deficiencies in the financial reporting process and corporate disclosure requirements of corporate organizations. This has had a negative and cumulative impact on the perceived credibility of financial reporting. This concern is now at the forefront of public debate about the accounting profession and its effectiveness (IFAC, 2003). There has been a decline in reporting credibility across capital markets worldwide, with the scale of the problem partly attributable to the unprecedented level of share prices in many markets.

In spite of the existence of research pointing to the link between corporate scandal and loss of public confidence, there is paucity of research focused on the future of the profession in the midst of these challenges. Steering and Working Committees on Accounting (2004) which examined how public confidence in financial reporting can be restored, noted that accounting and auditing systems and policy in the management process, requires a set of best practices for governance and financial reporting.

Bloom and Myring (2008) study, which examined the future of the auditing profession from the perspective of the employment status of future accountants, provided a significant contribution in this area. Dennis (2006) also provided empirical evidence on the need to understand the best and brightest future accountants. The study noted that succession plans must be developed if employees are to have successful career progress. There must be a transfer of knowledge from management to staff. However, these studies were focused on the training, recruitment and retention of good accountants for the auditing profession. The studies were not linked at all with corporate collapse or auditors' ethical conduct. Therefore, a research focusing on ethics and the impact of corporate scandals on the future outlook of auditing profession is overdue.

Aim and objectives of the study

The aim of this study is to provide information that may help improve the auditing profession in Nigeria from the perspectives of ethics. In order to achieve this aim, the research set out to:

i) Investigate the credibility of the auditing profession;

ii) Investigate the implication of accounting scandals on the auditing profession; and
iii) Examine whether any significant relationship exists among the perceptions of the respondent groups.

Research questions

This research attempted to provide answers to the following questions:

i) Is the auditing profession performing up to the expectation of the public in Nigeria?
ii) Has the response of the profession to contemporary challenges facing the auditing profession been proactive and adequate in restoring public confidence?
iii) Is the auditing profession still attractive to future professionals owing to ethical violations?
iv) Do respondents' perceptions about corporate scandal and the impact on auditing profession differ?

Research hypotheses

The hypotheses stated in the null form were tested in order to provide answers to the research questions mentioned above:

H_{01}: There is no significant difference in the perception of respondent groups regarding belief in the integrity of the auditing profession.
H_{02}: There is no significant difference in the perception of respondent groups on the need to restore public confidence in the auditing profession.
H_{03}: There is no significant difference in the perception of respondent groups on the effects of accounting scandals on the auditing profession.

Significance of the study

The auditing profession plays a significant role in making information available for decision making in the capital market (Healy, 2005). Therefore, this research is expected to be of benefit to financial reporting and auditing stakeholders in the Nigerian economy because accounting and indeed auditing play a fundamental role in the activities of a national economy.

This study is expected to reveal the outlook for the future of the auditing profession in Nigeria in relation to ethics from the perspectives of stakeholders. This is important because the IFAC places a lot of importance on the image of the profession. Finally, the research work is also expected to be of benefit to researchers and students of accounting since this is a profession that operates in a dynamic society. The outcome of the study will provide a reference point for future researchers and a blue-print for policy makers.

Scope of the study

This study is premised on the current state of the auditing profession, especially in Nigeria, and the future outlook in relation to the improvement of public confidence in the profession. Therefore, perceptions of selected stakeholders are sought in providing answers to the problems and questions that have been raised in this research work. The focus of the research in terms of study groups includes public accountants (external auditors - EA), industry accountants (IA), accounting educators (AA), and accounting students (who are believed to be the future practitioners - AS) in Lagos State, Nigeria. Responses from the subject groups were analysed to reveal how optimistic or pessimistic the stakeholders were on the future outlook of the auditing profession in Nigeria.

LITERATURE REVIEW

An overview of the attributes of a profession

Harvey (2009) described a profession as a group of people in a learned occupation, the members of which agree to abide by specified rules of conduct when practising the profession. It is further described by Wikipedia as a vocation founded upon specialized educational training, the purpose of which is to supply disinterested counsel and services to others, for a direct and definite compensation, wholly apart from expectation of other business gain. According to the Oxford English Dictionary (1989) and Perks (1993), professions involve the application of specialised knowledge of a subject, field, or science to fee-paying clientele. Southern Illinois University (2004) also noted that it is obvious that professional activity involves systematic knowledge and proficiency. In essence, professions are distinguished from other occupations represented by trade groups due to their level of legal recognition. The accounting profession in Nigeria is enjoying this status through the Institute of Chartered Accountants of Nigeria.

Boone (2001) opined that professions are based on scientific and philosophical facts acquired through scholarly endeavour. Individuals who enter a profession do so for reasons that distinguish them from other work or vocations. They understand that their work renders a unique public service with a scientific or philosophical basis and/or body of knowledge that requires an extended period of academic and hands-on preparation. Professions are also based on specialized skills necessary for the professional to perform the public service. This view is also consistent with the Australian Council of Professions (2004), Burbules and Densmore (1991) and Pratte and Rury (1991) viewed profession as a disciplined group of individuals who adhere to ethical standards.

It is inherent in the definitions of a profession that a code of ethics governs the activities of each profession. Such codes require behaviour and practice beyond the personal moral obligations of an individual. This explains the reason why the public has a level of expectation from the auditing profession.

Auditing as a profession

Napier and Carnegie (2007) noted that accounting has been described as an increasingly social practice rather than a technical practice as it competes with other professional groups and occupations to attract and retain talents. As a profession, auditing has come under scrutiny in many ways (Ajibolade, 2008; Adeyeye et al., 2010), particularly in eras of corporate collapse. These events lead some to question whether auditing meets the requirements of a profession.

In examining what distinguishes a profession from other occupations, West and Yee (2006) opined that occupational status is a matter of perception and is endowed by the society in which an occupational group is constituted. An aspect of the development of occupational status concerns the particular social and cultural values which abide within the society in which an occupation is situated. This high esteem arises primarily from the higher social function of their work, which is regarded as vital to society as a whole and thus of having a special and valuable nature. Abercrombie et al. (1984) suggested that a profession relies on performing services not for its own interest but for the public good. Therefore, if the interest of the public is to be served, the professional authority of accountants is justified when accounting information serves its stated purpose and functions.

It is clear from the various contributions in the literature that the auditing profession and indeed the entire accounting profession, as an occupational group, has after a while achieved an elevated level of authority over financial reporting practices that have been sourced from a coherent body of knowledge. In essence, the public ascribes the auditing profession a high social status, regard and esteem over financial information in corporate entities. Therefore, it can be said that the auditing profession evolved as a result of the social contract between it and the society.

The legitimacy of the auditing profession

Jackling and Watty (2008) opined that conferring legitimacy is not a one-off occurrence. It relies upon the concept of social contract. Matthews (1993) noted that social contract is used to define an arrangement between an organisation and members of the society. These studies considered that an organisation's survival will be threatened if society perceives that the organisation has breached its social contract. In a recent study by Deegan (2006), changing community expectations and society norms may dictate that what is considered legitimate at one specific point in time may not be considered legitimate at a future date. Therefore, the organisation's need for auditors, who represent the value system of the profession that they represent, is crucial to the maintenance of the social contract with the society.

Furthermore, there is an implicit assumption that the value system of the profession and the society are congruent. The society has an expectation that professional accountants (auditors) will work in the interest of the stakeholders by upholding the fundamental principles of professional conduct such as expertise, professional ethics, knowledge, competence and above all, integrity. According to Dellaportas and Davenport (2007), public interest is defined as "the collective well-being of people and institutions the profession serves and to protect the economic interest of third parties by facilitating an efficient economic decision making process through the provision of relevant and reliable economic data". The study concluded that professional accounting bodies in which the auditors belong are empowered with a responsibility to act on behalf of a public and to do whatever is necessary to protect and advance the interests of the public. In essence, it is expected that the auditing profession (as represented by the professional accounting bodies) recognises its responsibility to society as part of the social contract.

Where there is incongruence between the value system of the profession and the society, there is the likelihood that the social contract may be renegotiated. According to Lindblom (1994), this incongruence is referred to as "legitimacy gap". This may mean a re-assessment of the expectations of the skills and attributes that members of the auditing profession have in meeting various business challenges. Thus, this study examines the impact of these challenges on the continuous ability of the auditing profession to perform its roles on corporate financial data.

Ethics and the viability of the auditing profession

The future viability of any professional body is dependent upon its ability to continuously live up to the expectation required of it as an occupational status and its ability to attract new members. According to Theuri and Weickgenannt (2008), accounting scandals around the world have resulted in a wave of negative publicity for the auditing profession. The bankruptcies of Enron, Satyam, WorldCom, Sunbeam, and others, and the related accounting improprieties at these companies have led many in the business world (including students and professors) to question the viability of the auditing profession. The study noted that those already in the profession may be concerned about mechanisms to control damage and/or strategies to fix the problem, those who are preparing to enter the profession (for example, students), may be more concerned that the qualities that attracted them to pursue the profession may be eroding. According to The American Assembly (2005), the collapse of Arthur Andersen in 2002 created a new auditing landscape which has resulted in several mergers of audit firms. This has resulted into the emergence of only four firms perceived as being capable of serving the vast majority of United States' public companies. The current members are PricewaterhouseCoopers, Deloitte and Touche, Ernst and Young, and KPMG.

Arthur Andersen's collapse, together with the revelation of numerous accounting scandals, also created a new regulatory environment; the passage of the Sarbanes-Oxley Act of 2002; the attendant creation of the Public Company Accounting Oversight Board (PCAOB) to oversee the formerly self-regulating auditors of public companies; and the imposition of new regulations from the stock exchanges and the U.S. Securities and Exchange Commission (SEC).

These negative perceptions have been found to have effect on student enrolment for the accounting profession with a rippling effect on the number of audit trainees. According to Albrecht and Sack (2000), Ahmed et al. (1997), Tan and Laswad (2006) and Well (2005), students graduating from accounting degree programmes have been found to be declining. These studies have suggested that the reason for this decline include a negative perception of accounting, bad information about accounting, increasing academic requirements, a misunderstanding of accounting and the skills required, and narrow curricula at the high school and tertiary education level. This decline was described in these studies as being genuine. Williams (2001) noted that this decline is not likely to improve in the very near future.

The phenomenon captured in this section has been linked to the erosion of ethical values expected to guide the auditors and other accounting practitioners in meeting societal expectations. Adeyeye et al. (2010) undertook a study on the ethical challenges of practicing accountants in Nigeria. A number of factors that were assumed to influence the ethical behaviour of an auditor in the course of his audit assignments were examined. The influence of family background, religious belief, economic issues, familiarity issues and monitoring and regulatory issues were studied. The result of the study showed the interrelatedness of the identified variable. The researchers concluded that it is imperative to monitor and positively control these variables for audit profession to sustain its relevance in a dynamic business world.

MATERIAL AND METHODS

This section of the study describes the research design, population of the study, sampling, research instrument and the method of analysis.

Research design

Survey research design was used in this study. This research strategy was considered necessary because of its ability to view comprehensively and in detail the major questions raised in the study. According to Denscombe (2003), this research design is an efficient way of collecting information from a large number of respondents and the ability to use statistical techniques to determine statistical significance.

Study population

A population is the entire set of relevant units of analysis (Saunders et al., 2007). Since this study is on the auditing profession, population of the study is defined as all accountants in Nigeria. The choice of all accountants is hinged on the belief that all accountants have the knowledge of what the duties and roles of auditors are (Frankfort-Nachmias and Nachmias, 2006). Thus, accountants in all sectors of the Nigeria economy represent the population of the study.

Sampling frame and sampling technique

Sampling is the procedure for drawing units from a population. It results in the reduction of the amount of data to be collected, by considering only data from a sub-group rather than all possible elements. When data serving as the basis for generalisation is comprised of a subset or sub-group of the population, that subset or subgroup is called sample (Frankfort-Nachmias and Nachmias, 2006; Saunders et al., 2007). In the absence of an up-to-date list and sector category of accountants in Nigeria, 50 prospective respondents from industry accountants were drawn by using the official listing of companies quoted on the Nigerian Stock Exchange as at March 10, 2009 (The Punch 13, 2009). One hundred respondents consisting of 50 accountants in academics and 50 accounting students were drawn from tertiary institutions offering accounting programme in tertiary institutions in Lagos State, Nigeria while 50 public accountants (auditors) were drawn from accounting firms in the state. Therefore, the sample size was 200. All members in the sample were drawn randomly at various public fora where the respondents were approached for participation in the study.

Data type and data collection instrument

Primary data were collected for this study. The primary data was obtained from the targeted respondents through a carefully constructed questionnaire. The questionnaire was designed to capture the demographic data of the respondents and their opinions with respect to the research questions. The questionnaire was divided into two sections. Section one sought to obtain information on demographic details of respondents while Section two consisted of items measuring the perception of respondent groups on ethics and the future outlook of auditing profession. The questionnaire was constructed using a five-point likert scale.

Method of data analysis

The data collected were analysed using both descriptive and inferential statistics. The descriptive method described the demography of respondents and other variables in the study using percentages, frequency count, mean and standard deviation. The hypotheses formulated for this study were tested with the use of statistical tools for population means and level of significance tests. Thus, the four hypotheses proposed in the study were tested using

Table 1. Demographic details of respondents.

		Frequency	Percent	Valid percent	Cumulative percent
Gender	Male	103	72.0	72.0	72.0
	Female	40	28.0	28.0	100.0
Status	Single	48	33.6	33.6	33.6
	Married	95	66.4	66.4	100.0
Respondents category	Accounting Student (AS)	42	29.4	29.4	29.4
	Industry Accountant (IA)	38	26.6	26.6	55.9
	External Auditor (EA)	35	24.5	24.5	80.4
	Academic Accountant (AA)	28	19.6	19.6	100.0

Source: Field Survey, 2010.

F-test. These hypotheses tested whether the means from the perceptions of the four groups of respondents were the same. According to Bluman (2004), F-test is used to test a hypothesis concerning the means of three or more populations. This technique is also called analysis of variance (ANOVA). The hypotheses proposed in the study take the form that:

H_0: $\mu_1 = \mu_2 = \mu_3 = \mu_4$

H_1: At least one (1) mean is different from the others.
where: μ= mean, 1-4 = respondent groups.

RESULTS

This section of the research work deals with the analysis of the questionnaire, provision of answers to the research questions and the discussion of findings from the study.

Demographic data analysis

Out of the two hundred copies of the questionnaire administered, a total of one hundred and forty-three copies were returned. Hence, one hundred and forty-three usable copies of questionnaires were used for analysis. This represents an overall response rate of seventy-two per cent (72%) for all the groups. These responses were used in providing answers to the questions raised in the study.

Table 1 shows the breakdown of respondents by gender. One hundred and three male respondents representing seventy-two percent (72%) and forty female respondents representing twenty-eight percent (28%) were surveyed in this study. This shows that views of respondents were sought across the two genders. It also indicates that forty-eight respondents representing about thirty-four percent of respondents were single and ninety-five respondents representing about sixty-six percent were married. Hence, a higher number of respondents were matured individuals.

The study also made effort to describe the category of respondents used in the investigation. The results of respondents based on the category of groups are presented in Table 1. The Table shows that forty-two respondents representing twenty-nine percent are accounting students and thirty-eight (38) respondents representing about twenty-seven percent are industry accountants. Furthermore, thirty-five respondents representing (25%) are public accountants (external auditors) and twenty-eight respondents representing (20%) are academic accountants.

Research Question 1: Is the auditing profession living up to the expectation of the public in Nigeria?

In order to generate valid response to the first research question, analyses were carried out by using the responses from the questionnaire. Items 1, 8, 9, 10, 15 and 18 of the questionnaire were used in providing answers to this research question. The questions bordered on the opinion of the respondents on the integrity of auditing profession. The descriptive statistics of responses are presented in Table 2.

For example, the need for auditors to abide by a high ethical standard because of their responsibility to honour the public trust (Statement 1) has a high mean score of above 4.80 in each of the respondent groups. This shows that respondent groups are aware that auditors owe the public a duty to maintain a high standard of ethics which will accord them the integrity that the public repose on them. Furthermore, there appears to be a general consensus by respondent groups that shaping the views of the new entrants to the profession is an important step towards restoring the integrity of the financial reporting process (Statement 10). This is evidenced by a relatively high mean score of above 4.00 by all respondent groups. Respondents' opinion was also sought on the credibility

Table 2. Descriptive statistics on the integrity of the auditing profession.

No.	Statement		Mean	Std. deviation
1	Auditors must abide by high ethical standard because of their responsibility to honour the public trust..	SA	4.93	0.261
		IA	4.89	0.311
		EA	4.86	0.355
		AA	4.89	0.315
		Total	4.90	0.307
2	The auditing profession is loosing its credibility.	SA	4.00	1.126
		IA	1.82	1.062
		EA	3.51	1.314
		AA	2.64	1.193
		Total	3.03	1.451
3	The event surrounding the introduction of Corporate Governance Code in Nigeria and the United States Version of Sarbanes Oxley Act places the auditing profession at a crossroad.	SA	4.00	1.126
		IA	1.82	1.062
		EA	3.51	1.314
		AA	3.50	1.319
		Total	3.20	1.466
10	Shaping the views of students entering the profession is an important step to restoring the integrity of financial reporting process.	SA	4.57	0.501
		IA	4.34	0.481
		EA	4.54	0.561
		AA	4.68	0.476
		Total	4.52	0.515
15	It is impossible to properly integrate the responsibility of an external auditor who is paid by the client because he is licensed to protect the public trust.	SA	3.55	0.705
		IA	2.32	0.904
		EA	2.29	0.987
		AA	3.54	1.071
		Total	2.91	1.094
18	Compliance with ethics and cultural values of the profession has been on the declining state.	SA	3.95	0.987
		IA	2.79	0.935
		EA	2.26	0.886
		AA	2.82	0.983
		Total	3.01	1.141

Source: SPSS output.

of the profession through Statement 8. It appears that respondents have different perception of the current level of credibility accorded to the profession. Accounting students were of the opinion that the profession has in recent times lost its credibility while industry accountants have a totally different opinion. These opinions are evidenced by a mean score of 4.00 for accounting students and 1.82 for industry accountants. Therefore, hypothesis was proposed that there is no significant difference in the perception of respondent groups regarding the belief in the high integrity of the profession.

Hypothesis 1: There is no significant difference in the perception of respondent groups regarding the belief in the integrity of the profession.

Hypothesis 1 concerns the belief in the integrity of the auditing profession. Six items from the questionnaire are associated with this hypothesis. These are Statements 1, 8, 9, 10, 15 and 18. The result of the hypothesis proposed is shown in Table 2. Out of the six statements used in validating the proposition made on the integrity of the profession, significant differences were found for four

Table 3 Panel A. Results of ANOVA on the integrity of the profession.

		Sum of squares	df	Mean square	F	Sig.
	Between groups	1005.177	3	335.059	46.397	0.000
Integrity * Category	Within groups	1003.802	139	7.222		
	Total	2008.979	142			

Table 3 Panel B. Result of ANOVA on the need to restore public confidence in the profession.

		Sum of squares	df	Mean square	F	Sig.
	Between groups	0.079	3	0.026	0.179	0.910
Confidence * Category	Within groups	20.536	139	0.148		
	Total	20.615	142			

Table 3 Panel C. Result of ANOVA on the future existence of the profession.

		Sum of squares	df	Mean square	F	Sig.
The future * Category	Between groups	.110	3	.037	.240	.868
	Within groups	21.191	139	0.152		
	Total	21.301	142			

Source: Field Survey, 2010.

statements (items 8, 9, 15 and 18). Consequently, the conclusion was that there were significantly different perceptions among the groups regarding the integrity of the auditing profession in Nigeria. For example, on Statement 18, 'compliance with ethics and cultural values of the profession has been on a declining state', student accountants have a mean score of 3.95 while public accountants have a lower mean score of 2.26.

Panel A of the Analysis of Variance result in Table 3 shows that there is a significant difference in the perception of respondents. Overall, four of the statements have a high F-ratio of above 5.00 in Statements 8, 9, 15 and 18 with p-value less than 0.05. Hence, the proposition made on the integrity of the auditing profession is not accepted. However, the study also reveals that there are no significant difference in the perception of respondent groups on the need for auditors to abide by high ethical standard and the need to shape the views of new entrants to the profession (Statements 1 and 10).

Research question 2: Has the response of the profession to these challenges been proactive and adequate in restoring public confidence?

Table 4 shows the descriptive statistics for the five statements used for this research question. There are indications from the table that there are varying perceptions on the adequacy of the current regulatory framework being able to restore investors' confidence in the auditing profession in Nigeria (Statement 5).

This is evidenced by a mean score of 3.21 for industry accountants and a low mean score of 1.81 for student accountants. The Table also shows that ethics is believed to be a major issue in business and accounting. This is evidenced by a mean score above 4.20 in each of the groups being studied.

Hypothesis 2: There is no significant difference in the perception of respondent groups on the need to restore public confidence in the auditing profession

The result of the hypothesis is presented in Table 3 (Panel B). Item 12 of the questionnaire was used in testing the proposition made. There are indications from this Table that the statement used (Statement 12) is not significant with p-value less than 0.05. Therefore, respondents appear not to have significantly different perceptions of the need to restore investors' confidence. In essence, there is no significantly different perception of respondent groups on the need for the profession to take steps to restore investors' confidence in the profession in Statement 12 ($F_{(3, 139)} = 0.179$, p-value > 0.05).

Research questions 3 and 4: On the impact of audit challenges on the attractiveness of the profession

Items 2, 7, 11, 16, 19, 22 and 23 of the questionnaire

Table 4. Descriptive stats. on the need to restore public confidence in auditing.

No.	Statement		Mean	Std. deviation
4	Investors' confidence will not be restored by regulation of auditing alone.	SA	3.71	1.019
		IA	3.50	1.225
		EA	3.40	1.006
		AA	2.57	1.069
		Total	3.36	1.147
5	The present regulatory framework of the auditing profession is adequate in restoring investors' confidence.	SA	1.81	.890
		IA	3.21	1.234
		EA	2.23	1.140
		AA	1.89	1.197
		Total	2.30	1.239
12	The auditing profession must take steps towards restoring public confidence in the integrity of the profession.	SA	4.12	0.328
		IA	4.16	0.437
		EA	4.17	0.382
		AA	4.18	0.390
		Total	4.15	0.381
20	The crisis in investors' confidence towards the auditing profession is irrelevant in our economy.	SA	1.93	0.558
		IA	1.92	0.487
		EA	1.83	0.453
		AA	1.61	0.497
		Total	1.84	0.513
21	Ethics is a major issue that should be emphasised in the auditing profession.	SA	4.24	0.431
		IA	4.21	0.413
		EA	4.26	0.443
		AA	4.68	0.476
		Total	4.32	0.469

Source: Field Survey, 2010.

were used in providing answers to this research question. The questions bordered on the opinion of the respondents on the effect of business failure, accounting and ethical scandals on the future existence of the profession (Table 5).

It appears from Table 5 that respondent groups have varying perceptions of whether the profession has not taken sufficient steps to avoid corporate and ethical scandals as shown in Statement 7. Academic accountants appear to have the highest mean score of 3.54 while industry accountants have the lowest mean score of 2.45. The Table also shows that respondents have varying opinions on the decline of core values which attracted them to the profession (Statement 2) as evidenced by a mean score ranging between 3.6 and 2.8. Furthermore, the Table also shows that respondent groups have a high mean score above 4.00 on the opinion that the auditing profession will continue to play a key role in the future prosperity of the Nigerian economy (Statement 11).

Hypothesis 3: There is no significant difference in the perception of respondent groups on the effects of accounting scandals on the auditing profession

The hypothesis being no significant difference in the perception of respondent groups on the future existence of auditing profession was tested using item 11 of the questionnaire. The result of the hypothesis is presented in Table 3 (Panel C). There is an indication that respondents are not different in their perception that the profession will continue to play a key role in the future prosperity of the Nigerian economy.

DISCUSSION

The recent collapses of various companies around the world have led to increasing interest in the financial reporting process deficiencies and inadequacies in the corporate disclosure practices. This situation has had a

Table 5. Descriptive statistics on the future existence of the auditing profession.

Quest. Item	Statement		Mean	Std. deviation
2	The core values which attracted me to the profession have declined.	SA	3.62	.882
		IA	2.82	.982
		EA	2.80	.933
		AA	2.82	.905
		Total	3.05	.988
7	The auditing profession has not taken sufficient steps to avoid future corporate and ethical standards.	SA	3.21	1.094
		IA	2.45	1.108
		EA	2.74	.950
		AA	3.54	.793
		Total	2.96	1.080
11	The profession will continue to play active role in the future prosperity of the Nigerian economy.	SA	4.05	.439
		IA	4.11	.388
		EA	4.09	.373
		AA	4.04	.331
		Total	4.07	.387
16	I have noticed a decline in the ethics of the auditing profession more than it used to be.	SA	3.71	.805
		IA	2.32	.702
		EA	1.71	.458
		AA	2.25	.585
		Total	2.57	1.018
19	Fundamental changes must occur to restore the integrity of the financial reporting process.	SA	4.40	.627
		IA	2.55	.891
		EA	2.34	.765
		AA	3.50	.882
		Total	3.23	1.161
22	Am optimistic about the good future of the auditing profession.	SA	4.07	.601
		IA	4.21	.413
		EA	4.26	.443
		AA	4.68	.476
		Total	4.27	.533
23	Recent corporate and ethical scandals have really affected the perception of auditing as a profession.	SA	4.36	.656
		IA	3.95	1.229
		EA	2.14	1.264
		AA	3.93	1.303
		Total	3.62	1.403

Source: Field Survey, 2010.

negative and cumulative impact on the perceived credibility of financial reporting and has tarnished the perception of the future outlook of the profession amidst the various gaps in public expectations.

Survey research design was used in this study. The perceptions of 143 informed stakeholders out of the 200 respondents sampled were used. The respondents image of the auditing profession. The current study examined ethics of the auditing profession and consisted of four target groups: accounting students, industry accountants, external auditors and academic accountants. Primary data were obtained from the targeted respondents through a questionnaire. The data collected were analysed using both descriptive and inferential statistics.

The results of the first hypothesis show that there were significantly different perceptions among the groups regarding the integrity of the auditing profession in Nigeria. This result may be due to varied orientations and experiences. For example, respondents whose value system and upbringing have limited them to ethically inclined environments may not appreciate the perceived intensity of the fraudulent financial reporting and audit inadequacies. This result, however, is inconsistent with the findings in Bakre (2007) which indicted the accountants, auditors, and the accounting professional bodies in Nigeria for extremely poor level of integrity observed. The study also revealed that there were no significant differences in the perceptions of respondent groups on the need for auditors to abide by high ethical standard and the need to shape the views of new entrants to the profession. This result accords substantially with the view expressed in Ajibolade (2008) that future professional accountants should be properly groomed in ethical standards to maintain the respectability of the profession. In addition, the opinion expressed here is normal for professional growth and improvement of service delivery in financial reporting and auditing endeavours.

The study also made inquiries into the need for improved public confidence on the profession. Respondents appear to have no significantly different perception of the need to restore investors' confidence. Consequently, there is no significant difference in the perception of respondent groups on the need for the profession to take steps to restore investors' confidence in the profession. Results from the study also suggest that respondents have different perceptions on the decline of core values which attracted them to the profession. This result can also be viewed from the global popularity of the accounting discipline.

It also appears that perceptual differences existed on whether the profession has made sufficient efforts to avoid future corporate and ethical scandals. This result is mixed as the perceptions are likely to have been affected by respondents' activities. For instance, respondents who have lost substantial amounts of investment in the Nigerian capital market might have attributed the financial loss to the perceived unethical practices of management aided by the organisations' accountants and audit expectation gap. Nevertheless, respondents were not different in their perception that the profession will continue to play a key role in the future prosperity of the Nigerian economy.

Conclusions

This study sought to provide information that may help improve the auditing profession in Nigeria, by investigating the perception of selected stakeholders on recent corporate failures and ethical scandals as well as the effect of these on regulatory reforms and the future of auditing profession in Nigeria. Arising from the pursuit of this objective are specific recommendations which will improve the credibility of this profession.

There is the need for the profession to direct its efforts towards shaping the views of new entrants to the profession. This can be achieved through sound ethical training as results from the study suggested that this is an important step towards restoring the integrity of financial reporting process. Adherence and enforcement of high ethical standard for members of the profession will go a long way in maintaining diligence in the way members of the profession carry out their duties.

This study also recommends that regulatory agencies should be more proactive in their response to issues which affect the profession. While evidence exist in this study that there is the need for an improved regulation of the profession, such regulation should be targeted towards restoring confidence in the Nigerian capital market. Finally, the profession should make efforts to improve and uphold its cultural values at all times. It is believed that the profession of auditing has the potential to continue to play a significant role in the future prosperity of the Nigerian economy.

REFERENCES

Abercrombie N, Hill S, Turner BS (1984). Dictionary of sociology, Penguin Books, 2nd ed.

Adelaja SO (2009). An evaluation of the perception of auditors' independence in Nigeria. Niger. J. Manage. Stud., 10(1): 122-145.

Adeyeye GB, Adeyemi SB, Otusanya OJ (2010). Ethical challenges of practicing accountants in Nigeria. Nigerian J. Manage. Stud., 10(2): (290-326).

Ahmed K, Alam KF, Alam M (1997). An empirical study of factors affecting accounting students' career choice in New Zealand, Acc. Edu.: An Int. J., 6(4): 325-335.

Ajibolade SO (2008). A Survey of the Perception of Ethical Behaviour of Future Nigerian Accounting Professionals. Nig. Acctant., 43(3): 54-59.

Albrecht WS, Sack RJ (2000). Accounting Education: Charting the course through a perilous future, Acc. Edu. Series No. 16, American Acc. Ass., Sarasota, FL.

Australian Council of Professions (2004). About professions in Australia: Definition of a profession, available at http://www.professions.com.au/define profession.html (accessed 9 December 2010).

Bakre OM (2007). The unethical practices of accountants and auditors and the compromising stance of professional bodies in the corporate world: evidence from Nigeria. Accting. Forum, 31: 277-303.

Bloom R, Myring M (2008). Charting the future of the accounting profession: Recruiting and retaining the next generation, The CPA J., available at http://www.nysscpa.org/cpajournal/2008/608/essentials/p65.htm on 14/08/2009 (accessed 20 January 2011).

Bluman AG (2004). Elementary statistics: A step by step approach, (5th ed). McGraw-Hill.

Boone T (2001). Constructing a profession, professionalization of exercise Physiologyonline: An Int. electronic J. exercise physiologists, 4(5), available at http://www.css.edu/users/tboone2/asep/ ConstructingAprofession.html (accessed 20 January 2011).

Burbules N, Densmore K (1991). The limits of making teaching a profession, Edu. Policy, 5(1): 44-63.

Cogan M (1953). Toward a definition of profession, Harvard Edu. Rev.,

23(1): 33-50.
Degan C (2006). Legitimacy theory. In Hoque, Z. (Ed.) Methodological Issues in Accounting Research, Spirumus Press Ltd., London.
Dellaportas S, Davenport L (2007). Reflections on the public interest in accounting, Crit. Persp. in Acc., available at, http://doi:10.1016/j.cpa_2007.06.002 (accessed 6 January 2011).
Dennis A (2006). Understanding the best and brightest, J. Acc., 202(5): 41-47.
Denscombe M (2003). The good research guide for small-scale social research projects, (2nd Ed.), Open University Press Maidenhead-Philadelphia.
Frankfort-Nachmias C, Nachmias D (2006). Research methods in the social sciences. (5th Ed.), Hodder Arnold, London.
Goode W. (1957). Community within a community: the professions, American Soc. Rev., 22(2): 194-200.
Hale MW, Huston R, Smith ML (2005). The once and future accountants: Ethics and the future outlook of the US accounting profession, Inter. J. Acc., Aud. Perf. Eva., 2(4): 426-440.
Harvey L (2009). Analytic Quality Glossary, Quality research international, available at http://www.qualityresearchinternational.com/glossary/ (accessed 20 February 2011).
Healy PM (2005). The challenges facing auditors and analysts in U.S. Capital Markets, Available at http://newman.baruch.cuny.edu/digital/saxe/saxe_2005/healy_05.html. (Accessed 14, September, 2010).
Hines RD (1988). Financial accounting: In communicating reality, we construct reality, Acc. Org. Soc., 13(3): 251-261.
International Federation of Accountants Education Committee (2003). International education standards for professional accountants, available at http://www.ifac.org/Members/DownLoads/IES_1-6.pdf (accessed 6 January 2011).
Jackling B, Watty K (2008). The professional accountant of the future: Never mind the quality check the look!, paper presented at Critical Perspectives on Accounting Conference, New York, April.
Lindblom CK (1994). The implications of organizational legitimacy for corporate social performance and disclosure, paper presented the critical Perspective on Accounting Conference, NY, New York.
Mactosh MO, Francis WM, Ongocho S (2010). Public trust on auditors and the auditing profession among Cooperative Societies in Kisii-Kenya, Afric. J. Bus. M., 1: 274-281.
Matthews MR (1993). Socially responsible accounting, Chapman Hall, London.
Napier CJ, Carnegie GD (2007). The portrayal of accounting and accountants following the Enron collapse, paper presented at the EAA 30th Annual Congress, Lisbon, April.
Oxford English Dictionary (1989). (2ed.), Oxford University Press.
Perks RW (1993). Accounting and society, Chapman and Hall, London.
Punch Newspaper (2009). The Punch, June 13, 2009: 49.
Pratte R, Rury JL (1991). Teachers, professionalism, and craft, Tea. Co. Rec., 93: 59-72.
Sarbanes-Oxley Act (2002). Pub. L. No. 107-204, 116 Stat. 745 (2002).
Saunders MNK, Lewis P, Thornhill A (2007). Research methods for business students, (4th ed). FT Prentice Hall.
Smith LM (2002). Luca Pacioli: The father of accounting, available at http://acct.tamu.edu/smith/ethics/pacioli.htm, (accessed 26 March 2009).
Southern Illinois University (2004). Engineering as a profession, available at http://civil.engr.siu.edu/intro/profession.htm, undated page, (accessed November 2004).
Tan LM, Laswad F (2006). Students' beliefs, attitudes and intentions to major in accounting, Acc. Edu.: An Int. J., 15(2): 167-187.
The American Assembly (2005). The future of the accounting profession, American Assembly Report, 103rd American Assembly, Columbia University.
Theuri P, Weickgenannt A (2008). Maturity effects on students perception of how accounting scandals impact the accounting profession, J. Col. Teach. Learn., 5(1): 53-60.
Wells P, Fieger P (2005). High school teachers' perceptions of accounting: An international Study, paper presented at the AFAANZ Conference, Melbourne, Australia.
West B, Yee H (2006). Professionalisation and accounting in china: A historic and comparative review, proceedings of 8th Interd. Persp. Acc. Conf., Cardiff, July 10-12.
Williams P (2001). Who gets to speak and what must they say? A commentary on the Briloff affair, Crit. Persp. on Accting., 12: 213-219.
Wyatt AR (2004). Accounting professionalism - they just don't get it!, Acc. Horizons, 18(1): 45-53.

A critical review of Fischer tax compliance model: A research synthesis

Gerald Chau* **and Patrick Leung**

School of Accounting and Finance, the Hong Kong Polytechnic University, Hung Hom, Kowloon, Hong Kong.

The primary objective of this paper is to summarize and review extant literature concerning Fischer tax compliance model for a dual purpose. Firstly, the Fischer tax compliance model provides a framework for understanding the influence of those socio-economic and psychological components on tax payers' compliance decision. We suggest a partial refinement to this model by incorporating another important environmental factor - culture and the interaction effect between noncompliance opportunity and tax system/structure on tax compliance. Secondly, the review enables us to synthesize this topic so as to help researchers identify those gaps and consider promising future directions for further study.

Key words: Tax evasion, Fischer model, tax compliance determinants, Hofstede, cultural dimensions.

INTRODUCTION

Tax evasion is a universal phenomenon that takes place in all societies and economic systems including both developed and developing countries. In the US, it is estimated that the extent of tax gap (the difference between taxes owed and taxed filed) for 2001 were US$ 353 billion (IRS, 2006). This concern is particularly severe for developing countries given the rapid growth of investment in their economies and their lack of adequate experience in dealing with this problem. In China, the tax evasion by multinationals resulted in revenue loss amounted to US$ 3.88 billion each year (Asia Times, April 11 2007). In Hong Kong, the Inland revenue department reported that about US $ 1.15 billion was collected from 2003 - 07 back tax and penalties (IRD, 2007).

Thus, tax compliance is growing international concerns for tax authorities and public policy makers as tax evasion seriously threatens the capacity of government to raise public revenue.

Because of the significance of this issue, tax compliance determinants based on Fischer model(Fischer et al., 1992) have been an important subject of research in developed countries over the past couple of years (e.g. Andreoni et al., 1998; Ritsema et al., 2003; Houston and Tran, 2001; Richardson, 2006). So far, there has been no comprehensive review of the literature related to this issue so as to refine the Fischer model and identify those gaps for future research areas. Thus, the primary objective of this paper is to summarize and review extant literature concerning Fischer tax compliance model for a dual purpose, firstly, the Fischer tax compliance model provides a framework for understanding the influence of those socio-economic and psychological components on taxpayers' compliance decision. We suggest a partial refinement to this model by incorporating another important environmental factor - culture and the interaction effect between non-compliance opportunity and tax system/structure on tax compliance. Secondly, the review enables us to synthesize this topic so as to help researchers identify those gaps and consider promising future directions for further study.

FISCHER MODEL

Jackson and Milliron (1986) carry out a comprehensive review of the tax compliance literature and identify 14 key factors that have been studied by researcher on tax compliance. These factors are categorized by Fischer and associates (Fischer et al., 1992) into 4 groups in his expanded model (Fischer Model): (ii) demographic (e.g.-age, gender and education) (ii) noncompliance opportunity (e.g. income level, income source and occupation), (iii) attitudes and perceptions (e.g. fairness of the tax

*Corresponding author. E-mail:afgerald@polyu.edu.hk. Tel.: (852) 2766 7061. Fax: (852) 23309845.

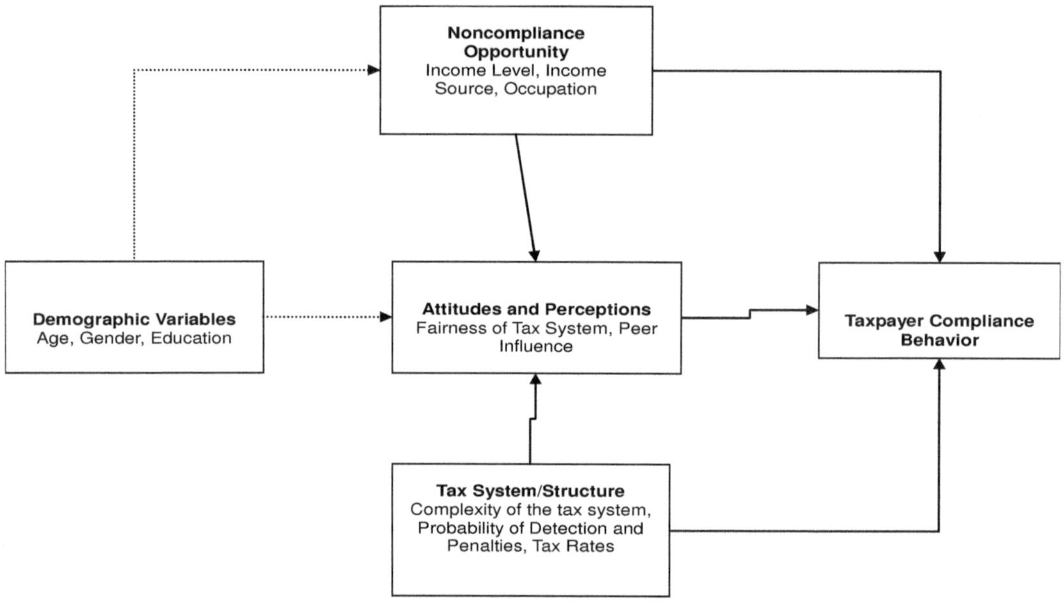

Figure 1. Fisher et al. (1992) tax compliance model.

system and peer influence) and (iv) tax system/structure (e.g. complexity of the tax system, probability of detection and penalties and tax rates). Thus Fisher model of tax compliance incorporates economic, sociological and psychological factors into a comprehensive one. The Fisher model is illustrated in Figure 1 and elaborated in the following sections.

DEMOGRAPHIC VARIALES

The relationship between demographic variables and tax compliance has long been of interest (Tittle, 1980). 3 major personal characteristics for which there is evidence of a relationship are age, gender and education (Jackson and Milliron, 1986). The Fischer model suggests that demographic variables indirectly affect taxpayer compliance by their impacts on noncompliance opportunities and attitudes and perceptions.

Age

A common demographic variable is the taxpayers' age. A positive link between age and taxpayer compliance is reported (Jackson and Milliron, 1986). In addition, data coming from the taxpayer compliance measurement program (TCMP) of the internal revenue service also indicate that "noncompliance is significantly less common and of lower magnitude among householders in which either the head or the head's spouse is over age 65" (Andreoni et al., 1998). In general, young taxpayers are more willing to take risks and are less sensitive to sanctions. Based on the 1997 Arkansas tax penalty amnesty program, Ritsema et al. (2003) also find that age is a factor for intentional evaders, with younger taxpayers less complaint.

Gender

Early research (Tittle, 1980) testing the tax compliance level of males versus females reports that females are more likely to tax compliance. Traditionally, "females have been identified with conforming roles, moral restraints and more conservative life pattern" (Jackson and Milliron, 1986). All these attributes may promote higher tax compliance. Experimental study conducted by Baldry (1987) also finds that females tend to tax compliance by more than males do. Jackson and Jaouen (1989) also reveal a significant gender difference by treatment group from a pool of potential jurors. However, the study by Houston and Tran (2001) indicates a higher proportion of tax evasion committed by women than men.

Education

Education, as a demographic variable relates to the taxpayers' ability to comprehend and comply or not comply with the tax laws (Jackson and Milliron, 1986). 2 aspects of education have been distinguished: "the general degree of fiscal knowledge and the degree of knowledge involving evasion opportunities" (Groenland and Veldhoven, 1983). This knowledge is considered to be important for attitudes towards tax compliance. Song and Yarbrough (1978) have included education as a background variable in their experiment.

They find that those with more fiscal knowledge had more positive tax ethics scores (attitudes towards tax compliance will be discussed below) than those with lower fiscal knowledge. Eriksen and Fallan (1996) also find that specific tax knowledge was positively linked to taxpayer attitude. The study conducted by Chan et al. (2000) reveal that higher education is directly linked to an increased likelihood of tax compliance. By using randomized response technique for a mail questionnaire survey of Australian individuals, Houston and Tran (2001) also find that taxpayers without tertiary education tend to have lower proportions of tax compliance than their counterparts with tertiary education. In addition, Richardson (2006) also reports that general education level is significantly related to tax evasion.

NON-COMPLIANCE OPPORTUNITY

In the Fischer model, noncompliance opportunity can affect taxpayer compliance directly through income level, income source and occupation and indirectly through attitudes and perceptions.

Income level

Almost all the theoretical model indicates that as income rises, tax evasions should increase over most ranges (Andreoni et al., 1998). Vogel (1974) finds that respondents who report an improvement in individual financial/income status during the past 5 years are more likely to commit tax evasion than those who report a deterioration of their financial/income status during the same period. Houston and Tran (2001) also reveal the respondents in the lower income group tend to have a lower proportion of tax compliance by under-reporting income and by over-claiming expenses than their counterparts in the higher income group. By investigating participants in the 1997 Arkansas Tax penalty amnesty program, Ritsema et al. (2003) also find that income level is positively related to the tax owed.

Income source

Tax payers vary in terms of the opportunities available to them to overstating expenses and understating incomes. Greater tax noncompliance opportunity is generally resulted from self-employment and income sources not subject to withholding taxes. In one of the first tax compliance studies, Groves (1958) argues that income source has a significant impact on tax compliance. Surveys by Aitken and Bonneville (1980) and Groenland and Voldhoven (1983) find that taxpayers who are self-employed are more likely to commit various forms of tax non-compliance. Houston and Tran (2001) also reveal a significantly higher proportion of tax evasion among respondents who are self-employed. In addition Vogel (1974) also reveals that 39% of Swedish respondents who acknowledged receiving additional income that was not taxable at the source also committed evading taxes in comparison with 21% of those acknowledging no such additional income. Based on the poll tax in Tanzania, Fjeldstad and Semboja (2001) find support for differences in opportunities for tax noncompliance. "Employees paying their head-tax through a tax withholding system have fewer opportunities to evade than the self-employed" (Fjeldstad and Semboja, 2001). Richardson (2006) also reports that income source is significantly related to tax evasion.

Occupation

This refers to an individual's employment or earnings activity (Jackson and Milliron, 1986). Sutherland (1949) argues that tax evasion is considered as a white-collar crime, committed by an individual of respectability and high social status in the course of performing his employment. In addition, TCMP data also indicate that "among all sole proprietors those who engaged in sales from fixed locations (car dealerships, stores, restaurants etc) understated taxes by the greatest percentage" (Andreoni et al., 1998).

ATTITUDES AND PERCEPTIONS

The Fischer model suggests 2 major considerations for altering taxpayers' attitudes and perceptions to tax compliance are the fairness of the tax system and peer influence.

Fairness of tax system

It is widely believed by tax administrators and the taxpayers that growing dissatisfaction with the fairness of tax system is the major causes for increasing tax noncompliance. Tax fairness consists of at least 2 different dimensions. "One dimension appears to involve the equity of the trade - the benefits received for the tax dollars given. The other dimension appears to involve the equity of the taxpayer's burden in reference to that of other individuals" Jackson and Milliron (1986, p. 137). Thus unfairness of the tax system may reflect taxpayers' perceptions that they are overpaying taxes in relation to the value of the services provided by government or in relation to what other taxpayers pay. Porcano (1984) finds that taxpayers' need and ability to pay are the most significant variables related to perceptions of fairness of the tax system. Other surveys conducted by Scott and Grasmick (1982) and Spicer and Lundstedt (1976) indicate that respondents who believe that the tax system is unfair are more likely to commit tax noncompliance behavior. Based on a quasi-experiment with pre-testing and post-testing of 2 student groups, Eriksen and Fallan (1996) also reveal that an important means of ensuring tax compliance is to provide more tax knowledge so as to improve people's perception of the fairness of the tax system. The study conducted by Richardson (2006) also indicates that perceived fairness of tax system is significantly related to tax evasion.

Peer influence

Peers are usually referred to taxpayers' associates and include friends, relatives and colleagues (Jackson and Milliron, 1986). The peer influence is reflected in an individual's expectations in relation to the approval or disapproval of that tax noncompliance behavior. Grasmick and Scott (1982) indicate that respondents with peers who practice tax noncompliance are more likely to commit as well. The survey conducted by Mason et al. (1975) finds that people committing tax noncompliance are more likely to discuss tax matters with their peers. The study conducted by Chan et al. (2000) also reveals that taxpayers may still commit noncompliance so long as this noncompliance is consistent with in-group expectations and norms.

TAX SYSTEM/STRUCTURE

It is widely acknowledged that the extent of tax compliance in many developing countries has been decreasing. The underdeveloped tax system/structure is one of the major causes for this phenomenon. In the Fischer Model, the effectiveness of tax system is affected by complexity of tax system, probability of detection and penalties and tax rates.

Complexity of tax system

As the tax law has become increasingly complex, complexity has come to be recognized as a possible reason for tax noncompliance (Jackson and Milliron, 1986). In the context of tax compliance decisions, complexity should include 2 dimensions, excessive detail in the tax rules and numerous computations required. Taxpayers should be able to understand the tax rules for computations by which they are to be taxed. These tax rules should aim to be simple, understandable and clear in order to enhance tax compliance. In general, complexity of tax system should increase as the number of criteria specified by tax laws increase. Clotfelter (1983) reveals that complexity of tax system has been associated with greater underreporting of tax. Milliron (1985) also finds that complexity has a significant effect on tax compliance decision. Richardson (2006) also reports that tax law complexity is significantly related to tax evasion.

Probability of detection and penalties

In general, higher audit probabilities and severe penalties encourage tax compliance. Probability of detection refers to the likelihood that the tax authorities will discover an individual's noncompliance and seek to remedy the evasion. Individuals normally would like to evade their tax liabilities entirely and the only reason they might not do so is that there is some non-zero probability of being caught (Massimo, 1993). Raising the probability of detection will increase tax compliance and tax audit represents one of the effective detective measures used by tax authorities (Alm, 1991). In fact, tax audits are considered to have both direct deterrent effect on the taxpayers actually audited and indirect deterrent effect on taxpayers not audited (Alm et al., 2004). Witte and Woodbury (1985) find a significant positive relationship between the risk of tax audit and the rate of voluntary tax compliance. However, the study by Beron et al. (1990) reveals that tax audit exert only a modest positive effect on tax compliance.

Another important factor affecting tax compliance is the relationship between tax compliance and the severity of sanctions. The idea is that fear of penalties prohibits tax noncompliance behavior. Establishing an effective system to penalize tax evaders is an important measure to encourage tax compliance. Taxpayers will be more likely to comply if noncompliance may result in severe penalties. According to the theoretical work conducted by Allingham and Sandmo (1972), tax compliance can be increased by increasing the penalties associated with it. To be effective, penalties must be applied speedily and forcefully. Witte and Woodbury (1985) report a significant relationship between the severity of criminal sanctions and tax compliance. Other studies by Grasmick and Scott (1982) and Tittle (1980) also indicate that respondents acknowledging some form of tax noncompliance are less likely if such acts would result in severe penalties. The experimental studies conducted by Hasseldine et al. (2007) also show that severity of sanctions has significant effects on tax compliance behavior.

Tax rates

The third major construct of tax system/structure in the Fischer model is tax rates. Empirical evidence has suggested that progressive versus flat tax rate is the significant structural variable in association with tax compliance behavior (Clotfelter, 1983). Research using experiments typically find that high tax rates are linked to less tax compliance (Friedland et al., 1978). Using the

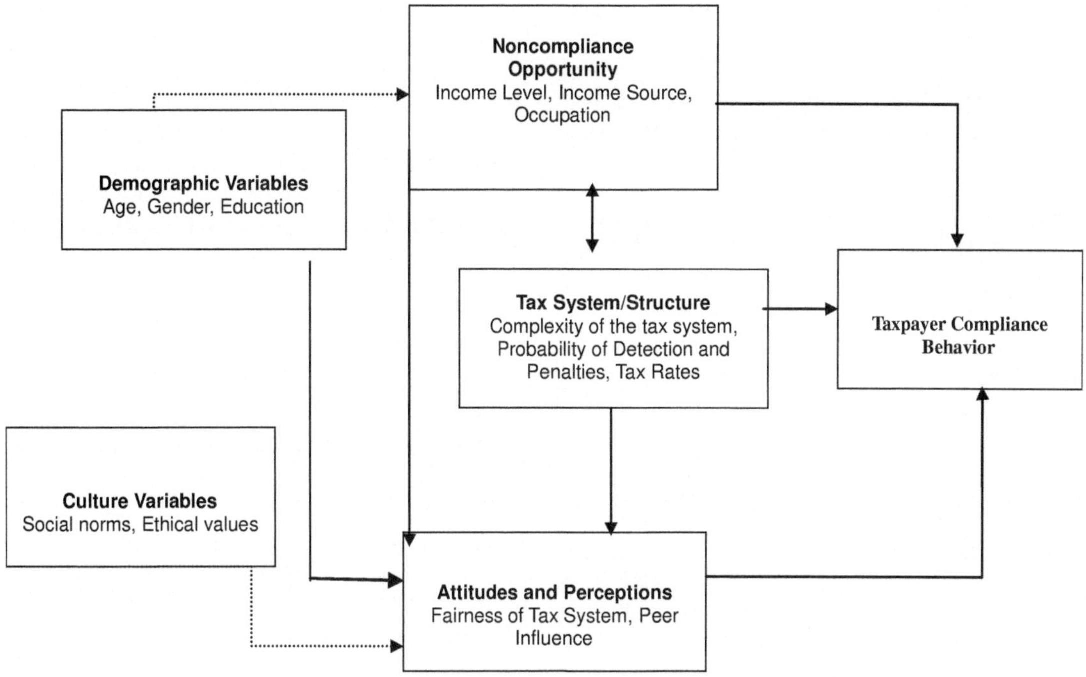

Figure 2. Modified fisher et al. (1992) tax compliance model.

audited tax returns for individual taxpayers in Jamaica, Alm et al. (1993) also reveal that the probability of underreporting and the level of underreporting are positively related to the marginal tax rate.

MODICICATIONS TO FISHER MODEL

The Fischer model provides a framework for understanding the influence of those socio-economic and psychological components on taxpayers' compliance decision. We suggest a partial refinement to this model by incorporating another important environmental factor - culture and the interaction effect between noncompliance opportunity and tax system/structure on tax compliance (Figure 2). We will illustrate this interaction effect by using income level and tax rates.

Culture

Culture is considered to be a powerful environmental factor that affects the taxpayer's compliance. Different social norms and ethical values will create different incentives for tax compliance. In fact, ethical values influenced by social norms may prohibit taxpayers from engaging in tax evasion (Blanthorne and Kaplan, 2008). The cultural framework most widely used is that of Hofstede (1980). Based on an attitude survey of about 116,000 IBN employees, Hofstede identifies 4 underlying societal values; individualism, power distance, uncertainty avoidance and masculinity. Cultural research has found significant differences between the US and Chinese citizens (Hofstede, 1991). Not all cultural dimensions affect taxpayers' compliance. Chan et al. (2000) suggests that the cultural dimension affecting tax compliance is collectivism and individualism. In Hofstede's model, individualism and collectivism refer to the degree of interdependence a society maintains among individuals (Hofstede, 1991). The cultural dimension of individualism relates to the degree of integration a society maintains among its members. A high individualism culture is signified by people focusing on themselves rather than on the group to which they belong. Under this perspective, an individual is seen as separable from and independent of a group affiliation. People in such low individualism culture as Chinese citizens, they tend to be collectivists who are expected to follow and subscribe to the values of their in-groups in order to gain peer acceptance and social status (Hofstede, 1991). In contrast, a high individualism culture such as US citizens is signified by people focusing on themselves rather than on the group to which they belong. Under this perspective, they view themselves as distinct entities and place great value on individual rights. These cultural differences may have a direct impact on ethical values and moral development and ultimately affecting tax compliance decisions. The study conducted by Chan et al. (2000) indicates that culture of the taxpayers has an impact on taxpayer compliance efforts.

Interaction effect between income level and tax rates

Income level and tax rates are found to be negatively related to tax-compliance (Andreoni et al., 1998; Houston and Tran, 2001). Further, these 2 variables may jointly have a negative interaction effect (that is, 2 variables considered together), which is over and above that of their individual impact, on tax compliance. A taxpayer with high income and high tax rates would have higher motivation to be aggressive in tax reporting. The case would be more noticeable if the taxpayer is facing a progressive tax system. On the other hand, a taxpayer with high income but low tax rates would have lower motivation to be aggressive in tax reporting.

Conclusions and suggestions for future research

This paper summarizes extant research on the tax compliance determinants based on Fischer's model. This synthesis should be of interest to academic researchers as identifying the tax compliance determinants and resolving tax compliance problems could provide challenging research opportunities in taxation. Despite the many studies as discussed above, much work remains to be done if we would like to develop fully understanding of this intrinsically complex subject and the means of promoting tax compliance. Based on the syntheses of research on tax compliance, our conclusions about those gaps on tax compliance determinants studies and areas for future research are as follows

As discussed above, existing research provides insights into the different components of Fischer's model without investigating their inter-relationship. Additional theory-building research to further extend Fisher model might be worthwhile. To be of practical relevance, such research should concentrate on identifying and understanding variables and their inter-relationship that act as key determinants of tax compliance.

Extant literature on the compliance including both analytical and empirical studies mainly focused on individual noncompliance. There is little or no research on corporate tax noncompliance. Greater attention should be paid to the complex corporate noncompliance. This area is of considerable significance for the function of fair tax systems between individuals and corporations.

Tax compliance research conducted so far is mainly focused on developed countries. In view of the inadequacies in the institutional framework and insufficient expertise and resources to monitor the intricacies of the tax compliance problems, developing countries are particularly vulnerable to tax noncompliance. There is an urgent need for more empirical and institutional research on the tax compliance behaviors in developing countries.

A final issue that warrants attention is the effect of culture on tax compliance. Although the tax compliance research in other cultures other than the Anglo-Saxon countries could provide insight into the cultural effects on tax compliance behavior; little work has been done on comparative tax compliance under different cultural environments. In fact different cultures will create different incentives and opportunities for tax compliance or evasion. Thus future work needs to incorporate cultural dimensions into tax compliance research. In addition, research based on a greater longitudinal emphasis could also be carried out so as to assess the impact of changes on cultural dimensions.

REFERENCES

Aitken SS, Bonneville L (1980). A general taxpayer opinion survey. Washington, DC: IRS, Office of Planning and Research.

Allingham MG, Sandmo A (1972). Income tax evasion: A theoretical analysis J. Public Econ. 1: 323-338.

Alm J (1991). A perspective on the experimental analysis of taxpayer reporting. Acc. Rev., 66: 577-593.

Alm J, Bahl R, Murray MN (1993). Audit Selection and Income Tax Under-reporting in The Tax Compliance Game. J. Dev. Econ., 42: 1-33

Alm J, Jackson B, McKee M (2004). Audit Information Dissemination, Taxpayer Communication, and Compliance: An Experimental Approach Paper prepared for 2004 IRS Research Conference.

Andreoni J, Erard B, Feinstein J (1998). Tax Compliance, J. Econ. Literature, 36: 818-860.

Baldry JC (1987). Income Tax Evasion and the Tax Schedule: Some Experimental Results. Public Financ. 42: 357-83.

Beron K, Tauchen HV, Witte AD (1990). The Effects of Audits and Socio-economic Variables on Compliance Working paper, University of North Carolina.

Blanthorne C, Kaplan S (2008). An egocentric model of the relations among the opportunity to underreport, social norms, ethical beliefs, and underreporting behavior. Account., Organizations Society 33: 684-703.

Chan CW, Troutman CS, O'Bryan D (2000). An Expanded Model of Taxpayer Compliance: Empirical Evidence from the United States and Hong Kong J. Int. Account., Auditing Taxation, 9: 83-103.

Clotfelter C (1983). Tax Evasion and Tax Rates: An Analysis of Individual Returns. Rev. Econ. Stat. August: 363-373.

Eriksen K, Fallan L (1996). Tax Knowledge and Attitudes Towards Taxation: A Report on a Quasi-experiment. J. Econ. Psychol. 17: 387-402.

Fischer CM, Wartick M, Mark M (1992). Detection Probability and Taxpayer Compliance: A Review of the Literature. J. Acc. Lit. 11: 1-46.

Fjeldstad OH, Semboja J (2001). Why People Pay Taxes: The Case of the Development Levy in Tanzania. World Dev. 29: 2059-2074.

Friedland N, Maital S, Rutenberg A (1978). A Simulation Study of Income Tax Evasion. J. Public Econ. 10: 107-116.

Grasmick H, Scott WJ (1982). Tax Evasion and Mechanisms of Social Control: A Comparison with Grand and Petty Theft. J Econ. Psychol. 2: 213-230.

Groenland E, Veldhoven GM (1983). Tax Evasion Behavior: A Psychological Framework. J. Econ. Psychol. 3: 129-144.

Groves H (1958). Empirical Studies of Income Tax Compliance. Natl Tax J. December: 291-301.

Hasseldine J, Hite P, James S, Toumi M (2007). Persuasive communications: Tax compliance enforcement strategies for sole proprietors. Contemp Account. Res. 24: 171-194.

Hofstede GH (1980). Culture's consequences: International differences in work-related values Sage Publications.

Hofstede GH (1991). Cultures and organizations: Software of the mind. McGraw-Hill International.

Houston J, Tran A (2001). A Survey of Tax Evasion Using the Randomized Response Technique. Adv. Taxation, 13: 69-94.

Inland Revenue Department (IRD) (2007). Annual Report, 2006-2007.

Inland Revenue Service (IRS) (2006). IRS updates tax gap estimates IR-2006-28.

Jackson BR, Jaouen PR (1989). Influencing Taxpayer Compliance

Through Sanction Threat or Appeals to Conscience. Adv. Taxation, 2: 131-147.
Jackson BR, Milliron VC (1986). Tax Compliance Research: Findings, Problems, and Prospects, J. Account. Lit. 5: 125-165.
Mason R, Calvin LD, Faulkenberry GD (1975). Knowledge, evasion and public support for Oregon's tax system. Corvallis, OR: Survey Research Center, Oregon State University.
Massimo B (1993). A Fairness Approach to Income Tax Evasion. J. Public Econ. 52: 345-362.
Milliron VC (1985). A Behavioral Study of the Meaning and Influence of Tax Complexity J. Account. Res. Autumn: 794-816.
Porcano T (1984). Distributive Justice and Tax Policy. Account. Rev. October: 619-636.
Richardson G (2006). Determinants of tax evasion: a cross-country investigation. J. Int. Acc. Auditing Taxation, 15: 150-169.
Ritsema CM, Thomas DW, Ferrier GD (2003). Economic and Behavioral Determinants of Tax Compliance: Evidence from the 1997 Arkansas Tax Penalty Amnesty Program Paper prepared for 2003 IRS Research Conference.
Scott WJ, Grasmick HG (1981). Deterrence and Income Tax Cheating: Testing Interaction Hypotheses in Utilitarian Theories J. Applied Behavioral Sci. 17: 395-408.
Song YD, Yarbrough TE (1978). Tax Ethics and Taxpayer Attitude: A Survey Public Administration Review September-October: 442-452.
Spicer MN, Lundstedt SB (1976). Understanding Tax Evasion. Public Financ. 31: 295-305.
Sutherland E (1949). White Collar Crime New York: Dryden.
Tittle C (1980). Sanctions and Social Deviance: The Question of Deterrence New York: Praeger.
Vogel J (1974). Taxation and Public Opinion in Sweden: an Interpretation of Recent Survey Data. Natl. Tax J. 27: 499-513.
Witte A, Woodbury D (1985). The Effect of Tax Laws and Tax Administration on Tax Compliance: The Case of the U.S. Individual Income Tax. Natl. Tax J. March: 1-13.

Capital market as a veritable source of development in Nigeria economy

Josiah Mary[1]*, Samson. A. Adedinran[1] and Akpeti. O. Elizabeth[2].

[1]Department of Accounting, College of Business Management Science, Igbinedion University Okada, Edo State, Nigeria.
[2]Department of Business Administration, College of Business Management Science, Igbinedion University Okada, Edo State, Nigeria.

This study takes a look at the impact of the capital market in the development of the Nigerian economy. The main objective includes; identifying the importance of the capital market. Data were collected from the Central Bank Statistical Bulletin from the period of 1992 to 2007 and the Ordinary Least Square and cochrane – Orcutt iterative methods were used to analyze the data. It was discovered that the capital market has not contributed positively to the development of the Nigerian economy. However, there is a positive correlation between the rate of transactions in the capital market and the development of Nigerian economy. It is recommended that stringent requirement for entry into the capital market should be relaxed and adequate publicity should be given to the activity at the capital market, it is believed that when these recommendations are implemented, the impact of capital market on the economy will be positive.

Key word: Capital market, economy, development.

INTRODUCTION

The capital market is the prime motor that drives any economy on its path to growth and development because it is responsible for long-term-growth capital formation. The money market only complements the capital market by providing the necessary working capital to support gross fixed capital formation. Unfortunately, the Nigerian capital market has not fully performed its natural function of funding investment. One of the major indicators of capital market development is the proportion of long-term fixed capital that is raise in relation to the gross domestic product. Between 1999 and 2004, capital formation in terms of long-term funds raised from the market through new issues of securities to the gross domestic product averages only 1.36%, while the new issues to gross fixed capital formation averages 16.0%. Market capitalization to gross domestic product also averaged only 14.25% during the same period. It is therefore not surprising that the Nigerian economy has only been growing at an average of 3.2% annum over the period. Most of the funds raised in Nigeria have been short-term from the money market and these are not growth funds. According to Mary et al. (2012). Financial institutions have not contributed much in financing capital investment but they have however contributed towards stock market development.

The capital market has not been a popular source of funds because of the instability in the economy, low yields to investors in capital market instruments, and government's overbearing presence in economic matters.

Objectives of the study

1) To provide special financing strategies for those projects with long-term gestation periods.
2) To create an appropriate mechanism for capital formation and efficient allocation of resources among competing projects.
3) To broaden share ownership practice and maintain fair prices for securities.

*Corresponding author. E-mail: majoel2003@yahoo.com

LITERATURE REVIEW

Capital market has important strategic roles for providing risk capital for long term structures that ensures the liquidity and stability of financial system. Thriving capital markets are often vibrant in private sector development and strong economic growth.

Within the broad classifications of capital market are the security market and non security market. The non security, which comprises of bank and bank related institutions mainly intermediate indebt and debt related instruments. This type of financial market institution performs mostly financial intermediation and is quite developed relative to the security market.

The capital market

One of the widely quoted definitions of the capital market is given by Nwankwo (1998: 246) who says that the capital market comprises the complex of institution and mechanism through which intermediate term funds and long term funds are pooled and made available to business, government and individual. They also asserted that the capital market comprises the process by which securities already outstanding are transferred. This definition is very embracing; it contains the fact that the capital market has no fixed location and deals on medium and long term funds, has government, individual and business firms as participants and ensures liquidity as it provides market for both new and old securities.

Also according to Alile (1986:154), the central task of the capital market is the mobilization of funds in the hands of individuals who save pool and channel such funds into productive uses.

Capital market instruments

The instruments are the securities that are traded in the stock market. They cannot be inspected or assessed the way electronics, tubers, apples, grapes etc are being assessed. The instruments can be categorized into three major groups of securities according to Herbert (2004:421). These are;

a) Ordinary shares
b) Preference shares
c) Debt instruments

Ordinary shares: They are issued to owners of the company. They are long term financing with a nominal value or face value. The memorandum and article of association of a company specified the number of authorized ordinary shares a company can issue. The ordinary shareholders of a company have a residual claim in the company, their claims to income and assets come after the creditors and preference shareholders have been paid in full. As a result, a shareholders return on investment is less than the return to a lender or preference shareholders. However, there is no limit to the return of ordinary shares.

Preference shares: This is another major source of long-term financing to a company. The holders of preference shares are entitled to a fixed percentage dividend before any dividend is paid to ordinary shareholders. However, preference dividend can only be paid if sufficient distributable profits are available, although with cumulative preference shares the right to an unpaid dividend is carried forward to later years. The arrears of dividend on cumulative preference shares must be paid before any dividend is paid to ordinary shares. For credibility sake, companies always try to pay the fixed dividend regularly.

Just like the debt instruments, a preference shares has a nominal value and dividend, which is paid at a fixed percentage of this amount. Preference shares can be redeemable or irredeemable.

Debt instrument: A bond represents a method of long term borrowing by corporation of government agencies, when a corporate bond is issued, it as a legal contract that goes with it which contains the provision of loans in terms of its amounts, interest and maturity period. Bonds are sold in multiples such as N1000. They are purchased by commercial banks, insurance companies, pension fund and even individuals. This form of financing is usually reserved for target companies or corporation. This is why they have prior claims on the firm's asset in the event of liquidating. There are different classes of bonds

Types of capital market

Primary market

According to Soyede (2005: 8) Primary market is a market for new securities. It is a platform where the company or government can raise money for investment or where already quoted companies can raise fresh funds for expansion. Both the Securities and Exchange Commission (SEC) and the Nigerian Stock Exchange (NSE) are involved in primary market activities. The issuing houses and stock brokers also play prominent roles. Until 1993, when deregulation of the capital market commenced, the SEC was responsible for pricing and allotment of new issues in the Nigerian capital market while the quotation committee of the Nigerian Stock Exchange approved only issue which is to be listed on the exchange's official list. The issuing houses and stockbrokers package issues for government and public companies.

However, the Central Bank of Nigeria acts as issuing

houses for federal government stocks when company wishes to sell such shares (offer for sale). If such company is already listed, the price is technically suspended to forestall any insider or abuse of classified information. This situation holds true reason for companies going into mergers and acquisition or rearrangement that may potentially have bearing on their price and the suspension is sustained by the Nigerian Stock Exchange until such exercise is completed.

For companies seeking listing for first time, the securities are listed with the offer price; soon after the offer exercise is completed instruments representing ownership are dispatched to the shareholders. It is of paramount important to mention here that hitherto, Securities and Exchange Commission was the sole body giving approval to offer price proposed by the Issuer in conjunction with Issuing Houses. However, under the present dispensation the issuing house proposes and defends a price at which it is willing to underwrite the entire securities to be issued. This becomes the offer price and entirely conforms to the price. While Securities and Exchange Commission examines the offer documents with a view to ascertaining the adequacy of price and conformity with statutory requirements among other things, the Nigerian Stock Exchange reviews the same documents to ensure the company or institution meets its listing requirements.

According to Alile (1997: 109) The primary market takes into representation the issuance which could be in form of any of the following:

Offer for sale: Public offers for shares in a company by existing shareholders, proceeds of which go to the vendors. This is a system by which existing shareholders offer their shareholding or part of them for public subscription. In other words, offer for sale is a transfer of ownership of shares from existing holders to new holders. Most of the public offers under the federal government privatization programmer under this category. It differs from offer for subscription in that the proceeds of an offer do not go to the company but to the selling shareholders.

Offer for subscription: This is a direct issue to the public by floating a number of shares of debenture stock. It carries the suppositions that the company is a public one and the proceeds of the issue go to the company to finance expansion or and modernalization. In other words, the company issues a prospectus inviting the public to its shares and it should be noted that the company cannot dictate who subscribes to its shares.

Stock exchange introduction: Where a company seeking quotation already has enough shares held in public hands, the council of stock exchange may permit its security to be introduced into and listed on the market, no new or existing shares to be sold. The added marketability to raise fresh funds in the future invariably at a lower price or cost.

Private placement: Securities are sold to the client of the Issuing Houses or Stockbrokers handling the issue instead of being offered directly to the general public. This is often necessitated by the desire to save time and cost of issue. The council of the Stock Exchange seldom grants such permission and this method is utilized by quoted Plc's. This differs from offer from the subscription and offer for sale in that it is not an invitation to the public to subscribe, rather, the shares or stocks are placed with a broker who then seeks out for the prospective purchasers.

Right issue: These involve offer to buy more shares generally made to existing shareholders and sometimes at concessionary price. Applications are considered by quotations committee of the exchange for ratification and avoid excruciating interest rate charged in the money market. The approval of the council gives the go ahead for the primary market activities before the commencement of the primary market activities; the Securities and Exchange Commission is given the application to determine the offer price of the security.

However, in view of favourable terms on which such issues are usually made, shareholders scarcely ever miss the opportunity. Underwriting of securities is an aspect of primary market. It is an intermediary process and it is far gaining ground in Nigerian Capital Market. They buy from the issuers at one and sell to the investors at a slightly higher price. The price differences referred to as "underwriters spread", represents compensation for absorbing the risk that goes along with guaranteeing the borrower, the expected proceed from sales before the securities are actually placed in the market or in hand of investors.

Secondary market

This enhances the new issue market in many ways, it provides the means by which investor can monitor the value of their shares and liquidate them when they wish to do so. According to Pandey (2006:4), it is a type of market where existing securities of a market are traded on daily and continuous basis. It is the market for existing securities. This consists of exchanges and over-the-counter markets where securities are bought and sold after their issuance in the primary market. It has little to do with influencing the way an economy allocates its capital resources or the way in which sailing surplus and savings deficit unit deal with one another. However, events in the secondary market frequently provide the basis for the terms and conditions that will prevail in the primary market. If there were no secondary market in which investors could turn investments in new issues back into cash when they choose, many investors would not buy new issues in first places. If any investors truly intend to make any irrevocable commitment of their funds, the availability of a secondary market is an absolute pre-requisite to the existence of a primary market in common stock. From the perspective of the overall economy, the secondary augmentation of the flow of funds into the new issue market is particularly important. It makes it possible for the economy to make long term commitment in real capital. This point is perhaps best illustrated by considering what would occur if the financial claims issued by firms and individuals could not be traded in the secondary market. The secondary market makes it possible for those who desire to make long term real investments to obtain the money capital of savers who have no intension of committing themselves for the long term. Thus, they provide the economy with the opportunity to consider entirely new approaches to building its capital stock. Market capitalization is the market value of a company's issued shares capital; it is the product of the current quoted prices of shares and the number of shares outstanding.

Opportunities in the capital market

According to Dozie (1996: 11) the capital market can be described as a place where a nation's wealth is bought and sold. It creates facilities for raising funds for investment in long term assets. The Nigerian capital market is no expectation to this global role. The opportunities that abound in our market can be looked at from three major perspectives.

Corporate finance benefits of the capital market

A unique benefit of stock market to corporate entities is the provision of long term, non-debt financial capital. Through the issuance of equity securities, companies acquire perpetual capital for development. Through the provision of equity capital the market enables companies to avoid over reliance on debt financing. Thus improving corporate debt to equity ratio.

Financing options in the capital market

The stock market offers an array of financing instruments that the long term investments that meets the long term investment needs of both government and private sector. The medium and long term corperate debt markets remain a critical element in the sustainable development of economics. Experience in Nigeria in the last decade, shows that the use of corperate bonds is a more prudent method of raising long term finance than bank loans. The advantages are that states or local government can implement their project quickly and at the same time avoid high interest rates in the bank loans.

Secondary market activities

The stock market is an important economic sector whose uses are best appreciated from the perspective of efficiency in capital formation and allocation. An efficient stock market mobilizes savings and allocates a greater proportion to those investments with the highest perspective rate of returns after giving due allowance for risk. Secondary market is synonymous with the NSE and does not create new securities.

The business in this market is triggered off when investors in the primary market decide to dispose their holdings. In effect, the issuing companies do not directly benefit from transactions in the secondary market. It is the original investors that benefits. Such benefits come in form of Okigbo (1981:1);

a) Dividend payment.
b) Stock splits.
C) Capital appreciation.
d) Long term hedge against trends.

ENVIRONMENTAL IMPERATIVES FOR CAPITAL MARKET SMOOTH FUNCTIONING

Before the objectives of capital market can be fully achieved for economic growth of any nation, the following environmental factors are imperative for its smooth functioning;

a) An economic and administrative central structure cum policy measures that allow an appropriate role for private sector enterprises: This refers to the encouragements and public enlightenments made to the members of the public or benefits to be derived by investing their savings in capital market and all other steps to boost development for the betterment of a nation.
b) A policy scheme that encourages price flexibility as reflected by the interplay of supply and demand factors. This is the work of the regulatory bodies like Nigerian Stock Exchange (NSE), Security and Exchange commission (SEC) and government can come up with any measures for its growth if the need arises.
c) A stable political environment: frequents changes of government and their policies cum decisions without due consideration of the importance of capital market will not augur well for development. Therefore a well defined and articulated programme coupled with a stable and organized political environment will have a positive effect on the activities and growth of capital market.

Conditions for establishing a capital market

According to Ekiran (1999: 267) the environment of a country plays a major role in the success or failure of a capital market development because if an environment is conducive, it will give room for the rapid growth of a capital market than in an environment that is hostile.

Political environment

This is the first to be considered in establishment of capital market. If there is enough political stability, it gives the investors' confidence that national policies will permit over time and that this policies will appropriate measures to encourage private savings of both the entrepreneurships and the investors. But in an unstable short term view, this causes a volatile market and does not encourage long term planning.

Economic environment

In an economy where market development becomes priority, government enterprise should not be pre dominant, otherwise capital market development becomes difficult.

Role of private sector

The role of a stock market within an economy as an engine for capital formation is intentioned with findings and positive constructive role for the private sector in general. To achieve thus, both the private sector and the capital market must be integrated into the country's overall development programme, both must know and be responsive to the needs of the population as a whole. In addition, microeconomics measures such as risk, yield and liquidity of capital must be adopted to encourage the greater channeling of saving through capital market.

Legal and regulatory environment

Regulation is necessary to protect the investors and in process increase their confidence. It is also necessary to ensure a fair and orderly security in the market to achieve these objectives, company laws must be modernized and the conditions granting the listing to companies seeking quotations must be clear and positive, there must be rules and regulations for the brokers, directors and also operators of the stock market. Also, there must be code of conduct for brokers, directors and managers of the stock exchange, stock broking firms and quoted companies.

Characteristics of capital market

According to Ekiran (2000: 268) the characteristics of capital market include:

Participant

The participants of capital market can broadly be classified into regulators and the operators. The regulators include an apex regulatory body usually a securities commission and the securities exchange itself which is usually self regulatory. The operators which are sometimes referred issuing houses, regulatory etc.

Commodities traded in the market

The commodities traded in the market are securities of medium and long term nature.

Scope and size

The scope and size of a capital markets are quite large and wide. The market thrive on movement of activities and dealing.

Organization

Most capital market though wide in scope are normally organized. This is necessary in order for them to command the respect of the public and at the same time guarantee a fair play to all the participants.

Flexibility and adaptability

One way by which the effectiveness of a capital market can be measured to examine its readiness to accept and take part in changes that may occur in the overall economy.

Mode of transaction

Transaction in the capital market involves the use of financial instruments such as corperate equities (shares), debentures, government bonds etc all in an effort to raise funds.

Duality on the transfer process

This feature is based on the fact that the capital market performs the dual role of raising funds through the issue of new instruments or selling existing ones to new investors. By this function, the market helps to ratio funds among numerous competing alternative uses.

ROLE OF CAPITAL MARKET

The main function of the capital market is to transfer from surplus (savings) sectors to the deficit (capital investment) sector of economy. Hence, we say that the capital market enables or facilities the transfer of funds from savers to users.

The various institutions which facilities the transfer of funds in the capital market includes; stock exchange, issuing houses, stock brokers, shareholders, share distribution agents (commercial banks), underwriters and institutional investors (e.g. pension funds, insurance companies and merchant banks) and the Nigerian Securities and Exchange commission as the apex regulatory body.

According to Muhammed (1988: 10) the function of an active market includes the followings:

a) The promotion of rapid formation.
b) The provision of sufficient liquidity for any investor or group of investors.
c) The mobilization of savings from numerous economic units for economic growth and development.
d) The provision of an alternative source of fund other than taxation for government.
e) The creation of a built in operational and creational efficiency within the financial system to ensure that resources are optimally utilized at relatively little costs.
f) The encouragement of a more efferent allocation of new investment through the pricing mechanism.
g) The broadening of the ownership base of asset and the creation of healthy private sector.
H) Provision of an efficient mechanism for the allocation of savings among competing productive investment projects.
i) The encouragement of a more efficient allocation of a given amount of tangible wealth through changes in wealth ownership and composition.
j) It is an avenue for effecting payment on debt.
k) It is a necessary liquidity mechanism for investors through a formal debt and equity mechanism.
l) It is machinery for mobilizing long term financial resources for industrial development.

LEVELS OF MARKET EFFICIENCY

A market is said to be efficient if it uses the information available correctly in setting and adjusting prices of securities. Inoga (1977: 24). Market efficiency refers to two essential ingredient of price adjustment to new information. Speed and quality (direction and magnitude) of the adjustment. The main effect of efficiency in capital market is that it precludes most investors from the capacity or ability to out-perform the market. But the market is deficient in term of speed and quality of it reaction, the sophisticated investors would have little difficulty in profiting from the situation.

Alile (1997: 105) and Pandel (2006: 419) made a distinction between three levels of market efficiency with each level relating to a specific set of information which is increasingly more comprehensive than the previous level. These are weak, semi strong and strong levels of efficiency.

Weak efficiency

A market is efficient in the weak form if share prices fully reflect the information implied by all prior price movements. Share price movements become totally independent of previous price movement implying the absence of only price pattern with prophetic significance. Prices would only respond to new information such as new economic event of new industry.

The implication of this is that historical price and returns information does not provide a basis for superior forecasting of future price or returns. Therefore past information cannot help investors beat the market and make excessive returns.

Semi strong efficiency

This is efficient on the semi strong sense if share price respond instantaneously and unbiased to new published information. The implication of semi strong efficiency is that current share prices would invariably represent the best interpretation of the information about the firm. Therefore, it becomes futile for investors to search for bargain opportunities from analysis of published data, such as annual reports or other corporate announcements designed to lure them to the market.

Strong efficiency

The market is efficient in the strong form if share prices fully reflect not only published information but also all relevant information including data not yet publicly available.

To conclude the review on the efficient capital market theory, it can be asserted that if prices and returns prevailing at any point in the capital market do reflect all available historic and current public information, it will be difficult for investors to achieve superior performance by judging that security market conditions may be better or worse in the future.

CAPITAL MARKET AND ECONOMY DEVELOPMENT

Economic development according to Kindler Berger means improvement in Nigeria welfare especially for persons with the lower incomes, the eradication of mass poverty, illiteracy, disease and early death, changes in the composition of input and output that include shift in the underlying structure of production away from agriculture towards industrial activities, the organization of the economy in such a way that productive employment is generally among the working age population rather than the situation of a privileged minority and the correspondence groups in making decisions about the direction, economic and otherwise in which they should move to improve their welfare.

Economic development involves a sustained growth in quality and quantity of the output over a period of time, thus leading to structural transformation of the economy.

This happens when store resources are saved from productive use and savings are channeled into the type of investment which will increase productive capacity. It is at this point that the facilities created by capital market come into play for the channeling of savings into investment.

Capital accumulation of formation, directions of flow as well as the mechanization and efficient utilization of capital are crucial to any economy. One of such mechanisms is the capital market. One might at this point ask the question "What is capital?"

According to Ekiran (2000: 253) capital is the portion of resources available to the current period which rather than being consumed, are being diverted to the creation of intermediate goods which in turn would be used in the production of other goods.

Alternatively capital may refer to those stock of finished goods produced at the current period but are put for further consumption. The essence of capital formation is therefore the postponement of consumption to some future date.

Development in the Nigerian capital market

The finance and insurance sector is the one that has experience about the highest growth on the Nigeria economy especially since after the introduction of the Structural Adjustment Programme (SAP). This has had positive implications on the activities of the capital market in Nigeria.

The total number of securities transacted in the capital market (both first and second tier) was 334 in 1961. Of this, government securities were 92 while industries were 342 (72.5% of the total). In 1965, the total number of transaction increased to 1018 (204.79% over the 1961 figure). Of this, industrial securities dominated with a percentage share of 61.6%.

The number of transactions however dropped in 1970 to 643 (47.8% of which were government securities). Again, the value of total transactions in the year was N16.6 million with government securities accounting for almost the total value (98.78). Industrial securities though more in number were valued at only N0.2 million.

From 1976 however, industrial share of both in number and value of transactions increased tremendously (from 97.0 and 2.03% for 1990 to 97.3 and 3.29% for 1985 and 98.85 and 11.11% respectively in 1987.

The sudden growth both in the total number and value of transaction in the market and in the share of industrial securities during these periods can be attributed to the positive effect of the Nigeria enterprise Promotion Decree of 1977 on the development of the private enterprise in Nigeria.

The same positive trend continued at even a faster rate in the late 1980's. The share of government securities in the number and value of transaction fall from 1.44% and 92.6, in 1985 to 1.15 and 88.9% respectively in 1987, falling further to 0.39 and 65.13% in 1990,0.10 and 10.4% in 1993 and 1995. This development is in line with Structural Adjustment Programmes' policy of allowing greater private sector participation in the economy.

Unlike the above picture, the trend in the total number and value of securities traded in the capital market over the same period as being erratic with decline in number 1990 and 1993 and the value in 1985. Both the secondary and primary market recorded massive growth in 1995 as a result of the relative calm in industrial environment (compared with 1993 and 1994), the repealing of the Nigeria enterprise promotion (NEP) Decree and Exchange Countries Act (ECA) of 1962. Another development that aided positive growth in 1995 was the promulgation of the Nigerian Investment Promotion commission (NIPC) Decree No. 16 and the Foreign Exchange provision decree No. 17 of 1995.

The stock exchange began its operation on 6th June, with 8 securities listed on it. Activities in the year 2001 shows that exchange as 282 securities made up of 19 government stock / bond, 49 industrial loan (debentures) or preferences. Six companies were listed on this segment of the stock market by 1988 and by 2002 over twenty-three companies had availed themselves of the opportunities offered by this market.

Over the years, the listing has increased and as at November 30th, 1985 there were 20 securities on the exchange official list, and increasing to 290 as at the end of April 2007. Although a small market by international standard, the Nigerian capital market is one of the leading markets in Sub-Saharan Africa and has made some notable strides in recent years. With a history of over 50 years (when the first public issue was floated) and 42 years of a stock exchange, equity listings and market capitalization are still relatively small, standing at 196 and US$7.0 billion respectively at the end of March 2003. The value of equities traded at year-end 2002 was US$0.5 billion, a much lower figure than market capitalization. As a result of this, turnover ratio of 7.9% was recorded at the end of 2002, higher than the average turnover ratio for 1998 to 2002. From a historical perspective, this figure except for 2001 is an improvement, evidencing the continued rise in activities in the market. The market has been quite active this year with traded equities of N10.8 billion (US$ 86 million) in January 2003, which represented about 18% of the total equity value in 2002. By end of March 2003, N24 billion (US$188.9 million) equities had been traded. It is important to point out that the depreciation of the local currency, the naira, has continued to impact on the size of the market in dollar terms. Between 1997 and December 2002, the naira lost over half its value to the dollar. As a result, while market capitalization witnessed impressive growth in local currency terms, this was not the case in dollar terms as a much slower growth was registered. For instance, in the five years ending 2002, equity market capitalization recorded almost three-fold increase from N256.8 billion in 1998 to N748.7 billion in 2002 or a 191.5% increase while it rose by 52.6% or from US$3.8 billion in 1998 to US$5.8 billion in 2002. The point being made is that, if the local currency had been strong, the dollar size of the market would have been larger.

In 2002, equity market capitalization grew by over N100 billion (US$794million) or 15% and has remained on the upward swing this year. In the month of January 2003, equity market capitalization rose by over 12.4% and by February 2003, it had gained N116 billion (US$0.9 billion) over December 2002 more than the increase in the whole of that year. However, in March 2003, market capitalization rose by N98.2 billion (US$0.8 billion) over December 2002. If this trend continues, market capitalization by year-end 2003 is likely to significant surpassing the gain recorded in 2002.

The impressive movement in market capitalization has been led principally, by new listings, and firmer prices arising from positive market sentiments. In 2004, the stock index rose by 10.7% albeit lower than the price increase of 35.2% in 2003 and 54.0% in 2000. In point of fact, the five years (2000 to 2005) average index growth of 33.3% was higher than the growth of inflation, which averaged 12.6% during the same period.

The impressive expansion of the capital market is also evident in the size (percentage) of market capitalization to gross domestic product (GDP). A look at this over the past decade shows that market capitalization represented 14.0% of GDP in 2002 in contrast to 12.0% in 2005, 9.4% in 1999 and 5.6% in 1992. The rising trend indicates that market capitalization is growing faster (in percentage terms) than GDP.

The commission believes that as the merits of the capital market become better appreciated, more initial public offerings (IPOs) would be induced. Furthermore, privatization and strong equity prices could further bolster the percentage of market capitalization to GDP. Indeed, the capital market has in recent times become a major source of funds to corporate entities and is increasingly becoming attractive to state governments. This is particularly obvious in the number and value of new issues as well as the variety of fundraisers in the market lately.

Year 2002 was a record year for the capital market with total flotation of N61.3 billion or US$0.483 million, the highest annual record ever posted in the capital market. This single year record surpassed the cumulative figure for the preceding two years. It is also significant that the total value of flotation last year 2006 represented 36.4% of flotation in the ten years ended 2002. It may be instructive to state that the commission actually received 46 new issue applications for N78 billion but only 33 applications had been cleared and opened by year-end. The 33 flotation's in 2004 compares favourably with 27 and 21 in 2001 and 2000 respectively. The listing as increased to over 290 securities as at 2007.

THE SECOND-TIER SECURITIES MARKET AND THE EXCHANGE

This market arose for various reasons. One of them was to encourage small firms in participating in the activities of exchange. Another was to increase the number of quoted companies. The Federal Government creates this market as a kind of solution to problems, which these small companies faced in gaining quotation in the exchange.

These companies faced high cost of seeking quotation with exchange. There was the fear of losing control of the business through going to the public. Also, it is known that Nigerians hate disclosing accurate financial information about their business. Also little or no knowledge of the capital market becomes a handicap to them.

Many companies in Nigeria are experiencing these problems. But the establishment of the second-tier securities market, it helped in solving most of these problems.

Information requirement are not as extensive as that of the stock exchange. The firms involved here are nurtured and helped to grow and graduate from second tier to the first tier security market.

Benefit of second tier security market

1) Reduced cost of quotation especially for small firms.
2) Enhanced ability to buy and sell shares.
3) Assurance of continuity of business even after death of founders.
4) Greater scopes of raising capital for the companies.
5) Growth through help of the exchange and certain schemes provided by government like the employees share scheme.
6) More knowledge in the capital market operation and benefits to be derived from it Inoga (1977:64).

RESEARCH METHODOLOGY

Data source

In the collection of data, the researcher made use of secondary data only as this study involves a time series analysis .The data used in the regression is presented in Table 1.

METHOD OF DATA ANALYSIS

The method to be adopted in this study requires the use of

Table 1. data used in the regression.

YEAR	BCE	GCE	IIP	SMD	INF
1992	171071.0	58640.3	136.2	491.7	44.5
1993	280697.6	80948.1	131.7	804.4	57.2
1994	439113.8	85021.9	129.2	985.9	57.0
1995	474361.4	114476.3	128.8	1838.8	72.8
1996	371079.0	172105.7	132.5	6979.6	29.3
1997	365870.6	205553.2	140.6	10330.5	8.5
1998	519510.6	192984.4	133.9	13571.1	10.0
1999	632010.1	175735.8	129.1	14072.0	6.6
2000	472011.7	268894.5	138.9	28153.1	6.6
2001	848992.8	371897.9	144.1	57683.8	18.9
2002	1311910.4	438114.9	145.2	59402.7	12.9
2003	1833694.8	429230.0	147.0	120402.6	14.0
2004	1993610.7	456970.0	151.2	225820.0	15.0
2005	22564117.7	561931.4	158.8	262935.8	17.9
2006	24739480.5	595821.6	151.5	470253.4	8.2
2007	107575717	634656.6	158.9	1076020.4	5.4

Source: CBN statistical bulletin, 2008.

empirical analysis of simple and multiple regression techniques meant to establish the impact of capital market on the economy. Regression analysis is concerned with the study of the dependence of one variable on other variables

Model specification

This study is on how capital market has not contributed positively to Nigeria economy. The model is thus specified as:

GDP = f(MCAP, VOT, NOD, NOL)

Where;
GDP = Gross domestic product
MCAP = Market capitalisation
NOL = Number of listing
VOT = Value of transaction
NOD = Number of deals

Specifying it in econometric form:

$$GDP = a0 + al\ MCAP + a2\ VOT + a3\ NOD + a4\ NOL + Ut$$

Where;
Ao = Intercept
A1 = Impact of market capitalization
A2 = Impact of value of transaction
A3 = Impact of number of deals
A4 = Impact of new listing
Ut = Error term.

Definition of variables

Gross domestic product

This is the totality of goods and services produced in Nigeria without regards to weather income generated during the reference period accrues to or are paid to nationals of foreign countries GDP is an economic indicator which measures the welfare and economic performance of a country.

Market capitalisation

This refers to the total market value of the equity in publicity traded entity. It also refers to the value of all listed securities based on their market prices.

Number of listed securities

This is the total number of corporate bodies that have issued shares to the investing public duly approved by SEC and traded on the floor of the stock exchange.

Number of deals

As the name implies it refers to the total transactions that took place in the capital market at a given period.

Test of hypothesis

In this study, we shall undertake a statistical evaluation of an analytical model so as to determine the reliability of the result obtained. The measures to be used include:

a) Co-efficient of correlation of the regression
b) Co-efficient of determination
c) The student T-test
d) The F-test

Hypothesis 1

H_0: Capital Market does not contribute to the development of Nigeria economy

H_1: Capital Market has contributed positively to the development of the Nigeria economy.

Co-efficient of determination

The co-efficient of determination measures the degree of relationship existing among the variables. It would show the percentage of total variation in dependent variable that is explained by the independent variables.

RESULT ANALYSIS AND INTERPRETATION

In analyzing the important of the capital market to the Nigerian economy, an ordinary least square technique was used in estimating the model which tries to establish the casual relationship between the dependent variables and independent variables. This will help us determine the structural coefficient and other summary statistics.

The result is presented as follows;

GDP	= -626254.9	- 2.2248MCAP	+ 20.1519VOT	+ 11.2864NOD	+ 11131.6NOL
	(478283.3)	(1.5548)	(24.5709)	(3.2431)	(4101.4)
T – Ratio	(-1.3094)	(-1.4310)	(0.82015)	(3.4801)	(2.7121)

R – Squared = 0.96551, R – Bar – Squared = 0.95924
S.E. of regression = 1247162, F-Stat = 153.9738
DW – Statistics = 1.2916

A close examination at the result of the equation shows that some signs were in line with the opinion expectation. From the result, VOT, NOD, and NOL satisfy this condition while MCAP which is expected to be positive is negative. In this case, MCAP is not in line with the expectation.

From the equation, the different co-efficient of the variables representing the capital show the different contributions of the respective variables to the economy which is being represented by the GDP. In this line, using the co-efficient, autonomous GDP is a negative 626254.9. This simply means that when all variables are held constant, there will be a negative variation up to the tune of 626254.9 units in GDP. Similarly, a unit changes in MCAP when all variables are held constant will lead to a decrease in GDP by 2.2248 units less the autonomous component.

However, a unit change in VOT will produce a positive impact on the growth of the Nigerian economy proxied by 20.1519 units. Similarly, if NOD alone change, GDP becomes 11.2864 of the changes in NOL less the autonomous component. When taken one at a time, with other variables being held constant, VOT, NOD, and NOL will each increase GDP by 20.1519, 11.2864 and 11131.6 respectively while MCAP will reduce GDP by 2.2248.

As for the test of significant, using the T-ratio, we find that only NOD and NOL are statistically significant. This is due to the fact that it observed T-values are either greater than the "Rule of thumb" of 2. All other variables are statistically insignificant as their observed T-values are either negative or far less than 2.

From the R-squared of 0.96551, the regression co-efficient of multiple determination is 0.96551, indicating that 97% of the changes in GDP is explained by the changes in the independent variables. The R-bar square shows that 96% of the systematic variation in GDP is explained by the independent variables.

Also, looking at the F-Test reveals that the calculated values of 153.97 is greater than the critical value which indicates that the F-Statistics is significant at 1% level of significance. The implication of this is that the explanatory variables combined explain the variation in the levels of growth in GDP within the period under consideration, which shows that the null hypothesis is accepted that capital market has not contribute positively to the development of the Nigeria economy.

Hypothesis 2

H_0: Value of traded or listed securities do not contribute to the development of the Nigeria economy
H_1: Value of traded or listed securities has contributed to the development of the Nigerian economy

The DW-statistics of 1.2916 shows that there is auto-correlation in the model which needs to be correlated using the Cochrane-orcutt method and the result is presented below:

GDP	= -1.20	- 0.49485MCAP	+ 17.2238VOT	+ 1.8815NOD	+ 91181.8NOL
	(2774835)	(0.92263)	(16.5781)	(4.2990)	(14042.0)
T – Ratio	(-4.3250)	(-0.53635)	(1.0389)	(-0.43767)	(6.4935)

R – Squared = 0.99467, R – Bar – Squared = 0.98734
F-Stat = 135.6927, DW – Statistics = 2.1527

The result of the Cochrane orcutt stated was achieved after 13 iterations. From the result, we see that VOT is positively correlated to GDP while others are negative.

Using the coefficient, GDP is negative 1.20 when all variables are held constant. Holding other variables constant with only MCAP changing, GDP becomes negative 0.49485 of the changes in MCAP. When only VOT changes, GDP becomes 17.2238 of the changes in VOT less the autonomous component. Where only NOD changes, GDP becomes negative 1.8815 of the changes in NOD less the autonomous components. Where only NOL changes, GDP becomes 91181.8 of the changes in NOL less the autonomous component.

Using the T-Ratio, we find that only NOL is statistically significant. This is due to the fact that its observed T-value is greater than the "Rule of thumb" of 2. Other variables such as MCAP, VOT, and NOD are insignificant because their observed T-values are either negative or less than 2.

The R-square is 0.99467, indicating that 99% of the changes in GDP are explained by the independent variables. The R-Bar-Squared is 0.98734 indicating that 98% of the systematic variation in GDP is explained by the independent variable.

The F-value of 135.69 shows that the joint significance of the parameter estimates cannot be dismissed at 5% level because the observed F-value is greater than the critical F-value. Even, at the stringent 1%, the parameter estimate is still acceptable reflecting the significance of the variables in predicting the dependent variables.

Also, the DW statistics has equally improved to 2.15. This signifies the correlation of the auto-correlation problem which existed under the ordinary least square estimation, the alternate hypothesis is accepted which state that value of traded or listed securities have contributed to development of the Nigeria economy

DISCUSSION

In the study, quantitative tools were brought to bear on the verification of impact of the capital market to the Nigerian economy. The model employed in this research is the multiple regression model. This model enables us to predict the relationship between the dependents variable and the independent variables. The equation is fitted with least squares to determine the parameters in the model. The auto-correlation that existed in the ordinary least square result was corrected through cochrane-orcutt iterative method.

The result obtained from the estimation exercise and the Cochrane-orcutt iterative methods is fairly satisfactory. Some of the coefficients have positive impact on gross domestic product (GDP) while others have negative impact. From the result obtained from analyzing the data, we can summarize our findings thus;

1) Market capitalization which represents the total market value of listed securities have not contributed positively to the development of Nigerian economy during the period understudy. This is revealed by the negative value of market capitalization both in the least square and Cochrane-orcutt methods. The implication of this is that the total market value of equity in the capital market is relatively small to contribute positively to GDP.
2) Value of transaction (VOT) which represents the volume of securities being traded in the capital market is positively correlated to GDP both in the least square and the Cochrane-orcutt methods. The implication of this is that the volume of transactions in the capital market has contributed positively to the development of the Nigerian economy. In explaining this findings relatively with the earlier one, we can conclude that despite the fact that the market capitalization has not contributed positively to the Nigerian economy, the rate and value of trade of these few listed securities have contributed to the development of the Nigerian economy.
3) Number of deals (NOD) which represents the total transaction that took place in the capital market during the given period is positively correlated to GDP under the ordinary least square but negatively correlated in the Cochrane-orcutt method after the absence of the auto-correlation in the error term of the regression. The implication of this is that the deals in the capital market have not made positive impact on the GDP. This findings is also in agreement with findings 1.
4) Number of listed securities (NOL) which represents the total number of listed securities traded on the floor of the stock exchange is positively correlated to GDP both in the ordinary least square and the Cochrane-orcutt method. The implication of this is that the listed securities although few are being traded upon thereby contributing to the development of the Nigerian economy. This findings is also in agreement with findings 2.

Conclusion

Nigeria is part of the global community and should imitate policies that have benefited other countries. The capital market is a veritable tool that can be used to enhance the development of Nigeria. Although, the country is making effort to come out of the effect of the global financial meltdown, adequate policies should be put in place to ensure that the capital market contributes its role towards the overall development of the economy.

RECOMMENDATIONS

Some of the stringent requirement for entry into the market should be relaxed to ensure that more companies are listed. This will further increase the market capitalization and contributes positively to GDP; the capital market network should be expanded to facilitate the mobilization of savings across the country for investment. There should be public awareness campaign by capital market operators especially now that the country is just coming out of the global economic crisis. There should be appropriate pricing of securities in the capital market. This will build the confident of potential investors in the market. Government should reduce the number of public and private sectorrepresentatives on the council of the Nigerian stock exchange who are not relevant to the day-to-day activities of the market.

REFERENCES

Alile JI (1997). CapitalMarket in Nigeria.West Africa Institute for financial and Economic Management volume 4.

Ekiran O (2000). Understanding the capital market.McGraw-Hill Publisher.

Herbert W (2004). Towards an Efficient Capital Market in Nigeria. This Day Newspaper Oct. 27 2004.

Inoga MA, Enuga CO (1997). Institutional, Traditional and Asset Pricing characteristics of the Nigerian Stock Exchange", African Economic

Research Paper.
Mary J, Samson AA, Kayode OS, Elizabeth AO (2012). Capital investment is finanaced by financial institution in Nigeria economy. Res. J. Bus. Manage., ISSSN 1819-1932/DOL:103923/rjbm.
Muhammed AS (1998). Scope and function of the Capital Market.Business Times.
Nwankwo GO (1988). The Nigeria Financial System. Macmillan Publishers Ltd.
Pandey IM (2006). Financial Management Concept, Vikas Publishing House PVT Ltd.
Soyede A (2005). The Role of Capital Market in Economic Developments. Secur. Mark. J., 6(3): 6-14.

18

The domination of the pure form of capitalism over the objectives of financial statements (reporting)

Bassam Abu-Abbass* and Riyadh Al-Abdullah

Department of Accounting, College of Business Administration, University of Bahrain, P.O. Box: 32038, Kingdom of Bahrain.

A careful analysis of four documents related to the formulation of objectives of financial statements (reporting) reveals that they are dominated by the pure form of capitalism. Two documents (the Trueblood Committee's Report and SFAC No.1) are constructed as normative theories based explicitly on the U.S. culture. The other two documents (the IASB's CF and the IASB-FASB's Joint CF) are not constructed in a theory form but implicitly based on the U.S. cultural background. The first two documents are more particular and clear regarding the formulation of the objectives of financial statements (reporting) and supporting arguments (logic). On the other hand, the other two documents are general and vague. Their generality and vagueness are attributed to the unnamed belonging to the cultural background on which the objective of financial statements (reporting) is based. The reason for not declaring the belonging of the cultural background is the fear that the objective of financial statements (reporting) and standards based on them might face an outright rejection by the overwhelming majority of countries in the world.

Key words: Objectives, pure form of capitalism, earning power, cash wealth maximization, financial statements, financial reporting.

INTRODUCTION

Accounting literature is replete with critical articles on various topics related to the relationships between capitalism and accounting. Accounting is characterized as having an obvious bias towards the interest of the capitalistic groups through its emphasis on representing a particular social and political climate (Cooper and Sherer, 1984). Financial reporting, in an endevour to promote profit maximization, contribute to many agonies and silences many injustices (Chwastiak and Young, 2003). The accountant himself is characterized as partisan (Tinker, 1991; Baker and Bettner, 1997). Thus, accounting and the accountant are consciously or are forced to create rather than reflect reality (Hines, 1988) which dispossesses accounting and the accountant of any claim of reporting reality objectively (Hines, 1991). The obvious consequences of all this bias are preserving the interest of the capitalistic groups; that is preserving the status–quo situation, a total neglect of many social dimensions of accounting worthy of reporting to many interested social groups in accounting information who have undisputable influential and decisive role in allowing a commercial entity to come into being and the continuity of this being (Puxty, 1986, 1991) and moral responsibility is, on many occasions, at stake (Watkins, 2003), manifested particularly in the provision of dishonest financial information (Chambers and Crowley, 2003). This bias is also extended to accounting standards designed for international purposes such as international accounting standards (Walker, 2010). Accounting education is blamed for this bias since it disseminates capitalism-based accounting values through marginalism (Tinker, 1980), accounting equation and disclosure (Kelly, 2001) and the goal of maximizing shareholder value (Ravenscroft and Williams, 2004).

However, the above studies lack the focus on three issues. First, they do not specifically reveal the type and characteristics of capitalism that accounting is required to serve. Second, they do not demonstrate how these

*Corresponding author. E-mail: abuabbas@buss.uob.bh.

characteristics are reflected in accounting. Third, they do not offer a detailed analysis on specific accounting constituents dominated by capitalism. We use the formulation of the objectives of financial statements (reporting) by professional bodies as a case in point.

The formulation of the objectives of financial statements (reporting) is used in our study to reveal how the characteristics of one form of capitalism (that is the pure form) are reflected. The stock market consists of four important constituents: participants, their decisions, their information needs and their goal. We argue that setting objectives of financial statements (reporting) also necessitate specifying four integrated ingredients: users of financial information, their decisions, their information needs and their goals. If users are mainly represented by shareholders, their decisions are assumed to be only cash-based economic decisions, their information needs are restricted to information useful for assessing the amounts, timing and uncertainty of cash flows of an entity and their goal is only wealth maximization, then these ingredients are exactly required by what we call "the pure form of capitalism"[1]. This form of capitalism best fits the U.S. culture that is characterized by the highest form of individualism in general (Hofstede, 1984), extreme individualism in economic matters (Keller, 2007), extreme self-interest (Friedman, 1970; Kelly, 2001), shareholder primacy (Kelly, 2001), an obsession with profit maximization (Nunan, 1988; Keller, 2007) and consequently with cash wealth maximization as the mantra of capitalism (Ravenscroft and Williams, 2004) or with what is called unlimited accumulation of wealth (Chiapello and Ding, 2005). This obsession is espoused by a professsional accounting body like the FASB which has an authorized responsibility for setting accounting standards in the U.S. All or some of these characteristics are taken for granted by economic theories (e.g. neoclassical economic theories), as well as by accounting theories (e.g. positive accounting theories) and indoctrinated by economics and accounting education (Ravenscroft and Williams, 2004).

Accounting is an ideal channel for fully absorbing and subsequently disseminating cultural values. Disseminating the cultural values of the pure form of capitalism through accounting enhances the current economic domination by the U.S. over the rest of the world. It is in the interest of the U.S., as the super power No. 1 in the world, that economic domination is supplemented by an accounting system saturated with the same doctrines of the dominating economic system. Accounting is more superior to economics in disseminating cultural values because accounting techniques and the figures based on them are born out of specifics values; yet these values cannot be easily felt and/or discovered. Values are masked by the impressively well-organized and sequentially arranged accounting procedures and the ostensible exactitude of neatly presented figures. The absorbent (the brain of the human being) has no choice but to fully take in what the eyes transform out of the picture presented. This exactly resembles anesthesia for an operation. The human being does not feel what is happening to his body (the brain in the case of accounting) until the job is perfectly done and the consequences, being negative or positive, cannot be reversed.

The objective of financial reporting established by the IASB-FASB's joint effort involves the positions of the two boards. Then, it is necessary to analyze their previous positions on the objectives of financial statements (reporting). Their previous positions represented by the Statement of Financial Accounting Concept (SFAC No. 1) issued by FASB in 1978 and amended and reissued again in 2008, and Framework for the Preparation and Presentation of Financial Statement issued in 1998 by International Accounting Standards Committee (IASC) and adopted by IASB in 2001 (hereafter International Accounting Standard Board's Conceptual Framework or IASB's CF). Moreover, we also analyze the report of the study group on the objectives of financial statements issued by the American Institute of Certified Public Accountants (AICPA) in 1973 (hereafter Trueblood Committee's Report). The reason for including the Trueblood Committee's Report is because it helps reveal whether there are historically cultural roots of the pure form of capitalism in the formulation of the objectives of the financial statements (reporting). The four documents are analyzed through three main topics: cultural background, theory structure and particularity versus generality and clarity versus vagueness.

THE IMPORTANCE OF THE OBJECTIVES OF FINANCIAL STATEMENTS (REPORTING)

It is difficult to imagine any action, activity or behavior by a human being or an organization without being based on and led by an objective or a group of objectives. An objective is simply a stimulus and a guide to action. An objective is supposed to be the sole determinant of all what occur subsequently. Once chosen, objectives practically direct and lead an action, activity or behavior. Therefore, it is imperative to carefully set the objectives because all processes subsequent to the choice of an objective might turn out to be destructive or at least a waste of time and resources.

Objectives do not spring from a vacuum. Objectives, particularly as social phenomena, are the results of a long history of interaction among various ideologies

[1]The pure form of capitalism imposes on a contemporary enterprise certain characteristics. Its environment is a pure economic one and based totally on cash transactions. Its stakeholders consist of only the owners group. The social entity is never thought of. Social responsibility is considered to be "fundamentally subversive doctrine" (Friedman, 1970, P. 6). Owners are assumed to only accept wealth maximization. Management is required to be just a replica of the owners. This is a type of metempsychosis world as far as the relationship and the allocation of functions are concerned among an enterprise, its management and its owners.

related to economics, politics, customs, religion, education etc. pervasive in a specific country. Actions subsequent to the objectives adopted are influenced by the same ideologies. It is supposed that based on the objectives chosen, the other elements of a conceptual framework are logically derived. Most importantly, the influence of the objectives is supposed to extend over the setting process of standards. Actually, there ought to be inseparability between accounting standards and the objectives chosen (Anton, 1976). This must be the real fear of the IASB-FASB's Joint CF.

An understanding of the choice of objectives must be based on a clear understanding of the cultural constituents (environment) in a particular country because it is impossible to determine the objectives of financial statements (reporting) without referring to a specific cultural background. Both the Trueblood Committee's Report (AICPA, 1973, p. 13) and the SFAC No. 1 (FASB, 2008, p. 6) make an explicit commitment to the culture (environment) of the U.S. when they formulate the objectives of financial statements (reporting). Both IASB's CF and IASB-FASB's Joint CF avoid an explicit commitment to a specific culture. However, the objectives of financial reporting in both ISAB's CF and IASB-FASB's Joint CF are not without a cultural background. It is only an implicit cultural background. Explicit or implicit, it is inevitable to base the objectives of financial statements (reporting) on a specific cultural background.

CULTURE, THEORY, PARTICULARITY AND CLARITY VERSUS GENERALITY AND VAGUENESS

The development of a conceptual framework is usually looked upon as the first step in the right direction to rationalize accounting standards. This is due to the derivative nature of the conceptual framework when it is based on or constitutes a deductively derived theory. All elements in the conceptual framework are assumed to be logically derived. In this case, it is supposed that less disagreement would occur among the various interested parties on various elements of a conceptual framework as well as on accounting standards.

The importance of a theory is that it allows building an integrated coherent (Hendriksen, 1970; Llewelyn, 2003) and harmonious whole (Kerlinger, 1964) with either less or perhaps no discrepancies among the various elements of a constructed whole, ensures logical sequence, and leads to more particularity and clarity versus generality and vagueness. The particularity and clarity are necessitated by the fact that scientific theories are simply abstractions in a sense that they are focus-oriented. A theory is supposed to represent a fruitful investigation into what perplexes human being about specific element of a specific phenomenon. This means a theory is about discovery (Ryan et al., 2002). To be useful, a discovery must have two characteristics; particularity and clarity, both of which eliminate the perplexities associated with any aspect of specific phenomenon. Particularity ensures sharpness and deepness. Clarity ensures unambiguity, and accordingly further enhances sharpness and deepness.

The first step in building any theory is an adequate choice of a number of premises. In accounting, like all other social sciences, the most important premises are those related to the culture comprising various economic, political and social values. The influence of culture on accounting is demonstrated theoretically, on a multi-nation approach (Gray, 1988; Nobes, 1998), on a specific-nation approach (Harrison and McKinnon, 1986), and empirically (Chanchani and Willett, 2004). Actually, the early development of double-entry system, the cradle of the contemporary financial accounting, is attributed to certain cultural factors (Sombart, 1915; Littleton, 1933; Kam, 1990). Even the relationship between accounting, as a field of inquiry, and values becomes indisputable when Watts and Zimmerman (1990), the godfathers of positivism in accounting and the promoters of value free-based research, modify their position after Tinker et al. (1982) convincingly demonstrate that positive accounting theories cannot be value free.

Formulating a theory for an objective of financial reporting without being based on a specific cultural background leads to abstractionism, resulting in a total lack of connectedness between an incubated (objective) and an incubator (culture) which an objective is supposed to serve. Besides, the lack of the necessary connectedness between an objective and the relevant cultural background does not allow the construction of a theory in social sciences.

On the other hand, it is impossible to formulate an objective of financial reporting without a cultural background. This means that the ISAB-FASB's Joint CF actually has a cultural background reference. However, to promote the IASB-FASB's Joint CF internationally, it would be unwise, as far as the real undeclared intentions and goals are concerned, to particularly (explicitly) specify the elements of the chosen cultural background and name its country of belonging. It is just unpalatable, and sometimes may lead to social upheavals or at least resentment, to declare explicitly that a specific objective of financial statements (reporting) adopted in a specific country is based on the cultural background of a different country. An explicit preference of a foreign culture to our own culture is usually taken as a sign of self-contempt and an inferiority complex. This is a natural predisposition of human beings.

An alternative is to implicitly base an objective of financial statements (reporting) on a specific cultural background. If the elements of the cultural background are not particularly (explicitly) specified and the specific cultural background represented by these elements are not determined, then there will be two consequences. First, a theory cannot be built. Second, generality and vagueness would prevail. As a result, we assume that the lack of an explicit cultural background reference in the derivation of an objective of financial reporting leads to an absence of a theory, and consequently more generality and more vagueness would prevail.

Since it is impossible to formulate objectives of financial statements unless they are connected to a specific cultural background, then the question is: what is the cultural background of the IASB-FASB's Joint CF?

TRUEBLOOD COMMITTEE'S REPORT

A brief introduction

The AICPA established the study group on the objectives of financial statements (usually known as the Trueblood Committee) with the responsibility of specifying the objectives of financial statements. The Trueblood Committee issued a report entitled "Objectives of Financial Statements" that contains twelve objectives (AICPA, 1973). Ten objectives are related to financial accounting of a commercial enterprise (1-10)[2], objective 11 is related to non-for-profit organizations and objective 12 is related to social goals. The objectives are related to financial statements rather than to financial reporting. The Trueblood Committee's Report does not discuss the differences between financial statements and financial reporting.

Cultural background

In 1972, the Trueblood Committee's report connects, in a clear and an explicit manner, its objectives to the U.S. cultural background. For example, the Trueblood Committee's report mentions the following: "...its members agreed to concentrate on the financial environ-ment of the United States" (AICPA, 1973, p. 9), "*In the United States,*-emphasis is added- where the economic system emphasizes private enterprise, individuals and enterprises generally attempt to maximize their own wealth...*In our economy,*-emphasis is added- the attainment of individual economic goals often is encouraged by laws, such as those that define property rights[3], promote competition, and establish efficient markets" (AICPA, 1973, p. 14).

In addition, the cultural dimension is used by the Trueblood Committee's Report as a justification to allow the domination of economic goals over social goals (AICPA, 1973, pp. 53-55). It is noteworthy that the whole U.S. environment is reduced to an economic environment. The use in the above quotation of the phrase "in our economy" is an evidence of this reductionism. This reductionism can be attributed to the type of a capitalistic atmosphere in the U.S. since economic consequences are the perspective through which all other elements of the U.S. environment are looked upon.

Theoretical structure

The Trueblood Committee's report represents a theory for the objectives of financial statements. It has all the required elements of a deductively derived normative theory including minor and major premises, logical sequence, derived conclusions (the objectives of financial statements), and a harmonious integrated whole. This theorization approach is used through the whole of the Trueblood Committee's report and for the derivation of each of the 12 objectives.

The more general premises related to the evolutionary and adaptive nature of accounting as a social system, the connection between objectives of financial statements and the goals they help achieve, the user's information needs, the connection between the objectives of financial statements and the economic environment, the environment of accounting in the U.S., the users and their general needs are first used. Then the Trueblood Committee's report moves to premises of less generality such as the allocation of resources in an efficient way, the role of information in making economic decisions and the maximization tenet.

The objectives of financial statements are formulated in the order from more general to more particular. Objective no. 1 is the most general, whereas objective no. 4 is more particular in specifying information about earning power as the sole information that ought to be provided. Objectives no. 6, 7, 8, and 9 are more particular and clear since the types of financial statements are specifically named and their role in providing information related to earning power is also specifically mentioned.

As an example of a more specific derivation, let us look at objective no. 4: "An objective of financial statements is to provide users with information for predicting, comparing, and evaluating enterprise earning power[4]". To derive this objective, the major premise, related to the primary goal of each commercial enterprise which is "to increase its cash wealth so that over time it can return the maximum amount of cash to its owners" (AICPA, 1973, p. 21), is used. This goal is repeated many times through different words and phrases in chapter 2 which lead to the derivation of objective 4 (AICPA, 1973, pp. 21-24). This is followed and concurrently accompanied by other

[2] The objectives are neither numbered in the Trueblood Committee's Report nor in the SFAC No. 1. We number them in the same order shown in both documents.

[3] This is also emphasized by Grady (1965, P. 24). Grady sets the basic concept of "A Society and Government Structure Honoring Private Property Rights" at the top of a ten basic concepts to which generally accounting standards are oriented.

[4] Earning power is usually used as a measure to check whether an enterprise maximize investors' wealth or not.

premises of less generality such as those related to measurement of the enterprise in terms of its goals, the role of accounting, accounting and economic earnings.

Particularity and clarity versus generality and vagueness

The construction of a deductively derived normative theory, the establishment of a clear-cut connection between the objectives of financial statements and the U.S. culture allow a clear specification in the Trueblood Committee's Report of the user groups, their decisions, their information needs and their goals in a particular and clear approach.

It is true that some generality and vagueness can be discerned in the first two objectives. Since these two objectives are the first in the list of 12 objectives, their generality and vagueness are expected. This is quite understandable since objectives 1-10 are derived in a descending order from more general specification to more particular specification. Objective No. 1 requires the provision of information useful for making economic decisions. Neither the types of economic decision nor the decision makers are identified. Objective No. 2 requires serving those users (that is decision makers) with limited authority, ability or resources to obtain information. Objective No. 3 names two groups, shareholders and creditors, as the prime users of financial information who are interested in predicting, comparing and evaluating potential cash flows in terms of amount, timing and uncertainty. The user groups is further reduced to only one group of users; that is, owners, since, according to the Trueblood Committee's Report, the "overall concept of earning power represents the enterprise's ability to achieve its *ultimate goal*-emphasis is added- of providing maximum cash to its *owners*-emphasis is added" (AICPA, 1973, p. 23).

If objectives Nos. 1, 2 and 3 are combined, then we can infer that providers of capital, owners in particular, are the prime users of financial statements. Also the type of decisions is restricted to be economic decisions. With owners as the prime users, the economic decisions related to publicly held enterprises are restricted within buy-hold-sell of shares in the stock markets.

Objective No. 4 requires the provision of financial information for the assessment of the entity's earning power (the prime focus of the objectives of financial statements). Objective No. 5 requires the provision of information for assessing management's ability to effectively utilize resources of the enterprise. Objective No. 6 requires the provision of both factual and interpretive information useful for predicting, comparing and evaluating enterprise earning power. It is interesting to note that the Trueblood Committee's Report insists on interpretive information, which means it seeks connecting factual information with a necessary supporting logic; that is, what is sought are interpretively derived figures. If objectives Nos. 4, 5 and 6 are combined, then the logically derived wealth maximization goal represents the prime or even the sole goal sought and all financial statements are required to provide information to assess an enterprise's ability in achieving this goal.

The type of information useful for this assessment is related to earning power. The Trueblood Committee's Report leaves no doubt about the focus of financial statements, and accordingly this focus is repeated many times to make its particularization loud and clear. The emphasis on earning power is repeated in objectives No. 7 (related to balance sheet), No. 8 (related to income statement) and No. 9 (related to cash flows statement). Objective No. 10 is related to the provision of forecasts as long as they enhance the reliability of users' prediction. Since users' prediction is based on earning power, then objective no.10 is a further evidence of the emphasis on earning power.

All these emphases on earning power are based, according to the Trueblood Committee's Report, on a tendency by users to "assess the earning power of publicly held enterprises virtually every day" (AICPA, 1973, p. 23). This demonstrates the insistence of the Trueblood Committee's Report on linking the objectives of financial statements with its surrounding environment.

The objectives formulated in the Trueblood Committee's report fit exactly the pure form of capitalism. Owners (shareholders) are the prime users groups. Cash-based buy-hold-sell decisions are the only decisions that must be served by the information provided. Information on earning power is the sole information that must be provided for continuous assessment of the amount, timing and uncertainty of an entity's cash flows. Cash wealth maximization is the ultimate goal of an entity's owners and must be the ultimate goal of the entity itself.

SFAC NO. 1

A brief introduction

The FASB issued in November 1978 the Statement of Financial Accounting Concepts (SFAC) No. 1: Objectives of Financial Reporting by Business Enterprises (amended and reissued in 2008). The SFAC No.1 includes 7 objectives. All these objectives are specifically related to financial reporting of a commercial enterprise. The FASB's seven members did not reach agreement on five of the 12 objectives of the Trueblood Committee's Report (FASB, 2008, p. 16). The seven objectives are related to financial reporting rather than to financial statements. Financial statements are considered as a central feature of financial reporting (FASB, 2008, p. 5) with the implication that more and better information is usually provided by financial reporting.

Cultural background

SFAC No. 1 establishes the following universally undisputed premise; "the objectives of financial reporting are not immutable- they are affected by the economic, legal, political and social environment in which financial reporting takes place" (FASB, 2008, p. 1). "The objectives in this statement are affected by the economic, political and social environment in the United States" (FASB, 2008, p. 6). To show a true allegiance to this premise, SFAC No.1 devotes a complete sub-section entitled "Environmental Context of Objectives" to the cultural background of the U.S. (FASB, 2008, pp. 6-7). The "United States" has been specifically mentioned four times in this subsection to clearly indicate that the objectives of financial reporting are related specifically to the economic, legal, political and social environment of the U.S.

Unlike the Trueblood Committee's Report, SFAC No.1 is more elaborate on the relationship between the objectives of financial reporting and the U.S. cultural background. However, it is stated that "the objectives in this statement are affected by the economic, legal and social environment in the United States", the focus of the SAFC No. 1 is only restricted to the economic cultural background. Again, there is a type of reductionism. The objectives of financial reporting are either assumed to be only influenced by the economic cultural background or the cultural background of the U.S. consists of only one element; that is economics. In eight paragraphs (9-16) in the SFAC No. 1, almost everything related to the U.S. economy including the main characteristics, stock markets, private enterprises and individuals' tendencies are mentioned. This focus allows more particularity and clarity in the derivation of the objectives of financial reporting.

Theoretical structure

SFAC No. 1 reflects a deductively derived normative theory. It has all the required elements of a deductively derived theory. It starts with major premises and moves in a descending order to minor premises. For example, in order to derive the general objective of providing financial information, "that is useful to present and potential investors and creditors and other users in making rational investment, credit, and similar decisions" (FASB, 2008, p. 11), certain major premises are used. Some of these premises are the nature of the U.S. economy, the role of business enterprises in the U.S. economy, the private ownership of the business enterprises, the owners (investors) of the business enterprises, the fate of management being totally handed over to owners (investors), the association between the effectiveness of all elements in the whole U.S. economy and the provision of information useful to those who make economic decisions and the centrality of financial information "that reflect the relative standing and performance in evaluating alternative courses of action and the expected returns, risks and cost of each" (FASB, 2008, pp. 6-7).

However, the deductive approach is also used before and after the section entitled "Objectives of Financial Reporting". In this section, each of the seven objectives of financial reporting is first formulated then followed by relevant premises. Actually, the SFAC No. 1 itself refers to the descending nature of its objectives from more general to more particular. Par. 33 states that "The following objectives of financial reporting flow from the preceding paragraphs and proceed from the more general to the more specific. The objectives begin with a broad focus on information that is useful in investment and credit decisions; then narrow that focus to investors' and creditors' primary interest in the prospects of receiving cash from their investments in or loans to business enterprises..." (FASB, 2008, p. 10).

Particularity and clarity versus generality and vagueness

In par. 24, before formulating the objectives, and under the section entitled "Potential Users and Their Interests", a comprehensive list that contains 23 interested groups in financial information is provided. When Objective No. 1 is formulated in par. 34, this comprehensive list is reduced to include only three groups: investors, creditors and other users. Thus, SFAC No. 1 moves from generality to particularity. However, there is still an element of generality represented by the use of "other users" This gives the impression that the other users need different information.

To avoid the dilemma of different information needs for different users, the hypothesis of common information needs based on common interest is used since it is assumed in par. 25 that all interested groups have common interest in the enterprise's ability to generate favorable cash flows (FASB, 2008, p. 9). This particularization is overemphasized and made imperative in objective No. 2 (par. 37) since "Financial reporting *should*-emphasis is added- provide information to help present and potential investors and creditors and other users in assessing the amounts, timing, and uncertainty of prospective cash receipts from dividends or interest and the proceeds from the sale, redemption, or maturity of securities or loans" (FASB, 2008, p.11). By mentioning only securities and loans, the particularization is very clear.

However, there are generalization and vagueness related to other users. It is unrealistic to make imperative that all other users are solely interested in financial information useful in assessing the amounts, timing, and uncertainty related to prospective cash receipts from dividends or interest and the proceeds from the sale, redemption, or maturity of securities or loans. Although the other users do not deal with securities and loans, they are assumed in an imperative way to be interested in cash flows related to securities and loans.

Objective No. 3 is about achieving efficiency related to an enterprise's economic resources, claims to those resources and changes in them. Changes in economic resources and claims on those resources are assumed to indicate the existence of efficiency. Objective No.4 is about the provision of information on the three constituents of a balance sheet: resources, obligations and owners equity. Information about these three constituents is assumed to be useful for identifying strengths and weaknesses and accordingly assessing solvency and liquidity, providing a basis for evaluating the performance during a period and providing "direct indications of the cash inflows potentials of some resources and of the cash needed to satisfy many, if not most, obligations" (FASB, 2008, p.12). Combining objectives 3 and 4 results in a direct emphasis on earning power, that is, the ability of generating and transferring earnings into cash, which reinforces what is required by objective No. 2.

As for the priorities of the financial information, it is clear that SFAC No. 1 gives greater weight to the income statement. This is emphasized at the beginning of SFAC No. 1 and with more particularity and clarity in Objective No. 5. It is stated, in the HIGHLIGHTS, that "The primary focus of financial reporting is information about earnings and its components" (FASB, 2008, p. 2). Paragraph 42 (P. 13) elaborates on the special status accorded to earnings. In particular, SFAC No. 1 restricts judgment on performance through only earnings and its components. The relationship between earnings, earnings power and cash wealth maximization is given an utmost priority in par. 43 based on the assumption that "investors, creditors and others who are interested with assessing the prospects for enterprise's net cash inflows and its ability to generate favorable cash inflows leads primarily to an interest in information about its earnings…" (FASB, 2008, p. 9).

This particularization of interest in earnings is further emphasized by SFAC No. 1, in par. 43, by giving information on earnings a very powerful role in *"assessing enterprise's ability to generate favorable cash flows–* emphasis is added- than that of the cash flows information itself*"* (FASB, 2008, p. 14).

Objective No. 6 is restricted to the provision of information on cash receipts and disbursements and its usefulness for "understanding the operations of an enterprise, evaluating its financing activities, assessing its liquidity or solvency, or interpreting earnings information provided" (FASB, 2008, p. 14). This is a type of particularization of the relationship between cash movements (cash inflows and outflows) and earning power.

In Objective No. 7, (p. 14), SFAC No. 1 becomes more particular in emphasizing the information on earning power for judging on management stewardship or accountability. Actually, judging on management stewardship is made a function of how owners are faring through assessing an enterprise earning power (FASB, 2008, pp. 14-15).

In par. 52, the whole process of management stewardship is solely based on how the interests of owners are served. All this leaves us with the impression that owners' satisfaction is the focus of the objectives of financial reporting. The initial emphasis on providing information for decisions by investors, creditors and others are replaced by an emphasis on providing information representing the extent to which the interests of owners are served.

What are emphasized by the seven objectives of financial reporting in SFAC No. 1 are owners as the prime users of accounting information, their information needs are mainly restricted to earnings and earning power, their decisions are buy-hold-sell shares in the capital market, and favorable cash flows or cash wealth maximization is their goal. Again, these are the main constituents of the pure form of capitalism.

IASB'S CF

A brief introduction

IASB did not issue a separate report, study or statement on the objectives of financial statements. Instead, the "framework for the preparation and presentation of financial statements" which was issued by IASC, was endorsed literally by IASB. Unlike both the Trueblood Committee's report and SFAC No. 1, IASB formulates the objective of financial statements separately from the users of financial statements. Therefore, there are two separate sections in the IASB's CF: The "Users and their information needs" and "The objectives of financial statements". This separation is unnecessary and unjustified since the objective of financial statements is alluded to in the section entitled "Users and their information needs", and users and their information needs are referred to many times in the section entitled "The objective of financial statements". IASB's CF establishes only one objective of financial reporting[5].

Cultural background

IASB did not discuss any element of the financial statements objectives' cultural background. IASB's standards are promoted for the implementation by various countries with different cultures. To explicitly connect its accounting system to a specific cultural background, IASB will perhaps find no country that would adopt its IFRS except the one whose culture background is favored by IASB. It is just not plausible to publicly favor and promote a

[5] This objective is stated in par. 12 in the following way: "The objective of financial statements is to provide information about the financial position, performance and changes in financial position of an entity that is useful to *a wide range of users*-emphasis is added- in making economic decisions" (IASB, 2008, P36).

specific culture by IASB as an international organization that is supposed to be serving the accounting information needs of users in all countries.

There are four elements discussed by IASB in the section entitled "Users and their information needs" and section entitled "The objective of financial statements", which can be attributed to a specific cultural background. These elements are the specific targeted group of users of financial statements, decisions made by the targeted group of users, information relevant to their decisions and their goals. In par. 10 of the section entitled "Users and their information needs", investors of risk capital (in par. 9/a investors are only represented by shareholders) are picked up by IASB's CF as the most important users of financial statements whose information needs must be satisfied (IASB, 2006, p. 35). In paragraphs 12, 13, 14 and 15 of the section entitled "the objective of financial statements"; only the "economic decisions" taken by the users of financial information are emphasized (IASB, 2006, p. 36). The assessment of the stewardship or accountability of management is assumed to be made under the umbrella of economic decisions. This indicates a declared bias to economic decisions. The accounting information relevant to their decisions is plainly stated in par. 15 as that information relevant to evaluate the ability of an entity to generate cash and cash equivalents and the timing and uncertainty of their generation. This is an emphasis on cash wealth. In paragraph 17, an emphasis is placed on their goals, which considers profitability as an important element of performance for its role in predicting the capacity of an entity to generate cash and cash equivalent (IASB, 2006, p. 37). This is an indirect way of requiring information to be useful only in assessing the "earning power" of an entity, and accordingly, conducive to cash wealth maximization.

The same four elements are particularly emphasized in both the Trueblood Committee's report and SFAC No.1. As a result, we can say that IASB's objective of financial statements does not lack a specific cultural background. It is the U.S. culture dominated by the pure form of capitalism. This means that IASB's CF assumes consciously or unconsciously that what is useful for the U.S. is also useful for the rest of the world. This is welcome by the U.S. accounting profession. It is only that IASB's CF cannot explicitly admit that it bases its objective of financial statements on the U.S. cultural background. If it does, it will enter its whole program in a dark tunnel. One element in this dark tunnel is the big question mark about the hegemony and sacredness of the U.S. cultural background.

Theoretical structure

There is no theory of whatever type through which the objective of financial statements is derived. Paragraphs 15 to 20, explain the role of three financial statements (balance sheet, income statement and statement of changes in financial position) individually and/or jointly in the attainment of the objective of financial statements (IASB, 2006, pp. 36-37). The explanations offered are simply in the form of justifying the emphasis, in an abstract manner, on the contribution of financial statements to provide information only useful for assessing an enterprise's ability in the generation of cash and cash equivalents including information on the amount, timing and uncertainty of their generation.

When each of the 15 to 20 paragraphs is deconstructed into separate sentences, these separate sentences neither constitute separate logical premises nor do they constitute a logically cohesive whole. For example, Par. 17 consists of the following four sentences: First, information about the performance of an entity (in particular, its profitability) is required in order to *assess potential changes in the economic recourses that it is likely to control in the future* –emphasis is added. Second, information about the variability of performance is *important* –emphasis is added- in this respect. Third, information about performance is useful in *predicting the capacity* of the entity to generate cash flows from existing resource base-emphasis is added. Fourth, it is also useful in *forming judgments about the effectiveness with which the entity might employ its additional* resources–emphasis is added. There is a total lack of a logical sequence between the above four sentences. What is, for example, the connection between the first and the second sentences? In addition, there is a mere repetition. What is the fundamental difference between "*assess potential changes in the economic recourses that it is likely to control in the future*" and "*forming judgments about the effectiveness with which the entity might employ its additional* resources"? These four sentences are, at best, disconnected descriptive statements; and, at worst, a collection of hotchpotch talks. This is a much lamented situation.

In addition, there is usually a lack of providing the necessary justifying logic in each paragraph, as well as a lack of the necessary connection among various paragraphs. For example, par. 12 spells out the objective of financial statements. The objective is neither preceded nor followed in par. 12 itself or in pars. 13 and 14, which are supposedly related to par. 12, by the necessary supporting logic which would lead to an integrated whole. Par. 13 is restricted to the hypothesis of common needs to justify the provision of information useful for economic decisions; and par. 14 is restricted to the provision of information relevant to assess stewardship or accountability of management with an assumption that information useful for decision making is also useful for assessing the stewardship for the accountability of management. There is a combination of what could be regarded as unconnected descriptions and/or assignment of duties or functions. There are also a large number of companies, professional accounting organizations and countries encouraged or coerced to promote and accept

IASB's standards. Yet, the objective of financial statements, which these standards are required to achieve is neither based on a theory nor, at least, supported by well-organized logic.

Particularity and clarity versus generality and vagueness

In the section entitled "Users and their information needs", IASB's CF provides a list of seven groups of users. These groups are ranked in the following order in paragraph 9: present and potential investors, employees, lenders, suppliers and other trade creditors, customers, governments and their agencies, and public (IASB, 2006, p. 35). The IASB's CF is very particular in equating investors with shareholders. Their decisions are also restricted to be buy-hold-sell. The ranking cannot be assumed without a purpose. Given the investors the top of the list indicates a preference or non-neutrality approach to the needs of one particular group of users.

In par. 10, IASB becomes more particular and non-neutral. It is states that *"....investors are providers of risk capital to the entity, the provision of financial statements that meet their needs also meet most of the needs of other users that financial statements can satisfy"* (IASB, 2006, p. 35). Therefore, the information useful for decisions making in capital markets are assumed to be equally useful for the needs of all other users. This requires excuses. Two excuses are presented in par. 10. First, investors are granted a privileged status for being "providers of risk capital". "Providers of risk capital" is used as a justification for the non-neutrality by IASB. Risk capital is assumed as the top of all altruisms and, accordingly, owners must be rewarded by providing them with the information that satisfies their needs. The second excuse is a very bizarre one. It replaces (or even imposes) a non-existential phenomenon (that is similarity of information needs of various groups of users) with (on) an existential phenomenon (that is dissimilarity of information needs of various groups of users). The use of the "most of the needs" in the previous quotation is a type of preemptive logic to avoid criticism for being unrealistic and biased.

In paragraph 12 of the section entitled "The Objective of financial Statements", IASB's CF switches from particularity and clarity to generality and vagueness. It is stated that "The objectives of financial statements is to provide information about financial position, performance and changes in financial position of an entity that is useful to *a wide range of users*-emphasis is added- in making economic decisions" (IASB, 2006, p. 36). "Wide range of users" and "economic decisions" are too general expressions since various and diverse users are interested in various and diverse economic decisions. On the other hand, these two expressions are incompatible. There are many user groups who are not interested in economic decisions. They might be interested in social and environmental decisions. In addition, this is a type of replacing the multi-faceted environment of accounting with only economic environment. Therefore, reductionism is resorted to.

In par. 14 (p. 36), IASB's CF adheres further to generality and vagueness by referring to both the importance of providing useful information for making economic decisions and in assessing the stewardship function of management or the accountability of management for the resources entrusted to it. Unlike both the Trueblood Committee's report and SFAC No. 1, IASB's CF does not clarify how information that is assumed to be useful for cash-based economic decisions to be made by investors (which is supposed to be requiring forward looking approach to the provision of information) can also be useful for judging on stewardship of management, or the accountability of management for the resources entrusted to it (which is supposed to require a backward looking approach to the provision of information). IASB' CF gives two examples falling within two different domains, economic decision making and judging on stewardship of management. Yet, it claims that both falls within the domain of making economic decision; these are hold or sale of investment and reappointment or replacement the management. The decisions related to hold or sell of investment are pure economic decisions which require forward looking information. The decisions related to the reappointment or replacement of management are more related to the governance structure and usually requires backward looking information useful for judging on how management has conducted its responsibilities. The generalization occurs because IASB's CF implicitly assumes that what is useful for cash-based economic decisions is equally useful for judging on stewardship of management. This means that all decisions are based on cash potentials. This is unprecedented generalization of cash capabilities. The vagueness is introduced through a lack of justification for this generality.

Regarding the type of information that must be provided by financial reporting, the IASB's CF is very particular and clear. It assumes that economic decisions are based on one type of information, that is "the ability of an entity to generate cash and cash equivalents and of the timing and uncertainty of their generation" (IASB, 2006, P. 36). Accordingly, the balance sheet (par. 16), the income statement (par. 17) and statement of changes in financial position (par. 18) are all required to provide information useful for assessing an entity's ability to generate cash and cash equivalents. However, IASB, in par. 15, introduces an additional particularity by mentioning four examples (payment to employees and suppliers, payment of interests, repayment of loans and payment of dividends) from which it can be inferred that the relationship between an entity and all users are based on cash payments and receipts. This is a type of particularity dictated by further reductionism of an entity's environment from an economic one to a pure cash environment. However, it is too vague to understand why all decisions made by and for an entity are of an economic nature and that all economic decisions made by and for an entity are only based on cash.

Despite the chaotic status of the IASB's CF (mixing particularity with generality and clarity with vagueness), there is one thing that is sure; shareholders are assumed to be the prime users of information provided by financial reporting, their decisions are cash-based economic decisions or buy-hold-sell decisions, their information needs are centered on the amount, timing and uncertainty of cash and cash equivalents. However, IASB's CF avoids explicitly specifying its position on the goal of the prime user. It is difficult to avoid the combination of shareholders, cash-based buy-hold-sell decisions, and the sole interest in cash and cash equivalents can lead to anything but the goal of cash wealth maximization. As a result, we can say that financial reporting is required to provide information compatible with pure form of capitalism.

THE IASB-FASB'S JOINT CF

A brief introduction

In May 2008, an "Exposure Draft of An Improved Conceptual Framework" was issued by both the IASB and FASB to establish joint conceptual framework. In September 2010 both the IASB and FASB jointly completed and issued the "Conceptual Framework for Financial Reporting". The FASB issued it as SFAC No. 8. The IASB issued it under the title "Conceptual Framework for Financial Reporting 2010". Both are identical with very minor differences. SFAC No. 8 is used in this paper. However, we prefer to use the title "IASB-FASB's Joint CF" because it is more expressive and indicative. The IASB-FASB's Joint CF consists of two chapters. Chapter 1 deals with the objective of financial reporting, and chapter 2 deals with qualitative characteristics and concepts. Our discussion is restricted to chapter 1. Chapter 1 consists of two main parts. The first part, the Objective of Financial Reporting (OBs), consists of 21OBs (OB1 – OB21). The second part is the "Appendix: Basis for conclusions for chapter 1", which consists of 35 bases for conclusions called (BCs), (BC1.1-BC1.35). The BCs includes "reasons for accepting some alternatives and rejecting others" (FASB, 2010, p. 6). Therefore, the BCs are further arguments to support of those in the OBs. The IASB-FASB's Joint CF establishes only one objective[6].

Cultural background

There is a lack of an explicit discussion of a cultural background in the IASB-FASB's Joint CF. This is replaced by an implicit cultural background references. There are certain repeated terms and expressions which allow the derivation of this implicit cultural background. For example, buying, holding and selling equity and debt instruments, equity investors, holders of debt instruments, participants in stock markets, efficient allocation of resources in capital markets, timing, amount and uncertainty of cash flows, cash, net cash inflows, future net cash inflows, future cash flows, cash returns, an enterprise's ability to generate cash flows, etc. All these indicate what is required by a cultural background favoring the pure form of capitalism.

Theoretical structure

To give the impression that the IASB-FASB's Joint CF is a scientific piece of work, OB1 suggests that the reason for starting with the objective of general purpose financial reporting is that the other elements of the conceptual framework (that is reporting entity, qualitative characteristics, the constraints, useful financial information, elements of financial statements, definition, recognition, measurement, and presentation and disclosure) are logically derived (FASB, 2010, p. 1). This is a promising statement and allows inferring that standards issued later on will be logically constructed through a deductive system.

On the other hand, what is said in OB1 is not followed in the construction of chapter 1 of the IASB-FASB's Joint CF. Surely; there is an absence of a theory. There is even an absence of a logically harmonious whole. This is in harmony with IASB's CF. This lack of a theory extends over pages (1 to 5), which are devoted to the OBs, and pages (6 to 14), which are devoted to BCs. For example, OBs (3 to 11) cannot be considered as a collection of major and minor premises leading to OB2 as a logically derived conclusion since there is no attempt to connect the OBs (3 to 11). Then a logical sequence among them cannot be distinguished. They represent more or less discussions on various unconnected, fragmented, topics. OB3 and OB4 represent discussions of the three groups of users and an emphasis on future net cash inflows to the entity. OB5, OB6, OB8 and OB10 represent discussions of the information needs of the primary users and an implicit reference to the "common information needs" hypothesis. OB7 is about providing information related to the value of reporting entity. OB9 is about the information needs of management. OB11 represents a discussion on the reality of financial statements in that they "are based on estimates, judgments and models rather than exact depictions" (FASB, 2010, p. 3).

[6]In OB2, the objective of financial reporting is set in the following way: "The objective of general purpose financial reporting is to provide financial information about the reporting entity that is useful to existing and potential investors, lenders, and other creditors in making decisions about providing resources to the entity. Those decisions involve buying, selling, or holding equity and debt instruments and providing or settling loans and other forms of credit" (FASB, 2010, p. 1).

Particularity and clarity versus generality and vagueness

The objective of financial reporting stated in OB2 contains two characteristics of a general nature (FASB, 2010, p. 1). First, the provision of financial information that is useful for making decisions. Thus, the types of decision are not specified; that is economic and/or otherwise. Second, the decision makers are divided into three groups: existing and potential investors, lenders and other creditors. None of these groups are identified. Obviously, clarity is missing in OB2.

The generalization in OB2 related to the group of investors is eliminated in OB3 through the identification of the economic decisions taken by this group that is some clarity is introduced. It becomes clear that the decisions are those related to buying, selling or holding shares and debt instruments. Accordingly, the decision makers can be easily identified. To some extent, the group of lenders is determined through identifying decisions made by them which include providing and settling loans. It is not known who make these loans; banks, financing houses, other institutions or individuals. The group of other creditors and their decisions are never identified. Thus, the IASB-FASB's Joint CF prefers particularity in case of equity investors and holders of debt instruments, mixing generality and particularity in case of lenders, and absolute generality in case of other creditors. This may give the impression that the emphasis of the objective of financial reporting is on investors' equity and debt instruments' holders and their decisions.

In BC1.15c, users are divided into two groups: primary users and all types of stakeholders (FASB, 2010, P. 9). However, the information needs of these two groups are not grouped into two types. There is only one type of information needs. It is the information needs of the primary users which are assumed to be likely useful to "all types of stakeholders". This type of generalizing the usefulness of information needs of one group to all other groups is not justified. Once groups are different, their information needs are also different.

The problem with satisfying the information needs of the primary users is that this group is looked upon as a cohesively intimate group (a totally single homogeneous group) rather than a collection of groups with diametrically opposing information needs. Actually, the IASB-FASB's Joint CF concedes to this fact in OB8 when it is stated that "Individual primary users have *different and possibly conflicting information needs and desires*"- emphasis is added- (FASB, 2010, P. 2). Bondholders prefer less courageous (less risky) decisions, modest profit and the availability of a minimum idle cash to insure the payment of interest and the repayment of principal on due dates. On the other hand, shareholders are interested in more courageous (more risky decisions) that bring the highest possible return to insure maximum dividends and appreciation in their shares in the stock capital markets. Then, the question is that: is it possible to satisfy the information needs of these two groups though information about returns that is useful for creation of perceptions related to an entity's ability to generate future cash inflows as is mentioned in OB3? Besides, this type of information is different from information required by the remaining groups, that is lenders and other creditors. For example, suppliers are not interested in this long-run approach. They are usually interested in information related particularly to the availability of cash, and less interested in whether an entity achieves profit or loss. Their focus is on short- run. This is diametrically opposite to the interest of both shareholders and holders of debt instruments.

To summarize, the formation needs of one sub-group within the primary group, that is shareholders and holders of debt instruments, is set at the particularity level. Their information needs are generalized. This generalization results from the assumption that their information needs are identical and specifically restricted within return (variability and components) that is useful for creation of perception about an entity's ability to generate future cash inflows. Once the information needs are particularized, then there must be a particular group interested in the particular information.

The IASB-FASB's Joint CF tries to be more general and vague as far as earning power is concerned. Earning power per se is never mentioned in the IASB-FASB's Joint CF. However, the elements constituting earning power are mentioned in many places in IASB-FASB's Joint CF. First of all, cash, cash flows, future cash flows and net future cash flows are mentioned 16 times in 11 OBs out of 21 OBs. This indicates again that economic decisions are about or based on cash. Thus, the whole financial reporting environment is reduced to cash-based economic decisions. In OB3, it is clear that cash return is the most important. It is stated that "Investors', lenders', and other creditors' expectations about *returns*–emphasis is added- depends on their assessment of the amount, timing, and uncertainty of (the prospects for) *future net cash inflows* –emphasis is added- to the entity. Consequently, existing and potential investors, lenders, and other creditors *need information* –emphasis is added- to help them assess the prospects for *future net cash inflows*- emphasis is added- to the entity" (FASB, 2010, pp. 1-2). In addition, the relation between financial position, income statement and changes in financial position and cash generation ability by an entity is also emphasized in OBs 4, 14, 15, 17, and 18.

Three elements of the pure form of capitalism are emphasized. These are the cash-based economic decisions (buy-sell-hold), information on earning power and cash wealth maximization.

It is true that IASB-FASB's Joint CF does not explicitly show any favoritism to shareholders. Since these three elements are more prominent and they fit the pure form of capitalism, then the explicit avoidance of favoring shareholders is necessitated by showing ostensible neutrality to facilitate the promotion of any subsequent pronouncements based on continuous joint efforts by the IASB and FASB. The IASB-FASB's Joint CF tries to be more general and vague because it is fully aware that the direct involvement of the FASB at the international arena requires giving the impression that it does not intend to promote the U.S. culture.

CONCLUSIONS

This paper develops a theory based on three complementary parts: culture, theoretical structure and particularity and clarity versus generality and vagueness. For any accounting theory, a culture reflected by a number of major premises represents the necessary threshold that directs the other parts of the theory. Thus, particularity is ensured since a theory is born out of a specific culture and accordingly could be regarded as constructive contributor to that culture. Clarity is also guaranteed since the connection between a specific culture and theoretical structure avoids unnecessary interpretations. This is because a specific culture (premises) leads to a specific conclusion. When formulating the objectives of financial statements (reporting), both the Trueblood Committee's report and the SFAC No. 1 make an explicit commitment to the culture (environment) of the U.S. This allows both documents to formulate objectives for financial statements (reporting) molded to serve the four elements of the pure form of capitalism: owners (shareholders), the cash-based economic decisions (buy-sell-hold), the provision of information on earning power and the goal of cash wealth maximization. The connection between a specific culture and the theoretical structure ensures specific conclusions (objectives) that fit the pure form of capitalism. Generality of a theory is restricted to a culture identical to that of the U.S. Thus, an objective of financial statements (reporting) based on the U.S. culture can be of no use in a different culture since the U.S. culture is unique as any other culture of any other country. U.S. exceptionalism is a clear reflection of this uniqueness (De Lange and Howieson, 2006). Particularity and clarity are necessary ingredients of both the Trueblood Committee's Report and the SFAC No. 1. The objectives in both the IASB's CF and IASB-FASB's Joint CF also reflect the four elements of pure form of capitalism. Yet these two documents avoid an explicit commitment to a specific culture. However, a careful analysis of these two documents clearly reveals that they do not lack a specific cultural background since it is inevitable to avoid leaning on a specific cultural background whenever an accounting concept is formulated. The characteristics of the economic setting provided by the IASB's CF and IASB-FASB's Joint CF leaves no doubt that the objectives formulated by them fit the U.S. culture. There are two main differences between the former two documents (Trueblood Committee's report and the SFAC No. 1), and the latter two documents (IASB's CF and IASB-FASB's Joint CF). First, in the former two documents, the U.S. cultural characteristics are formally discussed and logically connected among themselves and to the objectives of financial statements (reporting). In the latter two documents, the characteristics of the U.S. culture are scattered here and there in order to camouflage the true origin of the cultural background of the objectives of financial statements (reporting). Second, in the first two documents, a theoretical structure based on logical sequence is constructed. In the latter tow documents, a theory is naturally missing. The reason for this chaotic situation in both the IASB's CF and IASB-FASB's Joint CF is that they cannot explicitly admit that the formulated objectives are based on the pure form of capitalism which is born out of the U.S. culture. The doctrines of the pure capitalism in many countries around the globe are either weak or do not exist. One obvious consequence of adopting the objective of financial reporting formulated in the IASB-FASB's Joint CF and the subsequent implementation of IFRSs by these countries is the dissemination and domination of the doctrines of the pure form of capitalism. Ideological domination is the perfect tool for all political, economic and military hegemony.

REFERENCES

AICPA (1973). Objectives of Financial Statements. Report of the Study Group on the Objectives of Financial Statements.

Anton HR (1976). Objectives of Financial Accounting: Review and Analysis. J. Accountancy pp.40-51

Baker C, Bettner M (1997). Interpretive and Critical Research in Accounting: A Commentary on its Absence from Mainstream Accounting Research. Crit. Perspect. Account. 8(1):293-310.

Chambers V, Crowley P (2003). Capitalism and Accounting Reform. SAM Adv. Manage. J. pp.44-56.

Chanchani S, Willett R (2004). An Empirical Assessment of Gray's Accounting Value Constructs. Int. J. Account. 39(2):125-54.

Chiapello E, Ding Y (2005). Searching for accounting Features of Capitalism: An Illustration with economic Transition in Chain, http://en.scientificcommons.org/8108743.

Chwastiak M, Young JJ (2003). Silences in Annual Reports. Crit. Perspect. Account. 14 (5):533-552.

Cooper DJ, Sherer MJ (1984). The Value of Corporate Accounting Reports: Arguments for a Political Economy of accounting, Accounting. Organ. Soc. 9(3-4):207-232.

De Lange P, Howieson B (2006). International Accounting Standards Setting and U.S. Exceptionalism. Crit. Perspect. Account.17:1007-1032.

FASB (2008). Statement of Financial Accounting Concepts No. 1. Original Pronouncement as Amended. www.fasb.org/pdf/aop_CON1.pdf.

FASB (2010). Statement of Financial Accounting Concepts No. 8. Conceptual Framework for Financial Reporting. Chapter 1: The Objective of General purpose Financial Reporting. And Chapter 3: Qualitative Characteristics of Useful Financial Reporting. www.fasb.org/cs/blobserver?blobcol.

Friedman M (1970). The Social responsibility of Business is to Increase its Profits. The New York Times Magazine. September 13. (www.colorado.edu/.../friedman-soc-resp-business.ht...).

Gray SJ (1988). Towards a Theory of Cultural Influence on the Development of Accounting Systems Internationally. ABACUS 24(1):1-15.

Harrison GL, McKinnon JL (1986). Culture and Accounting Change: A New Perspective on Corporate Reporting Regulation and Accounting Policy Formulation. Account. Organ. Soc. 11(3):233-252.
Hendriksen E (1970). Accounting Theory. Homewood, IL: Richard D. Irwin.
Hines R (1988). Financial Accounting: In Communicating Reality, We Construct Reality. Account. Organ. Soc. 13(3): 251-261.
Hines R (1991). The FASB's Conceptual Framework, Financial Accounting and the Maintenance of Social World. Account. Organ. Soc. 16(4):313-331.
Hofstede G (1984). The Cultural Relativity of the Quality of Life Concept. Acad. Manage. Rev. 9(3):389-398.
IASB (2006). International Financial Reporting Standards (IFRSs). International Accounting Standards Foundation. IASCF Publication. London
Kam V (1990). Accounting Theory, Second Edition. John Wiley & Sons.
Keller AC (2007). Smith Versus Friedman: Markets and Ethics. Crit. Perspect. Account. 18:159-188.
Kelly M (2001). The Divine Right of Capital: Dethroning the Corporate Aristocracy. Berrett-Koehler Publishers, Inc. San Fransisco.
Kerlinger FN (1964). Foundations of Behavioral Research. New York: Holt. Rinehart and Winston.
Littleton AC (1933). Accounting Evolution to 1900, American Institute Publishing Co.
Llewelyn S (2003). What Counts as "Theory" in Qualitative management and Accounting Research? Account. Auditing Accountability J. 16(4):662-708.
Nobes CW (1998). Towards a General Models of the reasons for International Differences in Financial reporting. ABACUS pp.162-187.
Nunan R (1988). The Libertarian Conception of Corporate Property: A Critique of Milton Friedman's Views on the Social Responsibility of Business. J. Bus. Ethics. 7:891-906.
Puxty A (1986). Social Accounting as Immanent Legitimation: A Critique of a Technist Ideology. Adv. Public Interest Account. 4:95-112.
Puxty A (1991). Social Accountability and Universal Pragmatics. Adv. Public Interest Account. 4:35-46.
Ravenscroft S, Williams PF (2004). Conference Address: Considering Accounting Education in the USA Post-Enron. Account. Educ. 13(supplement 1): 7-23.
Ryan B, Scapens RW, Theobald M (2002). Research Method and Methodology in Finance and Accounting, 2nd Edition, South-Western Cengage Learning.
Sombart W (1915). The Quintessence of Capitalism, Dutton & Co.
Tinker AM, Merino BD, Neimark MD (1982). The Normative Origins of Positive Accounting Theories: Accounting Ideology and Thought. Account. Organ. Soc. 7(2):167-200.
Tinker T (1980). Towards a Political Economy of Accounting: An Empirical Illustration of the Cambridge Controversies. Account. Organ. Soc. 5(1):147-160.
Tinker T (1991). The Accountant as Partisan. Account. Organ. Soc. 16(3):297-310.
Walker M (2010). Accounting for Varieties of Capitalism: The Case against a Single Set of Global Accounting Standards. Br. Account. Rev. 42:137-152.
Watkins S (2003). Ethical Conflicts at Enron: Moral Responsibility in Corporate Capitalism. California Manage. Rev. 45(4): 6-19.
Watts RL, Zimmerman JL (1990). Positive Accounting Theory: A Ten Year Perspective. Account. Rev. 65(1):131-159.

19

The contextual framework of corporate income tax evasion

Paula Fukofuka

School of Business Administration, South China University of Technology, Wuhan, Tianhe District, Guangzhou, P.R. China 510640.

The Portfolio Investment Framework, the Principal Agent Framework and the Principal Two Agents Framework of tax evasion, individually or collectively, are inadequate to represent fairly the dynamics of corporate income tax evasion. These behavior based frameworks are for the prediction of tax evasion and their usefulness for identifying tax evasion is limited. To bridge the gap between the prediction and the identification aspects of corporate income tax evasion, this paper presents the Contextual Framework of Corporate Income Tax Evasion, structured with twelve ideas and thirty five dynamics to guide and direct future research. With a simple game theory model, the paper promotes the tax audit cut-off policy that incorporates a reward program for the agent of government, ensures audit frequency and tests independence of the agent from governance.

Key words: Portfolio Investment Framework, Principle Agent Framework, Principle Two Agent Framework, Tax Evasion, Corporate Income Tax Evasion.

INTRODUCTION

Tax evasion is a loss of government revenue and is a major concern across nations. Recently, the estimated loss to tax evasion is approximately (USD$) $21 billion in the next five years in the United States (Adams, 2013), $30 billion a year in Russia (Amos, 2013), $21 billion a year in the United Kingdom (Wright, 2013) and $30 billion a year in Greece (Daley, 2010). On the other hand, these estimations are the estimated tax saves of tax evaders. The opposing loss or benefit of tax evasion between government and tax evaders is the reason why tax evasion keeps recurring and has persisted.

A key aspect in the combat against tax evasion is the ability of tax collectors to detect evasion. This aspect was ignored in the development of theoretical frameworks and modeling of tax evasion. Theoretical inquiries, however, concentrated on the prediction of tax evasion based on the logic of evasion behaviors. The ignoring of the detection aspect of evasion limits the usefulness of the behavior based frameworks because the worth of the prediction is evaluated by the successful identification of evasion when it is executed.

The purpose of this paper is to present a contextual based approach, specifically, for corporate income tax evasion, to bridge the gap between the prediction and the identification of corporate income tax evasion. The main argument is that the context of tax evasion presents identifiable indicators of evasion that the behavior based approach ignored. And so, attentions are drawn herein to the dynamics of tax evasion in the corporate context that may indicate the existence of income tax evasion. This is essential for the correct understanding of the problem of corporate income tax evasion and is extremely important for strategizing of appropriate innovative actions in dealing with this problem. The intention is to offer a new framework to guide future research on this topic.

The remainder of this paper is structured in six sections. Section 2 describes the three commonly used tax evasion frameworks in the theoretical discussion of and modeling for corporate tax evasion and their inadequacies to the corporate setting. Section 3 describes the dynamics of the Contextual Framework of Corporate Income Tax Evasion (CFCITE). In Section 4, the basic ideas of the CFCITE are summarized. Section 5 provides a simple game theory model based on the CFCITE to explain tax audit strategies. In Section 6, the results and the practical applications of the basic model are discussed. Section 7 provides the conclusion remarks.

Three commonly used tax evasion frameworks

A tax evasion framework is a basic structure of ideas that provides the guiding principles and directions for constructing, analyzing and interpreting tax evasion. Because different frameworks offer different guidelines and directions, an inaccurate structure can cause us to make mistaken conclusions or attempt erroneous or impossible tasks. To avoid such problems, is to ensure the accuracy of the frameworks used for examining corporate income tax evasion.

Theoretical discussions and modeling of and for corporate income tax evasion are commonly based on three tax evasion frameworks – the 'Portfolio Investment Framework' (PIF), 'Principal Agent Framework' (PAF) and the 'Principal Two Agent Framework' (PTAF). These frameworks were developed originally to explain the tax evasion behavior of individual taxpayers but were later adopted or extended by researchers and economists to explain the tax evasion behavior of a corporation, which in fact does not exist.

The PIF was developed by Allingham and Sandmo (1972) to explain the evasion behavior of individual taxpayers as a portfolio investment decision that reflects taxpayer's rationality and response to punishment and uncertainty. The basic structure of this framework consisted of four ideas. First, tax evasion is an investment decision made under uncertainty circumstances. Second, punishment deters evasion behavior as in the economics of criminal activity proposed by Becker (1968) and by Tulkens and Jacquemin (1971). Third, uncertainty for detection and conviction promotes risk takings as in the economics of uncertainty explained by Arrow (1970) and Mossin (1968). Fourth, an individual is risk averse as in the axioms for behavior under uncertainty proposed by Von Neumann-Morgenstern (1947). With these ideas, Allingham and Sandmo (1972) showed that tax evasion of individual taxpayers is deterred by a higher probability of detection and encouraged by higher tax rates.

Reinganum and Wilde (1985) developed the PAF to determine the optimal audit policy of the IRS[1]. This framework is structured with five ideas. First, taxation is a Principal-Agent relationship between tax-collecting agency (principal) and taxpayer (agent). Second, income is a random variable. Third, the agent freely observes his or her true income but the principal can only observe it at a cost (audit costs). Fourth, this is a relationship of two parties with opposing interests where the principal seeks to maximize tax collected from the agent, net of audit costs, while the agent seeks to minimize tax paid to the principal. Fifth, the reported income of the agent conveys information about the agent's true income to the principal. In the Principal-Agent relationship, the principal asks the agent to report his or her income and then assesses the reported income to determine its truthfulness. If the reported income is deemed to be too low it triggers an audit (audit cutoff policy) at a cost to the principal.

Kim and Park (1990) departed from the PAF and proposed the PTAF, arguing that in the real world the tax collectors, who are different from government, collect the taxes from taxpayers on behalf of and for the government. This framework was developed to explain the possibility of bribery in the process of collecting taxes. The framework is structured with three ideas. First, tax collector (agent of government) collects taxes on behalf of government (the principal) from the taxpayer (who is also an agent of government). This gives the name *"Principal Two Agents"*. Second, tax reporting and tax auditing is a three-person game (a sequential game) in which the principal must induce the tax collector not to accept bribery and implement a system that discourages the taxpayer from evading taxes. Third, the players are intellectual rational individuals who behave strategically to maximize personal utility.

There are three major problems in the uses of the PIF, the PAF and the PTAF to explain corporate income tax evasion. First, identifying of the taxpayer as the tax evader is not the case with corporate income tax evasion. Second, these frameworks are behavior based but a corporation is an artificial person without evasion behavior. Third, these frameworks do not offer a just and fair representation of the dynamics of corporate income tax evasion.

First, the PIF, the PAF and the PTAF were framed with the assumption that the taxpayer is the tax evader. This is not so in corporate income tax evasion because a corporation is the taxpayer but is not the tax evader. An evader is "any person who knowingly makes a false or misleading statement or omits from such statement any material particular which lessens his tax liability" (Government of Tonga, 2002). A corporation, however, is a legal person[2] created by law (Friedman, 1970), distinct and separate from its individual owners or shareholders, who is incapable of knowingly evading tax.

Although a corporation has legal rights and obligations in the same way that a natural person does, it requires a

[1] The tax-collecting agency in Tonga is the Revenue Services Department.

[2] Commonly referred to as artificial person, fictitious person, legal entity or body corporate.

natural person, an agent, to act and make decisions on its behalf. And so, tax evasion decisions are decisions made by the agent[3] not the corporation. Therefore, the agent is the central party for the investigation of corporate income tax evasion. However, this does not free the corporation from the penalty of tax evasion because, as the principal, the corporation remains liable for the decisions of the agent.

Secondly, the behavior based approach examines the evasion behaviors of taxpayers identified by the PIF, PAF and PTAF as behaviors under uncertainty, towards risk and punishment, and the ability to make rational decisions. These are dispositions of a natural person not of a legal person. Just so, the behavior based approach is suitable for the investigation of individual tax evasion but is inappropriate for corporate income tax evasion.

In addition, tax evasion is commonly discussed as a moral choice. But such choice can only be made by a natural person because only a natural person has or lacks intrinsic qualities, that is, the virtues of prudence, temperance, fortitude, justice, charity, faith and hope which are the intrinsic qualities of a moral person identified by virtue ethics and Christianity. And so, to infer that a corporation is the tax evader advocates that a corporation is capable of making moral choices. Although a corporation has legal rights, privileges, responsibilities and liabilities, as an investor, a borrower, a customer and so forth that may associate a corporation with the morality of the choice (deontology), the consequence of the choice (consequentialism) and the moral consensus for the situation (situational morality), it is incapable of knowingly choosing right from wrong.

Further, the behavior based approach requires behavioral information. But information about the evasion behaviors of an evader is neither disclosed in a tax return nor possible to deduce from it. Therefore, the usefulness of the behavior based approach, by itself, for identifying tax evasion lacks merit.

Thirdly, the PIF, the PAF and the PTAF, individually or collectively, are inadequate to offer just and fair representations of the dynamics of corporate income tax evasion. The inadequacies relate to the ignoring of parties, like directors and auditors, who can significantly compel or constrain an evasion decision, the relationships between the parties in corporate settings and the influences of the environments.

Collectively, the PIF, the PAF and the PTAF identified four parties in the income tax relationship, who are the taxpayer, the agent of a corporation, the tax collectors as agent of government and the government or tax authorities. The power of the owners, the directors and other external parties to induce or discourage evasion decisions are ignored. As a result, these behavior based approach ignored the usefulness of third party information for identifying the existence of an evasion. But third party information, such as, the tax returns of the owners, the directors, a subsidiary of the corporation, and so forth of a corporation can be used to verify the truthfulness of the tax return of a corporation.

Further, the behavior based approach emphasized evasion behavior as a responding mode strictly based on rationalization of benefits and consequences. Social interactions and the influences of the environment are ignored. This paper argues that social factors or relationships and environmental factors are important elements of tax evasion. To ignore these elements from the constructions of evasion frameworks impaired the usefulness of a framework to drive theoretical discussions of and modeling for corporate income tax evasion.

The CONTEXTUAL FRAMEWORK OF CORPORATE INCOME TAX EVASION

The contextual based approach presents corporate income tax evasion as a strategic decision of a natural person (the agent) to evade the income tax of a legal person (the principal) in a contextual setting comprised seven parties, twenty four relationships and four environments. These formed the thirty five dynamics that framed the Contextual Framework of Corporate Income Tax Evasion as shown in Figure 1.

Parties are the persons, both natural persons and legal persons, who influenced directly or indirectly the decisions to evade corporate income taxes. They are denoted in Figure 1 as number (24), (25), (26), (27), (28), (29) and (30). Their involvement or influence exists either in the form of formal contracts or via professional or social associations. They[4] are the owner, the director, the corporation, the CEO, the government, the tax collector and the external parties. The owner is the investor who invests in the corporation with an intention to gain maximum returns on his or her investment. The owner appoints the director to govern the "affairs"[5] of the corporation and to ensure maximum returns on the owner's investment. The director then engages the CEO to manage the corporation under the directions and supervisions of the director. External parties refer to external auditors, competitors, financial institutions, other organizations and all those whose formal and social associations affect directly or indirectly the evasion decisions of the CEO and or the honesty of the tax collect taxes from all parties and thus employs the tax collector to collect the taxes on its behalf. Each party has

[3] Revenue Services Administration Act 2002, Section 2(1)(b) identify the agent of corporation as the "chief executive officer" synonymously referred to in Tonga as "general manager", "managing director" or "manager".

[4] For simplicity purposes, the parties are expressed in singular form.

[5] Companies Act 1995, Section 127(1)(2) and (3): "Management of the company: (1) The business and affairs of a company shall be managed by, or under the direction or supervision of, the board of the company. (2) The board of a company has all the powers necessary for managing, and for directing and supervising the management of, the business and affairs of the company. (3) Subjections (1) and (2) are subject to any modifications, exceptions or limitations contained in this Act or in the Company's constitution."

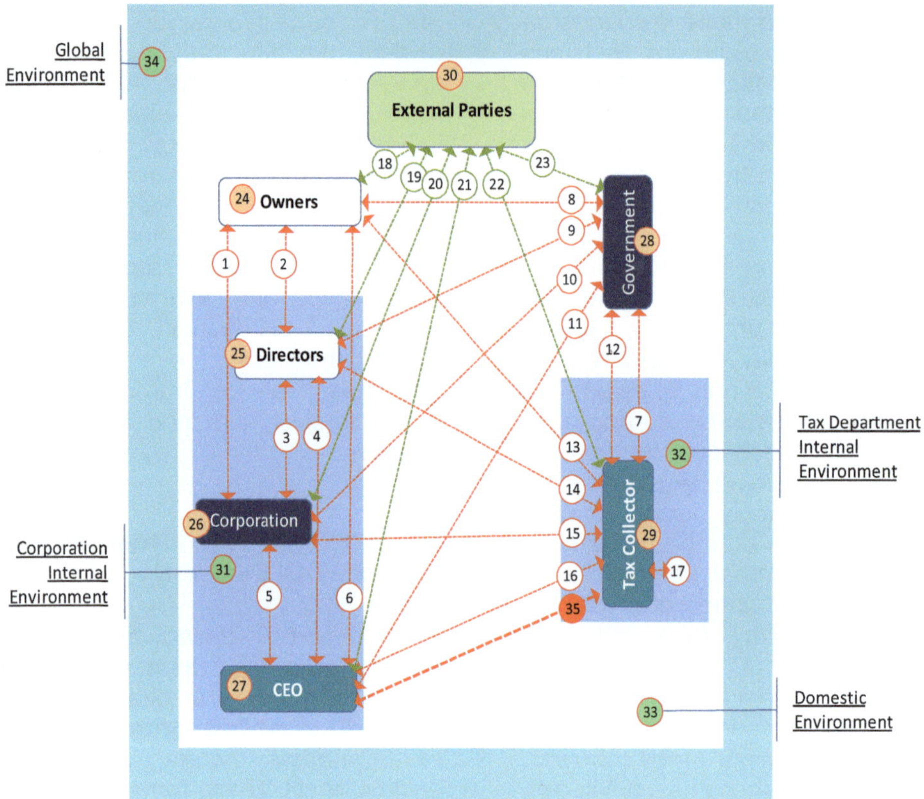

Figure 1. The context of corporate income tax evasion.

collector. The government has a constitutional right[6] to multiple roles and plays multiple positions. For example, the CEO is an individual, citizen of society, taxpayer, employee, tax agent of the corporation, a subordinator of the director and so on.

The characteristics of the individual party are important to the identifications of corporate income tax evasion. This requires information about the identity, size or numbers, status, type and authority of each party. Examples are: is the owner a legal or natural person, how many directors are in the board, is it a family or government or public corporation, and what is the degree of control or the percentage of the share-holdings? The characteristics of the parties provide information about how easy it is to induce and support an evasion decision, the costs for enticing an agent to evade tax and the degree of influence of each party on the agent. Example, if the corporation has one owner and this owner is the only director, then the difficulty that may involve in persuading other owners or members of the board to approve and support an evasion decision does not exist. And so, the influence of the owner/director on the agent is high. Another example, a public or government owned corporation is subject to a higher degree of scrutiny and accountability than a private or family corporation. And so, there is a higher possibility to evade corporate income tax in a family corporation than in a government owned enterprise. Another example, a tax return supported by financial statements audited by one of the big four auditors is more reliable than one supported by a newly established audit firm or a private auditor.

In relationships, Figure 1 identified twenty four relationships in corporate income tax denoted as numbers (1) to (23) and (35). For simplicity, the relationships within a corporation and within the Revenue Services Department are excluded but they are equally important. The twenty four relationships can be classified under eight groups as shown in Table 1.

Each relationship in Group 8 is determined by the role and position of the each external party to the owner, the director, the corporation and the CEO. Examples, the external party may be an investee, a family member, a lender, a supplier, a customer, an auditor or a subsidiary of the owner, the director, the corporation or the CEO.

Relationship (35) represents the game of corporate income tax evasion, a game between the agent of the

[6] Act of Constitution of Tonga, Clause 18 and Clause 19(b): "All the people have the right to expect that the Government will protect their life liberty and property and therefore it is right for all the people to support and contribute to the Government according to law…."; "The Treasurer, with the approval of Privy Council, shall have power to increase or decrease the taxes and/or customs duties and shall have power to levy new taxes and/or customs duties, and all such increase or decreases or new taxes or customs duties shall be published in the Gazette and shall have full force and shall remain effective from the date of publication in the Gazette until rescinded by the Legislative Assembly or by the Treasurer with the approval of Privy Council."

Table 1. Relationship groups.

Groups	Numbers
1. Investor – investee relationship	(1)
2. Principal – agent relationship	(2), (3), (5) and (7)
3. Agent – investee relationship	(4)
4. Agent – agent relationship	(4) and (35)
5. Investor – agent relationship	(6)
6. Citizen – government relationship	(8), (9), (10), (11), (12) and (23)
7. Taxpayer – tax collector relationship	(13), (14), (15), (16), (17) and (22)
8. Other relationships	(18), (19), (20) and (21)

corporation (the CEO) and the agent of government (the tax collector). In this relationship, the CEO seeks to minimize the income tax payments of the corporation thereby minimizing the tax revenue of the government and the tax collector seeks to maximize the revenue of the government by maximizing the income tax payments of the corporation. However, the results of this game can be influenced by the twenty four relationships of corporate tax evasion. Therefore, it is important to identify the relationship indicators that may encourage evasion decisions.

Lack of independence, conflict of interests and lack of segregation of duties are trademarks of corruption, theft and tax evasion but these are ignored by the PIF, PAF and PTAF. In corporate income tax evasion, the existence of these trademarks can be identified in the relationships between the multiple role play of the individual party and between the parties. Example, if the owner or the majority controlling shareholder is also the managing director, then conflict of interest is present as there is no independence and segregation of duties between ownership, governance and the agent. In this case, the cost for enticing an agent to evade tax is eliminated and the benefits derived by the owner/director/agent from an evasion are high and so the possibility to evade tax is also high. Another example, if the tax collector is an investor in the corporation or a friend or family of the agent or the director or the owner, the possibility for collusion between the tax collector and the agent to evade tax is high. Relationships between the parties can be easily established from the tax returns of the corporation or from third party information.

Several studies identified incentive structures and organizational culture (Ferrell et al., 1989; Travino, 1986), ambient lighting (Zhong et al., 2010), environmental wealth (Gino and Pierce, 2009) and moral standards of a society (Fukofuka, 2013) as environmental factors that influenced choice behavior. And so, the four environments that influenced evasion decisions are denoted in Figure 1 as numbers (31), (32), (33) and (34).

The internal environment consists of the employees, the physical environment, procedures and systems, internal controls, organizational culture and factors within a corporation that not only influence the activities and choices of the agent but may also indicate the possible existence of tax evasion. To falsify a tax return and financial statements, it requires an override of the accounting systems. And so, internal environmental indicators of evasion may include weak accounting internal control systems, lack of independence and segregation of duties within a corporation, reliance on cash transactions, poor record keeping, absence of a qualified in- house accountant, employees in the finance department are dominated by family members and high turnover of employees in the finance department.

The internal environment of the Revenue Services Department does not only affect the decisions of the tax collector but also influences the evasion decisions of the CEO. The perceived probability of detection refers to the CEO's perceptions of the ability of the Revenue Services Department to detect evasion. Ability includes competency level, efficiency level, effectiveness level and the internal environment of the Revenue Services Department. Therefore, the tax collector should likewise assess the ability of the CEO to evade tax. This requires an assessment of the internal environment of a corporation.

The domestic environment consists of domestic forces that affect the evasion decision of the CEO and the assessment and audit decision of the tax collector. These include technological force, sociocultural force, demographic force, political force and legal force. The global environment is the sum total of the domestic environments of the international communities. The domestic and global environments generally affect the parties. However, in spite of the general effect, they are important elements for the understanding of tax evasion. Example, the greater the differences between the income tax rate for corporation and the tax rates for withholding tax, PAYE tax and personal income tax, the greater the temptation to transfer corporate assets and income to a third party at a lower tax rate. Another example, the lower the economic condition in a country the greater the vulnerability of the parties for bribery and unethical conducts.

Now, the most common methods of corporate income tax evasions, listed in BizFilings Toolkit (2013), are (a) deliberately under-reporting or omitting income like not reporting sales; (b) keeping two sets of books and making false entries in books and records; (c) claiming false or overstating expenses like overstating travel expenses or paying family members for work they did not perform; (d) claiming personal expenses as business expenses; (e) hiding or transferring of assets or income to a third party; and (f) engaging in a sham transaction as in labeling a transaction as something it is not. Depending on the evasion method used by the evader, other forms of evasion are also performed as part of the cover up. Examples, the evading of consumption tax to cover up the under-reporting or omitting of sales or the evading of personal income tax to cover up personal income acquired from the evasion. In some cases, like the transferring of income to a third party at a lower tax rate, the evaded income may be reported by the third party to alleviate the suspicions of the tax collector.

The PIF, the PAF and the PTAF are limited for strategizing of appropriate innovative actions in dealing with these common corporate income tax evasion methods because these frameworks offered no indicators for identifying evasion. But with the contextual based approach, there is a better chance of being able to identify them by considering the existence of evasion indicators provided by the parties, their relationships and the environments.

The basic ideas of the contextual framework of corporate income tax evasion

To summarize the basic ideas, the Contextual Framework is structured with the following twelve ideas.

First, the corporation is the taxpayer but not the evader of corporate income tax because a corporation is a legal person who is incapable of making evasion decisions. The evader is the agent or the CEO of the corporation.

Second, a corporation, as a principal, passively shares the consequences of and perhaps the benefits from an evasion.

Third, corporate income tax is an Agent-Agent relationship between the agent of the corporation and the agent of government each represents and acts in the best interests of their respective principals. However, the agents will not always act in the best interest of the principals (Jensen and Meckling, 1976) because if the agents perceive that the probability of detection is low and the benefit acquired from an evasion is high, the agents will deviate from protecting the interests of the principal to maximize personal interests.

Fourth, since corporate income tax evasion is an agency relationship, it encourages tax evasion and "bribery" (Kim and Park, 1990).

Fifth, the agent of a corporation and the agent of the government are natural persons and risk averse individuals (Allingham and Sandmo, 1972).

Sixth, the agent of the corporation will evade the income tax of the corporation if and only if the agent perceives to personally benefit directly or indirectly from the evasion. Also, the agent of the government will accept bribes for the same reason.

Seventh, taxation is a game of information. The agent of a corporation submits a false or misleading corporate tax return or omits from such return any material particular which lessens the tax liability of the corporation. The tax collector then employs direct and indirect methods to assess the submitted tax return to identify evasion. Direct methods refer to the assessing of the accuracy and reasonableness of figures and information disclosed in a tax return. Indirect methods involve the determination of the correct taxable income by analyzing the contextual factors. Based on the evidence from the assessment, the tax collector accepts or amends the taxable income of the corporation or performs an audit thereon.

Eighth, a tax audit imposes audit costs on the principals but not on the agents. That is, government bears the costs of performing the audit and the corporation acquires the costs for accommodating the tax audit.

Ninth, certain characteristics of the individual parties, such as the size of a corporation, having offshore branches, size of the board of directors, type of ownership, and nature of the company, may indicate the presence of tax evasion or a specific method of evasion.

Tenth, tax evasion is influenced by both the personal morality of the agent and the consensus morality of situations or the context.

Eleventh, lack of independence, conflicts of interest and lack of segregation of duties between parties can be indicators of tax evasion.

Twelfth, the evasion decisions and tax assessments are influenced by the internal environment of the corporation, the internal environment of the taxation department, the domestic environment, and the global environment, particularly, those factors that esteem unethical conduct. Accordingly, there are indicators of tax evasion in the environments.

Basic model and the CFCITE

The basic model considers a two person game. One is the Agent of the Corporation (AC) and the other the Agent of the Government (AG). In this game, the AC is uncertain whether the AG will conduct a tax audit or not on the tax return of the Corporation filed by the AC. This uncertainty implies the equilibrium of the game is mixed strategy equilibrium and not pure strategy equilibrium.

The AC has two strategies: forge the tax return of the Corporation (t_1) at probability p_{t1} or lodge true return (t_2) at probability p_{t2}, and $p_{t1} + p_{t2} = 1$. The AG also has two strategies: conduct tax audit (a_1) at probability p_{a1} or no tax audit (a_2) at probability p_{a2}, and $p_{a1} + p_{a2} = 1$.

To assess the influence of independence, two cases will be assessed. Case one: the parties are independent of each other and case two there is no independence. In

Table 2. Case one strategies matrix.

	Player 2: AG	
Player 1: AC	**a_1 conduct tax audit**	**a_2 no tax audit**
t_1 *forge tax return*	$\mu_{ac} + \varepsilon - \varphi_{ac}$ β	$\mu_{ac} + \varepsilon$ $-\delta$
t_2 *lodge true return*	0 $-\propto$	0 0

case one, the costs of evasion to the corporation (C_μ) are shared between the parties collaborated in evading the income tax of the corporation. Assuming all parties involved with the exception of the AG, then C_μ = AC's share (μ_{ac}) + Owner's share (μ_o) + Director's share (μ_d) + Other Parties' share (μ_p). If the AG performed strategy a_1, the evasion will be discovered and the involved parties will be penalized. And so, the fines will be: the corporation = φ_{co} = tax rate (true income – underreported income), the AC = φ_{ac} = tax rate (μ_{ac}), the Owner = φ_o = tax rate (μ_o), the Director = φ_d = tax rate (μ_d), and the Other Parties = φ_p = tax rate (μ_p). Therefore, the expected returns of the parties in case one are as follows.

Corporation: Tax rate (true income – underreported income) – C_μ – tax audit assistance cost – φ_{co}

AC: μ_{ac} – evasion other related gain – φ_{ac}
Owner: $\mu_o - \varphi_o$
Director: $\mu_d - \varphi_d$
Other Party: $\mu_p - \varphi_p$
Government: $\varphi_{co} + \varphi_{ac} + \varphi_o + \varphi_d + \varphi_p$ – audit cost – AG bonus
AG: Bonus – $\propto - \delta$

where tax audit assistance cost, $\varphi_{co}, \varphi_{ac}, \varphi_o, \varphi_d, \varphi_p$, audit cost and AG bonus only if AG performed strategy a_1. The evasion other related gain (ε) refers to the AC other forged returns related gains (such as booking of personal expenses as company's expenses) and $\varepsilon \in [0, \varphi_{ac}]$. The AG bonus ($\beta$) is a percentage of the Government net income from strategy a_1, that is, $\beta = \pi\% \,(\varphi_{co} + \varphi_{ac} + \varphi_o + \varphi_d + \varphi_p - audit\ cost)$.
If the AG performed strategy a_1 whereas the AC performed strategy t_2, then the AG acquired an economic and social loss = $\propto$ for incurring an audit cost to the Government for no return. On the other hand, if the AG performed strategy a_2 whereas the AC performed strategy t_1, then the AG acquired an economic and social loss = δ for failure to recover the evaded tax and the penalties thereon.

The strategies matrix of the AC and the AG for case one are shown in Table 2.

The following calculations were conducted to identify the mixed strategies Nash Equilibrium of the game.

First, identify the AG's expected return p^*_{t1} from the strategies:

$$\begin{aligned}\mu_{AG1} &= (\beta).p_{t1} + (-\delta).p_{t2}\\ &= (\beta).p_{t1} + (-\delta).(1 - p_{t1})\\ &= \beta.p_{t1} - \delta + \delta.p_{t1}\\ &= p_{t1}(\beta + \delta) - \delta \qquad (1)\\ \mu_{AG2} &= (-\propto).p_{t1} + 0.p_{t2}\\ &= -p_{t1}.(\propto) \qquad (2)\end{aligned}$$

Let $\mu_{AG1} = \mu_{AG2}$ and solves for p^*_{t1}:

$$\begin{aligned}p_{t1}(\beta + \delta) - \delta &= -p_{t1}.(\propto)\\ p_{t1}(\beta + \delta + \propto) &= \delta\\ p^*_{t1} &= \frac{\delta}{\beta + \delta + \propto}\end{aligned}$$

This means, if the probability of adopting strategy t_1 by the AC is less than $\frac{\delta}{\beta+\delta+\propto}$, then the AG optimal selection is strategy a_2 (no tax audit). On the other hand, if the probability of adopting strategy t_1 by the AC is greater than $\frac{\delta}{\beta+\delta+\propto}$, then the AG optimal selection is strategy a_1 (conduct tax audit). However, if the probability of adopting strategy t_1 by the AC equals to $\frac{\delta}{\beta+\delta+\propto}$, then conducting a tax audit or no tax audit make no difference to the AG.

Second, identify the AC expected return p^*_{a1} from the strategies:

$$\begin{aligned}\mu_{AC1} &= (\mu_{ac} + \varepsilon - \varphi_{ac}).p_{a1} + (\mu_{ac} + \varepsilon).p_{a2}\\ &= (\mu_{ac} + \varepsilon - \varphi_{ac}).p_{a1} + (\mu_{ac} + \varepsilon)(1 - p_{a1})\\ &= (\mu_{ac} + \varepsilon - \varphi_{ac}).p_{a1} + (\mu_{ac} + \varepsilon) + p_{a1}(-\mu_{ac} - \varepsilon)\\ &= p_{a1}.(-\varphi_{ac}) + \mu_{ac} + \varepsilon \qquad (4)\\ \mu_{AC2} &= 0.p_{a1} + 0.p_{a2}\\ &= 0 \qquad (5)\end{aligned}$$

Let $\mu_{AC1} = \mu_{AC2}$ and solves for p^*_{a1}:

$$\begin{aligned}p_{a1}.(-\varphi_{ac}) + \mu_{ac} + \varepsilon &= 0\\ p_{a1}.(-\varphi_{ac}) &= -\mu_{ac} - \varepsilon\\ p^*_{a1} &= \frac{\mu_{ac} + \varepsilon}{\varphi_{ac}} \qquad (6)\end{aligned}$$

Table 3. Case two strategies matrix.

	Player 2: AG	
Player 1: AC	**a_1 conduct tax audit**	**a_2 no tax audit**
t_1 *forge tax return*	$\mu_{ac} + \mu_o + \mu_d + \varepsilon - \varphi_{ac} - \varphi_o - \varphi_d$ β	$\mu_{ac} + \mu_o + \mu_d + \varepsilon$ $-\delta$
t_2 *lodge true return*	0 $-\propto$	0 0

This means if the probability of the AG adopting strategy a_1 is less than $\frac{\mu_{ac}+\varepsilon}{\varphi_{ac}}$, then the AC optimal selection is strategy t_1 (forge tax return). On the other hand, if the probability of the AG adopting strategy a_1 is greater than $\frac{\mu_{ac}+\varepsilon}{\varphi_{ac}}$, then the AC optimal selection is strategy t_2 (lodge true return). However, if the probability of the AG adopting strategy a_1 equals $\frac{\mu_{ac}+\varepsilon}{\varphi_{ac}}$, then to forge tax return or lodge true return makes no difference to the AC.

Therefore, the Mixed Strategy Nash Equilibrium of this model is $\{p^*_{t1} = \frac{\delta}{\beta+\delta+\propto}$, and $p^*_{a1} = \frac{\mu_{ac}+\varepsilon}{\varphi_{ac}}\}$. Accordingly, in the case where the parties are independent of each other, the AG conducts tax audit at the probability of $\frac{\mu_{ac}+\varepsilon}{\varphi_{ac}}$, and the AC forges the tax return of the corporation at the probability of $\frac{\delta}{\beta+\delta+\propto}$.

In case two, assuming there is no independence between the Owner, the Director and the AC, that is, the Owner is the Director as well as the AC, then the expected returns of the parties in case two are as follows.

Corporation: Tax rate (true income – underreported income) – C_μ – tax audit assistance cost – φ_{co}
AC: $\mu_{ac} + \mu_o + \mu_d - \varepsilon - \varphi_{ac}$
Other Party: $\mu_p - \varphi_p$
Government: $\varphi_{co} + \varphi_{ac} + \varphi_p + \varphi_o + \varphi_d$ – audit cost – AG bonus
AG: $\beta - \propto - \delta$

Then the Strategies Matrix of the AC and the AG in case two are shown in Table 3.

First, identify the AG's expected return p^*_{t1} from the strategies. However, the AG's expected return in case two remains the same as in case one because $\beta, -\delta$ *and* $-\propto$ do not change. Therefore, the AG optimal selection strategies in response to the probability of adopting strategy t_1 or strategy t_2 by the AC are the same as in case one.

Second, identify the AC expected return p^*_{a1} from the strategies:

$$\mu 2_{AC1} = (\mu_{ac} + \mu_o + \mu_d + \varepsilon - \varphi_{ac} - \varphi_o - \varphi_d).p_{a1} + (\mu_{ac} + \mu_o + \mu_d + \varepsilon).p_{a2}$$
$$= (\mu_{ac} + \mu_o + \mu_d + \varepsilon - \varphi_{ac} - \varphi_o - \varphi_d).p_{a1} + (\mu_{ac} + \mu_o + \mu_d + \varepsilon)(1 - p_{a1})$$
$$= (\mu_{ac} + \mu_o + \mu_d + \varepsilon - \varphi_{ac} - \varphi_o - \varphi_d).p_{a1} + (\mu_{ac} + \mu_o + \mu_d + \varepsilon) + p_{a1}(-\mu_{ac} - \mu_o - \mu_d - \varepsilon)$$
$$= p_{a1}.(-\varphi_{ac} - \varphi_o - \varphi_d) + \mu_{ac} + \mu_o + \mu_d + \varepsilon \quad (7)$$

$$\mu 2_{AC2} = 0.p_{a1} + 0.p_{a2} = 0 \quad (8)$$

Let $\mu 2_{AC1} = \mu 2_{AC2}$ and solves for p^*_{a1}:

$$p_{a1}.(-\varphi_{ac} - \varphi_o - \varphi_d) + \mu_{ac} + \mu_o + \mu_d + \varepsilon = 0$$
$$p_{a1}.(-\varphi_{ac} - \varphi_o - \varphi_d) = -\mu_{ac} - \mu_o - \mu_d - \varepsilon$$
$$p^*_{a1} = \frac{\mu_{ac} + \mu_o + \mu_d + \varepsilon}{\varphi_{ac} + \varphi_o + \varphi_d} \quad (9)$$

This means if the probability of the AG adopting strategy a_1 is less than $\frac{\mu_{ac}+\mu_o+\mu_d+\varepsilon}{\varphi_{ac}+\varphi_o+\varphi_d}$, then the AC optimal selection is strategy t_1 (forge tax return). On the other hand, if the probability of the AG adopting strategy a_1 is greater than $\frac{\mu_{ac}+\mu_o+\mu_d+\varepsilon}{\varphi_{ac}+\varphi_o+\varphi_d}$, then the AC optimal selection is strategy t_2 (lodge true return). However, if the probability of the AG adopting strategy a_1 equals $\frac{\mu_{ac}+\mu_o+\mu_d+\varepsilon}{\varphi_{ac}+\varphi_o+\varphi_d}$, then to forge tax return or lodge true return makes no difference to the AC.

Therefore, the Mixed Strategy Nash Equilibrium of case two is $\{p^*_{t1} = \frac{\delta}{\beta+\delta+\propto}$, and $p^*_{a1} = \frac{\mu_{ac}+\mu_o+\mu_d+\varepsilon}{\varphi_{ac}+\varphi_o+\varphi_d}\}$. Accordingly, in this case where independence is lacking, the AG conducts tax audit at the probability of $\frac{\mu_{ac}+\mu_o+\mu_d+\varepsilon}{\varphi_{ac}+\varphi_o+\varphi_d}$, and the AC forges the tax return of the corporation at the probability of $\frac{\delta}{\beta+\delta+\propto}$.

DISCUSSION OF THE BASIC MODEL AND PRACTICAL APPLICATIONS

The strategies matrixes in Table 1 and Table 2 indicate that when $\mu_{ac} + \varepsilon > \varphi_{ac}$ and $(\mu_{ac} + \mu_o + \mu_d + \varepsilon) > (\varphi_{ac} + \varphi_o + \varphi_d)$ for case one and case two respectively, the AC's expected return from strategy t_1 is higher than the AC's expected return from strategy t_2. For these reasons, some of the ACs are motivated to forge tax returns in spite of the known penalties for doing so. Furthermore, if the AG decides not to conduct a tax audit when the AC selects t_1, the AG loss will be greater than zero because at $\{t_1, a_2\}$ the AG loss equals $-\delta$.

For practical applications, the model provides three strategies for tax audit policy. First, rewarding of the AG for the capturing of tax evasion reduces the tax evasion. Second, high frequency of tax audit reduces tax evasion. Third, lack of independence between the AC and the owner and/ or the director is indicator of tax evasion. To test the validity of these suggestions, the model must satisfy the following conditions.

Condition 1: if the rewarding of the AG for the capturing of tax evasion reduces corporate income tax evasion, then an increase of β should reduce the probability at which the AC evades the income tax of the corporation.

Condition 2: if the increase of tax audit frequency reduces tax evasion, then an increase of $\propto$ or a decrease of β should reduce the probability at which the AC evades the income tax of the corporation.

Condition 3: if the lack of independence between the AC and the owner and/or the director increases tax evasion, then $\frac{\mu_{ac}+\mu_o+\mu_d+\varepsilon}{\varphi_{ac}+\varphi_o+\varphi_d}$ is greater than $\frac{\mu_{ac}+\varepsilon}{\varphi_{ac}}$.

REWARD PROGRAM FOR THE AG

Reward program, particularly for whistleblower, has been regulated and implemented in the United States of America as one of the means of combating tax evasion. Since December 2006, Congress is willing to pay a minimum of 15% and a maximum of 30% of the amount that the IRS actually collects to an informant who provides "specific and credible" information that will "substantially" lead to the determination and collection of $2 million or more of tax (Tax Whistleblower Law Firm, 2013; IRS of the United States of America, 2013). The purpose of this new incentive is to encourage people who otherwise would not step forward and report tax fraud; and the program was estimated to raise approximately $182 million over 10 years (Herman, 2006). The basic premise of the reward program is that reward will attract whistleblowers because whistle-blowers are rational individuals who seek to maximize personal utility.

On this same premise, this paper suggests that since the AG is a rational person who seeks to maximize personal utility, the rewarding of the AG (β), based on the AG's ability to capture evasion, will encourage the AG's commitment to capture tax evasion; and since the AC is also a rational person, the AC's knowledge of such reward will reduce the probability at which the AC evades corporate income tax. Reward or bonus herein refers to the incentives offered on top of the AG's basic salary.

Since the model established β as one of the denominators in the AC's evasion probability $\frac{\delta}{\beta+\delta+\propto}$, it suggests that an increase of β, if δ and $\propto$ remain constant, will reduce the probability at which the AC evades corporate income tax. Alternatively, if β is eliminated from the model and then recalculate the probability at which the AC forges tax return, the new probability is $\frac{\delta}{\delta+\propto}$. And since $\beta > 0$, it means that $\frac{\delta}{\delta+\propto}$ is greater than $\frac{\delta}{\beta+\delta+\propto}$. Therefore, Condition 1 is supported.

Accordingly, the model shows that if Government implements a program that rewards the AG for the capturing of tax evasion, such program will reduce corporate income tax evasion.

Frequency of tax audit and audit policy

Prior studies about the best method for selecting of tax returns for auditing compared cut-off policy and random audit policy. Reinganum and Wilde (1985), through a simple model, showed that an audit cut-off policy is better than any random audit policy. Mookherjee and Png (1989), however, presented a model with sufficient conditions for random audits to be optimal. Pestieau et al. (2004), in a simple model, showed that government can significantly alter the tax audit results by adjusting the audit policy in response to the individuals' differences in risk preference and income. This paper draws attention to the frequency of performing a tax audit as an aspect of audit policy. Frequency refers to the number of times the AG audits the tax returns of a corporation.

This paper proposes that an increase in the number of times the AG audits the tax return of a corporation reduces the probability at which the AC of that corporation evades corporate income tax. This is so because the basic model established $\propto$ as one of the denominators in the AC's evasion probability $\frac{\delta}{\beta+\delta+\propto}$. And so, an increase in $\propto$, if β and δ remain constant, reduces the probability at which the AC evades corporate income tax. Even when performing a tax audit on a true return, the mere conducts of that audit negatively influence the decision of that AC to evade tax in the future. Further, the relationship between δ and $\frac{\delta}{\beta+\delta+\propto}$ suggests that if δ is high, then $\frac{\delta}{\beta+\delta+\propto}$ is high. This implies that failure to audit a forged return will motivate the AC to evade the income tax of their corporation. Therefore, Condition 2 is supported.

In order to ensure audit frequency, the audit policy must incorporate a set of audit frequency cut-off rules. Such rules may be based on the size of the corporation or the level of income or level of expenses or type of industry and so forth. For example, part of an audit frequency cut-off rules may be stated as: 'Every corporation with a total assets or total expenses or total sales that exceed one billion at any point in time during the year are subject to no less than three audits in every five years; and those corporations with a total assets or total expenses or total sales below one billion are subject to no less than two audits in every four years. The time of audit shall be determined by the AG'. The validity of the cut-off policy and the importance of increasing the risk faced by the AC are supported by Reinganum and Wilde (1985) and Mookherjee and Png (1989).

Lack of independence as an evasion indicator

Although the lack of independence, segregation of duties and conflict of interests between parties within a corporation are the indicators commonly used by internal and external auditors to identify control weaknesses, mismanagements and fraud in a corporation (Chinese Institute of Certified Public Accountants, 2008), their inclusion in tax evasion modeling or application is lacking. This paper advocates that the AG should also use the same principles, in particular, the relationships between the AC and the Owner and/ or the Director, for identifying evasion. This suggestion is supported if $\frac{\mu_{ac}+\mu_o+\mu_d+\varepsilon}{\varphi_{ac}+\varphi_o+\varphi_d} > \frac{\mu_{ac}+\varepsilon}{\varphi_{ac}}$.

From Section 5:
$\mu_o + \mu_d > 0$
$\varphi_o + \varphi_d > 0$ and
$\mu_o + \mu_d > \varphi_o + \varphi_d$

Therefore, $\frac{\mu_{ac}+\mu_o+\mu_d+\varepsilon}{\varphi_{ac}+\varphi_o+\varphi_d} > \frac{\mu_{ac}+\varepsilon}{\varphi_{ac}}$ and Condition 3 is supported. Accordingly, the AG's tax audit probability should shift from $\frac{\mu_{ac}+\varepsilon}{\varphi_{ac}}$ to $\frac{\mu_{ac}+\mu_o+\mu_d+\varepsilon}{\varphi_{ac}+\varphi_o+\varphi_d}$ when independence between the AC and the Owner and/or the Director is deprived. Further, when the AC knows that the lack of independence, in actuality and in appearance, will subject the corporation to a higher probability of being audited by the AG, the AC who is in such dilemma will be motivated to lodge true returns.

Therefore, the basic model promotes the cut-off policy and recommends the inclusion of independence tests as part of the audit selection process.

Conclusion

Theoretical researches on corporate income tax evasion have been disadvantaged far too long by the incompatibility and limitations of the PIF, the PAF and the PTAF to represent fairly the dynamics of corporate income tax evasion. These behavior based frameworks emphasized the logic of evasion behaviors for predicting tax evasion and ignored the identification aspect of tax evasion. This paper argues that in order to enhance the theoretical contributions to the problem of corporate income tax evasion, it requires a framework that bridges the gap between the prediction aspect and the identification aspects of corporate income tax evasion. For this purpose, the paper offered the CFCITE.

The paper identifies four aspects of audit policy that will reduce corporate income tax evasion. First, the cut-off policy is recommended over the standard random audit policy. Second, there should be a reward program to encourage the capturing of tax evasion and discourage it practices. Third, cut-off policy should include rules to ensure the frequency of tax auditing. Fourth, audit policy should include an independence test to ensure that corporate characterized by lack of independence between governance and the AC are subjected to a higher audit probability than those corporations without such characteristics.

The paper makes several significant contributions to academic knowledge of corporate income tax evasion. First, the paper departs from the traditional consensus that the corporation is the evader of corporate income tax and reveals that the agent of a corporation is the real evader. Second, the paper adds the characteristics aspect of the parties as important elements to the study of corporate income tax evasion. Third, the paper adds the dynamics of relationships and environments as indicators of tax evasion. Fourth, the paper departs from the traditional behavior based approach and offers a contextual based approach for the study of corporate income tax evasion.

Future study may focus on improving the basic model by considering additional factors such as bribery.

REFERENCES

Adams D (2013). Florida hit by "tsunami" of tax identity fraud. Reuter. 12 February 2013. Viewed 5 April 2013, http://www.reuters.com/article/2013/02/17/us-usa-tax-fraud-idUSBRE91G05M20130217?irpc=932.

Allingham MG, Sandmo A (1972). Income tax evasion: A theoretical analysis. J. Public Econ. 1:323-338.

Amos H (2013). Russia losses £52bn a year in tax evasion and illegal transfers, says bank chief. Guardian. 21 February 2013. Viewed 5 April 2013, http://www.guardian.co.uk/world/2013/feb/21/russia-loses-52-billion-tax-evasion.

Arrow KJ (1970). Essays in the theory of risk-bearing. North-Holland, ch.3.

Becker GS (1968). Crime and punishment: An economic approach. J. Political Econ. 76:169-217.

BizFilings Toolkit (2013). Tax avoidance is legal: Tax evasion is criminal. Fact checked on 28 January 2013. Viewed 22 April 2013, http://www.bizfilings.com/toolkit/sbg/tax-info/fed-taxes/tax-avoidance-and-tax-evasion.aspx.

Chinese Institute of Certified Public Accountants (2008). China standards on auditing, review, other assurance, related services and quality control. Standards CICPA. Dalian Publishing House. People's Republic of China.

Daley S (2010). Greek wealth is everywhere but tax forms. New York Times. 1 May 2010. Viewed 5 April 2013, http://www.havocscope.com/tag/greece/page/2/.

Ferrell OC, Gresham LG, Fraedrich J (1989). A synthesis of ethical decision models for marketing. J. Macromarketing 9:55-64.

Friedman M (1970). The social responsibility of business is to increase its profits. New York Times Magazine. 32FF.
Fukofuka P (2013). The effects of the moral standards of Tonga on government auditors' moral choice behavior, Master thesis. China University of Technology, China.
Gino F, Pierce L (2009). The abundance effect: Unethical behavior in the presence of wealth. Organ. Behav. Hum. Decis. Processes 109(2):142-155.
Government of Tonga (2002). Revenue Services Administration Act 2002.Kingdom of Tonga.
Herman T (2006). Tax report: Legislations raises the rewards for tips uncovering big fraud. The Wall Street Journal, 20 December 2006. Viewed 19 June 2013, http://www.lopds.com/pressnews-articles/#Tax Report.
Jensen M, William M (1976). Theory of the firm: Managerial behavior, agency costs and ownership structure. J. Financ. Econ. 3:305-360.
Mookherjee D, Png I (1989). Optimal auditing, insurance and redistribution. Q. J. Econ. 104:399-415.
Mossin J (1968). Taxation and risk-taking: an expected utility approach. Economica 35:74-82.
Pestieau P, Possen UM, Slutsky S M (2004). Jointly optimal taxes and enforcement policies in response to tax evasion. J. Public Econ. Theory 6(4):337-374.
Reinganum JF, Wilde LL (1985). Income tax compliance in a principal-agent framework. J. Public Econ. 26:1-18.
Tax Whistleblower Law Firm (2013). Tax whistleblower reward program. Reward Tax.Com. Viewed 29 June 2013, http://www.rewardtax.com.
The IRS of the United States of America (2013). Whistleblower – informant award. IRS Update 10 June 2013. Viewed 19 June 2013, http://www.irs.gov/uac/Whistleblower-Informant-Award.
Travino LK (1986). Ethical decision making in organizations: A person-situation interactionist model. Acad. Manage. Rev. 11:601-617.
Tulkens H, Jacquemin A (1971). The cost of delinquency: a problem of optimal allocation of private and public expenditure. CORE. Discussion Paper 7133.
Wright O (2013). CPS launched crackdown on middle-class tax evaders. Independence. 22 January 2013. Viewed 5 April 2013, http://www.independent.co.uk/news/uk/home-news/cps-launches-crackdown-on-middleclass-tax-evaders-8460891.html.
Zhong CB, Strejcek B, Sivanathan N (2010). A clean self can render harsh moral judgment. J. Exp. Soc. Psychol. 46(5):859-862.

The modern portfolio theory as an investment decision tool

Iyiola Omisore[1], Munirat Yusuf[2]* and Nwufo Christopher .I.[3]

[1]Senator, Federal Republic of Nigeria.
[2]Department of Business Administration, University of Abuja, Abuja, Nigeria.
[3]Department of Accounting, University of Abuja, Abuja, Nigeria.

This research paper is academic exposition into the modern portfolio theory (MPT) written with a primary objective of showing how it aids an investor to classify, estimate, and control both the kind and the amount of expected risk and return in an attempt to maximize portfolio expected return for a given amount of portfolio risk, or equivalently minimize risk for a given level of expected return. A methodology section is included which examined applicability of the theory to real time investment decisions relative to assumptions of the MPT. A fair critique of the MPT is carried out to determine inherent flaws of the theory while attempting to proffer areas of further improvement (for example, the post-modern portfolio theory [PMPT]). The paper is summarised to give a compressed view of the discourse upon which conclusions were drawn while referencing cited literature as employed in the course of the presentation.

Key words: Assets, beta coefficient, diversification, expected returns, investment, portfolio, risk, uncertainty.

INTRODUCTION

This paper presentation is an assessment of the modern portfolio theory as an investment decision tool. In the investment world, there exist different motives for investment. The most prominent among all is to earn a return on investment. However, selecting investments on the basis of returns alone is not sufficient. The fact that most investors invest their funds in more than one security suggests that there are other factors, besides return, and they must be considered. The investors not only like return but also dislike risk.

The financial market, despite the benefits and rewards, is a complexly volatile industry which requires critical analysis to adequately evaluate risks relative to returns to aid decisions as regards participation in the industry. Upon such premise, this research work is an academic insight into some analytics of the financial market. The presentation is an attempt to create foundation knowledge to understanding the workings of the financial market. Despite the span of the research, specific attention would be accorded to the Modern Portfolio Theory.

In the course of this discourse, some historical background to financial market analysis would be examined, related literature (to Modern Portfolio Theory) reviewed, its applications, pros and cons of the theory would equally be examined.

It is intended that this write-up would add to the existing pool of knowledge on the concept being investigated.

LITERATURE REVIEW

Investment portfolio theories guide the way an individual investor or financial planner allocates money and other capital assets within an investing portfolio. An investing portfolio has long-term goals independent of a market's day-to-day fluctuations; because of these goals, investment portfolio theories aim to aid investors or

*Corresponding author. E-mail: drmrsyusuf@yahoo.com.

financial planners with tools to estimate the expected risk and return associated with investments.

Passive portfolio theories, on one hand, combine an investor's goals and temperament with financial actions. Passive theories propose minimal input from the investor; instead, passive strategies rely on diversification, buying many stocks in the same industry or market, to match the performance of a market index. Passive theories use market data and other available information to forecast investment performance.

Active Portfolio Theories come in three varieties. Active portfolios can either be patient, aggressive or conservative. Patient portfolios invest in established, stable companies that pay dividends and earn revenue despite economic conditions. Aggressive portfolios buy riskier stocks, those that are growing, in an attempt to maximize returns; because of the volatility to which this type of portfolio is exposed, it has a high turnover rate. As the name implies, conservative portfolios invest with an eye on yield and long-term stability.

In any financial market analysis, if the objective of the analysis involves determination of stocks to buy and at what price, there are two basic methodologies: Fundamental analysis, which maintains that markets may misprice a security in the short run but that the "correct" price will eventually be reached. Profits can be made by trading the mispriced security and then waiting for the market to recognize its "mistake" and re-price the security. Technical analysis, maintains that all information is reflected already in the stock price. Trends 'are your friend' and sentiment changes predate and predict trend changes. Investors' emotional responses to price movements lead to recognizable price chart patterns. Technical analysis does not care what the 'value' of a stock is. Their price predictions are only extrapolations from historical price patterns.

Fundamental analysis of a business involves analysing its financial statements and forexhealth, its management and competitive advantages, and its competitors and markets. When applied to futures and, it focuses on the overall state of the economy, interest rates, production, earnings, and management.

Fundamental analysis is performed on historical and present data, but with the goal of making financial forecasts. There are several possible objectives:

1. To conduct a company stock valuation and predict its probable price evolution
2. To make a projection on its business performance
3. To evaluate its management and make internal business decisions
4. To calculate its credit risk

While fundamental analysts examine earnings, dividends, new products, research and the like, technical analysts examine what investors fear or thought of these developments and whether or not investors have the Where withal to back up their opinions; these two concepts are called psych (psychology) and supply/ demand.

Technical analysts use market indicators of many sorts, some of which are mathematical transformations of price, often including up and down volume, advance/decline data and other inputs. These indicators are used to help assess whether an asset is trending, and if it is, the probability of its direction and of continuation. Also, relationships between price/volume indices and market indicators are sought. Examples include the relative strength index, and MACD. Other avenues of study include correlations between changes in options (implied volatility) and put/call ratios with price. Also, important are sentiment indicators such as put/call ratios, bull/bear ratios, short interest, implied volatility, etc.

There are many techniques in technical analysis. Adherents of different techniques (for example, Candlestick charting, Dow Theory, and Elliott Wave theory), may ignore other approaches, yet many financial traders combine elements from more than one technique. Some technical analysts use subjective judgment to decide which pattern(s) a particular instrument reflects at a given time and what the interpretation of that pattern should be. Others employ a strictly mechanical or systematic approach to pattern identification and interpretation.

Technical analysis is frequently contrasted with fundamental analysis; the study of economic factors that influence the way investors price financial markets. Technical analysis holds that prices already reflect all such trends before investors are aware of them. Uncovering those trends is what technical indicators are designed to do, imperfect as they may be. Fundamental indicators are subject to the same limitations, naturally. Some traders use technical or fundamental analysis exclusively, while others use both types to make trading decisions.

THE MODERN PORTFOLIO THEORY (MPT)

Harry Markowitz 1991, an American economist in the 1950s developed a theory of "portfolio choice," which allows investors to analyse risk relative to their expected return. For this work Markowitz, a professor at Baruch College at the City University of New York, shared the 1990 Nobel Memorial Prize in Economic Sciences with William Sharpe and Merton Miller.

Markowitz's theory is today known as the Modern Portfolio Theory, (MPT). The MPT is a theory of investment which attempts to maximize portfolio expected return for a given amount of portfolio risk, or equivalently minimize risk for a given level of expected return, by carefully choosing the proportions of various assets. Although the MPT is widely used in practice in the financial industry, in recent years, the basic assumptions

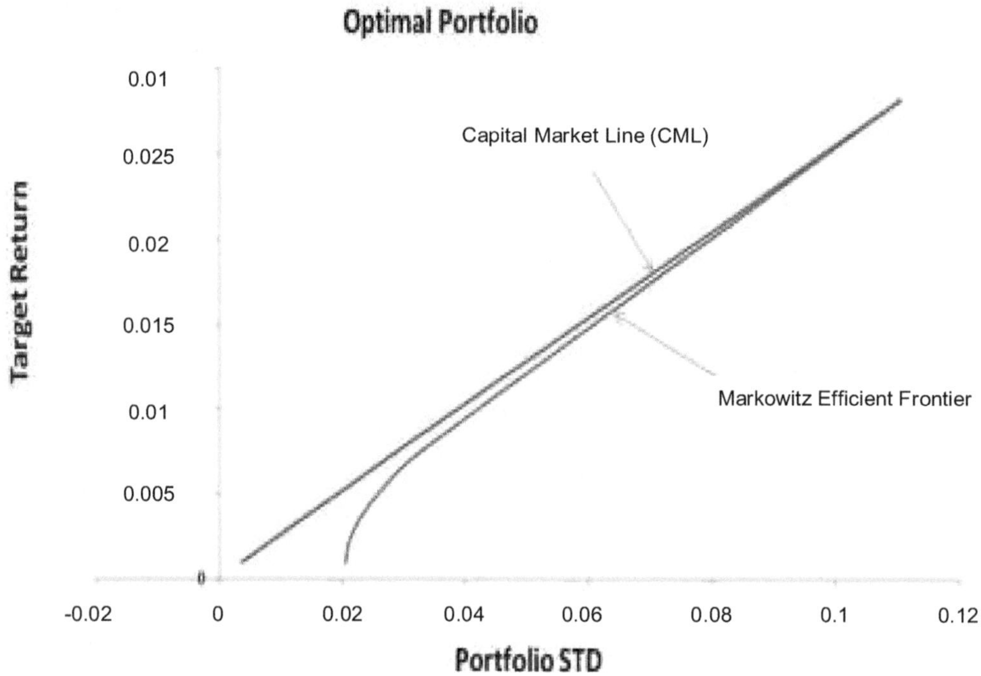

Figure 1. Markouwitz Modern Portfolio theory.

of the MPT have been widely challenged.

The Modern Portfolio Theory, an improvement upon traditional investment models, is an important advance in the mathematical modelling of finance. The theory encourages asset diversification to hedge against market risk as well as risk that is unique to a specific company.

The theory (MPT) is a sophisticated investment decision approach that aids an investor to classify, estimate, and control both the kind and the amount of expected risk and return; also called Portfolio Management Theory. Essential to the portfolio theory are its quantification of the relationship between risk and return and the assumption that investors must be compensated for assuming risk. Portfolio theory departs from traditional security analysis in shifting emphasis from analysing the characteristics of individual investments to determining the statistical relationships among the individual securities that comprise the overall portfolio (Edwin and Martins 1997).

The MPT mathematically formulates the concept of diversification in investing, with the aim of selecting a collection of investment assets that has collectively lower risk than any individual asset. The possibility of this can be seen intuitively because different types of assets often change in value in opposite ways. But diversification lowers risk even if assets' returns are not negatively correlated-indeed, even if they are positively correlated.

More technically, the MPT models an asset return as a normally distributed function (or more generally as an elliptically distributed random variable), define risk as the standard deviation of return, and models a portfolio as a weighted combination of assets so that the return of a portfolio is the weighted combination of the assets' returns. By combining different assets whose returns are not perfectly positively correlated, MPT seeks to reduce the total variance of the portfolio return. MPT also assumes that investors are rational and markets are efficient.

The fundamental concept behind the MPT is that assets in an investment portfolio should not be selected individually, each on their own merits. Rather, it is important to consider how each asset changes in price relative to how every other asset in the portfolio changes in price.

Investing is a trade-off between risk and expected return as shown in Figure 1. Generally, assets with higher expected returns are riskier (Taleb, 2007). For a given amount of risk, the MPT describes how to select a portfolio with the highest possible expected return. Or, for a given expected return, the MPT explains how to select a portfolio with the lowest possible risk (the targeted expected return cannot be more than the highest-returning available security, of course, unless negative holdings of assets are possible).

Concept of risk and expected return

Return

Return is the basic motivating force and the principal reward in any investment process. Returns may be defined in terms of realized return (that is, the return which has been earned) and expected return (that is, the return which the investor anticipates to earn over some future investment period). The expected return is a predicted or estimated return and may or may not occur. The realized returns in the past allow an investor to estimate cash inflows in terms of dividends, interest, bonus, capital gains, etc., available to the holder of the investment. The return can be measured as the total gain or loss to the holder over a given period of time and may be defined as a percentage return on the initial amount invested. With reference to investment in equity shares, return is consisting of the dividends and the capital gain or loss at the time of sale of these shares.

Risk

Risk in investment analysis, is the unpredictability of future returns from an investment. The concept of risk may be defined as the possibility that the actual return may not be same as expected. In other words, risk refers to the chance that the actual outcome (return) from an investment will differ from an expected outcome. With reference to a firm, risk may be defined as the possibility that the actual outcome of a financial decision may not be same as estimated. The risk may be considered as a chance of variation in return. Investments having greater chances of variations are considered more risky than those with lesser chances of variations.

Risk should be differentiated from uncertainty; Risk is defined as a situation where the possibility of happening or non-happening of an event can be quantified and measured: while uncertainty is a situation where this possibility cannot be measured. Thus, risk is a situation where probabilities can be assigned to an event on the basis of facts and figures available regarding the decision. Uncertainty, on the other hand, is a situation where either the facts and figures are not available, or the probabilities cannot be assigned.

Measurement of risk and the beta coefficient

No investor can predict with certainty whether the income from an investment will increase or decrease and by how much. Statistical measures can be used to make precise measurement of risk about the estimated returns, to gauge the extent to which the expected return and actual return are likely to differ. The expected return, standard deviation and variance of outcomes can be used to measure risk.

Beta coefficient

There is another measure of risk known as β which measures the risk of one security/ portfolio relative to market risk. The market risk is represented by fluctuation in the market benchmark, that is, market index. Shares whose β factor is more than 1 are considered less risky. It may be noted that β is a measure of systematic risk which cannot be diversified away.

The total risk of an investment consists of two components: diversifiable (unsystematic) risk and non-diversifiable (systematic) risk. The relationship between total risk, diversifiable risk, and non-diversifiable risk can be expressed by the following equation:

Total risk = Diversifiable risk + Non diversifiable risk

Assumptions of the modern portfolio theory

The framework of the MPT makes many assumptions about investors and markets. Some are explicit in MPT equations; such as the use of Normal distributions to model returns. Others are implicit, such as the neglect of taxes and transaction fees. None of these assumptions are entirely true, and each of them compromises the MPT to some degree. Predominant among the MPT assumptions is the efficient market theory.

The efficient market theory

The efficient market theory is widely referred to as a hypothesis, and thus efficient market hypothesis (EMH) asserts that financial markets are "informationally efficient". That is, one cannot consistently achieve returns in excess of average market returns on a risk-adjusted basis, given the information available at the time the investment is made.

There are three major versions of the MPT hypothesis: "weak", "semi-strong", and "strong". The weak EMH asserts that prices of traded assets (for example, stocks, bonds, or property) already reflect all past publicly available information. The semi-strong *EMH* opines that prices reflect all publicly available information and that prices change to reflect new public information. The strong EMH additionally claims that prices instantly reflect even hidden or "insider" information. There is evidence for and against the weak and semi-strong EMHs, while there is powerful evidence against the strong EMH (Andrei, 2000).

Extensive researches have revealed signs of inefficiency in financial markets. Critics have blamed the belief in rational markets for much of the late-2000s global financial crisis. In response, proponents of the hypothesis have stated that market efficiency does not mean having no uncertainty about the future, rather the market efficiency is a simplification of the world which may not always hold true, and that the market is practically efficient for investment purposes for most individuals (Chambernan, 1983).

Asset returns are (jointly) normally distributed random variables

Despite this assumption, evidence from frequent observations shows that returns in equity and other markets are not normally distributed. Large swings (3 to 6 standard deviations from the mean) occur in the market far more frequently than the normal distribution assumption would predict. While the model can also be justified by assuming any return distribution which is jointly elliptical, all the joint elliptical distributions are symmetrical whereas asset returns empirically are not.

Correlations between assets are fixed and constant forever

Correlations depend on systemic relationships between the underlying assets, and change when these relationships change. During times of financial crisis, all assets tend to become positively correlated, because they all move (down) together. In other words, the MPT fails to function when investors are most in need of protection from risk.

All investors aim to maximize economic utility

Investors aim to maximize economic utility in order to make as much money as possible, regardless of any other considerations. This is a key assumption of the efficient market hypothesis, upon which the MPT relies.

All investors are rational and risk-averse

This is another assumption of the efficient market hypothesis, but we now know from behavioural economics that market participants are not rational. It does not allow for "herd behaviour" or investors who will accept lower returns for higher risk. Even gamblers clearly pay for risk, and it is possible that some stock traders will pay for risk as well.

All investors have access to the same information at the same time

This also comes from the efficient market hypothesis. In-fact, real markets contain information asymmetry, insider trading, and those who are simply better informed than others.

Investors have an accurate conception of possible returns

The probability beliefs of investors match the true distribution of returns. A different possibility is investors' expectations being biased, causing market prices to be informationally inefficient. This possibility is studied in the field of behavioural finance, which uses psychological assumptions to provide alternatives to the capital asset pricing model (Owen and Rabinovitch, 1983).

There are no taxes or transaction costs

Real financial products are subject both to taxes and transaction costs (such as broker fees), and taking these into account will alter the composition of the optimum portfolio. These assumptions can be relaxed with more complicated versions of the model.

All investors are price takers

Their actions do not influence prices. In reality, sufficiently large sales or purchases of individual assets can shift market prices for that asset and others (via cross-elasticity of demand). An investor may not even be able to assemble the theoretically optimal portfolio if the market moves too much while they are buying the required securities.

Any investor can lend and borrow an unlimited amount at the risk free rate of interest.

In reality, every investor has a credit limit.

All securities can be divided into parcels of any size

In reality, fractional shares usually cannot be bought or sold, and some assets have minimum order sizes.
More complex versions of the MPT take into account a more sophisticated model of the world (such as one with non-normal distributions and taxes) but all mathematical models of finance still rely on many unrealistic premises as stated previously.

APPLICATION OF THE MODERN PORTFOLIO THEORY

The MPT assumes that investors are risk averse, meaning that given two portfolios that offer the same expected return, investors will prefer the less risky one. Thus, an investor will take on increased risk only if compensated by higher expected returns. Conversely, an investor who wants higher expected returns must accept more risk. The exact trade-off will be the same for all investors, but different investors will evaluate the trade-off differently based on individual risk aversion characteristics. The implication is that a rational investor will not invest in a portfolio if a second portfolio exists with a more favourable risk-expected return profile – that is, if for that level of risk an alternative portfolio exists which has better expected returns.

The MPT is therefore a form of diversification. Under certain assumptions and for specific quantitative definitions of risk and return, MPT explains how to find the best possible diversification strategy.

Applying the theory

The Portfolio theory (MPT) approach has four basic procedures: Security valuation-describing a universe of assets in terms of expected return and expected risk; asset allocation decision- determining how assets are to be distributed among classes of investment, such as stocks or bonds; portfolio optimization-reconciling risk and return in selecting the securities to be included, such as determining which portfolio of stocks offers the best return for a given level of expected risk; and performance measurement-dividing each stock's performance (risk) into market-related (systematic) and industry/security-related (residual) classifications (Brodie, 2009).

Step one: Data collection

Get historical data for all the selected equities. Determine the average weekly (or daily) returns and corresponding standard deviation in weekly returns. Find the correlation between selected assets.

Step two: Create a Markowitz efficient frontier

The portfolio standard deviation is provided by the follow equation:

σP = sqrt (∑square(wi). square(σi2) + ∑∑ wi .wj.Covij

Construct different portfolios with given target returns (0.001, 0.002, etc.) and use the "solver" in excel to find weights such that the standard deviation for the portfolio (expressed previously) is minimized. Then, plot these portfolios with return on y-axis and risk or standard deviation on x-axis. The resulting envelope curve is called the "Markowitz efficient frontier". All the portfolios on this frontier are efficient in the sense that any portfolio beneath this line will not provide a better risk-return alternative (either the portfolio will have lower return for given risk or higher risk for given return) (Markowitz, 1959, 1952).

Step three: Create the market portfolio

Market portfolio is defined as the portfolio with risky assets that provide highest expected return over risk-free rate per unit of risk for any available portfolio with risky assets. Or, a portfolio with the maximum Sharpe ratio.

Step four: Create the capital market line

According to capital market theory, investors who allocate their capital between a riskless security and the risky portfolio (M) can expect a return equal to the risk-free rate plus compensation for the number of risk units they accept. In other words;

Step five: The optimal portfolio

Finally, we are ready for our optimal portfolio. Optimal portfolio is represented by the point of tangency between the capital market line and the Markowitz efficient frontier.

The theory is a mathematical model that uses standard deviation of return as a proxy for risk, which is valid if asset returns are jointly normally distributed or otherwise elliptically distributed.

Under the model:

1. Portfolio return is the proportion-weighted combination of the constituent assets' returns.
2. Portfolio volatility is a function of the correlations ρ_{ij} of the component assets, for all asset pairs (i, j).

Expected return:

$$\mathrm{E}(R_p) = \sum_i w_i \mathrm{E}(R_i)$$

Where R_p is the return on the portfolio, R_i is the return on asset i and w_i is the weighting of component asset i (that is, the share of asset i in the portfolio).

Portfolio return variance:

$$\sigma_p^2 = \sum_i w_i^2 \sigma_i^2 + \sum_i \sum_{j \neq i} w_i w_j \sigma_i \sigma_j \rho_{ij},$$

Where ρ_{ij} is the correlation coefficient between the returns on assets i and j.

Alternatively the expression can be written as:

$$\sigma_p^2 = \sum_i \sum_j w_i w_j \sigma_i \sigma_j \rho_{ij},$$

Where $\rho_{ij} = 1$ for $i = j$.

Portfolio return volatility (standard deviation):

$$\sigma_p = \sqrt{\sigma_p^2}$$

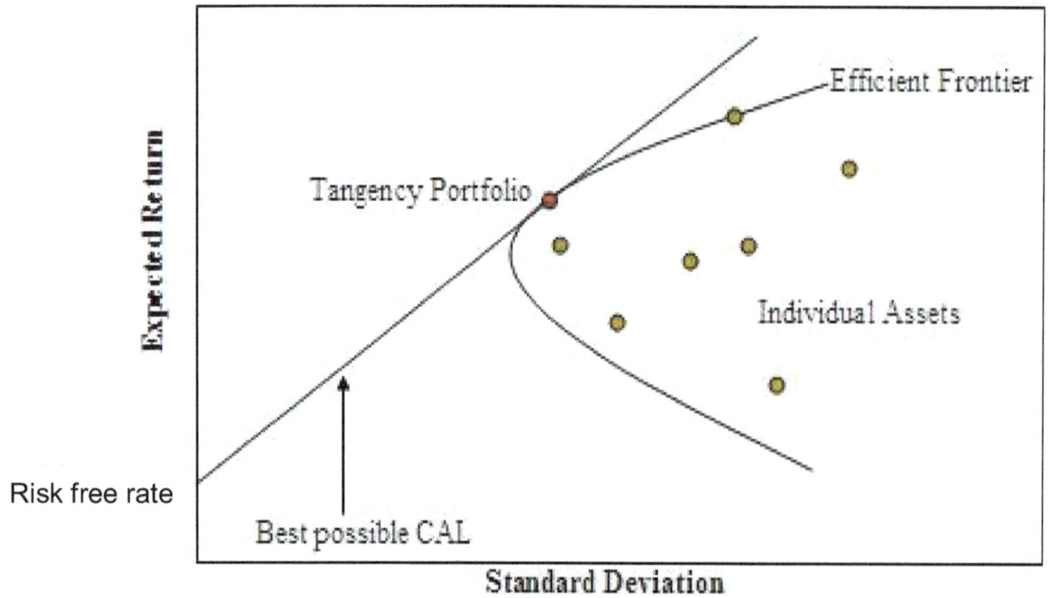

Figure 2. Efficient frontier. The hyperbola is sometimes referred to as the 'Markowitz Bullet', and is the efficient frontier if no risk-free asset is available. With a risk-free asset, the straight line is the efficient frontier.

For a two asset portfolio, we have the following:

Portfolio return:

$$\mathrm{E}(R_p) = w_A\mathrm{E}(R_A) + w_B\mathrm{E}(R_B) = w_A\mathrm{E}(R_A) + (1 - w_A)\mathrm{E}(R_B).$$

Portfolio variance:

$$\sigma_p^2 = w_A^2\sigma_A^2 + w_B^2\sigma_B^2 + 2w_Aw_B\sigma_A\sigma_B\rho_{AB}$$

For a three asset portfolio, we have the following:

Portfolio return:

$$w_A\mathrm{E}(R_A) + w_B\mathrm{E}(R_B) + w_C\mathrm{E}(R_C)$$

Portfolio variance:

$$\sigma_p^2 = w_A^2\sigma_A^2 + w_B^2\sigma_B^2 + w_C^2\sigma_C^2 + 2w_Aw_B\sigma_A\sigma_B\rho_{AB} + 2w_Aw_C\sigma_A\sigma_C\rho_{AC} + 2w_Bw_C\sigma_B\sigma_C\rho_{BC}$$

PRACTICAL APPLICATIONS OF THE THEORY IN INVESTMENT DECISION MAKING

Diversification

An investor can reduce portfolio risk simply by holding combinations of instruments which are not perfectly positively correlated (correlation coefficient $-1 \leq \rho_{ij} < 1$). In other words, investors can reduce their exposure to individual asset risk by holding a diversified portfolio of assets. Diversification may allow for the same portfolio expected return with reduced risk.

If all the asset pairs have correlations of 0—they are perfectly uncorrelated—the portfolio's return variance is the sum over all assets of the square of the fraction held in the asset times the asset's return variance (and the portfolio standard deviation is the square root of this sum) (Koponen, 2003).

The efficient frontier with no risk-free asset

As shown in Figure 2, every possible combination of the risky assets, without including any holdings of the risk-free asset, can be plotted in risk-expected return space, and the collection of all such possible portfolios defines a region in this space. The left boundary of this region is a hyperbola, and the upper edge of this region is the efficient frontier in the absence of a risk-free asset (sometimes called "the Markowitz bullet"). Combinations along this upper edge represent portfolios (including no holdings of the risk-free asset) for which there is lowest risk for a given level of expected return. Equivalently, a portfolio laying on the efficient frontier represents the combination offering the best possible expected return for given risk level (Kent et al., 2001).

Matrices are preferred for calculations of the efficient frontier. In matrix form, for a given "risk tolerance" $q \in [0, \infty)$, the efficient frontier is found by minimizing the following expression:

$$w^T\Sigma w - q * R^T w$$

Where, w is a vector of portfolio weights and $_i \sum w_i = 1$ (The weights can be negative, which means investors can short a security); Σ is the covariance matrix for the returns on the assets in the portfolio; $q \geq 0$ is a "risk tolerance" factor, where 0 results in the portfolio with minimal risk and ∞results in the portfolio infinitely far out on the frontier with both expected return and risk unbounded; and $R$is a vector of expected returns. $w^T \Sigma w$is the variance of portfolio return. $R^T w$ is the expected return on the portfolio.

The foregoing optimization finds the point on the frontier at which the inverse of the slope of the frontier would be q if portfolio return variance instead of standard deviation were plotted horizontally. The frontier in its entirety is parametric on q.

Many software packages, including Microsoft Excel, MATLAB, Mathematical and R, provide optimization routines suitable for the foregoing problem.

An alternative approach to specifying the efficient frontier is to do so parametrically on expected portfolio return $R^T w$. This version of the problem requires that we minimize;

$$w^T \Sigma w$$

Subject to:

$$R^T w = \mu$$

For parameter μ. This problem is easily solved using a Lagrange Multiplier (Merton, 1972).

Applications to project portfolios and other "non-financial" assets

The MPT is gradually being applied to portfolios of projects and other assets besides financial instruments. When applied beyond traditional financial portfolios, some fundamental differences between the different types of portfolios must be considered:

1. The assets in financial portfolios are, for practical purposes, continuously divisible while portfolios of projects are "lumpy". For example, while we can compute that the optimal portfolio position for 3 stocks is, say, 47, 30 and 23%, the optimal position for a project portfolio may not allow us to simply change the amount spent on a project. Projects might be all or nothing or, at least, have logical units that cannot be separated. A portfolio optimization method would have to take the discrete nature of projects into account.
2. The assets of financial portfolios are liquid; they can be assessed or re-assessed at any point in time. But opportunities for launching new projects may be limited and may occur in limited windows of time. Projects that have already been initiated cannot be abandoned without the loss of the sunk costs (that is, there is little or no recovery/salvage value of a half-complete project).

However, that neither of these cited differences necessarily eliminates the possibility of using the MPT and such portfolios. They simply indicate the need to run the optimization with an additional set of mathematically-expressed constraints that would not normally apply to financial portfolios.

Furthermore, some of the simplest elements of the modern portfolio theory are applicable to virtually any kind of portfolio. The concept of capturing the risk tolerance of an investor by documenting how much risk is acceptable for a given return may be applied to a variety of decision analysis problems. MPT uses historical variance as a measure of risk, but portfolios of assets like major projects do not have a well-defined "historical variance". In this case, the MPT investment boundary can be expressed in more general terms like "chance of a return on investment (ROI) less than cost of capital" or "chance of losing more than half of the investment". When risk is put in terms of uncertainty about forecasts and possible losses then the concept is transferable to various types of investment.

Application to other disciplines

As far back as the early 1970s, concepts from modern portfolio theory gained relevance in the field of regional science. In a series of seminal works, researchers, such as Michael Conroy, modelled the labour force in an economy using portfolio-theoretic methods to examine growth and variability in the labour force. This was followed by an extensive literature on the relationship between economic growth and volatility.

More recently, modern portfolio theory has been used to model the self-concept in social psychology. When the self attributes comprising the self-concept constitute a well-diversified portfolio, then psychological outcomes at the level of the individual such as mood and self-esteem should be more stable than when the self-concept is undiversified. This prediction has been confirmed in studies involving human subjects.

Recently, the theory has been applied to modelling the uncertainty and correlation between documents in information retrieval (Chandra and Shadel, 2007).

CRITICISM OF THE THEORY

Despite its theoretical relevance, the MPT has been highly criticised; its simplistic assumptions being a predominant bias. Critics question its viability as an investment strategy, because its model of financial markets does not match the real world in many ways. In recent years, basic underlying assumptions of the MPT have been grossly challenged by fields such as the behavioural economics.

Efforts to translate the theoretical foundation of the theory into a viable portfolio construction algorithm have been plagued by technical difficulties stemming from the instability of the original optimization problem with respect to available data. Recent research shows that instabilities of this type disappear when a regularizing constraint or penalty term is incorporated in the optimization procedure.

The theory does not really model the market

The risk, return, and correlation measures used by MPT are based on expected (forecast) values, which means that they are mathematical statements about the future (the expected value of returns is explicit in such equations, and implicit in the definitions of variance and covariance). In practice, investors must substitute predictions based on historical measurements of asset return and volatility for these values in the equations. Very often, such expected values fail to take account of new circumstances which did not exist when the historical data were generated.

More fundamentally, investors are stuck with estimating key parameters from past market data because the MPT attempts to model risk in terms of the likelihood of losses, but says nothing about why those losses might occur. The risk measurements used are probabilistic in nature, not structural. This is a major difference as compared to many engineering approaches to risk management.

The Theory does not consider personal, environmental, strategic, or social dimensions of investment decisions

It only attempts to maximize risk-adjusted returns, without regard to other consequences. In a narrow sense, its complete reliance on asset prices makes it vulnerable to all the standard market failures such as those arising from information asymmetry, externalities, and public goods. It also rewards corporate fraud and dishonest accounting. More broadly, a firm may have strategic or social goals that shape its investment decisions, and an individual investor might have personal goals. In either case, information other than historical returns (as suggested by the MPT) is relevant.

The MPT does not take cognisance of its own effect on asset prices

Diversification eliminates non-systematic risk, but, at the cost of increasing the systematic risk. Diversification forces the portfolio manager to invest in assets without analysing their fundamentals; solely for the benefit of eliminating the portfolio's non-systematic risk (the capital asset pricing investment in all available assets) (Chandra, 2003). This artificially increased demand pushes up the price of assets that, when analysed individually, would be of little fundamental value. The result is that the whole portfolio becomes more expensive and, as a result, the probability of a positive return decreases (that is, the risk of the portfolio increases).

The legitimacy of the modern portfolio theory has been challenged by financial analysts who often cite Warren Buffett as a rule breaker. Warren Buffett, a major financial market referral with successful financial takeovers in his resume, is not a typical investor. Unlike the average mutual fund manager, Buffet often buys companies and then manages them. He provides them with economies of scale, lower cost of capital and the benefits of his managerial wisdom. And when he takes large portions in companies, he often gets a board seat. So perhaps his great returns are more a result of his managerial skills than his investment skills, or some combination of both. This, obviously, is not congruent with the line of thought of MPT proponents (Sabbadini, 2010).

CONCLUSION

This paper presentation sought to review the relevance of the modern portfolio theory as an investment portfolio tool in portfolio decision making. In the course of the research, the relevance and applicability of the MPT was reviewed, however, it was also established that many inherent flaws of the theory have marred the efficacy of the theory. Among other things, its simplistic assumptions and direct correlation of risks and returns were identified as significant flaws.

Despite the limitations of the theory, it is still widely accepted and further research is being carried out on its principles. The post modern portfolio theory is a significant advancement of the theory. Post-modern portfolio theory encourages far greater diversification in an investment portfolio than does the MPT. By utilizing the alpha coefficient and the beta coefficient, each of which gauge an investment's performance, investors can engineer a portfolio's risk and returns to coincide with investment objectives. The alpha coefficient measures an investment's performance relative to its risk; the beta coefficient measures an investment's return relative to the market as a whole. The post-modern portfolio theory (PMPT) separates alpha- and beta-generated revenue, and then considers each individually to maximize their performance. The PMPT is more adaptable to the individual investor and can gauge risk relative to the investor's minimum acceptable return (MAR) for an asset.

REFERENCES

Andrei S (2000). Inefficient Markets: An Introduction to Behavioral Finance. Clarendon Lectures in Economics, p. 145.

Brodie DM, Daubechies G, Loris (2009). Sparse and stable Markowitz portfolios. Proc. Natl. Acad. Sci., pp. 106.
Chambernan G (1983). A characterization of the distributions that imply mean-variance utility functions, J. Econ. Theory, 29: 185-201.
Chandra S (2003). Regional Economy Size and the Growth-Instability Frontier: Evidence from Europe". J. Reg. Sci., 43(1): 95-122. doi:10.1111/1467-9787.00291.
Chandra S, Shadel WG (2007). Crossing disciplinary boundaries: Applying financial portfolio theory to model the organization of the self-concept. J. Res. Personal., 41(2): 346-373. doi:10.1016/j.jrp.2006.04.007.
Edwin JE, Martin JG (1997). Modern portfolio theory, 1950 to date. J. Bank. Fin., 21: 1743-1759.
Harry MM (1991). Autobiography, The Nobel Prizes 1990, Editor Tore Frangsmyr, [Nobel Foundation], Stockholm, pp. 56-70.
Kent D, Daniel DH, Avanidhar S (2001). Overconfidence Arbitrage, and Equilibrium Asset Pricing. J. F., 56(3): 921-965.
Koponen TM (2003). Commodities in action: measuring embeddedness and imposing values. Sociol. Rev., 50(4): 543-569.
Markowitz HM (1952). Portfolio Selection. J. Fin., pp. 120-131
Markowitz HM (1959). Portfolio Selection: Efficient Diversification of Investments. New York: John Wiley Sons, pp. 95-112. (reprinted by Yale University Press, 1970, ISBN 978-0-300-01372-6; 2nd ed. Basil Blackwell, 1991, ISBN 978-1-55786-108-5)
Merton R (1972). An analytic derivation of the efficient portfolio frontier, J. Fin. Quant. Anal., September, 7: 1851-1872.
Owen J, Rabinovitch R (1983). On the class of elliptical distributions and their applications to the theory of portfolio choice, J. Fin. 38: 745-752.
Sabbadini T (2010). Manufacturing Portfolio Theory. International Institute for Advanced Studies in Systems Research and Cybernetics. pp.120-160.
Taleb NN (2007). The Black Swan: The Impact of the Highly Improbable, Random House, pp. 80-120.

Evaluating taxpayers' attitude and its influence on tax compliance decisions in Tamale, Ghana

Abubakari Abdul – Razak[1] and Christopher Jwayire Adafula[2]

[1]Accountancy Department Tamale Polytechnic Tamale - Northern Region Ghana.
[2]Finance Department; Accountant Budgets, Bolgatanga Polytechnic, Sumbrungu – U/E Region, Ghana.

This research was conducted to provide an insight into the debate in Ghana - a developing country: the influence of attitudes of individual taxpayers on tax compliance decisions. Survey responses from questionnaires administered to operators of SMEs in Tamale, were quantitatively analysed. Both descriptive and inferential statistics were applied. The results indicated that, individuals are highly concerned with the amount of taxes they pay. The rates of income taxes in Ghana are generally perceived to be high. Furthermore, the burden of taxes paid affects the attitudes of individuals and this informs how they evaluate the tax system and consequently their compliance decisions. Individuals have little regard for the amount of taxes paid by them in comparison to amounts paid by higher income earners. It was further revealed that, the level of governmental accountability and transparency did not significantly impact taxpayers' attitudes. The perceived level of benefits derived from the provision of public goods and services particularly physical infrastructure was high. The results further indicated that, individuals did not clearly understand the tax laws. A significant positive statistical relationship (R=0.72) was found to exist between levels of understanding and tax compliance decisions.

Key words: Tax compliance, individual attitudes, planned behaviour, Tamale –Ghana.

INTRODUCTION

Achieving high levels of voluntary tax compliance and/or maintaining current compliance rates as well as increasing the marginal levels are issues of concern to fiscal policy makers in developed and developing countries alike. This is the case because, irrespective of the nature of the economy, the principal objective of taxation is one and the same: to raise revenue towards the financing of public goods and services, and funding of governments (Martina et al., 2008). Indeed taxes are a major part of the means through which monetary resources are mobilised by governments for the prosecution of projects and programmes. These projects and programmes are usually undertaken with the view to providing varied services to the citizenry ranging from; road infrastructure, internal security, protection against external aggression, sewage services, disaster management and to the new phenomenon of counterterrorism.

Ghana has recently achieved a lower middle income status; as a result of rebasing of the economy by the Statistical Services of Ghana in 2011(Francisco et al., 2013). Substantial investment in productive infrastructure is required to maintain this exalted status and to prevent the country from sliding. These infrastructural projects, as stated earlier are financed from a myriad of sources including taxation. To this end, taxpayers' attitude towards tax payment is seen as a major precondition for effective revenue mobilization in all countries and Ghana is not an exception. In spite of its current middle income status, Ghana continues to face challenges with regard to mobilisation of tax revenues, and there seems to be no end in sight in this regard. For example, only 1.5 million citizens out of the estimated taxable population of 6 million pay direct taxes (Ghana, 2011). This represents only 25% rate of compliance. The share of personal income tax to total tax revenue has been the lowest in the past 15 years (Ghana, 2012). Historically, Ghanaians vehemently resisted Act 486 of 1994, the law that initially introduced the Value Added Tax (VAT). The famous "Kumipreko" demonstrations and other resistance protests against the introduction of the tax were fierce (Ali-Nakyea, 2006). Quite recently, the general public's response to the introduction of the Communication Service Tax (CST) christened "Talk tax" was negative.

Tax research in Ghana, like other developing countries, seems to focus greater attention on the twin issues of administrative reforms of taxation and reduction of corruption (Richard, 2003). For example, Terkper (2007) explored ways of improving the tax accounting systems of SME's in Ghana while Ayee (2007) discussed strategies for achieving compliance through building and improving reciprocity with government. The study by Atuguba (2006) profiled the tax culture of Ghanaians. It however fell short of examining specific attitudinal antecedents of tax-paying behaviour. This study is hence carried out to examine the issue of tax payers' attitude effect on tax compliance. In view of that, this study sought to achieve the following objectives:

i. To assess the extent to which individual taxpayers' perceptions of the burden of tax influences the attitudes of income taxpayers in Tamale (Ghana).
ii. To assess the degree to which individual income taxpayers' levels of understanding of the tax law influences attitudes of taxpayers.
iii. To determine whether taxpayers' perceptions of accountability of government influences taxpayer's attitudes.
iv. To determine the extent to which the factors mentioned above influence individual taxpayer's compliance decisions.

Scope of the study

This study focused on individual income earners in the Tamale metropolitan area. These persons were informal self employed/petty traders and individuals engaged in small and medium scale enterprises located within the Tamale Metropolitan area. The meaning of small and medium scale enterprises in this study is based on the definition and classification given by Ayee (2007). The age of respondents, annual incomes, educational backgrounds and the type of enterprise operated were analysed. These factors were considered important because of their likely effects on the individual's compliance decision. Older business enterprises may have dealt with the tax authorities for a rather longer period than younger ones; thus the older business operators may better understand the tax laws, and consequently may be better positioned to evaluate their burden of taxes. Ghana's income tax regime is progressive; and thus taxpayers with varying levels of incomes will feel different about the distribution effects of the tax system. The gender and educational qualifications of respondents were also studied. The issue of feminine compliance influenced our decision to analyse the gender of the respondents. Educated people are more capable of comparing the benefits derived from government in relation to the amounts they contribute to the state, as compared to less educated people. It was therefore deemed necessary to evaluate the educational backgrounds of the respondents. The results of these are shown in (Annex Table 2).

Delimitations

i. Respondents whose incomes are exempted from tax by law were not included in this study.
ii. Also persons, whose income taxes (Pay As You Earn) are deducted at source, by the Controller and Accountant General Department, were not included in the population of this study.

Limitations of the study

(a) Due to the small sample size used for this study, results may not be generalized beyond the specific population from which the sample was drawn.
(b) Sampled respondents may not have answered all questions with candor, and therefore the results of this research based on the opinions of the sampled group might not accurately reflect the opinions of all members of the included population. This is more so because, people generally feel reluctant to divulge correct information about their incomes and tax positions (Coskun and Savasan, 2009).

REVIEW OF RELEVANT LITERATURE

All over the world, governments strive to achieve development goals that are set out in either their annual fiscal budget or in their medium term plans. These goals require huge capital outlay to be met from taxation and other revenue sources. Certainly, taxes are generally seen as the most convenient means through which the cost of governments is met albeit from the standpoint of government (Eshag, 1983). However, taxpayers' views appear not to take in with this notion. This assertion could be justified in the light of the various concerns regarding non-compliance to tax in the form of avoidance at the very least and outright evasion at the extreme (Coskun et al., 2009). Tax compliance has therefore generated huge international concerns for tax authorities and policy makers as tax evasion seriously threatens the capacity of governments to raise public revenue (Gerald et al., 2009). Developing and emerging economies are particularly vulnerable to tax evasion and avoidance activities of individual taxpayers and corporations... as the tax losses arising in course of tax evasion and avoidance activities do largely contribute to the poor performance of the state revenue mobilization in these countries... (GIZ, 2010).

In this regard, several attempts have over the years been made by both practitioners and academics to examine the issue of tax compliance from various angles including the behaviour of the taxpayer. For instance, Eshag (1983) argues that, the amount of tax revenue generated by a government for its expenditure programmes depends among other things, upon the willingness of the taxpayer to comply with the tax laws of the country. This willingness could also be attributed to the attitude that taxpayers demonstrate at any given point in time on the one hand and the purpose of the tax on the other hand (Noami and Joel, 2009).

Some of the empirical researches on tax compliance and evasion undertaken from various angles in the context of the business and economic environments of the developed countries of the world include those of: Andreoni, et al., (1998); Torgler (2003); Wenzel (2002); Diego and Luca (2011); Serdan et al. (2011) and Coskun et al. (2009). It has been argued that the findings of these works could not be favourably applied within the context of developing countries due mainly to the noticeable differences in the socio-political, cultural and even demographic constitution of the developed and developing economies (Alabede et al., 2011). Likhovsk (2010) also criticised some of these studies for their reliance on risk based neoclassical economics approaches to model the compliance decisions of individuals, particularly with reference to: (i) the level of actual income (ii) tax rate (iii) audit probability, and (iv) the magnitude of fines. Kircher et al. (2007) and Young et al. (2013) both faulted the economic approach to assessing tax compliance for its inability to provide extensive empirical explanations regarding tax compliance decisions on the one hand, and the constraint in methodology and the narrow scope applied to explain complex compliance behaviour on the other hand.

This gap therefore ushered in a new dimension to tax compliance research, aimed at identifying and explaining the other critical "*actors in the field*") which influence the individual's compliance decision (Alm et al., 2011). In line with this, Fischer et al. (1992) resorted to different non-economic factors such as demographic; non-compliance opportunity; tax payers' attitude and perceptions of tax system fairness; and various features of the tax system fairness have been proposed to affect tax compliance. Following the lead of Fischer et al. (1992), the Inland Revenue Service of USA outlined 64 factors that are related with tax compliance by taxpayers or companies (Young, 1994). Other behavioural based studies of tax compliance include that of: Modeo et al. (1987) and Harwood et al. (1993). Also moral reasoning was studied by Singh (2003) and tax penalty and sanctions by Davis et al. (2002) and Tittle (1997).

This paper explores within the context of a developing country the taxpayers' perceptions regarding the burden of taxes; taxpayers' level of understanding and their attitude to pay tax; perception of government accountability to tax payers and how all these factors influence tax compliance.

The extent which the tax payers perceive a tax system to be fair influences their attitude to pay their taxes (Coskun, 2009; Alm, et al., 2011). Alabede et al. (2011) postulated that, a tax payer whose motive is to demonstrate his beliefs in a system will evaluate the fairness of the systems with objectivity whereas the taxpayer whose attitude is motivated by what benefit to derive from the system may label the tax system fair only if he is benefiting from it. Also Richardson (2006) indicated that perceived fairness of tax system is significantly related to tax non-compliance. Roth et al. (1989) and Jackson and Milliron (1986) found that tax payers concerns about fairness have links with attitudes and behavioral intentions about tax compliance. Therefore, to understand a particular individual tax payer's behavior, it is important to identify the determining variable of behavioural intentions (Hanno and Violette, 1996).

Apart from individual tax payers' perception about the fairness of the tax system, its complexity or otherwise influences the compliance of tax payers. The Internal Revenue Act 2000 of Ghana (Act 592) as amended stated in section 1 (i) that "a person who has a chargeable income shall pay subject to this Act, for each year of assessment income tax as calculated in accordance with this Act"(Ghana, 2000). As a civic duty, the expectation is that citizens may comply with the Act, but that is not the case with some citizens (Alabede et al., 2011). Terkper (2007) advanced the reason that tax payers demonstrate various degrees of compliance owing to factors such as lack of understanding of the tax laws; improper book keeping and apathy towards government. Jackson and Milliron (1986) contended that the complexity of tax system has been considered as a possible reason for tax non-compliance. To Young et al. (2013), the rules should be simple and clear allowing

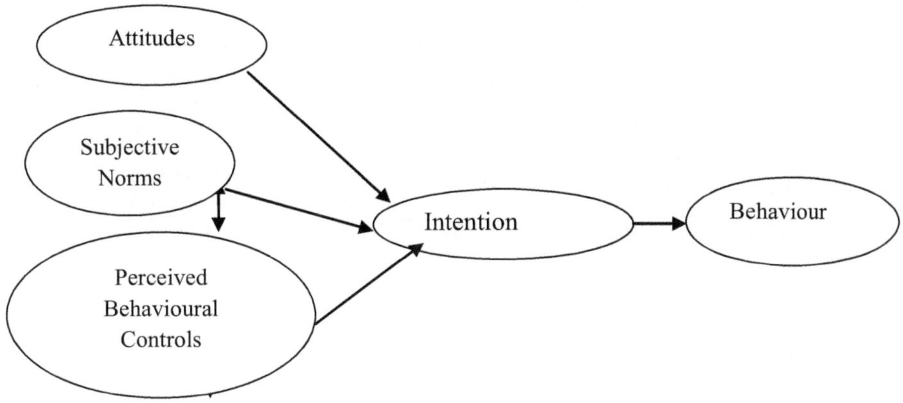

Figure 1. The theory of planned behaviour. *Source:* Ajzen (1991: 182).

taxpayers to read and understand the requirement and the rules they need to follow easily and quickly. Otherwise, tax payers' intentions of compliance may reduce. Beck et al. (1991) also concurred with this view by arguing that reducing tax complexity may lead to an increased perception of fairness on tax system and subsequent reduction of tax non- compliance.

Taxpayers' expectations are that the revenue generated from taxes should be spent and accounted for meaningfully by the state, (Young et al., 2013). Where this is lacking it can cause a slack in tax payers' commitment to pay their taxes. This is corroborated by Thorndike (2009) as he posited that citizens must comply with their obligations as part of their bargains, while governments are expected to secure the safety and security of individuals including the right to property. Braithwaite (2001) contended that the taxpayers' evaluation of local tax bureau's performance is proposed to affect tax compliance. Thus, the extent to which the tax office is delivering on its charter is suggested to be a factor affecting compliance. Young et al. (2013) concurred to this as they put it that as tax authority is fulfilling its promise their willingness to follow tax requirement may be higher.

The conceptual framework

This research is performed within the framework of the theory of planned behaviour. This model is shown in Figure 1.

From Figure 1, it can be seen that, the immediate antecedent determinant of behaviour is the intention behind that behaviour. Intentions are the motivational factors that influence behaviours that are under the volitional control of the individual (Ajzen, 1991). Volitional control behaviour is one in which the individual can decide at will to perform or not to perform the behaviour. Though taxes are the product of law which must be obeyed, the decision to obey or not to obey is a voluntary one. Thus the issue of voluntary tax compliance can be investigated within the theory of planned behaviour (Allingham and Sandmo, 1972).

The willingness to pay taxes or comply with the tax laws or to engage in the given behaviour in general terms is informed by the overall attitude of the individual given certain coperant factors (Pickens, 2005). Thus the factors forming the basis of this study have been considered as antecedents of an individual's taxpaying attitude and modelled as follows (Figure 2):

MATERIALS AND METHODS

Research hypothesis

Given the availability of prior literature on the phenomenon of tax compliance and the need to examine the other critical "actors in the field" (Alm et al., 2011) which influence the individual's compliance decision, particularly within the context of a developing country like Ghana, the following tentative hypotheses have been articulated and examined in this study.

Hypotheses 1: *Perception of the burden of tax does not significantly influence taxpayers' attitudes and does not positively correlates with tax compliance*. This hypothesis was applied to examine the relationship and for that matter the extent to which the taxpayer's views about the burden of tax predicts an individual's taxpaying attitude. Some previous research works for example; Alabede et al., (2011); Diego and Luca, (2011); Allingham and Sandmo, (1972) seem to support the view that, taxpayers have some concern for vertical and horizontal equity and that, some taxpayers compliance levels decreased with high levels of unfairness in the tax system. The findings of Atuguba (2006) that "Ghanaians can be tax loving" is profoundly exciting and thus should be tested empirically.

Hypotheses 2: *Taxpayers level of understanding of the tax laws does not significantly influence taxpaying attitudes and does not positively correlate the individual's tax compliance*. "Complexity is

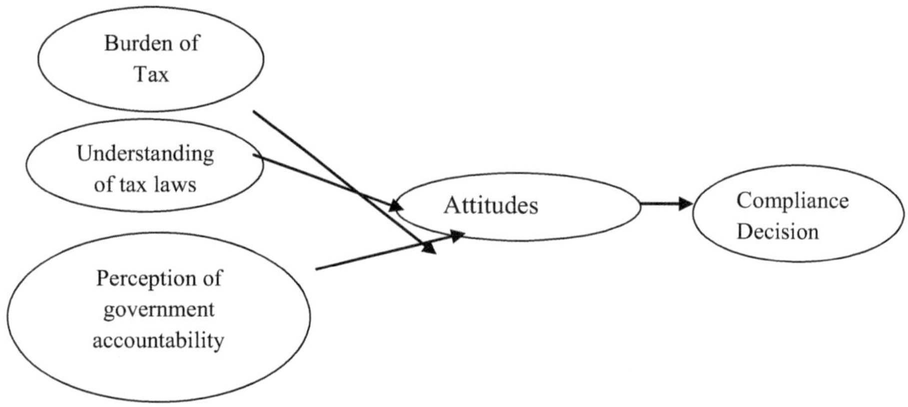

Figure 2. Researchers' model.

an unwanted feature of a tax system as it enhances the opportunity to avoid taxes" (Coskun and Savasan, 2009). The complexities in the system especially the use of legal verbiage could be an added ingredient in the milieu of noncompliance. The second hypothesis is thus meant to test whether there is any significant relationship between levels of understanding of the tax laws and tax compliance attitude

Hypotheses 3: *Taxpayers' perceptions of government accountability do not significantly influence taxpayers' attitudes and do not positively correlate with tax compliance decisions.* Underlying this hypothesis is the view that, when individuals voluntarily comply with their tax obligation, they are expectant that their contribution will yield some results. These results are viewed from different perspectives including the extent to which government is considered accountable to the people (Ayee, 2007). It is thus assumed that, if individuals perceive their government of the day to be accountable, they will in consequence comply voluntarily with their tax obligations.

Research design and methods

A survey involving individual income earners in the Tamale metropolitan area was conducted. A structured questionnaire containing a five point Likert scale test items was applied in soliciting the opinions of individual taxpayers who are engaged in active medium and small scale businesses in Tamale. These individuals were selected on the basis of convenience. Interviews were also utilised in obtaining the primary data for this research. The Cronbach alpha (α) was applied as the statistical measure of reliability. The reliability estimates indicated that, each test item had an alpha (α) value greater than the mostly recommended magnitude of 0.70 according to Pallant,(2005).

Population and sample size

Non-probability sampling method was applied in this study. The sampling technique used was purposive. According to Ayee, (2007) most Medium and Small Scale Enterprises in Ghana are managed by semi-literate individuals who are indifferent to proper record keeping. It would have therefore been inappropriate to randomly select respondents using probability sampling techniques as it is likely that a respondent may be randomly selected who cannot provide answers to the questions. The sample was drawn from a population consisting of the following business categories; hairdressers, vehicle mechanics, provision shop keepers, fuel station malls, other shopping malls, and bookshop keepers, vendors of small wares and market women and men. A total of 390 questionnaires were applied out of which 244 were successfully returned. The return rate was 62.56%. Out of the successful returns 11 questionnaire forms were omitted.

Presentation of data

The Spearman Rank correlation coefficient (R) was applied to explain the strength of the relationship between the three main factors in the hypotheses of this research and tax compliance. Rank correlation is used because of the measurement scale applied in assessing the opinions of respondents regarding their levels of agreement and disagreement. A one-way ANOVA was also applied in testing for significant differences between the means of attitudinal variables and tax compliance. These tools were primarily employed to explain the causal relationship between the three variables namely; perception of burden of tax, understanding of the tax laws, and perception of government accountability influence the tax compliance decisions of individuals.

Socio biographic profile of respondents

A total of 233 respondents were successful. Out of this the male respondents represented 45.06%, and the rest of the 54.94 %(128) were females. The mean age of business was 5 year (SD = 0.991). More than 61% of these businesses had been in operation above the mean of 5 years. Also 45% of respondents earned below GH₵6,500 in annual taxable incomes. The mean taxable income was GH₵9,750 with a standard deviation of 0.991. On the educational profile of respondents, 30.9% were senior high school leavers while only representing 9.7% had post first degree qualifications. In total more than half, that is 127 of the respondents did not have post secondary education. Sole proprietorship was the dominant type of business ownership with 82% of respondents operating this form of business while the second largest category was partnerships representing a total of 30 (12.9%). This situation appears to be the norm in most Ghanaian business ownerships (Ayee, 2007) owing to various socio-cultural factors. In regard to the

Table 1. ANOVA of individual taxpayer's perceptions of burden of taxes paid.

		Sum of squares	df	Mean square	F	*P - Value*
Burden of amount of taxes paid	Between groups	8.334	4	2.083	2.912	.000
	Within groups	163.117	227	.715		
	Total	171.451	233			
Opinion on rates of taxes generally	Between groups	37.242	4	9.310	11.728	.000
	Within groups	180.202	227	.794		
	Total	217.444	233			
Fairness of tax paid relative to higher income-earners	Between groups	23.565	4	5.891	3.255	.000
	Within groups	410.913	227	1.810		
	Total	434.478	233			

Source: Field Survey, January (2013).

TIN status about 79% of respondents have had their businesses registered with the Domestic Tax Revenue Division of the Ghana Revenue Authority. Indeed technical compliance in this regard is clearly very high. When this data was further cross analysed according to the gender of respondents, the results showed that, 91% of females had registered their businesses as opposed to 66% for their male counterparts. Statistics on the biographic profile of respondents are illustrated in Table 2 in the annexure section of this paper.

Inter-item correlation matrix

Partial correlations were also calculated and analysed with the view to determining the magnitude and direction of relationship between the various attitudinal factors. The result of this is shown in the correlation matrix in Table 2 in the annex. Almost all underlying attitudinal variables showed significant inter-item correlations. Five major items stood out clearly in terms of their partial/inter-item correlation coefficients. These are (1) the perception of the burden of taxes paid (2) the opinion about the rate of taxes generally, (3) the legal language used in structuring the tax laws (4) the likelihood of compliance given an increase in ones level of income in the future and (5) perceptions of benefits derived from governments' use of public funds. All these variables have significant inter-item correlation coefficients greater than 0.3. This is indicative that, there is a higher degree of interdependence between the various items, thus justifying their inclusion in measuring the construct, that is, tax compliance decisions. This conclusion is further corroborated by the Spearman's correlation matrix of the weighted means of these variables shown in Table 4.

DISCUSSION OF RESULTS

Perceptions of burden of taxes

From Table 3 it has been revealed by the ANOVA that, there was no significant difference between the means of the three response items (all critical $P < 0.05$) which are applied in measuring the burden of tax. Most people appear slightly indifferent to the amount of taxes they paid relative to those paid by higher income earners. This is indicative that, the compliance decision of the sampled individuals in this study is not influenced by concerns of vertical equity. This finding is rather diametrically opposed to the conclusions of (Coskun and Savasan, 2009) regarding vertical and horizontal equity. The Spearman Rank correlation coefficient ($R = 0.720$) reveals a strong statistical positive relationship between burden of tax and voluntary compliance. The coefficient of determination (R^2) = 0.5184 or 51.84% also reveals a greater degree of the measured variable. This result is in tandem with prior research for example, (Alabede et al., 2011; Serdan et al., 2011; Torgler, 2003; Alm, et al., 2011; Atubuga, 2006) whose works concluded among others thing that, tax payers have concerns for fairness and take seriously their burden of tax in forming their tax compliance attitudes.

Taxpayers' levels of understanding of the tax laws

On the issue of understanding of the tax laws, a greater number of people demonstrated poor understanding of the tax laws. There was strong agreement that, the tax laws are written in a language that is difficult to understand and to apply. The respective means and standard deviations of 2.80, 1.135 and 3.230, 1.170 for statement of LU1 and LU3 as shown in Table 1 clearly attest to this conclusion. As evidenced by the review of literature, notably by Atuguba (2006), Alabede et al. (2011) and Diego and Luca (2011) the extent to which taxpayers understand the tax laws affects tax compliance. The results of the ANOVA presented in Table 4 also did not indicate the existence of any significant statistical difference as all P values were < 0.05.

Perception of government's accountability

Individuals indicated that they are moderately benefiting from governments use of public funds. The level of government accountability was also somewhat low. This is also demonstrated in Table 1 (annexure) by the mean scores above 3.1 for all statements. The Spearman

Table 2. ANOVA of taxpayers levels of understanding of tax laws.

		Sum of squares	df	Mean square	F	*P - salue*
Understanding rate of the tax law	Between groups	11.853	4	2.963	2.353	.000
	Within groups	287.066	228	1.259		
	Total	298.918	233			
Legal language affecting understanding of tax laws	Between groups	9.866	4	2.467	1.380	.000
	Within groups	407.404	228	1.787		
	Total	417.270	233			
Declaration of ALL sources of incomes	Between groups	5.670	4	1.418	1.036	.002
	Within groups	311.815	228	1.368		
	Total	317.485	233			

Source: Field Survey, January (2013).

Table 3. ANOVA of perception of government's accountability.

		Sum of square	df	Mean square	F	*P-value*
Level of transparency and accountability in the use of public funds in Ghana	Between Groups	10.134	5	2.027	1.858	.000
	Within Groups	247.668	227	1.091		
	Total	257.803	233			
Usage of public funds influencing willingness to pay taxes	Between Groups	16.092	5	3.218	3.061	.001
	Within Groups	238.689	227	1.051		
	Total	254.781	233			
Perception of benefits derived from government use of public funds	Between Groups	10.779	5	2.156	2.530	.002
	Within Groups	193.436	227	.852		
	Total	204.215	233			

Source: Field Survey, January (2013).

Ranked correlation coefficient for perception of government accountability also shows a rather slightly significant positive relationship ($R = 0.534$; $R^2 = 29.7\%$). Taxpayers however did not consider the issue of government accountability to be of essence in making their tax compliance decisions. This result is very profound given that, in a civic society, citizens most of the time will hold their governments accountable, where they seem to have notions that they are not getting their fair share of the bargain (Feld and Bruno, 2009). An argument could however be made that, this suggestion is very idealistic in assuming that, there is a high level of awareness or consciousness in the citizenry regarding their rights and obligations under the social contract (Thorndike, 2009). The results of this study rather suggest the contrary. Sampled respondents did not consider government accountability in forming attitudes towards the tax system.

SUMMARY AND CONCLUSION

This study evaluated taxpayers' attitude and its effects on

Table 4. Spearman rank correlation coefficients between individual attitudinal factors and tax compliance.

	Burden of Tax	Understanding of tax laws	Perception of government accountability	Tax compliance
Burden of Tax	1	0.665*	0.514**	0.720**
Understanding of tax laws	0.665*	1	0.635*	0.626**
Perception of government accountability	0.514**	0.635*	1	0.534**
Tax compliance	0.720**	0.626**	0.534**	1

Source: Field Survey, January (2013) **. Correlation is significant at the 0.01 level (2-tailed). *.Correlation is significant at the 0.05 level (2-tailed).

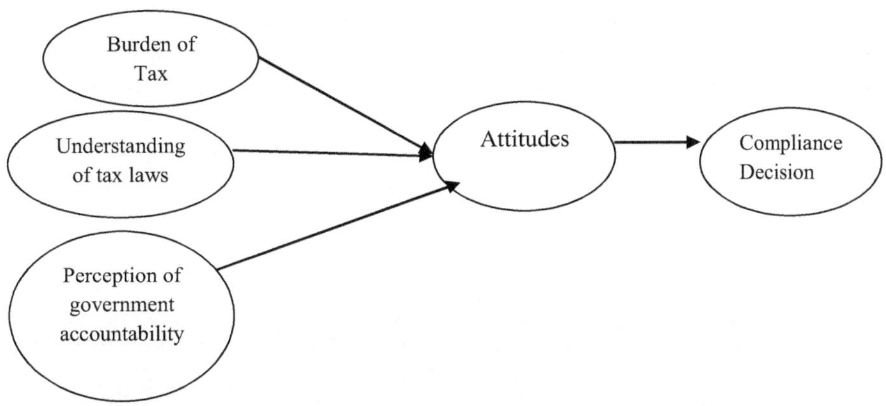

Figure 3. Summary of results of the model - correlation coefficients; Source: Researchers' Model: January 2013.

tax compliance decisions in Tamale – Ghana. Three major factors were hypothesised and tested. These were: perception of burden of tax, respondents' level of understanding of the tax laws and respondents' perceptions of governments' accountability (Figure 3).

Perception of burden of tax

Individual taxpayers had concern for the amount of taxes they pay. Female taxpayers were more sensitive to the amount of taxes they pay as pointed out earlier. A strong positive correlation exists between perceived levels of tax burden and compliance decisions. The policy implication of this is for the tax authorities to adopt strategies towards making the tax system more equitable taking the taxpayers views into account. After all, the issue of equity is one of the cardinal cannons of taxation identified by Adams Smith, an 18th century economist and political philosopher whose cutting edge economic and political economy theories have remained relevant till this day. Taxpayers perceive that, they were receiving some benefits from the government. They indicated that they may continue to comply with their tax obligations if the perceived benefits from government increased, even though their tax burdens were high. This conclusion was reflected in the inter-item correlation coefficient between burden of tax and perception of government's accountability. The partial correlation coefficient between burden of tax and perceive level of benefits derived (0.325) is significant.

Levels of understanding of the tax law

The study further established that taxpayers did not clearly understand the tax laws. The tax laws are written in a language that is very difficult to understand and to apply (Table 2). The levels of understanding of the tax laws influenced to a significant degree the attitudes of taxpayers. Taxpayers' levels of understanding positively correlated to a significant degree with their tax compliance decisions. These conclusions had been confirms the evidences in extant studies (Alabede et al., 2011; Atubuga, 2006; Everest, 2008).

Perception of Government's Accountability

Levels of accountability and transparency in governance are matters that taxpayers have less regard for in their compliance decisions. This conclusion is in line with Atuguba (2006). That study concluded in part that people doubted the real benefits of paying taxes. Tax education is very crucial as the levels of transparency in the government use of revenue affects tax compliance. Atubuga (2006) captured this notions succinctly when he concluded in part "the transparency of the tax system is directly proportional to people's willingness to pay taxes and hence the amount of taxes that may be mobilised"

RECOMMENDATION

It is recommended that, the Domestic Tax Division of the Ghana Revenue Authority should revamp and revitalise the taxpayer award scheme. The aim should be to award consistency and faithfulness in income declaration and prompt payment of taxes. This will encourage other taxpayers not to indulge in tax evasion.

Individuals will continue to willingly pay their taxes if they know that their taxes are being put to good use (Atubuga, 2006; Ayee, 2007). It is therefore recommended that the government through the ministry of information should continuously educate the taxpaying public about ongoing projects which are being financed from their taxes. When taxpayers get feedback from their governments in connection with the use to which their taxes are put, their voluntary compliance levels may increase as a result.

The National Board for Small Scale Industries (NBSSI) in collaboration with national bodies such as National Commission for Civic Education, Rural Enterprise Foundation, and other allied bodies to carryout business education fairs with the view to promoting joint venturing. This will likely widen the current envelop of taxable incomes and in consequence increase the amount of tax revenues to be generated by government for development purposes.

It is worth reiterating that there is the need for government through the National Commission on Civic Education in collaboration with the ministry of information to undertake sensitization programmes aimed at educating the public about their fundamental obligations as citizens. The operations and client service units of the Domestic Taxes Division of the Ghana Revenue Authority should adopt mechanisms aimed at clarifying the tax laws. New legislative instruments for the implementation of any budget or fiscal policy should be promptly disseminated and the taxpaying public clearly educated. This will deal with the problem of low levels of understanding of the tax laws. When this is achieved it will conceivably help to increase the amount of revenue mobilised from direct taxation. *If possible tax education should be introduced at the basic school level with the view to making the population a very conscious taxpaying mass.*

Suggestions for further research

The sample size used was not very large due to financial resource constraints. Further research could therefore by conducted into the phenomenon using a larger sample size. Preferably the study could be conducted across the 10 regions of Ghana to find out whether there are regional differences in attitudes with regard to tax compliance. This could be an important step is clarifying and updating extant knowledge about the tax culture and morale of Ghanaians.

The religious denominations of respondents were not analysed. A comparative study on tax compliance based on religion might be worth exploring.

There also is the need to explore further on why female taxpayers have greater concern for equity and the burden of tax than male taxpayers. Some studies have tried to look at feminine compliance to tax within the context of the Western developed countries. This is worthy of replication in a developing country like Ghana

REFERENCES

Ajzen I (1991). *Organisational and Human Decision Processes: The Theory of Planned Behaviour.* Massachusetts: Academic Press Inc.

Alabede OJ, Ariffin ZZ, Kamil MI (July 2011). Individual Taxpayers' Attitutes and Compliance Behaviour in Nigeria: The moderating Role of Financial Condition and Risk Preference. *J. Account. Taxat. Vol 3(5).*

Alabede OJ, Zainol A, Kamil MI (2011). Determinants of Tax Compliance Behaviour: A Proposed Model for Nigeria . *Inter. Res. J. Financ. Econ. p.* 122.

Ali-Nakyea A (2006). *Taxation in Ghana; Priniciples Practice and Planning; Page 273.* Accra: Black Mask Limited.

Allingham G, Sandmo A (1972). Income Tax Evasion: A Theoritical Analysis. *J. Pub. Econ.* 323 - 338.

Alm J, Kirkchler E, Muehlbacher S, Gangl k, Hofmann E, Kogler C (2011). Rethinking the Research Paradigms for Analysing Tax Compliance Behaviour. *"The Shadow Economy, Tax Evasion and Money Laundering"* (p. 34). Munster: FOCUS.

Andreoni J, Erard B, Feistein J (1998). Tax Compliace. *J. Econ. Lit. Vol 36.*

Atubuga R (2006). *The Tax Culture of Ghanaian: A Research Report Prepared for the Revenue Mobilisation Support (RMS).* Accra: Legal Resource Centre; GTZ.

Ayee JR (2007). Building Tax Compliance Through Reciprocity with Government. *Enterprise Formalization in Africa* (pp. 6 - 7). Accra: Foreign Investment Advisory Service of the World Bank Group.

Beck P, Davis J, Jung W (1991). Experimental Evidenceon Tax Compliance reporting under uncertainty. *Accounting Review.*

Braithwaite V, Reinhart M, Graham R (2001). *Preliminary findings from the Community Hopes, Fears and Actions Survey.*

Coskun CA, Savasan F (2009). Tax Morale: Empirical Evidence from Turkey. *Annual Meeting of the European Public Choice Society.*

Davis J, Hecht G, Perkins JD (2002). Social Behaviours,Enforcement and Tax Compliance Dynamics. *The Accounting Review.*

Diego L, Luca Z (2011). Happiness and Tax Morale: An Empirical Analysis. *Working Paper Serie. WP 4.*

Eshag E (1983). *Fiscal and Monetary Policies and Problems in Developing Countries.* Cambridge: Cambridge University Press.

Everest PM (2008). Business Tax as State-building in Developing Countries: Applying governance principles in Private Sector Development. *Inter. J. Regulat. Gov. 8(2)*: 123 -154.

Feld LP, Bruno SF (2009). Tax Evasion in Switzerland: The Roles of Deterrence and Tax Morale. *Working Paer Series. Working Paper No. 284, Institute for Empirical Research in Economics. University of Zurich.*

Fischer C, Wartick M, Mar M (1992). Detection Probability and Taxpayers Compliance: A Review of Literature. *IIJ Accounting Literature*.

Fishbein M, Ajzen I (1975). Belief, Attitude, Intention and Behaviour: An Introduction to Theory and Research- Reading. *Reading, MA - Wesley.*

Juan AMM, María GR, Francisco SG (2013). *Ghana's Advance to Middle-income Status Requires Firm Policies.* Retrieved from IMFSurvey Magazine: http://www/imf.org/external/pubs/ft/survey/so/2013/car061213a.htm

Frank VO, Frank S (2005). A Connectionist Model of Attitute Formation and Change. *Personal. Soc. Psychol. Rev. 9(3)*231-274.

Gerald C, Leung P (2009). A Critical Review of Fischers Tax Compliance Model: A Research Synthesis. *J. Taxat. Account.*

Ghana RO (2000). Internal Revenue Act, Act 592 2000. Accra: Assembly Press.

Ghana RO (2011). *Budget Statement and Economic Policy.* Accra: Assembly Press.

GIZ (2010). *Addressing Tax Evasion and Avoidance in Developing Countries.* Deutsche Gessellschaft fur Internationale Zusammenarbeit (GIZ) GmbH.

Harwood G, Larkins E, Vazques J (1993). Using a Randomised response methology to collect data for tax compliance. *The J. Am. Taxat.*

Isaac W, Ajay M, Mehrotra PM (2009). *The Thunder of History: The Origins and Development of the New Fiscal Sociology.* Cambridge: Cambridge Press.

Jackson B, Milliron V (1986). Tax Compliance Research Findings, Problems and Prospects. *Journal of Accounting Literature.*

Kirchler, E., & Hoelzl Wahl, E. (2008). The Slippery Slope Framework. *Journal of Economics and Psychology*, 210 -225.

Kristina M (2004). *Moving towards a more effective model of regulatory enforcement in the Australian Taxation Office.*

Kristina M (2004, November). An Examination of Taxpayers' Attitudes Towards the Australian Tax System: Asurvey of Tax Scheme Investors.Working Paper 46. *Centre for Tax System Integrity;Australian National University*, p. 2.

Likhovsk A (2010). Is Tax Law Culturally Specific? Lessons from the history of income tax law in Mandatory Palestine. *Theoritical Inquiries in Law*, 725-763.

Lumumba, O. M., Magutu, P. O., Wanjohi, S. M., & Mokoro MJ (2010). Taxpayers' Attitutes and Tax Compliance Behaviour in Keyna. *African Journal of Business and Management.*

Margaret M, Evans C (2009). Sustaining Growth in Developing Economies through Improved Taxpayer Compliance: Challenges for Policy Makers and Revenue Authorities. *eJouranl of Tax Research; Volume 7 Number 2.*

Martina H, Silvia R, Eric K, Alfred S (2008). Procedural Fairness and Tax Compliance. *Econ. Analy. Tax Policy, 38(1)*: 137.

Modeo S, Schepanski A, Uecker V (1987). Modelling of Judgement of Taxpayers' Compliance:. *Account. Rev.* 323-342.

Noami F, Joel S (2009). War and Taxation: When Does Patriotism Overcome the Free-Rider Impluse? *The New Fiscal Sociology. Taxation in Coparative and Historial Perspectives*, pp. 143-156.

Pallant J (2005). *SPSS Survival Manual: A step by Step Guidde to Data Analysis Using SPSS for Windows.* Maidenhead: Open University Press.

Pickens J (2005). *Organisational Behaviour for Health Care: Attitudes and Perceptions, Page 44.* Miami Florida.

Richardson D (2006). Determinants of Tax Evasion. A cross-country investigation. *International Journal of Accounting, Auditing and Taxation*, 150-169.

Sandmo A (2006). The Thoery of Tax Evasion: A Retrospective View. *National Tax J., 58*: 642 - 663.

Serdan B, Ahmet FC, Tamer B (2011). An Investigation of Tax Compliance Intentions: A Theory of Planned Behaviour Approach. *European J. Econ. Financ. Admin. Sci.*

Singh V (2003). Tax Compliance and Ethical Decision-making. A Malaysian Perspective. *1st Edu.l Pearson Malaysia Sdn.Bhd.*

Terkper S (2007). Improving Taxpayer Acconting for SMEs and Individuals. *Andrew Young School of Policy Studies; Annual Conference on Public Finance Issues:Alternative Methods of Taxing Individuals* (pp. 22-23). Georgia State: Georgia State University.

Thorndike JJ (2009). The Unfair Advantage of the Few: The New Deal Origins of "Soak the Rich" Taxation. *The New Fiscal Sociology: Taxation in Comparative and Historical Perspectives*, pp. 26 - 28.

Tittle C (1997). Sanction, Fear and the Maintenance of Social Order. *Social Forces,55(3/*, 579-596.

Torgler B (2003). The Importance of faith. *Centre for Research in Economics, Management and the Arts (CREMA).*

Wenzel M (2002). *An Analysis of Norm Processing in Tax Compliance.* Canbera: The Australian National University, University Tax Office. Centre for Tax Integrity.

Young A, Danny C, Daniel H (2013). A Study of the Impace of Culture on Tax Compliance in China. *International Tax Journal;CCH Incorporated.*

22

Do the changes in tax incentives encourage direct investment in China by Taiwanese enterprises?

Wan-Ying Lin[1] and Jui-Chih Wang[2]

[1]Department of Accounting, National Chengchi University, Taiwan.
[2]Department of Accounting Information, National Taipei University of Business, Taiwan.

This study examined the association between tax incentives of China's 2008 Enterprise Income Tax Law (the 2008 tax law) and inflows of foreign direct investments from Taiwanese enterprises (TDI) to China. In addition, this study also investigated the effects of industry and location on TDI. This study showed that reduced tax rate concessions for foreign enterprises and increased tax rate considerably reduced TDI inflow to China. Furthermore, industry-specific tax incentives became more favorable than location-specific tax incentives after the new tax laws were introduced. The results of joint tests of tax reform and tax incentives indicated that the 2008 tax law did not provide location-specific tax incentives for TDI, while industry-specific tax incentives appeared to be more attractive to TDI. Moreover, Taiwanese enterprises with intensive indirect investment in China as well as with higher shareholdings were inclined to have higher TDI. The implications of these findings implied that foreign direct investment strategy in accordance with industry-specific and location-specific tax incentives can enhance the competitive advantages of multinational companies.

Key words: Tax incentives, the 2008 tax law, Taiwanese direct investment (TDI).

INTRODUCTION

Since China implemented its economic reform and opening-up policy, the Chinese government has addressed the country's financial and technological shortfalls by encouraging the inflow of foreign capital and technology to facilitate China's industrialization and urbanization. In 2013, China's gross domestic product (GDP) was USD 9,185 billion,[1] and the mean economic growth rate from 2007 to 2013 was 9.74%, indicating that China's economy has undergone rapid and stable growth. The value of foreign investment by the top ten countries or regions neighboring China accounted for 91.61% of all foreign direct investment (FDI) in China. Taiwanese enterprises were the second-largest investor in China, indicating its influence on China's market.[2] China approved almost 730,000 FDI enterprises, with a total value of USD 1.2 trillion. Because of this rapid growth, China has become the second-largest recipient of FDI in the world. Based on the inflow of foreign investment, China is currently the world's largest developing country.

Taiwanese enterprises were the pioneers of FDI in China. Since the initial economic reform and opening-up policy initiated during the 1980s, Taiwanese businesses have invested in China. China began promoting its economic reform and opening-up policy in the late 1970s, and the investment environment in its coastal cities has continually improved, effectively becoming outposts for

[1] Please refer to the PRC State Administration of Taxation statistical data.

[2] For further information, please refer to the website: http://www.fdi.gov.cn.

FDI enterprises. During the 1980s, Taiwanese enterprises established labor-intensive industries in the four economic development zones of Shenzhen, Zhuhai, Xiamen, and Shantou. In the early 1990s, the economic reform and opening-up progressed northward to Shanghai, and later, to more cities along the Yangtze River, as well as in coastal areas and border regions. Consequently, Taiwanese investment moved northward and shifted from labor-intensive industries to technology- and capital-intensive industries. The Investment Commission of the Ministry of Economic Affairs, ROC (MOEA) reported that since China implemented the opening-up policy in 1991, the Taiwanese government has approved 237 investments in China, with a value of USD 174 million. In 2013, 40,762 investments worth USD 133.7 billion were approved, accounting for more than 62% of Taiwan's total outward direct investment. Thus, Taiwanese enterprises clearly occupy a key economic position in China.

Previous studies have primarily investigated the macroeconomic factors affecting FDI in China. Limited extant studies have discussed the effect of tax incentives for investing in specific locations and industries on FDI. This study explores the effect of tax reform incentives on FDI in China after controlling the effect of macroeconomic factors on FDI. We performed a regression analysis to examine the effect of tax incentives on Taiwanese direct investment (TDI) in China. The empirical results of this study suggest that by reducing tax rate concessions for foreign enterprises and increasing the tax rate to 25%, the 2008 tax law effectively decreased the level of TDI in China. After the 2008 tax law was enacted, TDI in Western China was taxed at a reduced rate of 15%, primarily because TDI in that area accounted for only 3% of all TDI in China. Despite attempts to encourage foreign investment in China's western regions, the appeal of tax incentives was limited. Hence, our results show that the increase in TDI was not significant. Furthermore, after promulgating the 2008 tax law, tax incentives for investing in high-tech electronic industries became more favorable than those investing in western China. Because Taiwanese businesses investing in high-tech electronic industries were taxed at a rate of 15%, more Taiwanese enterprises invested in these industries. This study performed joint tests on the 2008 tax law and tax incentives, and the joint test results indicate that the 2008 tax reform did not provide tax incentives encouraging TDI in western China, although it provided effective tax incentives for investing in high-tech electronic industries. The results also show that higher TDI in China and comparatively higher *tax rates* for holding shares facilitated an increase in TDI in China. These two factors were critical tax incentives for TDI enterprises in China.

The contributions of this study are three-fold. First, the validity of this research is strengthened by using a large firm-year sample (from 2001 to 2013) of subsidiaries operating in China. Second, this study incorporated a more comprehensive set of control variables to better investigate the effect of tax incentive on FDI. In addition to controlling the effect of the 2008 China new income tax law on FDI, we also controlled the macroeconomic factors influencing China's overall FDI, including the economic growth rate, consumer price index, employment rate, and the market size of securities to enhance the breadth of this research. Finally, this study provides empirical evidence on the implication of tax reform on industry-specific and location-specific FDI managerial decisions. Specifically, the results provide strategic perspectives for Taiwanese enterprises, one of the largest FDI inflow regions in China, to focus on west-bound and new-high-tech industry investment in China. The findings therefore can also shed light on other inflow sources with respect to FDI inflow investment decisions.

The remainder of this paper is organized as follows. Section 2 details the background of tax reforms in China. Section 3 describes previous studies that are relevant to developing our hypotheses. Section 4 describes the research methodology of the empirical model employed in this study, *including* the empirical variables and sample selection method. Section 5 reports the empirical results and presents additional analyses, and finally, Section 6 *presents* our conclusion, limitation and the implications of our findings.

Institutional background and tax reform in China

Since China's economic reform and opening up to foreign trade, foreign direct investment enterprises in China have played a crucial role in facilitating China's economic development and levitating the development of industries. Table 1 listed the top-ten FDI inflow countries (regions) in China. Asian countries (regions) accounted for the top six due to geographical reason. Hong Kong has long been China's largest source of FDI inflow. The amount of Hong Kong's investment in China has accumulated to USD 420 billion over the period of 2001 to 2012. Japan is China's second largest source of FDI in China which the amount had accumulated to USD 59 billion. South Korea is the fastest growing and also the third largest country (region) FDI inflow source. Prior to 1995, Taiwan was the second largest FDI inflow source next to Hong Kong. However, with China's opening up policy, more and more countries invested in China. Taiwan became the fourth largest source of FDI in 2002. After 2003, Taiwan became China's

Table 1. FDI Inflows in China.

Year	Hong Kong	Japan	Macao	Singapore	Korea	Taiwan	USA	Germany	France	UK
2001	1,671,730	434,842	32,112	214,355	215,178	297,994	443,322	121,292	53,246	105,166
2002	1,786,093	419,009	46,838	233,720	272,073	397,064	542,392	92,796	57,560	89,576
2003	1,770,010	505,419	41,660	205,840	448,854	337,724	419,851	85,697	60,431	74,247
2004	1,899,830	545,157	54,639	200,814	624,786	311,749	394,095	105,848	65,674	79,282
2005	1,794,879	652,977	60,046	220,432	516,834	215,171	306,123	153,004	61,506	96,475
2006	2,023,292	459,806	60,290	226,046	389,487	213,583	286,509	197,871	38,269	72,610
2007	2,770,342	358,922	63,700	318,457	367,831	177,437	261,623	73,397	45,601	83,094
2008	4,103,640	365,235	58,161	443,529	313,532	189,868	294,434	90,049	58,775	91,401
2009	4,607,547	410,497	81,471	360,484	270,007	188,055	255,499	121,657	65,365	67,902
2010	6,056,677	408,372	65,524	542,820	269,217	247,574	301,734	88,840	123,820	71,032
2011	7,050,016	632,963	68,043	609,681	255,107	218,343	236,932	112,896	76,853	58,152
2012	6,556,119	735,156	50,556	630,508	303,800	284,707	259,809	145,095	65,242	40,960
Total	42,090,175	5,928,355	683,040	4,206,686	4,246,706	3,079,269	4,002,323	1,388,442	772,342	929,897

Source: National Bureau of Statistics of China, 2001-2012. (USD 10,000).

fifth-largest FDI inflow source. In 2012, Taiwan invested in China amounted to USD 2.8 billion. Furthermore, Table 1 also indicated that Germany, United Kingdom, France, United States and Canada also in the top-ten list.

The 1991 tax reform on FDI in China

China's open door policy, which was adopted in 1979, initiated long-term socioeconomic change after 30 years of economic stagnation. With it came the flow of FDI during the early 1980s, which was followed by the proliferation of income tax laws, including the Income Tax Law Concerning Joint Ventures with Chinese and Foreign Investment (the 1980 tax law), which was designed to govern equity joint ventures, and the Income Tax Law Concerning Foreign Enterprises (the 1981 tax law), which concerned contractual joint ventures and wholly foreign-owned enterprises. Throughout the 1980s, these two laws imposed various tax rates and incentives on these three types of FDI (Cho et al., 1998).

The 1991 tax reform, which lowered the marginal tax rate from 40 to 30% and expanded the range of tax preference, resulted in positive changes in foreign investment flows between China and its competitors. China's Income Tax Law for Foreign Investment Enterprises included many tax incentives, such as a 5-year tax holiday, 40% income tax refund for profits from reinvesting in China for a minimum of 5 years, 50% income tax refund for over 70% of export-oriented FIEs in any year, and the designation of investment incentive zones with a tax rate of 15 or 24%, which was less than the statutory rate (30%), and a local surtax (10%). In addition, China designated special economic zones *with* the lowest tax rate (15%) and more tax incentives, and they were thus ranked as a highly favored tax group. Furthermore, coastal open cities were designated with a concessionary (after the tax-holiday) tax rate (24%), and they were accordingly ranked as a moderately favored tax group.

The 2008 tax reform on FDI in China

Before 2008, foreign-funded companies in China were taxed at a relatively low rate, and a series of preferential policies were implemented to encourage FDI in China. Most foreign-invested enterprises were taxed at a rate (15% or 24%) that was almost 10% less than that for domestic enterprises (33%). On March 16, 2007, China passed the new Enterprise Income Tax (EIT) Law (the 2008 tax law), which will come into effect on January 1, 2008. This was the first law in China's history that imposed an income tax on all *types of enterprises,* and it replaced the Foreign Invested Enterprises (FIE) Income Tax Law (which applied to FDI enterprises) and Interim EIT Regulations (which applied to Chinese-owned enterprises). The 2008 tax law unified the income tax system imposed on foreign and domestic enterprises in China, and it provided a single statutory rate of 25% on business profit. The legislation integrated the taxation of local and foreign firms by consolidating the domestic and foreign EIT laws.

The 2008 tax law removed various tax incentives for foreign investors establishing factories in China *to manufacture* exportable goods. The 2008 tax law was anticipated to have a profound impact on foreign-based investors who had already established manufacturing operations in China under the old tax system that favored the production of exportable goods. However, these changes also offered opportunities for technology or service companies to expand their operations in China by providing new tax incentives and domestic market opportunities.

Taiwanese enterprises investments in China

Taiwanese investment in China has promoted China's economic development and Taiwan's industrial upgrade. Taiwanese enterprises were the pioneers of FDI in China, and they occupy a key economic position in the country. During the 1980s, they established labor-intensive industries in China's four economic development zones (Shenzhen, Zhuhai, Xiamen, and Shantou). In the early 1990s, the opening-up policy was progressively implemented northward to Shanghai, and subsequently in more cities along the Yangtze River, as well as in coastal areas and border regions. Consequently, Taiwanese FDI enterprises moved northward and shifted from labor-intensive industries to technology-intensive and capital-intensive industries. According to the Investment Commission of the MOEA statistical data show that in 1991, the Taiwan government approved 237 investment projects in China (valued at USD 174 million). Subsequently, the number of investments increased rapidly, and 40,762 projects were approved *up to 2013* (valued at USD 133.7 billion). TDI in China accounted for more than 60% of total TDI. The amount of direct and indirect investments in China between 1993 and 2012, the Taiwanese government approved USD 27,477 million direct investment and USD 80,831 million indirect investments in China. This shows that approximately 75% of Taiwanese enterprises invested China indirectly.

Between 1952 and 2013, *the TDI* was primarily located in China's coastal areas, including Jiangsu Province (32.6%), Guangdong Province (20.3%), and Shanghai (15.61%). By contrast, considerably fewer TDI was located in China's western regions, including Sichuan Province (2.2%) and Chongqing (1.53%). The remaining TDI was located in the western area of Guangxi Zhuang Autonomous Region, Northwestern China, Guizhou Province, Yunnan Province, and Tibet Autonomous Region, accounting for less than 1% of TDI. To balance the disparity between developments in China's eastern and western regions, the 2008 tax law offering tax concessions to encourage FDI in Western China. The table also shows that Taiwanese FDI enterprises in the coastal cities in Eastern China[3] accounted for 71.58% of all approved investments, primarily because of geographic, transportation infrastructure, and climate factors in that region. In addition, investments in Northern[4] and Central China[5] respectively accounted for 5.01 and 22.92% of all approved investments.

At the end of 2013, the top three industries for TDI in China were electronic components manufacturer (19.08%), computers, electronics, and optical products manufacturer (13.74%) and electrical equipment manufacturer (7.32%). These industries collectively accounted for 40.14% of TDI in China.

LITERATURE REVIEW AND HYPOTHESES DEVELOPMENT

Tax incentives for FDI

Before 1979, FDI was not allowed in China. In 1979, China opened its economy to foreign investors, and FDI in China grew to USD 133 billion by the end of 1995. In the previous 15 years, China has actively opened its regional markets to foreign businesses, and progressively opened inland areas to foreign trade. Consequently, substantial changes have been implemented regarding the size, source, and type of investment for introducing foreign capital and technology. Because of China's foreign investment policy for coastal areas, foreign businesses have invested approximately four times more in coastal provinces than they have in inland provinces. Furthermore, FDI inflow to China increased considerably after China's *entry* into the World Trade Organization in 2001. At the end of 2010, the cumulative FDI inflow to China peaked at USD 1,047 billion. Since 1979, China has formulated a series of tax incentives, including tax exemptions and lower tax rates, through tax laws for foreign enterprises. These laws were drafted in accordance with the principle of minimum tax burden and maximum preferential tax treatment, and to further open China's markets to foreign trade. These tax incentives are industry-specific, location-specific, and enterprise-specific. The tax incentives include partial tax concessions, such as reduced tax rates, tax holidays, tax refunds, depreciation, and loss carry backs and carry forwards, with a particular focus on enterprise income tax.

Previous studies have shown that most developing countries use tax incentives to attract FDI (Hadari, 1990; Usher, 1977). However, previous studies have yielded conflicting results regarding the effectiveness of using tax incentives to attract FDI. One view is that Chinese tax policies have had a decisive influence on foreign investment in China. Between 1979 and 1995, the coastal regions, which were given more tax preferences, attracted approximately 83% of foreign investment (compared which only 17% for the inland regions). Policies offering greater tax preferences in the coastal regions are a critical factor in the recent rapid absorption of FDI in those regions. Specifically, if foreign enterprises investing in China intended to increase their after-tax returns, increased FDI would be anticipated in the special tax incentive zones that offer concessionary rates (15 or 24%), compared with that in other areas where FDI is subject to higher statutory tax rates. Attitudinal and empirical studies on the effect of tax incentives on FDI have been inconclusive. Some studies (Fortune, 1977; Root and Ahmed, 1978; Hartman, 1984; Boskin and Gale, 1986; Papke, 1987; Young, 1988; Slemrod, 1990; Grubert and Mutti, 1991; He and Guisinger, 1993; Swenson, 1994;

[3] This includes the six provinces and one municipality: Shandong, Zhejiang, Anhui, Fujian, Jiangxi, Jiangsu and Shanghai.

[4] This includes Beijing, Tianjin, Hebei, Shanxi and Inner Mongolia.

[5] The region includes Henan, Hubei, Hunan, Guangdong and Hainan.

Hines, 1996) have shown that tax incentives are a critical factor for attracting FDI and for making regional investment decisions; however, other studies (Forsyth, 1971; Carlton, 1983; Lim, 1983; Yelpaala, 1984; Moore et al., 1987; Ernst and Young International, 1994) have presented opposite conclusions. This inconsistency may partially be the result of the various tax measurements employed in these studies. Hartman (1984), Boskin and Gale (1986), and Young (1988) measured the influence of effective tax rates on FDI. Grubert and Mutti (1991) empirically showed that statutory tax rates are stronger determinants of income shifting than effective tax rates.

China provides an ideal opportunity for testing these assertions because of its relatively high FDI, as well as the various tax incentives that China has offered to attract FDI during the previous two decades. China's total FDI has grown annually at an average rate of 41%; specifically, it has increased from USD 1.26 billion in 1984 to USD 41.73 billion in 1996 (China State Statistical Bureau, 1983–1997). By 1993, China had become the second-largest recipient of FDI in the world (second to the United States), and the largest beneficiary in the developing world.

Tax incentives have been adopted worldwide to attract foreign direct investment (FDI) and its superior technology. Deng et al. (2012) develop a static computable general equilibrium (CGE) model of China to explore it. Their results suggest that abolishing differential tax system leads to weaker FDI spillovers in the short term. Park et al. (2013) examine how a tax regime, composed of a host country's corporate taxes and tariffs, affects inbound and outbound FDI. Their empirical results of this study intensify the opinion that tax burdens or incentives are deeply associated with inbound or outbound FDI, and imply that the adjusted outbound FDI gravity model is helpful to examine determinants of FDI or tax effects on FDI. Klemm and Parys (2012) prepared a new dataset of tax incentives in over 40 Latin American, Caribbean and African countries for the period 1985-2004. They found evidence that lower rates and longer tax holidays are effective in attracting FDI in Latin America and the Caribbean but not in Africa. An (2012) examined whether FIEs are responding to the 2008 tax reforms in China by reducing their investment in China. This study found that FIEs are reducing their investment in China and the magnitude of the response is larger for Hong Kong-Macau-Taiwan (HMT) investment enterprises. The evidence of An (2012) supports the claim that some Chinese investors engaged in "roundtripping" FDI.

Based on the aforementioned studies, China's tax policies do have impact on DFI. According to An (2012), the influence of tax incentives under 2008 tax reforms was a reducing effect. As one of the top-ten FDI inflow source, it is expected that Taiwanese direct investment (TDI) inflow to China would decrease after the new tax laws were enacted. Accordingly, this study proposed the following hypothesis:

H1: *Ceteris paribus*, after the 2008 tax laws were implemented in China, tax incentives for foreign investors were reduced, and TDI is decreased.

Tax incentives on FDI types.

In China, there are three types of FIE on FDI: equity joint ventures, contractual joint ventures, and wholly foreign-owned enterprises. Equity joint ventures are limited liability corporations (there is a minimal requirement of 25% foreign participation) in which Chinese and foreign partners jointly invest and manage the operations. Contractual joint ventures may or may not form as legal entities, and there is no minimal foreign participation requirement. In addition, the profits and losses are shared in accordance with the terms and conditions stipulated in the venture contract. Wholly foreign-owned enterprises may be established by foreign companies using their own capital, technology, and management. Moreover, foreign investors are responsible for all risks, gains, and losses. In 1991, the Income Tax Law for Foreign Investment Enterprises and Foreign Enterprises (the 1991 tax law) were simplified, and all types of FDI were granted identical tax benefits.

Under the 1991 tax law, all three types of FDI were treated identically, and they were subjected to the same tax rates and incentives. Two major differences exist in the tax provisions for the three types of FDI. First, the 1991 tax law replaced the progressive tax rates of the 1981 tax law with a flat income tax rate (30%) and local tax (3%) on all types of FDI. Consequently, the tax liability of large contractual joint ventures and wholly foreign-owned enterprises was reduced, whereas the small and medium enterprises, which previously paid lower taxes, were liable to pay a higher tax rate. Second, the 1991 tax law unified tax exemptions, reductions, and refunds for all types of FDI. Regarding the choice of investment type, foreign investors considered both tax and nontax factors. To compare the governing laws and regulations, legal liability, duration, approval and registration, capital requirements, profit/loss distribution, management and ownership control, and termination of business of the three types of FDI in China. Tung and Cho (2000) explored whether the various types of FDI were affected differently. They showed that China's tax reforms in 1979–1991 provided more tax incentives for equity joint ventures than they did for contractual joint ventures and wholly foreign-owned enterprises; moreover, most types of FDI in China were equity joint ventures. After the 1991 tax reform, the effect of tax incentives on the type of investment was insignificant.

Tax incentives based on FDI zone

Location theory purports that multinational enterprises (MNEs) maximize their FDI potential by selecting an FDI location that is close to their market or *to their source of* raw materials. When an investment location attracts increasingly more FDI, it becomes an agglomerated location. Moreover, the agglomeration effect is typically associated with externalities. Operating in concentrated production or population areas facilitates the rapid spillover of knowledge and access to joint networks of suppliers and distributors. Consequently, firms can enhance their technology level to acquire economies of scale and scope. Investing in regions featuring substantial industrial clustering is likely to involve relatively lower costs than *in regions* with a dispersed manufacturing sector. Regarding the agglomeration effect, Krugman (1991) considered clustering as a form of economic activity resulting from historical contingencies. Because of contingencies, some locations became clustering sites for specific industries; for example, manufacturing firms that minimize their transportation costs can attain economies of scale. Thus, they typically select locations with aggregated industries.

Previous studies have shown that most developing countries use tax incentives to attract FDI (Hadari, 1990; Usher, 1977). However, previous studies have yielded conflicting results regarding the effectiveness of using tax incentives to attract FDI. Tung and Cho (2000) assessed whether preferential tax treatment was an effective method for attracting FDI to China, and whether it influenced the organizational structure of FDI enterprises. Consistent with previous research, their results indicate that concessionary tax rates and incentives were effective for attracting FDI into the designated special tax incentive zones in China. Consistent with Scholes and Wolfson (1992), they showed that the increased inflow of FDI into these zones was the result of concessionary tax rates enhancing the after-tax return on investments.

In China, from the early 1980s to the early 1990s, special tax incentive cities and zones emerged, spanning from the south to the north areas and from the coastal regions to the inner areas of China. All provinces and autonomous regions (except for Tibet) were opened to FDI. These cities and zones offered various tax concessions to foreign investors (Cho and Tung, 1998). The open door policy began in 1980 when China opened four special economic zones in comparatively less developed rural areas of Southern China. The local governments of these zones were given autonomy over their economic development and, a 15% tax rate has been available to foreign investors operating in these areas since 1984. The success of the special economic zones led to the further opening up of China to foreign investment. In 1984, 14 Coastal Open Cities were designated to attract foreign capital and technology to improve local industries.

In 1992, the Chinese government opened up 18 provincial capitals, six cities along the Yangtze River, and 13 border open cities. Hence, the development of special tax incentive zones was further extended to inner parts and border regions of China. Simultaneously, the government undertook various measures to facilitate the inflow of FDI, such as developing an institutional infrastructure and adopting laws to regulate the legislative, administrative, and judicial operations of government. To attract FDI into the special tax incentive zones, generous tax incentives were offered to investors. Specifically, FIEs operating in the zones were granted concessionary tax rates of either 15 or 24%, which was comparatively lower than the statutory tax rates (33%) levied on FIEs outside of these areas.

The theory of location advantages considers the dispersion of resources and markets, international transport, trade barriers, infrastructure, cultural and psychological gaps, and political factors. Manufacturers typically select their preferred regions based on their characteristics. Crow (1979) indicated that many countries could achieve regional industrial development by offering additional incentives to attract business to designated regions. Scholes and Wolfson (1989, 1992) also indicated that tax rules jointly influence investment decisions and organizational form. If tax factors are critical investment decisions, China's concessionary income tax rates (15 or 24%) would be adopted in the different special tax incentive zones. Dunning (1988) stressed the importance of location selection for FDI, and indicated that the factors requiring consideration are ownership structure, investment location, and the degree of internationalization. Klimberg and Ratick (2008) indicated that a suitable investment location should be determined based on the location configuration, optimal applicability, and equipment performance. Pan and Chi (1999) showed that FDI MNEs in Beijing, Shanghai, Tianjin, and other coastal metropolitan cities exhibited optimal production efficiency. Li et al. (2003) reported that the performance and invest- ment location of enterprises did not differ significantly between coastal and inland cities.

Buettner and Ruf (2007) investigated the impact of taxation on the decision of German multinationals to hold or establish a subsidiary in other European countries or abroad. Taking account of unobserved local characteristics as well as firm-specific preferences for potential locations, their findings confirmed that there are significant effects of tax incentives on cross-border location decisions. Azemar et al. (2007) measured the effects of taxation on FDI and estimated the impact of tax sparing provisions on Japanese outbound FDI between 1989 and 2000. They found that a positive relation exists between the tax sparing provision and the location of Japanese FDI. Parys and James (2010) investigated to what extent tax incentives are effective in attracting investment in Sub-Saharan Africa and found no robust positive relation between tax holidays and investment in the tax incentives zone. Guo (2010) examined the relation between taxes and the distribution of FDI in China. The results show that taxes have a significantly negative effect on the location. Foster (2011) showed that FDI in China was markedly skewed in favor of the richest east region, whereas the western region was the weakest attractor. Chen and Yeh (2012) examined variations in the preferences of location antecedents and the rate of FDI by MNEs in relation to increased FDI experience and evolved strategic intentions.

Taiwanese FDI enterprises prefer certain economic regions. The eastern region of China, which has the longest coastline, is nearest to Taiwan, and it features extensive internal and external links, convenient transportation, and advanced communications infrastructure, all of which attract foreign companies. Currently, Shanghai Pudong New District, which was expanded into an open economic zone, is the largest base of Chinese industrial technology, and it is a crucial international port city in the Western Pacific region. Therefore, most Taiwanese FDI is concentrated in Eastern China, accounting for 71.58% of all investments. With increasingly more foreign companies entering Eastern China, the infrastructure has advanced, and the quality of workers and employees has improved. However, the labor and land tax costs have increased accordingly. The 2007 *Report on the Operating Conditions of China Investment Undertakings* showed that the strongest incentive for Taiwanese FDI in China is cheap labor. Moreover, increasing labor costs has a negative impact on the business performance.

Regarding the 2008 tax law, China's central government revised the List of Industries for Foreign Investment in Mid-west China to develop the country's eastern regions, which gradually became critical bases for MNEs investing in China. With China's economic development, the costs of land, labor, and other factors in Eastern China have increased recently. Certain industries became less competitive, and the declining economic efficiency caused companies operating in Eastern China to become inefficient.

To minimize the gap between the eastern and western regions of mainland China, China's government implemented the China Western Development Program to relocate some manufacturing industry chains operating near China's coastal region to the western region, thereby attracting *Notes Book (NB)* industry clusters to Chongqing and Chengdu, Sichuan Province, to establish factories. Chongqing and Chengdu are competing aggressively to become leaders of the NB industry chain through internal competition for resources, and external competition for positive investment opportunities. In addition to the environmental advantages of the investment location, new railroad infrastructure can significantly reduce the time and cost of transportation. Successful investment in Chongqing, Taiwanese FDI enterprises to the free trade zone investment enjoys state subsidies of 10 years and 15% income tax for export tax rebates.

To continue encouraging economic developments in Western China, the Ministry of Finance, General Administration of Customs, and State Administration of Taxation jointly issued the 58th Notice on the Indepth Implementation of the Western Development Strategy on Tax Policy in July 2011. The 58th Notice extended the tax preferential policies of the western development period from January 1, 2011 to December 31, 2020. The 58th Notice made provisions for enterprises operating in preferred industries in the western area of China, as well as provisions encouraging industrial projects for the main business in China. After companies have been audited by tax authorities, they are required to pay a reduced corporate income tax rate of 15% in Taiwan. Thus, since 2008, China's tax concessions have favored businesses operating in the country's western regions, and they have also encouraged Taiwanese FDI in China's northwestern and southwestern regions. Hence, this study expected that the implementation of the 2008 tax law will increase FDI in Western China. Accordingly, we proposed the following hypothesis:

H2: *Ceteris paribus*, after the 2008 tax law implementation, the TDI enterprises in Western China have the higher TDI.

Tax incentives based on the FDI industry

The 1991 tax law provides many tax incentives for FDI enterprises in China; such as a 50% reduction in the tax rate for income from exportable products or high-technology enterprises, 40% income tax refund for reinvesting in China. After implementing the 2008 tax law, the principle of providing favorable tax concessions for location-specific investment has shifted to favor more for industry- specific investment. Thus, high-technology enterprises were taxed at a rate of 15% instead of the standard rate of 25%. However, new high-technology enterprises were required to meet stringent requirements, including the core intellectual property, research and development expenditure exceeding a specific threshold, and reach the required proportion of scientific and technical personnel. High-tech enterprises can enjoy other tax breaks including 50% additional deduction or amortization of development costs, small and medium high-tech enterprises can be offset part of the taxable investments and accelerated or shorten the depreciation of fixed assets. Hence, Taiwan businessmen invest in high-tech industry of emerging technologies to China, higher the amount of their investment. The hypothesis is proposed as follows:

H3: *Ceteris paribus*, after the 2008 tax law implementation, the TDI enterprises belonging to high-tech and new technology industries have higher TDI.

Non-tax incentives factors

Types and holding shares of FDI flow

Taiwanese FDI enterprises typically invest in China either

directly or indirectly. Direct investments include remittance of investments to subsidiaries in China either through companies operating in a third region or via direct remittance. Indirect investments are made either through investment companies or through existing companies registered in a third region, which accounted for one-third of TDI in China. Currently, most Taiwanese businesses invest in China through investment companies operating in Hong Kong and Macau. Moreover, because the tax rates in Hong Kong and Macau are relatively low, large shareholders can increase their profits through tax savings. Furthermore, in 2008, Taiwan's tax authorities drafted an amendment of Article 24 of the Relations between Peoples of the Taiwan Area and the Mainland China Area. The article states that proceeds (i.e., dividend revenues) received by Taiwanese FDI enterprises in China that have been subjected to a 10% tax are considered an income item that can be deducted from their taxable income when the dividend is paid to Taiwan.

Because most Taiwanese FDI enterprises operating in China involve indirect investments, Taiwanese enterprises benefit from paying less tax. Article 24 also states that most of Taiwanese companies using investment companies (or subsidiaries) operating in a third region to invest in enterprises in mainland China, in accordance with Taiwan's Income Tax Law, declare the investment proceeds *from* third-region companies derived from investing in companies in mainland China as investment returns, *because this income is considered as taxable income*. However, the portion of returns on investments in third-region areas (or in mainland China) that have already been subjected to income tax can be deducted from their tax payable in Taiwan. Draft amendments to the general relaxation of investment Taiwanese businessmen on the mainland China taxation provisions to reduce tax duplication, thereby encouraging companies to return their dividends to their parent company in Taiwan. Therefore, this study controlled the effect of the type of investment on FDI behavior.

Rates of the holding shares

Taiwanese parent companies' holding shares in subsidiaries represented various decision-making power which will affect the TDI decisions in China. Regardless of whether Taiwanese enterprises invest directly or indirectly in subsidiaries in China, up to 25% of shares held by parent companies are considered gains (or losses) on equity investments. Although Taiwanese parent companies can repatriate their investment income, because no tax agreement exists between Taiwan and China, repatriated profits are subject to a 10% withholding tax. According to the current tax conventions of the Organization for Economic Cooperation and Development, if Taiwan signed a tax agreement with mainland China, the withholding tax rate on repatriated investment profits would be reduced to 5%, provided that the Taiwanese shareholders held more than 25% of shares. Because of the tax incentives for holding more than 25% of shares, we controlled the tax incentives for stock ownership to control the effect of holding shares on Taiwanese FDI in China.

Macroeconomic factors

Numerous empirical studies have discussed the determinants of regional FDI distribution in China. Cheng and Kwan (2000) examined data from 29 provinces from 1985 to 1995, and they observed the agglomeration effects from the rate of foreign capital stocks. They showed that larger markets, perfect infrastructures, preferential policies, and lower wages exerted a positive effect on FDI. In addition, *they* reported that although education exerts a positive influence on FDI, the effect was non-significant. Coughlin and Segev (2000) used data of regional provinces in China from 1990 to 1997 to examine the mode of the determinants of FDI in China. They showed that market size, labor productivity, and location (i.e., coastal versus inland) exerted a positive effect on FDI. Conversely, higher wages and illiteracy rates negatively influenced FDI. Wei and Liu (1999) reported that lower wage rates and higher GDP growth rates have a positive effect on attracting FDI. Furthermore, high levels of international trade have a positive effect on FDI. *Ceteris paribus*, the higher the research and development manpower, the more attractive a region would be to foreign investors. Moreover, a positive relationship exists among infrastructure, preferential policies, and FDI. In addition, areas that are geographically closer to the main sources of FDI have a positive effect on pledged FDI.

Sun et al. (2002) examined the changes in importance of FDI determinants over time. Among the various determinants for attracting FDI, wages exhibited a positive relationship with FDI before 1991, although the relationship was negative following 1991. In addition, labor quality and infrastructure were crucial determinants of FDI distribution. Buettner and Ruf (2007) investigated the impact of taxation on the decision of location for investments. The results confirmed a significant effect of market size on cross-border location decisions.

Liu et al. (2012) analyzed the relative importance of the potential determinants of FDI inflow across the coastal, northeastern, central, and western regions in China between 2001 and 2009. Specifically, they examined market size, labor cost, labor quality, physical infrastructure development, telecommunications, and the degree of economic openness and government incentives to attract FDI. This study used the employment rate, economic growth rate, inflation price index, and market size to control the effect of macroeconomic factors on FDI.

Naveed et al. (2013) found that economic growth was the most dominating factors of FDI. Khan et al. (2014) analyzed the relationship between macroeconomic factors (e.g. economic growth, consumer consumption index) and FDI in South Asia. Similar to Naveed et al. (2013), Khan et al. (2014) also found that economic growth is an important factor.

RESEARCH DESIGN

Regression model

This study investigated the impact of tax incentives on TDI in China by controlling the effect of macroeconomic factors on TDI. The multiple regression equation is expressed as follows:

$$
\begin{aligned}
TDI_{it} = {} & \alpha_0 + \alpha_1 DY08_{it} + \alpha_2 DY08 \times AREA_{it} + \alpha_3 DY08 \times ELEC_{it} + \alpha_4 AREA_{it} \\
& + \alpha_5 ELEC_{it} + \alpha_6 TYPE_{it} + \alpha_7 HOLD_{it} + \alpha_8 INVREV_{i,t-1} + \alpha_9 EMPLOY_t \\
& + \alpha_{10} GDP_t + \alpha_{11} CPI_t + \alpha_{12} INDEX_t + \varepsilon_{it} \quad \text{(1)}
\end{aligned}
$$

Measurement variables

Dependent variables

TDI_{it} was measured using the natural logarithm of the value (in NTD 1,000) of Taiwanese FDI in China's subsidiaries of firm *i* at year *t*.

Hypothesis variables

$DY08_{it}$ is a dummy variable for the year; if the year was between 2008 and 2012, then *DY08* = 1 (otherwise, *DY08* = 0). It is not uncommon to use Year dummy to capture the effect of tax reform on business decisions in related articles. For instance, previous studies adopted year-dummy variable to explore the effect of USA TRA 1986 tax reform on dividend policy (Burman et al.1994; Papaioannou and Savarese, 1994; Schulman et al., 1996; Casey et al., 1999; Casey and Dickens, 2000) and domestic income shifting behavior (Shevlin et al. 2012). Wang and Chen (2004) used the dummy-year variable to examine the implementation of 1998 Taiwan imputation tax system on cash dividend payout ratios and capital structure (Wang and Chen, 2007). Tung and Cho (2000, 2001) also employed the year dummy variable to examine whether concessionary tax rates and tax incentives under 1991 China tax reforms attract FDI into certain designated areas. This study anticipated that a negative correlation would exist between TDI and the 2008 tax law enacted.

$AREA_{it}$ is a dummy variable denoting location; if a Taiwanese subsidiary firm *i* was located in Western China, then AREA = 1 (otherwise, AREA = 0). We anticipated that preferential tax treatment was given to enterprises operating in Western China *when* the 2008 tax law was enacted. We hypothesized that the correlation between *TDI* and *AREA* would be positive.

$ELEC_{it}$ is a dummy variable representing specific industries; if a Taiwanese subsidiary firm *i* invested in a high-technology electronics industry, then *ELEC* = 1, (otherwise, *ELEC* = 0). We anticipated that the preferential tax rate of 15% was applied to FDI enterprises operating in high-technology electronics industries after the new tax laws were enacted. We hypothesized that the correlation between *TDI* and *ELEC* would be positive.

Control variables

$TYPE_{it}$ is a dummy variable denoting the investment type. If a Taiwanese parent firm *made either through investment companies or through existing companies registered in a third region* to indirectly invest China subsidiary *i*, then *TYPE* = 1 (otherwise, *TYPE* = 0; i.e., a direct investment). We anticipated that preferential tax treatment was given for indirect investments, and we hypothesized that the correlation between *TDI* and *TYPE* would be positive.

$HOLD_{it}$ is a dummy variable for the rate of holding shares; if a subsidiary firm *i* received more than 25% of its investments from a Taiwanese parent firm, then *HOLD* = 1 (otherwise, *HOLD* = 0). We anticipated that less tax was withheld when invested holding shares exceeded 25%. We hypothesized that the correlation between *TDI* and *TYPE* would be positive.

$INVREV_{i,t-1}$ denotes the preceding period ($t-1$) investment revenue for firm *i* in year *t* in China. Most subsidiaries retain the profits as savings in the host country, and they do not return it back to their parent firm. We controlled this effect on *TDI*, and we anticipated that the correlation between *TDI* and *INVREV* would be positive.

$EMPLOY_t$ represents the rate of employment at year *t* in China; we expect there is positive correlation between *TDI* and *EMPLOY*.

GDP_t denotes the real GDP per person at year *t* in China. China's GDP growth has been relatively high in these years; however, this study controls the impact of *GDP* on *TDI*.

CPI_t denotes the consumer price index (CPI) at year *t* in China; we anticipated that the correlation between *TDI* and *CPI* would be positive.

$INDEX_t$ is the weighted stock market index of the Shanghai Stock Exchange at year *t*. We anticipated that the correlation between *TDI* and *CPI* would be positive.

Research sample data

Because *of the unavailability of* financial statements of Taiwanese FDI enterprises in China, we used data from a

Table 2. Taiwan FDI Amount in China.

Panel A: Types of investment						
Variables	**Mean**	**Minimum**	**Q1**	**Median**	**Q3**	**Maximum**
direct remittance (n=617)	1025016.72	1892	85300	252736	1054245	19087152
third-region remittance (n=714)	2134082.91	34	127709	531296	1753314	27359037
through investment companies (n=25,688)	2107739.72	40	175985	542832	1624459.50	73505945
through existing companies (n=12,400)	3027295.64	656	197834	665734	1988625	55000000
Panel B: Areas of investment						
Variables	**Mean**	**Minimum**	**Q1**	**Median**	**Q3**	**Maximum**
East China Area (n=24,346)	2361558.49	136	188594	605535	1859995	73505945
South China Area (n=10,917)	2048339.20	40	157310	445079	1341520	73505945
Central China Area (n=797)	3898000.79	6978	434199	989769	2885863	73505945
North China Area (n=2,789)	2104046.55	527	153836	536979	1321990	73505945
Northwest Area (n=310)	3477419.68	4278	205934	852459	1929755	27359037
Southwest Area (n=913)	5105919.41	6990	476742	1205485	5339966	73505945
Northeast Area (n=610)	3458906.80	9731	435979	1205485	1783951	73505945

Firm-Year/NTD1,000.

TEJ database (specifically, parent company financial information, location, FDI type, rate of holding shares, and value of investments from parent companies investing in China). Initially, we obtained a sample comprising 43,138 observations samples from the *TEJ*. After removing 2,418 missing data, this study analyzed the remaining 40,720 firm-year observations. Subsequently, we deleted 23,523 observations *for* outliers and missing data due to the use of one-period-lagged values. The final samples of 17,197 observations were used in the correlation and regression analyses.

EMPIRICAL RESULTS

Descriptive statistics and *correlation coefficients analyses*

Table 2 (Panel A) reports investment types for TDI in China. Investment types include direct- and indirect-investment. Direct investments include remittance of investments to subsidiaries in China either through via direct remittance (direct remittance) or via companies operating in a third region (third-region remittance). Indirect investments are made either through investment companies (through investment companies) or via through existing companies registered in a third region (through existing companies), which accounted for one-third of TDI in China. Panel A shows that 671 firms direct remittance invested in China subsidiaries between 2001 to 2012. The mean of these investments is NTD 1,025 million. There are 714 China subsidiaries firms received remittance investments from a third-region company, and the mean is NTD 2,134 million. There are 25,688 firms used investment companies to invest indirectly in subsidiaries, which was the most commonly used approach, and the mean is NTD 2,108 million. Panel A also indicates that 12,400 firms used existing companies in third-region to invest indirectly in China subsidiaries, and the mean is NTD 3,027 million. Based on the TEJ database, we divided the investment areas into eight areas (East China, South China, Central China, North China, Northwest, Southwest, Northeast, and other regions). Table 2 (Panel B) shows that between 2001 and 2012, most TDI in China was primarily in the coastal regions of East China Area, with 24,346 firm-year observations, accounting for 60% of the entire sample. The mean of these investments is NTD 2,362 million. The number of observations of South China Area is 10,917, and the mean is NTD 2,048 million. The number of observation of North China Area is 2,789 and the mean is NTD 2,104 million. After implementing the 2008 tax law, China government encouraged FDI inflow into Western China to balance the disparity in economic development between China's eastern and western regions. The TDI accounted for only 310 firm-year observations for Northwest Area, and the mean investments for this region is NTD 3,477 million. Panel B shows that there were 913 firm-year observations for Southwest Area, but the mean investments is NTD 5,106 million. The data in Table 2 show that TDI inflow to China's western region increased slowly over time, because the opened up years are shorter and the costs of property, equipment are larger, the returns on investment are stagnant. Table 3 reports the descriptive statistics of research variables. The Panel A of Table 3 shows the mean investment (*TDI*) is NTD 2,852 million. In addition, the analysis shows that regarding the location of foreign-invested firms (*AREA*), only 3% were located in

Table 3. Regression variables descriptive statistics result.

Panel A: Total Sample (n=17,197)						
Variable	**Mean**	**Minimum**	**Q1**	**Median**	**Q3**	**Maximum**
Investment Amount	2852227	350	220449	709680	2269071	73505945
TDI	13.44	5.86	12.30	13.47	14.63	18.11
DY08	0.57	0	0	1	1	1
AREA	0.03	0	0	0	0	1
ELEC	0.60	0	0	1	1	1
TYPE	0.94	0	1	1	1	1
HOLD	0.98	0	1	1	1	1
INVREV (t-1)	9.65	0	8.31	9.78	11.11	16.96
EMPLOY	95.87	95.7	95.80	95.90	95.90	96.40
GDP	3476.60	1038	2064	3404	5434	6076
CPI	2.96	-0.4	1.9	2.5	4	7
INDEX	2482.26	1161.06	1820.81	2269.13	2808	5262

Panel B: Pre-2008 (n=7,343)						
Variable	**Mean**	**Minimum**	**Q1**	**Median**	**Q3**	**Maximum**
Investment Amount	1571813	350	152197	494176	1322017	30522129
TDI	13.03	5.86	11.93	13.11	14.09	17.23
DY08	0.03	0	0	0	0	1
AREA	0.57	0	0	1	1	1
ELEC	0.95	0	1	1	1	1
TYPE	0.99	0	1	1	1	1
HOLD	9.51	0	8.2607514	9.6524588	10.94	16.55
EMPLOY	95.91	95.7	95.8	95.9	96	96.4
GDP	1817	1038	1270	1726	2064	2645
CPI	3	-0.4	1.6	2.8	3.20	6.50
INDEX	2488	1161.06	1266.5	1497.04	2675.47	5261.56

Panel C: Post-2008 (n=9,854)						
Variable	**Mean**	**Minimum**	**Q1**	**Median**	**Q3**	**Maximum**
Investment Amount	3806366	527	294308	938022	2985448	73505945
TDI	13.75	6.27	12.59	13.75	14.91	18.11
DY08	0.04	0	0	0	0	1
AREA	0.61	0	0	1	1	1
ELEC	0.93	0	1	1	1	1
TYPE	0.98	0	1	1	1	1
HOLD	9.76	0	8.3416486	9.8845595	11.2458431	16.9622158
EMPLOY	95.85	95.70	95.80	95.90	95.90	95.90
GDP	4713	3404	3740	4423	5434	6076
CPI	2.98	1.20	1.90	2.50	4.10	4.60
INDEX	2478	1820.81	2199.42	2269.13	2808.08	3277.14

Variable definitions: *Investment Amount*it: this is measured by the investment amount of Taiwan FDI in China's subsidiaries firm *i* at year *t* in NTD. *TDI*it: this is measured by the natural logarithm of investment amount of Taiwan FDI in China's subsidiaries firm *i* at year *t* in NTD. *DY08*it: this is the dummy variable of year, if the year is 2008 to 2012 then *DY08*=1; o.w. then *DY08*=0. *AREA*it: this is the dummy variable of location, if the China's subsidiaries firm *i* invested in location of western China then *AREA*=1; o.w. then *AREA*=0.*ELEC*it: it is the dummy variable of industry, if the China's subsidiaries firm *i* invested in high-tech electronic industries then *ELEC*=1; o.w. then *ELEC*=0.*TYPE*it: it is the dummy variable of investing type, if a Taiwanese parent firm made either through investment companies or through existing companies registered in a third region to indirectly invest China subsidiary i, then TYPE = 1 (otherwise, TYPE = 0; i.e., a direct investment).*HOLD*it: it is the dummy variable of holding share rate, if the China's subsidiaries firm i is invested by Taiwan parent firm more than 25% then *HOLD*=1; o.w. then *HOLD*=0.*INVREV*i,t-1: it is the last period (*t-1*) investment revenue for firm *i* at year *t* in China. *EMPLOY*t: it is the rate of employment at year *t* in China. *GDP*t : it is the real GDP per person at year t in China. *CPI*t : it is the Consumer Price Index at year *t* in China. *INDEX*t : it is the weighted stock index of Shanghai at year *t* in China.

Western China, whereas almost 50% of Taiwanese FDI enterprises invested in high-technology electronics industries (*ELEC*). Regarding the preferred investment type, 94% of Taiwanese FDI enterprises invested indirectly in China (*TYPE*), with 98% of parents' firms holding more than 25% of subsidiaries shares (*HOLD*). Regarding the macroeconomic factors, both the mean and median rate of employment (*EMPLOY*) in China is 96%. In addition, the mean (median) of GDP per person (*GDP*) and CPI is RMB 3,477 (RMB 3,404) and 2.96% (2.5%), respectively.

Finally, the mean (median) of index of the capital (securities) market is 2,482 (2,269). We divided the sample into the following two groups based on when the 2008 tax law was enacted: the pre-enactment group (2001–2007; *DY08* = 0); and the post-enactment group (2008–2012; *DY08* = 1). Table 3 (Panels B and C) show that the mean investment (*TDI*) of the pre-enactment group is NTD 1,572 million, whereas that of the post-enactment group is NTD 3,806 million. It appears that the mean TDI increased by 1.42 times after the 2008 tax law was enacted.

The statistical analysis for the research variables are detailed as follows. The mean *AREA* increased from 3 to 4%, and only 1% of TDI were located in Western China after the 2008 tax law was enacted. The mean *ELEC* increased from 57 to 61%, and only 4% TDI were in the high-technology industries after the enactment of the new tax law. Table 4 presented both Pearson and Spearman correlation coefficient matrixes. Based on the Pearson correlation coefficient matrix, the correlation coefficient is 0.86 between DY08 and GDP. Unexpectedly, the enactment of 2008 tax reform in China (DY08) is positively correlated with TDI. Furthermore, *DY08*, *TDI* are positively correlated with *DY08*×*AREA* and *DY08*×*ELEC*, as expected. The results indicated that the 2008 tax law did provide location-specific and industry-specific tax incentives for FDI. The inter-correlation among the independent variables suggests that a multivariate analysis is further required to consider the effect of enactment of 2008 tax reform on TDI decisions by simultaneously incorporating all the independent variables. The Spearman correlation coefficients matrix provides similar results. The Variance Inflation Factor (VIF) test shows that the values are all below 4, which implies they may not exit serious multicollinearity problems.

Regression analyses

Before 2008, foreign-funded companies in China were taxed at a relatively low rate, and a series of preferential policies were implemented to encourage FDI inflow to China. Most foreign-invested enterprises were taxed at almost 10% less than that applied to domestic enterprises. On March 16, 2007, the National People's Congress of China promulgated the 2008 tax law (effective as of January 1, 2008). This was the first law in China's history imposing an income tax on all forms of enterprise, and it replaced the FIE Income Tax Law and Interim EIT Regulations. The EIT unified the income tax system imposed on foreign and domestic enterprises operating in China, and it provided a single statutory rate of 25% on business profit. The 2008 tax law removed various tax incentives for foreign investors establishing factories in China for producing exportable goods. The 2008 tax law was anticipated to have a profound impact on foreign-based investors who had already established manufacturing operations in China under the old tax system that favored the production of exportable goods. However, these changes also offered opportunities for technology industries to expand their operations, and for factories to relocate to Western China by providing new tax incentives and domestic market opportunities.

Table 5 shows the result of the Taiwanese FDI (*TDI*) regression model. The coefficient of *DY08* is significantly negative, indicating that implementing the 2008 tax law, which reduced tax concessions for Taiwanese FDI and increased tax rates to 25%, resulted in a significant reduction in *TDI* (t =-2.38, p <0.0174); thus, H1 is supported. For the period after the new tax laws were enacted, the *DY08* × *AREA* regression coefficient is positive (t = 1.15, p = 0.2516), but lacks statistically significance, indicating that the *TDI* in Western China capitalized on the reduced tax rate of 15%, which was a 10% reduction (25%-15%=10%). Because *TDI* in Western China was only 3%, despite China's tax incentives encouraging *TDI* inflow to the western regions, the appeal of tax incentives for investing in this region was limited. Hence, although we observed an increase in *TDI*, the difference is not significant; thus, H2 is unsupported. Furthermore, for the period after the 2008 tax law was enacted, the *DY08* × *ELEC* regression coefficient is positively significant (t = 7.90, p < 0.0001), indicating that industry-specific tax incentives were preferable to location-specific tax incentives. Taiwanese FDI enterprises investing in high-technology electronic industries capitalized on the tax rate 15%, and *TDI* in high-technology electronics industries increased; thus, H3 is supported. This finding is consistent with the results reported by Liu et al. (2012).

Table 5 shows the variables for controlling the effect of nontax factors on *TDI*. The regression coefficient of *AREA* (0.295) is statistically significant (t = 2.47, p= 0.0136), indicating that Taiwanese FDI enterprises located in Western China (i.e., Northwestern and Southwestern China in this study) were offer greater tax incentives by China's government. Since 2008, China's tax concessions for developing the western region has provided enterprises this region belonged to the encouraged industry catalogue and located in the western area. There are provisions encouraging industrial project for the main business in China; and its main business income total income exceeds 70% business that year, as well as the

Table 4. Correlation coefficients statistics result.

Variables	*TDI*	*DY08*	*DY08*×*AREA*	*DY08*×*ELEC*	*AREA*	*ELEC*	*TYPE*	*HOLD*	*INVREV*	*EMPLOY*	*GDP*	*CPI*	*INDEX*
TDI	1	0.203***	0.072***	0.120***	0.060***	-0.056***	0.068***	0.045***	0.325***	-0.037***	0.228***	0.104***	0.086***
		(<.0001)	(<.0001)	(<.0001)	(<.0001)	(<.0001)	(<.0001)	(<.0001)	(<.0001)	(<.0001)	(<.0001)	(<.0001)	(<.0001)
DY08	0.199***	1	0.114***	0.636***	0.015*	0.042***	-0.046***	-0.016**	0.058***	-0.250***	0.864***	0.011	-0.007
	(<.0001)		(<.0001)	(<.0001)	(0.0575)	(<.0001)	(<.0001)	(0.0330)	(<.0001)	(<.0001)	(<.0001)	(0.1473)	(0.3397)
DY08×*AREA*	0.069***	0.114***	1	0.056***	0.780***	-0.012	-0.002	-0.004	0.019**	-0.018**	0.113***	0.007	-0.006
	(<.0001)	(<.0001)		(<.0001)	(<.0001)	(0.1313)	(0.7904)	(0.6129)	(0.0124)	(0.0192)	(<.0001)	(0.3913)	(0.4188)
DY08×*ELEC*	0.117***	0.636***	0.056***	1	-0.004	0.606***	-0.019**	0.006	0.069***	-0.155***	0.555***	0.014*	-0.004
	(<.0001)	(<.0001)	(<.0001)		(0.5964)	(<.0001)	(0.0119)	(0.4651)	(<.0001)	(<.0001)	(<.0001)	(0.0787)	(0.6182)
AREA	0.058***	0.0145*	0.780***	-0.004	1	-0.038***	-0.008	-0.001	-0.002	0.004	0.021***	-0.002	-0.013
	(<.0001)	(0.0575)	(<.0001)	(0.5964)		(<.0001)	(0.3059)	(0.8571)	(0.8034)	(0.5714)	(0.0052)	(0.7744)	(0.1085)
ELEC	-0.049***	0.043***	-0.012	0.606***	-0.04***	1	0.007	0.011	0.050***	-0.027***	0.048***	0.025***	0.015*
	(<.0001)	(<.0001)	(0.1313)	(<.0001)	(<.0001)		(0.3859)	(0.1537)	(<.0001)	(0.0004)	(<.0001)	(0.0011)	(0.0506)
TYPE	0.063***	-0.046***	-0.002	-0.019**	-0.008	0.007	1	0.009	0.027***	-0.009	-0.057***	0.008	0.017**
	(<.0001)	(<.0001)	(0.7904)	(0.0119)	(0.3059)	(0.3859)		(0.2602)	(0.0006)	(0.2600)	(<.0001)	(0.3124)	(0.0288)
HOLD	0.049***	-0.016**	-0.004	0.006	-0.001	0.011	0.009	1	0.004	-0.005	-0.015**	-0.001	0.002
	(<.0001)	(0.0330)	(0.6129)	(0.4651)	(0.8571)	(0.1537)	(0.2602)		(0.6163)	(0.5049)	(0.0442)	(0.8761)	(0.7538)
INVREV	0.324***	0.056***	0.018**	0.069***	0.001	0.052***	0.024***	0.002	1	0.011	0.062***	0.041***	0.043***
	(<.0001)	(<.0001)	(0.0193)	(<.0001)	(0.9900)	(<.0001)	(0.0020)	(0.8325)		(0.1509)	(<.0001)	(<.0001)	(<.0001)
EMPLOY	-0.004	-0.201***	-0.009	-0.122***	0.006	-0.007	-0.009	-0.003	0.018**	1	-0.041***	0.132***	0.203***
	(0.5688)	(<.0001)	(0.2320)	(<.0001)	(0.4611)	(0.3800)	(0.2213)	(0.6758)	(0.0183)		(<.0001)	(<.0001)	(<.0001)
GDP	0.226***	0.861***	0.111***	0.553***	0.019**	0.050***	-0.053***	-0.015**	0.061***	0.090***	1	0.270***	0.139***
	(<.0001)	(<.0001)	(<.0001)	(<.0001)	(0.0117)	(<.0001)	(<.0001)	(0.0444)	(<.0001)	(<.0001)		(<.0001)	(<.0001)
CPI	0.097***	0.037***	0.012	0.032***	0.000	0.024***	0.001	-0.007	0.035***	0.430***	0.342***	1	0.728***
	(<.0001)	(<.0001)	(0.1216)	(<.0001)	(0.9945)	(0.0020)	(0.9458)	(0.3961)	(<.0001)	(<.0001)	(<.0001)		(<.0001)
INDEX	0.134***	0.267***	0.022***	0.171***	-0.011	0.024***	0.004	-0.007	0.045***	0.263***	0.399***	0.593***	1
	(<.0001)	(<.0001)	(0.0033)	(<.0001)	(0.1473)	(0.0019)	(0.6098)	(0.3306)	(<.0001)	(<.0001)	(<.0001)	(<.0001)	

a. The upper right corner is Pearson Correlation Coefficients; the lower left corner is Spearman Correlation Coefficients. b. ***, **, and * denote significance at the 0.01, 0.05, and 0.10 level, respectively. c. Variable definitions: *TDI*it : this is measured by the natural logarithm of investment amount of Taiwan FDI in China's subsidiaries firm *i* at year *t* in NTD. *DY08*it : this is the dummy variable of year, if the year is 2008 to 2012 then *DY08*=1; o.w. then *DY08*=0. *AREA*it : this is the dummy variable of location, if the China's subsidiaries firm *i* invested in location of western China then *AREA*=1; o.w. then *AREA*=0. *ELEC*it :it is the dummy variable of industry, if the China's subsidiaries firm *i* invested in high-tech electronic industries then *ELEC*=1; o.w. then *ELEC*=0. *TYPE*it : it is the dummy variable of investing type, if a Taiwanese parent firm made either through investment companies or through existing companies registered in a third region to indirectly invest China subsidiary i, then TYPE = 1 (otherwise, TYPE = 0; i.e., a direct investment). *HOLD*it : it is the dummy variable of holding share rate, if the China's subsidiaries firm i is invested by Taiwan parent firm more than 25% then *HOLD*=1; o.w. then *HOLD*=0. *INVREV*i,t-1: it is the last period (*t-1*) investment revenue for firm *i* at year *t* in China. *EMPLOY*t : it is the rate of employment at year *t* in China. *GDP*t : it is the real GDP per person at year t in China. *CPI*t : it is the Consumer Price Index at year *t* in China. *INDEX*t : it is the weighted stock index of Shanghai at year *t* in China, we expect there is positive correlation between *TDI* and *CPI*.

Table 5. Regression analysis result.

Variables	Pred. Sign	Parameter Estimate	t-Value	Pr > |t|
Intercept	?	50.456	4.67	<.0001
DY08	-	-0.163**	-2.38	0.0174
DY08×AREA	α_2 +	0.170	1.15	0.2516
DY08×ELEC	α_3 +	0.398***	7.90	<.0001
AREA	α_4 +	0.295**	2.47	0.0136
ELEC	α_5 +	-0.522***	-13.75	<.0001
TYPE	+	0.489***	9.57	<.0001
HOLD	+	0.330***	3.47	0.0005
INVREV	+	0.261***	47.17	<.0001
EMPLOY	+	-0.427***	-3.78	0.0002
GDP	+	0.000***	10.61	<.0001
CPI	+	0.002	0.17	0.8659
INDEX	+	0.000***	4.32	<.0001

Adj. R-Sq. 17.52%; F-Value 305.46 (p value <.0001); Test 1: H0 $\alpha_2=\alpha_4$; F Value 0.24 (p value =0.6222) Accept Ho; Test 2: H0 $\alpha_3=\alpha_5$; F Value 123.42 (p value <.0001) Reject Ho; *INVREV*t-1: Due to one lag period missing data 23,523 firm-year, this paper use n=17,197 to follow-up regression analysis. b. *** and ** denote significance at the 0.01 and 0.05 level, respectively. c. Variable definitions: *TDI*it : this is measured by the natural logarithm of investment amount of Taiwan FDI in China's subsidiaries firm *i* at year *t* in NTD. *DY08*it : this is the dummy variable of year, if the year is 2008 to 2012 then *DY08*=1; o.w. then *DY08*=0. *AREA*it : this is the dummy variable of location, if the China's subsidiaries firm *i* invested in location of western China then *AREA*=1; o.w. then *AREA*=0. *ELEC*it : it is the dummy variable of industry, if the China's subsidiaries firm *i* invested in high-tech electronic industries then *ELEC*=1; o.w. then *ELEC*=0. *TYPE*it : it is the dummy variable of investing type, if a Taiwanese parent firm made either through investment companies or through existing companies registered in a third region to indirectly invest China subsidiary i, then TYPE = 1 (otherwise, TYPE = 0; i.e., a direct investment). *HOLD*it : it is the dummy variable of holding share rate, if the China's subsidiaries firm i is invested by Taiwan parent firm more than 25% then *HOLD*=1; o.w. then *HOLD*=0. *INVREV*i,t-1: it is the last period (*t-1*) investment revenue for firm *i* at year *t* in China. *EMPLOY*t : it is the rate of employment at year *t* in China. *GDP*t : it is the real GDP per person at year t in China. *CPI*t : it is the Consumer Price Index at year *t* in China. *INDEX*t : it is the weighted stock index of Shanghai at year *t* in China.

$$TDI_{it} = \alpha_0 + \alpha_1 \mathrm{DY08}_{it} + \alpha_2 \mathrm{DY08} \times \mathrm{AREA}_{it} + \alpha_3 DY08 \times ELEC_{it} + \alpha_4 AREA_{it} + \alpha_5 ELEC_{it} + \alpha_6 \mathrm{TYPE}_{it} + \alpha_7 HOLD_{it} + \alpha_8 INVREV_{i,t-1} + \alpha_9 EMPLOY_t + \alpha_{10} \mathrm{GDP}_t + \alpha_{11} CPI_t + \alpha_{12} \mathrm{INDEX}_t + \varepsilon_{it} \quad (1)$$

implementation of enterprise applications and management audits by tax authorities. After companies have been audited by tax authorities, they are required to pay a reduced corporate income tax rate of 15% in Taiwan. Thus, these tax incentives encouraged TDI to flow from the southeastern region to the southwestern region. Furthermore, relative to the financial services industries, the high-technology electronics industries require more capital, land, and plant equipment. Recently, TDI inflow to China's high-technology electronics industries has decreased. The regression coefficient of *ELEC* (-0.522) is statistically significant. The F values in the last row of Table 5 shows the joint test results of the effect of tax reform and tax incentives. The result of Joint Test 1 is not significant, indicating that the 2008 tax reform did not provide tax incentives for FDI in specific locations. However, the result of Joint Test 2 is significant, indicating that industry-specific tax incentives following the 2008 tax reform were effective. The type of investment and ratio of holding shares are critical factors for Taiwanese FDI inflow to China. The *TYPE* and *HOLD* regression coefficients are positively significant, indicating that Taiwanese FDI enterprises invested indirectly in China to decrease the amount of payable income tax, hence the increase in *TDI*. This study also controlled the investment revenues from the preceding period; most Taiwanese FDI subsidiaries retained their investment income in China to minimize their payable income tax for remittances on dividends, and to reinvest in China. The regression coefficient of *INVREV* (0.261) is statistically significant ($t = 47.17$, $p < .0001$).

With respect to macroeconomic factors, the regression coefficient of *EMPLOY* is significantly negative; because the increased employment rate decreased *TDI*, it did not conform to this study. The higher *GDP* and *INDEX* values indicate that more foreign funds are required to increase *TDI* in China. This finding is in agreement with the findings reported by Sun et al. (2002) and Liu et al. (2012).

Conclusion

Since China's reform and opening up, Chinese government has aggressively introduced foreign capital and technology to promote China's industrialization and urbanization. The China 2008 tax law decreased tax concessions and raised tax rates to 25% for FDI. Under the 2008 tax law reform, the FDI invested in Western China and high-technology industries will enjoy the 15% tax rate which decreased tax burden by 10% (from 25 to 15%). This study used official macroeconomic data to explore the association between the tax incentives of China 2008 tax law on TDI in China. This study also performed tests on the effect of tax incentives of 2008 new tax law on FDI in specific locations and industries.

The empirical results showed that the enactment of 2008 tax reform was associated with significant reduction in TDI in China. As to location specific tax concessions, we failed to find significantly positive relation between TDI invested in western China after the 2008 tax law was enacted. This may be due to the proportion of TDI invested in Western China was only about 3%; although China encourages FDI bounded toward the western area, the aggregate tax incentive is still limited. In addition, after promulgating the 2008 tax law, tax incentives for investing in high-technology industries are more favorable than non-high-technology industries.

Taiwanese businesses investing in high-technology electronic industries were taxed at a rate of 15%, thus more Taiwanese enterprises invested directly in those industries after the 2008 tax law was enacted. In other words, the test results indicated that the 2008 tax reform did not provide tax incentives for FDI in specific locations, although it provided effective tax incentives for FDI in specific industries. This finding supports the goals of the China 2008 tax reform which emphasizes tax incentives more on industry-specific than on location-specific. The results of this study have rendered implications for government policy making and investment strategies formation for management of enterprises. Given an increasing competitive environment, how to save tax burden via the choices of the location and industries is imperative for enterprises. It is therefore essential to be knowledgeable about tax incentives of FDI in China as well as the impacts on the parent company and factors that may improve or exacerbate investments.

There are some research limitations to this study. First of all, due to the inherent difficulties in obtaining the financial statements of subsidiaries in China, we can only use data from their parent companies. Secondly, the incorporation of macro-economic and tax incentives variables cannot be all inclusive. There are some factors we cannot control. For instance, the political factor sometimes could be the most influential factor on FDI. In the future, the disclosure of subsidiaries data in China could enhance the in-depth research on FDI study.

ACKNOWLEDGEMENT

We thank the editor and two anonymous reviewers for providing helpful comments. We also acknowledge financial support from the Ministry of Science and Technology, Taiwan (NSC 99-2410-H-141-006).

Conflict of Interests

The authors have not declared any conflict of interests.

REFERENCES

An Z (2012). Taxation and foreign direct investment (FDI): empirical evidence from a quasi-experiment in China. Int. Tax Pub. Finance 19(5):660-676.

Azemar C, Desbordes R, Mucchielli JL (2007). Do tax sparing agreements contribute to the attraction of FDI in developing countries? Int. Tax Pub. Finance 14(5): 543-562.

Boskin MJ, Gale WG (1986). New results on the effects of tax policy on the international location of investment. National Bureau of Economic Research Working Paper. Washington, DC: NBER.

Buettner T, Ruf M (2007). Tax incentives and the location of FDI: Evidence from a panel of German multinationals. Int. Tax and Public Finance 14(2):151-164.

Burman L, Clausing K, O'Hare J (1994). Tax reform and realizations of capital gains in 1986. Natl. Tax J. 47 (1):1-18.

Carlton DW (1983). The location and employment choices of new firms: An econometric model with discrete and continuous endogenous variables. Rev. Econ. Stat. 65:440–449.

Casey M, Anderson D, Mesak H and Dickens R (1999). Examining the impact of the 1986 tax reform act on corporate dividend policy: A new methodology. Financ. Rev.34 (3):33-46.

Casey M, Dickens R (2000). The effects of tax and regulatory changes on commercial bank dividend policy. Q. Rev. Econ. Finance 40(2):279-293.

Chen C, Yeh C (2012). Re-examining location antecedents and pace of foreign direct investment: Evidence from Taiwanese investments in China. J. Bus. Res. 65(8):1171-1178.

Cheng LK, Kwan YK (2000). What are the determinants of the location of foreign direct investment? The Chinese experience. J. Int. Econ. 51:379–400.

Cho S, Chow L, Tang XL (1998). The 1991 income tax law for foreign investment in China: Changes and implications for foreign investors, in S. Cho (Ed), Taxation Reforms in China, The Hong Kong Polytechnic University. p.14-20.

Cho S, Tung S (1998). Special tax incentive zones and regional tax incentive policy in the People's Republic of China. Int. Tax J. 24(4):81–91.

Coughlin CC, Segev E (2000). Foreign direct investment in China: A

spatial economic study. World Econ. 23:1-23.
Crow RT (1979). Output determination and investment specification in micro- economics models of open regions. Regional Sci. Urban Econ. 9: 141–158.
Deng Z, Falvey R, Blake A (2012). Trading market access for technology? Tax incentives, foreign direct investment and productivity spillovers in China. J. Policy Mode.34 (5): 675-690.
Dunning JH (1998). Explaining international production, London: Unwin Hyman.
Ernst & Young International (1994). Report of a survey of the strategic investment of global 1000 companies: Investment in emerging markets, opportunity versus risk. Ernst & Young International, Ltd.
Forsyth D (1971). US investment in Scotland. New York: Praeger.
Fortune (1977). Facility location decisions survey. New York: Fortune.
Foster M (2011). Distribution of FDI across China - Common policies but differing impacts by region. J. Chin. Econ. Foreign Trade Stud. 4(2):125-138.
Grubert H, Mutti J (1991). Taxes, tariffs and transfer pricing in multinational corporate decision making. Rev. Econ. Stat. 73(2):285-293.
Guo J (2010). The effects of tax rates on foreign direct investment in China. J.Inter. Manage.Studies 5(1): 31-37.
Hadari Y (1990). The role of tax incentives in attracting foreign investments in selected development countries and the desirable policy. The International Lawyer, 24(1): p.121-152.
Hartman D (1984). Tax policy and foreign direct investment in the United States. Natl. Tax J. 37(4):475–488.
He X, Guisinger S (1993). Taxation of U.S. foreign direct investment abroad: Effective tax rates and tax policy competition in developed and developing countries. J. Int. Account. Audit. Tax. 2(2):215–229.
Hines J R (1996). Altered States: Taxes and the location of foreign direct investment in America. Am. Econ.Rev.86:1076–1094.
Khan MA, Khan MZ, Zaman K (2014). Questing the three key growth determinants: Energy consumption, foreign direct investment and financial development in South Asia. Renew. Energy 68:203-215.
Klemm A, Parys S (2012). Empirical evidence on the effects of tax incentives. Int.Tax Pub.Finance 19(3):393-423.
Klimberg RK, Ratick SJ (2008). Modeling data envelopment analysis (DEA) efficient location/allocation decision. Comput.Res.35: 457-474.
Krugman P (1991). Increasing returns and economic geography. Journal of Political Economy, 99(3):483-499.
Li J, Qian G, Lam K,Wang D (2003). Firm resource and first mover advantages: A case of foreign direct investment (FDI) in China. Int. Bus. Rev. 12:625–645.
Lim D (1983). Fiscal incentives and direct foreign investment in less developed countries. J.Dev. Stud. pp.207–212.
Liu K, Daly K, Varua ME (2012). Determinants of regional distribution of FDI inflows across China's four regions. Int. Bus. Res. 5(12):119-126.
Moore ML, Steece BM, Swenson CW (1987). An analysis of the impact of state income tax rates and bases on foreign investment. Account. Rev. 62(4): 671-685.
Naveed IC, Mehmood A, Mian SM (2013). Empirical relationship between foreign direct investment and economic growth. China Finance Rev. Int. 3(1) : 26-41.
Pan Y, Chi SK (1999). Financial performance and survival of multinational corporations in China. Strat. Manage. J. 20:359-374.
Papaioannou GJ, Savarese CM (1994). Corporate dividend policy response to the tax reform act of 1986. Financ. Manage. 23(1):56-63.
Papke LE (1987). Subnational taxation and capital mobility: Estimates of tax-price elasticities. Natl. Tax J. 40 (2):191-203.
Park J, Kim C, Yang D (2013). An Empirical Study of the Impact of a Host Country's Tax Regime on Inbound and Outbound Foreign Direct Investment. J. Korea Trade 17(2): 21-51.
Root FR, Ahmed AA (1978). The influence of policy instruments on manufacturing direct foreign investment in developing countries. J. Int. Bus. Stud. 9(3):81-93.
Scholes MS, Wolfson MA (1989). Issues in the theory of optimal capital structure. In: S. Bhattacharya & G. Constantinides (Eds), Frontiers of modern financial theory pp.49–74.
Scholes MS, Wolfson MA (1992). Taxes and business strategy: A planning approach. Englewood Cliffs, NJ: Prentice-Hall.
Schulman CT, Thomas DW, Sellers KF, Kennedy DB (1996). Effects of tax integration and capital gains tax on corporate leverage. Nat. Tax J. 49 (1):31-55.
Shelvlin T, Tang YH, Wilson RJ (2012). Domestic income shifting by Chinese listed firms. J. Amer. Tax. Assoc. 34(1):1-29.
Slemrod J (1990). Tax effects on foreign direct investment in the United States: Evidence from a cross-country comparison. In: A. Razin & J. Slemrod (Eds), Taxation in the global economy: 79–122. Chicago: National Bureau Economic Research.
Sun Q, Tong W and Yu Q (2002). Determinants of foreign direct investment across China. J. Int. Money , Finance 21(1):79-113.
Swenson DL (1994). The impact of U. S. tax reform on foreign direct investment in the United State. J. Pub. Econ.54 (2):243–266.
Tung S, Cho S (2000). The impact of tax incentives on foreign direct investment in China. J.Inter. Account., Audit. Tax. 9(2):105-135.
Tung S, Cho S (2001). Determinants of Regional Investment Decisions in China: An econometric model of tax incentive policy. Rev. Quantit. Finance Account. 17:167-185.
Usher D (1977). The economics of tax incentives to encourage investment in less developed countries. J. Develop. Econ.4: 119-149.
Parys S, James S (2010). The effectiveness of tax incentives in attracting investment: Panel data evidence from the CFA Franc zone. Int. Tax. Pub. Finan. 17(4):400-429.
Wang JC and Chen MC (2007). An empirical investigation of impacts of the integrated income tax system on corporate financing decisions. Chiao Da Manage. Rev. Chin. 27(1):221-246.
Wang JC, Chen MC (2004). An empirical investigation of impacts of the imputation tax system on corporate dividend payouts. J. Manage. 21(2): 257-277.
Wei Y, Liu X (1999). The regional distribution of foreign direct investment in China. Regional Stud. 33(9):857-867.
Yelpaala K (1984). The efficacy of tax incentives within the framework of the neoclassical theory of foreign direct investment: A legislative policy analysis. Taxes Int. Law J. 19:365-414.
Young KH (1988). The effect of taxes and rates of return on foreign direct investment in the United States. Nat.Tax J. 41(1):109-121.

Enhanced relationship preparedness in a dutch multinational context: A tax control framework

D.W. Colon and D.M. Swagerman

University of Groningen, the Netherlands.

This paper deals with enhanced relationship participation in an international context. The purpose of this paper is to present insight into the essentials for implementing a Tax Control Framework (TCF) and to present incentives to participate in an enhanced relationship. First, the relevant guidance for implementing a TCF is described. Second, based on a survey with tax directors of the largest Dutch multinational organizations quoted on the Dutch stock exchange incentives for participating in an enhanced relationship are investigated. Performing an analysis on the results identifies two important incentives for organizations to participate in an enhanced relationship.

Key words: Controlling, corporate governance, enhanced relationship, Tax, OECD, internal control

INTRODUCTION

Tax compliance and tax accounting are radically changing in most countries worldwide as part of an initiative of the Organization for Economic Co-operation and Development (OECD). Information notes published by the OECD stimulate the implementation of risk concentrated tax authorities resulting in an "enhanced relationship". The aim is that companies organize their tax structure risk base (OECD, 2010), comparable with the overall internal control systems emphasized after the Enron failure. The tax structure should give tax authorities insight into the largest tax risks. Based on the OECD initiative countries all over the world implemented enhanced relationship policies in their national regulations (Bakker and Kloosterhof, 2010). In 2005 the Dutch tax authorities introduced a version of the tax based regulation proposed by the OECD, "horizontal monitoring".

From the year 2007 horizontal monitoring is official policy in the Netherlands (Belastingdienst, 2008; Van Daelen and Van der Elst, 2010). Horizontal monitoring changes the relation of the tax authorities and companies. On one hand, the tax authority has to stimulate an environment of trust and close cooperation. On the other hand companies are expected to contact the tax authorities whenever there is ambiguity about the tax obligation resulting from activities.

The advantage for the tax authorities is a better allocation of resources as it can focus on the organizations and/ or parts of organizations with the highest perceived risk. The advantage for companies is a

Less intensive tax investigation by the tax authorities at year end (Kemp and Verbakel, 2010). To reach these advantages the tax authorities needs insight into the risks of companies. To fulfill this requirement the Dutch tax authorities obliged companies who want to participate in horizontal monitoring to set up a Tax Control Framework (TCF).

However, only limited Dutch guidance for a TCF is available; the Dutch Tax Authorities have no mandatory framework. The OECD offers some general guidance. Besides, well known models are present from controlling process other than tax, for example COSO and COBIT. A TCF model fulfilling the requirements of the OECD, COSO, COBIT and the Dutch Tax Authorities is the Tax Management Maturity Model (T3M). This model identifies tax risks in six specific tax related subjects: Business and (Tax) environment, Business operations, Tax Operations, Tax Risk Management, Monitoring/Testing and Tax assurance. These broad areas are divided into more specific factors which are the fundaments for the judgment of a subject.

This paper focuses on the fundaments for implementing a TCF and the main incentives for companies to participate in an enhanced relationship. First, relevant TCF guidance will be stated. As a TCF should fulfill requirements by relevant authorities, understanding this requirements is important. The question that will be answered is *what guidance is in place by the OECD, Dutch tax authorities, COSO and COBIT for implementing a TCF?* Second, focusing on practitioners in Dutch multinational firms answer will be given to the research question *what are the main incentives for multinationals to participate in an enhanced relationship?* Specifically, the focus will be on three possible incentives: effect on the business environment, new rules and policies in the short term, and the Netherlands as a tax haven.

This paper continues with the scientific relevance. Then the relevant TCF guidance from the OECD, the Dutch tax authorities, and controlling models will be discussed. The last part of this paper focuses on the results and analysis of a survey with Dutch multinationals quoted on the largest Dutch stock exchanges.

Scientific relevance

Enhanced relationships[1] are regularly discussed in the scientific literature (eSimonis, 2008; De Groot and Van de Enden, 2010). However, the (international) guidelines existing for a TCF have been rarely discussed in the literature. Tax controlling - and a TCF as a part of it - is a portion of the organization's corporate governance. So, research on the implementation of a TCF is rewarding for the controlling literature as well for company's best practices. The first important contribution of this paper to the literature is the creation of a universal guideline for the development of a TCF. The Dutch focus of this paper could be easily changed to another country focus by replacing the Dutch tax law factors by other countries' tax laws factors.

The second important contribution of this paper is the focus on practitioners. An enhanced relationship could not be entirely based on theoretical concepts, but practitioners should contribute to enhanced relationship policies as this will overcome problems not recognized when focusing solely on theories. Only limited research concerning an enhanced relationship focused on practitioners (Freedman et al., 2009).

The survey results presented in this paper show companies' incentives for participating in an enhanced relationship. As willingness by companies to participate in an enhanced relationship is essential for the success of this policy, this paper exposes important insights for further implementation of enhanced relationship laws and regulations worldwide.

Guidance

OECD

The OECD introduced the concept of an enhanced relationship. After years of discussion with the member states and the draft of many papers 35 economies signed in 2006 the Seoul declaration (OECD, 2006): the commitment for cooperation on efficient and international orientated tax authorities. In 2008 this commitment has been followed up by the Cape Town Communiqué (OECD, 2008). Representatives of 45 economies discussed the application of risk management to taxes. Understanding the risk management of companies gives the tax authorities the possibility to allocate their resources to parts of organizations with higher risks (less effective risk management) and companies not in control for their taxes at all.

In the years after Cape Town the OECD introduced reports giving participating economies high-level input for enhanced relationship implementation (OECD, 2010; 2011; 2012). The main guidance consists of four aspects: real-time contact with companies about tax issues, focus on tax related processes, make tax compliance easier, and stimulate a good cooperation between the tax authorities and companies and their stakeholders.

Dutch tax authorities obliged implementing a TCF for horizontal monitoring participation but supported the interpretation of a TCF only with limited guidance (Belastingdienst, 2008). The horizontal monitoring documentation published by the Dutch tax authorities states that practitioners have to develop a TCF from their own knowledge and experience. Limited guidance is given in this documentation by referencing COSO as possible tool for implementing a TCF.

[1] As mentioned the Dutch form of a "enhanced relationship" is "horizontal monitoring". For the ease of reading in this paper the term "enhanced relationship" is used when the Dutch form is concerned.

COSO (ERM)[2]

COSO is a model developed to support companies in setting their internal control frameworks (COSO, 2004). It consists of four company goals. These goals are linked to four organizational levels and eight risk and control components. Besides the model COSO publishes additional reports which can be used by practitioners as best practice: the reports anticipate on new challenges companies encounter (e.g. COSO, 2009). So, usage of the COSO model requires also the application of the COSO reports.

COBIT

Information technology (IT) has a great impact on the functioning of most organizations. The processes concerning IT (IT governance) should be in control. A model supporting this purpose is COBIT[3] developed by ISACA[4]. COBIT consists of five principles which are the fundaments of the model: meeting stakeholder needs, covering the enterprise end-to-end, applying a single integrated framework, enabling a holistic approach, and separating governance from management. This leads to the practical implementation by the "key areas" defined in COBIT: plan, build, run, monitor, and governance.

Combining the guidance given in the sections above creates a framework for implementing a TCF. This framework can be easily internationally implemented, as only the guidance of the Dutch tax authorities has to be replaced to make it fit for other countries than the Netherlands. As mentioned before, a model fulfilling the (international) requirements for setting a TCF is the Tax Management Maturity Model (Colon, 2012).

Large multinationals

This part of the paper contains findings of a survey with tax directors of large multinationals. The results of the survey are further analyzed to find the incentives that are the most important for large multinationals to participate in an enhanced relationship. First the hypotheses will be rationalized, which form the input for our survey. Second the analysis and results will be discussed. Research on enhanced relationship with surveys is very limited. In the paper is referenced Freedman et al. (2009). The only relevant survey in relation to enhanced relationships is our focus. In this research the UK practice has been examined. As there is limited relevant research specific for an enhanced relationship, hypotheses are framed partly by (indirect) related literature and commons sense. Considering the limited research with surveys specific for enhanced relationships, it is not possible to add more relevant literature and we consider literature that is only very limited not as value adding.

Hypotheses

Organizational goals are not only limited to the interest of shareholders. Organizations have to consider the interests of all the stakeholders. Corporate social responsibility (CSR) has an important impact on modern societies. A description of CSR is (Jones et al., 2009): the integration of social, economic, ethical and environment considerations into the organizational strategy and operational activities. So transparency about taxes is also a part of this description.

Not every society organizations' operations require the same strictness of CSR. The strictness of CSR could be an incentive for organizations to settle in a specific country. Of importance is the perception of the relevant society: does the society perceive the organization in performing their activities regarding CSR. Specific for taxes, this could entail an in-control statement for the TCF (De Groot and Van der Enden, 2010). However, it is important for companies to consider an enhanced relationship relevant for their business. If companies consider an enhanced relationship as positive for their business one could expect them to be more positive in the implementation of an enhanced relationship.

Hypothesis 1

The perception of a better business environment by an enhanced relationship is positively related to the willingness to participate in an enhanced relationship.

Not every company implements the same level of CSR. Some companies are more prepared to implement high level CSR than others. Currently an enhanced relationship is no obligation. However, when companies expect new compliance rules to be applied in the near future, companies have to consider how this impacts their activities. For an enhanced relationship this could mean that companies are more willing to participate immediately.

Hypothesis 2

The expectation of a short term (five years) international obligation to participate in an enhanced relationship is positively related to the willingness to participate in an enhanced relationship.

Some companies present themselves to the society as part of their CSR policy. If companies could be expected to be more society concerned regardless of the reputational effects and possible higher profits,

[2] Committee of Sponsoring Organizations of the Treadway Commission (Enterprise Risk Management). For a detailed background see: www.coso.org
[3] Control Objectives for Information and related Technology
[4] Information Systems Audit and Control Association

companies are expected to be more willing to pay taxes. Following this rationale, companies of the opinion that taxes can easily be avoided should be more convenient with an enhanced relationship as these present themselves more positively than relative less paying companies.

Hypothesis 3

The perception of the Netherlands as a tax haven is positively related to the willingness to participate in an enhanced relationship.

METHOD

The assumed relations will be tested by a survey with a selection of companies. The selection of companies is limited to Dutch multinationals quoted on the largest Dutch stock exchanges (AEX and Midkap). No difference was made to industry or the quotation on only the Dutch or also other stock exchanges. The Dutch multinationals quoted on the Dutch stock exchanges concern the most relevant sample as the Dutch tax authorities focused initially on the these companies before implementing enhanced relationships at other companies. Therefore these companies have more experience with an enhanced relationship than other companies in the Netherlands. For the selected companies a survey had been sent to the company's tax director. The relevant period of the survey is March to May 2012. The operational numbers are extracted from the relevant annual reports (2012). The sample is states of twenty companies.

Measures

Dependent variable - The measure for the willingness to participate in an enhanced relationship has been measured by a number given by the tax directors scaled from one to five (one is no willingness and five is the opposite).

Independent variables - The effect on the business environment has been determined by questioning respondents considering an enhanced relationship to be negative (one), with no effect (two) or positive (three) for the business environment.

The expectation that an enhanced relationship will be an obligation on the short term (five years) has been measured on a five point scale (five is an enhanced relationship is highly expected). Respondents were questioned to consider the short term obligation of an enhanced relationship in an international context.

The perception of the Netherlands as a tax haven has been EU centered. The tax directors were questioned to consider the taxes in comparison to the other EU member states. Number one indicates low tax avoidance while five indicates that the Netherlands is considered as a tax haven.

In addition, a control variable has been put into the sample to exclude the possible impact of other factors on the hypotheses. As larger companies have a larger impact on their environment; more pressure exists on a company to have more CSR. This possible impact has to be excluded. So, a control variable for the number of employees of a company has been adopted. The number of employees is measured by a logarithm of the actual number of employees.

Method of analysis

Relations will be considered by using SPSS. In SPSS the relations are tested with linear regression. With this method the relations between the first three mentioned independent variables and the dependent variable as described above (conform the hypotheses formulated above) are tested.

RESULTS

The descriptive statistics (Table 1) show no indication for an exceptional sample. The willingness for an enhanced relationship (4.100 out of 5) is high in the sample. Besides, an enhanced relationship is considered to be positive for the business environment (2.421 out of 3). The perception of an enhanced relationship obligation in the short term and the perception of the Netherlands as a tax haven are neither considered to be positive or negative by the tax directors (3.000 and 2.500 out of 5 respectively). The number of employees in the sample is considered to be high (9.548 after using a logarithm) compared to other research, for example Gallo and Christensen (2011) who found an average of 2.28. However, this is plausible as our sample consists only of the largest Dutch multinationals.

The Pearson correlation (Table 2) shows only one notable outcome. Tax directors who are of the opinion that an enhanced relationship is positive for the business environment are expecting an enhanced relationship to be obliged in the short term. So, based on this finding, logically, it could be expected that these variables are either or neither related to the willingness to participate in an enhanced relationship. No other correlations were found in the sample.

Hypothesis 1 suggested a relation between the perceived (positive) effect on the business environment and the willingness to participate in an enhanced relationship. The regression results (Table 3) presented a significant relation on 1% level (coefficient of 0.729). Based on the sample the perceived effect on the business environment is a major incentive for companies to participate in an enhanced relationship. Hypothesis 1 is accepted.

Hypothesis 2 suggested a relationship between the obligation to participate in an enhanced relationship in the short term (less than five years) and the willingness to participate in an enhanced relationship. The regression results presented a significant relation on 5% level (coefficient 0.336). Based on the sample the perception of the short term obligation of an enhanced relationship is an incentive for companies to participate in an enhanced relationship. Hypothesis 2 is accepted.

Hypothesis 3 suggested a relationship between the perception of the Netherlands as a tax haven and the willingness to participate in an enhanced relationship. The regression results presented no significant relation for this hypothesis. Based on the sample the perception of the Netherlands as a tax haven is no incentive for companies to participate in an enhanced relationship. Hypothesis 3 is rejected.

Table 1. Descriptive statistics for dependent and independent variables.

	Average	Min	Max	Std. Dev.
Dependent variable				
Willingness	4.100	3	5	0.788
Independent variables				
Business environment	2.421	1	3	0.838
Short term	3.000	1	4	1.076
Tax haven	2.500	1	4	0.889
Control variable				
Number of employees	9.548	5.74	12.47	1.661

Table 2. Pearson correlation with independent variables.

Variabe	Business environment	Short term	Tax Haven	Employees
Business environment	1.000			
Short term	0.712***	1.000		
Tax haven	0.131	0.275	1.000	
Number of employees	0.154	0.047	0.061	1.000

*** Correlation is significant on the 1% level, (two-way).

Table 3. Enhanced relationship willingness regression results.

	(1)	(2)	(3)	(4)	(5)
Constant	2.813 (1.039)	1.395 (0.645)	1.483 (0.833)	2.260 (1.109)	0.701 (0.556)
Number of employees	0.135 * (0.107)	0.093 * (0.063)	0.120 * (0.079)	0.127 (0.106)	0.106 * (0.051)
Business environment (H1)	--	0.729 *** (0.128)	--	--	0.435 *** (0.146)
Short term (H2)	--	--	0.336 ** (0.117)	--	0.293 ** (0.115)
Tax haven (H3)	--	--	--	0.252 (0.197)	0.152 (0.096)
R-squared	0.081	0.704	0.530	0.161	0.837
Adjusted R-squared	0.030	0.667	0.474	0.063	0.791
F-value	1.580	18.997 ***	9.569 ***	1.635	18.029 ***

The dependent variable in every regression is enhanced relationship willingness. ***, **, * Coefficient is statistical significant at respectively 1, 5, and 10% level.

DISCUSSION

The first part of this paper discussed relevant guidelines for implementing a TCF. International guidelines were described and Dutch guidelines for an enhanced relationship were mentioned. It was noticed that the Dutch guidelines stated could easily be replaced by another national guideline for having a universal framework for implementing TCF. Important contributions to the literature have been made by giving an overview of the relevant literature usable universally. For every company implementing a TCF, the guideline mentioned is the basis for implementation.

The second part of this paper presented the analysis of a survey with tax directors employed at Dutch multinationals quoted on the largest Dutch stock exchanges. Two important incentives influencing the willingness of companies to participate in an enhanced relationship has been identified: a (perceived) positive impact on the business environment and the expectation that an enhanced relationship will be an obligation in the short term (less than five years). This finding is very important for tax authorities and scholars. For the tax authorities the fundamental has been put for a tax policy stimulating large multinationals to participate in an enhanced relationship. Future regulations should focus more on the benefits for companies to stimulate participation in an enhanced relationship. First we recommend that a financial incentive be given to companies, for example, by lower compliance cost for government regulations charged to companies. Second, we recommend that a reputation incentive be put in place, for example, by obliging the disclosure of the state of the TCF in the annual report. For scholars an important insight has been presented: not a purely theoretical approach has been used for the explanation why an enhanced relationship is or is not a success in a country; but with this paper the beginning of an understanding of company perception/ motivation towards an enhanced relationship has been presented.

This paper has limitations giving possibilities to further scientific research. First, as this paper is limited to the relevant framework for an enhanced relationship in the Netherlands, further investigation could focus on another country or identify the differences between the national guidelines to build further on a (international) framework for a TCF. Second, this paper focused only on a limited amount of incentives influencing the willingness of companies to participate in an enhanced relationship. Additional incentives could be the topic of further research. Besides, the context could also be chanced; this paper focused on the largest organizations, while it is possible smaller organizations or organizations in other countries would give other outcomes. Third, the sample in this paper is small (2o). A small sample is very sensitive for movement in the outcome of one or more items limiting the generalization of this paper. Further research could be focused on overcoming this limitation.

Conclusion

This paper presented the relevant guideline for implementing a TCF with a focus on the Netherlands. Besides, this paper identified two important incentives for companies to participate in an enhanced relationship: the perception of a positive effect on the business environment and the expectation that an enhanced relationship will be an obligation in the short term.

Conflict of Interests

The authors have not declared any conflict of interests.

REFERENCES

Bakker A, Kloosterhof S (2010). Tax Risk Management: From Risk to Opportunity. Amsterdam: International Bureau of Fiscal Documentation.

Belastingdienst (2008). Tax Control Framework: van risicogericht naar "in control": het werk verandert'. Policy paper Belastingdienst. available at www. belastingdienst.nl, http://download.belastingdienst.nl/belastingdienst/docs/tax_control_framework_dv4011z1pl.pdf, last accessed on 30 September 2013.

Colon DW (2012). Toetsing van het Tax Management Maturity Model en horizontaal toezicht bereidheid in Nederland. Working paper University of Groningen. Available at http://irs.ub.rug.nl/dbi/50bf518a7e54f, last accessed on 30 September 2013.

COSO (2004). Enterprise Risk Management: Integrated Framework. Committee of Sponsoring Organizations of the Treadway Commission. Available at http://www.coso.org/documents/coso_erm_executivesummary.pdf, last accessed at 30 September 2013.

COSO (2009). Strengthening Enterprise Risk Management for Strategic Advantage. Committee of Sponsoring Organizations of the Treadway Commission. Available at http://www.coso.org/documents/COSO_09_board_position_final102309PRINTandWEBFINAL_000.pdf, last accessed at 30 September 2013.

Daelen M, van Elst, C van der (2010). Risk Management and Corporate Governance. Edgard Elgar, Cheltenham.

Freedman J, Loomer G, Vella J (2009). Corporate Tax Risk and Tax Avoidance: New Approaches' Bri. Tax Rev. (1):74-116.

Gallo P, Cristensen L (2011), Firm Size Matters: An Empirical Investigation of Organizational Size and Ownership on Sustainability-Related Behaviors. Bus. Soc. 50(2):315-349.

Groot J, Enden E, van der (2010). Verantwoording over interne beheersing onder Horizontaal toezicht. Weekblad voor Fiscaal Recht 6851:375-382.

Kemp J, Verbakel R (2010). Knelpunten van horizontaal toezicht bij middelgrote ondernemingen. Weekblad voor Fiscaal Recht 6844:124-130.

Organisation for Economic Co-operation and Development, (2006). Seoul Declaration. OECD declaration. Available at www.oecd.org/dataoecd/49/28/40839436.pdf, last accessed at 30 September 2013.

Organisation for Economic Co-operation and Development, (2008). Cape Town Communique. OECD communique. Available at www.oecd.org/dataoecd/26/43/39886621.pdf, last accessed at 30 September 2013.

Organisation for Economic Co-operation and Development, (2010). Tax Compliance and Tax Accounting Systems. Information note OECD. Available at www.oecd.org/dataoecd/42/37/45045662.pdf, last accessed at 30 September 2013.

Organisation for Economic Co-operation and Development, (2011). Tackling Aggressive Tax Planning Through Improved Transparency and Disclosure. Information note OECD. Available at www.oecd.org/dataoecd/13/55/48322860.pdf, last accessed at 30 September 2013.

Organisation for Economic Co-operation and Development, (2012). Right from the start: Influencing the Compliance Environment for Small and Medium Enterprises. Information note OECD. Available at www.oecd.org/site/ctpfta/49428016.pdf, last accessed at 30 September 2013.

Simone L, Sansing R, Seidman J (2011). When are Enhanced Relationship Tax Compliance Programs Mutually Beneficial? Working paper SSRN. Available at http://ssrn.com/abstract=1954823, last accessed at 30 September 2013.

Determinants of gift tax compliance among employees of the formal sector in Kumasi Metropolis, Ghana

Frank Yao Gbadago[1] and Dadson Awunyo-Vitor[2]

[1]Department of Accounting Studies Education, College of Technology Education
University of Education, Winneba, Kumasi, Ghana.
[2]Department of Agricultural Economics, Agribusiness and Extension, Faculty of Agriculture, College of Agriculture and Natural Resources, Kwame Nkrumah University of Science and Technology, Kumasi, Ghana.

The study examined the awareness and level of compliance with gift tax by formal sector employees in Kumasi Metropolis Ghana. Two hundred and fifty-two respondents were sampled for the study using the purposive sampling method. Questionnaire was used to solicit data and information from the respondents. Data collected were analyzed using descriptive statistics and probit regression model. The results of the study revealed that the level of compliance with the gift tax is very low. The key reason identified in the study for the low level of compliance with gift tax among Ghanaian taxpayers is unawareness of gift tax obligations. The probit regression result revealed that level of education, knowledge of tax law, and penalty for non- compliance significantly influence respondents' decision to comply with the gift tax law .Hence, the low level of education offered by the Ghana Revenue Authority on the gift tax and non-enforcement of the law have contributed to the low level of compliance. The study therefore recommends that the Ghana Revenue Authority should step up education on the gift tax law and enforce penalty for non- compliance to improve revenue from gift tax.

Key words: Gift tax, tax compliance, Kumasi Metropolis, Tax payers, Ghana.

INTRODUCTION

Since taxation is a compulsory levy on individuals, entities and property by a tax authority (the government of a tax jurisdiction) for the purposes of supporting its expenditure (Sally, 1999; Nakyea, 2008; Alabede, 2014; Bruce-Twum, 2014), incomes and/or gifts are usually the subject matter of taxation. Incomes are usually paid openly and directly to the beneficiaries (that is the person earning the income) and are, most of the time, documented. Hence, they are easily identified and assessed for tax. However, that is not the case of gifts received or receivable. According to Part V- Interpretation Section 110 (1) of the Internal Revenue Act, 2000 (Act 592 as amended), a gift is a receipt without consideration or inadequate consideration. In other words, a gift is something one receives without adequate compensation paid to the giver by the receiver. Further, Section 105(1) of the Internal Revenue Act, 2000 (Act 592 as amended) provides that a gift, which is taxable under the Act, shall be taxed at the specified rate on the total value of taxable gifts received by a person within a year of assessment.

Although the tax laws of Ghana, specifically Internal Revenue Act, 2000 (Act 592 as amended), provides for this, in practice compliance is almost non-existence (Terkper, 2003; Gatsi and Acquah, 2010 and Bruce-Twum, 2014). Interestingly, this observation was also made by Tusubira and Nkote (2013) in Uganda, suggesting that non-compliance is a problem (Andreoni et al., 1998) in taxation systems in other parts of the world (Abdul-Razak and Adafula, 2013). To the researcher, compliance with gift tax is both statutory and a civic obligation. Accordingly, non-compliance may result in liability. The purpose of this paper therefore is to educate the public on the provisions of the tax law relating to gift tax and the responsibilities of the taxpayers or the citizenry of Ghana to abide by the law, whilst recommending ways of improving the collection rate. As observed by Gatsi and Acquah (2010), Bruce-Twum (2014) and others around the world, notably McKerchar and Evans (2009), Tusubira and Nkote (2013) and Alabede (2014), lack of knowledge of tax law and its provisions account for the non-compliance with tax among tax payers. Currently, the level of compliance is almost non-existing; meanwhile it is perceived that people do receive gifts almost on daily basis ranging from cash gifts, hampers, cars and other tangible assets.

The aim of the study is to assess the level of gift tax provisions compliance among formal sector employees in Kumasi Metropolis.

REVIEW OF RELEVANT LITERATURE

Since tax revenue has been accepted as the most important source of revenue for governments (Sally, 1999; Nakyea, 2008; Martina et al., 2008; Brautigam, 2008; McKerchar and Evans, 2009; Abdul-Razak and Adafula, 2013; Bruce-Twum, 2014), every effort should be made to assist the government, not only to maintain the level of tax revenue, but also to create voluntary compliance among taxpayers or citizenry of a country like Ghana. To the researcher, this is very important in the advent of the current financial situation facing developing nations after the financial crunch from the western world leading to massive reductions in donations and grants emanating from the developed world to the developing world, mostly Africa, for which Ghana is not an exception (OECD, 2014). Many scholars and analysts assert that for Ghana to have adequate financial resources to finance its developmental programs and agenda (Moss and Majerowicz, 2012), it needs to properly develop its taxation systems in order to rake in more tax revenue (Nakyea, 2008; Martina et al., 2008; Brautigam, 2008; McKerchar and Evans, 2009; Gatsi and Acquah, 2010; Abdul- Razak and Adafula, 2013). This accounts for the recent moves by the government of the day to introduce new taxes to raise tax revenues for development projects and financing of recurrent budget items. In assessing a taxpayer's tax liability, incomes are usually and easily identified and assessed for tax even if the taxpayer attempts not to disclose it (Dressler, 2002; Akhand, 2012). This may be partly because income is mostly paid by one party to the other leaving a trail; also, it is paid in the open directly to the beneficiary (that is the person earning the income); in addition, most of the time, the income received is usually documented.

Gifts of a certain nature are the subject matter of tax laws of Ghana specifically Internal Revenue Act, 2000 (Act 592) as amended. According to Part V-interpretation Section 110 (1) of Act 592 (amended), a gift is a receipt without consideration or inadequate consideration. Section 105(1) of the Act, Act 592 (as amended) further provides that, a gift which is taxable under the Act, shall be taxed at the specified rate on the total value of the taxable gifts so received by a person within a year of assessment. Section 106 of the Act, (Act 592 as amended) defines "taxable gift" to mean,

(a) Any of the following assets situated in Ghana:

i. Building of a permanent or temporary nature;
ii. Land;
iii. Shares, bonds and other securities;
iv. Money, including foreign currency;
v. Business and business assets;
vi. Any means of transportation (that is, by land, air or sea);
vii. Goods or chattels not included in the means of transportation; and
viii. Part of, or any right to or interest in any of the assets referred to above

(b) An asset or a benefit, whether situated in Ghana or outside Ghana, received by or for the benefit of a resident person as a gift where the asset has been or is credited in an account or has been or is invested, accumulated, capitalized or otherwise dealt with in the name of or on behalf of or at the direction of the person

(c) A favour in money or money's worth or a consideration for an act or omission or the forbearance of an act or omission that inures for or to the benefit of a resident person.

It is worthy of note that it is immaterial whether or not the person being taxed physically received the asset, so long as the act, omission or transaction is inured to the benefit of that person (Internal Revenue (Amendment) Act, 2003 (Act 644).

The provision of the tax law in respect of gift is, however, liberal requesting voluntary compliance from the taxpayer. Thus, the law provides that under procedure relating to gift tax (S.108) a person who receives a taxable gift shall, within thirty (30) days of receipt, furnish the Commissioner General of Ghana Revenue Authority with a return in writing containing the following information:

1. the description and location of the taxable gift;
2. the total value of the gift, how it is calculated and tax payable with respect to that gift;
3. the full name and address of the donor of the gift; and
4. any other information required by the Commissioner.

A skimpy and sketchy opinion is that in Ghana, although people do receive gifts on a daily basis ranging from cash (Gatsi and Acquah, 2010; Bruce-Twum, 2014) in the form of local and foreign currency to landed property as well as means of transportation to mention but few, they do not honour their gift tax obligation thereon (Bruce-Twum, 2014). Consequentially, in compliance with the provisions of the tax law, especially in respect of gifts, these should be subject to taxation. It is, however, worthy to mention that it is not every gift received that are taxable. Under section 105(2) gifts received by a person under or for the following reasons are exempt from tax:

1. by a person under a will or upon intestacy;
2. by a person from that person's spouse, child, parent, brother, sister, aunt, uncle, nephew or niece;
3. by a religious body which uses the gift received for the benefit of the public or a section of the public; or
4. for charitable or educational purposes.

In assessing the value of the gifts subject to tax, the market value of the gift received or receivable is usually used.

The few empirical studies on gift tax in Ghana attempted to provide some answers to the above questions as follows: Gatsi and Acquah (2010), in their study on information asymmetry and gift tax, concluded that gift tax is one of the conduits through which tax revenue can be enhanced for development with a call on Ghana Revenue Authority for better education on the tax. Later, Bruce-Twum (2014) tried to determine the extent of knowledge about gift tax especially in the Accra-Tema metropolis and reached the conclusion that the level of awareness is very low, resulting in non-compliance with gift tax in Ghana. Empirically, there were a series of research studies on taxation and tax compliance in general; for example: enhancing voluntary tax compliance by reducing compliance costs (Jenkins and Forlemu, 1993); tax compliance costs for the SMEs business sector (Evans et al., 2013); investigating tax compliance (Myles et al., 2013); and social norms and tax compliance (Onu and Oats, 2014), all undertaken in advanced economies. In addition to the above, there have been studies undertaken on making large corporations tax compliance in other developing economies like Bangladesh (Akhand, 2012); and income tax compliance among SMEs in Uganda (Tusubira and Nkote, 2013). In Ghana, income tax non-compliance among Ghanaian self employed (Baba and Asante, 2012), and taxpayers' attitude and its influence on tax compliance decisions (Abdul-Razak and Adafula, 2013) are some of the available compliance studies; however they failed to estimate the level of non-compliance. Although some levels of research works have been done on gift tax compliance, notably Gatsi and Acquah's (2010) study 'Information Asymmetry and Gift Tax in Ghana' and Bruce-Twum's (2014) 'Gift Tax Compliance in Ghana, an Empirical Study', the researchers, in determining the level of awareness and/ or compliance with gift tax, did not use a very large sample size. For example, Bruce-Twum (2014) only used one hundred and sixty-seven respondents in his analysis. Further, it was found from the literature review that most studies undertaken in the area of tax in Ghana were on income tax and not gift tax. Therefore, this research aims to fill this research gap by assessing the level of compliance with gift tax among the Ghanaian taxpayers generally.

METHODOLOGY

The general approach adopted for this research was a survey. A questionnaire was used as the data collection instrument; it was administered to the respondents. The population for the study was basically formal sector employees in Kumasi Metropolis. The formal sector workers were selected and used for this research because it is assumed that, as they are in formal employment and are mostly literates, they might have had some level of knowledge about tax and hence provide an opportunity to measure the level of compliance among them. However, due to the vastness of the population, a purposive sampling approach was adopted to sample the respondents. In all 252 respondents were sampled for the study.

Analytical framework

Descriptive and inferential statistics with the help of SPSS and STATA econometric package were used to analyze the data. The respondents' decision to comply with the gift tax Act (provisions under the Internal Revenue Act, 2000 as amended) can be said to be dichotomous involving two mutually exclusive alternatives. The respondents may comply with the Act or may not comply with the Act. This results in a binary dependent variable. The framework for estimating models with binary dependent variables has its root in the threshold theory of decision making in which a reaction occurs only after the strength of a stimulus increases beyond the individual's reaction threshold (Hill and Kau, 1981). Therefore, the respondent when faced with a choice to comply with the gift tax Act has a reaction threshold which is influenced by several factors. Based on the reaction threshold the respondent may either comply or may not comply, leading to binary dependent variable y_i which takes on the values of zero (not comply with the Act) and one (comply with the Act)

The probability of observing a value of one is:

$$P_r = \left(y_i = \frac{1}{x_i\beta_i}\right) = 1 - F(x_i\beta_i) \qquad 1$$

where $F(.)$ is a cumulative distribution function; it is a continuous, strictly increasing function that takes a real value and returns a value which ranges from 0 to 1. Then, it follows that the probability of observing the zeros is:

$$P_r\left(y_i = \frac{0}{x_i\beta_i}\right) = F(-x_i\beta_i) \qquad 2$$

Table 1. Variables for the probit model.

Variables	Description	Measurement	Expected sign
AgeR	Age of the respondents	Age in years	+
AgeB	How low respondents have been in business	Age in years	+
Edu	Number of years spent in formal school	In years	+
Asso	Does the respondent belong to any association	dummy (1= if respondent belong to association ; 0 otherwise)	+
KnoTaxL	Knowledge of tax laws	Dummy variable ; 1 = has knowledge; 0 = Otherwise	+
Gender	gender of the business operator	dummy (1 = Male 0 = Otherwise)	+
Perp	Perception of filling procedures	dummy (1 = Cumbersome; 0 = Otherwise)	+
Size	Size of the business	that the net asset in Ghana Cedis	+
Aware	awareness of offences and penalties	dummy (1 = aware of the penalty, 0= Otherwise)	+
Dist	Distance to the nearest tax office in kilometres	Kilometres	-

Given such a specification, we determine the parameters for estimating this model using the maximum likelihood estimation approach. The dependent variable is an unobserved latent variable that is linearly related to by the equation:

$$y_i = \beta_i x_i + \mu_i \tag{3}$$

Where μ_i is a random disturbance term and x_i is independent variable which influences respondents' compliance decision. The observed dependent variable is determined by whether y_i exceeds a threshold value or otherwise:

$$y_i = \begin{cases} 1 if\ y_i^* > 0 \\ 0\ if\ y_i^* \leq 0 \end{cases} \tag{4}$$

where y_i^* is the threshold value for y_i and is assumed to be normally distributed. Common models for estimating such parameters include probit (standard normal), logit (logistic) and tobit (extreme value) (Madala, 2005).

The model

This study adopted the probit model partly because of its ability to constrain the utility value of the decision to join variable to lie within 0 and 1, and its ability to resolve the problem of heteroscedasticity. Following Madala (2005), the probit model adopted for the study is specified as:

$$P_i = P(y_i^* < y_i).$$
$$P_i = P(y_i^* < \beta_0 + \beta_i x_i) = F(y_i) \tag{5}$$
$$P_i = F(y_i) = \frac{1}{\sqrt{2\pi}} \int_{-\infty}^{Z_i} e^{\frac{S^2}{2}} dS.$$

where P_i is the probability that a respondent will comply with gift tax act or not; S is a random variable which is assumed to be normally distributed with mean zero and unit variance; y_i is the dependent variable (decision to comply); y_i^* is as defined above. To obtain an estimate of the index Z_i , the inverse of the cumulative normal function is used:

$$y_i = F^{-1}(P_i) = \beta_0 + \beta_i x_i + \mu_i \tag{6}$$

$$y_i = \beta_0 + \beta_i x_i + \mu_i \tag{7}$$

Where $\beta_0, \beta_1, \beta_2 \ldots \beta_{14}$ are parameters of the probit model; however, these parameters do not provide direct information about the effect of the changes in the independent or explanatory variables on the probability of respondents complying with the gift tax Act. The relative effect of each explanatory variable on the likelihood that a respondent will comply with the gift tax Act is given by:

$$\frac{\partial P_i}{\partial x_i} = \beta_i * \int(Z_i) \tag{8}$$

Where P_i is the mean dependent variable whose value is given in the probit results as:

$$\int(Z_i) = F^{-1}(P_i) \tag{9}$$

Guided by related studies (Toumi, 2007; Jackson and Milliron, 1986), the following factors are identified to influence compliance with gift tax by the respondents (Table 1).

The empirical model is specified as:

$$y_i = \beta_0 + \beta_1 \text{AgeR}_i + \beta_2 \text{AgeB}_i + \beta_3 \text{Edu}_i + \beta_4 \text{Asso}_i + \beta_5 \text{KnoTaxL}_i + \beta_6 \text{Gender}_i + \beta_7 \text{Perp}_i + \beta_8 \text{Size}_i + \beta_9 \text{Aware}_i + \beta_{10} \text{Dist}_i + +\mu_i \tag{10}$$

RESULTS AND DISCUSSION

The result of the study revealed that out of the sample of 252 respondents studied, 131 (being 51.98%) were males, while 121 (48.02%) were females (Table 2), indicating that there were more males than females.

The age characteristics of the sample studied revealed that those between the ages of 20-29 were about 50.00%; 30-39 formed about 28.97%; followed by those above 40 representing 21.03% (Table 3). Interestingly, this observation is similar to that of the observations in the 2010 Ghana National Population and Housing Census (GSS, 2013).

An attempt was made to ascertain the educational background of the respondents as it does have an impact

Table 2. Gender distribution of respondents.

Gender	Frequency	Percentage (%)
Male	131	51.98
Female	121	48.02
Total	252	100.00

Source: Field Survey, July, 2014

Table 3. Age of respondents.

Age	Frequency	Percentage (%)
20-29	126	50.00
30-39	73	28.97
40-49	36	14.29
50 & above	17	6.75
Total	252	100.00

Source: Field Survey, July, 2014

Table 4. Educational background of the respondents.

Education	Frequency	Percentage (%)
SSCE	57	22.62
O' Level	12	4.76
A' level	7	2.78
Diploma	39	15.48
Degree	112	44.44
Not Applicable	25	9.92
Total	252	100.00

Source: Field Survey, July, 2014

on the level of compliance with the tax in question; it was observed that about 90% of the respondents are literates and only about 10% have not had formal education. The details are shown in Table 4.

From Table 4, those respondents who possess degrees represent 44.44% followed by those with SSCE (22.62%), diplomas (15.48%), O' and A' levels (7.54%); 9.92% have no educational qualifications.

Besides the demographic characteristics discussed above, the researcher was quick to dive into the working experience of the respondents. This is partly because it was assumed that those who have worked for some time may have had some experience of paying taxes including gift tax. Interestingly, although those who have been working between 1 to 5 years dominate with 46.83%, those who have worked for more than 5 years were in the majority (Table 5).

Thus, those with work experience ranging between 1 to 5 years dominated the respondents while those with work experience of 31 years and above formed the smallest part of the population; though 1.98% did not indicate their number of working years experience.

Table 5. Years of working experience of the respondents.

Years of working experience	Frequency	Percentage (%)
1-5 yrs	118	46.83
6-10 yrs	59	23.41
11-15 yrs	27	10.71
16-20 yrs	17	6.75
21-30 yrs	19	7.54
31 & above	7	2.78
No response	5	1.98
Total	252	100.00

Source: Field Survey, July, 2014

Compliance with gift tax has been explained to the respondents as submission of returns on gifts received and receivable and paying the gift tax thereon in accordance with Section 108 of Internal Revenue Act, 2000 (Act 592 as amended). In this case a question was post as to whether the respondents have ever paid taxes. About 90% indicated that they had paid tax in the form of direct tax such as Pay As You Earn (PAYE) on employment income, as well as Indirect tax such as VAT. Out of 252 respondents, 226 responded in the affirmative (about 89.68%); 19 respondents (being 7.54%) indicated not ever having paid any tax; while 7 respondents (making up 2.78%) were not sure if they have ever paid any tax (Table 6).

Narrowing further to gift tax, the researcher attempted to find out whether the respondents have ever received gifts since if one does not receive gift, there is no likelihood of being liable to gift tax. The research revealed that while about 81% of the respondents have received gifts, 11% have not received gifts; about 4% were not sure whether they have received gifts or not, while further 4% respondents did not indicate any response as shown in Table 7.

The main sources or donors of the gifts as per the research findings were mainly from parents, children and other close relatives to business contacts as well as friends as depicted in Table 8. In some cases, the gifts were from a combination of the above mentioned sources.

The research revealed that even though a good number of the respondents received gifts, 80.95% (Table 9), being the majority, do not regularly submit returns on the gifts so received as required by the tax law.

The result indicates that 71.43% do not regularly submit returns on the gifts they do receive and only 6.75% do submit returns on gifts they receive. However 21.83% were not sure whether they do submit returns or not on the gifts they receive as shown in Table 10. This means non-compliance in terms of non-submission of returns on gifts is very high. This indicates, in other words, that compliance is very low.

Table 6. Whether respondents have ever paid tax.

Have You ever paid tax	Frequency	Percentage (%)
No	19	7.54
Yes	226	89.68
Not Sure	7	2.78
Total	252	100.00

Source: Field Survey, July, 2014

Table 7. Whether Respondents Have Received Gifts.

Have you ever receive any gift	Frequency	Percentage (%)
No	27	**10.71**
Yes	204	**80.95**
Not Sure	11	**4.37**
No response	10	**3.97**
Total	252	100.00

Source: Field Survey, July, 2014

Table 8. Donors of Gifts Received.

Donors of gifts received	Frequency	Percentage (%)
Parents	28	9.59
Uncles / aunts	14	4.79
Brother / sister (biological)	21	7.19
Spouse	13	4.45
Children	5	1.71
Friends	77	26.37
Business contacts	16	5.48
Employer	4	1.37
Combination of more than one donor	84	28.77
No response	30	10.27
Total	292	100.00

Source: Field Survey, July, 2014

Table 9. Whether the respondents submit tax returns on gifts received.

Do you regularly submit return on taxable gifts received?	Frequency	Percentage
No	180	**71.43**
Yes	17	**6.75**
Not Sure	55	**21.83**
Total	252	100.00

Source: Field Survey, July, 2014

As a follow up to this the researcher sought to find out whether gift taxes are regularly paid on gifts that the respondents received regularly; and it came to light that only 15 respondents (making 5.95%) responded yes, 31 respondents (being 12.30%) said no, and a large number of 206 respondents (being 81.75%) were not sure as shown in Table 11. This still indicates very low compliance in terms of payment of gift tax.

In an attempt to find out the reasons for the non-compliance among the respondents, the respondents

Table 10. Whether respondents pay gifts tax on gifts received regularly.

Have you ever paid tax on taxable gifts received	Frequency	Percentage (%)
No	31	**12.30**
Yes	15	**5.95**
Not Sure	206	**81.75**
Total	252	100.00

Source: Field Survey, July, 2014

Table 11. Why respondents do not pay gift tax on gifts received.

Why not pay tax on taxable gifts received?	Frequency	Percentage (%)
Not aware of gift tax	179	**71.03**
Just do not want to pay	23	**9.13**
Commissioner has never asked for it	20	**7.94**
Have never receive gifts	9	**3.57**
Value of gift below threshold amount	21	**8.33**
Total	252	100.00

Source: Field Survey, July, 2014.

Table 12. Awareness of the Tax Laws Requirement for the Submission of Gift Tax Return on Gifts Received Within 30 Days after Receipt of the Gift.

Are you aware of the gift tax?	Frequency	Percentage (%)
No	186	73.81
Yes	31	12.30
Not Sure	23	9.13
No response	12	4.76
Total	252	100.00

Source: Field Survey, July, 2014

were asked to indicate the reasons why they were not paying the gift tax on the gifts they received: 71.03% indicated that they were not aware of the gift tax, 9.13% said they just did not want to pay, 8.33% indicated that the values of the gifts they received were below the threshold amount, 7.94% pointed out the Commissioner General of the Ghana Revenue Authority in charge of the Collection and administration of the tax has never asked for it, while 3.57% revealed that they had never received gifts.

Following the responses above, the research put across a follow up question as to whether the respondents were aware of the requirement of the tax law for the submission of return on gifts received or receivable within 30 days of receipt. The results were as depicted in Table 12. About 74% claimed they were not aware of the requirement; 12% indicated their awareness; 9% were not too sure if they were aware; and about 5% did not give a response. This revealed a very high level of unawareness of the gift tax requirement and hence the high level of non-compliance in terms of submission and non-payment.

Besides the low level of compliance, it was surprising and more confusing to find out at this point that the respondents were aware of their obligation under gift tax law, and that more than 60% of the respondents are not willing to comply as shown in Table 13.

While 34.52% of the respondents indicated their readiness to honour the gift tax henceforth, 38.49% said no, 18.25% said they are not sure while 8.73% did not give a response.

Regression results of determinants of gift tax compliance

The result of the factors influencing gift tax compliance by formal sector employees in Kumasi Metropolis is presented in Table 14. Out of the 10 variables 4 of them have significant relationship with gift tax compliance.

Table 13. Whether respondents will pay the gift tax any time they receive a taxable gift henceforth.

Are willing to pay gift tax	Frequency	Percentage (%)
No	97	**38.49**
Yes	87	**34.52**
Not Sure	46	**18.25**
No response	22	**8.73**
Total	252	100.00

Table 14. Probit estimates for determinants of gift tax compliance.

Variables	Coefficient	t-statistic	Marginal Effect
Age of the respondents (AgeR)	0.006	1.264	0.002
How low respondents have been in business (AgeB)	0.036	0.782	0.014
Number of years spent in formal school(Edu)	0.057***	5.000	0.022
Does the respondent belong to any association (Asso)	0.055	1.155	0.017
Knowledge of tax laws (KnoTaxL)	0.289**	2.210	0.050
gender of the business operator(Gender)	0.278	1.408	0.073
awareness of offences and penalties(Aware)	1.587***	5.843	0.396
Perception of filling procedures (Perp)	0.488***	3.492	0.052
Size of the business(Size)	0.099	0.807	-0.038
Distance to the nearest tax office in kilometres(Dist)	-0.055	-0.453	-0.022
Constant	0.671	0.624	-

Note: *** indicates the variable is statistically significant at 99% confidence level, ** indicates the variable is statistically significant at 95% confidence level, and * indicates the variable is statistically significant at 90% confidence level. Log likelihood = -344.01797; Number of obs = 238; LR chi2(10) = 103.46; Prob > chi2 = 0.0000; Pseudo R2 = 0.1307.

Number of years spent in formal school has positive and significant relationship with gift tax compliance.

This implies that respondents who attained higher level of formal education are more likely to comply with gift tax Act as compared to those with low level of formal education. The reason for this observation might be the fact that with higher level of formal education the respondents can read and write and understand the implication of non compliance with the law. The marginal effect revealed that additional year spent in formal schools would increase the likelihood of compliance by 2%.

Respondent's knowledge of tax laws has positive and significant relationship with compliance. Individuals who have knowledge about the law are more likely to comply with the gift tax law as compared to their counterparts who do not have knowledge about the law.

Similarly, respondents who are aware of the penalty for non compliance are more likely to comply. This may be attributed to the fact that those with knowledge of the tax law and or have idea about the penalty for non compliance may be able to assess the risk of being caught for non compliance and consequent cost they have to incur. This may influence their decision to comply. Based on the marginal effect those with knowledge about the law are 5% more likely to comply compared with those who do not have knowledge about the law. Whilst those who are aware of the penalty are 39% more likely to comply with the law compared to their counterparts who are not aware of the penalty for non compliance.

Perception of procedures of filling of gift tax returns has positive and significant relationship with respondents' decision to comply with the law. The respondents may assess the cost of complying with the law, not only tangible cost but also intangible cost. Regarding gift tax return filing procedures, once they perceive it as cumbersome or time consuming they are likely to shy away from complying with the law as it may increase their cost of compliance.

CONCLUSION AND RECOMMENDATIONS

This study revealed that, although the taxation of gifts is provided for in the tax laws of Ghana specifically Internal Revenue Act, 2000 (Act 592 as amended), making compliance both statutory and civic obligations, the level of non-compliance is very high among the Ghanaian taxpayers. Some of the reasons identified by the study for the low level of compliance with gift tax among Ghanaian taxpayers are: unawareness of gift tax obligations, those taxpayers who are aware do not feel obliged to pay; the non-enforcement by the tax officials; some taxpayers simply never receive taxable gifts; or the value of the gift is not above the exempt threshold. It was obvious from the study that the low level of education provided on the gifts tax by the tax officials and non-enforcement on their part coupled with the unwillingness by the taxpayers to voluntarily comply largely account for the very low level of compliance with gift tax among taxpayers in Ghana, specifically in the Kumasi metropolis. The above findings are very striking as Ghana, like all other developing countries, needs to exploit taxation as a means of sourcing revenue to finance developmental programmes and activities, as donor funds and grants are not forthcoming due to the economic challenges facing various nations after the financial meltdown in the west.

From the foregoing, it is therefore recommended that the Domestic Tax Revenue Division of the Ghana Revenue Authority intensifies tax education especially on the gifts tax obligations immediately, and puts in place measures to enforce such obligations.

Conflict of Interests

The authors have not declared any conflict of interests.

REFERENCES

Abdul-Razak A, Adafula CJ (2013). Evaluating taxpayers' attitudes and its influence on tax compliance decisions in Tamale, Ghana. J Account. Tax., 5(3) : 48-57.

Akhand MZH (2012). Coercion or Persuasion? Making Large Corporations Tax Compliant in Bangladesh. International Development Department School of Government and Society University of Birmingham.

Alabede JO (2014). An Exploratory Analysis of Individual Taxpayers' Compliance Behaviour in Nigeria: a Study of Demographic Differences and Impact. Int. J Account. Tax. 2(2): 39-64.

Andreoni J, Erard B, Feinstein J (1998). Tax Compliance. J Econ. Lit. 36(2):818-860.

Baba SA, Asante S (2012). Sanctions: Panacea for Income Tax Non-Compliance Among Ghanaian Self-Employed? Eur. J. Bus. Manage. 4:7.

Brautigam D (2008). Introduction: Taxation and State-Building in Developing Countries. In Brautigam D, Fjeldstad OH, Moore M (Eds), Taxation and State-Building in Developing Countries: Capacity and Consent, Cambridge University Press, Cambridge, pp. 1-33.

Bruce-Twum E (2014). Gift Tax Compliance in Ghana, an Empirical Study. J. Finan. Account., 2(1):1-7. Science and Education Publishing. [Online] Available: Website: http://www.pubs.sciepub.com/jfa/2/1/1 (July, 16, 2014).

Dressler J (2002). *Encyclopaedia of crime and justice.* Michigan: MacMillan.

Evans C, Lignier P, Tran-Nam B (2013). Tax Compliance Costs for the Small and Medium Enterprise Business Sector: Recent Evidence from Australia. TARC, School of Taxation and Business Law, University of New South Wales, Australia (*Discussion Paper*).

Ghana Statistical Service (2012). 2010 Population & Housing Census Summary Report of Final Results. Accra, Ghana Statistical Service.

Gatsi JG, Acquah SI (2010). Information Asymmetry and Gift Tax in Ghana. Social Science Research Network.

Jenkins GP, Forlemu EN (1993). Enhancing Voluntary Compliance by reducing compliance costs: A taxpayer Service Approach.

Martina H, Silvia R, Eric K, Alfred S, (2008). Procedural Fairness and Tax Compliance. Economic Analysis. Tax Policy, 38(1).

McKerchar M, Evans C (2009). Sustaining Growth in Developing Economies through Improved Taxpayer Compliance: Challenges for Policy Makers and Revenue Authorities. eJournal of Tax Research December 2014, 7(2): 171-201.

Moss T, Majerowicz S (2012). No Longer Poor: Ghana's New Income Status and Implications of Graduation from IDA. CGD Working Paper 300. Washington, D.C.: Center for Global Development. [Online] Available: http://www.cgdev.org/content/publications/detail/1426321.

Myles G, Hashimzade N, Rablen MD, Page F (2013). The Use of Agent-Based Modelling to Investigate Tax Compliance. Tax Administration Research Centre (Discussion Paper: 004-13).

Nakyea AA (2008). Taxation in Ghana, Principles, Practice & Planning, 2nd Edition, Accra, Black Mask Ltd.

OECD (2014). Development Aid at a Glance Statistics by Region 2. Africa 2014 Edition.

Onu D, Oats L (2014). Social Norms and Tax Compliance. Tax Administration Research Centre (Discussion Paper: 006-14).

Sally MJ (1999). Principles of Taxation for Business and Investment Planning. (1999 Edition), New York, Irwin / McGraw-Hill

Terkper S (2003). Managing small and medium-size taxpayers in developing economies. Tax notes international, 211-234.

Tusubira FN, Nkote IN (2013). Income Tax Compliance among SMEs in Uganda: Taxpayers' Proficiencies Perspective. Int. J Bus. Soc. Sci., 4(11) 113-143.

Toumi M (2007). Persuasive communications: tax compliance enforcement strategies for sole proprietors. *Contemporary Accounting Research,* 24(1): 171-94.

Jackson B, Milliron V (1986). 'Tax Compliance Research: Findings, Problems, and Prospects' J. Account. Liter. 5:125-165

LEGISLATION

Internal Revenue Act 2000 (Act 592 as Amended).
Internal Revenue Regulations 2001 (LI1675 as Amended).
Internal Revenue (Amendment) Act, 2002 (Act 622).
Internal Revenue (Amendment) Act, 2003 (Act 644).

25

An empirical analysis of taxpayers' fairness preferences from Canada's Taxpayer Bill of rights

Jonathan Farrar

Ryerson University, Canada.

Many countries have adopted a taxpayer charter or equivalent, which governs the relationship between taxpayers and tax authorities. However, little is known about the extent to which these charters are constructed in accordance with widely accepted fairness dimensions, as well as the relative importance of taxpayer charter rights within each fairness dimension. This research investigates the Canadian taxpayer charter (the Taxpayer Bill of Rights) using a trio of fairness dimensions that are known to influence tax compliance and the tax assessment process: procedural fairness, interpersonal fairness, and informational fairness. Rights classified as interpersonal or informational fairness were significantly underweight relative to procedural fairness. Furthermore, taxpayers rated data privacy, tax authority's accountability, and comprehensive communication of information as the most important aspects of their service relationship with the tax authority. Implications for tax policy makers and tax researchers are discussed.

Key words: Fairness, tax compliance, charter.

INTRODUCTION

Taxpayer charters summarize taxpayers' rights and obligations pertaining to their tax affairs and dealings with tax authorities. The Organisation for Economic Co-operation and Development (OECD), which is an international economic organization with a focus on the role and importance of tax policies, and informal world tax authority, has suggested that tax authorities issue a taxpayers' charter, and that a taxpayers' charter should cover basic taxpayers' rights and obligations (OECD, 1990). The United Kingdom was the first to adopt a taxpayers' charter, in 1986. A number of countries have subsequently adopted taxpayer charters, including Australia, Canada, France, India, Italy, Ireland, New Zealand, South Africa, Pakistan, the Philippines, Russia, Spain, Uganda, and the United States (CIOT, 2008).

Taxpayer charters, or equivalents, such as a Taxpayer Bill of Rights, may improve taxpayers' trust and confidence in tax authorities, which in turn may improve tax morale, and subsequently tax compliance. A taxpayer charter symbolizes the partnership between taxpayers and tax authorities, which helps to address the unequal balance of power between these parties, and may instil trust in taxpayers (Unger, 2014). There is also a wide literature on the association between fairness and compliance (Verboon and Goslinga, 2009), which supports the premise that taxpayers who perceive a tax authority to be fair are more likely to be compliant. A taxpayer charter is a way for a tax authority to establish fairness in its dealings with taxpayers, and as such, may be one way for tax authorities to improve compliance through fairness. Alm and Torgler (2011) contend that a "full house" of compliance strategies is needed to combat tax evasion, which includes deterrence activities such as audits and penalties, but also a more service-oriented administrative focus, which includes fairness-based approaches.

Although tax research has examined the historical development of the content of some taxpayer charters (Doern, 1993; McLennan, 2003), the suitability of taxpayer charters as a dispute resolution mechanism (Mookhey, 2013), the legal status of taxpayer charters (Dawe, 2014), and a comparative analysis of different countries' charters (Unger, 2014), there is a dearth of theoretically based empirical research regarding the propriety of the contents of taxpayer charters. The purpose of this research is twofold. First, it will analyze the contents of the taxpayer charter in Canada – the Taxpayer Bill of Rights – using Colquitt's (2001) theoretical fairness framework, which encompasses procedural fairness, interpersonal fairness, and informational fairness, to determine the extent to which different aspects of fairness are present in the taxpayer charter. Second, it will identify taxpayer's preferences for the contents in this charter according to each fairness dimension. By recognizing which aspects of each dimension of fairness are most important to taxpayers, tax authorities may be able to refine their compliance strategies, and tax researchers may be able to focus their research on previously unexplored aspects of fairness and compliance. Canada was chosen, as its taxpayer charter has received minimal attention in the tax literature (Li, 1998), and its charter has undergone several major revisions, making it a timely case study.

The Canadian Taxpayer Bill of Rights contains sixteen items. These items were classified as procedural fairness, interpersonal fairness, and informational fairness (Colquitt, 2001). The item classification was validated by an expert panel. A survey was administered to a sample of 606 Canadian taxpayers, who ranked each right according to order of importance for each fairness category. Statistical analysis was then performed on the ranked data. Results indicated that items comprising interpersonal fairness and informational fairness were decidedly underweight relative to procedural fairness. The most important procedural fairness item was, *The right to privacy and confidentiality*, whereas the most important informational fairness right was, *The right to complete, accurate, clear, and timely information*. No interpersonal fairness items were significantly preferred over each other.

The remainder of this paper is structured as follows. In the next section, Colquitt's (2001) framework is presented, along with empirical evidence on the association between each fairness dimension and compliance. Next is a brief overview of the Canadian Taxpayer Bill of Rights, followed by the research methodology and results. The paper concludes with a discussion of the implications for tax researchers and tax authorities.

Tax fairness and tax compliance

Fairness is a judgment arising from actual or imagined comparisons involving oneself or oneself and others. Fairness was initially conceptualized as distributive fairness, which is concerned with outcome allocations. Later, the conceptual understanding of fairness was broadened to include procedural fairness, which is the fairness of procedures that lead to decision outcomes, and interactional fairness, which is concerned with the quality of the treatment individuals receive when procedures are enacted. Subsequently, interactional fairness was split into two distinct elements: interpersonal fairness and informational fairness. Interpersonal fairness refers to sensitivity and respectful treatment shown during decision processes, whereas informational fairness refers to the adequacy of explanations given during decision processes. The fairness literature thus recognizes these four distinct but related categories of fairness: distributive, procedural, interpersonal, and informational (Colquitt, 2001).

These four factors are generalizable to contexts where authority figures make decisions that impact one or more members of a collective (Colquitt et al., 2005). Therefore, applying this framework to the tax context is appropriate, since in the tax context tax authorities make decisions that impact individual taxpayers (a collective). The focus of this paper is on procedural, interpersonal, and informational fairness, since this trio encompasses the fairness of the tax assessment process, which is informally governed by taxpayer charters. In the tax context, procedural fairness is concerned with administrative protocol leading to taxpayer outcomes (Wenzel, 2002); interpersonal fairness refers to the relational aspects of the tax authority-taxpayer relationship; and informational fairness refers to the adequacy of explanations given to taxpayers by tax authorities (Wenzel, 2006). Situations involving an interaction between taxpayers and a tax authority, such as a taxpayer inquiry, or a taxpayer-tax authority dispute, will have all three dimensions of fairness present concurrently, since the tax authority has procedures to follow, the taxpayer will have a relational encounter with a tax authority through a tax agent or other channel, and the tax authority will provide some degree of explanation during the encounter. What remains to be discovered is the degree to which taxpayer charters comprise each of these three dimensions of fairness, and within each dimension, which taxpayer rights are most important to taxpayers, and therefore might be most relevant for compliance.

There is a significant body of literature that documents a significant and positive association between each of procedural fairness, interpersonal fairness, and informational fairness, on tax compliance (Farrar et al., 2015). However, only a few studies are able to provide insights into the nuances of each type of fairness, and how these nuances influence tax compliance. Regarding procedural fairness, Worsham (1996) investigated accuracy and consistency of tax procedures on tax compliance, and Hogan et al. (2013) investigated the effect of taxpayer voice on tax compliance. Wenzel and Taylor (2004), Wenzel (2006), and Doyle et al. (2009) investigated the respectful tone of tax authority letters, and the information quality of tax authority letters. Van Dijke and Verboon (2010) investigated how the clarity of explanation impacted tax compliance. By classifying taxpayer charters according to each dimension of fairness, and subsequently identifying the items that are most relevant to taxpayers, tax researchers may be able to identify additional nuances of fairness that are likely to impact compliance, which tax researchers could further investigate, thereby extending the tax fairness-tax compliance literature. There are also tax policy implications arising from this classification and ranking, since by knowing which aspects of each type of fairness are most important to taxpayers, tax authorities can better focus their service delivery strategies to ensure the needs of taxpayers are met, which may in turn improve compliance.

OVERVIEW OF CANADA'S TAXPAYER BILL OF RIGHTS

The genesis of the Canadian Taxpayer Bill of Rights began in 1984, when a task force issued a report with 76 recommendations as to how Canada's tax authority (the Canada Revenue Agency; CRA) could improve service to taxpayers. The following year, a *Declaration of Taxpayer Rights* was issued, containing eight rights taxpayers had in their dealings with the CRA (Li 1998). It was not until 2007 that an official Taxpayer Bill of Rights was introduced in Canada, which contained fifteen rights. Also in 2007, the Office of the Taxpayers' Ombudsman was created, with a mandate to uphold the rights in the Taxpayer Bill of Rights, and assist taxpayers who have grievances about their dealings with the CRA. A sixteenth right was included in 2013 (CRA 2013).

RESEARCH METHODOLOGY

The research method consists of three steps. First, the sixteen rights were classified according to whether each was related to procedural fairness, interpersonal fairness, or informational fairness. This classification was validated with an expert panel of tax academics and tax practitioners. Second, a survey was administered to a large sample of taxpayers, in which they ranked each right in order of importance, across each dimension of fairness. Third, statistical analysis was performed on the data to determine if and where there were significant differences in preferences for each right within each dimension of fairness.

Step 1: Classification of rights

All sixteen rights were classified according to whether each was related to procedural fairness, interpersonal fairness, and informational fairness. This classification is contained in Table 1. Each are listed in the order in which they appear in the Taxpayer Bill of Rights, and are labelled as 'PRO' (procedural fairness), 'INT' (interpersonal fairness), or 'INF' (informational fairness).
In most cases, the wording of each right was clear and unambiguous. For example, a clearly worded right is, *You have the right to have the law applied consistently*. Consistency was the only focus of this particular right. Other rights were somewhat ambiguous, since they contained elements that could have spanned multiple fairness dimensions. For example, an ambiguous right is, *You have the right to complete, accurate, clear, and timely information*. The notion of timeliness could be procedural, since a delay in the execution of a procedure could relate to procedural fairness, or it could relate to the adequacy of explanations (informational fairness). Since the overall context of this right was about the provision of information to taxpayers, it was classified as relating to informational fairness.

Three of the rights had similar language, but each captured a different dimension of fairness. The right, *You have the right to a formal review and subsequent appeal*, relates to a tax procedure. The right, *You have the right to lodge a service complaint and request a formal review without fear of reprisal*, relates to interpersonal treatment following the procedure. The right, *You have the right to lodge a service complaint and to be provided with an explanation of our findings*, relates to informational fairness. No other right used language that had cross-similarities.

The expert panel consisted of four tax academics and two tax practitioners. Members of the panel were given the definitions for each dimension of fairness, and were asked for input on the classifications, and whether they would suggest any changes. There were no changes to the initial classifications, nor did any member of the panel disagree with the underlying classification itself.[1]

[1] One member of the panel commented that the right, *You have the right to expect us to be accountable*, which was classified as relating to procedural fairness, could be an item relating to informational fairness, since by providing information to taxpayers, a tax authority is being accountable. Nevertheless, informational fairness in the tax context relates to the adequacy of explanations, rather than a tax authority's willingness to make an explanation, which is more of a procedural concern. By providing an explanation, regardless of its adequacy, the tax authority is being accountable. Therefore,

Step 2: Administration of survey

Participants were Canadian taxpayers recruited from a consumer research firm that has a database of 200,000 Canadians. To be representative of a typical taxpayer population, participants were randomly selected using two parameters: gender and age. The sample was restricted to taxpayers between the ages of 25 to 80, and was evenly distributed across age groups and gender. 637 respondents completed the survey, at which point the data collection was terminated. Of these, 31 contained missing data and were deleted, leaving 606 usable responses.

Potential participants received an email invitation from the firm to participate in a questionnaire about income taxes. Individuals willing to complete the survey clicked on a web link, and were directed to the survey. Respondents had a unique user ID and password provided by the firm, which ensured that they could not respond to a survey more than once. Participants were incentivized using a point system specific to the firm.

Participants read an introductory screen, which provided a brief overview of the Taxpayer Bill of Rights. They were told that on the following three screens, they would see these rights listed, and would be asked to rank them in order of their importance. To minimize order effects, i.e., the tendency for respondents to rank the first item in the list as the most important, etc., the lists of rights were randomly ordered for each participant. Demographic information was collected at the end of the survey, and included gender, age, income, education, tax preparer, whether the respondent had ever had an unpleasant encounter with the tax authority, and whether the respondent had ever had a tax dispute with the tax authority. Demographic data are reported in Table 2.[2]

Step 3: Statistical Analysis

To perform statistical analysis on the sample, statistical tests were conducted to determine if there were any significant differences in the rankings within each fairness dimension. Then, if a test result was significant, further post-hoc statistical tests were conducted to understand and isolate where the significant differences in rankings occurred within each dimension.

Testing for overall differences in the rankings within each fairness category

The first test requires testing for significant differences in the rankings for each fairness dimension. The Friedman test was used, which is appropriate for testing differences in ranked data between conditions when there are more than two conditions and the same participants have been used in all conditions (Field, 2009). Since one fairness category (interpersonal fairness) had two conditions, the Friedman test cannot be used. In this instance, the binomial test is appropriate (Field, 2009). A significant test result indicates that there are significant differences in rankings of the rights within a fairness category, but it cannot identify where the differences occur.

Results are as follows. For the ten rights pertaining to procedural fairness, the test result was significant (χ^2 = 786.69, $p<0.001$), which indicates that there were significant differences in terms of how these 10 rights were ranked. For the two rights pertaining to interpersonal fairness, the test result was not significant ($P_{binomial}=0.49$), which indicates respondents did not prefer one right over another. For the four rights pertaining to informational fairness, the test result was significant (χ^2 = 450.65, $p<0.001$), which also indicates that there were significant differences in terms of how these four rights were ranked. Thus, there were significant differences in rankings within the procedural fairness and informational fairness dimensions. Subsequent statistical analysis can isolate which rights are ranked significantly different from each other, within each of these two categories.

Understanding the differences in rankings within each fairness category

Since there were two significant test results, it is necessary to do further statistical analysis to determine which rights were ranked significantly different from each other. The Wilcoxon signed-rank test (Field, 2009) is appropriate for this purpose. One-tailed tests are used, since the test is whether one mean is higher than another. A Bonferroni correction is applied to the significance level, according to the number of pairwise comparisons (Field, 2009).

Within procedural fairness and informational fairness, the rights were ranked according to their mean rank, in order of preference, beginning with the most preferred right. Wilcoxon signed-rank tests were performed on each pair of rights to determine if the order of preferences differed significantly. Table 3a reports the results for the rights classified as procedural fairness, and Table 3b reports the results for the rights classified as informational fairness. Each table shows the rights ranked in order of

since the notion of accountability is broader than just the adequacy of an explanation, it was retained as relating to procedural fairness.

[2] According to the most recent Canadian income statistics published by Statistics Canada (http://www.statcan.gc.ca/tables-tableaux/sum-som/l01/cst01/famil105a-eng.htm), the sample was similarly weighted to that of the Canadian population with respect to income, except that the income category below $25,000 was underweight (by about 15%), and the income categories above $50,000 and $75,000 were overweight by 6% and 4%, respectively. Furthermore, 8.4% of the sample chose not to disclose their income, which may have been the lowest income respondents. Although the sample might be slightly less representative of the lowest income Canadians, given that the population of the income category below $25,000 is the one least likely to pay tax, the sample is likely to be representative of the broader population of Canadian taxpayers. The median age of the sample was 51, which compares favorably with the median age in Canada in the 25 to 80 age group (http://www.statcan.gc.ca/pub/91-215-x/2012000/part-partie2-eng.htm).

Table 1. Classification of taxpayer rights by category of fairness.

Taxpayer Bill of Rights		
Procedural fairness	**Interpersonal fairness**	**Informational fairness**
PRO1. You have the right to receive entitlements and to pay no more and no less than what is required by law. PRO2. You have the right to service in both official languages. PRO3. You have the right to privacy and confidentiality. PRO4. You have the right to a formal review and subsequent appeal. PRO5. You have the right, unless otherwise provided by law, not to pay income tax amounts in dispute before you have had an impartial review. PRO6. You have the right to have the law applied consistently. PRO7. You have the right to have the costs of compliance taken into account when administering tax legislation. PRO8. You have the right to expect us to be accountable. PRO9. You have the right to relief from penalties and interest under tax legislation because of extraordinary circumstances. PRO10. You have the right to be represented by a person of your choice.	INT1. You have the right to be treated professionally, courteously, and fairly. INT2. You have the right to lodge a service complaint and request a formal review without fear of reprisal.	INF1. You have the right to complete, accurate, clear, and timely information. INF2. You have the right to lodge a service complaint and to be provided with an explanation of our findings. INF3. You have the right to expect us to publish our standards and report annually. INF4. You have the right to expect us to warn you about questionable tax schemes in a timely manner.

preference, beginning with the most preferred right, the mean rank of each right, and the results of the Wilcoxon signed-rank test.

Results are as follows. Of the ten procedural fairness rights, the most preferred right was PRO3, *You have the right to privacy and confidentiality*, with a mean rank of 4.09 out of 10, followed by PRO8, *You have the right to expect us to be accountable*, with a mean rank of 4.28 out of 10. Although these two rights were not ranked significantly different from each other (Z=-1.208, p=0.114), the rank scores of PRO8 and the next-highest ranked right (PRO1; mean score of 4.90 out of 10) were significantly different (Z=-3.881, p<0.001), which indicates that the two highest-ranked rights were significantly more preferred than any other procedural right.

There were no other significant differences in mean rank scores, except for the two least-preferred rights, PRO10, *You have the right to be represented by a person of your choice*, with a mean rank of 6.34 out of 10, and PRO2, *You have the right to service in both official languages*, with a mean rank of 8.16 out of 10. PRO10 was significantly different than the right ranked next in highest importance to it, PRO7 (Z=-3.167, p=0.001), and PRO2 was ranked significantly different than PRO10 (Z=-10.987, p<0.001). Thus, respondents made a significant distinction between their two least-preferred procedural fairness rights, and also made a significant distinction between their two least-preferred procedural fairness rights and all other procedural fairness rights. Respondents did not make a significantly different distinction in preference rankings amongst the remaining six procedural fairness rights.

Of the four rights associated with informational fairness, there was a clear distinction in preferences for each right, since all of the statistical test scores were statistically significant. The most preferred right was INF1, *You have the right to complete, accurate, clear, and timely information* (mean rank of 1.78 out of 4), followed by INF2, *You have the right to lodge a service complaint and to be provided with an explanation of our findings* (mean rank 2.28 out of 4), followed by INF4, *You have the right to expect us to warn you about questionable tax schemes in a timely manner* (mean rank 2.63 out of 4), and finally the least-preferred right, INF3, *You have the right to expect us to publish our service standards and report annually* (mean rank 3.31 out of 4).

Sensitivity analysis

Although not tabulated, sensitivity analysis was conducted on each mean rank score. Differences in rank scores across dichotomous demographic variables (gender, whether the respondent had ever had an unpleasant encounter with the tax authority, and whether the respondent had ever had a tax dispute with the tax authority) were analyzed using two-tailed Mann-Whitney tests (Field, 2009). Although there were a few significant differences in rank score by gender and whether the respondent had ever had a tax dispute, the overall rankings of preferences within fairness dimensions did not change, nor their statistical significance relative to each other. Consequently, respondents' gender, having had an unpleasant encounter with the tax authority, and having had a tax dispute with the tax authority do not appear to influence overall preferences for taxpayer rights.

Differences in ranked scores across demographic

Table 2. Demographic profile statistics.

Sample size	**n = 606**
Gender	
male	n = 304 (50.2%)
female	n = 302 (49.8%)
age	mean = 50.3 years
	std dev = 15.1 years
Income:	
less than $25,000	n=145 (23.9%)
between $25,000 and $50,000	n=163 (26.9%)
between $50,001 and $75,000	n=125 (20.7%)
between $75,001 and $100,000	n=71 (11.7%)
greater than $100,000	n=51 (8.4%)
prefer not to answer	n=51 (8.4%)
Highest level of education completed	
high school	n = 150 (24.8%)
community college	n = 176 (29.0%)
undergraduate degree	n = 141 (23.2%)
graduate degree	n = 115 (19.0%)
other	n = 24 (4.0%)
Tax preparer	
Taxpayer	n = 312 (51.5%)
Taxpayer's spouse/partner	n = 46 (7.6%)
Paid preparer	n = 195 (32.2%)
Other	n = 53 (8.7%)
Had an unpleasant encounter with CRA	
yes	n = 116 (19.1%)
no	n = 490 (80.9%)
Had a tax dispute with CRA	
yes	n = 139 (22.9%)
no	n = 467 (77.1%)

Table 3a. Rank order preferences for procedural fairness rights.

Right, ranked by order of preference*		**Mean rank score (out of 10)**	**Pairwise comparisons**	**Statistical Analysis**	
				Wilcoxon signed-rank test score	**Significance (one-tailed)**
1	PRO3	4.09	PRO3 – PRO8	-1.208	0.114
2	PRO8	4.28	PRO8 – PRO1	-3.881	<0.001 ♦
3	PRO1	4.90	PRO1 – PRO6	-1.829	0.033
4	PRO6	5.15	PRO6 – PRO5	-1.055	0.146
5	PRO5	5.34	PRO5 – PRO9	-0.564	0.287
6	PRO9	5.42	PRO9 – PRO4	-0.368	0.357
7	PRO4	5.48	PRO4 – PRO7	-2.287	0.011
8	PRO7	5.84	PRO7 – PRO10	-3.167	0.001 ♦
9	PRO10	6.34	PRO10 – PRO2	-10.987	<0.001 ♦
10	PRO2	8.16	♦ statistically significant		

* from most preferred to least preferred, where 1=most preferred and 10=least preferred. ♦ 0.0056 is the critical level of significance with Bonferroni correction (i.e., 0.05/9, for 9 pairwise comparisons).

Table 3b. Rank order preferences for informational fairness rights.

Right, ranked by order of preference*		Mean rank score (out of 4)	Pairwise comparisons	Statistical Analysis	
				Wilcoxon signed-rank test score	Significance (one-tailed)
1	INF1	1.78	INF1 – INF2	-7.612	<0.001 ♦
2	INF2	2.28	INF2 – INF4	-5.193	<0.001 ♦
3	INF4	2.63	INF4 – INF3	-9.797	<0.001 ♦
4	INF3	3.31	♦ statistically significant		

* from most preferred to least preferred, where 1=most preferred and 4=least preferred. ♦ 0.016 is the critical level of significance with Bonferroni correction (i.e., 0.05/3, for 3 pairwise comparisons).

variables with more than two conditions (education, income, tax preparer) were analyzed using Kruskal-Wallis tests (Field, 2009). Although there were a few significant differences for income and tax preparer, the overall rankings of preferences within fairness dimensions did not change, nor their statistical significance relative to each other. Consequently, respondents' education, income, and choice of tax preparer do not appear to influence overall preferences for taxpayer rights.

The sensitivity analysis suggests that the overall preference rankings within fairness categories appear to be robust, even after considering the influence of demographic variables.

IMPLICATIONS AND CONCLUSION

Although it is not publicly documented how the contents of the Taxpayer Bill of Rights were chosen, it is unlikely that a theoretically based fairness framework was explicitly or implicitly considered. Given the importance of fairness to taxpayers' compliance, it is useful to consider rights under a taxpayer charter with respect to fairness. One broad finding that emerges from this study is the unequal distribution of rights according to dimensions of fairness, since ten of the sixteen rights were related to procedural fairness, four were related to informational fairness, and only two were related to interpersonal fairness. The emphasis on procedural fairness may not be misplaced, since there are likely to be more nuances with respect to administrative procedures rather than how information is conveyed to taxpayers, or with respect to the relational aspects of the taxpayer-tax authority encounter. Nevertheless, it is likely that the interpersonal and informational aspects of the taxpayer-tax authority relationship deserve greater emphasis, especially given the empirical findings with respect to their positive impact on tax compliance. Thus, these results suggest that policy makers should give greater consideration to interpersonal and informational fairness when crafting or revising taxpayer charters. Future research could also consider the extent to which other countries' taxpayer charters have an unequal distribution of fairness dimensions.

While academic research has suggested revisions to existing taxpayer charters (Unger, 2014), and while professional tax bodies have developed model taxpayer charters (CFE, 2014; OECD, 1990), the underlying fairness dimensions have not been explicitly considered in the construction of these charters. Given that procedural fairness, interpersonal fairness, and informational fairness occur concurrently in tax practice, tax policy makers could consider how their taxpayer charters reflect the multidimensionality of tax fairness.

Results from this study also have implications for tax authorities. Since there were two procedural fairness rights ranked significantly higher than all other procedural rights, it is possible that tax authorities should give greater attention to them, as they may be likely to influence compliance directly, or indirectly through trust. Future research could investigate these possibilities. Specifically, taxpayers' right to privacy and confidentiality was the most preferred procedural fairness right, followed by the right for the tax authority to be accountable. Pragmatically, not only could the tax authority emphasize the confidentiality of taxpayer-tax authority transactions and its accountability to taxpayers on its websites, correspondence, and other channels of communication, but where breaches of privacy or confidentiality occur, or where there is a perception that the tax authority failed to be accountable, it may be especially important for tax authorities to take transparent and reparative actions, as subsequent compliance may be impacted.

Results from this study also suggest that information provided by tax authorities to taxpayers is important, especially as it relates to completeness, accuracy, clarity, and timeliness. Future research could consider how these elements impact compliance concurrently, or indirectly through trust. Given the low number of interpersonal fairness rights, it may not be surprising that one right was not significantly preferred over another, but this does not mean that interpersonal fairness is not important to taxpayers. The empirical research on the association between interpersonal fairness and compliance, cited earlier, suggests otherwise. However, future research could identify other aspects of interpersonal fairness that may be relevant to taxpayers with a view to understanding which aspect(s) is(are) most valued by taxpayers.

Implications of these results for tax researchers are that issues in the most preferred procedural and informational rights could be investigated further to determine their impact on tax compliance. Specifically, tax researchers could consider how privacy or confidentiality of taxpayer information, or lack thereof, impacts compliance; how accountability of tax authorities, or lack thereof, impacts compliance; and how the quality of the information provided to taxpayers with respect to accuracy, completeness, clarity, and delay, impacts compliance.

There are several limitations to this study. First, the results are tested on taxpayers from Canada, and although there is no reason to believe they would not generalize to taxpayers from other countries, results should be applied with care. Second, given the nature of the data and the categorization framework, it was not possible to assess the relative rankings of rights from one category with the rankings of rights from another category. It may be useful to know, for example, if the lowest ranked right from one dimension is ranked higher than the highest ranked right from another dimension. Future research could examine this possibility.

In Canada, approximately 5,400 complaints are received each year in Canada by the Office of the Taxpayers' Ombudsman, and it conducts investigations on about 1,000 of these, pertaining to the Taxpayer Bill of Rights (OTO, 2013). Therefore, the rights under this taxpayers' charter are of importance. Furthermore, the Canadian tax authority is planning to cut 3,100 full-time positions by 2017-18, and in 2013 closed payment and enquiry service counters in its Tax Services Offices across Canada (Fekete, 2013; Rankin, 2014). Thus, the quality of customer service has likely suffered and will likely suffer further. There has also been a recent series of Canadian cases where taxpayers alleged negligence by tax agents (Bevacqua, 2013). Consequently, understanding key aspects of the tax authority-taxpayer service relationship should be important to tax authorities, who may be better able to channel their resources to prioritize a customer service focus on the attributes of the tax assessment process that are valued most by taxpayers, thereby improving compliance directly, or indirectly through other means, such as trust.

Globally, since tax authorities in advanced economies have been subject to significant budget cuts (OECD 2012), low-cost ways to improve compliance will only increase in importance, and taxpayer charters may be instrumental in ensuring smooth interactions between tax authorities and taxpayers. This research has highlighted several items relating to procedural fairness and informational fairness that appear especially important to taxpayers. This research also suggests that tax policy makers should give greater consideration to interpersonal fairness and informational fairness when constructing taxpayer charters, and in particular, identify other aspects of interpersonal fairness that could be incorporated into taxpayer charters.

Conflict of Interests

The author has not declared any conflict of interests.

REFERENCES

Alm J, Torgler B (2011). Do ethics matter? Tax compliance and morality. J. Bus. Ethics 101(4): 635-651.

Bevacqua J (2013). Suing Canadian tax officials for negligence: An assessment of recent developments. Can. Tax J. 61(4):893-914.

CFE (2013). A model taxpayer charter. Confederation Fiscale Européenne.

CIOT (2008). A taxpayers' charter for the United Kingdom. Chartered Institute of Taxation.

Colquitt J (2001). On the dimensionality of organizational justice: A construct validation of a measure. J. App. Psych. 86(3):386-400.

Colquitt J, Greenberg J, Scott B (2005). Organizational justice: Where do we stand? ("Handbook of organizational justice", Erlbaum Associates pp. 589-619).

CRA (2013). Taxpayer Bill of Rights Guide: Understanding your rights as a taxpayer. Retrieved 30 April 2015, from: http://www.cra-arc.gc.ca/E/pub/tg/rc17/rc17-11-13e.pdf.

Dawe R (2014). A legal duty to provide accurate information to the public? J. Parl. Pol. Law 8(1):187-208.

Doern G (1993). The UK Citizen's Charter: Origins and implementation in three agencies. Policy Politics 21(1):17-29.

Doyle E, Gallery K, Coyle M (2009). Procedural justice principles and tax compliance in Ireland: A preliminary exploration in the context of reminder letters. J. Fin. Man. Publ. Serv. 8(1):49-62.

Farrar J, Massey D, Thorne L (2015). Tax fairness and tax compliance: A literature review and tax fairness scale development study. Working paper.

Fekete J (2013). Federal government plans to slash millions, hundreds of staff from Canada Revenue Agency compliance programs. Retrieved 30 April 2015, from: http://o.canada.com/business/federal-government-plans-to-slash-millions-hundreds-of-staff-from-canada-revenue-agency-compliance-programs/

Field A (2009). "Discovering Statistics Using SPSS". (3rd Edition), Sage Publications, Thousand Oaks, California.

Hogan B, Maroney J, Rupert T (2013). The relation among voice value, policy outcomes, and intensity of support on fairness assessments of tax legislation. J. Am. Tax. Assoc. 216(4):209-217.

Li J (1998). Taxpayers' Rights in Canada. ("Taxpayers' Rights: An International Perspective", Queensland, Revenue Law Journal, School of Law, Bond University pp.89-137.

McLennan M (2003). The principles and concepts in the development of the Taxpayers' Charter. Austr. Tax Rev. 32(1):22-50.

Mookhey S (2013). Tax disputes system design. J. Tax Res. 11(1):79-96.

OECD (1990). Taxpayers' rights and obligations – practice note. OECD Committee of Fiscal Affairs Forum on Tax Administration.

OECD (2012). Working smarter in structuring the administration, in compliance, and through legislation. Forum on Tax Administration, Information note.

OTO (2013). Annual Report. Office of the Taxpayers' Ombudsman. Retrieved 30 April 2015, from: http://www.oto-boc.gc.ca/rprts/nnl/rprt1213-eng.pdf

Rankin M (2014). CRA Service Cuts. Retrieved 30 April 2015, from: http://murrayrankin.ndp.ca/changes-at-the-canada-revenue-agency.

Unger K (2014). Ethics codes and taxpayer charters: Increasing tax morale to increase tax compliance. J. Tax Res. 12(2):483-498.

Van Dijke M, Verboon P (2010). Trust in authorities as a boundary condition to procedural fairness: effects on tax compliance. J. Econ. Psych. 31(1):80-91.

Verboon P, Goslinga S (2009). The role of fairness in tax compliance. Neth. J. Psych. 65(1):136-145.

Wenzel M (2002). The impact of outcome orientation and justice concerns on tax compliance: The role of taxpayers' identity. J. App. Psych. 87(4):629-645.

Wenzel M, Taylor N (2004). An experimental evaluation of tax-reporting schedules: a case of evidence-based tax administration. J. Pub. Econ. 88(12):2785-2799.

Wenzel M (2006). A letter from the tax office: Compliance effects of informational and interpersonal justice. Soc. Just. Res. 19(3):345-364.

Worsham R (1996). The effect of tax authority behavior on taxpayer compliance: a procedural justice approach. J. Am. Tax. Assoc. 18(2):19-39.

26

Employees' compensation: Do taxes play any role? Evidence from the compensation-taxation literature

Akinloye Akindayomi[1] and Adesola Adeduro Ogunmakin [2]

[1]Accounting and Business Law, College of Business Administration, University of Texas - Pan American, 1201 W. University Drive Edinburg, TX 78539-9999, U.S.A.
[2]Department of Accounting, Faculty of Management Sciences, Ekiti State University, Nigeria.

Compensation incentive schemes are mainly driven by the need to align owner-manager interests in the real corporate world of separation of ownership and control. We find that the role of taxes and its implication for employees' compensation is, at best, evidently inconclusive in the compensation-taxation literature. Using a literature review/synthesis of the existing research approach, we begin by identifying three distinct forms of employees' compensation. Then, we examine developing and current state of extant research in order to review the role of taxation and its implication in the corporate choice, and magnitude of remuneration packages. In particular, we highlight the units of investigation in those studies, contextualize their findings, identify gaps or areas that have not been accorded much research attention, and offer suggestions for future analysis and research in this area of taxation vis-à-vis compensation packages.

Key words: Employees' compensation, taxes, incentive alignment.

INTRODUCTION

Compensation incentive schemes are mainly driven by the need to align owner-manager interests in the real corporate world of separation of ownership and control (Jensen and Meckling, 1976). While there is a long strand of research documenting positive earnings-compensation relation (Chan et. al., 2014), the role of taxes and its implications for employees' compensation (i.e. compensation-taxation relation) is, at best, evidently inconclusive in the literature. An Increasing number of research in the empirical domain integrates agency theory into the investigation of corporate tax avoidance. Their findings however are inconclusive. Even taxed-based accounting research has consistently been providing mixed evidence in the literature as to the relevance of taxation to employees' compensation. While some find taxes to play significant roles, others find no direct or demanding role or significant implication of taxation in the corporate choice or decision regarding employees' compensation (Dechow et al., 2010). Therefore, the extent firms consider taxation as an input in their choices of compensation packages remains an empirical question, especially since at a macro level, Frydman and Molloy (2011) find "...no relationship between changes in tax rates and changes in pay" and that this lack of relationship or negligible effect of taxes on compensation dates back to 1980s.

At the top management level, it is not uncommon to find some forms of compensation packages that are tied to cost reduction. In fact, Ittner et al. (1997) report that some bonus contracts reward "cost reduction". It can thus be argued that many executives may see tax expense (within a profit center) as a cost to be cut in their overall cost minimization strategy. Very recent studies such as Schmittdiel (2014) show that through compensation contracts, executives (CEOs in particular) are encouraged ("incentivized") to engage in aggressive tax planning (avoidance) activities. In fact, Schmittdiel suggests that CEO's bonuses should be tied directly to tax payments. Armstrong et al. (2012) also show that firms explicitly reward tax directors to incentivize them to "reduce the level of tax expense reported in the financial statements". This suggests that firms use compensation to reward tax aggressiveness especially as it relates to GAAP effective tax rates. However, it must be noted that such a practice could backfire as such tax aggressiveness can invite increased scrutiny from tax authorities which may cost the firm future large cash outflow (in the form of back taxes, penalties and fines) when earlier tax positions cannot be sustained upon the Internal Revenue Service (IRS) audit. Schmittdiel writes, "shareholders reward income increase that comes from tax savings more strongly than other net income increases", thereby concluding that CEOs are "incentivized" to pursue aggressive tax avoidance strategies for favorable compensation contracts. If this is true, then it extends research into the realm of reality that investors not only incentivize tax aggressiveness but also reward earnings management. Clearly more research is needed to 'legitimize' this assertion.

Researchers find that managers are less likely to manage compensations accounts for 'contracting reasons' because most compensation contracts are generally based on pretax earnings (Hanlon and Heitzman, 2010). In fact, Desai and Dharmapala (2008) report a negative relationship between equity-based compensation and book-tax difference (a proxy for tax avoidance). They also show that firms use ownership structures to minimize the effect of taxes on compensation. For example, partnership tax status in the U.S. allows preferential tax treatment on partner's carried interest compensation as this is taxed at tax-favored capital gains tax rates and not ordinary income tax rates. We must note that this relates mostly to partners in private equity firms and not employees. It should be noted that employees' compensation[1] can be cash-based, equity-based[2] or deferred. The cash-based compensation could be of many kinds which include, but not necessarily limited to, regular wages and salaries, and stock appreciation rights. On the other hand, stock-based compensation is primarily in the form of employees' stock options, which can also include performance motivated stock appreciation rights[3]. Deferred compensations are mainly in the form of pensions or pensionable benefits.

The paper proceeds as follows: the methodology is presented in the next section. In section three, each of these employees' compensation packages is discussed in sequence vis-à-vis the developing and current state of extant research reflecting on tax role and its implication in the corporate choice, and magnitude of these remunerations. Concluding comments are provided in the last section (Figure 1).

METHODOLOGY

Due to the perceived importance of taxation and its ramifications on the dynamics of employees' compensation, we provide a synopsis of a review and synthesize existing research on the compensation-taxation relation. A review of hundreds of identified papers that contextualize compensation-taxation relation was performed to examine the role (if any) that taxation plays in employee compensation. After extensive review of studies in this area, we identify studies that precisely examine corporate taxation and employee compensation (i.e. connecting compensation with taxation). The publication dates for these studies range between 1988 and 2014. The sample of the publications is tabulated below in terms of the units of investigation examined, methodologies employed, and findings obtained.

Each of the two researchers involved in the current review independently sampled and reviewed at least 100 academic publications in accounting, finance and related literatures. The articles reviewed focus on compensation-taxation relation vis-à-vis the three distinct forms of employees' compensation (cash-based, equity-based, and deferred). After extensive review, both researchers mutually agreed on the identified units of investigation in the sampled studies and then evaluate their findings which produce the basis for further analysis in our study.

Within the compensation –taxation framework, the analysis constructively categorizes the forms of employees' compensation packages into cash compensation, equity-based compensation and pension plans. Cash compensation primarily includes salaries and bonuses. Equity-based compensation focuses on stock options and the pension plans primarily examine defined benefit pension plans. The emerging issues for future academic studies are identified and discussed to advance knowledge in this important area of accounting and taxation research (Table 1).

[1] Except otherwise stated, employees' compensation is meant to include all employees (top management and CEOs inclusive). Although, the fact that stock-based compensation is commonly applied to CEOs and top management for strategic motivational/incentive reasons, middle or lower-level employees generally are seldom given such a booty especially in the form of stock appreciation rights. This is not an assertion!

[2] This categorization could be arbitrary in that stock-based compensation could be transformed into cash for employees even directly from the company in the form of stock appreciation right. Notwithstanding, a general purpose categorization could be made for intellectual curiosity.

[3] It should be noted that there is also Employee Stock Ownership Plans (ESOP). It is not considered in this discussion.

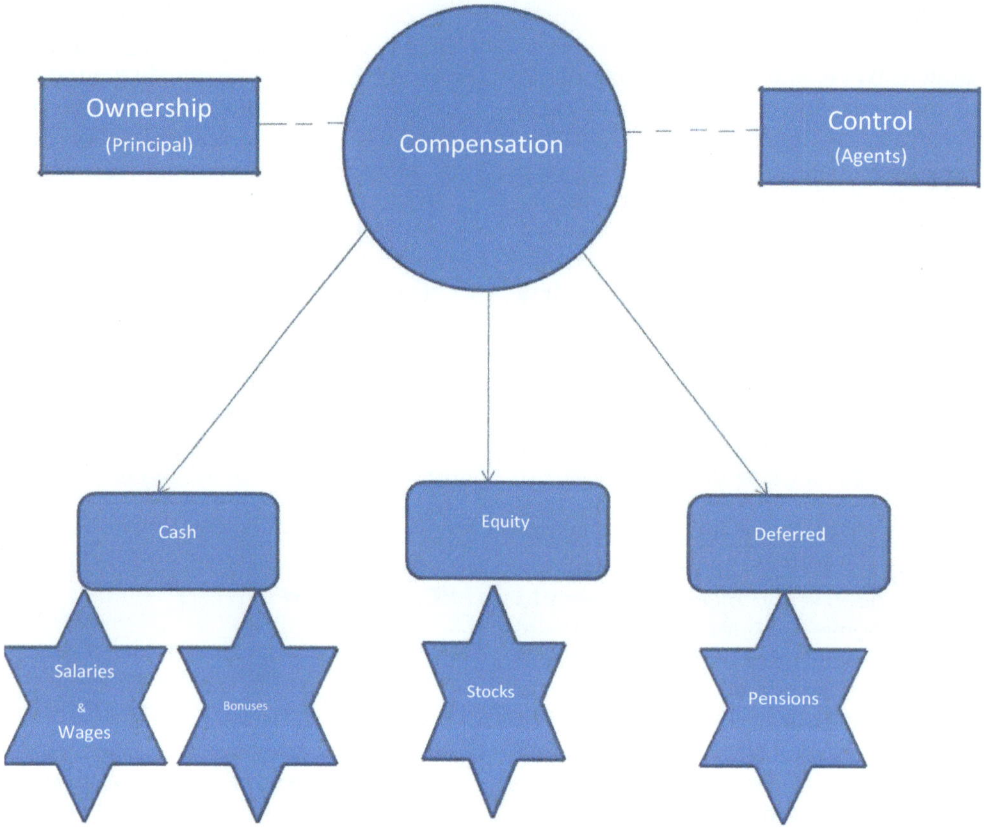

Figure 1. Separation of ownership – control. This figures shows compensation bridging the gap between ownership and control in a typical publicly traded organization in order to align the principal- agent interests.

RESULTS/DISCUSSIONS

Salaries and wages or other regular remunerations

This form of employee's compensation is not expected to have direct impact on tax related corporate decisions when it comes to employee/executive compensation. Common opinion perceives this compensation expense as a given and that corporations' commitment on meeting this obligation might be highly inflexible or involuntary. This translates to the fact that limited manipulations could be made for corporate tax-arbitrage.[4] It is therefore, not surprising that its consideration in the literature is almost nonexistent or at best passive with related studies consistently finding no or mixed results when it comes to its compensation-taxation relation. However, a study that can fit into this category is the one by Philips (2003) who investigates the effectiveness of corporate tax planning vis-à-vis the role of compensation-based incentives and firms' choice to using pre or after-tax basis for employees' compensation. He finds that "compensating business-unit managers, but not executive officers, on an after-tax basis leads to lower effective tax rates".[5]

A different but related study by Ke (2001) documents that the interconnectivity between individual tax rates and corporate tax rates (within a time period) is capable of influencing the character of managerial compensation in terms of such compensation's tax-deductibility. It is important to interpret the findings of the study in its context in that the study is based on privately held insurance companies. Therefore, the incentives for aggressive tax planning cum financial reporting strategies generally embarked upon by publicly quoted corporations are virtually nonexistent within the context of that study. Notwithstanding, the study is valuable in enhancing researchers' appreciation of the tax planning opportunities and strategies pursuable in privately held organizations. Some research questions that require further exploration include the sensitivity of compensation packages to a firm's foreign presence, leverage, and capital investment

[4] This does not mean that this form of employees' compensation is completely tax irrelevant. Usually, corporate tax arbitrage intentions might significantly impact the magnitude (and not the choice) of this form of compensation especially within the context of substitution dynamics.

[5] Without prejudice to the rigorous analysis methodologically displayed in the study, it is worthy to mention that this study is an empirical survey and so the findings need to be cautiously interpreted especially in term of its generalizability.

Table 1. Sample of prior research on compensation-taxation relation.

Year of publication	Author(s)	Compensation Type(s)	Research unit(s) of investigation**	Methodology	Findings
1988	Thomas J. K.	Defined Benefit Pension Plans.	Funding levels of DBP and the tax status of the firm.	Archival/ Empirical	Pension funding and tax status are related.
1989	Thomas J. K.	Defined Benefit Pension Plans.	The role of taxation in the termination of overfunded plans?	Archival/ Empirical	Termination of overfunded pension plans is not motivated by taxation.
1995	Yermack D.	Stock Options and Cash Compensation (Salary and Bonus).	Corporate tax status should influence mix of CEOs' compensation.	Archival/ Empirical	No support for corporate tax reduction regarding compensation mix (i.e. stock-based or salary & bonuses).
1998	Austin J.R.; Gaver J.J. and Gaver K.M.	Stock Options	Corporate marginal tax rates determine firm's choice between Incentive Stock Options and Nonqualified Options.	Archival/ Empirical	Conditional on executives holding period, tax influences the choice of stock options between Incentive Stock Options and Nonqualified Options.
2000	Klassen K. J. and A. Mawani	Stock Options and Cash Compensation (Salary and Bonus).	Effects of financial and tax reporting incentives on executive stock option grants	Archival/ Empirical	Firms trade-off financial reporting and tax incentives but that this is more pronounced in Canadian setting relative to the U.S.
2001	Bin Ke	Cash Compensation (Salary and Bonus).	Effect of taxes on managerial compensation for privately held insurers.	Archival/ Empirical	The level of compensation-taxation relation depends on the degree of management ownership in privately held companies.
2002	Frank M. M.	Defined Benefits Plan	Allocation of defined benefits plan assets between equity and bonds	Archival/ Empirical	No tax effect with respect to equity, but significant tax effects with respect to bond.
2003	Philips J.D.		Using after tax measure in compensating employees.	Survey/Empirical	Compensating business-unit managers versus CEOs on after-tax basis produces lower effective tax rates.
2003	Mawani A.	Employee Stock Options	Tax deductibility of employee stock options	Literature Review	Employee stock options are not effective tax savings compensation package, but good at aligning employee-shareholder interests. agency
2011	Frydman, C., & Molloy, R. S	Cash Compensation (Salary and Bonus).	The effect of tax policy on executive compensation.	Archival/ Empirical	There is no relationship between changes in tax rates and compensation.
2012	Armstrong, C.S., Blouin, J.L., &Larcker, DF	Cash Compensation (Salary and Bonus) as well as stock-based compensation	The relationship between tax director compensation and corporate effective tax rates (both GAAP and Cash rates).	Proprietary Data/ Archival/Empirical	Tax directors are incentivized to reduce GAAP effective tax rates.

Table 1. Contd.

2014	Schmittdiel, H.	Bonus Contracts	The effect of compensation choice on corporate tax avoidance	Archival/ Empirical	Mixed results found as there is heterogeneity in effects across industries.

**We do not suggest that the unit(s) of investigation is exclusive as some studies that we reviewed examine a variety of research questions/hypotheses. However, as long as there is a clear and concise contribution(s) to the entire study, we focus on those unit(s) of investigation that squares with the objective of our study which is to examine the role (if any) of taxation in the compensation-taxation relation.

intensity. Schmittdiel (2014) explores those but only within the realm of bonus contracts and finds mixed or inconclusive results.

Equity-based employees' compensation

Unlike the form of compensation discussed above, stock-based employees' compensation has enjoyed much (if not most) of researchers' attention in tax-based accounting research (Hanlon and Heitzman, 2010). Some of the research outputs in this area are now reviewed to understand the developing state of the debate and the prospect for future academic development in this important area of tax and accounting research.

Individuals, firms, and even non-tax sensitive institutions engage in tax avoidance strategies because of its value-creation potentials. It is, therefore, expected that firms should be willing to compensate employees using after-tax remuneration incentives. Phillips (2003) finds results consistent with this proposition, but Desai et al. (2007) show that Phillips' finding did not hold for equity-based remunerations.

Tax and non-tax factors as well as Pareto optimal considerations usually drive corporations' decisions to employ this form of compensation (Thornton, 1999; Scholes et al., 1992). Therefore, it will not be out of place to reason that corporations will want to make voluntary stock-based employees' compensation to minimize tax liability. While it is generally believed that taxes do play a significant role in the design, choice, and mechanics of stock-based compensation (Graham, 2008), the interesting conclusion regarding its (optimum) magnitude so far is inconclusive with mixed evidence in the literature as to the role or implication of taxation in this regard.

In what appears as a rather intellectual discomfort with the use of stock options as compensation for managers, Johnson (2003) believes that using stock options to compensate managers and CEOs could turn out inimical to the corporation's strategic existence and thus run contrary to shareholders' interests. For example, the author asserts "managers with significant options have an incentive to take the company into suicidal risks because option holders do not participate in the shareholders' losses" (see also Akindayomi, 2006). It can be argued (in our opinion) that while the former part of the Johnson statement could be true, the latter part is much of a stretch. This is because employees/executives with substantial wealth tied to the company (i.e. 'wealth specificity') could face considerable erosion of wealth if stock prices significantly drop over a long period of time.

Our understanding of Johnson's contention in this study is that stock options could be a bad corporate idea, not necessarily because it could not lead to minimization of corporate tax liability (i.e. it could be tax-relevant), but that their use could further precipitate agency problems as managers could selfishly engage in the pursuit of sub-optimal goal(s) which may deceptively signal corporate long-term prospects given its short-term success.[6] Similarly, compensating employees/executives with stocks instead of cash could further increase free cash flow available to managers. Jensen (1986) expresses concerns that such free cash flows are susceptible to diversion towards maximizing managers' utility at the potential huge costs to shareholders.

It can be argued that Johnson's 'dislike' for the use of stock options within a compensation package, as documented in the literature, offers vital opportunity for future empirical studies. Studies aimed at empirically documenting the relationship between corporate use of stock-based compensation and corporate failure will interestingly confirm or disconfirm Johnson's anxiety in this regard and shows if his contention is appropriately placed. This is important in that Klassen and Mawani (2000) provide statistics that stock options are increasingly becoming a significant part of executives' compensation package both in Canada and the U.S. Yermack (1995) earlier raised concerns as to the high probability that stock options are being abused by managers who engage in "managerial self-interest, or rent-seeking behavior by senior management."[7]

In what seems like contemporaneous study, Mawani

[6] There are other implications and potent inferences that could be drawn from the Johnson study. For example, he sees stock options as flamboyant accounting terminology/technology to cosmetically give deceptive financial information. He vigorously asserts that stock options are not free.

[7] Yermack's concern appears the same with Jensen's concern. However, both concerns are different if one contextualizes the possible cause of the abuse. Jensen considers free cash flows while Yermack looks at no- free cash flow contexts, but still maintains that managers can still be self-seeking. Therefore, it is not tautological to mention both.

(2003) portrays stock options in a more positive light claiming, for example, that instead of stock options widening the incentive asymmetry gap between managers and the shareholders, they can actually be used to align "the employees' interests and long-term incentives with those of shareholders" thus potentially reducing agency costs. Klassen and Mawani (2000), in their study of option grants to Canadian CEOs, examine the relationships and interrelationships between financial reporting and tax reporting incentives vis-à-vis stock-based compensation.[8] They find that there is a significant relationship between their "proxies for short-run financial reporting incentives and the observed option grants." Relatedly, they find evidence that "option granting behavior is correlated with proxies for tax incentives." The significance of their study is that both financial reporting and tax reporting incentives impact the option granting behaviors of corporations. This finding is not that surprising in that given Canadian institutional tax context regarding option granting,[9] one would expect corporations to trade-off between both (financial versus tax) incentives compared to their counterparts in the U.S.

The Klassen and Mawani findings above are markedly in contrast with Yermack (1995)'s findings which, among others, do not find either financial reporting or tax status of corporations influencing their option granting behaviors. Matsunaga (1995) also contributed to the intellectual unease by showing that there is a positive relationship between a firm's financial reporting costs and the likelihood of granting stock options to employees. In fact, apparently expressing frustrated satisfaction on the inconclusive or mixed evidence with respect to the role of taxes on stock options, Shackelford and Shevlin (2001) are forced to conclude (in their judgment) that taxes are not an important determinant of individual firm's choice between Incentive Stock Options (ISOs) and Non-Qualified Stock Options (NQSOs).

In the current study's assessment, the controversies appear not much to be on the use of stock options by corporations, but on what the mechanism should be such that corporation boards can effectively control managerial self-interest seeking or "rent" seeking behavior. This will "prevent wealth transfer from other shareholders to executives"; moreover that stock options bestow on executives or employees what Mawani termed 'upside gains' without any downside risks.

Prior to 2006, the complexity surrounding the use of stock options is somehow exacerbated by the decision of accounting standards not to recognize expensing options granted to employees which Mawani (2003) referred to as "technical valuation issues." However, some scholars continue to argue in favor of expensing option grants to employees (Bodie et al., 2003). The sustained intellectual arguments surrounding this issue could have prompted the Financial Accounting Standard Board (FASB) to agree to the new expensing regime since 2006, and also the IASB's intentions to sponsor global debate on the possibility of *income-statementalizing* stock option grants.[10] Furthermore, Mawani (2003), referring to the literature, documents the widening gap between book-tax conformity[11] in the U.S. such that it has attracted the legislative attention in the U.S. Congress. A bill sponsored by Levin-McCain in February 2002 is an important point of reference. The contention of Congress is that if corporations enjoy tax deductions with respect to option grants to employees, such an amount should be expensed in the financial statement with the consequence of reducing reported profits, thus impacting the stock market valuation of such corporation.[12] This non-conformity of the book-tax conformity is presently less of an issue in Canada.

Mawani (2003) argues that expensing stock options will "restore accounting neutrality" vis-à-vis option grants. Such could also enhance the competitiveness of the stock market as the disappearance of the financial accounting reporting benefits could cause more private placements of shares thus making the stock market more active. This is true since extant literature cannot conclusively find evidence in support of the capability of employees' stock options to effectively and desirably align seemingly conflicting incentives between the employees and their shareholders.

However, the findings of Austin et al. (1998) call for cautious optimism as to the possibility of corporate reluctance to use option grants if there is tax-book conformity. Austin et al. document that despite the corporate tax disadvantage of ISOs, their sampled corporations use ISOs or a combination of both ISOs and NQSOs predominantly. This, therefore, suggests that CEOs and boards might not be deterred in their decision towards the continued use of stock options. This view is consistent with the conjecture of Austin et al. that "...option choice is made to minimize the executive's tax burden, without regard for the corporate tax implications." Therefore, future studies to empirically document whether stock options actually reduce the effective marginal tax rates will valuably add to the literature as to whether or not stock options are actually a bad idea from the corporate tax point of view.

[8] This study has consistent objectives with similar studies like Yermack (1995) and Matsumaga (1995) in the U.S. except for the context differences between US and Canada, which of course is research sufficient for rich empirical investigations.

[9] For example, while in the U.S. the option benefits of Non-Qualified Options (NQSO) are tax deductible, in Canada, such benefits are not tax deductible.

[10] For further discussion on this, see "International Accounting Board Plans To Treat Options as Costs," *Wall Street* Journal Europe's edition of November 7, 2002. The real outcome and effect of such debates is yet to be measured.

[11] Shackelford and Shevlin (2001) note that "pensions are another form of compensation that has attracted book-tax analysis." This is further explored in the proceeding section.

[12] While we are not particularly convinced of the value-relevance of this argument, we notwithstanding support it in the interest of fairness, in that all corporations will be assessed on an equal or equivalent level field by the market and not that option granting corporations, while eating their cake in the form of tax deductions, will still have it in the form of otherwise higher reported profits.

In what appears as an empirical documentation of Pareto methodology which is widely applied by Thornton (1999), Mawani (2003) investigated the cancellation of executive stock options in Canada vis-à-vis tax and accounting income considerations. He operationalized the trade-off between financial reporting costs and tax costs in a multilateral framework using insider-trading data. He finds that tax benefits and reported income are taken into account by Canadian public corporations in their decisions of whether or not executive stock options should be cancelled. It is, however, not clear if the capital market will not see such a cancellation as a dis-appointment with its negative valuation impact. The validity of this thinking can be assessed if one considers the positive information value in the form of expectations of future rise in earnings and thus stock price that the granting of the option had initially signaled to the market.[13] Such a market reaction can be captured by examining the abnormal returns of the stocks of such firms engaged in the cancellation around the cancellation announcement period.

Hitherto, the conceptual methodology gap in the study of stock options is the (near) accurate or approximate measure that could effectively capture the holding period's behaviors of executives. For example, Austin et al. note that "consistency of our results with the joint tax minimization hypothesis requires that all executives of high tax firms have long holding periods. If there is diversity in executive preferences for holding stock *(options)*, this situation will not hold." This warning statement simply accentuates the importance for future research to find a proxy that can closely approximate this reality. Further, without a definite conclusion on the tax-efficiency status of the equity-based form of compensation, research in this area remains actively open.

Pension plans-based employees' compensation

We must mention that there is a scarcity of theoretical and empirical literature relevant to pension plans especially within the domain of taxation. We see few studies on pension plans. We hope that our discussion in this review will fruitfully advance the state of research efforts in this form of deferred employee compensation.

Pensions are generally deferred employees' compensation, which means that the values are cashable in the future. Therefore, given multi-period tax planning perspectives, one would expect taxation to play a prominent role in both corporate and employees' attitudes towards the pension plans.[14] It is no wonder that the Internal Revenue Code (IRC) 409A imposes an election and documentation requirement on the firms using deferred compensation packages.

There appears to be less controversial evidence in the literature on pension plans and the role of taxation or its implication for those plans. Many studies, as cited in Thomas (1988), acknowledge the fact that tax arbitrage could be the reason for increasing existence and survival of defined benefit pension plans, hence its growing prominence in the corporate cycle. In fact, Thomas categorically states that the findings of his study "reject the view that pension funding and tax status are unrelated." However, it is not yet clear in the literature as to the limit of tax arbitrage that corporations can engage in given other moderating and related issues of pension and non-pension shields. Notwithstanding, the reality-gap in Thomas' finding begs the question as to why do tax-exempt institutions continue to use defined benefit plans? This suggests that there could be a bunch of nontax factors driving organizations' preference for choice of pension plans. To further underscore the possible significance of nontax factors in the corporate operationalization of pension plans, Thomas (1989)'s study reveals that firms' termination decision with respect to defined benefit plans could be driven primarily by factors other than taxation excepting in special cases which simply are difficult to empirically identify or justify.

One area that appears controversial with its indirect but potentially considerable effect on the employees and their eventual pension claims is the asset allocation vis-à-vis defined benefit plan and the impact of taxation in this corporate investment choice. Frank (2002) notes and contributes to this inconclusiveness in the literature. The findings of her study provide inconsistent flow to prior empirical work by documenting that "firms' tax benefits are positively and significantly associated with the percentage of their pension assets invested in bonds." In other words, tax is important in corporate allocation decision of assets from defined benefit plan to investment opportunities and alternatives.

Conclusion

Depending on the type of compensation package used by a company, the role of taxes remains painfully unclear. The theoretical and empirical research in taxation, accounting and finance on employees' compensation is commendably intuitive, relevant and thought provoking. However, the commonality in those streams of research suggests inconclusive findings with regards to the role

[13] Alternatively, if granting stock options signaled positive information to the market as documented in the literature, then executives could grant options to take undue advantage of such an announcement to the market with an upfront knowledge of the intentions that the option will be cancelled and redeemed for cash. Therefore, what cash compensation cannot get from the market on its own, granting options and then converting it into cash by cancellation could. Insider trading on the market!

[14] For example, the significance of pension plans and management can be appreciated if one considers its strategic roles and continued mention of pensions in corporate reorganizations. Recent debates in Canada on Air Canada and General Motors in the U.S. regarding reorganization strategies readily come to mind.

and implication of taxation in corporate choice of employees' compensation as well as employees' preference among alternative compensation packages. The discussions above project the fact that considerable research improvement is required to actually bring to the fore the desired commonality and conclusiveness. With cautious optimism, the current study hopes that such an intellectual congruence will occur, except for the fact that there will be continued refinements and improvements of research that will usually breed further dimensions for active need for more research. This can then enlarge the coast for intellectual prospects in this important area of financial accounting and taxation research.

It is worthy to mention the possible role of methodologies and proxies for constructs in the empirical studies around the tax relevance of employees' compensation packages. For example, while some studies have been unfortunately 'forced' to calculate corporate effective tax rates using information in the financial statements, others have used the simulated marginal tax rates. There is no doubt that methodological differences could unintentionally drive research findings. For example, the sample periods may need to be longer than the ones widely used in many of the prior studies as the treatment may lag/lead the effects, that is, the effect of taxation on compensation may take years to manifest. In addition, the research contexts and databases used by many studies in this area of accounting and taxation research could limit the generalizability of findings. Therefore, in addition to highlights above, the current study calls for new and improved creative efforts to broaden the scope of investigations and methodological specifications in the domain of compensation-taxation research. This is particularly important if one considers the unique concerns of (reverse) causality, omitted variables and endogeneity issues that pervade tax-related compensation research.

Conflict of Interests

The author has not declared any conflict of interest.

REFERENCES

Akindayomi A (2006). "An Empirical Investigation on the Impact of Executive Stock Options on Firm Valuation". Dissertation, University of Calgary (Alberta, Canada).

Armstrong CS, Blouin JL, Larcker DF (2012). The incentives for tax planning. J Account. Econ. 53(1):391-411.

Austin JR, Gaver JJ, Gaver KM (1998) The choice of incentive stock options vs. nonqualified options: A marginal tax rate perspective". J Am. Tax. Assoc. 20(2):1-21.

Bodie ZR, Kaplan S, Merton RC (2003). For the last time: stock options are an expense. Harvard Bus. Rev. 81(3):62-71.

Chan LH, Chen KC, Chen TY, Yu Y (2014). Substitution between Real and Accruals-Based Earnings Management after Voluntary Adoption of Compensation Clawback Provisions. Account. Rev. 90(1):147-174.

Dechow P, Ge W, Schrand C (2010). Understanding earnings quality: A review of the proxies, their determinants and their consequences. J Account. Econ. 50(2):344-401.

Desai MA, Dyck A, Zingales L (2007). Theft and taxes. J. Financ. Econ. 84(3):591-623.

Desai M A, Dharmapala D (2008). Tax and corporate governance: An economic approach in tax and corporate governance. Springer Berlin Heidelberg.

Frank MM (2002). The impact of taxes on corporate defined benefit plan asset allocation. J Account. Res. 40(4):1163-90.

Frydman C, Molloy RS (2011). Does tax policy affect executive compensation? Evidence from postwar tax reforms. J Public Econ. 95(11):1425-1437.

Graham J (2008). Taxes and corporate finance. In: Eckbo, E. (Ed.), Handbook of Corporate Finance; Empirical Corporate Finance Amsterdam. Elsevier Science.

Hanlon M, Heitzman S (2010). A review of tax research. J Account. Econ. 50(2):127-178.

Ittner CD, Larcker DF, Rajan MV (1997). The choice of performance measures in annual bonus contracts. Account. Rev. 72(2):231-255.

Jensen M (1986). Agency costs of free cash flow, corporate finance and the market for take-overs. Am. Econ. Rev. 76(Papers & Proc.):323-328.

Jensen MC, Meckling WH (1976). Theory of the firm: Managerial behavior, agency costs and ownership structure. J. Financ. Econ. 3(4):305-360.

Johnson CH (2003). Stock and Stock Option Compensation: A Bad Idea. Can. Tax J. 51(3):1259-90.

Ke B (2001). Taxes as a determinant of managerial compensation in privately held insurance companies. The Accounting Review. 76(4):655-74.

Klassen KJ, Mawani A (2000). The impact of financial and tax reporting incentives on option grants to Canadian CEOs. Contemp. Account. Res. 17(2):227-62.

Matsunaga SR (1995). The effects of financial reporting costs on the use of employee stock options. Account. Rev. 70(1):1-26.

Mawani A (2003). Tax Deductibility of Employee Stock Options. Can. Tax J. 51(3):1230-58.

Mawani A (2003). Cancellation of executive stock options: Tax and accounting income considerations. Contemp. Account. Res. 20(3):495-517.

Philips JD (2003). Corporate tax-planning effectiveness: The role of compensation-based incentives. Account. Rev. 78(3):847-874.

Schmittdiel H (2014). Are CEOs incentivized to avoid Corporate Taxes?-Empirical Evidence on Managerial Bonus Contracts. Tinbergen Institute Discussion Paper. http://papers.ssrn.com/sol3/papers.cfm?abstract_id=2436101.

Scholes M, Wolfson A, Erickson M, Maydew E, Shevlin T (1992). Taxes and business strategy: A planning approach. Prentice-Hall. New Jersey.

Shackelford DA, Shelvlin T (2001). Empirical tax research in accounting. J Account. Econ. 31(1):321-387.

Thomas JK (1988). Corporate taxes and defined benefit pension plans. J Account. Econ. 10(3):199-237.

Thomas JK (1989). Why do firms terminate their overfunded pension plans? J Account. Econ. 11(4):361-98.

Thornton DB (1999). Managerial tax planning – A Canadian perspectives. Revised Second Edition.

Yermack D (1995). Do corporations award CEO stock options effectively? J. Financ. Econ. 39(2):449-476.

Permissions

All chapters in this book were first published in JAT, by Academic Journals; hereby published with permission under the Creative Commons Attribution License or equivalent. Every chapter published in this book has been scrutinized by our experts. Their significance has been extensively debated. The topics covered herein carry significant findings which will fuel the growth of the discipline. They may even be implemented as practical applications or may be referred to as a beginning point for another development.

The contributors of this book come from diverse backgrounds, making this book a truly international effort. This book will bring forth new frontiers with its revolutionizing research information and detailed analysis of the nascent developments around the world.

We would like to thank all the contributing authors for lending their expertise to make the book truly unique. They have played a crucial role in the development of this book. Without their invaluable contributions this book wouldn't have been possible. They have made vital efforts to compile up to date information on the varied aspects of this subject to make this book a valuable addition to the collection of many professionals and students.

This book was conceptualized with the vision of imparting up-to-date information and advanced data in this field. To ensure the same, a matchless editorial board was set up. Every individual on the board went through rigorous rounds of assessment to prove their worth. After which they invested a large part of their time researching and compiling the most relevant data for our readers.

The editorial board has been involved in producing this book since its inception. They have spent rigorous hours researching and exploring the diverse topics which have resulted in the successful publishing of this book. They have passed on their knowledge of decades through this book. To expedite this challenging task, the publisher supported the team at every step. A small team of assistant editors was also appointed to further simplify the editing procedure and attain best results for the readers.

Apart from the editorial board, the designing team has also invested a significant amount of their time in understanding the subject and creating the most relevant covers. They scrutinized every image to scout for the most suitable representation of the subject and create an appropriate cover for the book.

The publishing team has been an ardent support to the editorial, designing and production team. Their endless efforts to recruit the best for this project, has resulted in the accomplishment of this book. They are a veteran in the field of academics and their pool of knowledge is as vast as their experience in printing. Their expertise and guidance has proved useful at every step. Their uncompromising quality standards have made this book an exceptional effort. Their encouragement from time to time has been an inspiration for everyone.

The publisher and the editorial board hope that this book will prove to be a valuable piece of knowledge for researchers, students, practitioners and scholars across the globe.

List of Contributors

N. S. Bonu
Faculty of Business, University of Botswana, Gaborone, Botswana

P. Pedro Motau
Faculty of Business, University of Botswana, Gaborone, Botswana

Tao Zeng
Accounting School of Business and Economics, Wilfrid Laurier University, Waterloo, Ontario, Canada, N2L 3C5

Seyed Mohammad Mousavi Shahroodi
Faculty of Industrial Engineering and Management, Shahroud Industrial University, Iran

Jr. Gil B. Manzon
Fulton Hall 536, Boston College. Boston, MA

George Plesko
University of Connecticut, School of Business 2100 Hillside Road, Unit 1041A Storrs, CT 06269-1041

James O. Alabede
College of Business Universiti Utara Malaysia, Sintok, Kedah State-Malaysia

Zaimah Zainol Ariffin
College of Business Universiti Utara Malaysia, Sintok, Kedah State-Malaysia

Kamil Md Idris
College of Business Universiti Utara Malaysia, Sintok, Kedah State-Malaysia

Priyesh Sharma
Hidaytullah National Law University (HNLU), Raipur, India

Siddharth Dang
Hidaytullah National Law University (HNLU), Raipur, India

Ravindra Tripathi
Department of Humanities and Social Sciences, Motilal Nehru National Institute of Technology, Allahabad, India

Ambalika Sinha
Department of Humanities and Social Sciences, Motilal Nehru National Institute of Technology, Allahabad, India

Sweta Agarwal
Department of Humanities and Social Sciences, Motilal Nehru National Institute of Technology, Allahabad, India

Danie Schutte
North West University, Private Bag X6001, Potchefstroom, 2520, South Africa

Pieter Buys
School for Accounting Sciences, Faculty of Economic and Management Sciences, North West University

Srinvas Gumparthi
SSN School of Management and Computer Applications, Chennai, India

Swetha Khatri
SSN School of Management and Computer Applications, Chennai, India

V. Manickavasagam
Department of Corporate Secretaryship Alagappa University, Karaikudi, India

A.S. Norman
Tumaini University, Tanzania or Kampala International University, Tanzania

Marcos Cintra
Rua Cesar Valejo 360, ap.191-A, São Paulo, 05685-000, São Paulo, Brazil

Arturo José Galindo
Inter-American Development Bank, Washington, DC, USA

Cristina Pombo
Inter-American Development Bank, Washington, DC, USA

John McDonald
Flinders Business School, Flinders University, GPO Box 2100, Adelaide 5001, Australia

Seyed Mohammad Mousavi Shahroudy
Shahrood University of Technology, Iran

Semiu Babatunde ADEYEMI
Department of Accounting, University of Lagos, Lagos, Nigeria

Temitope Olamide, FAGBEMI
Department of Accounting and Finance, University of Ilorin, Ilorin, Kwara State, Nigeria

Gerald Chau
School of Accounting and Finance, the Hong Kong Polytechnic University, Hung Hom, Kowloon, Hong Kong

Patrick Leung
School of Accounting and Finance, the Hong Kong Polytechnic University, Hung Hom, Kowloon, Hong Kong

Josiah Mary
Department of Accounting, College of Business Management Science, Igbinedion University Okada, Edo State, Nigeria

Samson. A. Adedinran
Department of Accounting, College of Business Management Science, Igbinedion University Okada, Edo State, Nigeria

Akpeti. O. Elizabeth
Department of Business Administration, College of Business Management Science, Igbinedion University Okada,Edo State, Nigeria

Bassam Abu-Abbass
Department of Accounting, College of Business Administration, University of Bahrain, P.O. Box: 32038, Kingdom of Bahrain

Riyadh Al-Abdullah
Department of Accounting, College of Business Administration, University of Bahrain, P.O. Box: 32038, Kingdom of Bahrain

Paula Fukofuka
School of Business Administration, South China University of Technology, Wuhan, Tianhe District, Guangzhou, P.R. China 510640

Iyiola Omisore
Senator, Federal Republic of Nigeria

Munirat Yusuf
Department of Business Administration, University of Abuja, Abuja, Nigeria

I. Nwufo Christopher
Department of Accounting, University of Abuja, Abuja, Nigeria

Abubakari Abdul-Razak
Accountancy Department Tamale Polytechnic Tamale - Northern Region Ghana

Christopher Jwayire Adafula
Finance Department; Accountant Budgets, Bolgatanga Polytechnic, Sumbrungu - U/E Region, Ghana

Wan-Ying Lin
Department of Accounting, National Chengchi University, Taiwan

Jui-Chih Wang
Department of Accounting Information, National Taipei University of Business, Taiwan

D. W. Colon
University of Groningen, the Netherlands

D. M. Swagerman
University of Groningen, the Netherlands

Frank Yao Gbadago
Department of Accounting Studies Education, College of Technology Education
University of Education, Winneba, Kumasi, Ghana

Dadson Awunyo-Vitor
Department of Agricultural Economics, Agribusiness and Extension, Faculty of Agriculture, College of Agriculture andNatural Resources, Kwame Nkrumah University of Science and Technology, Kumasi, Ghana

Jonathan Farrar
Ryerson University, Canada

Akinloye Akindayomi
Accounting and Business Law, College of Business Administration, University of Texas - Pan American, 1201 W. University Drive Edinburg, TX 78539-9999, U.S.A

Adesola Adeduro Ogunmakin
Department of Accounting, Faculty of Management Sciences, Ekiti State University, Nigeria